New Exodus in John

Kyungu Ra

WIPF & STOCK · Eugene, Oregon

Wipf and Stock Publishers
199 W 8th Ave, Suite 3
Eugene, OR 97401

New Exodus in John
By Ra, Kyungu
Copyright©2018 Apostolos
ISBN 13: 978-1-5326-6978-1
Publication date 9/23/2018
Previously published by Apostolos, 2018

Acknowledgements

Above all, I give great thanks and glory to God our Savior the Lord.

I acknowledge my debt of gratitude to all who have contributed to the completion of this work.

I am particularly grateful to Dr. Tom Holland of UST (Union School of Theology, Oxford) and Prof. D. P. Davies of St. David's College, the University of Wales, Lampeter (now University of Wales, Trinity Saint David's), who were my supervisors for my Ph.D. dissertation submitted to the University of Wales, Lampeter in September 2008. Dr. Holland supervised my research through all its challenges with great forbearance. He has often advised me to publish the work and has introduced me to some publishers. He also gives a high recommendation for this book without hesitation. Prof. D. P. Davies guided this research with his thorough reading and encouragement.

I am also grateful to Dr. Eryl Davies, the previous principal of ETCW (Evangelical Theological College of Wales, now Union School of Theology), for his patience and thoughtful encouragement. Also, I am thankful for the sincere guidance of Dr. Stephen Smalley and Dr. Paul Middleton in the oral defence of my dissertation.

This book also has great debts, in prayer and financial support, to churches and communities, such as Sarang Community Church, Jeon-Ju Yeol-Lin-Moon Presbyterian Church, Kimje Bongwal Presbyterian Church, Global Mission Society, and Food and Nutrition for Good News (cf. Wholistic Interest Through Health) in South Korea, Gilgal Baptist Church Porthcawl in Wales, and Calvin Theological College under Korea Church Mission in Tanzania.

In particular, I must thank my father, Mr. Yeon-Jong Ra and my wider family for their unfailing prayers, encouragement and financial support. My great thanks are to my wife, Mijung and my daughters, Haein and Chongin who have encouraged me to publish this work.

Last of all, I would like to say deep thanks to Mathew Bartlett and Apostolos Publishing team, who edited and published the work in better English expressions.

This book is dedicated to my dear mum, the late Sa-Yi Ra, who passed away in an unexpected accident in September 2009 and who now rests with her Lord and Saviour.

Abbreviations

ACNT: Augsburg Commentary on the New Testament

ACTSTJ: ACTS (Asian Center for Theological Studies and Mission) Theological Journal

ANTC: Abingdon New Testament Commentaries

ATR: Anglican Theological Review

BBR: Bulletin for Biblical Research

BDB: Brown-Driver-Briggs, Hebrew and English Lexicon of the Old Testament

Bib: Biblica

BJRL: Bulletin of the John Rylands University Library of Manchester

BS: Bibliotheca Sacra

BST: The Bible Speaks Today

BT: Banner of Truth

BTB: Biblical Theology Bulletin

CBQ: Catholic Biblical Quarterly

CTJ: Calvin Theological Journal

CUP: Cambridge University Press

DR: Downside Review

EA: Exod Aditu

ETL: Ephemerides Theologicae Lovanienses

EQ: Evangelical Quarterly

ExpT: The Expository Times

GTJ: Grace Theological Journal

HBT: Horizons in Biblical Theology

HeyJ: Heythrop Journal

HT: Hebrew Text

HTR: Harvard Theological Review

IBS: Irish Biblical Studies

ICC: The International Critical Commentary

IRT: Issues in Religion and Theology

IVP: Inter-Varsity Press

JBL: Journal of Biblical Literature

JETS: Journal of the Evangelical Theological Society

JJS: Journal of Jewish Studies

JSJ: Journal for the Study of Judaism

JSJ Supp: Journal for the Study of Judaism, Supplement

JSNT: Journal for the Study of the New Testament

JSNT Supp: Journal for the Study of the New Testament, Supplement

JSOT: Journal for the Study of the Old Testament

JSP: Journal for the Study of the Pseudepigrapha

JSP Supp: Journal for the Study of the Pseudepigrapha, Supplement

JTS: Journal of Theological Studies

LXX: Septuagint

MT: Masoretic Text

NCB: New Century Bible

NCBC: New Century Bible Commentary

Neot: Neotestamentica

NIBC: New International Bible Commentary

NICNT: The New International Commentary on the New Testament

NIDNTT: New International Dictionary of New Testament Theology

NIDOTTE: New International Dictionary of Old Testament Theology and Exegesis

NIGTC: The New International Greek Testament Commentary

NIV: New International Version

NovT: Novum Testamentum

NovT Supp: Novum Testamentum, Supplement

NT: The New Testament

NTS: New Testament Studies

OT: The Old Testament

OUP: Oxford University Press

RB: Revue Biblique

RE: Review and Expositor

RQ: Restoration Quarterly

RTR: The Reformed Theological Review

SAP: Sheffield Academic Press

SB: Scripture Bulletin

SCJ: Stone-Campbell Journal

SNTSMS: Society for New Testament Studies Monograph Series

STB: Studies in Biblical Theology

SJT: Scottish Journal of Theology

Str-B: H. Strack and P. Billerbeck. *Kommentar zum Neuen Testament*

TDNT: Theological Dictionary of the New Testament

TDOT: Theological Dictionary of the Old Testament

Tg: Targum

TynB: Tyndale Bulletin

TT: Theology Today

TrinJ: Trinity Journal

VoxE: Vox Evangelica

VT: Vetus Testamentum

WBC: Word Biblical Commentary

WTJ: Westminster Theological Journal

WUNT: Wissenschaftliche Untersuchungen zum Neuen Testament

ZNW: Zeitschrift für die neutestamentliche Wissenschaft

ABBREVIATIONS OF NON-BIBLICAL SOURCES

Old Testament Apocrypha and Pseudepigrapha

Bar.: Baruch

Sir. : The Wisdom of the Son of Sirach (Ecculus: Ecclesiasticus)

Tob.: Tobit

Wis.: Wisdom of Solomon

1 Macc.: 1 Maccabees

2 Macc.: 2 Maccabees

3 Macc.: 3 Maccabees

4 Macc.: 4 Maccabees

1 En.: 1 Enoch (Ethiopic Apocalypse of Enoch)

2 En.: 2 Enoch (Slavonic Apocalypse of Enoch)

3 En.: 3 Enoch (Hebrew Apocalypse of Enoch)

2 [Syr. Apoc.] Bar.: 2 [Syriac Apocalypse of] Baruch

4 Bar.: 4 Baruch

Apoc. Abr.: Apocalypse of Abraham

Apoc. Mos.: Apocalypse of Moses

Jub.: Jubilees

Sib. Or.: Sibylline Oracles

Pss. Sol.: Psalms of Solomon

Test. Mos.: Testament of Moses (Ass. Mos.: Assumption of Moses)

Test. Lev.: Testament of Levi

Test. Jud.: Testament of Judah

Test. Jos.: Testament of Joseph

Test. Ben.: Testament of Benjamin

DEAD SEA SCROLLS

CD: Cairo (Genizah text of the) Damascus (Document)

1QM: War Scroll

1QS: Community Rule

1QH: Thanksgiving Hymns

1QSa (=1Q28a): Appendix A (Rule of the Congregation) to 1QS

1QSb: Appendix B (Benedictions or Blessings) to 1QS

1QpHab: 1QpHabakkuk (Commentary on Habakkuk)

4QpsDanA[a] (=4Q246): 4QAramaic Apocalypse

4Q225: 4QPseudo-Jubilees

4QFlor. (=4Q174): 4QFlorileguim

4QDibHam [4QDibHam^a] (=4Q504): Words of the Heavenly Lights [Luminaries^a]

4QPBless (= 4Q252, frag.1, VI); 4QGenesis Commentary on Gen 49:10

4QpIsa^a (= 4QIsa^a or 4Q16): 4QCommentaries on Isaiah

4QS: Community Rule manuscripts from Cave 4

4Q521: 4QMessianic Apocalypse

4QShirShab (=4Q400–407): 4QSongs of the Sabbath Sacrifice

Masada ShirShab: Masada Songs of the Sabbath Sacrifice

11QMelch. (=11Q13): 11QMelchizedek (Heavenly Price Melchizedek)

11QShirShab: 11Q Songs of the Sabbath Sacrifice

11Q Temple: 11Q Temple Scroll

11Q18: 11Q New Jerusalem (Description of the New Jerusalem)

PHILO'S WORKS

Conf. Ling.: De Cofusione Linguarum

Fuga: De Fuga et Inventione

Leg. Alleg.: Legum Allegoriae

Mosis: De Vita Mosis

Op. Mund.: De Opificio Mundi

Plant.: De Plantatione

Qius. Rer. Div.: Quis Rerum Divinarum Heres

Quaest. Ex.: Quaestiones et solutiones in Exodum

Quaest. Gen.: Quaestiones et solutiones in Genesim

Quod Det. Pot. Insid. Sol.: Quod Deterius Potiori Insidiari Soleat

Quod Deus Immut.: Quod Deus Immutabilis Sit

Somn.: De Somniis

Spec. Leg.: De Specialibus Legibus

JOSEPHUS' WORKS

War (or J.W.): Jewish War

Ant.: Antiquities of the Jews

Bell.: Bellum Judaicum

Life: The Life

RABBINIC SOURCES

MISHNAH

m. Ker.: Keritot

m. Ket.: Ketuboth

m. Mid.: Middot

m. Nid.: Niddah

m. Pesah.: Pesahim

m. Sheb.: Shebuot

m. Sheq.: Sheqalim

m. Sukk.: Sukkah

m. Yom.: Yomah

TOSEFTA

t. Ket.: Ketuboth

t. Men.: Menahoth

t. Sukk.: Sukkah

t. Yad.: Yadayim

BABYLONIAN TALMUD

b. Ber.: Berakhot

b. 'Erub.: 'Erubin

b. Gitt.: Gittin.

b. Hag.: Hagiga

b. Hul.: Hulin

b. Ker.: Keritot

b. Ket.: Ketuboth

b. Pesah.: Pesahim

b. Sanh.: Sanhedrin

b. Shab.: Shabbat

b. Sukk.: Sukkah

b. Taan.; Taanit

b. Yeb.: Yebamoth

PALESTINIAN TALMUD

y. Ber.: Berakhot

y. Hag.: Hagiga

MIDRASHIM

Gen R.: Genesis Rabbah

Exod R.: exodus Rabbah

Lev R.: Leviticus Rabbah

Num R.: Numbers Rabbah

Deut R.: Deuteronomy Rabbah

Eccl R.: Ecclesiastes Rabbah

Song R.: Song Rabbah

Lam R.: Lamentation Rabbah

Hekhaloth R.: Hekhaloth Rabbah

Cant. R.: Canticles Rabbah

Midr. R.: Midrash Rabbah

Midr. Sam: Midrash Samuel

Midr. Ps: Midrash Psalm

Shemot R.: Shemot Rabbah

Pesiqta R.: Pesiqta Rabbati

Pesiqta R. Kah.: Pesiqta de Rab Kahana

Pirqe R. Eliezer: Pirqe de Rabbi Eliezer

Sifre on Deut; Sifre on Deuteronomy (Sifre Deuteronomy)

Mek. Ex: Mekhilta exodus

TARGUM

Tg. Neof. Gen [Tg. Neof. 1] : Targum Neofiti Genesis

Tg. Onk.: Targum Onkelos

Tg. Jon.: Targum Jonathan

Tg. Num: Targum Numbers

Tg. Job: Targum Job

Tg. Ps: Targum Psalm

Tg. Isa: Targum Isaiah

Tg Jer: Targum Jeremiah

Tg Ezek: Targum Ezekiel

Tg. Mic: Targum Micah

Tg. Zech: Targum Zechariah

Fragment Tg.: Fragment Targum

Tg. Cant.: Targum of Canticles

GRAECO-ROMAN, EARLY CHRISTIAN AND GNOSTIC WRITINGS

Pliny, Nat. Hist.: Natural history

Irenaeus, Adv. Haer.: Adversus Haereses

Justin, Dial.: Dialogue

Barnabas: Epistle of Barnabas

Thomas: Gospel of Thomas

SAMARITAN LITERATURE

M.M.: Memar Marqah

Abstract

This book explores Christ's identity and his works in John's Gospel in the light of the predicted new exodus and eschatological Passover. It further explores the relationship that exists between the Passover and the firstborn, who in the Passover was substituted by the paschal lamb.

The idea of the firstborn—especially the death of the firstborn—is reflected in some major Christological titles: the only Son, the beloved Son, the Davidic Messianic King, the Deutero-Isaianic suffering servant of the Lord and the Son of Man. Themes related to the paschal/new exodus/firstborn motif are abundantly reflected in the narratives of John 1–4.

Above all, the Johannine Logos, who is introduced as the only Son of God and as the Son of Man in John's Gospel (cf. John 1:14, 18, 51; 3:13–18), probably alludes to the idea of the firstborn and the Danielic Son of Man figure (based on the idea of the firstborn). This figure fulfils the calling of the Deutero-Isaianic suffering servant of the Lord for the restoration of Israel from exile and for the salvation of the gentiles as the sons of God.

Even though the Johannine Jesus, as the Logos, the only Son of God and the Danielic Son of Man, is ontologically the divine Son, enthroned in heaven, he is also the Danielic Son of Man, who, as the symbolic representative of the saints of the Most High (the Ancient of Days), will be enthroned on a heavenly thrones. That is, the Johannine Jesus will functionally accomplish the restoration (ascension) of the Israelites from exile to the throne of God through the work of the Isaianic servant of Yahweh. Therefore, by a vicarious atoning death as the guilt-offering for sinful Israel, and all the nations, acting as the ransom in order to redeem them from condemnation at the last judgment.

The Johannine Jesus is also the eschatological fulfilment of the Davidic covenant. As the Son (firstborn/paschal lamb/only Son) of God and the King of Israel, Jesus builds the eschatological new Temple through his vicarious atoning redemptive death and resurrection against the background of the Passover feast. The building of the new eschatological Temple is related to the expectation for the new exodus.

This book conclusively shows that the paschal/new exodus motif is an important prism for interpreting John's Gospel and Johannine Christology.

Contents

Introduction 14

Chapter 1: The Prologue (John 1:1–18) 38

Chapter 2: Some Testimonies (John 1:19–51) 72

Chapter 3: Water into Wine Miracle John 2:1–11 112

Chapter 4: Jesus's Action in the Temple John 2:12–25. cf. Matt 21:12–13; Mark 11:15–17; Luke 19:45–46 126

Chapter 5: Jesus and Nicodemus (John 3:1–21) and, Jesus and John the Baptist (John 3:22–36) 160

Chapter 6: Jesus and the Samaritan Woman (John 4:1–42) and Jesus's Healing (John 4:43–54) 242

Chapter 7: Conclusion 289

Bibliography 292

Introduction

i) The Significance of the Exodus to Israel and the Expectation for the New Exodus

The exodus was the most crucial event in Israel's history and is deeply engraved in her memory. It became the ideology which guided Israel's whole life. The exodus, through the Passover, was not only the day of Yahweh's deliverance for Israel out of Egypt, the land of slavery (Exod 13:3), but also the starting point of Israel as a national community.[1] Yahweh commanded Israel to commemorate the Passover in the generations to come by celebrating it as a national festival to the Lord—a lasting ordinance (Exod 12:14). Through observing the festivals of the Passover and Tabernacles (Lev 23:4, 43), Israel celebrated and remembered what Yahweh had acheived through the Passover and their wanderings in the wilderness. Even those who were unclean because of touching a dead body or were away on a journey, still had to celebrate it on the fourteenth day of the second month at twilight (Num 9:9–11).

Further, Yahweh asked Israel to teach their descendants in the promised land about all that Yahweh had done during the exodus.[2] At the Passover feast, the exodus was re-enacted through the ritual and became a living reality to each generation of the Israelites for whom her future second exodus deliverance was anticipated (cf. *m. Pesah.* 10:5; Ps 113–118).[3] Yahweh also commanded Israel to redeem every firstborn, which would be commemorated as a sign on their hands and a symbol on their foreheads to show that the Lord had brought them out of Egypt with his mighty hands (Exod 13:14–16). The significance of the Passover is presented in the regulations of the firstborn (Exod 13:1–16) and the Levites who redeem the firstborn (Num 3:12–13, 40–51; 8:14–19. cf. the redemption money). Furthermore, the significance of the deliverance by Yahweh is reflected in the first and fourth of the Ten Commandments (Exod 20), in which Yahweh introduces himself as the one who delivered Israel out of Egypt.[4] In addition, the exodus was the basis of Israel's social and economic

---

[1] T. F. Glasson, *Moses*, 15; R. E. Nixon, *Exodus*, 5, who says that, 'Israel's history had its true beginning in a crucial historical experience that made her a self-conscious historical community – an event so decisive that earlier happenings and subsequent experiences were seen in its light.' Cf. Exod 12:2.
[2] Cf. Exod 12:24–27.
[3] Nixon, *Exodus*, 8; A. C. Brunson, *Psalm 118*, 69–82, esp. 71–72, 74; J. A. Dennis, *Gathering*, 172 n. 265.
[4] Nixon, *Exodus*, 7. Cf. Exod 20:2; Lev 11:45; 19:37; 22:33; Deut 5:6, 15b; 11:1–4; 26:8; Num 15:41; Josh 24:5–7; Jud 2:12; 1 Sam 12:8.

structures.[5] Thus, the first exodus event itself became an important archetype in the biblical tradition, a means of telling and retelling God's acts of deliverance.[6]

According to Holland,[7] this historical pattern of the deliverance of Israel out of Egypt, with Yahweh's mighty power displayed in the signs and wonders and the promises of a deliverance from Babylon, became the basis of the expectation of the eschatological redemption, that is, the new exodus. Marshall[8] also argues that the concept of redemption in the NT originates from the divine act of deliverance of Israel from Egypt, which is the type for understanding God's future salvation for his people.

The prayer in Isa 63:7–19 recalls Yahweh's deliverance of Israel in the days of Moses and Israel's rebellion during the wilderness period. Together with this is their prayer to Yahweh for his return for the sake of Israel, the new exodus, in order to restore the Temple and Jerusalem. The prophets at the time of Jerusalem's destruction by Babylon proclaimed the exiled Israel's return to their own land after payment for their sins had been made (Isa 40:2). After Yahweh restored them to Jerusalem, he would give to them peace according to the covenant of peace, i.e. the new covenant.[9] The restoration of peace and salvation in Zion would be fulfilled by the kingly reign of Yahweh (Isa 52:7), with the rebuilding of the Temple (Hag 2:6–9; Zech 8:9–13). When Yahweh would raise Zion up and the glory of Yahweh would rise upon Zion at the eschaton, all nations would forsake their idols and weapons, bring their treasures to Zion, worship Yahweh, and join the peace of Yahweh with Israel (Isa 60). At that time, Yahweh would create a new heaven and a new earth.[10] For the accomplishment of the eschatological redemption of Yahweh, i.e. the new exodus, the Davidic Son,

---

[5] Nixon, *Exodus*, 7. Cf. Lev 25:37–42, 55; 26:13; Deut 10:18; 24:17–18; 24:21–22.
[6] T. Longman III and D. G. Reid, *Warrior*, 32. Cf. Neh 9; Pss 78; 105; 106; 136.
[7] T. S. Holland, *Motif*, 9. See Holland, *ibid.*, 9–16, for some references including new exodus theme in the Old Testament (esp. in the Prophets), the Dead Sea Scrolls, Josephus, *Jubilees*, *Psalms of Solomon*, Rabbinic sources, and the New Testament. See also, B. W. Anderson, 'Exodus,' 177–195; Nixon, 'Exodus,' 8–32; Brunson, *Psalm 118*, 69–82; J. T. Dennison, 'Exodus,' 6–11 (esp. 8); M. Fishbane, *Text*, 121ff; P. B. Harner, 'Creation,' 300–306; J. J. Enz, 'Afterlife,' 29–39; D. Daube, *Exodus*; G. R. Beasley-Murray, 'Christology,' 28.
[8] I. H. Marshall, 'Development,' 153–169. Cf. Exod 13:13; 34:19; Num 3:44–51; 8:16–19; Isa 43:1; Luke 24:21; 1:68–69; 2:25, 38; Gal 3:13; 4:5; Rom 8:21; 1 Cor 7:22f; Col 1:14; 1 Tim 2:6; Heb 9:11ff, 15; 2 Pet 2:1; Rev 1:5; 5:9; 14:3; Acts 20:28. Also, J. Jeremias, *Eucharistic*, 225; *idem.*, *TDNT*, I, 340; J. D. G. Dunn, 'Understanding,' 133.
[9] Cf. Isa 54:10–13; 55:12; Jer 29:11; 33:6ff; Ezek 3:25; 37:26ff.
[10] Cf. Isa 65:17–25; 11:1ff; Ezek 24:25ff; Hos 2:18ff.

the Messiah would play the central role according to the promise of 2 Sam 7:12ff.[11]

This messianic expectation was also richly reflected in extra-biblical Jewish literature. For example, *4QFlor.* 1:1–13, which contained the tradition of 2 Sam 7:12ff, shows that Yahweh promised David that he would establish his kingdom for ever, where the branch of David would be enthroned. It also interpreted the Qumran Community in terms of the Temple.[12] *Pss. Sol.* 17:23ff; 32:16 also shows the hope of a prayer as follows: the enthronement of the Davidic Son over Israel, the destruction of the unrighteous rulers by him, and the cleansing of Jerusalem by him.[13] This points to the prophetic expectation of the new exodus with the coming of the Son of David, the Messiah.[14] Further, *1 En.* 90:28f reflects the expectation of the restoration of the Temple and religious cults in the messianic age, and *1 En.* 46:51–53 shows that the Messiah, the Son of David, would defeat the gentiles and bring peace for the people of Yahweh.[15] This messianic expectation is shown in *4 Ezra* 12:31–34; 13:1–13; *2 Bar.* 40:1–3.[16]

The NT, especially Luke 1–2, clearly illustrates that some godly Jews anticipated the day of salvation with the coming of the Messiah. In particular, Jesus proclaimed that the eschatological salvation predicted by Isa 61:1–2 (Luke 4:18–19) had been fulfilled in him, which, according to Holland, was the new exodus of Isaiah.[17] The resurrected Jesus himself said the fulfilment of all the Scriptures were through his coming and his work (Luke 24:27, 44, 45). In John's Gospel, messianic expectations are reflected in some references (cf. John 1:19–27, 45; 6:14–15; 7:40–42). Brunson defines the new exodus (the restoration) of Israel as follows:

> The widespread and general hope of deliverance and restoration can be divided into three distinct yet interlinked categories which account for all of the expectations: the return from exile; the defeat of Israel's enemies; and the return of Yahweh to live and reign among his people. I will refer to this complex of restoration hope as the *new exodus*, a phrase which although not specially found in the ancient texts yet adequately describes the eschatological program

---

[11] Cf. Isa 9:6ff; 11:1ff; 55:3–5; Mic 5:1ff; Jer 23:5f; Ezek 34:23ff; 37:24ff; *Ps. Sol.* 11:2–5; 17:21–46; 4 Ezra 13. Holland, *Motif*, 14–15; Marshall, 'Development,' 155; M. L. Strauss, *Davidic*, 292–297.
[12] N. T. Wright, *People*, 310f.
[13] F. F. Bruce, *History*, 119f.
[14] Holland, *Motif*, 12f.
[15] S. Kim, 'Peace,' 281.
[16] Kim, 'Peace,' 281.
[17] Holland, *Motif*, 13f.

presented by the Prophets and also ties these longings to the paradigmatic deliverance in Israel's past.[18]

Ideas related to the end of the exile or to the return (the restoration) from exile played central roles in understanding the eschatological affliction in both Second Temple Judaism and the teachings of Jesus.[19] According to Wright,[20] even though Israel in the Second Temple Judaism had returned from the exile in Babylon several hundred years ago, they had nevertheless remained under the continuous rule of the gentiles. Thus, they had a great expectation of real restoration through the Davidic Messiah. In this historical context, as Holland states:

> the identification of Jesus with the promises relating to the Davidic deliverer is crucial for appreciating the early church's understanding of the person and work of its saviour.[21]

ii) Studies of the New Exodus Motif in John's Gospel[22]

Studies of the new exodus in John have generally been limited to the perspectives of the original exodus and thus to Moses who has been regarded as the great deliverer in the original exodus. J. J. Enz[23] has argued that the Fourth Gospel reflects many instances of typology relating to the exodus traditions and alludes to the deliberate literary pattern of exodus.

---

[18] Brunson, *Psalm 118*, 153–154 (original emphasis); Dennis, *Gathering*, 141 n. 106, for whom the new exodus is the whole complex of hopes such as 'the gathering of the exiles, the return of Yahweh, Israel's deliverance from their enemies, and a new Temple.' Also, Holland, *Motif*, 9 for whom the new exodus is 'eschatological redemption.' N. T. Wright, *Victory*, 201 for whom the new exodus is 'the return from exile, the defeat of evil, and the return of YHWH to Zion.'

[19] See J. M. Scott (ed.), *Exile*; idem., *Restoration*; Wright, *People*, 268–272; idem., *Victory*, xvii-xviii, 126–127, 203–204, 248–250; M. Bryan, *Jesus*, 12–20; C. A. Evans, 'Jesus,' 77–100; M. A. Knibb, 'Exile,' 253–272; P. R. Ackroyd, *Exile*.

[20] Wright, *Victory*, 94f; idem., *People*, 280–338, esp. 269–272.

[21] Holland, *Motif*, 14.

[22] Cf. Wright, *People*; idem., *Victory*. Strauss, *Davidic*, studies Luke and Acts in the light of Isaianic new exodus and regards the Davidic messianic King in first Isaiah as the same figure as the suffering Servant of Yahweh in second Isaiah. With his supposition that the unity of Isaiah was accepted in the first century A.D., Strauss argues that the eschatological deliverer is the Davidic messianic King (cf. Isa 9:1–7; 11:1–16) who leads an eschatological new exodus of God's people through suffering as the Servant of Yahweh of the servant songs. However, Strauss did not note how the two figures are interrelated with each other. R. E. Watts, *Isaiah's*, studies Mark's Gospel in connection with the Isaianic new exodus, although he recognizes the influence of the original exodus to the Isaianic new exodus. Similarly, D. Pao, *Acts*, argues that the Isaianic new exodus influenced Acts. Holland, *Motif* studies the paschal-new exodus motif in Paul's Epistle to the Romans, where he first indicates the importance of the death of the firstborn against the background of the Passover. Also, see T. S. Holland, *Contours*.

[23] J. J. Enz, 'Exodus,' 208–215.

Enz further suggests that the Johannine Jesus recognized his identity and work in the light of the ministry of Moses, namely, the new Moses.

R. H. Smith[24] suggests the four basic requirements for a typological analysis and compares, on this basis, the signs (and wonders) performed by Moses in Egypt in Exod 2:23–12:51 with the signs performed by the Johannine Jesus. Smith argues that the signs of the Johannine Jesus allude to the signs of Moses, however, inverting the nature of the signs significantly from Moses' works of destruction to Jesus's works of life-giving.[25]

T. F. Glasson[26] presents parallels between Moses and Jesus, and defines Jesus as a second Moses leading God's people in a new exodus. That is, for Glasson, Jesus as the new Moses fulfils the messianic hope and brings about the long expected deliverance.

R. E. Nixon[27] shows the presence of the original exodus themes in John, without considering the Isaianic new exodus in John. This is despite the fact that he recognizes that the original exodus motifs were developed in Isaiah, especially in Isa 40–55.

J. K. Howard[28] studied the significance of the Passover in the Fourth Gospel. Howard points out that the exodus (and the Passover in it) is the basis of a messianic deliverance in later Judaism and the NT. Howard argues that:

> Jesus is pictured both as a second Moses leading his people forth from a bondage far greater than the slavery of a human despot, from the thraldom of sin and death, and as the Antitype of the very

---

[24] R. H. Smith, 'Exodus,' 329–342.

[25] Smith, 'Exodus,' 333–340. Cf. Moses' turning water into blood (Exod 7:14–24) and Jesus's miraculous changing of water into wine (John 2:1–11), a plague upon the domestic animals of Egypt (Exod 9:1–7) and Jesus's healing of the official's son (John 4:46–54), the affliction of the Egyptians with a disease which produces sores on the body (Exod 9:8–12) and Jesus's healing of the lame man at the pool of Bethesda (John 5:2–9), the thunder storm and devastating hail (Exod 9:13–35) and Jesus's stilling of the storm on the Sea of Galilee (John 6:16–21), locusts upon the foliage and fruit of Egypt (Exod 10:10–20) and Jesus's feeding of the multitude with bread (John 6:1–15), the thick darkness in Egypt (Exod 10:21–29) and Jesus's healing of the blind man (John 9:1–41), the slaughter of the firstborn of Egypt (Exod 11:1–12:32) and Jesus's raising of Lazarus (John 11:1–44). Smith, *ibid.*, 337 recognized that the death of the firstborn in the tenth plague is reflected in the death of Jesus as the firstborn, but he did not explore this observation.

[26] Glasson, *Moses*.

[27] Nixon, *Exodus*, 5–10, 20–21.

[28] J. K. Howard, 'Passover,' 329–337.

Passover sacrifice itself, through which the redemption of the New Israel was effected.[29]

Howard correctly asserts that the Lamb of God in John 1:29 alludes to the Isaianic suffering servant of God (cf. Isa 53:7) and to the paschal lamb. However, Howard disregards 'the Son of God' as the one upon whom the Spirit comes down and remains and who will baptize with the Holy Spirit. Also, he does not consider the interrelationship between the Passover Lamb and the Isaianic suffering servant of Yahweh. Further, Howard[30] finds the messianic significance of the Temple incident in John 2:13–25 (cf. Mal 3:1; *Ps. Sol.* 17:32ff) and argues that the coming Messiah will establish the messianic community, that is, the new Temple or the eschatological congregation of the righteous, through the death of Christ as the fulfilment of Isa 53:7 and the original Passover who is the paschal victim. However, Howard does not explain how the Davidic messianic King will build the new Temple, the eschatological messianic community through his death as the paschal victim.

There are even Johannine scholars who ignore the new exodus motif in John, who nevertheless argue for the significance of Moses to understand the Johannine Jesus's identity and his works.[31] For example, M. E. Boismard[32] understands the Johannine Jesus as the new Moses on the basis of 'the prophet like Moses' in Deut 18:18, which is reflected in John 1:25, 45; 5:46; 6:1–15 (esp. v. 14); 7:40, 52. Furthermore, in Nathanael's confession in John 1:49, Boismard relates 'the King of Israel' to the kingship of Joseph the patriarch, without considering 'the Son of God.'

W. A. Meeks[33] defines Moses as the archetype of the prophet-king based on Deut 18:15, 18 (cf. John 1:21; 6:14; 7:40) and some Mosaic traditions in Jewish literature. Meeks argues that Jesus's identity and his works must be interpreted as the new Moses, the prophet-king. Juxtaposing John 6:14f ('the prophet who is coming into the world') and John 18:37 ('I have come

---

[29] Howard, 'Passover,' 329.
[30] Howard, 'Passover,' 333.
[31] So, R. N. Longenecker, *Christology*, 32–39, esp. 36–37; M. Davies, *Rhetoric*, 70–76.
[32] M.-E. Boismard, *Moses*, 1–67. Boismard, *ibid.*, 42–59 argues that Moses' signs in Exod 4:1–9 are alluded to in the three signs performed by Jesus in Galilee [cf. the water changed into wine at Cana in Galilee (2:1–12), the healing of the son of the royal official at Capernaum (4:46–54), and the miraculous catch in the sea of Galilee (21:1–14)]. Further, Boismard, *ibid.*, 18–20 argues that the fact that Jesus was crucified with two others – one on each side and Jesus in the middle- in John 19:17–18 alludes to Exod 17:8–13, where Moses' hands were extended and supported by Aaron and Hur at the battle against the Amalekites.
[33] W. A. Meeks, *Prophet-King*. However, Meeks' argument for Moses' kingship in Jewish sources and Samaritan sources has been criticized by Brunson, *Psalm 118*, 229–231.

into the world' and 'to testify to the truth'), Meeks[34] advances the idea of combining the prophet and the king. Meeks[35] presents some references concerning Moses's role as the intercessor for Israel. In John 1:49; 18:28–19:22, Meeks[36] recognizes the two important Christological titles, Son of God and King of Israel, but fails to note that the titles are clearly related to the Davidic messianic king. Meeks[37] points out that the crucified Jesus who as the King of Israel is paradoxically enthroned is identified with the paschal lamb in John 19:36, but fails to note the relationship of the titles. Meeks[38] further discusses the motifs of scattering, dispersion (exile and judgment) and gathering (restoration) into one the scattered children of God in John 11:50–52. He argues that the work of gathering the scattered children of God is related to Moses, not to David. He develops this theory because he suggests that there is no tradition saying that the Davidic Messiah will die for his people.

P. N. Anderson[39] suggests that 'the Prophet coming into the world' in John 6:14 alludes to 'the Prophet like Moses' in Deut 18:15–22, and thus argues that the Johannine Jesus has to be understood in the light of Moses rather than the Davidic Messiah.

S. Harstine[40] examines the function of Moses as a character in the Fourth Gospel, that is, Moses's relationship to the narrative plot of the Gospel, and then Moses's relationship to the protagonist, Jesus. Dealing with seven references related to Moses (1:17; 1:45; 3:14; 5:45–46; 6:32; 7:19–23; 9:28–29), Harstine concludes that:

> Moses functions as a historical anchor, a witness, and an authoritative figure. The portrayal of Moses as a legendary figure in the narrative has been shown to be an ingredient for the development of the plot, namely the recognition of Jesus' identity.[41]

---

[34] Meeks, *Prophet-King*, 24–25.
[35] Meeks, *Prophet-King*, 118, 160–161. Cf. Philo, *Mosis* 2.166; *Jub.* 1:18–21; *Ass. Mos.* 11:17; 12:6; 1:14. Furthermore, in the Qumran document and Rabbinic sources, Meeks, *ibid.*, 174, 200–204 says that Moses' role as intercessor and mediator between Israel and God and Moses' great act of propitiation stands as the model for intercession and the basis for hope for forgiveness in 4QDibHam 2:5–12 ('*The Words of the Heavenly Lights*' (=4Q504)), cf. G. Vermes, *Complete*, 364); *Yalkut Shimoni*, 852 on Deut; *b. Sota* 13b, 14a; *b. Ber.* 32a; *Midr. R.* on Exod 32:11; *Shemot R.* 43.
[36] Meeks, *Prophet-King*, 72, 82–83, 89.
[37] Meeks, *Prophet-King*, 76–77.
[38] Meeks, *Prophet-King*, 96–98.
[39] P. N. Anderson, *Christology*, 170–193, 256, 260f.
[40] S. Harstine, *Moses*, 40–75.
[41] Harstine, *Moses*, 74–75.

From these references, we can recognize that Moses has been regarded as the crucial character for understanding Jesus in John whether in connection with the new exodus motif or not.

More recently, A. C. Brunson[42] and J. A. Dennis[43] have researched John's Gospel in the light of the new exodus motif, with the consideration of the original exodus and the Passover. Brunson has researched the presence of the new exodus motif in John on the basis of the Johannine narrative of Jesus's triumphal entry into Jerusalem against the background of the Passover feast in John 12:13 alluding to Ps 118:25–26. Brunson[44] argues that in John's Gospel the original exodus motif has to be interpreted in connection with the eschatological new exodus portrayed in the Prophets, because John quotes from Second Isaiah three times and from Zechariah once (cf. Zech 9:9 in John 12:14–15). Brunson[45] correctly argues that among the NT texts, John's Gospel emphasizes the Passover supremely. The Passover is referred to ten times in John (John 2:13, 23; 6:4; 11:55 (twice); 12:1; 13:1; 18:28, 39; 19:14; cf. 4:45; 5:1), compared with the Synoptics (cf. seven times in Luke and four times in Matthew and Mark respectively).

> The Passover theme that began at the outset of Jesus' ministry closes with him replacing the Passover lamb as the ideal sacrifice… Just as the initial Passover sacrifice brought redemption for Israel in Egypt and was the defining moment preceding the exodus, in the Fourth Gospel Jesus' sacrifice redeems the new Israel and provides a new or second exodus.[46]

In particular, Brunson[47] points out that 'the coming of God' cannot be separated from the hope of full restoration, the return (restoration) of the exiles, and the end of the exile. He states:

> The expectation was that Yahweh would return to reign in Jerusalem, gathering the exiles and once again living amongst them. The Prophets looked to the coming of God for the judgment

---

[42] Brunson, *Psalm 118*.
[43] Dennis, *Gathering*.
[44] Brunson, *Psalm 118*, 155 n. 55.
[45] Brunson, *Psalm 118*, 156; S. E. Porter, 'Traditional,' 396–428; Davies, *Rhetoric*, 234–235; Howard, 'Passover,' 329–337.
[46] Brunson, *Psalm 118*, 157; cf. Wright, *Victory*, 577.
[47] Brunson, *Psalm 118*, 174–175 (quoted from p. 174); G. R. Beasley-Murray, *Jesus*, 11–25, 348 n. 22; Wright, *Victory*, 206. Cf. Isa 24:23; 25:9; 31:4; 33:17–24; 35:2–10; 40:1–5, 9–11; 42:13–16; 43:1–5; 51:4–5, 11–12; 52:7–12; 54:1–8; 59:19–20; 60:1–4; 62:10–12; 63:1; 66:10–16; Jer 3:17–18; Ezek 43:1–7; Joel 3:1–2, 16–21; Mic 4:1–7; Hag 2:6–9; Zech 1:16–17; 2:4–13; 8:2–3, 8–9; ch 14; Mal 3:1–5; *1 En.* 1:3–10; 25:3–5; 90:15; 91:7; *Test. Mos.* 10:1–10; *Wis.* 3:7; *Jub.* 1:26–28; *Test. Lev.* 8:11; *2 En.* 32:1; *1QM* 6:4–6; *1QS* 3:18; 4:19; *CD* 7:9; 8:2–3.

of the wicked and deliverance of his people, with the post-exilic prophets especially emphasizing the coming for salvation.[48]

Against this OT background, Brunson[49] argues that 'the Coming One' in John means 'the enfleshment of the Isaianic Yahweh,' that is, the Johannine Jesus, 'actualizes Yahweh's return to Zion.' In the Johannine baptism pericope, he interprets 'the Lamb of God who takes away the sin of the world' (John 1:29, 36) as 'the paschal lamb,'[50] and 'the Coming One' (John 1:27) as 'the enfleshment of Isaianic Yahweh' in connection with Isa 40:3 quoted in John 1:23.[51] Here, identifying 'the sin-removing Lamb of God' in v. 29 with 'the Coming One' in v. 27, Brunson argues that Jesus bears the work of the Isaianic Yahweh, that is, 'the removal of Israel's sin, which had kept them in exile.'[52] I concur with Brunson who interprets the Johannine Jesus presented in this narrative as the Passover Lamb and the enfleshment of Isaianic Yahweh. Brunson[53] however, rejects the view that Jesus is to be understood as the Davidic messianic King and rather argues that Jesus is the coming of Yahweh who brings about the new exodus.

However, Brunson fails to note other titles, 'Son of God' (1:34) and 'the one on whom the Spirit comes down and remains and who will baptize with the Holy Spirit' (1:32–33). Another problem in his argument is that even though he[54] recognizes the importance of the idea of the Davidic Messiah in connection with the eschatological salvation (the new exodus) in the OT,

---

[48] Ibid.
[49] Brunson, *Psalm 118*, 179, 223–239. See pp. 240–264 for a detailed discussion of 'the Coming One' in John.
[50] Brunson, *Psalm 118*, 156–157 argues that 'the Lamb of God' means 'the Passover Lamb,' which is clearly supported by the narrative of the crucifixion in John 19 (vv. 29, 36) and that some references relating to the Passover describe Jesus as the Passover victim and thus invest the death of Jesus with new exodus significance (cf. John 2:13–25; 6:4–59; 11:55; 12:1; 18:28, 39). Brunson, *ibid.*, 158–159 presents other parallels evoking the Exodus in John. Also, Dennis, *Gathering*, 168, 172, 352.
[51] Brunson, *Psalm 118*, 242.
[52] Ibid.
[53] Brunson, *Psalm 118*, 231–234, 225–227. Cf. 'The title ['king of Israel' in John 12:13] would necessarily evoke the messianic Davidic king, and indeed Jesus fulfils this expectation: he is the messianic king from the House of David. However, it appears that John does not want to present Jesus primarily as the Davidic king, for although he is that, he is also much more. Similarly, the title functions to evoke the ideal eschatological king of the Psalms and the Prophets, but there is a disjunction: although Jesus comes as the ideal king, the reader must recognize that Jesus's kingship is of a higher order. I suggest that the title 'king of Israel' primarily points to Yahweh, and provides a bridge between the eschatological ideal king of Ps 118 and Yahweh's kingship that links Jesus's royal entry to Jerusalem with the coming of Yahweh.' (*ibid.*, 233–234, [] added by this writer). Also, Meeks, *Prophet-King*, 17, 20; Anderson, *Christology*, 229–230; Davies, *Rhetoric*, 212.
[54] Brunson, *Psalm 118*, 26–45.

Judaism and the NT, he[55] fails to note the idea of the Davidic messianic king, which is clearly reflected in John.[56]

J. A. Dennis[57] argues that the death of Jesus should be placed in the context of his rejection by Israel and against the background of the prophecy of Caiaphas in John 11:47–52. Dennis further argues that it must also be considered through the motifs of Israel's plight and restoration; it is the means by which the restoration (gathering) of the true children of God is made possible. Dennis employs a combination of narrative and social-historical methodologies. He surveys the evidence for the restoration of Israel in the OT and Jewish literature up to the first century CE in chapter 3 of his work, and then the motifs of the restoration of Israel presented in John's Gospel itself in chapters 4–6 of his work.

In particular, for Dennis, the reference that the Johannine Jesus would die not only for the Jewish nation but also for the scattered children of God, to bring them together and make them one is apparent in John 11:51b–52. For Dennis this reminds the reader of the classical hope of the eschatological 'gathering' and 'unification' of Israel; and thus the inauguration of the long awaited promise of Israel's restoration.[58] Here, Dennis argues that the expectation of gathering and unification in John 11:52 is related to the restoration of the Assyrian exile and to the unification of Judah and Ephraim rather than to the restoration of the gentiles.[59] Dennis interprets the Johannine Jesus's death in the light of the paschal lamb[60] or of the Deutero-Isaianic suffering servant of Yahweh,[61] for the restoration of Israel, namely, the gathering of true Israel.[62] Dennis[63] concludes that dealing with

---

[55] Brunson, *Psalm 118*, 184, 189, who argues that Jesus is the enfleshment of Yahweh on the basis of 'the King of Israel,' without considering 'the Son of God' in Nathanael's confession as well.

[56] Cf. Nathanael's confession ('the Son of God' and 'the King of Israel') in John 1:47, the Temple builder as the Son of God in John 2:12–25, the Passion narrative ('the Son of God' and 'the King of Jews') in John 18–19, Jesus's proclamation as 'the light of the world' against the background of the Jews' dispute as to that Jesus came from Galilee in John 7:41–42, 52; 8:12 (cf. Isa 9:1–2; Matt 4:12–16). For Jesus's Davidic kingship, see E. Hoskyns, *Fourth*, 324; G. R. Beasley-Murray, *John*, 118–119; C. K. Barrett, *John*, 330; R. E. Brown, *John I-XII*, 329–330; R. Schnackenburg, *John*, II, 158; D. A. Carson, *John*, 329–330.

[57] Dennis, *Gathering*.

[58] Dennis, *Gathering*, 331.

[59] Dennis, *Gathering*, 84–88. Also, B. Pitre, *Tribulation*, 31–40; S. McKnight, *Vision*, 10–11, 19.

[60] Dennis, *Gathering*, 21–24, 168, 168 n. 240, 172, 352.

[61] Dennis, *Gathering*, 205–206, 324–325, 352. Cf. ὑψωθῆναι in John 3:14–15; 8:28; 12:32–33; Isa 52:13. cf. Isa 27:9; 40:2; 43:24–25; 53:5–6, 8, 11–12.

[62] Dennis, *Gathering*, 187–209, who points out the interrelationship between Jesus's death and the gathering of true Israel in the Temple incident (John 2:13–22), Caiaphas' prophecy (John 11:50–52), the Feeding narrative (John 6:12–13, 51), the Good shepherd (John 10:15–16) and the kernel parable (John 12:24, 32).

the sin of God's people, Jesus's death as the vicarious atonement reflected in *hyper* texts brings about the second exodus restoration of the true Israel. However, Dennis has not noted the relationship between the paschal lamb and the Deutero-Isaianic suffering servant of the Lord.

From the baptism narrative in John (John 1:19–34), Dennis[64] argues that Jesus plays the role of the Isaianic Yahweh in Isa 40:3–4 (cf. John 1:23) and the Davidic Messiah in Isa 11:2–3 (cf. John 1:33), bringing about the Isaianic restoration. Thus, Dennis assumes Jesus's identity in John 1:29, ('the one who takes away the sin of the world') as fulfilling Yahweh's role in Isa 40:3–4, who comes to release Israel from sin and exile by means of a new or second exodus. Here, Dennis fails to note other Christological titles, 'Son of God' (v. 34), 'the one upon whom the Spirit comes down and remains' and 'the one who will baptize with the Holy Spirit.' These titles could allude not only to the Davidic Messiah (Isa 11:1–2; 61:1) but also to the Deutero-Isaianic suffering servant figure (Isa 42:1). Furthermore, from the Johannine Temple narrative (John 2:13–22), set against the background of the Passover (vv. 13, 23), Dennis recognizes Jesus as the Davidic Messiah ('branch')[65] on the basis of the OT and Judaism, but spends more space dealing with the death of the paschal lamb.[66] Dennis does not question why the Davidic Messiah died as the Passover Lamb, nor why the Davidic Messiah could build a new Temple (the eschatological people of God), that is, bringing about Israel's new exodus restoration, *through his death and resurrection.*[67]

iii) Jesus and the New Exodus

This book examines the identity of Jesus, and his works, in the light of the new exodus (based on the Prophets) and the Passover (the original exodus) in the Gospel of John 1–4. Here, the Passover is related particularly to the the death of the firstborn[68] who is to be understood as the same entity as

---

[63] Dennis, *Gathering*, 352–353.
[64] Dennis, *Gathering*, 336–337. On the other hand, Dennis, *ibid.*, 21–24 points out the vicarious and atoning effects of the death of Jesus as the Passover Lamb.
[65] Dennis, *Gathering*, 161–164.
[66] Dennis, *Gathering*, 168, 168 n. 240, 170–172.
[67] Cf. Dennis, *Gathering*, 172 says that 'Jesus as the eschatological Temple for the new Israel (that is, his sacrificial 'consumption' functions as the eschatological apex of the Temple cult and his 'rebuilding' from the grave effects the new Temple) should be interpreted in light of the second exodus deliverance that the Passover festival commemorated and re-enacted. As such, the Passover celebration fuelled hopes for a future deliverance.' Also, Howard, 'Passover,' 333.
[68] Cf. Holland, *Motif*. In connection with this research, some points of Holland's work have to be briefly introduced with regard to the idea of the firstborn. Traditionally, NT scholars have been observing only the death of the paschal lamb at the Passover for the original exodus, but Holland notes the importance of the death of the firstborn behind the death of the paschal

the paschal lamb, on the basis of Exod 4:22f; 12:1–51; 19:5f. Moses and the Passover Lamb have generally been accepted as the central characters in the original exodus. Therefore, they were regarded as the archetypes to explain the identity of the Deutero-Isaianic suffering servant for the Isaianic new exodus (restoration) and Jesus's identity in terms of eschatological redemption (new exodus). The death of the paschal lamb is accepted as the decisive basis for understanding Jesus's identity, who was crucified against the background of the Passover feast. On the other hand, in the new exodus motif based on Isaiah (esp. Deutero-Isaiah), Jesus's death is explained by the suffering servant of the Lord. Scholars generally point out that the forgiveness of sin is a prerequisite for the restoration (new exodus) of Israel from exile, and interpret the death of Jesus in the light of the paschal lamb or the Isaianic suffering servant. However, the relationship of the two figures has not been properly explained.

Moses was the deliverer leading the first exodus and his prophecy in Deut 18:15, 18, is interpreted to mean that Jesus is the new Moses ('the Prophet like Moses'), who will bring about the new exodus. However, the Davidic messianic figure is frequently presented as the central figure for the new eschatological salvation, the new exodus, in the Prophets, Jewish literature and the NT. So, there is a tension as to whether the deliverer for the new-eschatological exodus is the new Moses or the Davidic Messiah.

It must be noted that in the Johannine passion narrative, set against the background of the Passover feast, Jesus was crucified not only as 'the paschal lamb' (cf. John 19:29, 36) but also as 'the Son of God' (John 19:7) and 'the King of the Jews' (i.e. King of Israel, cf. John 18:33, 37, 39; 19:3, 15, 19, 21). The two titles ('the Son of God' and 'the King of the Jews') remind us of the Davidic messianic king based on Nathan's oracle in 2 Sam 7:12–16 (Pss 2:7; 89:1–51). It is also noteworthy that Jesus's action in the Temple is set against the Passover feast in John 2:13–23. This hints at the death of Jesus as the Davidic messianic figure, who will build the new Temple through his death and resurrection: 'the suffering Davidic messianic king.' Furthermore, John 3:14–16 (cf. Mark 10:45) shows that Jesus has to be

---

lamb. He has argued for the centrality of the idea of the firstborn who was killed against the background of the first Passover, for the interpretation of Jesus's death in the NT. For him, the firstborn (not the father) as the representative of his family has to bear the judgment of God vicariously, has the same entity as the paschal lamb, and includes the priesthood as well. Also, presenting some evidence in the OT, he argues that the death of the firstborn (the paschal lamb) has the effects of atoning redemption. He also points out the importance of the Davidic messianic King for the new exodus, on the basis of the idea of the firstborn. Conclusively, he argues that the research of Jesus's identity and the eschatological new exodus motif in the NT has to be done in the light not only of Isaianic new exodus but also of the original Passover, namely, the death of the firstborn/the paschal lamb. See also Holland, *Contours*.

crucified ('has to be raised,' ὑψωθῆναι δεῖ as 'the Son of Man,' as 'the Deutero-Isaianic suffering servant of the Lord' (cf. Isa 52:13 ὑψωθήσεται καὶ δοξασθήσεται) and as the only Son (τὸν υἱὸν τὸν μονογενῆ) of God' (cf. 'gave,' ἔδωκεν alluding to δῶτε [Isa 53:10] and παρεδόθη [Isa 53:12]). The title, 'the Son of Man' is often referred to with the death of Jesus (cf. the crucifixion, John 3:14; 6:53; 8:28; 12:23–24, 32–34; 14:31). As has been pointed out, the baptism narrative testifies Jesus as 'the Lamb of God' who takes away the sin of the world; an allusion to 'the paschal lamb' and 'the suffering servant of Yahweh.' Further the reference to 'the Son of God' and the Spirit-baptizer alludes to the Davidic messianic figure and the Isaianic servant of Yahweh in Isa 11:1–16; 42:1; 61:1.

On the original Passover night, the firstborn (the paschal lamb instead of the firstborn in the Israelite family) as the representative of his family vicariously bore the judgement of God. The firstborn is identified with the paschal lamb as the central figure whose death brought about the first exodus of Israel. Accordingly, the firstborn (subsidiary the paschal lamb) as the representative of his family bore a vicarious atoning redemptive death for the judgment of God.[69] The idea of the death of the firstborn is alluded to in the suffering and death of the Davidic messianic king (cf. Ps 89:1–51; Dan 9:24–26), in the Deutero-Isaianic suffering servant (who is the same figure as the Davidic messianic king in Isa 52:13–53:12; 9:1–7; 11:1–16; 55:3; 61:1–11), and in the suffering and death of the Son of Man based on Dan 7:13–14; 9:24–26. These are briefly introduced in the next section.

iv) Summary of the Study of Old Testament Christological Development[70]

The study of some Christological titles, the origin of each title, and the relationship between them, in realtion to the exodus-new exodus theory can be summarized as follows. Firstly, the dual concepts (firstborn son of God and the servant of God) have their origins simultaneously in the original exodus (Exod 4:22–23; 12:1–51) and in the Sinaiatic covenant (Exod 19:5–6; cf. Exod 24:1–11). The purpose of Yahweh who had first chosen

---

[69] Cf. Moses as the great leader for the first exodus (the deliverance) can be regarded as a model for Jesus who is the deliverer of the eschatological new exodus, but Moses cannot be a proper model for the vicarious atoning redemptive death of Jesus. Also, since we have great OT background for the deliverance of Israel from her sin and its consequence by the death of the firstborn as a propitiatory (or expiatory) offering to God ('the judgment of God'), we do not need to depend on the theology of martyrdom. Cf. Marshall, 'Development,' 160, 163, 166–168; Wright, *Victory*, 595–597; Dunn, 'Understanding,' 131–132; Brunson, *Psalm 118*, 178 n. 120; Dennis, *Gathering*, 127.

[70] For the detailed discussion, see Kyungu Ra, *Old Testament Christological Development* (Forthcoming: Apostolos).

Israel as the Son of God and the servant of God was reflected in the idea of the *firstborn son* of Yahweh and in the idea of *the priestly kingdom of Yahweh*, through whom all the nations had to be restored as the sons of Yahweh. Generally, the idea of the Son of God could contain the idea of the firstborn Son of God (Exod 4:22–23). Furthermore, the idea of the firstborn includes the priesthood. These dual concepts of sonship and servanthood in the Bilical narrative cannot be separated from each other. That is, sonship paradoxically includes servanthood, and *vice versa*.

Secondly, the central figure of the original exodus was not Moses but the firstborn. Its subsidiary, the paschal lamb killed on the Passover night, was the decisive event for the deliverance/redemption. The death of the firstborn of Pharaoh, the Egyptians, and of all their cattle, was an indispensable element for the exodus of Israel. As with the Egyptians, the firstborn of the Israelites were not excluded from the judgment of Yahweh on the Passover night, saved only by the blood of the paschal lamb. The only one who could suffer Yahweh's judgementon the Passover night was the firstborn son as the representative of his family. It was only the death of the paschal lamb that protected the life of the firstborn from the angel of death. Hence, in the original Passover, it was not the paschal lamb but the firstborn son who was the preferential focus of judgement. The death of the firstborn of the Israelite family was substituted by the death of the paschal lamb. Each paschal lamb slaughtered in each family of Israel bore the judgement of Yahweh which the firstborn of each Israeli family should have borne. This action brought about the exodus of Israel, accompanied by *a mixed multitude* (עֵרֶב רַב/ἐπίμικτος πολύς). Therefore, the death of the firstborn was identified with the death of the paschal lamb.

The fact that the firstborn son was the central figure at the Passover exodus is clearly alluded to in Yahweh's regulations concerning the redemption for the firstborn. These regulations pertained to man or animal (cf. Exod 13:1–2, 11–16), and concerned the Levites who were taken from among the Israelites in place of the firstborn Israelite males (cf. Num 3:12–13, 40–51; 8:14–19). This paradigm is based on the original exodus, particularly on the death of the firstborn male in the context of the Passover. The tradition of the death of the firstborn is reflected in Exod 20:5; 34:7; Ps 78: Mic 6:6–7; Zech 12:7–10; Ezek 45:25; Gen 22. The central figure of the Passover was the firstborn son whose death brought about not only the exodus of Israel from the bondage of Egypt (deliverance/redemption as a ransom), but also the expiation (atonement as a guilt offering reflected in Exod 4:24–26; Num 8:19) of the sin of the nation of Israel, corporately, the firstborn son of Yahweh. The image of redemption in both Old and New Testaments originated in the divine act of deliverance of Israel from Egypt. This is often recalled against the background of the expectation of the restoration, the new exodus, of Israel from exile among the gentiles (cf. Pss 113–118; *m. Pesah.* 10:4–7).

The individual firstborn son, who was replaced by the paschal lamb in the Israelite family, was the representative of its family and was vicariously killed *in the form of servant*. This firstborn must be distinguished from *the corporate son/firstborn son* of God, the nation of Jacob-Israel. The nation was, by the vicarious death of the firstborn son through the paschal lamb, delivered (redeemed) from Egypt to be the corporate servant of Yahweh (Exod 4:22–23, more clearly, 'the priestly kingdom of Yahweh' in Exod 19:5–6), so that all nations could be restored as the sons of Yahweh. The central figure of the Passover which brought about the exodus of Israel from the bondage of Egypt was not Moses, but the firstborn son, and the paschal lamb.

Thirdly, the dual status (son/firstborn of Yahweh and the servant of Yahweh including the priesthood) was applied to the enthroned Davidic king as the representative of Israel, the corporate son of God, on the basis of Yahweh's covenant with David (cf. 2 Sam 7:12–16; 1 Chron 17:13; 22:10; 28:6; Pss 2:7; 89:1–37; 132:12; 110:1, 4). The Davidic king had to obey Yahweh totally and was given a mission, the building of the Temple for Yahweh (cf. 1 Kings 8:1–66; 2 Chron 6:1–42; Isa 56:7–8). This task was first fulfilled by Solomon, the seed of David. Solomon's prayer at the dedication of the Temple (1 Kings 8:1–66; 2 Chron 6:1–42) shows how this building was intimately related to the history of the exodus of Israel. Further, it is related to the restoration of Israel from exile, and even to the restoration of the gentiles as God's sons—through Israel, his corporate firstborn/son, the priesthood (cf. 1 Kings 8:41–43; Exod 19:5f).

Furthermore, the priesthood of the firstborn is reflected in the status of the Davidic king who plays the central role in the celebration of the Passover (cf. 2 Kings 23:21–23; 2 Chron 30:1–27; 35:1–19; Ezek 45:21–25) and is the priest after the order of Melchizedek (cf. Ps 110:1–4; 2 Sam 5:1–12). In particular, in Ps 89, 'the new messianic David' as the firstborn/servant of Yahweh would accomplish the works of Yahweh: creation, the deliverance of Israel from Egypt, ruling over the surging sea and its waves, and crushing Rahab and Israel's enemies (cf. sea-monster, Leviathan, symbolizing Pharaoh or Egypt). Further alluding to Yahweh's rule over chaotic water, Yam (sea), the raging sea in the creation (cf. Gen 1:6–10; Exod 14:1–15:21; Pss 89:9–10, 25; 74:12–14; 87:4; Isa 30:7; 51:9–10; Job 7:12; 26:12; Isa 26:19–27:1; Ezek 32:1–6). This Psalm highlights the role of the Davidic messianic king who would accomplish the (new) creation and redemption.

Furthermore, Ps 89:38–51 reflects the suffering and death of the Davidic messianic king as the firstborn/servant of God (cf. Dan 9:24–26).

Fourthly, the importance of the idea of the son (the firstborn son/the only son) of God based on Exod 4:22–23; 2 Sam 7:12–14; Ps 2:7 can be recognized against the expectation of the restoration from exile in Judaism.[71] In the OT and Jewish literature, the three titles: firstborn of God, the only son of God, the beloved son of God, described the status of Israel, and were intimately related to one other. They substantially have the same meaning. Above all, they are based on the idea of the firstborn in Exod 4:22–23 (cf. Hos 11:1, 3, 8, 9, 12; Jer 6:26; 31:9, 20 (38:9, 20 in the LXX); Amos 8:10; Zech 12:10; *Pss. Sol.* 18:4; 13:9; *4 Ezra* 6:57–59).

Fifthly, in Deutero-Isaiah, the individual servant figure, who innocently and obediently suffers for the transgression of the people, to restore Jacob-Israel from exile and bring salvation to the gentiles, is recorded in the four servant songs (cf. Isa 42:1–4; 49:1–6; 50:4–9; 52:13–53:12). However, this figure must be distinguished from the corporate servant of Yahweh, that is, the nation Jacob-Israel. Since the idea of the servant of Yahweh is not separated from the idea of the son of Yahweh in the Scripture, the servant (the individual servant figure or the corporate servant, Jacob-Israel) of Yahweh in Deutero-Isaiah includes the status of the son/firstborn of Yahweh. Also, the suffering servant of Yahweh in Deutero-Isaiah is the same figure as the new Davidic king in the first part of Isaiah. This argument is strongly supported by the dual idea of sonship and servanthood, and by the close parallel between the new David (David *redivivus*, the Davidic royal figure) in the first part of Isaiah (cf. Isa 1–39) and the servant of Yahweh (also, the Anointed One of Yahweh) in the second part of Isaiah (cf. Isa 9:1–7; 11:1–16; 55:3; 61:1–11). The Isaianic suffering servant of Yahweh bears death for the vicarious atonement (guilt-offering and ransom) and covenant, to bring about the new exodus restoration of the exiled Israel and the salvation of the gentiles. Moses never bore vicarious suffering and death for the atonement (as a guilty offering, אָשָׁם, Isa 53:10) and deliverance/redemption (as a ransom, כֹּפֶר, Isa 43:3) of Israel from the bondage of Egypt at the Passover. The works of atonement and redemption that the firstborn or the paschal lamb bore at the Passover is the basis of the work of the Isaianic-suffering servant of Yahweh in the new exodus (Isa 52:13–53:12; 43:3–7, 22–24; 42:6; 49:8. cf. the light of the gentiles in Isa 9:1–2; 42:6; 49:6). Therefore, the death of the firstborn son is

---

[71] Cf. *Tob.* 13:4–5; *Jub.* 1:22–25; 2:20; *4 Ezra* 6:58; 7:28–29; *Sir.* 36:11; 4:10; 23:1, 4; 51:10; *Pss. Sol.* 13:9; 17:26–27; 18:4; *Wis.* 14:3; *3 Macc.* 6:3,8; 4QFlor. 1:11f; 4QpsDanA^a 1:7–21; 4Q504 3:1–9; *Pesiqta R.* 37; *Tg.* Ps 89:27; *Exod R.* 19:7; *3 En.* 44:10; *Midr. Ps* 2:9 on Ps 2:7; *Conf. Ling.* 62f; 145ff; *the Prayer of Joseph.*

the conceptual, theological basis of the idea of the suffering and death of the Davidic Messiah. This is reflected in the Isaianic suffering servant (the Davidic messianic king) of Yahweh in Isa 52:13–53:12; Ps 89:1–52 (esp. vv. 38–49); Dan 9:24–26; Zech 12:9–13:9 (esp. 13:7–9. cf. Zech 9:9–10; 11:4–14).

The epithets of the *Ebed Yahweh* in Jewish apocalyptic literature (cf. *Enoch, Ezra, Baruch*) were applied to the Messiah. However, the vicarious suffering which was an essential task of the *Ebed Yahweh* was absent from the messianic expectation, hence, no vicarious atoning death of the Messiah was envisaged (cf. *Test. Ben.* 3:8). Nonetheless, the servant of Yahweh of Isa 53 was interpreted as the Davidic messianic royal figure in the light of the exaltation and glorification (*Tg. Isa* 52:13. cf. 'the Temple builder' in *Tg. Isa* 53:5).

Sixthly, for the OT background of the Son of Man, בַּר אֱנָשׁ in Dan 7:13f and בֶּן אָדָם in Pss 80:17; 8:7 (cf. Ps 110:1, 4) have to be studied in connection with the firstborn son and the enthronement of the Davidic king. In Dan 7 the 'one like a son of man,' who appears with the heavenly clouds, receives the everlasting dominion and kingdom from the Ancient of Days, is seated on one of the throne-chariots beside the Ancient of Days, and is worshipped by all peoples and nations, is ontologically the divine Son of God. Also, he is, functionally and symbolically, the inclusive representative (head, firstborn) of the saints of the Most High, the true corporate son/firstborn of God (cf. Exod 4:22–23). Thus, the Danielic Son of Man plays the role of the firstborn of God, the representative of the sons (the faithful Israelites) of God. The enthronement of the 'one like a son of man' in Dan 7:13f means the enthronement of the saints (Israel) of the Most High, presenting the restoration or the new exodus of Israel, the corporate son of God and the covenantal people of God, from exile (cf. Exod 4:22f). Also, the enthronement of the Danielic Son of Man figure who is the firstborn/son of God and the inclusive representative of the saints of God in Dan 7:13f alludes to the enthronement of the Davidic king who as the firstborn/servant of God is the representative of Israel, the people (sons, the corporate son) of God. (cf. Pss 2:7; 89:3–4, 19–29; 110:1; Exod 4:22f).

The Danielic humanlike figure, who is related to the idea of the firstborn (son) of God, cannot be separated from the idea of the servant based on Exod 4:22f, which could include the concept of the (suffering) servant of God. This could be supported by the belief that the Danielic Son of Man in Dan 7 is identified as the Anointed One (the Davidic messianic figure) who is cut off in Dan 9:24–26 (cf. Ps 89:38–51), 'the suffering and death of the Son of Man' in Daniel. Since these dual ideas, the firstborn/son of God and the servant of God, including the priesthood, and especially the death of the firstborn as the form of the suffering servant could be the basis of the idea of the Danielic Son of Man. Furthermore, it could be the crucial context for the emergence of the idea of the Son of Man as the suffering servant of God in the NT (cf. Mark 10:45; John 3:13–16). The Son of Man, who as the kingly messianic figure of Dan 9:24–26, deserved to be served in Dan 7:13f; however, he paradoxically took the role of the suffering Servant, the same figure as the Davidic messianic king in Isa 9:1–7; 11:1–16; 55:3; 61:1–11, for the restoration or the new exodus of Israel from exile and even for the restoration of the gentiles in Deutero-Isaiah (cf. Isa 52:13–53:12).

Seventhly, in Ps 80:17 'the son of man' (בֶּן־אָדָם) is related to Israel's status as firstborn son in the context of the exodus (cf. the vine [shoot] brought out of Egypt and planted in Canaan in Ps 80:8ff, 14f; Exod 15:17; 23:28ff; 2 Sam 7:10; Pss 44:2; 78:55; Isa 5:1–7; 27:2–6; Jer 2:21; 12:10; Ezek 15:1–8; 17:1–10; 19:10–14; Hos 10:1; Amos 9:15; John 15:1) and to Israel, 'the man' (אִישׁ), 'the son of man' (בֶּן־אָדָם) in Ps 80:17, sitting on the throne beside Yahweh's throne in the context of the restoration. The imageries of Yahweh as the divine king enthroned over the cherubim and surrounded by the heavenly council (cf. Yahweh Elohim Sabaoth in Ps 80:1, 4, 7, 9) in the context of the expectation for the restoration, or new exodus, of Israel from exile in Ps 80 show the same tradition of the theophany-*merkabah* background related to the restoration of Israel, the saints of the Most High, in Dan 7. Thus, the two references (Dan 7:13 and Ps 80:17) are not different from each other in connection with the sonship of Israel based on the first exodus (Exod 4:22f). On the basis of this, the expectation for the restoration, the new exodus, of Israel is portrayed. Furthermore, as in Dan 7, the enthronement of 'the son of man' ('the man') as the son of God to be seated at the right hand of Yahweh's throne in the heavenly council in Ps 80 alludes to the enthronement of David or the Davidic king in Pss 2:7; 89; 110:1. This fits in with the concept of the firstborn as the representative, which originated from the Passover exodus (Exod 4:22f) and was applied to the Davidic king on the basis of Nathan's oracle in 2 Sam 7:12–16; Pss 2:7; 89:3f, 20–29 (cf. Isa 9:1–7; 11:1–16; 52:13–53:12; 55:3; 61:1–11).

Eighthly, 'the man' and 'the son of man' in Ps 8:4; 80:17 referring to *the man* (אֱנוֹשׁ) and *the son of man* (בֶּן אָדָם) has to be considered. 'The son of man' in Ps 8:4, alluding to Gen 1:26ff, is not a messianic title, but we have to note the idea of Adam or the first man who, as the image of God, had been crowned with his kingship and sovereignty of glory and honour to rule the created universe ('the Last Adam' cf. 1 Cor 15:24–27; Eph 1:19–22; Heb 2:5–9; Matt 21:16). 'The son of man' ('the man') was installed with God's authority and kingship in Ps 8:4 as the representative of God to accomplish God's will for the created world, thus, alluding to the idea of the servant of God. However, 'the son of man' ('the man') is the representative of the whole creation, alluding to the firstborn; in this case the firstborn of the whole creation of God. The fall of 'the son of man' ('the man') brought about the fall of all creation in Gen 3 (cf. 1 Cor 15:21ff). Furthermore, the roles of the servant and the firstborn, including the priesthood, were given to 'the son of man' ('the man'), which explains man's position between God and the rest of creation. Therefore, 'the son of man' ('the man') in Ps 8:4 reflects the themes of firstborn, servanthood, representative, priesthood and kingship, found in the first man, Adam in Gen 1–2. These are important descriptions of the status of Israel, the Davidic king, the Isaianic suffering Servant, Davidic messianic king, and the Danielic Son of Man figure.

However, if 'the man' ('the son of man') of *Yahweh's right hand* in Ps 80:17 is also related to the tradition of Ps 110:1f, the priesthood of 'the man' ('the son of man') in Ps 80:17 has to be considered, because the Israelite king, David, in Ps 110 clearly includes the thought of the priesthood after the order of Melchizedek in Ps 110:1, 4. This reveals the dual offices of kingship and priesthood bestowed on David or the Davidic king in the context of the coronation in Zion (Jerusalem/Salem) (cf. 2 Sam 5:1–12). In Ps 110:1, David or the Davidic king reigns over the kingdom of Israel, alluding to Ps 2:7; Dan 7:13f. In Ps 110:4, David or the Davidic king at the enthronement was installed as the high priest after the order of Melchizedek (cf. Gen 14:17–24; Ezek 45:21ff; Heb 5–7; Exod 19:5f).

Ninthly, the Son of Man texts in Dan 7:1–28: Pss 80:1–19; 8:1–9 show the antithesis between 'the man' ('the Son of Man') and other creatures. Dan 7 presents the antithesis between the four beasts in the setting of the great sea and the humanlike figures (the Ancient of Days and the 'one like a son of man') in the setting of the theophany-*merkabah* of the heavenly assembly. The four beasts symbolize the four gentile kingdoms or their four gentile kings. The four beasts that *came up out of the great sea* could symbolize the chaotic powers or the sea-monsters (cf. Rahab or Leviathan) who fought against Yahweh in the creation narrative (Job 26; cf. Job 12; 7:12). Further the same motif could be found in the narrative of the crossing of the Red Sea in Exod 14:1–15:21, when the Egyptians and the Pharaoh were destroyed by Yahweh. In particular, Rahab, the dragon-like chaotic sea-monster (cf. Leviathan) was often used as the name for the Egyptians or the Pharaoh in the context of the exodus and of the restoration (new exodus) of Israel from exile (cf. Isa 51:9–11; 26:20–27:1; Pss 74:12–14; 89:9–10; Ezek 32:1–6). In Ps 80, Israel and her enemies respectively symbolize 'the son of man' ('the man') and the beasts against the background of the expectation of deliverance of Israel from exile. This is similar to the contrast between the human figures and the four beasts in Dan 7. Further, the antithesis between humanity ('the son of man,' 'the man') and the animals including birds and fish ruled by him ('the son of man,' 'the man') in Ps 8:4–8, could be reflected in the contrast between Israel and the nations in Ps 80:13–17; Dan 7:1–14. The antithesis in these Son of Man references illustrates the intimate relation between the (new) creation and the restoration (the new exodus).

Tenthly, *merkabah*-theophany traditions in Jewish Apocalyptic Literature show the importance of Ezek 1:26ff; Dan 7:13 (9–28); Exod 4:22f (19:5f); Ps 80:17; 2 Sam 7:14; Pss 2:7; 89:3f, 19–29; 110:1, 4. The main concern of the *merkabah* tradition is the expectation that Israel, as the firstborn of God, is sitting on the throne set among the heavenly assembly (cf. targumic-rabbinic traditions on Gen 28:12; *The Prayer of Joseph*; *Conf. Ling.* 146). This deification (*apotheosis*) of Jacob-Israel means the restoration of the nation Jacob-Israel (as the firstborn of God) afflicted by the gentiles (cf. Exod 4:22f). In the *merkabah*-theophany scene of Dan 7, at the coronation where the heavenly humanlike figure as the son/firstborn of God sits on a heavenly throne-chariot is being given royal authority or royal honour, this reminds the reader of the enthronement of the Davidic prince based on Yahweh's covenant with David (2 Sam 7:12–16; Pss 2:7; 89:26–29; 110:1; cf. *Metatron* in *3 En.*; Rabbinic Controversy about Two Powers [Thrones]; *4QFlor.*; *4QPsDanA*ª). These interpretations of the identity of the heavenly humanlike figure appearing in Dan 7:13 support my argument regarding the dual concepts (the son/firstborn of God and the servant of God) based on Exod 4:22–23; 19:5–6 (cf. Ps 80:1–19) and its development with reference to the Davidic messianic king based on 2 Sam 7:12–16; Ps 89:26–29 (cf. Isa 9:1–7; 11:1–16; 55:3; 61:1–11). Further to this, *Midr. Ps* 2:9 on Ps 2:7 quoting Exod 4:22; Isa 42:1; 52:13; Pss 2:7f; 110:1; Dan 7:13–14, shows the intimate interrelationship of the Firstborn (Son) of God, the suffering servant of God, the Davidic king, the Son of Man, and the High Priest, in the light of the dual concepts (the son/firstborn of God and the servant of God) based on the death of the firstborn (the paschal lamb) in Exod 4:22f; 19:5f.

This ten point summary of the development of Old Testament Christological development has presented a number of important issues in relation to this study. The fact that diverse and paradoxical Christological titles can be combined with one other is explained by the dual concepts (the son/firstborn of God and the servant of God including the priesthood) and by the idea of the firstborn (esp. the death of the firstborn) in Exod 4:22f; 19:5f. These are reflected in the Davidic king (cf. 2 Sam 7:12–16; Pss 2:7; 89:1–37), the Isaianic suffering servant of God (who is the same figure as the Davidic messianic king, cf. Isa 9:1–7; 11:1–16; 52:13–53:12; 55:3; 61:1–11; Ps 89:38–51), and the Danielic Son of Man figure (cf. Dan 7:13–28; 9:24–26). The theme of the firstborn and especially the death of the firstborn is the basis that some, paradoxical or seemingly irrelevant, Christological titles can be combined with one other in the NT (cf. Mk 10:45; John 1:29–34; John 3:13–18). The death of the firstborn or the paschal lamb set against the background of the original Passover is a crucial key to unlock some Christological questions against the background of the eschatological restoration. These questions revolve around, the death of the Son (πρωτότοκος μονογενής ἀγαπητός) of God, the suffering of the Davidic Messianic King, the identity of the enigmatic Isaianic suffering servant of the Lord, and the passion of the Son of Man. Therefore, we can recognize the importance of the paschal-new exodus motif for understanding the identity of Jesus and his works reflected in some major Christological titles in the NT.

v) Basic Presuppositions for My Argument

a) Continuing Exile

I concur with Wright, who argues that most Jews living in Palestine in the Second Temple period regarded their plight under the gentiles as a continuing exile:

> Most Jews in this period [Second Temple period]... believed that, in all the senses that mattered, Israel's exile was still in progress. Although she had come back from Babylon, the glorious message of the prophets remained unfulfilled. Israel still remained in thrall to foreigners; worse, Israel's god had not returned to Zion.[72]

Brunson also argues that the OT (the Prophets) after the Babylonian exile and the Second Temple Jewish literature show:

> a widespread view that Israel remained in a state of exile well after the sixth century, and that this would continue until Yahweh

---

[72] Wright, *People*, 268–269 (my addition); *idem.*, *Victory*, 126–127, 203–204. Also, Brunson, *Psalm 118*, 63–69, 153–154; C. A. Evans, 'Jesus,' 77–100; J. M. Scott, 'Galatians 3.10,' 187–213; The Collection of Essays in J. M. Scott (ed.), *Exile*; E. P. Sanders, *Jesus*, 77–119; M. A. Knibb 'Exile,' 253–272; Ackroyd, *Exile*, 242–243. *Contra* B. Pitre, *Tribulation*, 31–40, who criticizing Wright's view of a continuing exile, argues that 'For while *no* first-century Jew living in the land would have considered themselves to still be in exile, *every* first-century Jew would have known that the ten tribes of the northern kingdom were still in exile... In other words, the glorious message of the prophets of necessity awaited the end of the Assyrian Exile. For it was the Assyrian Exile of ten of the twelve tribes which has scattered the greater part of Israel among the Gentiles, never to be gathered again.' (p. 38, original emphasis). Also, Dennis, *Gathering*, 80–88; J. D. G. Dunn, 'Jesus,' 21–26; Bryan, *Jesus*, 12–20; S. Kim, *Paul*, 136–141; K. R. Snodgrass, 'Reading,' 61–76; M. Casey, 'Where,' 99–100; B. W. Longenecker, *Triumph*, 138; I. H. Jones, 'Disputed,' 401–405. Cf. S. McKnight, *Vision*, 6, 10–11; D. H. Stern, *Restoring*, 26, 34–43. Cf. for the references concerning the restoration of the twelve tribes in the OT and Jewish literature, Pitre, *ibid.*, 37 nn. 130–131; Dennis, *ibid.*, 85 nn. 34–35; J. M. Scott, 'Rom 11:26,' 519 n. 79.

intervened decisively to inaugurate the eschatological era, restore his people and return to reign as king amongst them.[73]

The destruction of the Temple, and the dispersion and deportation of Israel, are very closely related to Israel's various exiles throughout history and particularly the Babylonian exile, in the OT and Second Temple Judaism. However, the reversal of these tragedies being Israel's deliverance from foreign domination, the establishment of a new Temple, and Israel's return to the land are key elements in the restoration ideas of both the OT and the Second Temple texts.

b) The Sin-Exile-Restoration Pattern

I agree with Dennis who proposes the theory of the so-called Sin-Exile-Restoration pattern based on the covenantal blessings and curses in Deut 4:27–31. As that which 'provided the historical and theological framework in which to interpret Israel's pattern of sin, punishment and hope for full renewal and restoration throughout its history' (sin, judgment [exile/dispersion] and restoration [gathering/return]) in the OT and Judaism.[74] Brunson further argues that:

> The curse of exile as a consequence for sin, warned of in Deut 8, had taken place, but the prophets expected a restoration from exile as promised in Deut 30:1–10.... Because exile is the consequence of sin, restoration depends on the removal of this state of guilt.[75]

The removal of Israel's sin through forgiveness is the crucial prerequisite for the restoration of Israel from exile.[76] As Brunson further comments: 'Thus when Jesus forgives it is an effecting of the restoration. When he

---

[73] Brunson, *Psalm 118*, 63–69, quoted from 68–69. Cf. Hag 2:6–7; Ezra 3:10–13; Neh 1:5–9; 9:36; Zech 1:12, 16–17; *Jub.* 1:1–14, 22–25; *2 Macc.* 1:27–29; 2:7–8, 18; *Tob.* 14:5–7. Also, see R. E. Watts, 'Consolation,' 31–32. Even Dennis, *Gathering*, 89–116, 350 recognizes this, after surveying Jewish literature up to the late first century CE: 'Israel remains under the curses of the covenant, or the age of wrath, in which foreign domination and exile/dispersion constitute Israel's present plight.' (p. 116).

[74] Dennis, *Gathering*, 89–127, esp. 89–93 (quoted from 90); Wright, *People*, 261; Brunson, *Psalm 118*, 63–64, 163–179; Scott, 'Galatians 3.10,' 195–213.

[75] Brunson, *Psalm 118*, 63–64; Scott, 'Galatians 3.10,' 205–206.

[76] Wright, *Victory*, 268–274; Dennis, *Gathering*, 125–129; Brunson, *Psalm 118*, 166–167, who also points out that it is reflected in John 20:23, where the resurrected Jesus commissioned his disciples to proclaim the message of the forgiveness of sin. Cf. Isa 1:25–27; 4:3–4; 53:4–12; Jer 31:31–33; Ezek 36:24–29, 33; 37:23–28; *Bar.* 1–3; 5:6; *Tob.* 3:4; 13:5–9; 14:4; *1 Macc.* 1:6–13, 64; 8:18; *2 Macc.* 4:13–17; 5:15–20; 6:12–17; 7:32; *4 Macc.* 7:21; *4 Ezra* 5:28; 10:19–22; *2 Bar.* 8:1–2; 13:9; 64:4–7; 80:1–7; *Tg. Isa* 8:7–8; 28:2; 32:14. Also, S. McKnight, *Vision*, 44–45 argues that, through table fellowship, Jesus symbolizes the end of exile, restoration, forgiveness and social acceptance, as in the case of Jehoiachin in 2 Kings 25:27–30.

speaks of forgiveness, he is speaking the language of the return, a language the exiles understand well.'[77]

c) Old Testament Use in John

Regarding the interrelationship between the OT and the NT, I basically follow the position of C. H. Dodd.[78] He argued that the NT writers highly respected the original context of the OT references which they used (quoted or alluded to). Following Dodd's standpoint, Holland argues that:

> there was an established hermeneutic in the early church which centred around the fulfilment of the new exodus promises and that within that context the NT writers show a strict respect for the original meaning and setting of the OT texts which they used.[79]

Having the same viewpoint as this, Brunson[80] argues how the OT was used in John:

> The Formula quotations show that even the most formal use of Scripture in John is allusive, that he refers primarily to those sections of the OT that were interpreted eschatologically, and that he appeals most often to the Psalms. Although not as obvious as formal quotations, the Fourth Gospel is also replete with OT themes, imagery, and symbols—an OT bedrock that is no less real for being subtle. John employs the feasts and other Jewish institutions to provide structure and plot development. The replacement theme situates John's Jesus firmly in Judaism, so that his ministry and identity are understood vis-à-vis Jewish practice and belief.[81]

Also, Ng argues that the OT in John was used 'to show the identity of Jesus as Christ, to explain his acts as messianic, and to interpret the details of his

---

[77] Brunson, *Psalm 118*, 167; Dennis, *Gathering*, 125.
[78] C. H. Dodd, *According*; idem., 'Testament,' 167–181, followed by I. H. Marshall, 'Assessment,' 195–216; Brunson, *Psalm 118*, 19–20; Holland, *Motif*, 33–48. *Contra* B. Lindars, 'Place,' 137–145.
[79] Holland, *Motif*, 47.
[80] Brunson, *Psalm 118*, 19–20, 141–153. For studies of OT quotations (and allusions to) in John, see Brunson, *ibid.*, 141–144; C. K. Barrett, 'Testament,' 155–169; D. A. Carson, 'John,' 245–264; A. T. Hanson, 'Scripture,' 358–379; M. Hengel, 'Gospel,' 380–395; Porter, 'Traditional,' 396–428; W. Y. Ng, *Symbolism*, 156–159; E. D. Freed, *Quotations*; M. J. J. Menken, *Quotations*.
[81] Brunson, *Psalm 118*, 152–153. Cf. the Lamb of God (1:29, 36); the shepherd imagery and sheep (10:1–16); the vine and branches (15:1–8, 16); allusions to Abraham (8:33, 39, 40, 52, 53, 56, 57, 58); Jacob (1:51; 4:6, 12); Joseph (4:5) and Elijah (1:21; 4:25); 'I Am' sayings; the concept of Wisdom/Logos; Sabbath (5:9, 10, 16, 18; 7:22, 23; 9:14, 16; 19:31) and the Law (1:17, 45; 7:19, 23, 49, 51; 8:5, 17; 10:34; 12:34; 15:25; 19:7); King of Israel (1:49; 12:13); Messiah (1:41; 4:25); Moses (1:17, 45; 3:14; 5:45, 46; 6:32; 7:19, 22 (twice), 23; 8:5; 9:28, 29); extensive exodus themes; OT institutions; OT feasts (Passover, Tabernacle), a Jewish feast (Dedication).

life and death as being anticipated in the Old Testament.'[82] Porter rightly points out that the Passover theme is the 'one that in conjunction with the OT fulfilment motif binds together the entire Gospel.'[83]

d) Research Area

This book aims to discover the paschal-new exodus motif of John's Gospel, by focussing on the first four chapters of that Gospel. Other than to limit book size, there is no specific reason for confining my study to the first four chapters. However, on the whole I agree with B. H. Throckmorton,[84] who suggests that one of main themes of John 2–4 is the new religious order replacing the old Jewish religious order, with the appearance of Jesus. This appearance ushers in, 'the new Temple' (2:13–22), 'the new generation' (3:1–10), and 'the new water' (4:1–42). I will therefore examine John 1–4 by dividing it into the following headings: the Prologue (John 1:1–18), Some Testimonies (John 1:19–51), Water into Wine Miracle (John 2:1–11), Jesus's Action in the Temple (John 2:12–25), Jesus and Nicodemus (John 3:1–21), Jesus and John the Baptist (John 3:22–36), Jesus and the Samaritan Woman (John 4:1–42) and Jesus's Healing (John 4:43–54).

---

[82] Ng, *Symbolism*, 158; Carson, 'John,' 246–247.
[83] Porter, 'Traditional,' 397.
[84] B. H. Throckmorton, *Creation*, 102. Also, C. H. Dodd, *Interpretation*, 297; F. F. Bruce, *John*, 77; B. Lindars, *John*, 133.

Chapter 1: The Prologue (John 1:1–18)

1.1 Introduction

1.1.1 The Origin of the Prologue

Discussions about the Prologue of John's Gospel have often concentrated on historical, theological and literary questions. Such questions relate to the origin of the Prologue, its authorship, literary styles, and its composition stages. Further questions are raised as to the relationship between it and the rest of the Gospel, its OT background, particularly the origin of the concept of 'the Logos,' the incarnation of the Logos, and its theological meaning. In order to discover the background and the meaning of the Johannine Logos, theologians have often studied Hellenistic Philosophy, Gnosticism, the OT, Jewish Wisdom literature, Targum and Rabbinic sources, and Philo's works, but have not reached any clear consensus. What is the background of John's usage concerning 'the Logos' and the incarnation of the Logos as a separate, real person? By employing this term, what is it that John describes about Jesus's identity and about the distinction of his work as regards the history of salvation?

The arguments of Johannine scholars concerning the origin of the Prologue of the Fourth Gospel can be divided into two main groups. First, some argue that the Evangelist uses a source hymn(s) with some additions and redaction of especially the passages concerning John the Baptist (vv. 6–8, 15). However, there are various opinions about the extent of the source poem's origin and content, and about additions and redaction.[85] Based on Mandaean literature and *the Odes of Solomon*, Bultmann[86] contends that the Evangelist used a source hymn where the sect of John the Baptist praised the Baptist as the revealer of Gnosticism. However, pointing to the parallelism, the pairing of similar sounding clauses, the call and response structure, Jeremias argues that 'the Prologue is a powerfully contrived song, an early Christian religious poem, a psalm and a hymn to the Logos, Jesus Christ.'[87] Dodd[88] argues that the Prologue of John's Gospel shares

---

[85] E.g., R. E. Brown, *John I-XII*, 18–23; R. Schnackenburg, *John*, I, 224–232, esp. 221–229; D. Lee, *Flesh*, 30.

[86] R. Bultmann, *John*, 13–17. However, E. Harris, *Prologue*, 19 says Bultmann's argument concerning the Evangelist's interpolation is not convincing. J. Jeremias, 'Revealing,' 72 also criticizes Bultmann's basic argument that the Prologue originated from a circle of the followers of John the Baptist.

[87] Jeremias, 'Revealing,' 72 also says that the Prologue could be divided into four strophes, 1–5/6–8/9–13/14–18 and that it could be distinguished into two between the original Prologue composed in Greek by Christians and the comments of the Evangelist about it (pp. 74f). J. Painter, 'Christology,' 460–474, esp. 466–468 also says that the original hymn had a wisdom (*sophia*) tradition of a Hellenist community, and that the Evangelist modified from wisdom

common ideas with the Poimandres tractate (Hermetic Writings). Brown[89] reconstructs an original hymn composed of 4 strophes, 1–2/3–5/10–12b/14–16. He thinks that to this original hymn, there were some additions of vv. 9, 12c–13 and 17–18 for explanation and then vv. 6–8 and 15 concerning John the Baptist. Rissi[90] and Deeks[91] think that the Prologue was composed of two separate source hymns.

Secondly, there are other Johannine theologians who argue that the Prologue as it now stands was written by the Evangelist and has a literary and theological unity.[92] Barrett says that, even though there have been diverse attempts to recover the original poetic structure of the Prologue by the supporters of the source hymn theory, the original poem does not actually exist. He rejects the suggestion that the Prologue was composed of poetic structure and contends it has just 'prose rhythm.' He argues that 'the whole passage shows, on careful exegesis, a marked internal unity, and also a distant unity of theme and subject-matter with the remainder of the Gospel.'[93] That is to say, the Prologue and the rest of the Gospel are one piece of theological writing. Dunn also comments that:

> I find it impossible to regard the Prologue of John's Gospel as redactional (i.e. added after the Fourth Evangelist put the Gospel into its present form); the themes of the Prologue are too closely integrated into the Gospel as a whole and are so clearly intended to

---

Christology to Logos Christology in the context of conflict between the early Jewish Christianity and the synagogue.

[88] C. H. Dodd, *Interpretation*, 10–53.

[89] Brown, *John I-XII*, 18–23. E. Kasemann, *Testament*, 138–152 says that vv. 1–13 is a Christian hymn, v. 12 is the climax of the hymn and v. 13 as a note is added by the author, and vv. 14–18 is an epilogue. S. Kim, *Exposition*, 33–34 assumes that the Prologue of John's Gospel, like in the Synoptics (cf. the narrative of the genealogy of Jesus was added to the testimony of the Baptist in Matthew and Luke), originally started with the testimony of the Baptist in vv. 6–8, 15, 19 to which the account concerning the Logos was added to help the Greek audience understand the Gospel (esp. concerning the divine Logos and his incarnation for God's revelation and salvation), who were familiar with the philosophical concept of logos.

[90] M. Rissi, 'John 1:1–18,' 394–401 says that the Johannine author adopted and expanded two hymns from the liturgy of his church. The first hymn was made up of vv. 1–2, 3–4, 5–10 and 11–12ab with the background of Gen 1, and the second one was vv. 14–18 in the light of the Exodus of the OT (Exod 33; 34; Ezek 37; 43; 48).

[91] D. G. Deeks, 'Prologue,' 62–78 proposes that source A, 'a Christian Gnostic hymn' was originally formed with 1ab, 3–5, 9–13, and source B, 'a creed' which probably belonged to the Evangelist's own community, 14abc, 16a, 18. At first, these two sources were adopted and constructed by the Evangelist with redaction and interpolation, and further modified by post-Johannine scribes for diverse ecclesiastical readers.

[92] E.g., C. K. Barrett, *John*, 149–151; E. Harris, *Prologue*; T. L. Brodie, *John*, 134; P. Borgen, 'True Light,' 115–130; R. A. Culpepper, 'Pivot,' 1–31; N. T. Wright, *People*, 416; S. R. Valentine, 'Johannine,' 291–304; A. B. Alexander, 'Logos,' 394–399, 467–472, esp. 470f.

[93] Barrett, *John*, 149ff, quoted from p. 150. Also, D. A. Carson, *John*, 111–112.

introduce these themes that such a conclusion is rendered implausible.[94]

The central subject of the controversy between the Jews and Jesus and of the subsequent discourse focussed on the origin of Jesus. The conclusion of the dispute was usually because of their lack of knowledge about Jesus sent from God; as Hooker[95] concludes, 'without it [the Prologue] the chapters which follow are incomprehensible to us, as to the Jewish opponents in the story.'

As Barrett has pointed out, the results of attempts to recover an original poem seem to depend on the presupposition or the imagination of those who try to do it.[96] I believe it is better to study the Prologue as it now stands. The important thing is that the Prologue has its literary and theological unity with the body of the Gospel, composed by the Evangelist. Here, Hooker's observation needs to be noted. Without a clear knowledge about the Logos's identity from the Prologue, we cannot completely understand Jesus's identity and his work in the body of the Gospel of John. If the Prologue has an absolutely intimate relationship to the rest of the Gospel according to the purpose of the writing of the author, sometimes the unclear part in the Prologue can be understood in the light of the remainder of the Gospel.

1.1.2 The Central Passage of the Prologue

What is the central passage and theme of the Prologue? Recently, concerning the literary structure of the Prologue, Endo[97] rejects chiastic structural understandings or symmetric parallel structural understandings, and suggests a tripartite parallel structure. Endo[98] divides the Prologue into three narratives—the first stanza (vv. 1–5), the second stanza (vv. 6–13), and

---

[94] J. D. G. Dunn, 'John,' 366 n. 78. See also J. A. T. Robinson, 'Relation,' 121–129, who has the same opinion and presupposes the written order of the Johannine writings as follows; the body of the Gospel, the Epistles, the Epilogue and the Prologue of the Gospel. Cf. R. N. Longenecker, *Christology*, 57. Ed. L. Miller, 'Johannine,' 445–457 also thinks that according to the written order of the Johannine writings themselves, the Logos concept in the Prologue could be developed from just 'word' or 'words' as the saving truth discoursed by Jesus in the Fourth Gospel proper, and then 'the Word of life' in the First Johannine Epistle, lastly to 'the Word' as a full-blown Christological title in the Gospel Prologue.

[95] M. D. Hooker, 'Prologue,' 40–58, quoted from 51 ([] added by this writer). Cf. John 5:37; 8:58; 10:34–36.

[96] Barrett, *Prologue*, 13–17; Robinson, 'Relation,' 120–129, esp. 122; E. Harris, *Prologue*; M. Endo, *Creation*, 184, 230–248. C. R. Koester, *Dwelling*, 101 says that 'even though the evangelist may have used a logos-hymn as a source, the present form of the prologue can be treated as a unified composition and an integral part of the gospel.' Also, Dennis, *Gathering*, 137 n. 86.

[97] Endo, *Creation*, 195–205.

[98] Endo, *Creation*, 203–204.

the third stanza (vv. 14–18)—and argues that important theological motifs are repeated, enlarged and developed in each stanza. These important motifs are the divine identity of the Logos, namely, the pre-existence of the Logos, the intimacy of the Logos with God (or oneness motif), the lordship of the Logos as the Creator (vv. 3, 10, 14c–15), and the coming (the incarnation) of the Logos and the response of the world against the Logos (vv. 5, 9, 14).

Traditionally, the Logos and his incarnation are thought of as the important doctrine, the climax of the Prologue, therefore being v. 14.[99] However, Culpepper[100] criticizes the argument that the central verse of the Prologue is v. 14. By analysing the literary structure of the Prologue, he states that the pivotal verse, the climax of the Prologue, is v. 12b (cf. 'he gave them the right to become children of God'), with which the Prologue has chiastic structure. Kasemann[101] also suggests that v. 12 is the climax of the Christian hymn in vv. 1–13 in the context of eschatological salvation. N. W. Lund[102] offers v. 13 as the central verse of the Prologue. And Dennis[103] argues that vv. 12–13 are the central passages of the Prologue, functioning as a theological/soteriological pivot. Further, P. Lamarche[104] contends that vv. 10–13 are the central passages of the Prologue made within a chiastic frame in the context of the plan of salvation for all; vv. 1–9 for the gentile and vv. 14–18 for the Jew. It is right that these theologians argue the significance of v. 12b or v. 12 or v. 12 or vv. 12–13 or vv. 10–13 in the light of eschatological salvation, even though it is difficult to accept Lamarche's argument about the division of the Prologue into two sections, one for the gentiles and the other for the Jews. Verses 12–13 disclose the importance of salvation as a theme of the Gospel. Dennis writes that:

> Verses 1–13 of the prologue narrate, in concise form, the eternal Logos' salvific mission, from before creation (v. 1), to his rejection by his creation and 'his own' (vv. 10–11), to the reception by those who became the children of God, the 'new creation' (vv. 12–13). There is a sort of spiralling downward motion detected in the portrayal of the Logos: from the general (creation/world) to the

---

[99] I. H. Marshall, 'Incarnational,' 2; Robinson, 'Relation,' 124; G. R. Beasley-Murray, *John*, 4.
[100] Culpepper, 'Pivot,' 1–31, esp. 13–15 says that the incarnation of the Logos is referred to in vv. 9–10 as well as v. 14, and that the structure of the Prologue is not chronicle but chiastic. Also, D. M. Smith, *John*, 48; Carson, *John*, 113; Dennis, *Gathering*, 137.
[101] Kasemann, *Testament*, 150–152, esp. 165 concludes that the emphasis of the Prologue is not the salvation that happened in the past but the eschatological presence of salvation through the Christ as the creator of eschatological sonship to God and of the new world.
[102] N. W. Lund, 'Influence,' 41–46.
[103] Dennis, *Gathering*, 138–140; J. Staley, 'Structure,' 241–246.
[104] P. Lamarche, 'Prologue,' 36–52.

specific (Israel) and then finally at the 'bottom' the focus on the restored Israel begins to point up again. In a sense, the whole story is present in 1.1–13 — from creation to redemption.[105]

The passage links the idea of becoming children of God with being 'born of God.' Thereby salvation is expressed with the image of 'generation' (or 'spiritual regeneration'). This image of generation can be fully noted in Jesus's conversation with Nicodemus in John 3.[106] Further, if the Prologue and the rest of the Gospel are one piece of writing elaborately designed by the Evangelist, then the purpose of writing foreseen in the Prologue as the introduction to the body of John's Gospel ought to be manifested in the conclusion of the Gospel. In this respect, it is first necessary to look at the purpose of the Fourth Evangelist stated in John 20:30–31. From this passage, it is not difficult to recognize two main things: first, the christological purpose; secondly the soteriological purpose. These two are intimately combined, and hence are difficult, and I suggest unnecessary, to separate. The first purpose of the writing is to help the reader to believe that Jesus is the Christ (Messiah), the Son of God. The second purpose is that, by believing him as the Christ and the Son of God, the believer has confidence that he/she has 'life' in his name. What must not be ignored in these verses is that the Evangelist expresses salvation as being bestowed with life. From many references in the Gospel, salvation is expressed with this concept of life or eternal life (cf. John 3:16). Salvation is referred to as the having of eternal life in the dialogue between Jesus and Nicodemus in John 3.

Furthermore, in v. 14 the incarnation of the Logos, which is mainly interpreted as a christological title, has to be interpreted in the context of salvation found in vv. 12–13. We cannot sharply divide the Prologue into the pre-existent Logos in vv. 1–13 and the incarnate Logos in vv. 14–18. Therefore the incarnation of the Logos should be interpreted not only in the light of Christology but also of Soteriology.

In this chapter, I will survey the overall identity of the Logos and his work, which are reflected in 1:1–13. I will then interact with the incarnate Logos and his works as highlighted in vv. 14–18, as these relate to the rest of the Gospel, but especially 3:13–18. I will then discuss the Logos in light of the OT (cf. Isa 55:11 and the Son of Man in Dan 7:13) and some other materials, and thereby find the meaning of the Johannine incarnate Logos and the identity of the Logos and his works. Further, I will discuss some suggestions about the background of the Johannine Logos and propose a

---

[105] Dennis, *Gathering*, 138–139.
[106] D. Wilkinson, *Creation*, 137.

theory about the Johnnine Logos in connection with the dual concepts of sonship and servanthood based on Exod 4:22–23; 19:5–6; the only (firstborn/beloved) Son of God, the Deutero-Isaianic suffering servant of the Lord, the Davidic messianic king, and the Danielic Son of Man (cf. the theophany-*merkabah* tradition).

1.2 The Logos and his Works (John 1:1–13)

The opening verse of the Gospel of John clearly recalls the first verse of Genesis, because 'In the beginning' (בְּרֵאשִׁית / ἐν ἀρχῇ) is not only the first phrase of the Bible, but the title of the first book of the Bible. Jeremias[107] suggests that the first few verses of the Prologue intentionally alludes to the first few words of the Bible, although the beginning of the Prologue means eternity before all creation, and the beginning of Genesis designates the creation. Further, Borgen [108] states that John 1:1–5 is a targumic reinterpretation against the beginning and the first day of creation in Gen 1:1–5. Even Bultmann [109] admits the relationship between the creation account in Genesis and the first few verses of the Johannine Prologue as well. Nevertheless, he[110] argues that the Gnostic Logos doctrine influenced not only the Johannine Logos but also other Logos ideas in Philo, the Jewish wisdom literature and the rabbinic writings.

Firstly, we can understand the pre-existence of the Logos and his identity as God the creator. Before the universe was created by God, there was only God. Therefore, the existence of the Logos before the creation of the world discloses his divine deity as God (cf. μονογενὴς θεός in v. 18). Since the first few verses allude to the creation narrative of Genesis, Johannine scholars think the identity of the Logos could be discussed against the background of the OT and Judaism. Also, the Logos could be understood in the light of creation (John 1:3–4). In v. 3 (cf. v. 10b), the role of the Logos as the agent in the creation of the heavens and the earth is repeatedly emphasized: 'through him' (the Logos), or 'without him.' Verse 3 further emphasises that all creatures without exception were created by means of the Logos:

---

[107] Jeremias, 'Revealing,' 79; O. Cullmann, 'Word,' 249–269; P. Borgen, 'Logos,' 92; *idem*., 'Targumic,' 288–295; *idem*., *Logos*, 15–18; Kim, *Exposition*, 35–38; Wilkinson, *Creation*, 129, 132; M. Hengel, *Christology*, 371–372; Lee, *Flesh*, 31; J. B. Polhill, 'John 1–4,' 446; W. Y. Ng, *Symbolism*, 157; M. Davies, *Rhetoric*, 81–82; W. S. Kurz, 'Intertextual,' 179–190; Endo, *Creation*, 206–208; M. L. Coloe, *Dwells*, 23; Brown, *John I-XII*, 217; *idem*., *John XIII-XXI*, 908; F. F. Bruce, *John*, 28–29.
[108] Borgen, 'Logos,' 92; *idem*., 'Targumic,' 288–295; Endo, *Creation*.
[109] Bultmann, *John*, 6–10; *idem*., *Theology*, II, 64.
[110] Bultmann, *John*, 8.

'all things,' 'nothing.'[111] The Logos is the mediator of creation. So, Bruce writes that:

> it is not by accident that the Gospel begins with the same phrase as the book of Genesis. In Gen 1:1 'In the beginning' introduces the story of the old creation; here it introduces the story of the new creation. In both works of creation the agent is the Word of God.[112]

Therefore, with reference to 'in the beginning' (vv. 1–2), the Evangelist discloses the direction or the main focus of the Fourth Gospel in the light of the creation of Genesis; that is, the new creation story in connection with Jesus's works (cf. John 20:30–31). Hengel [113] points out that 'in the beginning' (Ἐν ἀρχη) of John 1:1 alludes to Gen 1:1, and 'It is finished' (τετέλεσται) the shout of the victor in John 19:30 set against the background of the crucifixion to the completion of creation by God in Gen 2:1f, 'which signifies the finishing of the work of *new* creation, at the eve of the sixth day.' Here, the Logos who was the agent of the old creation works again as the agent for the new creation, namely, the eschatological salvation.[114]

Further, the Logos is the bearer of life, life and the giver of life. This image of the incarnate Logos, Jesus, as life and the giver of life is seen throughout the Gospel of John.[115] 'He [the Logos] is the source of divine life and power both in the old and in the new creation.'[116] Even though every step of the creation narrative reveals that God gave life to all creatures, the creation of humankind illustrates a significantly more powerful picture of God as the life-giver. The climax of the work of the Logos in creation is that God breathed his breath or spirit/life into the lifeless body so that it became a living being (Gen 2:7).[117] In the OT, there are numerous references to the Israelites praising God as the author of life.[118] Humanity by itself cannot become a viable living being; only God controls life and death.[119]

Becoming the children of God, that is receiving salvation, is the gift given by the Logos to those who believe in and accept the Logos. Those who are

---

[111] Wilkinson, *Creation*, 132.
[112] Bruce, *John*, 28–29; Cullmann, 'Word,' 250.
[113] Hengel, *Christology*, 371–372 (original emphasis). Also, Ng, *Symbolism*, 157; Coloe, *Dwells*, 23; Brown, *John I-XII*, 217; idem., *John XIII-XXI*, 908; Endo, *Creation*, 207–208; W. Meeks, *Prophet-King*, 304.
[114] Ng, *Symbolism*, 163; L. Goppelt, *Typos*, 181; M. Hengel, 'Gospel,' 393; Endo, *Creation*, 208.
[115] Cf. John 6:33, 35, 48, 68; 8:12; 10:10, 28; 11:25; 12:50; 14:6; 17:2.
[116] H.-G. Link, *NIDNTT*, II, 482 ([] added by this writer).
[117] von Rad, *TDNT*, II, 844. Cf. Deut 30:15–20; 32:47; 8:3; Amos 8:1ff; Ezek 37:1–14.
[118] Cf. Jer 17:13; Ps 36:9; 139:13ff.
[119] Cf. Exod 32:32; Mal 3:16; Ps 69:28; Isa 4:3.

'born of God' (ἐκ θεοῦ ἐγεννήθησαν in v. 13) are the children of God.[120] In John 1:13, the Evangelist clearly states that rebirth comes about not by the will or the decision of mankind but only by God. Rebirth[121] is the work of God, beyond the ability of mankind. This is understood in the light of new birth in John 3:3, 5. In this respect, Goppelt[122] rightly observes that one feature of the Gospel of John is that of its emphasis on regeneration, life and eternal life. Here, recognition is made of the vital relationship between rebirth and salvation. God's eschatological salvation is expressed in the light of rebirth or new creation.

Further, several references about 'resurrection' in the Gospel[123] have to be noted with relation to resurrection passages in the Prophets.[124] One of the powerful and creative references of God's spoken word and breath (πνεῦμα/רוּחַ) appears in the vision of the raising of the dry bones in Ezek 37:4ff, 9ff. Through this vision of the resurrection of the dead nation from its grave, God promised Israel deliverance from Babylon (Ezek 37:11–14). This two-step recreation through God's spoken word and breath (πνεῦμα/רוּחַ) alludes to the original creation of humanity in Gen 2:7. The valley of dry bones vision represents God's vital word and breath (πνεῦμα/רוּחַ) in bringing about the new creation or the new birth from the dead.[125] This vision could be understood in the light of the new creation and the new exodus-salvation; the restoration of Israel, the people of God, from exile. This is reflected in the resurrected Jesus's breathing the Holy Spirit to the disciples in John 20:22.[126]

According to Anderson,[127] the message of the new exodus-salvation in Deutero-Isaiah was expressed in the concept of a new creation. That Yahweh is the creator of the world (esp. Israel) is repeatedly referred to within the context of the expectation of the restoration of Israel from exile

---

[120] Cf. Some Johannine scholars, such as L. Sabourin, 'Begotten,' 86–90, interpret 'birth by God' not as 'the birth of the Christian' but as 'the virgin birth of Jesus,' namely, the incarnation of the Logos. However, this is not acceptable. See J. W. Pryor, 'Birth,' 296–318.
[121] A. Ringwald, *NIDNTT*, I, 179.
[122] L. Goppelt, *Theology*, I, 14. See also S. S. Smalley, *John*, 231, who says that 'John's distinctive description is 'eternal life' (ζωή αἰώνιος)' (John 3:15, 16; 5:24ff; 6:68; 10:28; 12:50; 17:2; 20:31), 'the bread of life' (6:35, 48), 'the resurrection and the life' (11:25), 'the way, the truth and the life' (14:6), 'the new-birth' (3:3, 5). Also, Endo, *Creation*, 217.
[123] Cf. John 5:25–29; 6:39, 40, 44, 54; 11:25, 38–44; cf. 20:21.
[124] Cf. Hos 6:1–3; 13:14; Isa 26:19; Dan 12:2; Ezek 37:1–14.
[125] B. Klappert, *NIDNTT*, III, 1100. Cf. Link, *NIDNTT*, II, 480.
[126] Endo, *Creation*, 246–247. Cf. Isa 42:5.
[127] Anderson, *Creation*, 25; Endo, *Creation*, 220–221; P. B. Harner, 'Creation,' 298–306; C. Stuhlmueller, 'Theology,' 429–467. Cf. Ng, *Symbolism*, 163; Hengel, 'Gospel,' 393.

in the OT and Jewish traditions.[128] The idea of the children of God, namely, the begetting children of God in John 1:12–13, is understood as the new creation, which means the eschatological expectation of the restoration of the covenantal people of God.

Above all, as Endo[129] has pointed out, the idea of 'the children of God' in v. 12 alludes to the idea that Israel was corporately chosen as the son of God, the firstborn of God in Exod 4:22–23 (Deut 14:1; 32:6) in the OT. The Father-son relationship between Yahweh and Israel is recalled against the background of the expectation of the restoration of Israel from exile (Hos 11:1; Jer 3:19; Isa 1:2, 4; 30:1; 45:11–12; 63:8–10 [16]; 64:8).[130]

In particular, Dennis[131] points out that, in John's Gospel, the phrase, 'the children of God' of John 1:12 reappears only in John 11:52, and is set against the background of Caiaphas' prophecy about the death of Jesus and the Jewish religious leaders' conspiracy to kill him. The Evangelist interprets Caiaphas' prophecy (John 11:50) about the death of Jesus as follows: 'Jesus would die for the Jewish nation (ὑπὲρ τοῦ ἔθνους), and not only for that nation but also for the scattered children of God, to bring them together and make them one' (vv. 51–52). Thus, the creation of children of God, namely, the begetting of the children of God in John 1:12–13 is presented as the salvation of the Jewish nation and the restoration of the scattered children of God in John 11:51–52. Dennis[132] points out 'the fact that the Logos' sojourn in the world and among his own will be characterized by rejection and will ultimately result in his death,' and argues that 'the goal of Jesus' ministry as that of begetting children of God in 1.12–13 will become a reality by means of his death.' The Logos who became flesh (ὁ λόγος σὰρξ ἐγένετο) dwelling among the restored people of God is clearly presented as the μονογενής of God the Father (μονογενοῦς παρὰ πατρός) in John 1:14. We can thus recognize the father-son relationship between God and the Logos. That the Logos (the μονογενής of God the Father) came to his own (τὰ ἴδια) but was not received by his own people (οἱ ἴδιοι) could intimate that the Logos, the only Son of God will suffer and be killed by his own people.[133]

---

[128] Endo, *Creation*, 220; Harner, 'Creation,' 298; Stuhlmueller, 'Theology,' 429–467. Cf. Isa 43:1–7; 45:11–13; 64:8; *4 Ezra* 6:55–59; 8:45; *2 Bar.* 14:15–19.
[129] Endo, *Creation*, 221–222.
[130] Endo, *Creation*, 221–222.
[131] Dennis, *Gathering*, 47–48.
[132] Dennis, *Gathering*, 52–54.
[133] Cf. Dennis, *Gathering*, 49, 51 thinks that τὰ ἴδια in v. 11a means 'the Logos' homeland of Israel, in the broad sense of the term (namely, Palestine), that is, the promised land the centre of which is Judea and Jerusalem, the 'place' where YHWH's Temple dwelled' and οἱ ἴδιοι in v. 11b, generally, 'God's historic covenant people,' primarily, 'the Jewish religious leaders' who

In particular, Endo[134] understands 'his (the Logos') name' of John 1:12 within the context of Exod 33–34, where Yahweh proclaimed his name in Exod 33:19 against Moses' begging to show his glory in Exod 33:18. Here, for Endo, Yahweh's name proclaimed to Moses recalls the name revealed to Moses in Exod 3:14 ('I am who I am'/אֶהְיֶה אֲשֶׁר אֶהְיֶה) against the background of the exodus and the Sinai incident. So, Endo argues that the name of the Logos, the Son (μονογενής) makes the restoration of God's people possible. This name (אָנֹכִי אָנֹכִי/ἐγώ εἰμι) often appears as Yahweh's name within the context of the restoration or the new exodus of Israel from exile in Deutero-Isaiah (e.g., Isa 43:11), and is one of the important Christological titles in John. So, the incarnate Logos can be understood as the enfleshment of the Deutero-Isaianic Yahweh.[135]

However, it must be noted that the creation of the new covenantal people of God (namely, the restoration of the people of God) will be made possible by the death of the Logos, the μονογενής (the only/firstborn) Son of God in vv. 12–14 (cf. the paschal lamb and the Son of God in John 1:29, 34; 19:29, 36). This could point to the work, the death, of the firstborn or the paschal lamb in Exod 4:22–23; 12:1–51, which brought about the exodus of Israel, the people of God, who became corporately the son of God, the firstborn of God and the servant of God.

The interpretation that the Johannine Jesus (μονογενής) can be understood as the firstborn of God could be supported by John 20:17. For it is here that the resurrected Jesus called his disciples his brothers, namely, the sons of God. The disciples were restored as the sons of God through the death of Jesus, the Logos, the μονογενής (the only Son) of God, the firstborn of God.[136] Here, we hardly deny the ontological divine deity of the Logos, the μονογενής of God the Father. In vv. 12–13, to all those who received the Logos (the μονογενής of God the Father with regard to v. 14), to those who believed in his name, the Logos gave the right to become children of God. In John 1:13, the becoming of the children of God is explained as divine birth, with the picture that bestows the life of the Holy Spirit. This is reflected in the new birth of water and the Spirit in John 3:1–9 (cf. Ezek 36:24–28; 37:1–28).[137]

---

rejected Jesus (the chief priests, the Pharisees in John 11:47–50, 53). Also, J. W. Pryor, 'Jesus,' 210–214; Carson, *John*, 124; Brown, *John I-XII*, 10; Wilkinson, *Creation*, 132. Kim, *Exposition*, 38–39 and Lee, *Flesh*, 168 think that 'his own' in v. 11 means not only, generally, humankind (the world) in connection with God's creation, but also, particularly, Israel in connection with God's election.

[134] Endo, *Creation*, 222–223.
[135] Brunson, *Psalm 118*.
[136] Endo, *Creation*, 246–247. Cf. C. S. Keener, *John*, 309, following M. J. Harris, *Jesus*, 282–283, says that NT Christology is mainly functional rather than ontological.
[137] Polhill, 'John 1–4,' 447.

Thus, both the becoming of the children of God in v. 12 and the begetting of the children of God in v. 13 mean the creation (the restoration) of the new people of God on the basis of the covenant.[138]

Furthermore, John 1:4–9 could be considered alongside John 8:12, 'I am the light of the world. Whoever follows me will never walk in darkness, but will have the light of life.' This proclamation of Jesus was issued at the Jewish Feast of Tabernacles (John 7–8).[139] It supports the identity of the Logos and his work as the life-giver which is fully understood against the background of the Feast of Tabernacles. In this Feast the Israelites commemorate God's guidance in the wilderness following the first exodus. Glasson concludes that 'the light of the world' points to the pillar of cloud and fire being expected to return at the end-time.[140] Jeremias[141] also says that here the light was not the inner light (the light of reason and of insight) but the light of the new creation, namely, the eschatological light as the saving light. Dennis[142] adds that the comment that John as the forerunner of the Logos testified to the light in John 1:6–8 (esp. v. 7), is related to the Isaianic voice in the wilderness who prepares for the coming of the Lord of Israel in John 1:23, 31. For Dennis this alludes to the restoration as portrayed in Isa 40:3. In Isaiah, the Davidic messianic king, the suffering servant of the Lord, is presented as the light of the gentiles (cf. Isa 9:2; 42:6; 49:6; 51:4; 60:1–2), which is reflected in the words of Jesus in John 8:12 'I am the light of the world.' This is set against the background of the dispute among the Jews as to whether Jesus who came from Galilee is the Davidic Messiah as recorded in John 7:41f, 52 (cf. Matt 4:12–16).

In John 1:1–13, the identity of the Johannine Logos and his work can be summarized as follows. The Logos is the pre-existent God, the creator, the life, the life-giver, namely, the agent of not only the old creation but also the new creation (Gen 1:1; 2:1f; John 1:1; 19:30). It is the Logos who can give humanity divine life (Gen 2:7; Ezek 37:1–14; John 20:22) and lead them to be reborn; being born of God and becoming 'children of God' (John 1:12–13). Also, he is the μονογενής of God the Father (John 1:14, 18) and the only Son of God (μονογενὴς θεός), the enfleshment of Yahweh (Exod 3:14; 33:19; Isa 43:11). Above all, the idea of the creation or the restoration of the children of God (namely, begetting children of God) through the death of the Logos, in John 1:12–14 (cf. John 3:13–18; 11:51–52) could allude to the exodus and

---

[138] Kim, *Exposition*, 38–40.
[139] Glasson, *Moses*, 64. Cf. Isa 4:5f; *Bar.* 5:8f; *Song R.* on 1:8 (R. Akiba).
[140] Glasson, *ibid.*,
[141] Jeremias, 'Revealing,' 80.
[142] Dennis, *Gathering*, 138; Brown, *John I-XII*, 27–28; Endo, *Creation*, 198, 219–220, 244–245; C. R. Koester, *Symbolism*, 123–154, esp. 124–125. Cf. Lee, *Flesh*, 168.

especially the Passover, in Exod 4:22–23; 12:1–51. For, it was through the death of the firstborn, or the paschal lamb, that Israel was corporately chosen as the son/firstborn/servant of God, that through her the whole world might become sons of God.

1.3 The Incarnation of the Logos (John 1: 14–18)

1.3.1 The Incarnate Logos and his Works

To assist in understanding the background of John 1:14–18, several passages in the OT are suggested as important by Johannine theologians,[143] mainly Exod 33–34; Ps 85:7–10; Joel 3:17; Zech 2:10 (2:14 LXX); Ezek 37:27–28. Concerning these passages, Goppelt[144] claims that the incarnation, the en-fleshing of the Logos, alludes to the theophany, the glory of God coming down to the first-exodus community Israel, particularly to Moses on Mount Sinai in Exod 33–34.

Several parallels could be drawn between John 1:14–18 and Exod 33–34.[145] Firstly, the Greek verb σκηνόω ('dwelling') in v. 14 means that the Logos pitched his tabernacle and lived in it among us. This term could recall the σκηνή (the tabernacle), where God met with Israel during the wilderness life of the first-exodus community (Exod 33:9; 25:8). The Hebrew word for 'to dwell' is שׁכן, which is used to denote God's 'dwelling' with Israel (Exod 25:8).[146]

Secondly, in v. 14, the term δόξα ('glory') in the LXX, generally renders Hebrew כָּבוֹד, which is used to denote God's visible manifestation in a theophany (Exod 33:22; 40:35). This visible divine presence manifested by the cloud was associated with the tabernacle (Exod 33:7–11) and with the Temple (1 Kings 8:10f).[147] This led to the *Shekinah* which was sometimes used as a synonym of God himself in the Targums.[148]

---

[143] See Hanson, *Prophetic*, 21f; idem., 'John 1:14–18,' 90–101; Goppelt, *Typos*, 181f; Carson, *John*, 127ff; Beasley-Murray, *John*, 14f; Bernard, *John*, I, 19ff; Wilkinson, *Creation*, 130; Koester, *Dwelling*, 100–115; idem., *Symbolism*, 125 n. 3; Rissi, 'John 1:1–18,' 394–401; Lee, *Flesh*, 35; Dennis, *Gathering*, 136–164; Coloe, *Dwells*, 23–27, 31–63; Endo, *Creation*, 201–202, 223–226; Boismard, *Moses*, 11 who argues that John 1:14–18 is the Johannine version of the Synoptic narrative of the transfiguration.
[144] Goppelt, *Typos*, 181f; Hooker, 'Prologue,' 53ff; E. F. Harrison, 'John 1:14,' 26; Rissi, 'John 1:1–18,' 399–400; Wilkinson, *Creation*, 134; Dennis, *Gathering*, 137, 142; Coloe, *Dwells*, 26–27; Endo, *Creation*, 201–202, 224–225.
[145] Koester, *Symbolism*, 125 n. 3; idem; *Dwelling*, 103–104; Dennis, *Gathering*, 142; Evans, *Word*, 79–81; Hanson, 'John 1:14–18,' 90–101; Endo, *Creation*, 225.
[146] Glasson, *Moses*, 65f; W. Michaelis, *TDNT*, VII, 368–394; M. J. Harris, *NIDNTT*, III, 811.
[147] Lee, *Flesh*, 34–35; Witherington, *Wisdom*, 55; Kittel, *TDNT*, II, 245; Dennis, *Gathering*, 137.
[148] Glasson, *Moses*, 66. Cf. Lev 26:12– 'I will cause my *Shekinah* to dwell among you.'

A third parallel could be found in a reference to the goodness of God, 'full of grace and truth.' Hanson [149] suggests that the Evangelist directly translated the Hebrew וְרַב־חֶסֶד וֶאֱמֶת ('abounding in steadfast love and faithfulness') in Exod 34:6b, which denotes the goodness of God, into πλήρης χάριτος καὶ ἀληθείας ('full of grace and truth') in v. 14b (cf. v. 17).

Furthermore, two more decisive references to 'the law and Moses' and 'no one has ever seen God' in vv. 17–18 could allude to Exod 33:20–23 and Exod 34:1–4 respectively. Therefore, according to these observations, it is probable that the narrative of the incarnation of the Logos recalls the revelation of the glory of God in the first exodus and the background is the so-called Mosaic covenant making on Sinai.[150]

The incarnation of the Logos, *dwelling among his people* and *showing the glory* of the only Son of the God in John 1:14, means the presence or return of God among his covenant people. This further alludes to the eschatological Temple, promised in the context of the restoration or the new exodus of Israel from exile (Ezek 37:27–28; 43:1–27; Isa 6:1ff; 40:5; 66:1ff).[151] Namely, the incarnation of the Logos means the eschatological fulfilment of the promise of the new Temple and the inauguration of the new exodus-salvation.[152] In other words, the incarnation of the Logos, Jesus's body is the new Temple and the place of God's presence among his covenant people (cf. John 2:21). Brunson[153] understands the incarnation of the Logos in v. 14 to mean the presence of Yahweh, which is the core of the entire complex of restoration; Jesus, as the Son of God the Father, 'carried out the work reserved to Yahweh—gathering the exiles, defeating the enemies of Israel, and embodying—not symbolically, but in reality – the return of Yahweh.' Therefore, the incarnation of the Logos, the presence of God dwelling among the restored people of God, showing the glory of God the Father means the inauguration of the eschatological restoration era.

Further, John 1:14–18 needs to be interpreted in the light of the covenant. The passage is definitely based on Exod 34, in which Yahweh renewed his covenant with Moses after the Israelites' idolatry of the golden calf. Yahweh's renewal of the broken covenant is based on 'his steadfast love and faithfulness' (cf. Yahweh's חסד).[154] Thiselton[155] says that God's covenant

---

[149] Hanson, *Prophetic*, 21; D. A. Baer and R. P. Gordon, *NIDOTTE*, II, 211–218; Dennis, *Gathering*, 143; Carson, *John*, 130–131; A. C. Thiselton, *NIDNTT*, III, 889.
[150] Beasley-Murray, *John*, 14; Koester, *Symbolism*, 125 n. 3.
[151] D. E. Holwerda, *Jesus*, 74–75; R. J. McKelvy, *Temple*, 75–76; Wilkinson, *Creation*, 130; D. Lee, *Flesh*, 29, 35; Dennis, *Gathering*, 136–164 (esp. 137, 144), 182 n. 318.
[152] Dennis, *Gathering*, 137–144; Endo, *Creation*, 202–202, 223; Beasley-Murray, *John*, 14.
[153] Brunson, *Psalm 118*, 388.
[154] Baer and Gordon, *NIDOTTE*, II, 211.

faithfulness is reflected in the context of the Incarnation of the Logos in John 1:14, 17.

In particular, vv. 16–17 makes known this covenantal background. Edward,[156] followed by Carson,[157] argues that to understand the meaning of 'χάριν ἀντὶ χάριτος' in v. 16, it should be considered with v. 17 in which syntactically there are parallels: the law/grace and truth, and through Moses/through Jesus. That is to say, as a grace, the law given through Moses was replaced by the new grace and truth which is superior to the old. Here, 'another blessing' (ἀντὶ χάριτος) clearly denotes 'the law' bestowed on the first-exodus community, through Moses in the light of the old covenant on Sinai. Therefore, 'one blessing' (χάριν) which replaced 'the law' and 'the old covenant,' definitely means 'grace and truth' given through Jesus Christ (Messiah) on the background of the new covenant.

Bruce[158] rightly claims that, 'Moses was the mediator of the law; Jesus Christ is not only the mediator but the embodiment of grace and truth.' No covenant was made with Moses, as it was with Abraham and David. Moses was simply the mediator of the Sinai covenant. So, what is the new covenant? I think it is not too difficult to understand the new covenant proclaimed through the Prophets in the context of the restoration (the new exodus) of Israel from exile.[159]

It is now necessary to turn to Isa 55 in order to understand the incarnation, descent of the Logos of God and the new covenant.[160] It could be further supported from my argument about the Logos in John 1:1–13, in which the Logos is the agent of the new creation in the light of the new exodus-salvation.[161] According to Isa 55:3, the new covenant called 'the covenant of peace' (Isa 54:10) and 'the everlasting covenant' (Isa 55:3) will be made on

---

[155] Thiselton, *NIDNTT*, III, 890.
[156] Edward, 'ΧΑΡΙΝ,' 3–15; Coloe, *Dwells*, 28.
[157] Carson, *John*, 132–134. However, I think a typological comparison between Moses and Jesus Christ seems to be very limited in John's Gospel, even though Moses seems to be paralleled with Jesus in v. 17, and he was the agent of God for the first Exodus and was also thought as a model of the agent for the new exodus at least in Judaism. In the Gospel of John, Moses seems to be not typologically compared to Jesus. God's gift given to the Israelites through Moses are typologically compared to Jesus; the snake (3:14), manna (6:32f), the light (7:37f) and the water (8:12). Also, Keener, *John*, 281–282, 291. Cf. Jeremias, *TDNT*, IV, 872f understands Jesus as the New Moses: 'As a mediator of revelation he [Moses] is thus a type of Him [Jesus] who brought the full revelation of God.' ([] added by this writer). Also Dennis, *Gathering*, 143–144; Koester, *Dwelling*, 104.
[158] Bruce, *John*, 44.
[159] Cf. Isa 54:10; 55:3; Jer 31:31–34; Ezek 16:8.
[160] Cf. 1.4.7. A Proposition.
[161] Cf. 1.2. The Logos and His Works (John 1:1–13).

the basis of the Davidic covenant: 'I will make an everlasting covenant with you, my faithful love promised to David' (Isa 55:3b). Baer and Gordon assume that:

> the assurance given in Isa 55:3 is, then, that the divine undertaking to David has not collapsed with the fall of his dynasty, but may now be made effective for a wider circle of potential beneficiaries who respond to the invitation issued in the preceding verses.[162]

Here, Yahweh proclaimed the everlasting-new covenant according to his חסד promised to David in 2 Sam 7:12–17 (v. 15); Ps 89. The new-everlasting-peace covenant was promised not so much upon the Mosaic covenant as upon the Davidic covenant,[163] in the context of the new exodus, a new salvation of God. To accomplish God's purpose of new salvation with the new covenant, he will send his Word, that is to say, the incarnation of the Logos. In Isa 55:12, God's purpose of the new salvation is denoted as the new exodus out of Babylon, with the restoration of all creation to its pre-fallen state. Also, in Isa 55:13, the new salvation will result in a new creation, in which 'the disappearance of thornbush and briers symbolizes the removal of the curse (and death) that followed sin (Gen 3:17f).'[164]

In particular, the goal of the incarnate Logos is fully reflected in μονογενής,[165] which could be interpreted with John 3:16, 18 and 1 John 4:9. God's eschatological salvation will be disclosed not only by the sending of the μονογενής Son into the world, but also ultimately by the crucifixion of the μονογενής Son. The climax of the Incarnation of the Logos is on the cross. In John 3:13–18, the only Son of God (τοῦ μονογενοῦς υἱοῦ τοῦ θεοῦ), the incarnate Logos, is the same figure as the Danielic Son of Man in Dan 7:13–14, who will bear the works or the death of the Deutero-Isaianic suffering servant of the Lord in v. 14 (ὑψωθῆναι δεῖ, cf. Isa 52:13) and in v. 16 (ἔδωκεν, cf. παρέδωκεν / הקרִיאם in Isa 53:6, 12), who is the same figure as the Davidic messianic King (cf. Isa 9:1–7; 11:1–16; 55:3; 61:1–11; 2 Sam 7:12–16; Pss 2:7; 89).[166] The death of the Davidic messianic king/Deutero-Isaianic suffering

---

[162] Baer and Gordon, *NIDOTTE*, II, 217. Cf. *1QS* 2:1; *1QM* 12:3.
[163] Cf. John 1:49–50, in which Nathanael's confession and Jesus's acceptance of it clearly depends on the Davidic covenant and the new covenant, even though reference of the Davidic Messiah is rare in the Gospel of John.
[164] Motyer, *Isaiah*, 458.
[165] Cf. 1.2. The Only One Son (the Only-Begotten Son), the Beloved Son, and the Firstborn Son of Ra, *Christological*, and 5.2.4.4. The Son of Man (Dan 7:13) and the Servant of Yahweh (Isa 52:13–53:12) and 5.2.5.1. 'The only Son' and the 'the Servant of Yahweh' (cf. vv. 16–18) of this work. Cf. John 1:14, 18; 3:16, 18; 1 John 4:9; Luke 7:12; 8:42; 9:38; Heb 11:17.
[166] Cf. 2.3. The Suffering Servant of Yahweh and the Davidic King (the New David) of Ra, *Christological*.

servant of the Lord is for atonement, redemption, and covenant-establishing to bring about the restoration of Israel from exile and to restore the gentiles to the sons of God (cf. the light for the gentiles, Isa 9:1–2 (Matt 4:12–16; John 7:41f, 52; 8:12); Isa 42:6; 49:6; 56:1–8; Mark 11:17).[167] Also, the death of the only Son of God for the salvation of the world in vv. 16–18 alludes to the death of the firstborn or the paschal lamb for the exodus of Israel accompanied by the multitude in Exod 4:22–23; 12:1–51 (cf. Exod 19:5–6). The salvation of God is connected with the μονογενής; the exaltation of the μονογενής Son on the cross, in which the Glory of God is paradoxically revealed, which definitely is a distinctive Johannine point (cf. Isa 52:13). The Glory of God prophesied by the Prophets[168] is fully revealed in the eschatological salvation of God, which was accomplished by the crucifixion of God's μονογενής Son. So, it could be said that the main theme of the Gospel, the exaltation and glorification of the μονογενής Son, the incarnate Logos on the cross, is stated in the Prologue of the Gospel. So, Kruijf[169] concludes that 'the term μονογενής as used in the Fourth Gospel is more of a soteriological than of a christological nature.'

Furthermore, the manifestation of God's glory and God's tabernacling does not relate to the first-exodus community but to the Johannine community, as a people of the new covenant.[170] The incarnation of the Logos in relation to the term σκηνόω (שכן, 'to dwell') could be understood in the light of the great expectation of the restoration of Israel out of Babylon, on the basis of God's faithful promise.[171] God's returning to the Israelites and his dwelling among them vividly denotes the restoration of Israel. God's returning[172] is intimately associated with the glory of God.

Further, the term 'glory' was used to denote the visible manifestation of the glorious status of God's people restored by the returning of God in the Prophets, especially, in Deutero-Isaiah.[173] The coming of the glory of God will result in the restoration of the glory of Israel. In the eschatological time, a full manifestation of the כבוד of God will not only bring salvation to Israel but also convert the gentiles.[174] It has also to be understood not only with

---

[167] Cf. 2.4. The Suffering Servant and 'the Firstborn Son'/'the paschal lamb' of Ra, *Christological*.
[168] Cf. Isa 60:1f; Ezek 39:21f; Zech 2:5–11.
[169] Kruijf, 'Glory,' 117–123, quoted from 123. However, I disagree with his argument based on the Isaac-Jesus typology. Cf. Holland, *Motif*, 121.
[170] 'His own (οἱ ἴδιοι)' in the OT is connected to God's own special covenant people, so his own possession; Exod 19:5; 23:22; Deut 7:6; 14:2; 26:18; Isa 43:21; 31:5; Ezek 13:18f; Mal 3:17. See E. Harris, *Prologue*, 23; Brown, *John I-XII*, 10; Borgen, 'Targumic,' 292; Pryor, 'Jesus,' 210–218.
[171] Cf. Zech 2:10 [LXX 2:14]; Jeol 3:17; Ezek 37:27–28.
[172] Cf. Isa 35:2; 40:5; 44:23; 66:18.
[173] Carson, *John*, 128. Cf. Isa 60:1. See also von Rad, *TDNT*, II, 241–242.
[174] S. Aalen, *NIDNTT*, II, 45. Cf. Isa 60:1f; Ezek 39:21f; Ps 96:3–9; Zech 2:5–11 [MT 2:9–15].

the glory of God, but with the glory of humankind in creation.[175] Then, in creation, humankinds possessed this כבוד of God and in the eschatological time, with the returning of God, this כבוד of God will be restored to them. Similar references are found in the Dead Sea Scrolls,[176] which show the great expectation of the restoration of Adam's glory. Apocalyptic literature also pays special attention to these kinds of traditions: 'at the fall man was alienated from the glory of God,' Apc. Mos. 20f.[177] In addition, in Philo's works, S. Kim[178] observes a parallel between the creation of the world and God's selection of Israel, and between the natural law God established for the world and the law revealed by God on Sinai.

To sum up, the narrative of the incarnate Logos in 1:14–18 is based on the glory of God revealed to the first exodus community on Sinai against the background of the Mosaic covenant (Exod 33–34). The incarnation of the Logos, namely, dwelling among his people and showing the glory of the μονογενής of God the Father in John 1:14 means the presence (the returning) of God among his covenant people and alludes to the eschatological Temple; the eschatological fulfilment of the promise of the new Temple and the new exodus-salvation (Ezek 37:27–28; 43:1–27; Isa 6:1ff; 40:5; 66:1ff). Both the incarnation (descent) of the Logos (John 1:14) and the new covenant (cf. 'χάριν ἀντὶ χάριτος' in John 1:16–17) can be understood against the background of Isa 55, in which the new-everlasting-peace covenant is based on the Davidic covenant. The Logos, the one and only God, sent from God accomplished God's purpose (Isa 55:11), namely, the new exodus and the new creation (Isa 55:12–13), revealing paradoxically the glory of God through his exaltation on the cross (John 3:13–18; Dan 7:13–14; Isa 52:13). Most importantly, in John 3:13–18, for the salvation of the world, the death of the Incanate Logos, the the only Son of God, who is the same figure as the Danielic Son of Man bearing the work or the death of the suffering

---

[175] Aalen, *NIDNTT*, II, 45. Cf. Ps 19:1 [MT 19:2]; Isa 6:3; Ps 8. von Rad, *TDNT*, II, 242, says that the manifestation of the glory of God denotes the final actualisation of His claim to rule the world. See also Kittel, *TDNT*, II, 246, who says that 'The restoration of dominion to Israel can be expressed as follows: 'When the Israelites keep the Torah in their midst, God will cause them to possess the throne of glory.' (*Num R.* 11 on Num 6:22).'

[176] Cf. *1QS* 4:23; *1QH* 17:15. See Kim, *Origin*, 187, 260; Aalen, *NIDNTT*, II, 45. Cf. 'Those who hold fast to it are destined to live for ever and all the glory of Adam shall be theirs.' (*CD* 3:20).

[177] Kittel, *TDNT*, II, 247; Aalen, *NIDNTT*, II, 45. Cf. *4 Ezra* 7:42, 91, 97; *2 Bar.* 21:23; 30:1; 51:10f; *Ps. Sol.* 17:34f.

[178] S. Kim, *Origin*, 236. Cf. *Quaest. Ex.* 2.46 on Exod 24:16. For Rabbinic sources, see Kim, *ibid.*, 260–62; Kittel, *TDNT*, II, 246–247; Aalen, *NIDNTT*, II, 45. Cf. In *Gen R.* 11 on 2:3, a significant rabbinic thought is that the first man Adam in paradise had a part of כבוד of God but he lost this 'radiance' through the fall. Therefore, in *Gen R.* 12 on 2:4, they hope the Messiah who will eventually restore all of these lost by the first man Adam.

servant of the Lord, alludes to the death of the firstborn or the paschal lamb in Exod 4:22–23.

1.3.2 The Revealer

What does the Evangelist disclose of the identity of the Logos in terms of salvation history? Here, the incarnation of the Logos is described as the revelation of God. V. 14 clearly means that the incarnate Logos has shown the glory of God the Father, full of grace and truth. In v. 18, the incarnate Logos, Jesus Christ, the one and only God (μονογενὴς θεός)[179] has revealed God the Father. V. 18 means that 'he exegetes (interprets) God to humankind.'[180] Also, the phrase, 'No one has ever seen God' (v. 18) alludes to Exod 33:20–23.[181] The main emphasis is that God is holy, spirit and invisible, and therefore, the invisible God the Father has shown himself through his self-revelation in the only begotten Son who is at his side.[182]

Thus, what Moses and the first exodus community Israel saw at the theophany on Sinai, was the Logos. 'Now that glory has been manifested on earth in a human life, 'full of grace and truth.''[183] Thus, Hanson rightly says that:

> when God appeared to Moses in Sinai as related in Exod 34:5–9, it was not God the Father who appeared, but the Word of God. It was the pre-existent Christ whom Moses saw; he did not see God, for no man has ever seen God.[184]

Therefore, the Logos is always the revelator of any theophany, the glory of God. The Logos is the visible revelator of the invisible God the Father.[185] In light of this point of view, we can understand the meaning of 'With him I speak mouth to mouth [face to face], clearly and not in riddles; he [Moses] sees the form (תְּמוּנָה) of Yahweh' in Num 12:8.

---

[179] Dennis, *Gathering*, 139 n. 97 thinks that μονογενὴς θεός v. 18 is right and this parallels 'the Logos God' in v. 1. Also, Endo, *Creation*, 202.

[180] Polhill, 'John 1–4,' 448 ([] added by this writer). Also, Dennis, *Gathering*, 143; Kurz, 'Intertextual,' 181–182; Endo, *Creation*, 202, 226.

[181] Borgen, 'Agent,' 129. Cf. John 6:46; Deut 4:12; Ps 97:2. See Borgen, *ibid.*, 121–129, for '*halakah* principle,' the Jewish thought about agent.

[182] Jeremias, 'Revealing,' 85.

[183] Bruce, *John*, 42; Thiselton, *NIDNTT*, III, 889.

[184] Hanson, *Prophetic*, 21.

[185] Kim, *Exposition*, 42. For the study concerning the revelator of a theophany, see Kim, *Origin*. While he studies Paul's Christology (Cf. Chap. VI), Kim discusses in detail a very important subject, 'ἡ εἰκὼν τοῦ θεοῦ' (the image of God), which is the core in Adam-Christology and Wisdom-Christology. He argues that 'ἡ εἰκὼν τοῦ θεοῦ' (the image of God) is the revelator or the bringer of theophany. Cf. Col 2:15–18. See also Holland, *Contours*, 275–286; *idem., Motif*, 185–198.

Endo[186] points out that the roles (works) played by the μονογενοῦς υἱοῦ τοῦ θεοῦ for God the Father are reflected in the rest of John's Gospel. These works perfectly reveal God the Father to the world, and thus he fulfills the works of Israel as the firstborn/servant/priest of God in Exod 4:22–23; 19:5–6, through whom God planned to restore the gentiles as his sons.

Furthermore, concerning 'the only God who was in the bosom of God the Father' in John 1:18 (μονογενὴς θεὸς ὁ ὢν εἰς τὸν κόλπον τοῦ πατρός, cf. μονογενοῦς παρὰ πατρός in v. 14), Borgen correctly states that:

> John adds that one heavenly figure has had this full vision of God, namely the divine Son, the one who is from God. The closest parallel to this heavenly figure is the idea of the heavenly Israel, he who sees God.[187]

Also, for Borgen,[188] the Jewish tradition of the heavenly model of Jacob-Israel who sees the face of God is the basis of the reference to the Son of Man in John 1:51.

To sum up, the incarnation of the Logos in v. 18 (v. 14) reveals God the Father, alluding to Exod 33:20–23; 34:5–9. What Moses and the exodus community saw at the theophany on Sinai was the pre-existent Logos, the μονογενὴς θεός. That the μονογενοῦς υἱοῦ τοῦ θεοῦ (the μονογενὴς θεός) reveals God the Father and fulfills his purpose and alludes to the works of Israel as the firstborn of God the Father in Exod 4:22–23; 19:5–6, which is the basis of the idea of the heavenly figure (esp. the Son of Man) of the theophany-*merkabah* mysticism tradition.

1.4 Some Suggestions on the Background of the Johannine Logos

1.4.1 Greek Philosophy

Milne[189] suggests that since logos has a wide usage in the first-century Hellenistic world, to relate to various of his audiences in a cultural and

---

[186] Endo, *Creation*, 210. Cf. John 12:45; 14:7, 9; 15:24; 6:38; 8:29; 9:33; 10:32, 37; 14:10, 31; 3:11; 8:26, 28; 12:49; 14:24; 17:14.
[187] Borgen, 'Agent,' 129. Cf. Gen 32:30.
[188] Borgen, 'Agent,' 129–130. Cf. *Conf. Ling.* 146; *Leg. Alleg.* 1.43. For the importance of the idea of the firstborn in the Jewish theophany- *merkabah* tradition against the background of the expectation of the restoration, see 3.3. The Theophany-*Merkabah* Tradition in the Jewish Apocalyptic Literature of Ra, *Christological*.
[189] B. Milne, *John*, 31; Kim, *Exposition*, 33–34 assumes that John's use of the Logos idea based on the Greek Philosophy (Platonic or Stoic) is to help the Greek audience understand the Gospel, who were familiar with the philosophical concept of logos. Nonetheless, Kim, *ibid.*, 35–37 argues that the Johannine Logos concept originated from the OT and Judaism (cf. 'the word (*dabar/logos*) of God' or 'the wisdom (*khokma/sophia*) of God') rather than Greek Philosophy. For Kim, the Evangelist integrated the Logos concept (e.g., the word of God or the wisdom of God)

philosophical context, John would use the term in introducing Jesus. Generally, in Greek literature and the Hellenistic world the term logos was frequently used to denote reason, the inward thought, and speech, the outward expression of its thought.[190] For Heraclitus, logos was the general universal law that does not change. For the Stoics, logos was the rational principle in accordance with which the universe existed and which is the essence of the rational human soul. The Stoics regarded logos as god who incarnates in every man and animal, and manifests itself throughout the world. For them, the logos as god of the universe was the soul of the material world.[191]

However, fundamentally, the logos of the Stoics is very pantheistic. Their logos does not have the personal character of the Logos and the concept of the world resisting the Logos as presented in the Prologue of John's Gospel. Their concept of the Logos incarnation is completely different from the incarnate Logos in the Gospel, where it is seen as one particular person at a given date in history.[192]

1.4.2 Gnosticism

Some theologians argue that the Johannine Logos concept originated in Gnosticism which is regarded by them as a pre-Christian movement. Bultmann,[193] a representative of this view, claims that the Prologue of the Gospel of John employs the language of Gnostic myths found especially in the *Odes of Solomon* and some of the Mandaean literature. He[194] argues that the shift from wisdom to Logos cannot be satisfactorily explained from OT or Jewish Wisdom source, and concludes that the Johannine Logos concept can be found in the Mandaean myth of the Primal Man. He[195] says that the Logos in the Johannine Prologue has as its sources the intermediary Gnostic figure between God and the world, who is very important cosmologically and soteriologically. The discovery of Coptic Gnostic Codices in the Nag Hammadi Library provoked a new interest in Bultmann's hypothesis. In

---

of the OT and Judaism with the Hellenistic Logos concept. See also Wilkinson, *Creation*, 125–139.

[190] For more detailed discussion, see G. Fries, *NIDNTT*, III, 1081–1087; H. Kleinknecht, *TDNT*, IV, 79–91; Morris, *John*, 102–111; Carson, *John*, 114–116; Smalley, *John*, 46–47; Bruce, *History*, 39–52; Manson, 'Logos,' 136–140; Kim, *Exposition*, 34f; Alexander, 'Logos,' 394–395; Wilkinson, *Creation*, 133.

[191] Cf. Carson, *John*, 114; G. H. Clark, *Logos*, 17; Smalley, *John*, 47; Kim, *Exposition*, 33ff.

[192] Clark, *Logos*, 17; E. Harris, *Prologue*, 197; Manson, 'Logos,' 140.

[193] Bultmann, *John*, 13–35; *idem.*, *TDNT*, I, 689–719; *idem.*, 'Prologue,' 18–35; *idem.*, *Theology*, II, 6–14.

[194] Bultmann, 'Prologue,' 18–35.

[195] Bultmann, *John*, 28; *idem*, 'Prologue,' 19.

particular, J. M. Robinson[196] supports Bultmann's basic argument about John's Gospel with some references from the Dead Sea Scrolls and the Nag Hammadi Codices, and concludes that these documents give evidence of a 'gnosticizing trajectory,' from which the Gospel of John has its religious background.

However, Evans makes the criticism that Robinson depends on very selective sources to support Bultmann's hypothesis, and claims that, according to broader and more inclusive surveys, 'the Gnostic redeemer hypothesis is improbable and unhelpful.'[197] Further, although Gnostic literature and the Gospel seem to share some linguistic commonplace terms, the concept of logos, the soteriology and the world-view of Gnosticism are totally different from the Gospel. For Gnostics, the logos is one of emanation between the supreme God and the created material world, and is sent not to redeem the world but to set the soul free from the bondage of the dark, lower material world.[198] For John, the way of rebirth is not by a gnostic vision, but by seeing (believing) that Jesus of Nazareth is the Christ (John 20:13) and receiving life through his name.[199] After comparing the dualistic language usage, and the concept of salvation, the flesh and the material world between Gnosticism and the Gospel of John, Lieu concludes that, 'the parallels of language with Gnosticism do not extend to parallels of fundamental meaning.'[200] Moreover, Dunn[201] also criticizes as an anachronistic interpretation Bulmann's and Robinson's argument concerning the existence of a pre-Christian Gnostic redeemer myth. Furthermore, Dunn[202] says that not only hellenistic religion and philosophy but also Gnosticism of the second and third century which are based on a dualistic thought system, have to be understood as 'divine indwelling' *in* the flesh rather than as 'divine incarnation' *as* the flesh.

1.4.3 Targum

There is an argument that the Aramaic מימרא (word) is frequently used to render the word of God in Targums of the OT. With several parallels

---

[196] J. M. Robinson, 'Trajectory,' 232–268, esp. 266; *idem.,* 'Gnosticism,' 125–143.

[197] Evans, *Word*, 15. See chapter 1and 2 for a fully detail discussion about Coptic Gnosticism and Syrian Gnosticism. See also Carson, *John*, 114; Kasemann, *Testament*, 150; Jeremias, 'Revealing,' 82; Hengel, *Son*, 73; Endo, *Creation*, 1–3; E. M. Yamauchi, *Pre-Christian Gnosticism*; Brown, *John I-XII*, lii-lxiv; Beasley-Murray, *John*, liii-lxvi.

[198] Cf. Goppelt, *Theology*, II, 298.

[199] Smalley, *John*, 53. Cf. Schnackenburg, *John*, I, 229ff, 238ff, 543–557; Beasley-Murray, *John*, 7.

[200] J. M. Lieu, 'Gnosticism,' 233–237, quoted from 234.

[201] Dunn, 'John,' 345–375, esp. 347-349; Carson, *John*, 114; Yamauchi, 'Pre-Christian Gnosticism,' 70; Wright, *People*, 415; Ashton, *Studying*, 6; Harrison, 'John 1:14,' 24; Beasley-Murray, *John*, liii-lxvi; Evans, *Word*, 198.

[202] J. D. G. Dunn, 'Incarnation,' 30–47, esp. 32 (original emphasis).

between the targumic and midrashic exegesis and the Gospel of John, Evans [203] suggests that some parallels disclose the same idea and background between them. Hanson[204] writes:

> *Pseudo-Jonathan* also, like *Onkelos*, avoids the anthropomorphism of the reference to God's hand in Exodus 33:22. Substitutes 'I will overshadow thee with my word.' This cannot be a mere periphrasis for 'God.' The whole point is that Moses will not be allowed to see God directly. The word is the substitute for God in the Targum, as the Logos is the substitute for God the Father in John 1:14–18.

However, Manson contends that:

> it [*Memra*] is not used then as the name for a hypostatized attribute of God, but simply as one of the many ways of avoiding the utterance of the divine name that was too sacred for utterance.[205]

Therefore, the word (מימרא) in the Targum does not have any divine hypostasis but is just a means of speaking about God without using his name to avoid the numerous anthropomorphisms of the OT.[206]

1.4.4 Philo of Alexandria

Philo was deeply influenced by Hellenistic philosophy, particularly Platonism and Stoicism, as well as by Judaism, and attempted to express or to interpret OT thought in terms of Greek philosophy. [207] Philo's interpretation of the OT has to be noted, because (from about 20 BCE to about 50 CE) he was one of the most important Jewish authors of the Second Temple period and was a contemporary of both Jesus and Paul in Greco-Roman times. [208] Bruce [209] states that Philo's thought is decisively helpful in understanding the Gospel of John, even though it is basically

---

[203] Evans, *Word*, 114–120. However, he also recognizes that only the incarnate Logos in the Johannine Prologue does not find any parallel in the מימרא of the Targum (p. 121). Also, Morris, *John*, 105.
[204] A. T. Hanson, *Prophetic*, 21–23 (quoted from 22); M. McNamara, 'Logos,' 115–117; Morris, *John*, 105f; W. E. Albright, *Horizons*, 45; Endo, *Creation*, 6–7. Cf. Str-B, II, 302–333.
[205] Manson, 'Logos,' 147–148 ([] added by this writer).
[206] Barrett, *John*, 153; Cullmann, 'Word,' 256; Klappert, *NIDNTT*, III, 1116.
[207] Cf. Smalley, *John*, 61; Morris, *John*, 107f; Barrett, *John*, 153f; Carson, *John*, 115; Jeremias, 'Revealing,' 87–88.
[208] E. Harris, *Prologue*, 199. Cf. Morris, *John*, 107 observes that Philo used the term 'logos' over 300 times. Bruce, *History*, 78 claims that the entire Mediterranean area as well as Palestine of the pre-Christian era had been under the influence of Greek philosophy and thought for several centuries. It is therefore difficult to separate Hellenistic thought and Hebraic thought within early Christianity. Also, Hengel, *Judaism*; Davies, 'Reflections,' 43–64.
[209] Bruce, *History*, 77;

different from John's Logos. Kim[210] particularly interprets in detail *Somn.* I, 227–241 which is Philo's exegesis about the theophany appeared to Jacob in Gen 31:12, and he concludes that Philo thought that Jacob did not see God directly in Bethel, but rather the image of God (cf. Col 2:15).

> For as those who are not able to look upon the sun itself, look upon the reflected rays of the sun as the sun itself, and upon the halo around the moon as if it were the moon itself; so also do those who are unable to bear the sight of God, look upon his image, his angel, word (logos), as himself. (*Somn.* 1.239).

> But if there be any as yet unfit to be called a son of God, let him press to take his place under God's firstborn, the Logos, who holds the eldership among the angels, an archangel as it were. Any many names are his, for he is called 'the Beginning' and the Name of God and his word and the Man after his image and 'he that sees,' that is, 'Israel.'(*Conf. Ling.* 146).[211]

For Philo, the image of God revealed to Jacob at the theophany was logos, the angel of God. Philo understood theophany as the appearance of the image of God, the Logos. Kim[212] further states that Philo describes wisdom as the image and the sight of God. Borgen[213] also assumes the possibility that the Johannine Logos concept could be developed from Philo's interpretation concerning Gen 1:3 in *Somn.* 1.75; *Conf. Ling.* 146.

In *Conf. Ling.* 146–147, with the application of some important titles (God's logos, his firstborn, his image, the beginning, the eldership among the angels, archangel, the one who sees God, Israel) to Jacob-Israel, the inclusive forefather of the people of Israel, Philo discloses the Jewish expectation to be exalted (or restored) to the sons of God in heaven, through (or by being included to) Jacob-Israel who as the inclusive (or representative) of the people of Israel is originally the firstborn of God

---

[210] Kim, *Origin*, 220–223.
[211] Quoted from Kim, *Son*, 29.
[212] Kim, *Origin*, 219f, 223. Cf. *Leg. Alleg.* 1.43– 'For he [God] called that divine and heavenly wisdom by many names; and he made it manifest that it had many applications; for he [God] called it the beginning, and the image, and the sight of God…' Philo diversely describes logos as follows: the image of God (*Conf. Ling.* 97, 147; *Fuga* 101; *Somn.* 1.45; *Leg. Alleg.* 1.43; 3.96; *Plant.* 18–20; *Op. Mund.* 24); the agent of creation, the image of God, according to and by which man is created (*Leg. Alleg.* 3.96; *Quis Rer. Div.* 230f; *Op. Mund.* 25, 69, 139; *Plant.* 19f; *Quaest. Gen.* 2.62); the bring-er of a theophany (*Quaest. Ex.* 2.13); an archangel, the son of God (*Conf. Ling.* 62f); the bring-er of a theophany and the second God (*Quaest. Gen.* 2.62); the image of God, through whom the whole universe was framed (*Spec. Leg.* 1.81); the firstborn (*Conf. Ling.* 146). See also Alexander, 'Logos,' 395–396.
[213] Borgen, 'Targumic,' 290.

(Exod 4:22f. cf. Gen 32:28–20; Ps 80:1–19).²¹⁴ Hengel²¹⁵ observes, from *Conf. Ling.* 145–147, the saving function of the Logos who as 'the firstborn of God' makes people worthy of being called 'sons of God' through spiritual rebirth. H. Schlier²¹⁶ argues that in *Conf. Ling.* 62–65, the 'ἀνατολή is used to mean the Branch 'ἀνατολή / צֶמַח) of Zech 6:12 (cf. *Conf. Ling.* 62) or 'the eldest son' or 'the firstborn' (cf. *Conf. Ling.* 63). This could reflect the importance of the idea of the firstborn in connection with the restoration of Israel in the theophany-*merkabah* tradition in Philo. Beasley-Murray ²¹⁷ says that the similarity of the logos concept of both Philo and the Evangelist has to be noted in the dimension of the independence of the two authors, for they reflect commonplace traditions and modes of thinking.

However, even though some Johannine scholars generally draw some parallels between the concept of the Logos in the Gospel of John and that of Philo, they point out that the Philonic Logos is quite different from that of the Gospel. ²¹⁸ Although the Philonic Logos could shed light on the interpretation of the Johannine Logos because both of them use the same term 'logos' with similar Logos concepts in the light of their common cultural, historical, religious and philosophical contexts, the former as a personified one is quite different from the latter who is a separated person. Any speculation concerning Logos cannot fully explain the incarnation of the Logos in the Gospel of John, because the Johannine Logos' incarnation is a historically unique salvation event.

1.4.5 The Wisdom of God in Wisdom Literature and Judaism

Some Johannine scholars²¹⁹ suggest that the concept of wisdom in Jewish wisdom literature could be the background of the Johannine Logos; Prov 1:7; 8:22–36; 30:4; 14; *Sir.* 24:1–28; *1 En.* 42; *Wis.* 8:3–4; 9:1–2, 18. In this

---

²¹⁴ See, e. *Conf. Ling.* 146 of 3.3. The Theophany-*Merkabah* Tradition in the Jewish Apocalyptic Literature in Chapter 3. The Son of Man of Ra, *Christological*, for a study of the theophany-*merkabah* tradition and the restoration of Israel on the basis of the concept of the firstborn (cf. Exod 4:22f; Ps 80:1–19; Dan 7:13f).
²¹⁵ Hengel, *Son*, 52–55, esp. 53–54; Kim, *Son*, 29; *idem.*, *Origin*, 245.
²¹⁶ H. Schlier, *TDNT*, I, 352f.
²¹⁷ Beasley-Murray, *John*, 6; Wilson, 'Philo,' 47–49; Alexander, 'Logos,' 394–399, 467–472; Manson, 'Logos,' 140.
²¹⁸ Carson, *John*, 115; Jeremias, 'Revealing,' 87–88; Endo, *Creation*, 5, 178–179; Boismard, *Moses*, 109.
²¹⁹ See Evans, *Word*, 83–94, esp. 83–92 for detailed parallels between wisdom in the Jewish wisdom source and the Johannine Logos. Also, Barrett, *John*, 153f; Morris, *John*, 106f; Carson, *John*, 115f; Wright, *People*, 410–417; Dodd, *Interpretation*, 274–277; Goppelt, *Theology*, II, 290; R. Harris, *Origin*; Kim, *Exposition*, 35ff; Koester, *Dwelling*, 108–110; Manson, 'Logos,' 142–144; R. N. Longenecker, *Christology*, 58; Hengel, *Christology*, 116–117; Lee, *Flesh*, 32; Witherington, *Wisdom*, 20–27; M. Davies, *Rhetoric*, 82; Keener, *John*, 300; Dunn, *Christology*, 163–268; Dennis, *Gathering*, 149; J. Ashton, *Studying*, 13–15.

wisdom literature, Wisdom was created in the beginning before all else, exists independently, eternally in the presence of God, stands in close relationship to God, and participates in the creation of the world. She is also described as the personified breath and word of Yahweh. Strikingly, she descended from heaven to dwell among the children of God but was rejected by the world, his own. So, she returned to her place.[220] Hengel[221] says that in Prov 8:22ff, 'before and during the creation, the personified Wisdom was a child playing beside his father,' which is reflected in John 1:18, and in Prov 30:4 the description of 'son of God' is reinterpreted as Wisdom. In *Wis.* 10, Wisdom is described as God's agent having watched over some patriarchs of Genesis, and having led the Israelites during the first exodus.[222] From some parallels to the Gospel of John in Jewish wisdom literature, it could be said that the concept of wisdom in Jewish wisdom literature may have much in common with the Johannine Logos. Hengel[223] assumes that the functions of wisdom (pre-existence, mediation of creation, mission into the world and means of revelation) is transformed into the Logos, God's creative Word in the Prologue of John's Gospel. Endo[224] argues that the word of God and the wisdom of God were used to emphasize the unique identity of God as the unique Creator and the unique ruler in 2 *En.* 33:3–4 ('There is no adviser and no successor to my creation …. Because wisdom is my adviser and my word is an agent [lit. *doer* or *deed*]').

In particular, Dunn[225] believes the most significant point of Johannine Christology could be the descent/ascent motif which he suggests may be understood in the light of apocalyptic and *merkabah* mysticism traditions, which were the important distinction in post-70 Judaism. Both traditions disclose the current pursuit of 'a direct knowledge of heavenly mysteries' through a vision or an ascent to heaven. In pointing out that the descent/ascent tradition often appears in Jewish wisdom literature, Dunn[226] identifies the Johannine Logos with Wisdom in the Jewish wisdom sources. Moreover, in rabbinic literature,[227] the Torah was created by God in the beginning, participated in the creation of the heaven and the earth, and was the life and the light of Israel. *Gen R.* 1 says, 'through the beginning God created the heaven and the earth.' Here, the beginning denotes the Torah.

---

[220] Ashton, *Studying*, 15; Wright, *People*, 415.
[221] Hengel, *Christology*, 116.
[222] Kim, *Origin*, 219f; Ashton, *Studying*, 15; Lee, *Flesh*, 32.
[223] Hengel, *Christology*, 116–117, 366. Also, *idem.*, *Son*, 73; Lee, *Flesh*, 32; Davies, *Rhetoric*, 82.
[224] Endo, *Creation* 209.
[225] Dunn, 'John,' 357–369.
[226] Dunn, 'John,' 369–372; Hengel, *Christology*, 149.
[227] Hengel, *Christology*, 116. Cf. Str-B, II, 353ff. Endo, *Creation*, 209 n. 10.

However, Goppelt[228] claims that these rabbinic teachings concerning the Torah were mostly written in the post-Christian era and that there is no connection between the Johannine Logos and the speculation of the Torah, because Judaism has never used the term logos. Goppelt nevertheless argues that the Johannine Logos is mostly related to Wisdom in Jewish wisdom literature. E. Harris also agrees that:

> there are here close similarities between the character and functions of the figure of Wisdom and those ascribed to the Logos, and also a greater degree of personification or hypostatization than in the case of 'the Word of God.'[229]

Nonetheless, Harris[230] states that wisdom tradition hardly explains the incarnation of the Logos, and further, questions if the Johannine Logos concept was based on the Jewish wisdom tradition. Harris raises the question that if wisdom was the essential issue, why did John's Gospel not start with, 'in the beginning the Wisdom?' Marshall[231] also assumes that the idea that the wisdom concept of Jewish wisdom literature could be the origin of the concept of the incarnation is just all probability. Boismard[232] argues that both the Wisdom in the wisdom literature (Prov 8:23–25; Sir. 24:3) and the Johannine Logos commonly come out of the mouth of God, meaning that they are begotten by God. However, Boismard points out that the Johannine Logos (as θεός in v. 1 or as μονογενὴς θεός in v. 18) rejects the idea that he was created, which is quite different from the Wisdom who remains a creature (cf. Prov 8:22; Sir. 24:8).

1.4.6 The Word of God in the Old Testament

According to Klappert,[233] the expression 'word of God' (דבר־יהוה) in the OT quite frequently appears, and this expression is emphasized in the prophetic times (93% in the OT). Carson[234] observes that דבר־יהוה is related to God's powerful activity in the creation,[235] the revelation[236] and the

---

[228] Goppelt, *Theology*, II, 298f.
[229] E. Harris, *Prologue*, 198.
[230] Harris, *ibid.*,
[231] Marshall, 'Incarnational,' 15f; Evans, *Word*, 94; Carson, *John*, 115f; Koester, *Dwelling*, 110; Boismard, *Moses*, 108–109.
[232] Boismard, *Moses*, 108–109. Cf. Davies, *Rhetoric*, 82.
[233] Klappert, *NIDNTT*, III, 1087.
[234] Carson, *John*, 115; Morris, *John*, 104; Kim, *Exposition*, 35–37; Wilkinson, *Creation*, 133; Hengel, *Christology*, 117, 366; Kurz, 'Intertextual,' 181–182; Endo, *Creation*, 210–216; Jeremias, 'Revealing,' 87–88; Davies, *Rhetoric*, 81.
[235] Cf. Gen 1:3ff; Ps 33:6. See Endo, *Creation*, 210–212
[236] Cf. Jer 1:4; Isa 9:8; Ezek 33:7; Amos 3:1, 8.

deliverance.[237] He further claims that, 'the personification of that "Word" makes it suitable for John to apply it as a title to God's ultimate self-disclosure, the person of his own Son.'[238] Goppelt[239] also suggest that the first sentence of the Prologue reminds us of the word of God in the OT who created the heavens and the earth. Cullmann[240] states that in the OT, there are many references to the creation story in Gen 1, in which the Word of God seems to have an independent identity having its own powerful effect in creation, although it may be personified. The powerful creative work of 'the Word of God' is recalled in Pss 33:6; 107:20; 147:15.

In particular, Cullmann thinks Isa 55:10ff seems to disclose the personification of the Word of God which could also occur in *Wis.* 18:15. *Wis.* 18:14–18 which has the Passover motif, shows that God's all-powerful Word [Logos] instead of God from heaven struck the firstborn of the Egyptians. Here, the Word is personified and divinely hypostatized as a stern warrior.[241]

> For while deep silence enveloped all things and night in its swift course was at midway, your [God's] all-powerful Word [Logos], from heaven, out of the royal throne, leaped like a stern warrior into the midst of the deadly land, bearing the sharp sword of your irrevocable commandment. Standing, it filled all things with death, and touched heaven though it stood upon the earth. Then at once visions of terrible dreams dismayed them, and unexpected fears came upon them, and one here and another there, thrown down half dead, made known the cause of their dying. (*Wis.* 18:14–18).

Cullmann[242] further contends that to understand the hypostatic aspect of the Logos or the Wisdom, it has to be first considered against the background of the creation story of Genesis and OT references reflecting the operation of the word of God. Jeremias[243] thinks that as the mean of God's revelation the personified Logos concept might appear in the LXX (Hab 3:5) which is older than Philo's materials. Jeremias argues that

---

[237] Cf. Ps 107:20; Isa 42:1–9; 44:24–28; 45:7–8; 46:8–13; 48:12–15; 55:11; Ezek 37:4. See Endo, *Creation*, 212–216, who points out that Isaiah often developed the motif of the creative word into God's redemptive works.
[238] Carson, *John*, 116; Endo, *Creation*, 215–216.
[239] Goppelt, *Theology*, II, 296; Wilkinson, *Creation*, 129; Kim, *Exposition*, 35–37; Hengel, *Christology*, 371–372; idem., *Son*, 73; Evans, *Word*, 77–79.
[240] Cullmann, 'Word,' 255–256; Harrison, 'John 1:14,' 24; Manson, 'Logos,' 146; Carson, *John*, 115–116; M. Davies, *Rhetoric*, 81; Endo, *Creation*, 215–216.
[241] Cheon, *Wisdom*, 85; Kim, *Origin*, 220; Manson, 'Logos,' 144.
[242] Cullmann, 'Word,' 255–256.
[243] Jeremias, 'Revealing,' 87–88; M. Davies, *Rhetoric*, 81.

'Pestilence (*debher*) marched ahead of God (v. 5).' The Hebrew was wrongly translated into 'before God shall come word (*dabhar*)' in the Septuagint, and it is thought that the Word as God's precursor could influence to 'God's Logos' in *Wis*. 18:15 and 'the Logos of God' in Rev 19:13.

However, Manson[244] writes, 'the word of God is here personified, but not personalized, spoken of as if it were a person, but not actually thought of as a person.' Pointing to the difficulty to explain the incarnation of the Logos, Marshall says:

> We shall do better to seek the origin of the doctrine in the church's knowledge of the filial consciousness of Jesus. The recognition that Jesus was the Son of God was the starting-point for reflection which made use of Wisdom and Logos language.[245]

From the discussion concerning the origin or the background of the Johannine Logos, a few issues need to be highlighted. Generally, Johannine scholars seem not to accept the logos concept of Greek Philosophy, Gnosticism, Rabbinic literature and Targum, as the background of the Johannine Logos. Rather than these sources, they have argued that the Logos concept has its origin in the word of God of OT, Philonic logos, and the wisdom of God in the Jewish wisdom literature. They emphasize the importance of 'the OT word of God' in connection with creation, revelation and salvation. Some theologians relate the word of God to 'wisdom' (*sophia*) of the Jewish wisdom literature, or to the Philonic logos.

Nonetheless, concerning the incarnation of the Logos as a historic person, almost all of them hesitate to suggest any proper documentary evidence. This discussion about the origin of the Johannine Logos, particularly the incarnate Logos, seems to be endless. In this situation, I think that the Gospel of John itself has to be considered in an attempt to find the background of it.

1.4.7 A Proposition

I have discussed the theological meanings of the Evangelist in connection with the Logos and his incarnation in the Prologue. In those verses the identity of the Johannine Logos is diversely presented as follows. The Logos is the pre-existent God (vv. 1–2, 18), the creator in the creation and the new creation (vv. 1, 3, 10–13; John 19:30; Gen 1:1; 2:1f), the life (the life-bearer, the life-giver, vv. 4, 13; Gen 2:7; Ezek 37:1–14; John 20:22; 3:1–9), and

---

[244] Manson, 'Logos,' 147. Goppelt, *Theology*, II, 296; E. Harris, *Prologue*, 197.
[245] Marshall, 'Incarnational,' 16.

the light of the world (vv. 4–9; John 8:12; Isa 9:1–2; 42:6; 49:6; 56:1–8; Matt 4:12–16).

The eschatological salvation of God is expressed by becoming the children of God (v. 12) and being born of God (v. 13), namely, the new birth, the new creation, which allows for the making of the family of God. Above all, the principles of the new creation or the restoration of the children of God (namely, the begetting of the children of God) was brought about through the work (the death) of the Logos, the μονογενής of God in John 1:1–14 (cf. John 3:13–18; 11:51–52). This alludes to the exodus and especially the Passover in Exod 4:22–23; 12:1–51, in which Israel was corporately chosen as the son/firstborn of God and as the servant of God through the death of the firstborn or the paschal lamb as the representative of each family (cf. John 1:29, 34; 19:29, 36; 20:17).

In particular, v. 14 (μονογενοῦς παρὰ πατρός) and v. 18 (μονογενὴς θεὸς ὁ ὢν εἰς τὸν κόλπον τοῦ πατρὸς ἐκεῖνος ἐξηγήσατο) show that the Logos is *the only Son of God* the Father. Only the Logos, who was in the bosom of God the Father, had the full vision of God the Father, has made God the Father known to the world and has accomplished the purpose of God the Father. Here, it must be noted that the Logos is the Son of God, more clearly, the only Son (firstborn/beloved) of God, not only functionally but also ontologically.

In John 3:13–18, the Johannine Logos, the only Son of God (τοῦ μονογενοῦς υἱοῦ τοῦ θεοῦ) is the same figure as the Danielic Son of Man (John 3:13–14. cf. Dan 7:13), the one who came from heaven to the world (v. 13), the one whom God sent into the world (v. 17). That is the incarnation (the descent) of the heavenly Danielic Son of Man, the only Son of God, the Johannine Logos. In Dan 7:13–28, the Danielic Son of Man ('one like a son of man') is functionally the inclusive representative (the firsborn) of the saints of the Most High, the Ancient of Days. The enthronement of the heavenly divine figure is the enthronement of the faithful Israel, meaning the eschatological restoration of Israel from exile. Also, the Danielic Son of Man is ontologically the divine figure as the Son/firstborn of God, the Most High, the Ancient of Days, since he came with the clouds, was given with authority, glory and sovereign power, and was worshipped by all peoples, nations and humankinds of every language. The Danielic Son of Man as the Son of the Ancient of Days sat on one of the glorious *merkabah*-thrones (cf. כָּרְסָוָן in Dan 7:9) set among the heavenly assembly. The heavenly Danielic Son of Man, the Logos, the only Son of God the Father should bear the work (the death) of the Deutero-Isaianic suffering servant of God in John 3:13–15 (ὑψωθῆναι δεῖ alluding to Isa 52:13. cf. John 11:51–52). This is the heavenly secret (רָז/סוֹד/μυστήριον) which will be revealed against the background of the expectation for the eschatological restoration: the new exodus of Israel.

The argument that the Son of Man who came from heaven in John 3:13-14 was based on the theophany-*merkabah* tradition of the Jewish Apocalyptic literature can be supported by John 12:41 (cf. John 1:51). Here, there is an alluding to the Isaianic *merkabah* tradition in Isa 6, the Evangelist testifies that 'These things Isaiah said because he saw his [Jesus's] glory, and he spoke of him [Jesus].' The Johannine Evangelist witnesses that the glory of Yahweh seated on the throne that Isaiah saw in Isa 6 is none other than the glory of Jesus. Namely, for John, Yahweh who Isaiah saw in the vision of Isa 6 is Jesus. Thus, the Johannine Logos, the only Son of God the Father is the same figure as the Danielic Son of Man, namely, the Son of the Ancient of Days (son/firstborn of God), the heavenly divine figure who is revealed with the contours of a human being ('one like a son of man') in the theophany-*merkabah* tradition.

Furthermore, the phrase, 'No one has ever seen God' in John 1:18a alludes to the fact that Moses was not allowed to see the face of God in Exod 33:20-23. Thus, that 'God the one and only, who is at the Father's bosom, has made him (God the Father) known' in John 1:18b could be interpreted as the Yahweh whom Moses had met on Sinai in Exod 34:6, 29-35 is none other than the only Son of God (μονογενὴς θεός).

In support of this position, the name of Yahweh proclaimed to Moses in Exod 34:5 could be related to Yahweh's name (cf. 'I am who I am') revealed to Moses in connection with the divine plan of the exodus of Israel in Exod 3:14. This name is often referred to in Deutero-Isaiah against the background of Yahweh's promise for the restoration (new exodus) of Israel from exile (cf. Isa 43:11-12). The name is reflected as the name of the Logos, the only Son of God in John 1:12 ('to all who received him, to those who believed in his name, he gave the right to become children of God'), and, similarly, as the name (ὄνομα) of the only Son of God' (τοῦ μονογενοῦς υἱοῦ τοῦ θεοῦ) in John 3:18. This name (ἐγώ εἰμι) is one of the distinctive Christological titles in John. Therefore, the Logos is God, the only Son of God, the enfleshment of Yahweh. This is clearly shown by John 1:14, where the incarnation of the Logos, dwelling among his people and showing the glory of the μονογενὴς θεός of God the Father, means the presence (the returning, the enfleshment) of Yahweh among his covenant people, alluding to the theophany in Exod 33-34 and the eschatological Temple expected in the prophets (cf. Ezek 37:27-28; 43:1-27; Isa 6:1ff; 40:5; 66:1ff).

Thus, the Johannine Logos is the pre-existent God, the creator and the provider of the new creation, the life, the life-giver, the light for the world, the revealer of God, the bringer of the restoration (the new exodus), the only Son of God the Father, the Son/firstborn of God, the Danielic Son of Man, namely, the Son/Firstborn of God (the Most High, the Ancient of Days), and, the enfleshment (the eschatological presence or returning) of Yahweh. Above all, the Johannine Logos, the only Son of God, the Danielic Son of Man, as the divine figure is ontologically the Son of God and also bears functionally the work of the Deutero-Isaianic suffering servant of God. As such he is the same figure as the Davidic messianic King, based on the thought of the firstborn/only Son (the paschal lamb) of God (Exod 4:22–23).

The theories that the Son of Man, as the Son of God, was sent by God the Father to the world to accomplish God's will through his death, namely, the bestowal of the eternal life, the resurrection life to those who believe in him, are abundantly presented in John 6:22–71, which alludes to Isa 55:11 (vv. 1–2, 10). John 6:22–71 has as its background the Passover feast (v. 4) and Jesus's miraculous signs (the feeding of the five thousand people in vv. 5–15, the walking on the water and the stilling of the storm in vv. 16–21). In these passages, the Son of Man is mentioned three times (vv. 27, 53, 62). The Son of Man is presented as the Son of God the Father (vv. 27, 32, 37, 40, 44, 45, 46, 57, 65), the one who was sent to the world (vv. 29, 39) or descended from heaven (v. 38), so as to fulfill the will of God (vv. 38–40) through his death (vv. 53–56), to give eternal life to those who believe in him and to raise them at the last day (vv. 39, 40, 44, 54). That the Son of Man as the Son of God the Father will fulfill the will of God alludes to the dual concepts of the sonship and servanthood based on Exod 4:22–23; 19:5–6.

Further, the Son of Man is the true bread from heaven 6:32, the bread of God (v. 33), the bread of life (vv. 35, 48), the living bread that came down from heaven (vv. 41, 50, 51, 58). He will ascend to where he was before v. 62 (cf. John 3:13–15). In v. 46, 'No one has seen the Father except the one who is from God; only he has seen the Father' is related to the Son of Man as the Son of God, alluding to the identity of the Logos, the μονογενὴς θεός in John 1:18 ('No one has seen God at any time; the only begotten God who is in the bosom of the Father, he has explained *Him*').

Interestingly, for some Johannine scholars, Isa 6:22–71 alludes to Isa 55. As was mentioned above, while Johannine theologians could follow diverse opinions concerning the original source of the Johannine Logos, some of them agree that the word of God of the OT, particularly, in Ps 33:6[246] or Isa

---

[246] Cf. 2.2.1. John the Baptist's Identity, in which Ps 33:6 and Isa 40:7–8 have been studied with reference to 'the word of the Lord' and 'the breath of our God' in the context of the first creation, the new creation and the new exodus. Cf. Endo, *Creation*, 158

55:10–11, is quite possibly a background to the Johannine Logos.[247] Also, if the Prologue and the rest of the Gospel, as one piece of work, have a literary and theological unity, they could reciprocally shed light on each other. Burkett's argument,[248] that John 6:26–65 is directly dependent on Isa 55:10–11, must also be noted.[249] Burkett[250] argues:

> The numerous and close parallels ... indicate that John 6:27ff is directly dependent on Isa 55:1–3, 10–11. The central theme of this discourse, the bread of life, which has descended from heaven, stems from an identification of Jesus with the word of God of Isaiah 55. This identification accounts for the central ideas that Jesus is sent by God, descended from heaven as bread, gives bread or food (his words) to eat and drink in order that those who receive them may have life, and returns to heaven to the one who sent him.

Burkett suggests the following evidences to support his conclusion.[251] Firstly, Isa 54:13, which is the only OT text quoted in this discourse (John 6:45), is near to Isa 55. Secondly, John 6:27 in which Jesus admonishes the people, recalls Isa 55:2.[252] Thirdly, the food in John 6:27 which the Son of Man will give the people is the bread given by the Word of God in Isa 55:10, as the rain or the snow come down from heaven to give bread to the eater. The words given by the Word of God is food itself and gives life to the listener in Isa 55:1–3. Fourthly, what it means to eat the flesh of the Son of Man and to drink the blood of the Son of Man figuratively means to accept words spoken by Jesus, that is the life-giving spirit (John 6:63), which can be understood in the light of Jesus's breath (John 20:22) and of the breath of God (Gen 2:7). Burkett concludes that, 'As the Word of God, he descends from heaven as living bread, gives the bread of life, and ascends back to the one who sent him' (Isa 55:10; John 6:62).

I have briefly introduced Burkett's arguments; however, I would like to add to Burkett. First of all, both John 6:38 and Isa 55:11 emphasize the

---

[247] Burkett, *Son*, 48; Manson, 'Logos,' 148–149; Evans, *Word*, 198; Carson, *John*, 115f; Cullmann, 'Word,' 255–256; D. M. Swancutt, 'Hungers,' 218–251; F. W. Young, 'Study,' 228; J. W. Dahms, 'Isaiah 55:11,' 78–88; Endo, *Creation*, 215–216, 241–242; Boismard, *Moses*, 92.

[248] Burkett, *Son*, chaps. 1 and 8; Endo, *Creation*, 241–242.

[249] Burkett, *Son*, 46–48, thinks that there is no reference to the 'manna's returning' to where manna came in Num 11:9 (pp. 46–47) and that 'a repeated or continuous process of eating the instruction of Wisdom' of *Sir.* 24:1 is basically different from 'one-time satisfaction of hunger' of John 6:35 (p. 129).

[250] Burkett, *Son*, 132 (cf. pp. 131–132).

[251] Burkett, *Son*, 134–141; Swancutt, 'Hungers,' 234–248; Endo, *Creation*, 241–242.

[252] Cf. Isa 55:2 – 'Why spend money on what is not bread, and your labour on what does not satisfy? Listen, listen to me, and eat what is good, and your soul will delight in the richest of fare.'

accomplishment of the purpose or the will of the sender, who is God. In John 6:38, Jesus has come down from heaven not to do his own will but to do the will of him who sent him.[253] In Isa 55:11, the word of God which goes out from the mouth of God will accomplish the purpose of God. This could remind us of the dual concepts (cf. the son/firstborn of God and the servant of God) which was based on the exodus (the Passover) in Exod 4:22–23; 19:5–6 and applied to the Davidic king (2 Sam 7:12–16; Pss 2:7; 89), even to the Deutero-Isaianic suffering Servant-Davidic messianic King (Isa 9:1–7; 11:1–16; 42:1–9; 52:13–53:12; 55:3; 61:1–11) against the background of the restoration of Israel and the gentiles.

Further, the function that, 'the word of God is the unfailing agent of the will of God'[254] in Isa 55:11 seems to be alluding to the task of Jesus endowed by the Father in John 6:39. This is the central idea of the sonship (and the servanthood as well) of Jesus in John.[255] If these arguments above are correct, that is to say, if in the discourse of John 6:25–71 Jesus discloses a part of his identity in the light of Isa 55, we could relate Jesus, 'the living bread from heaven' to 'the word of God' sent from God in Isa 55:10–11.

This could be supported by the argument of Endo[256] who says that the description of the works of the Son of God in John 4:34 alludes to the ministry of the (personified) word of God in Isa 55:11. For Endo, the combination of 'to do' (ποιήσω) and 'to accomplish' (τελειώσω) appears three times in the NT (cf. John 4:34; 5:36; 17:4), all of which are related to the work of the Son of God. In the OT, the combination of the two terms (ποιέω for עשה, τελειόω for צלח) comes out six times (cf. Ps 37:7; Dan 8:12, 24; 11:36; Isa 55:11; 2 Chron 31:21), among which only Isa 55:11 is related to the work of God.

Further, the motifs of food and water in connection with the work of the Son of God in John 4:14, 34 could allude to Isa 55:1–2, 10, in which God would offer drinks and food to the people in the end. Furthermore, Endo observes that in *4 Ezra* 6:38, 43; *2 Bar.* 54:3; 56:4, 'the personified word appears in both creational and eschatological contexts, and it is described as an agent to accomplish the will of God.'[257] For Endo, this is reflected in the ministry of Jesus as the Son of God. Anderson contends that, 'it is clear that

---

[253] Endo, *Creation*, 242.
[254] Motyer, *Isaiah*, 458; Swancutt, 'Hungers,' 239, 245. Cf. John 6:39 – 'And this is the will of him who sent me, that *I shall lose none of all* that he has given me, but raise them up at the last day.'
[255] Endo, *Creation*, 240. Cf. John 3:16; 4:34; 5:21, 26, 36; 6:33, 38–40; 8:29; 9:33; 10:32, 37; 12:50; 14:10, 31; 17:4.
[256] Endo, *Creation*, 240–241.
[257] Endo, *Creation*, 242, 215–216.

the Word is not a sound or even an idea. God's Word is an act, an event, a sovereign command, which accomplishes a result.'[258]

To sum up, in understanding the origin of the idea of the Johannine Logos (the incarnate Logos), one can recognize the significance not only of the Danielic Son of Man figure in the theophay-*merkabah* mysticism tradition, but also of the word of God in Isa 55:10–11 (vv. 1–3) reflected in John 6:22–71 and John 4:34. The Logos, the only Son of God in John 1:1–18 is presented as the Danielic Son of Man in John 3:13–18 and John 6:22–71. In John 6:22–71. The work of the Son of Man as the Son of God is described as the work of the personified and hypostatized Word of God against the background of the restoration or the new creation in Isa 55:10–11, alluding to the creation through the word of God in Genesis (cf. the restoration of the creation). Regarding the Logos, the μονογενὴς θεός, the descent (the incarnation) of the heavenly divine figure, the Danielic Son of Man is related to the creative and eschatological divine word of God of Isa 55:11.

1.5 Conclusion

We have studied the Johannine Logos concept (the incarnated Logos) in John's Prologue and other Johannine references (John 3:13–16; 6:22–71; 4:34). We have also examined their OT backgrounds, especially the Son of Man in Dan 7 and the personified and hypostatized word of God in Isa 55:10–11.

The Prologue presents the inauguration of the eschatological salvation, the restoration or the new exodus through the work or the death of the Logos. Further, this allows for the creation (the restoration) of the children (eschatological people) of God (the begetting of the children of God), namely, the building of the eschatological Temple.

The Johannine Logos as the μονογενὴς θεός and the Son of Man is ontologically the divine Son (the only Son) of God. As such the Logos also bears functionally the work by his death of the firstborn (the paschal lamb, the Deutero-Isaianic suffering servant of the Lord who is the same figure as the Davidic messianic King), which is based on the concept of the death of the firstborn and the dual concepts of sonship and servanthood including priesthood in Exod 4:22f; 19:5f.

---

[258] Anderson, *Creation*, 29.

Chapter 2: Some Testimonies (John 1:19–51)

2.1 Introduction

Long before the beginning of the baptismal works of John the Baptist, with his message urging repentance, there were already messianic expectations concerning Israel's deliverance (cf. Luke 2:38). This early messianic hope can be quite clearly seen in many parts of the Fourth Gospel itself, particularly in some of the questions posed by the delegations sent from Jerusalem, as well as in testimonies from the Baptist, Andrew, Philip, and Nathanael in John 1:19–51.[259] Bruce explains the historical situation at that period as follows:

> Less than a century before (63 BC) the native Hasmonaean dynasty had fallen and the land of Israel was incorporated in the Roman Empire. This loss of independence and the failure of the hopes that had been pinned to the Hasmonaean priest-kings brought about a revival of the ancient hope of a Messiah from the line of David…In any case, there was a wide variety of messianic hope, and alongside the expectation of a Messiah of David's line there is evidence of the expectation in some quarters of an 'anointed one' of Aaron's line.[260]

An example of this hope is found in the Qumran scrolls.

> They shall depart from none of the counsels of the Law to walk in all the stubbornness of their hearts, but shall be ruled by the primitive precepts in which the men of the Community were first instructed until there shall *come the Prophet and the Messiahs of Aaron and Israel.* (1QS 9:11)

Even though there are few references in the Fourth Gospel, the influence of the Baptist's baptismal work upon Jewish society in the Synoptics is clear. For example, his powerful message about repentance, eschatological judgement and restoration in the wilderness,[261] his life-style reflecting Elijah,[262] many Jewish people coming to him to be baptized.[263] Furthermore,

---

[259] Cf. D. Neufeld, 'When,' 120ff says that many messianic titles in John are intimately connected to contemporary Jewish messianic expectation, which is not ubiquitous and consistent but fluid and diverse: for example, royal-Davidic Messiah, priestly Messiah, anointed prophet, a heavenly figure. See also J. J. Collins, *Scepter*, 195; Kim, *Exposition*, 45.
[260] Bruce, *John*, 46–47. Cf. Carson, *John*, 142–143; Morris, *John*, 115, 117; J. R. Michaels, *John*, 29; B. Milne, *John*, 53.
[261] Cf. W. Howard-Brook, *Becoming*, 66.
[262] See C. E. B. Cranfield, *Mark*, 17. *Contra.* R. A. Guelich, *Mark 1–8:26*, 21. Cf. Mark 1:4–8; 2 Kings 1:8.
[263] Cf. Josephus, *Ant.* 5.2.

the official representatives sent from Jerusalem to investigate clearly shows that the Baptist's baptismal work influenced the Jews.

John 1:19–51 illustrates at least some of the messianic titles in the Jewish society at the time of Jesus.[264] Before the narratives of the public ministry of Jesus, the Evangelist introduces him as being the Messiah. Kim[265] claims that the testimony of Nathanael in John 1:49 ('the Son of God and the King of Israel') is the climax of the testimonies confessed by the Baptist and by the first disciples of Jesus. Jesus himself accepted Nathanael's confession and gave a prophetic promise. Nathanael's confession should be understood in the light of God's covenant to David in 2 Sam 7:12–16; Pss 2:7; 89. The self-understanding of the Baptist gives reference against the clear background of Isa 40:3 and suggests investigation of this passage in the light of the Isaianic new exodus would be rewarding.

Therefore, this passage will be discussed in the light of the new exodus. I will concentrate on the identity of John the Baptist and his work of baptism; on his testimonies and on Nathanael's confession. Further consideration will be given to Jesus's prophetic promise in terms of 'the Son of Man,' his own self-designation which he links with Jacob's vision in Gen 28:12.

2.2 John the Baptist's Identity and his Baptism (John 1:19–28)

2.2.1 John the Baptist's Identity

The key point of the questions of the official deputation[266] sent from the priests and Levites in Jerusalem was about the identity of the Baptist. At first, they asked if he was the Christ or Elijah or the Prophet. When John denied being any of these figures and identified himself according to Isa 40:3, they re-questioned why he baptized people with water. From the conversation between the Baptist and the representatives, it can be recognized that three aspects of his identity are interwoven; messianic expectation, the eschatological deliverance, and baptismal repentance.

---

[264] Kim, *Exposition*, 45–47.

[265] Kim, *Exposition*, 45–47. Further, Kim, *ibid.*, 45, 47, 52–54 says that, in John 1:51, Jesus's prophetic promise against Nathanael's testimony is the conclusion of the first chapter of the Gospel of John and the programmatic statement of the main body which will be developed in John 2–20.

[266] Cf. Carson, *John*, 142 thinks that the official representatives, priests and Levites, were sent by the Sanhedrin Council in Jerusalem, which was controlled by the family of the High Priest. See also Morris, *John*, 116. Carson, *John*, 144, also assumes that some Pharisees in v. 24 were a part of the official inspectors in v. 19, because Pharisees were influential enough in Jewish religious society to send their own representatives. Also, Bruce, *John*, 49; Morris, *John*, 122.

Neufeld says that, 'the question put to the Baptist implies that the Messiah, Elijah and the Prophet were expected to baptize.'[267]

Before the identity of the Baptist is discussed in the light of Isa 40:3, I will concentrate on Elijah and 'the Prophet' as raised by the delegation. Firstly, some Johannine scholars[268] accept that the identity of the Baptist as Elijah could be derived from Mal 4:5 and *Sir.* 48:10, on the basis of which, there was a tradition regarding the re-appearing of Elijah as the forerunner of the Messiah who would bring about eschatological deliverance. But John himself denied being Elijah, which was quite different from Jesus's understanding about him in the Synoptics. [269] Some Johannine commentators[270] have tried to harmonize these two perspectives concerning John's identity, between by himself in the Fourth Gospel and by Jesus in the Synoptics. None of them seems to be satisfactory. On the contrary, it suggests that the tradition, particularly with reference to the Baptist and Elijah, in the Fourth Gospel is independent of the Synoptics.

Secondly, Johannine scholars suggest that the question concerning 'the Prophet' was developed from Moses's prophecy in Deut 18:15–19. Bruce[271] argues that Moses's words were understood to point to the coming of a special prophet, the second Moses based on Deut 34:10, who would accomplish the mediatorial function Moses had exercised. Bruce[272] further says the Samaritans identified this Mosaic prophet with the eschatological Messiah, who could also be recognized from John 4:19, 25. Moreover,

---

[267] Neufeld, 'When,' 128. See also Barrett, *John*, 174; Bruce, *John*, 50; Beasley-Murray, *John*, 24; R. A. Whitacre, *John*, 65; B. J. Malina and R. L. Rohrbaugh, *John*, 43; Howard-Brook, *Becoming*, 63–64.
[268] Cf. Bruce, *John*, 47; Carson, *John*, 143; Morris, *John*, 118; Beasley-Murray, *John*, 23; Michaels, *John*, 29–30.
[269] Cf. Mark 9:13 ('Elijah has come, and they did to him whatever they pleased'); Matt 11:14; 17:12; Luke 1:17.
[270] J. A. T. Robinson, 'Elijah,' 264f, 270 assumes that the Baptist denied being Elijah, because he thought he himself was to prepare for the coming of Elijah, which means Elijah was a messianic figure. This argument was rejected by Beasley-Murray, *John*, 24. Also, Michaels, *John*, 29–30 says that the Baptist's denial was because he thought the one coming after him would be 'the prophet,' 'the Messiah' and 'Elijah.' Further, Morris, *John*, 118–119 says that 'He [the Baptist] fulfilled all the very real sense Jesus could say that he was Elijah. But the Jews remembered that Elijah had left the earth in a chariot of fire without passing through death (2 Kings 2:11), and they expected that in due course the identical figure would reappear. John was not Elijah in this sense, and he had no option but to deny that he was. And, of course, we must bear in mind the possibility that John may not have known that he was Elijah.' ([] added by this writer). See also Howard-Brook, *Becoming*, 65; Bruce, *John*, 47.
[271] Bruce, *John*, 48; Carson, *John*, 143.
[272] Bruce, *John*, 48; Carson, *John*, 143; Morris, *John*, 120.

Neufeld[273] argues that the Johannine messianic concept is connected to the prophetic Messiah (cf. the prophet like Moses in Deut 18) rather than the royal Messiah (cf. the Davidic messianic King). Some Johannine commentators[274] argue that the Johannine messianic concept is based on the prophetic Messiah like Moses, which was influenced by the Samaritan theology concerning the coming Messiah. Actually, Moses was mentioned several times and some signs performed by Jesus seem to allude to signs bestowed through Moses in the wilderness of the first exodus. Moreover, the crowd who saw the miracles of Jesus understood them in the light of Moses's miracles (John 6:14. cf. Acts 3:22). The crowds' thoughts about Jesus in the Fourth Gospel could reflect the messianic expectation of Jewish society at that time.

However, the messianic thought which Jesus or John the Evangelist disclosed rather than the crowds' idea must be noted. Some Johannine commentators argue that the Johannine messianic expectation is the prophetic Messiah like Moses being influenced by only the Samaritan messianic expectation. Above all, it needs to be noted that the Gospel of John clearly discloses the Davidic messianic expectation, especially, John 1:19–51; 2:13–22; 7:40–44 and 8:12 (cf. Isa 9:1–7).

After the Baptist denied being the Christ, Elijah, and the Prophet, he disclosed his identity and the background of his baptismal work, quoting the words of Isaiah 40:3. According to Snodgrass,[275] Isa 40:1–5, which was understood and distinctively adapted by the OT itself, the LXX, Targum, Dead Sea Scrolls, some Intertestamental literature, and rabbinic sources, was a classic statement of God's consolation against the background of eschatological salvation. Isa 40:3 was also one of the quotations, and furthermore, a unique formula quotation, in the four Gospels. This may mean that Isa 40:3 was a very important verse for the Evangelist to disclose the identity and the work of John the Baptist in relation to Jesus. Snodgrass recognizes the importance of this verse for understanding the Qumran community:

---

[273] Neufeld, 'When,' 130; Meeks, *Prophet-King*; Boismard, *Moses*, 66–67; Collins, *Scepter*, 205–207. Further, Neufeld, *ibid.*, 127 thinks that some messianic movements written in Josephus's writings seem to be understood against the background of 'the prophet like Moses' in Deut 18. Cf. Judas Son of Hezekiah (*Ant.* 17.271-272; *War* 2.56); Simon (*Ant.* 17.273-276); Judas the Galilean (*Ant.* 18.3–9, 23–25; *War* 2.118); Menahem, son of Judas the Galilean (*War* 2.433–434); Simon bar Giora (*War* 4.503); Athronges in 4 B.C. (*Ant.* 17.278-285); Samaritan prophet in 26–36 A.D.; Theudas in 44–46 A.D.
[274] Dennis, *Gathering*, 161, 177; E.D. Freed, 'Samaritan,' 243.
[275] K. R. Snodgrass, 'Streams,' 24–45; Cf. *1QS* 8:12–16; 9:17–20; 10:21; *Bar.* 5:7; *Ass. Mos.* 10:1–5; *1 En.* 1:6; *Ps. Sol.* 8:16 (18)-17 (19); *Lev R.* 1:14; 10:2; 21:7; *Deut R.* 4:11; *Midr. Ps* 4:8; 22:27; *Sir.* 48:24; Str-B, I, 96f.

> the Qumran community viewed their right living in the wilderness as the means of preparation for the soon coming of God ... the community viewed itself as fulfilling what was necessary to prepare the way for God's redemption, and they did so because of their interpretation of Isa 40:3.[276]

The Qumran community thought the preparation of the way of the Lord in the wilderness was the study of the law given through Moses.

> To go to the wilderness to prepare there the way of the Lord; as it is written, 'In the wilderness prepare the way of the Lord; make straight in the desert a highway for our God'. This is the study of the law, as he commended through Moses. (1QS 8:14)

> That is the time of clearing the way to the wilderness (1QS 9:20)

ἐγὼ φωνὴ βοῶντος ἐν τῇ ἐρήμῳ· εὐθύνατε τὴν ὁδὸν κυρίου (John 1:23)

φωνὴ βοῶντος ἐν τῇ ἐρήμῳ ἑτοιμάσατε τὴν ὁδὸν κυρίου εὐθείας ποιεῖτε τὰς τρίβους τοῦ θεοῦ ἡμῶν (Isa 40:3 LXX)

φωνὴ βοῶντος ἐν τῇ ἐρήμῳ· ἑτοιμάσατε τὴν ὁδὸν κυρίου, εὐθείας ποιεῖτε τὰς τρίβους αὐτοῦ. (Matt 3:3; Mark 1:3; Luke 3:4)

It is not difficult to recognize that every word except just one (εὐθύνατε) in John 1:23 is the same as Isa 40:3 in the LXX, and that the Synoptics are exactly the same as the LXX. So, Barrett[277] assumes that John the Evangelist translated just one word פנו directly into εὐθύνατε and that the rest of it was taken from the LXX. In the Fourth Gospel, Isa 40:3 is quoted by John the Baptist himself; however, in the Synoptics the Evangelists cite Isa 40:3 to refer to John the Baptist. The Baptist clearly believed that his identity and baptismal work was the fulfilment of Yahweh's prophetic promise given in Isa 40:3.

The context of Isa 40:3, and particularly 40:1–11, is the prologue to Isa 40–66, the second Isaiah, whose main subject is the comfort of Israel by Yahweh and the restoration of his exiled people.[278] Isa 40:1–2 shows

---

[276] Snodgrass, 'Streams,' 30.
[277] Barrett, *John*, 28–29, 173. M. J. J. Menken, *Quotations*, 21–35 (originally published as 'Isa 40:3,' 190–205), who argues that 'The reason for this change is to be looked for on the level of Johannine redaction: the evangelist wanted to avoid the idea that the task of John the Baptist had been accomplished when Jesus appeared on the scene. He intentionally changed the OT text, to bring out his own view of the relationship between John the Baptist and Jesus; the Baptist was not so much Jesus's precursor as a witness to Jesus being contemporaneous with him.' (p. 35). See also, E. D. Freed, *Quotations*, 1–7.
[278] Snodgrass, 'Streams,' 25; Carson, *John*, 144; Bruce, *John*, 49; Beasley-Murray, *John*, 20. Cf. Isa 49:8–13; 51:11–16; 52:7–10; 57:14; 62:10; 66:13–14. Cf. A. Motyer, *Isaiah*, 298ff.

Yahweh's comfort because his punishment against Israel's sin was finished by the Babylonian exile. Isa 40:3–5 shows a calling for the preparation of the way for Yahweh's triumphant return to his people. Isa 40:6–8 points out the eternal supremacy of Yahweh's word over the grass-like Babylonian idols. Isa 40:9–11 is a command to Jerusalem to announce to the cities of Judah the news of Yahweh's return. Here, in particular, Yahweh is described as the mighty warrior and as a shepherd bringing his flock to Jerusalem. Therefore, Carson says:

> In the original context, the Old Testament prophet is calling for a (metaphorical) improvement in the road system of the desert to the east, a levelling of hills and valleys and a straightening of the curves, to accommodate the return of the covenant people from exile. But even in Isaiah, the end of the exile begins to serve as a model, a literary 'type', of the final return to the Lord far greater than a return to geographical Jerusalem. If Isaiah 40–66 begins by announcing good news to Zion (Jerusalem), it goes on to anticipate a still greater redemption effected by the suffering servant of the Lord (Isa 52:13–53:12), climaxed by a new heaven and a new earth (Isa 65–66). It is this 'typological' connection, already established in the book of Isaiah, that the New Testament writers take up and understand to be fulfilled in the voice of John the Baptist, who cried in the desert, preparing a way for the Lord, and thereby announcing the coming of Jesus Messiah.[279]

Throckmorton[280] claims that the re-creation will be accomplished by God the Creator again at the end as he did at the beginning, and so will be understood in the light of eschatological salvation. Particularly in pointing out the parallel between 'the word of the Lord' and 'the breath of his mouth' in Ps 33:6, Throckmorton argues that both 'word' and 'breath' mean 'God's creative activity.'[281] With reference to 'breath' and 'word,' we should note Ps 33:6 and Isa 40:7–8. Even though, in this Isaianic reference, 'the breath of the Lord' and 'the word of our God' (God's everlasting glory) is contrasted with the grass and the flower, which represent human fragility. These two terms, 'breath' and 'word,' disclosing God's creative power in Ps 33:6 reflecting the first creation in Gen 2:7, were re-used to show Yahweh's great power and glory in the context of the restoration (the new exodus), the eschatological salvation in Isa 40:7–8 as well. The word of God can conclusively be understood in the context not only of the first creation in

---

[279] Carson, *John*, 144.
[280] B. H. Throckmorton, *Creation*, 55.
[281] Throckmorton, *Creation*, 57.

Gen 2:7 and Ps 33:6 but also of the new creation and the new exodus-salvation in Deutero-Isaiah, particularly Isa 40:7–8, and the Fourth Gospel. Therefore, Carmichael rightly argues that the new exodus patterned from the first exodus is a major motif in the Second Isaiah which is intimately connected to creation,[282] and John the Baptist's self-introduction using Isa 40:3 has to be understood in the context of new creation in Isa 40:12–31.[283]

In particular, pointing to ἐγὼ οὐκ εἰμὶ ὁ χριστός in John 1:20 which could reflect Jesus's distinctive use of ἐγώ εἰμί in the Gospel of John. Howard-Brook[284] says that the holy phrase has to be understood as Yahweh's name revealed to Moses in Exod 3:14. Freed[285] suggests that ἐγώ εἰμί in John 1:20 and 4:25 reflects Jesus's identity as the Messiah based on Isa 52:6. If these arguments are valid, the two references (Exod 3:14 and Isa 52:6) as the OT background of ἐγώ εἰμί could be respectively understood in the context of the first exodus from the bondage of Egypt and the new exodus from Babylonian exile.

Conclusively, the identity of John the Baptist which has to be grasped against the background of Isa 40:3, the context of the new exodus of the exiled people of God in Babylon, discloses that the Isaianic restoration (the new exodus, the eschatological salvation) has already started and will be climaxed in the new creation.

2.2.2 The Baptism of John the Baptist

Several possibilities concerning the origin of John's baptism could be suggested, such as the ritual washings in the OT law (Lev 15:5, 8, 13, 16), the imagery of washing in connection with repentance (Isa 1:16), Jewish proselyte-baptism,[286] and the initiation rite of the Qumran community. Witherington[287] argues that John's baptismal work was influenced not by the OT Prophets but by the baptism of the Qumran community or some other baptism-sect. Nonetheless, he also suggests that John's baptism was different from the purification rite of the Qumran sectarians, which was repeated, but was similar to the Jewish proselyte baptism, which was not repeated but was once and for all. However, Goppelt says that, 'in terms of its meaning however, John's baptism comes closer to the concept of the Essenes because these ablutions were united with repentance.'[288]

---

[282] C. M. Carmichael, *Creation*, 37. Cf. Isa 41:17–20; 42:5–17; 43:15–21; 51:10.
[283] Carmichael, *Creation*, 43.
[284] Howard-Brook, *Becoming*, 64.
[285] E. D. Freed, *'Ego Eimi,'* 288–291.
[286] T. W. Manson, *Servant-Messiah*, 42–44. cf. Str-B, I, 102–113.
[287] Witherington, *Wisdom*, 62.
[288] Goppelt, *Theology*, I, 37.

Nonetheless, Goppelt[289] recognizes that in spite of some overlap with the Qumran sectarians' baptism or the Jewish proselyte baptism, John's baptism had its own uniqueness and distinctiveness in the Jewish world. Further, Bruce [290] contends that the purification rite in the Qumran community by daily water bathing could be related to Ezek 36:25. However, the Qumran community's water bathing was repeatedly performed by them and they also thought the Holy Spirit was already present in their community.

Above all, John 1:33 clearly says that John's baptism by water had a divine origin, so it must not be thought that it was simply imitated from some other baptism performed at the time of Jesus. Although, there were some similarities to Jewish proselyte baptism and the water baptism of the Qumran community. What then was the origin of John's baptism by water? To begin with, the Baptist understood his identity and baptismal work in the light of Isa 40:3, which had as its background the prophetic promise about the new exodus from the Babylonian exile. Thus it can at least be assumed that he did baptize people with water as a work of preparation for the new exodus. If so, in regard to the new exodus, what is the most probable OT background concerning water baptism? Secondly, the comparison between John's water baptism and the Spirit-baptism of 'the Coming One' Jesus, has to be noted in John 1:26, 33 in the context of the new exodus as well. Jones writes:

> In all of this, John's water baptism announces the arrival of something new in the world; that is, it facilitates his work of preparing 'the way of the Lord' (1:23). The narrative focuses on this function in a way that diminishes, if not excludes, any purification or initiation of the baptisands. This applies as well to the relationship of water baptism with the Spirit baptism Jesus will offer. The narrative clearly places the emphasis on the baptism in the Spirit.... Thus far in the narrative, water does little more that signify the arrival of something new. John's water baptism indicates the imminent appearance of one far superior to John, one who will conduct his own baptism in the Holy Spirit.[291]

Therefore, the most probable reference in the OT, in relation to the baptism with water, the coming of the Spirit, and the baptism with the Spirit in the

---

[289] Goppelt, *Theology*, I, 37; Carson, *John*, 145.
[290] Bruce, *John*, 50; Goppelt, *Theology*, I, 39 n. 21; J. Jeremias, *Theology*, I, 80–82; Koester, *Symbolism*, 161.
[291] L. P. Jones, *Symbol*, 50–51; Koester, *Symbolism*, 157; Polhill, 'John 1–4,' 448; Ng, *Symbolism*, 68.

context of the new exodus, could be Ezek 36:25–35.[292] This is accepted by many Johannine scholars as the most likely background to John's water baptism.[293] From this passage, some valuable references can be noted, such as, the promise of the new exodus, the water sprinkling to cleanse, a new heart and a new spirit, putting the Spirit in God's people, the restoration to the promised land, the new covenant, the abundance in the restoration, the restoration of creation which is the new creation.

Therefore, it can be concluded that on the basis of Ezek 36:24–25, John offered water baptism to cleanse people as the first part of Ezekiel's prophecy and to prepare for the coming of the second part of the promise; namely, the renewing bestowal of the Spirit administered by Jesus, the Coming One, in the light of the eschatological new exodus, which was also symbolically expressed as the new creation and the messianic abundance in the eschatological time.

2.3 John the Baptist's Testimony to Jesus (John 1:29–34)

2.3.1 The Lamb of God (John 1:29, 36)

There have been many studies concerning the background of 'the Lamb of God who takes away the sin of the World,' [294] in the light of the OT. Johannine commentators suggest this title could be based on the Apocalyptic lamb, the Passover lamb, the Isaianic servant of Yahweh in Isa 53:7, the *Aqedah* based on Gen 22:8, the Scapegoat at the Day of Atonement, the daily offerings, and the guilt offerings in the OT. As to the importance of this passage, Turner says that 'John 1:29–34 is part of the Chap 1–2 which together have programmatic significance for the whole Gospel.' [295] In particular, John 1:29 is 'a doorway to the Johannine understanding of the cross,'[296] which could reflect the identity of Jesus and the direction of his work. The majority of Johannine scholars argue that the culmination of John 1:29 could be the crucifixion of Jesus (John 19:28–37). Before considering 'the Lamb of God' in the light of the cross, I will survey the ongoing theological debate over the background to it.

---

[292] Howard-Brook, *Becoming*, 64.
[293] Jones, *Symbol*, 48 n. 27; G. R. Beasley-Murray, *Baptism*, 31ff; Bruce, *John*, 50; Carson, *John*, 145; Morris, *John*, 123; Kim, 'Baptism,' 14; Goppelt, *Theology*, I, 36–39; Koester, *Symbolism*, 161; Ng, *Symbolism*, 67; Jeremias, *Theology*, I, 44.
[294] Cf. Morris, *John*, 126–131; Carson, *John*, 149–151; Marshall, 'Lamb,' 432–434; M. Turner, 'Atonement,' 99–122; C. K. Barrett, 'Lamb,' 210–218; G. L. Carey, 'Lamb,' 97–122; S. E. Porter, 'Traditional,' 396–428; J. C. O'Neill, 'Lamb,' 2–30; S. S. Smalley, 'Salvation,' 324–329; B. H. Grigsby, 'Cross,' 51–80; Hengel, *Atonement*, 46.
[295] Turner, 'Atonement,' 121.
[296] Turner, 'Atonement,' 122; Koester, *Symbolism*, 157.

It is necessary to consider the title with other titles the Son of God and the Spirit-Baptiser attested by the Baptist in the same context. Also, the Baptist's baptismal work based on Isa 40:3 in John 1:23 has to be taken into account. How can these titles, the Lamb of God, the Son of God, and the Spirit-baptizer, which seemingly have nothing in common, be simultaneously applied to Jesus in the same context? Through the following discussion, we shall recognize the interrelationship between these titles and with other Christological titles, on the basis of the firstborn idea against the background the Passover and the exodus.

2.3.1.1 The Apocalyptic Lamb

The argument that the apocalyptic lamb could be the background to the Lamb of God, was suggested by Dodd. Dodd[297] argues that the background to the Lamb of God could be found in the description of the apocalyptic lamb of Revelation and apocalyptic literature,[298] in which the Messiah was described as having the appearance of a horned ram or lamb. In Revelation, the lamb was slain, whereby it brings salvation for many, and victory against evil forces and sins. The apocalyptic lamb, the Messiah, will purge the sin of the world and destroy evil forces in the eschatological judgement. Although there are some arguments because of a linguistic difference between ἀμνός in John 1:29 and ἀρνίον in Revelation, it is not a major problem, because these terms have the same meaning.[299]

---

[297] Dodd, *Interpretation*, 230–238; Witherington, *Wisdom*, 66–67; Michaels, *John*, 36; Barrett, 'Lamb,' 213; Malina and Rohrbaugh, *John*, 50–52.

[298] Cf. Rev. 5:6, 8, 12, 13; ch.6; 7:14, 17; 14:1, 4, 10; 15:5; *1 En.* 90:9–12; *Test. Jos.* 19:8; *Test. Ben.* 3:8. In particular, O'Neill, 'Lamb,' 2–30 argues that the phrase 'the Lamb of God' was already used by Jewish scribes in the Testaments of the 12 Patriarchs, before it was used in Christian literature, and, in particular, *Test. Jos.* 19:11 showed the Jewish thinking of two anointed figures (the anointed priest and the anointed king), which was added by non-Christian Jewish scribes who had the concept of two Messiahs coming out of the tribe of Levi. O'Neill continues that 'The Testaments as a whole were put together into one connected document by compilers who were not Christians, for the document as a whole was transmitted by various scribes who were not Christians before it was transmitted as a whole by scribes who were Christians. It is almost certain, then, that Jews before Jesus Christ looked for the Messiah who would be called the Lamb of God.' (pp. 26–27). See also Turner, 'Atonement,' 199–120; Carson, *John*, 150; Beasley-Murray, *John*, 24f. However, Barrett, 'Lamb,' 215 says that *1 En.* 90:38 and *Test. Jos.* 19:8 could be corrupted or interpolated by Christian scribes. See also Smalley, 'Salvation,' 326; Morris, *John*, 126–127.

[299] Cf. Bruce, *John*, 52 points out that it has to be noted that the two Johannine literatures are the only sources in the NT, which use terms (*amnos* and *arnion*) meaning 'lamb' as the title of the Christ. Further, Turner, 'Atonement,' 120, argues that these terms are synonyms, in spite of observing that the Passover lamb was *probaton*, the apocalyptic lamb in Revelation was *arnion*, the victorious-apocalyptic lamb in *Test. Jos.* 19:6f was *amnos*, and lamb in John 1:29, 36 was *amnos*. See also Marshall, 'Lamb,' 433; Morris, *John*, 126; Carson, *John*, 150–151; R. N. Longenecker, *Christology*, 49–50. *Contra* Smalley, 'Salvation,' 326.

Barrett[300] suggests that at first John the Baptist understood this title in terms of the apocalyptic lamb as a messianic title before the start of Christianity; but John the Evangelist used this title in the light of the Passover Lamb. Barrett's argument is supported by Carson,[301] who argues that the Baptist's message about the work of the Coming One, the Messiah described in the Synoptics (cf. Mark 3:10–12) could accord with the description of the work of the Lamb of God, the Messiah in apocalyptic perspectives. Mark 3:10–12 clearly shows that the Baptist introduced the Messiah in terms of judgment, purification and salvation, which seems to be quite different from the Johannine narrative of the Baptist concerning the work of Jesus.[302]

Furthermore, Dodd[303] thinks αἴρω in John 1:29 means 'remove,' 'take out of the way' rather than 'bear,' 'take upon oneself.' So, Dodd[304] continues, it is not cultic and sacrificial but apocalyptic. However, some Johannine scholars[305] argue that this verb could contain both meanings. Jeremias states:

> In both cases it is a matter of setting aside the guilt of others. In the former, however, the means of doing this is by a substitutionary bearing of penalty; in the latter sin is removed by means of expiation.[306]

Carey rightly criticizes Dodd who too narrowly interprets the meaning of the phrase ('to takes away the sin of the world') as simply 'removal of evil' and ignores the obvious relationship between the removal of sin and the death of the Lord for others in Rev 7:14. Carey argues that Rev 7:14 clearly says that, 'the victorious lamb is he who overcomes death by his sacrifice and those who overcome are those who have washed their robes white in the blood of the lamb.'[307]

In particular, we have to recognize that a theophany-*merkabah* tradition of Rev 5:1–14 shows that the apocalyptic lamb is the same figure as the

---

[300] Barrett, 'Lamb,' 213; Porter, 'Traditional,' 408–409.
[301] Carson, *John*, 150.
[302] Turner, 'Atonement,' 119; Marshall, 'Lamb,' 432–434; Beasley-Murray, *John*, 24f; Carson, *John*, 150–151; E. W. Burrow, 'Lamb,' 245–247; Porter, 'Traditional,' 409. Cf. The understanding of the disciples about Jesus's action in the Temple in John 2:20–22, the theological comment of the Evangelist about Caiaphas' conspiracy to kill Jesus in John 11:49–52, and the disciples' post-resurrection understanding of Jesus's entry to Jerusalem and the crowds' shouting and behaviour in John 12:16.
[303] Dodd, *Interpretation*, 237.
[304] Dodd, *Interpretation*, 233.
[305] Cf. Bruce, *John*, 53; Marshall, 'Lamb,' 433; Morris, *John*, 130; Jeremias, *TDNT*, I, 185–186; Carey, 'Lamb,' 119; Carson, *John*, 150–151.
[306] Jeremias, *TDNT*, I, 186; MacGregor, *John*, 28.
[307] Carey, 'Lamb,' 104. See also Smith, *John*, 69; Smalley, 'Salvation,' 326.

Davidic messianic king (cf. the Lion of the tribe of Judah, the Root of David). In Rev 5:9–10, the apocalyptic lamb, namely, the Davidic messianic king is praised as the eschatological redeemer who with his blood (his death) purchased (redeemed, ransomed) people from the gentiles (cf. every tribe and language and people and nation) and restored them to God and made them to be a kingdom and priests to serve God and to reign on the earth. This clearly alludes to the identity of the people of God, Israel who is corporately chosen as the son of God, the firstborn of God and as the servant of God (Exod 4:22–23), as the kingdom of priest (Exod 19:5–6).

Also, the apocalyptic lamb is the same figure as the paschal lamb, since the identity of the apocalyptic lamb (the Davidic messianic king) and his works in Rev 5:1–10 are paralleled with the identity of the firstborn (the paschal lamb) and his works in Rev 1:4–8, being accompanied with the Danielic Son of Man ('one like a son of man'), against the background of a theophany-*merkabah* tradition in Rev 1:7, 13 (Dan 7:13–14).

2.3.1.2 The Aqedah Motif

On the basis of a reference to Abraham in John 8:56, some Johannine commentators argue that the *Aqedah* motif, the binding of Isaac in Gen 22:8, was the background of 'the Lamb of God' in John 1:29 (cf. John 3:16). For some scholars,[308] that God gave the only Son of God (τὸν υἱὸν τὸν μονογενῆ), which is a distinctive Johannine Christological title in John 3:16 (cf. John 1:14, 18), alludes to a sacrifice in the story of Abraham and Isaac, the only son (the beloved son) of Abraham in Gen 22:2, 8, 12 (cf. Rom 8:32). Brown says that:

> Even the mention of 'the world' fits in with this background, for Abraham's generosity in sacrificing his only son was to be beneficial to all the nations of the world (Gen 22:18; *Sir.* 44:21; *Jub.* 18:15).[309]

Vermes[310] thinks that all sacrifices in relation to the lamb originated in the *Aqedah*, which had the effect of deliverance, forgiveness and messianic salvation, and he continues that, 'the association of the *Aqedah* with

---

[308] B. Lindars, *John*, 159; Brown, *John I-XII*, 147; R. A. Rosenberg, 'Jesus,' 381–388, esp. 386; M. Davies, *Rhetoric*, 167; Hengel, *Atonement*, 61–62; *idem.*, *Son*, 11–12; Kim, 'Interpretation,' 215; Bretscher, 'Exodus 4:22–23,' 305; Keener, *John*, 415–416; K. H. Bartels, *NIDNTT*, II, 725; J. M. Bulman, 'Only,' 65; Beasley-Murray, *Life*, 39.
[309] Brown, *John I-XII*, 147. Cf. John 19:17.
[310] G. Vermes, *Scripture*, 225.

Passover was well established before the beginning of the Christian era.'[311] Grigsby even argues that Jesus is a new Isaac.[312]

However, Bruce[313] argues that Isaac's binding was not a sin offering. Carey[314] also points out that if the *Aqedah* was an important concept for NT Christology, Isaac typology should have appeared frequently in the NT. Furthermore, Holland concludes that, 'the most dominant model for the NT writers was not the *Aqedah* itself, but the Passover with the death of the firstborn.'[315] To sum up, the *Aqedah* motif could have been developed especially by Rabbinic sources before the beginning of the Christian era; however, it is not the basis of NT Christology nor the background to 'the Lamb of God' in John 1:29.

2.3.1.3 The Servant of the Lord

Jeremias[316] claims the lamb in Isa 53:7 could be one source of the background of 'the Lamb of God' of John 1:29. Above all, Jeremias[317] points out that the servant of Yahweh compared to a lamb (*amnos*) in Isa 53:7, was clearly linked to Jesus in Acts 8:32. This could reflect the first century identification whereby the work of Jesus was interpreted in the light of the Isaianic servant of God who was compared to a lamb. Secondly, by observing that the Aramaic *talya* which corresponds to *ebed* (servant) in Hebrew has the twofold significance of lamb (*amnos*) and servant or boy

---

[311] Vermes, *Scripture*, 200, 215; Rosenberg, 'Jesus,' 381–388. See also Holland, *Motif*, 115–121; Marshall, 'Lamb,' 433; Morris, *John*, 129; Glasson, *Moses*, 98–99; C. R. T. Hayward, 'Sacrifice,' 292–306; M. R. J. Bredin, 'Influence,' 26–43; B. N. Fisk, 'Offering,' 481–507; J. A. Fitzmyer, 'Sacrifice,' 211–229, esp. 228–229; Hengel, *Atonement*, 61–63; *idem.*, *Son*, 11–12; Kim, 'Interpretation,' 215; Bretscher, 'Exodus 4:22–23,' 305; Keener, *John*, 415–416; R. T. France, *Mark*, 81; Grigsby, 'Cross,' 59; Beasley-Murray, *Life*, 39. Cf. *Jub.* 18:26; *Ant.* 1.227–232; *Pseudo-Philo* (*Liber Antiquitatum Biblicarum*) 18:5; 32:2–4; 40:2; *Tg. Neof. Gen* 22:14; *Cant. R.* 1.14 §1; *Sifre* on Deut 32; *Gen R.* 55:5; 4Q225 (4QPseudo-Jubilees), Frag 2, cols i and ii; *4 Macc.* 13:12; Heb 6:13–14; 11:17; James 2:2; Rom 8:32. Contra B. D. Chilton and P. Davies, 'Aqedah,' 517; P. R. Davies, 'Passover,' 59–67; B. D. Chilton, 'Isaac,' 78–82; Carey, 'Lamb,' 103; Smith, *John*, 69; Fisk, 'Offering' 506 n. 85 criticizes Vermes' argument; 'Vermes presses expiatory function of the Aqedah in Pseudo-Philo's work beyond the evidence.'
[312] Grigsby, 'Cross,' 60–61; Rosenberg, 'Jesus,' 385–388.
[313] Bruce, *John*, 52; Morris, *John*, 129; Turner, 'Atonement,' 120 n. 49.
[314] Carey, 'Lamb,' 103; Smith, *John*, 69; Holland, *Motif*, 115–121; France, *Mark*, 81–82; Bretscher, 'Exodus 4:22–23,' 305.
[315] Holland, *Motif*, 121; Bretscher, 'Exodus 4:22–23.'
[316] Jeremias, *TDNT*, I, 339–340; *idem.*, V, 702; *idem.*, *Theology*, I, 53–55; Cullmann, *Christology*, 70–71; Beasley-Murray, *Life*, 39; Endo, *Creation*, 231; Bruce, *John*, 52–53; Marshall, 'Lamb,' 433; Polhill, 'John 1–4,' 449 argues that the Johannine lamb of God contains the paschal lamb and the Isaianic suffering Servant of the Lord. Also, R. B. Edwards, 'Christological,' 382. Cullmann, *Christology*, 71–72 think that the 'lamb' of Isa 53:7 alludes to the Passover lamb. Cf. R. T. France, 'Servant,' 26–52.
[317] Jeremias, *TDNT*, I, 339; *idem.*, *Theology*, I, 53–55.

(*pais*), Jeremias[318] assumes that John the Baptist used *talya* in terms of *pais* (servant), but later the Christian church reinterpreted *talya* in terms of *amnos* (lamb) in order to draw on the double meanings (*amnos* and *pais*) in the light of Isa 53. I feel that Jeremias' linguistic argument is a possibility but unconvincing. This linguistic argument was criticized by Morris,[319] who points out that the well-known expression, 'the servant of the Lord' could not be translated 'the Lamb of God,' which was a difficult and rare title.

Nonetheless, as a background to the Johannine Lamb of God, the Isaianic servant of the Lord could not be lightly dismissed. Porter[320] correctly points out that 'to take away the sin of the world' could reflect the substitutionary sacrificial death of Jesus, which could depend upon the expiatory efficacy accomplished through the substitutionary suffering of the servant of the Lord (Isa 53:10, 12). If, John the Baptist understands his baptismal work as the fulfilment of Isa 40:3 in John 1:23 and the descent of the Holy Spirit upon Jesus in John 1:32f it could be based on Isa 42:1 (cf. Isa 11:2; 61:1).

Also, the importance of the Isaianic servant of the Lord in John could be further supported by John 12:37–43. The Evangelist interprets the unbelief of the Jews as the fulfilment of Isa 53:1 in John 12:38, and the reason that they could not believe in Jesus as the fulfilment of Isa 6:10 in John 12:39–40.

Above all, ὑψωθῆναι δεῖ in John 3:14 (cf. John 8:28; 12:32, 34) shows that the Johannine Lamb of God, the Johannine Logos, the only Son of God as the Danielic Son of Man must bear the work (the death) of the Isaianic suffering servant of the Lord (cf. יָרוּם וְנִשָּׂא וְגָבַהּ מְאֹד / ὑψωθήσεται καὶ δοξασθήσεται in Isa 52:13).[321] Also, Jesus's servanthood (the suffering Servant) is shown by John 13, where Jesus washed the disciples' feet, symbolizing atonement of sin (cf. vv. 8–11), and gave them a new commandment (cf. the establishment of the new covenant) at the Last Supper against the background of the Jewish Passover feast.

These show Jesus's identity as the Isaianic suffering servant of the Lord, who is a guilt-offering, a ransom, a covenant, and the light of the gentiles against the background of the restoration of Israel and the gentiles (Isa

---

[318] Jeremias, *TDNT*, I, 339; *idem.*, *TDNT*, V, 702; *idem.*, *Theology*, I, 53–55; Cullmann, *Christology*, 70–71; Michel, *NIDNTT*, III, 611–612.
[319] Morris, *John*, 128. See also I. H. Marshall, *Christology*, 116–117; *idem.*, *Luke*, 381; Dodd, *Interpretation*, 235–236; Smalley, 'Salvation,' 325. Morris also argues that there was no clear evidence Isa 53 was applied to the Messiah before the Christian era. However, this argument seems to be unacceptable (cf. Acts 8:32).
[320] Porter, 'Traditional,' 410–411; Bruce, *John*, 52–53; Marshall, 'Lamb,' 433; Carey, 'Lamb,' 106; Jeremias, *TDNT*, I, 339–340.
[321] Edwards, 'Christological,' 382. See also R. Maddox, 'Function,' 118 n. 1. Cf. ἔδωκεν in John 3:16 could allude to παρέδωκεν/παρεδόθη in Isa 53:6, 12.

53:1–12; 43:3; 42:6; 49:6, 8; 9:1–2). Jesus clearly proclaimed that his death was for atonement, redemption and covenant, to create (restore) the eschatological people of God. In particular, the descent of the Holy Spirit upon Jesus in John 1:32–33 alludes to Isa 11:2; 42:1; 61:1.

2.3.1.4 The Passover Lamb

The majority of Johannine commentators[322] accept that one of the main theological backgrounds to 'the Lamb of God' is the Passover Lamb, even though some are not confident about the expiatory effect of the Passover lamb. This argument can be supported not only from the Fourth Gospel itself but also from other literature in the NT. Firstly, interpreting the crucifixion of Jesus in the light of the Passover lamb can be found in other references in the NT, such as 1 Cor 5:7; 1 Pet 1:19; Acts 8:32. So the use of the Passover lamb was not unknown as a description of Jesus in primitive Christianity.[323] Barrett comments:

> The probable source of John's thought and language is the paschal interpretation of the last supper and the Eucharist. The Eucharist is a paschal meal and in it the death of Christ for the remission of sins is portrayed.[324]

Bruce further argues that:

> The presentation of the redemptive work of Christ in terms of the exodus motif in so many strands of the New Testament teaching shows how primitive was the Christian use of this motif-going back, quite probably, to the period of Jesus' ministry …. The coincidence of Jesus' death with the Passover season no doubt helped the interpretation of his work as a new exodus.[325]

Secondly, the Gospel of John in itself clearly shows the richness of the Passover motif. Basically, it has to be noted that the Passover feast which featured just once at the end of Jesus's public ministry in the Synoptics, was

---

[322] Cf. Porter, 'Traditional,' 403–427; Barrett, *John*, 176–177; idem., 'Lamb,' 218; Brown, *John I-XII*, 61–63; Lindars, *John*, 109; Carson, *John*, 150; Evans, *Word*, 181–182; Grigsby, 'Cross,' 54; M. W. G. Stibbe, *Storyteller*, 35; Marshall, 'Lamb,' 433; idem., 'Development,' 160 n. 4; Morris, *John*, 127; Carey, 'Lamb,' 107, 111, 118–119; Turner, 'Atonement,' 120; F. F. Bruce, 'Saviour,' 64; Whitacre, *John*, 67; Goppelt, *Typos*, 189–190; Jeremias, *Eucharistic*, 146; Hengel, *Atonement*, 46; Polhill, 'John 1–4,' 449; G. R. Beasley-Murray, *Life*, 38; Longenecker, *Christology*, 49–50; Edwards, 'Christological,' 382; Lee, *Flesh*, 167; Davies, *Rhetoric*, 234–235. Contra Dodd, *Interpretation*, 233–235 says that the Passover motif is not clear in the Fourth Gospel. Also R. Kysar, *Fourth*, 140.

[323] Hengel, *Atonement*, 46.

[324] Barrett, *John*, 147; Hengel, *Atonement*, 46; Marshall, *Supper*, 57–75.

[325] Bruce, 'Saviour,' 64.

included at least three times in the Fourth Gospel, which could reflect the prominence of the Passover motif concerning the work of Jesus. Theologically, very notable things happened to Jesus at the centre of each of the Passover feasts.[326] Particularly in the passion narrative, the time Jesus was crucified on the cross was identified with the time the Passover lamb was slaughtered in the Temple at the day of preparation of Passover celebration (John 18:28; 19:14, 31). Also, the reference to 'hyssop' in 19:29 seems to recall one of the items used at the Passover festival in Exod 12:22. Furthermore, the fact that Jesus's legs were not broken in John 19:36 reflects the injunction that the legs of the Passover lamb must not be broken in Exod 12:46. Therefore, Porter rightly emphasizes the centrality of the Passover theme in the Fourth Gospel:

> The Passover theme essentially states that Jesus is seen by the author of the Fourth Gospel as the suitable and in fact ideal or perfect Passover victim. Since the animal sacrificed at Passover symbolized deliverance from the angel of death as well as redemption from the oppression of Egypt, which leads to the exodus and, eventually, entrance into Canaan, there are several supporting themes in the Fourth Gospel that could be cited as giving further support for the Passover theme.[327]

The argument that the Lamb of God is the Passover Lamb is supported by another title, 'the Son of God' attested by the Baptist at the same context (v. 34). The two titles ('the Lamb of God' and 'the Son of God') are simultaneously applied to Jesus. This reminds us of the vicarious atoning death of the firstborn, who was substituted by the paschal lamb in each Israelite family, as the representative of his family. At the Passover as set against the background of the exodus (deliverance, redemption),[328] through which Israel was corporately chosen as the son/firstborn of God and as the servant of God (Exod 4:22–23; 12:1–51), namely, as the kingdom of priests at the Sinai covenant (Exod 19:5–6), in order to restore the gentiles (including all creation) as the sons of God.

However, there are some conflicting arguments about the expiatory effect of the Passover victim.[329] Barrett[330] is not convinced by the expiatory

---

[326] Cf. Jesus's Temple accident in John 2:12–25/Jesus's feeding of five thousand people in John 6:1–15/Jesus's passion narrative in John 18–19. Further, the term, 'Passover' is mentioned about 10 times in John's Gospel. Cf. John 2:13, 23; 6:4; 11:55 (twice); 12:1; 13:1; 18:28, 39; 19:14 (19).
[327] Porter, 'Traditional,' 403–427, quoted from 406.
[328] Cf. Holland, *Contours*, 239; idem., *Motif*, 97; B. Pitre, *Tribulation*, 448. See 1.3. The Firstborn Son/the paschal lamb and the Exodus of Ra, *Christological*.
[329] For detail, see Holland, *Motif*, 62–63 n. 305.

function of the Passover lamb, and instead prefers the vicarious atonement of the servant of the Lord in Isa 53:12. Barrett's argument is supported by Marshall.[330] Nevertheless, Marshall[331] admits that the original Passover victim had a redemptive effect in delivering Israel from Egypt.

Carey[333] claims that the Passover offering in first century Judaism might not have had an expiatory function. However, for Carey, the original paschal sacrifice obviously had vicarious and expiatory power, in which the first Christians understood the death of Jesus, who had himself first connected his death to the Passover against the background of the Last Supper. After the examination of the Last Supper, Jeremias[334] concludes that Jesus understood his death as a redemptive, vicarious sacrifice, and goes on to say that the original Passover was accepted as an atonement. Morris[335] argues that all sacrificial offerings including the Passover offering had this expiatory efficacy. As has already been discussed,[336] the vicarious death of the firstborn male (the paschal lamb) as the representative of each family in the context of the original Passover brought about not only the exodus of Israel from the bondage of Egypt (cf. redemption/deliverance), but also the expiation of the sin of the nation of Israel, the son of God, the firstborn of God (cf. atonement).

Holland[337] argues that the value of the vicarious, redemptive atoning death of the firstborn, the paschal lamb, is shown by Yahweh's regulations that the first male offspring of every womb must be sacrificed to Yahweh. As a result, each firstborn of the Israelites had to be redeemed by the lamb (Exod

---

[330] Barrett, 'Lamb,' 217–218. See also Smalley, 'Salvation,' 326; Bultmann, *John*, 96; Brown, *John I-XII*, 68; Dodd, *Interpretation*, 233, who accepts that only the first Passover had expiatory efficacy.

[331] Marshall, 'Lamb,' 433.

[332] Marshall, 'Lamb,' 433; idem., *Supper*, 77. Cf. *m. Pesah.* 10:6. See also Porter, 'Traditional,' 411, who assumes that the original Passover offering was not sacrificial, even though he admits that the sacrificial concept of the Passover victim was apparently developed early on (Num 28:22; Ezek 45:21–25). Grigsby, 'Cross,' 53 says that the original paschal victim did not have expiatory power, but the expiatory effect of the paschal sacrifice was accepted by the time of the Fourth Gospel's composition. Also, Lee, *Flesh*, 167.

[333] Carey, 'Lamb,' 118–119.

[334] Jeremias, *Eucharistic*, 146, 225.

[335] Morris, *John*, 127; Schnackenburg, *John*, I, 299–300; Smith, *John*, 69; Whitacre, *John*, 67; Beasley-Murray, *Life*, 38. Cf. Josephus, *Ant.* 2.312; *Exod R.* 15; 'I see the paschal blood and propitiate you' (35b), and 'I mercifully take pity on you by means of the paschal Blood and the blood of circumcision, and I propitiate your souls.' (35a). See further Str-B, III, 699; IV, 40.

[336] See 1.3. The Firstborn Son/ the paschal lamb and the Exodus and 2.4. The Suffering Servant of Yahweh and the Firstborn Son/the paschal lamb of Ra, *Christological*.

[337] Holland, *Contours*, 241–242; idem., *Motif*, 100–101. See also Pitre, *Tribulation*, 406–412; I. H. Marshall, *Supper*, 77; idem., 'Development,' 153–169, esp. 154, 160; Cullmann, *Christology*, 71; Brown, *John I-XII*, 62; Jeremias, *Eucharistic*, 225f; idem., *TDNT*, I, 340; Dodd, *Interpretation*, 234.

13:1–2, 11–16; 34:19–20) and that the Levites had been taken in place of Israel's firstborn (cf. ransom money) (Num 3:12–13, 40–51; 8:14–19). Holland [338] points out that the vicarious atonement of the firstborn is reflected in the Levites' substitution for the firstborn in Num 8:16–19 (Num 1:53). At this juncture, Holland's argument concerning Ezek 45:17–23 has to be introduced. From this passage, Holland [339] observes the raising of a Davidic prince, whose main function was to provide abundant sacrifices for the sins of the covenant community not during the Day of Atonement but during the Passover, is against the background of the eschatological Temple and the eschatological new exodus. Therefore, Holland[340] rightly emphasizes that in Ezekiel the Davidic prince executed the paschal sacrifice, which absorbed the expiatory function of the Day of Atonement. Also, J. K. Howard [341] claims that John 1:29 recalled Ezekiel's statement concerning the eschatological paschal offering making atonement for the people's sins.

This argument could be supported by Kim[342] who claims that, in John 11:49, 51; 18:13–14, 24, Caiaphas's conspiracy to kill Jesus for the nation against the background of the Passover seems to reflect the eschatological fulfilment of the sacrifice offered on the Day of Atonement—on which day the high priest made atoning sacrifice for the sins of the nation in the OT (Lev 16).

Therefore, in the light of the atoning sacrificial efficacy of Jesus as the paschal lamb, it is difficult to accept the arguments of some Johannine commentators.[343] They claim that in the Fourth Gospel the salvation of God is fulfilled not by a vicarious and expiatory death for sin, redemption, the work of Jesus's atoning significance on the cross, but by God's gracious self-disclosure, revelation, the demonstration of God's love on the cross. However, this theological argument has been severely criticized.[344]

---

[338] Holland, *Contours*, 245–247; idem., *Motif*, 105–106. Cf. For some references regarding the idea of the vicarious atonement of the death of the firstborn (such as, the second commandment of the Decalogue (Exod 20:5); Exod 4:24–26; Ps 78:38, 49–52; Mic 6:6–7; Zech 12:10; Ezek 45:18–23), see Holland, *Motif*, 100–114; idem., *Contours*, 242–253.
[339] Holland, *Motif*, 63–65. Cf. Ezek 34:23–24; 37:24–25; 44:3; 45:7, 22; 46:2, 4, 8. Also, Porter, 'Traditional,' 411.
[340] Holland, *Motif*, 63, 111. See also J. D. G. Dunn 'Understanding,' 133.
[341] J. K. Howard, 'Passover,' 332.
[342] Kim, *Exposition*, 154–157.
[343] Cf. Bultmann, *Theology*, II, 15–92, esp. 54; J. T. Forestell, *Word*, 157–166; Whitacre, *John*, 68. Nevertheless, Forestell admits that John 1:29 describes Jesus as the Passover lamb, possibly regarded as an expiatory sacrifice in Judaism in the first century (ibid., 162).
[344] Carson, *John*, 152–153. For detail discussion, see also Turner, 'Atonement,' 99–122; Grigsby, 'Cross,' 51–80.

Furthermore, I submit that an examination of Zech 12:10, which was recalled after the passion narrative (par. John 19:37) represents the climax of John 1:29. From Zech 12:10, Holland[345] observes a reference concerning 'the death of a firstborn son/only one son,' which obviously recalled the Passover event to the Jews. Holland continues to indicate Yahweh's judgement against the nations to protect Israel, which echoed the first exodus events (Zech 12:7–9). Jesus's death by being pierced with a spear was the fulfilment of the death of the firstborn being pierced. Therefore, the death of Jesus represented the eschatological fulfilment of the Passover, which was intimately connected to the firstborn. Jesus's death by being pierced with a spear was the fulfilment of the death of the firstborn. Hence, the death of Jesus represented the eschatological fulfilment of the Passover Lamb, which was the substitute for the firstborn.

To sum up, as a result of my examination of the Johannine Lamb of God, the Passover Lamb seems to be the strongest background for it. This conclusion is supported by the centrality of the Passover theme of the Fourth Gospel. Further, the Johannine Lamb of God could be based on the suffering Servant, the same figure as the Davidic messianic King, of the Lord in Deutero-Isaiah. As we saw earlier, the vicarious, redemptive atoning death of the firstborn or the paschal lamb is the basis of the works of the Isaianic-suffering servant (Davidic messianic king). This is set against the background of the restoration of Israel from exile and the restoration of the gentiles to the sons of God.[346] Furthermore, the Johannine Lamb could depend on the concept of the apocalyptic lamb, who is the same figure as the Davidic messianic king (Rev 5:1–14) and as the firstborn (the paschal lamb) and the Danielic Son of Man (Rev 1:4–8, 13. cf. Dan 7:13–14).

Conclusively, through the discussion of some Christological titles used by the Baptist in John 1:29–34, we can again recognize the interrelationship between the firstborn/Son of God, the paschal lamb, the apocalyptic lamb, the Davidic messianic king, the suffering servant of God, the Spirit-Baptizer.[347]

2.3.2 The Spirit-Baptiser and the Son of God (John 1:32–33)

In the Gospel of John there is no clear comment about Jesus's baptism with water. However, it can be assumed that since, in the Synoptics (Matt 3:16; Mark 1:10; Luke 3:22), John the Baptist saw the Spirit coming down upon

---

[345] Holland, *Motif*, 110.
[346] See 2.4. The Suffering Servant and the Firstborn Son/the paschal lamb of Ra, *Christological*.
[347] C. Bennema, *Power*, 161 n. 1 thinks that the Lamb of God in John 1:29 includes the suffering Servant of the Lord (Isa 53), the paschal lamb (Exod 12), and the victorious Apocalyptic Lamb (*1 En.* 90:38; *Test. Jos.* 19:8).

Jesus in the context of Jesus's water baptism in the river Jordan, the descending of the Holy Spirit upon Jesus happened after Jesus's water baptism. Although there are some differences concerning the description of the baptismal setting between John's Gospel and the Synoptics, the descending of the Holy Spirit upon Jesus is a common statement in the four Gospels, and particularly the Holy Spirit came down like a dove. The opening of heaven and the voice from heaven (cf. Mark 1:11) only appear in the Synoptics, and instead, that Jesus was 'the Son of God' was testified to by the Baptist in the Fourth Gospel. In the light of the new exodus, I shall now discuss what is meant by the Spirit's coming and dwelling upon Jesus, of the Spirit's coming down as a dove, and, of 'the Son of God.'

Firstly, what is meant by the Spirit coming down and remaining upon Jesus? Boismard [348] understands that at the moment of Jesus's water baptism, the Holy Spirit's descending and remaining upon him reflected the divine ordinance of prophets through the Holy Spirit in the OT (Num 11:16–17, 24–29). Boismard suggests that it also meant the fulfilment of the Isaianic prophecies concerning the Messiah in Isa 42:1; 11:2; 61:1. He further states that:

> Jesus possesses in himself the Spirit which he received at his baptism; he can thus by a singular privilege be at once the Prophet like Moses announced in Deut 18:18 and the King of Israel, descendant of the patriarch Joseph and heir of his kingdom.[349]

Boismard interprets Jesus's signs and discourses in the light of the new Moses, the fulfilment of Deut 18, and as a descendent of the patriarch Joseph, the fulfilment of Gen 41:38, which represented the influences of Samaritan theology upon the Gospel of John.

However, regarding Isa 40:3 quoted in John 1:23, Isa 11 is clearly connected to the Baptism with the Holy Spirit of the Davidic Messiah expressed as the Root of Jesse, in the context of the restoration of the exiled people of God (cf. Isa 9:1–7; 55:3; 61:1).[350] Bruce[351] thinks that the descending and dwelling of the Holy Spirit on Jesus was the fulfilment of God's promise to pour out the Spirit upon the coming Davidic messianic King against the background of Isa 11:1–2, and, therefore one who baptizes people with the Spirit in

---

[348] Boismard, *Moses*, 40, 114–115.
[349] Boismard, *Moses*, 40.
[350] Koester, *Symbolism*, 159; Brown, *John I-XII*, 66; W. Russell, 'Holy,' 230; Beasley-Murray, *Life*, 63–64; Bennema, *Power*, 161–163; Burge, *Anointed*, 54–56. Cf. *1 En.* 49:3; 62:2; *Test. Jud.* 24:2; *Ps. Sol.* 17:37, 42; 18:7; *Sir.* 4:12, 24; *Jub.* 25:14.
[351] Bruce, *John*, 53–54. Cf. Acts 10:38. See also Carson, *John*, 151; Koester, *Symbolism*, 159; Whitacre, *John*, 69; Schnackenburg, *John*, I, 305; Morris, *John*, 133–134.

terms of eschatological salvation, the new exodus. Bruce[352] goes on to say that the background of v. 33 could be Ezek 36:25–27, in which God promised to cleanse his exiled people with water sprinkling and to give the Holy Spirit to them in the light of the restoration, and therefore the anointing of the Spirit upon Jesus was the fulfilment and the announcement that the promised eschatological age was coming.

Jeremias[353] particularly observes that some Jewish literature and the NT show the idea that the Spirit is quenched because of the sin of Israel. Despite this the Qumran sectarians thought of the presence and the working of the Holy Spirit among themselves.[354] From here, Jeremias[355] further indicates that the idea of the quenching of the Spirit and the absence of the Spirit represented alienation from God, which meant the judgement of God, and that people longed for the eschatological return of the Spirit, showing his dwelling among his community forever to complete his saving work.

Secondly, what is meant by the coming down of the Spirit from heaven *as a dove* upon Jesus? It needs to be noted that the Spirit's descent like a dove is referred to not only in the Gospel of John but also in the Synoptics. This is not by chance. Thinking that the symbol of 'dove' could be understood against the background of Gen 1:2 in the OT and Judaism, Smalley[356] suggests that the creation motif by God was being used again in the Gospel of John (cf. John 1:1, 14). Smalley further relates 'the dove' of Jesus's Spirit-baptism to 'the dove' in the Flood of Noah in Gen 8:8–12, and, therefore the water in which Jesus was baptized could be understood in the light of judgement and salvation (cf. 1 Pet 3:20–21). Carmichael also states that the relationship of the Holy Spirit to 'dove' can be found in the Dead Sea Scrolls and rabbinic sources.[357] If the returning and dwelling of the Spirit as

---

[352] Bruce, *John*, 54; Koester, *Symbolism*, 161; Carson, *John*, 152. Cf. Joel 2:28–29; *1QS* 4:20–21; *Jub.* 1:23. Cf. W. A. VanGemeren, 'Spirit,' 81–102; R. J. Sklba, 'Spirit,' 1–17. Cf. Isa 32:15.
[353] Jeremias, *Theology*, I, 80–81; Turner, 'Atonement,' 116. Cf. *1 Macc.* 4:46; 9:27; 14:41; 2 [*Syr. Apoc.*] *Bar.* 85:3; Str-B, I, 127–134; II, 128–34; *t. Sota* 13:2; Acts 2:17; Rom 8:23; 2 Cor 1:22; 5:5; Eph 1:4; 1 Thes 4:8; Heb 6:4f; John 7:39.
[354] Cf. *1 QH* 12:11f; 13:19; 14:13; 16:11.
[355] Jeremias, *Theology*, I, 82. Cf. Str-B, II, 134.
[356] Smalley, 'Salvation,' 327. See also G. Johnston, *Spirit-Paraclete*, 20–21; P. Garnet, 'Baptism,' 53–55; L. E. Keck, 'Spirit,' 51.
[357] Carmichael, *Creation*, 44ff. See also D. C. Allison, *Moses*, 200. Cf. 'The Spirit of God was borne over the water, as a dove which broods over her young.' (*b. Hag.* 15a; *y. Hag.* 77b). Carmichael especially notes that the verb 'hover' used to depict the descending of the Holy Spirit like dove is the same verb describing the Spirit's hovering over water in the creation narrative (Gen 1:2). This verb was used by Moses to describe Yahweh's guiding of the first Exodus people in the wilderness to the promised land in terms of an eagle's flight, hovering over its young (Deut 32:11) (p. 45).

a dove in the baptismal setting could be understood against the background of the Spirit-Creation motif in Gen 1:2 and of the judgement and salvation motif in Gen 8:8 in the light of the eschatological time, Jeremias' conclusion could be right, 'The eschatological presence of the Spirit thus represents a new creation.'[358]

Isa 42:1 shows that the servant of Yahweh, the same figure as the Davidic messianic King, upon whom Yahweh put his Spirit is the agent for the new creation, which means the restoration or new exodus, is reflected in the narrative of Jesus's baptism (cf. Mark 1:9–11; Matt 3:13–17; Luke 3:21–22).[359] The relationship between the coming of the Spirit and the new creation in the light of the eschatological time is particularly well supported by the testimony of John the Baptist concerning Jesus, 'he who will baptize with the Holy Spirit' (John 1:33). Jesus is the baptizer who will baptize the eschatological people of God with the Holy Spirit. This image appears in the Gospel of John.[360]

Thirdly, 'the Son of God'[361] requires some comment in the context of a baptismal setting. Concerning the Lamb of God who is based on the Passover Lamb, 'the Son of God' alludes to the firstborn of Exod 4:22–23. Further, as Bruce[362] suggests, 'the Son of God' is understood from Ps 2:7 (2 Sam 7:14), which denoted the inauguration of Jesus as the Davidic Messiah. However, Burge[363] and Carson[364] argue that this title could be based on Isa 42:1, which emphasizes Jesus, the servant of God, as the Anointed One empowered by the Spirit. However, if it is noted that in the Synoptics, the voice concerning Jesus's identity at the baptismal setting was proclaimed from heaven, but in the Fourth Gospel John the Baptist himself testified to Jesus after the bestowal of the Spirit to him, the title ('the Son of God') mentioned by the Baptist could be the Johannine version of the voice from heaven in the Synoptics (see Mark 1:11). Thus, taking all this evidence

---

[358] Jeremias, *Theology*, I, 82, 85.
[359] Cf. Marshall, *Luke*, 153–154. See b. The Heavenly Voices at the Baptism (Matt 3:17; Mark 1:11; Luke 3:22; cf. John 1:29, 34, 36) and the Transfiguration (Matt 17:5; Mark 9:7; Luke 9:35; 2 Pet 1:17) of 2.5.2.1. Jesus as the Servant of Yahweh in the New Testament of Ra, *Christological*.
[360] Cf. the new creation or the newborn with the Holy Spirit (John 3:1–10), Jesus's bestowing of the Holy Spirit to His disciples after Easter (John 20:21–23; Gen 2:7; Ezek 37:1–14). Cf. Koester, *Symbolism*, 161.
[361] Some Johannine scholars argue 'the Chosen One of God' is the original one rather than 'the Son of God.' Cf. Carson, *John*, 152; Morris, *John*, 134; Smalley, 'Salvation,' 328. But it is not clear. Cf. Koester, *Symbolism*, 159–160; F. Pack, 'Holy,' 139–140 says that 'the Son of God' is the decisive one of the Baptist's testimony.
[362] Bruce, *John*, 55; Koester, *Symbolism*, 159.
[363] Burge, *Anointed*, 61.
[364] Carson, *John*, 152.

together, the voice should be understood in the light of Exod 4:22–23; Ps 2:7; Isa 42:1.[365]

Psalm 2:7 is one of the coronation Psalms, in which Yahweh proclaimed to a Davidic king who is enthroned as Israel's king, 'you are my son, whom I have begotten today,' which is the fulfilment of Yahweh's promises to David in 2 Sam 7:12–16.[366] Here the Davidic king becomes the Son of God, the representative of Israel, the people of Yahweh, who is the true king over them. Isa 42 is the first of the Songs of the servant of Yahweh (Isa 42–53; 61:1–3), who is the Agent of the new exodus in Isaiah. Interestingly, Isaiah itself introduced the agent of the new exodus as the Davidic messianic king in Isa 9:1–7; 11:1–16; 55:3; 61:1–11. Isa 42:1 in particular describes the pleasure of Yahweh in his chosen Servant, his bestowing of the Spirit on him, and his commissioning him to deliver people under the exile in the eschatological time. Actually, the Isaianic suffering servant of the Lord is the same figure as the Davidic messianic King, alluding to the dual status of Israel as the son/firstborn of God and as the servant of God in Exod 4:22–23.

On the other hand, Brunson[367] understands 'the Coming One' (v. 30) as the enfleshment of Yahweh, the sin-removing Lamb of God (v. 27), the Son of God (v. 34), the one who will bring the eschatological blessing of the Holy Spirit (v. 33). Brunson mentions the removal of Israel's sin as the function of Yahweh, the Isaianic coming of Yahweh. Similarly, following Brunson, Dennis[368] also identifies Jesus with Yahweh who comes to release Israel from sin (Isa 40:3–4; John 1:29) and the messianic branch on whom the Spirit of the Lord will rest (Isa 11:1–4; John 1:31–33), for the fulfilment of the Isaianic restoration. Dennis[369] then argues for the Lamb of God (1:29) as the Passover Lamb (John 19), and points out the vicarious atonement of Jesus's death in the Johannine *hyper* texts, bringing about a second exodus deliverance. However, both Brunson and Dennis fail to give any proper explanation about the interrelationship of these Christological titles especially between the [Passover] Lamb of God and the Son of God, the Davidic messianic King, the suffering servant of the Lord.

---

[365] Cf. P. Bretscher, 'Exodus 4:22–23,' 301–311; R. E. Watt, *Isaiah's*, 110ff; J. Marcus, *Way*, 61ff; S. Kim, 'Baptism,' 17–20; I. H. Marshall, 'Reconsideration,' 326–336.

[366] Cf. Boismard, *Moses*, 100–102, recognizes that the OT background of 'the Son of God' could be related to the Davidic covenant in 2 Sam 7:9–16, nonetheless, strangely, tries to understand this title from the viewpoint of the rite of adoption in Ancient Asia and to emphasize the concept of God's protection in the light of the relationship between father and son.

[367] Brunson, *Psalm 118*, 240–264, esp. 242.

[368] Dennis, *Gathering*, 336–337.

[369] Dennis, *Gathering*, 352–353. See also, Brunson, *Psalm 118*, 157.

To sum up, the Spirit's coming down and remaining upon Jesus and 'the Son of God' was the fulfilment of God's promise to pour out the Spirit upon the coming Davidic messianic King (the suffering servant of the Lord). This is set against the background of Isa 11:1; 42:1; 61:1 and Ezek 36:25–27, and the announcement of the arrival of the promised eschatological salvation, the new exodus, the new creation. The reference to dove which could be based on the Spirit-Creation motif in Gen 1:2 and of Judgement and the Salvation motif in Gen 8:8–12 could also be understood in the light of the new eschatological creation.

2.4 Disciples' Testimonies and Jesus's Promise (John 1:35–51).

The overall atmosphere of this part seems to reflect the coming of the Messiah who was eagerly expected, even though some of the disciples and the people who met Jesus used several, diverse messianic titles. In particular, the testimony of Nathanael about Jesus seems to be the climax of the messianic titles of Jesus. As a response to Nathanael's testimony, Jesus promised that the disciples, including Nathanael, would see heaven open and the angels of God ascending and descending on the Son of Man.

2.4.1 Disciples' Testimonies

Concerning Philip's testimony to Jesus as 'the one of whom Moses and the Prophet wrote,' some commentators [370] assume it shows a messianic expectation based on the prophetic promise by Moses in Deut 18:15–19. Boismard[371] divides this passage into two parts: Moses's prophecy and the Prophet's prophecy. Boismard presents Gen 49:10, Num 24:17 and Deut 18:18 as candidate verses from the Pentateuch (Moses) in support of this, but he thinks that since the first two verses are the promise about the king coming from a descendant of the patriarch Judah, they could not be the background of Philip's messianic expectation. On the presupposition that the Fourth Gospel was strongly influenced by Samaritan theology, [372] Boismard argues that not only is Deut 18:18 the basis of Philip's

---

[370] Cf. Bruce, *John*, 59; Carson, *John*, 159; Boismard, *Moses*, 25.

[371] Boismard, *Moses*, 26–31.

[372] Boismard, *Moses*, 31 argues that all concepts about Moses, Joseph, prophet and king can be found in Samaritan Tradition, *Memar Marqah* (4 A.D.) and *Durran* 22. Cf. 'The *Taheb* will come in peace to reign over the place which God has chosen for pious people. Joseph came, he was rewarded with a kingdom after his enslavement and those who oppressed him sought his favors.... There is no one like *Joseph the king*, and no one like *Moses the prophet*. Both of them possessed an elevated position: Moses possessed prophecy and Joseph possessed the good mountain (i.e. Garizim). There is no one greater than these two (*Memar Marqah*, 4:12)' ... 'And after his death, Joseph was glorified, his bones were carried back by the great Prophet (i.e., Moses) who had been called 'god' by him who reigns. Two men in whom God was well pleased: *Joseph the king and Moses the Prophet* (*Durran* 22).' (quoted from Boismard, *Moses*, 31).

understanding about Jesus, but also of Nathanael's testimonies of Jesus in John 1:45 (cf. the Son of God and the King of Israel). For Boismard, Jesus has to be considered in the light of a prophet like Moses in the Gospel of John and this is also supported by Jesus's supernatural knowledge about Nathanael, [373] reflecting the tradition that prophets had supernatural knowledge in the OT.

Furthermore, Boismard[374] tries to connect the miracle of Jesus changing water into wine in Cana, to Joseph in Gen 41 giving provisions to the starving Egyptians and unjustifiably asserts that Jesus is not only a prophet like Moses but also the King of the line of the patriarch Joseph. Later, however, Boismard[375] rightly recognizes that Nathanael's testimony ('the Son of God and the King of Israel') reflected the Davidic covenant in 2 Sam 7:9–16 (cf. 1 Chron 17:3–14, Pss 2; Ps 89). However, he understands it in the light of the adoption rite in Ancient Asia. Further, he argues that it emphasizes the protection of the father in the relationship between son and father, and that this relationship is not limited to the Davidic kings but extended to all those who keep the law of God.

However, the majority of Johannine commentators [376] recognize that Nathanael's confession was based on the Davidic messianic expectation, which can be extensively found not only in the Old and New Testaments but also in extra-biblical literature. Also, as Boismard recognizes, a messianic figure of whom Moses wrote could be related not only to the Prophet like Moses of Deut 18 but also the Davidic messianic king of Gen 49:10. 'The Son of God' [377] can be basically thought of as one of the expressions of covenant thought with God in the OT (Exod 4:22–23), which was the background to the first exodus. Howton[378] suggests that this title could be taken from Hos 11:1, in the light of the new exodus reflecting the first exodus.

Above all, it has to be noted that in the testimony of Nathanael, sonship was connected with kingship. This link between sonship and kingship can

---

[373] Cf. There are some arguments about the identity of Nathanael. Carson, *John*, 159 thinks Nathanael is identified with Bartholomew, because Bartholomew came out with Philip in the Synoptics (cf. Matt 10:3; Mark 3:18; Luke 6:14). *Contra* Smith, *John*, 75; Morris, *John*, 143–144. However, C. E. Hill, 'Nathanael,' 60–61 says that Nathanael was James, son of Alphaeus, according to *Epistula Apostolorum*.

[374] Boismard, *Moses*, 32–34.

[375] Boismard, *Moses*, 100–112.

[376] Cf. Bruce, *John*, 61; Carson, *John*, 162; J. J. Collins, 'Son,' 65–82; Michaels, *John*, 41; Smith, *John*, 77; Whitacre, *John*, 74–75; Kim, *Exposition*, 46; C. R. Koester, 'Messianic,' 23–34; *idem*., *Symbolism*, 40–41.

[377] Cf. D. J. Howton, 'Son,' 227–237; Bretscher, 'Exodus 4:22–23,' 301–311.

[378] Howton, 'Son,' 230.

be appropriately understood against the background of the Davidic covenant in 2 Sam 7:12–14.[379] Here the Davidic king becomes the Son of God, the representative of Israel who are the people of Yahweh, the sons of God. Also, the Davidic king as the servant of God will build the house for God, the Temple. This Davidic covenant is everlasting, so it is never cancelled in spite of the Babylonian captivity of Israel (cf. Isa 55:3). The eschatological fulfilment of the Davidic covenant, which was called the new covenant or the covenant of peace,[380] is promised by God in the Prophets against the background of the new exodus.[381] This messianic expectation was also richly reflected in extra-biblical Jewish literature.[382]

Furthermore, in v. 46, Nathanael's scornful affirmation against 'Jesus of Nazareth' could reflect to some extent a sign of Nathanael's messianic expectation, in which the Messiah would come from somewhere other than Nazareth.[383] If we observe a reference to the Davidic messianic expectation of some people in the light of David's hometown Bethlehem, rather than Galilee in the Gospel of John, Nathanael's negative response against Nazareth could be based on the Davidic messianic hope in relation to Bethlehem[384] (cf. John 7:41–42, 52), David's hometown, according to the Prophet Micah's prophecy in Mic 5:2, which could probably be harmonized with his testimony- the Son of God and the King of Israel.

In John 8:12, Jesus proclaimed himself as the light of the World against the background of the dispute among the Jews (John 7:41–42) as to whether Jesus, who came from Galilee, was the Davidic Messiah. This could allude to Isa 9:1–7 (esp. v. 2) (cf. Isa 42:6; 49:6; 51:4; 55:3; 60:1–2), through which Jesus disclosed that he is the very Davidic messianic king, who is the same figure as the suffering servant of Yahweh.

The supernatural knowledge of Jesus about Nathanael sitting 'under the fig tree' could also be considered in terms of the Davidic messianic expectation (cf. Mic 4:4; Zech 3:10). Some commentators[385] believe the incident shows his supernatural knowledge concerning Nathanael's behaviour. But, based

---

[379] Carson, *John*, 162; Koester, *Symbolism*, 40–41. Cf. Pss 2:7; 89.
[380] Cf. Isa 54:10–13; 55:3; Jer 31:31–33; 33:15–17; Ezek 34:23–25; 37:23–28.
[381] Cf. Isa 9:1–7; 11:10–12; 55:3; Jer 23:5f; Ezek 34:23ff; 37:24ff; Amos 9:11.
[382] S. Kim, 'Interpretation,' 229; idem., 'Temple,' 87–131; idem., 'Stone,' 134–148; Koester, *Symbolism*, 40–41; idem., 'Messianic,' 23–34. Cf. 4QFlor. 1:1–13; 1QSa 2:11ff; 4QpsDanA^a; 4QPBless; Ps. Sol. 17–18; 1 En. 90:28f; 105:2; 4 Ezra 7:28–29; 12:31–34; 13:52; 14:9; 2 Bar. 40:1–3; Tg. Zech 6:12; Tg. Isa 53:5.
[383] Morris, *John*, 145; Kim, *Exposition*, 45.
[384] Kim, *Exposition*, 45.
[385] C. F. D. Moule, 'Fig Tree,' 211. Cf. Bruce, *John*, 61; Carson, *John*, 161.

on a rabbinic source[386] saying that 'under the fig tree' symbolized domestic tranquility, other commentators[387] connect this to the place for the study of the Torah, and argue that Nathanael was probably meditating on messianic prophecies in the OT.

On the other hand, other scholars understanding this in the light of Hos 9:10, relating Israel to figs, assume it implies that a new Israel—represented by Nathanael—was found by Jesus.[388] It could imply that Nathanael was called out from 'under the fig tree' symbolizing the old-Israel community, into a new community centred around Jesus.[389]

Other Johannine commentators argue that Jesus's comment recalled the vision of 'every man under his vine and under his fig tree' in the OT. For example, Koester argues that his mention is the fulfilment of Zech 3:10 with 1 Kings 4:25, Mic 4:4, *1 Macc.* 14:12. After pointing out 'the Branch' in the context of Zech 3:10 with Zech 6:12–13, Koester emphasizes that the image of calling under the fig tree implied peace and prosperity, with the advent of the Branch, the Davidic Messiah.[390]

To sum up, Nathanael's confession about Jesus can be considered against the background of the eschatological fulfilment of God's covenant to David in 2 Sam 7:12–14, which was repeatedly promised through the Prophets. Therefore, the coming of the Davidic Messiah could mean the beginning of eschatological salvation, the restoration, the new exodus.

2.4.2 Allusion to Jacob's Vision and the Son of Man (John 1:51)

As a response against Nathanael's testimony, Jesus promised him that he would see heaven open, and the angels of God ascending and descending on the Son of Man. Most Johannine commentators seem to accept Jacob's dream in Gen 28:12 as a background to Jesus's promise here. There are several opinions to be considered in understanding this promise.

---

[386] Cf. Str-B, I, 858; III, 371. 1 Kings 4:25; Isa 36:16; Mic 4:4; Zech 3:10.
[387] Morris, *John*, 146; Witherington, *Wisdom*, 71; Malina and Rohrbaugh, *John*, 56; R. F. Collins, 'Representative,' 35. However, this is rejected by Koester, 'Messianic,' 24, who says that it is very speculative.
[388] Michaels, *John*, 41.
[389] Burkett, *Son*, 114. Jer 24:1–8; 29:17; 8:13.
[390] Koester, 'Messianic,' 30; idem., *Symbolism*, 40–41; Dennis, *Gathering*, 162–163. See also L. P. Trudinger, 'Israelite,' 117–120; Howard-Brook, *Becoming*, 74. Cf. Isa 11:1; Zech 3:8; 6:12; Jer 23:5; 33:15; 4QFlor. 10–12a; 4QPBless; 4QpIsa^a 8–10; *Test. Jud.* 24; *y. Ber.* 5a; *Gen R.* 98:8; *Num R.* 18:21; *Lam R.* 1:51; *Midr. Ps* 21:1; *Pirqe R. Eliezer* 48; Rev 5:5.

Firstly, some Johannine scholars[391] suggest that Jesus, 'the Son of Man' should be understood in relation to the ladder of Jacob's vision in Gen 28:12. Morris assumes that the common thread between Jacob's dream and Jesus's promise concerning 'the Son of Man' is 'the thought of communication of the heavens and earth,' and so the role of the ladder is taken by 'the Son of Man,' Jesus, who will be the link between heaven and earth. Morris concludes, 'Jesus is indeed the fulfiller of prophecy, but he is also the Son of Man, the revealer of God, the means of establishing communication between earth and heaven.'[392] Derrett[393] argues that the ladder is replaced by the cross, on which 'the Son of man' is lifted up.

Secondly, some consider that Jacob corresponds to the disciples, or to Nathanael as a representative of the disciples, rather than to the Son of Man, Jesus. This view is offered, since both Jacob and the disciples were receivers of visions from Jesus, the bestower of the revelation,[394] and they were also compared with each other. Jacob-Israel was deceitful but Nathanael as a true Israelite was guileless. Jesus, the Son of Man who will be presented in a vision to the disciples is identified as the Lord in Jacob's dream. Neyrey says that:

> the heavenly Jesus corresponds to the appearing Lord in Gen 28:12. Thus far the allusion to Gen 28:12 in John 1:51 suggests that the focus is on a vision of a heavenly figure; that the angels ascend/descend toward this heavenly figure, not on a ladder; and

---

[391] Cf. Bruce, *John*, 62–63; Morris, *John*, 149–150; J. Ashton, *Understanding*, 347; Milne, *John*, 60; R. V. G. Tasker, *John*, 54; Malina and Rohrbaugh, *John*, 57, 62; Barrett, *John*, 187; B. Lindars, *John*, 122; Carmichael, *Creation*, 60; W. O. Walker, 'John 1:43–51,' 41; Whitacre, *John*, 75–76; Polhill, 'John 1–4,' 449–450; J. A. Drapper, 'Temple,' 279–280; Trudinger, 'Israelite,' 117–120; C. Ham, 'Son,' 78–79; Burkett, *Son*, 117–118, who says that 'Since where Gen 28:12 has 'on it' (ladder), John 1:51 substitutes 'on the Son of the Man'…. Hence, the angels ascend and descend *on* the Son of the Man. The Son of the Man is put in place of the ladder.' (original emphasis). However, Carson, *John*, 163 thinks that the בו in Gen 28:12 has to be translated into 'on him' (Jacob) rather than 'on it' (ladder). Michaels, *John*, 44 argues that 'ἐπί + accusative case' could mean the movement toward a target, that angels ascended from the Son of Man and descended toward the Son of Man in this vision. That is, it means 'on him.' Actually, it is unclear whether בו indicates Jacob or the ladder in the Hebrew Text, even though it was rendered into ἐπ᾽ αὐτῆς ('on it'), pointing to 'ladder' in the Greek version (LXX), Josephus (*Ant.* 19:1) and Philo (*Somn.* 1.3). The rabbis generally seemed to read it as 'on him' (Jacob). From this observation, Lindars, *John*, 122 admits the probability that בו was already rendered 'on him' when the Gospel of John was written, before this usage was adopted to be written by later rabbis. See also C. C. Rowland, 'John 1:51,' 501–502.

[392] Morris, *John*, 149–150, quoted from p. 150; Drapper, 'Temple,' 280; Milne, *John*, 60.

[393] J. D. M. Derrett, *Law*, 416. Cf. John 3:14; 8:28; 12:32, 34. However, this argument has been criticized by Carson, *John*, 163; Barrett, *John*, 187.

[394] Burkett, *Son*, 112, 116; Drapper, 'Temple,' 280; Maddox, 'Function,' 191; Kanagaraj, *Mysticism*, 189.

that Jesus corresponds to the appearing Lord in Jacob's theophany. This implies that Jesus will appear to his disciples in a theophany, just as the Lord appeared to Jacob.[395]

Neyrey believes that his argument is supported by the claim, 'No one has ever seen God' (1:18; 3:13; 6:46), and consequently it was the heavenly Jesus who appeared to the Patriarchs (cf. Abraham, John 8:58) and the Prophets (cf. Isaiah, John 12:41) in their theophanies in the OT; i.e., they were actually Christophanies. It is possible that even Moses was not excluded from this (John 1:18).[396] Further, Neyrey[397] believes that this theological idea can be found in Philo[398] and Justin.[399]

Thirdly, some Johannine commentators[400] link Jesus, the Son of the Man to the place of Jacob's dream, Bethel (which means, 'the house of God' and 'the gate of heaven'). Goppelt[401] thinks that Jesus is compared with the place the ladder stood rather than with Jacob. Similarly, Davies says that:

> in John 1:51 Jesus is not to be set over against Jacob or the ladder of his dream, but over against the sanctuary at Bethel itself, which had been a link between heaven and earth and the place of God's habitation on earth.[402]

Further, Carson[403] argues that Jesus the Son of Man has to be considered as the replacement of Jacob and Bethel: the new Israel, the new Bethel, the new house of God, the new gate of heaven, through whom God is revealed. Whitacre[404] thinks that Jesus as the new Jacob-Israel is the source of the true people of God, the locus of divine glory, and the meeting-place between heaven and earth, the real Temple (cf. John 2:19–21) and the gate (John 10:7), replacing Bethel, which was 'the house of God' and 'the gate of heaven,' exclaimed by the old Jacob.

However, most importantly, before moving to the next argument as to the use of the *merkabah* tradition and of rabbinic interpretations of Jacob's vision, we have to ask the following question. What is the main focus of

---

[395] J. H. Neyrey, 'Jacob,' 586–590, quoted from 590; Kanagaraj, *Mysticism*, 187, 192–194. Cf. Ezek 1:26; Isa 6:1. See also Carmichael, *Creation*, 65.
[396] Cf. 1.3.2. The Revealer
[397] Neyrey, 'Jacob,' 590–594.
[398] Cf. For the relating references in Philo, Neyrey, 'Jacob,' 592 nn. 29–30.
[399] Cf. Justin, *Dial*. 56.
[400] Cf. Carson, *John*, 163–164; Goppelt, *Typos*, 186; W. D. Davies, *Gospel*, 298–299; Smith, *John*, 78; Whitherington, *Wisdom*, 73; Drapper, 'Temple,' 280; Burge, *Anointed*, 86–87.
[401] Goppelt, *Typos*, 186.
[402] Davies, *Gospel*, 298.
[403] Carson, *John*, 163–164; Drapper, 'Temple,' 280; Maddox, 'Function,' 190.
[404] Whitacre, *John*, 75–76.

Jesus's words in the context of Nathanael's confession in relation to the eschatological fulfilment of the Davidic covenant, which is the climax of the messianic expectations of several disciples? The advent of the Davidic Messiah who was repeatedly promised by Yahweh through the Prophets can be intrinsically connected to the eschatological salvation, the new exodus. In this context, the focus could very well be Jesus himself depicted as the Son of Man in the light of Jacob's vision, and so the Son of Man needs essentially to be compared with Jacob rather than any thing else, such as ladder, Bethel, 'the house of God' and 'the gate of heaven.' This argument is supported by Carson, who writes:

> Because Jesus explicitly alludes to these experiences in Jacob's life, it becomes clear what kind of vision he is promising .... After all, the explicit parallel is drawn between Jacob and Jesus: the angels ascend and descend on the Son of Man, as they ascended and descended on Jacob (for clearly that is how John understands Gen 28:12).[405]

From this point of view, the first three arguments seem to miss the target, even though they could partly contribute to an understanding of Jesus's identity and his works. Furthermore, these arguments just define the relationship between Jacob and the Son of Man, the new Israel, without discussing why Jesus used a title the Son of Man in the light of Jacob and his vision to disclose his identity and works. To understand the relationship between Jacob and the Son of Man in the prophetic sayings of Jesus, we need to study this verse in the light of Jewish apocalyptic, and of targumic and rabbinic tradition about Gen 28:12, as some Johannine commentators[406] have already done, even though some[407] raise its chronological problem. Further, regarding other references such as 'heaven's opening,'[408] the Son of

---

[405] Carson, *John*, 163; O. Michel, *NIDNTT*, III, 630. *Contra.* Burkett, *Son*, 116.
[406] C. F. Burney, *Aramaic*, 115–117; H. Odeberg, *Fourth Gospel*, 35ff; Bultmann, *John*, 105 n. 3; Dodd, *Interpretation*, 245–246; R. H. Lightfoot, *John's*, 104; Lindars, *John*, 122; R. H. Strachan, *Fourth Gospel*, 9–10; Rowland, *Influence*, 141–151; *idem.*, 'John 1:51,' 498–507; Kim, *Son*, 82f; *idem.*, *Origin*, 239–256; *idem.*, *Exposition*, 47–54; N. A. Dahl, 'Johannine,' 136. Also see Neyrey, 'Jacob,' 598–603; Burkett, *Son*, 116–117; J. Kugel, 'Ladder,' 209–227; C. Milikowsky, 'Exile,' 265–296. See b. Targumic-Rabbinic Traditions on Gen 28:12 of 3.3. The Theophany-*Merkabah* Tradition in the Jewish Apocalyptic Literature of Ra, *Christological*.
[407] Cf. Burkett, *Son*, 116; Neyrey, 'Jacob,' 604; J. J. Kanagaraj, *Mysticism*, 189–190.
[408] In the OT and NT, 'the heavens' is in an intimate relationship with God as the divine realm such as the location of God's throne or His throne itself. Above all, at the heavenly assembly, God as the King sat on the heavenly throne and planned His government of the world, particularly of Israel, with the heavenly host. In connection with this, the expression 'the opening of the heavens' could be understood as meaning that God's plans regarding eschatological salvation, which was concealed in the heavens, is revealed and comes into force. Concerning this, see D. T. Tsumura, *NIDOTTE*, IV, 160–166, esp. 163–164; H. Bietenhard,

Man and the promise of vision in that verse, the apocalyptic-*markabah* mysticism in the OT and the Jewish literature has to be considered (cf. Ezek 1:1; Acts 7:56).[409]

Firstly, Rowland[410] has traced the development procedure of the *merkabah*-vision tradition coming out in Ezek 1:26ff to the OT and the Jewish apocalyptic literature. In particular, Rowland[411] disclosed that a part of the *merkabah*-vision tradition could be found in some interpretations of Jacob's vision in Gen 28:12 in the targumic and rabbinic literature. According to the traditions of Jacob's vision, since angels in heaven were prohibited from seeing the image (איקון or איקנין) of Jacob being engraved, or sitting, on the throne of the divine glory, angels came down to earth to see the face or image of Jacob as he slept at Bethel. From this observation, Rowland suggested that the image of Jacob engraved on the divine throne in the targumic and rabbinic tradition concerning Gen 28:12 was identified with 'a figure like that of a man' (דמות כמראה אדם) sitting on the divine throne in Ezek 1:26ff, which developed into the figure 'one like a son of man' (כבר נאש) appearing in Dan 7:13; *1 En.* 46ff; *4 Ezra* 13.[412]

Rowland[413] argues that the development of the targumic and rabbinic tradition about Jacob's איקנין in the light of the *merkabah* tradition might assist in understanding the meaning of Jesus's prophetic promise of John 1:51. Rowland[414] then concludes that in John 1:51, John the Evangelist

---

NIDNTT, II, 190–196; G. von Rad, *TDNT*, V, 504–509; H. Traub, *TDNT*, V, 513–535; S. Kim, *Son*, 31–32; *idem.*, 'Baptism,' 15; G. Bornkamm, *TDNT*, IV, 813–824, esp. 814f; Beasley-Murray, *Jesus*, 104f; *BDB*, 691; M. N. A. Bockmauehl, *Revelation*, 15f; Rowland, *Open*, 126, 359; L. C. Allen, *Ezekiel 1–19*, 22; R. Watt, *Isaiah's*, 102–104; W. Schweizer, *TDNT*, VIII, 368; J. Nolland, *Luke 1–9:20*, 160–161; D. A. Hagner, *Matthew 1–13*, 57; R. Gundry, *Mark*, 48; Marcus, *Way*, 48ff; Guelich, *Mark 1–8*, 26; Marshall, *Luke*, 152.

[409] Kim, *Exposition*, 47–54; S. Motyer, *Father*, 46; Dunn, 'John,' 357–366; Drapper, 'Temple,' 279–280; Kanagaraj, *Mysticism*, 186–194, esp. 188; J. B. Pryor, 'Johannine,' 341–351, esp. 342; P. Borgen, 'Agent,' 129–132; *idem.*, *Bread*, 175–177; Dahl, 'Johannine,' 136; E. M. Sidebottom, *Christ*, 76; Rowland, 'John 1:51,' 507; Nolland, *Luke 1–9:20*, 160; Watts, *Isaiah's*, 102 n. 63. *Contra* Burkett, *Son*, 115. Cf. See 3.3. The Theophany-*Merkabah* Tradition in the Jewish Apocalyptic Literature of Ra, *Christological*. Also, Kim, *Son*, 15–32.

[410] Rowland, *Influence*; *idem.*, 'John 1:51,' 498–507; *idem.*, *Open*; Kim, *Origin*, 254–255; *idem.*, *Son*; Kanagaraj, *Mysticism*, 49; H. Ridderbos, *John*, 93. Cf. *1 En.* 14; Dan 7; *Apoc. Abr.* 17f; *4 QS* 1; Rev 1.

[411] Rowland, *Influence*, 141–151; *idem.*, 'John 1:51,' 498–507; Kim, *Son*, 82–86; *idem.*, *Origin*, 242–243; *idem.*, *Exposition*, 47–49.

[412] Rowland, *Influence*, 141–151, esp. 148. Cf. *Tg. Jon.*; *Tg. Onk.*; *Tg. Neof.* 1; *Fragment Tg.*; *Gen R.* 68:12, 13, 18; 69:3; 70:12; *Exod R.* 42:2; *b. Hul.* 91b; *Hekhaloth R.* 9.

[413] Rowland, 'John 1:51,' 503. See also Kim, *Origin*, 254–255; *idem.*, *Son*, 82–86; *idem.*, *Exposition*, 47–54; Whitacre, *John*, 76. *Contra* Burkett, *Son*, 116–117.

[414] Rowland, 'John 1:51,' 505; *idem.*, *Open*, 22, 274; Drapper, 'Temple,' 280; Pryor, 'Johannine,' 342; Neyrey, 'Jacob,' 589–594.

emphasized that Jesus is the embodiment of the revelation of the divine glory. That is, Jesus the Son of Man whom Nathanael had acknowledged as the Son of God and the King of Israel, actually is the very one whom the angels of God wanted to look upon in Jacob's vision. However, he has not gone further to study the reason for the replacement of Jacob by the Son of Man, or the theological meaning of Jesus's promise in terms of the Son of Man in the context of the coming of the Davidic Messiah reflected in Nathanael's testimony.

Secondly, we shall concentrate on what was meant by 'the Son of Man.'[415] So far, the heavenly figure כבר נאש ('one like a son of man') appearing in Dan 7:13ff (cf. Ps 80:17) seems to be quite a plausible OT background to 'the Son of Man' in the NT.[416] Above all, in connection with John 1:51 in the light of the *merkabah* tradition, Kim's argument should be noted that 'the Son of Man' in the four Gospels is based on the *merkabah*–vision tradition in the Jewish apocalyptic literature.[417] Further, through *4QpsDanA*ᵃ; *4QFlor.* 1:1–3, some Greek versions of Dan 7:13 and some *merkabah* traditions of the Jewish Apocalyptic literature, he[418] argues that there is a possibility of messianic interpretation of the heavenly figure כבר נאש ('one like a son of man') of Dan 7:13 in the Judaism of the pre-New Testament era. Here, he[419] has pointed out that the heavenly figure כבר נאש ('one like a son of man') in Dan 7 is not only the symbol, but also the inclusive representative, of the saints of the Most High, who will be elevated as the sons of God to the divine throne at the eschatological time.

Furthermore, Kim[420] strengthens his argument with further apocalyptic literatures including the *merkabah* tradition, such as, '*The Prayer of Joseph*'

---

[415] See 3.2. The (Firstborn) Son of God and the Son of Man of Ra, *Christological*.
[416] Cf. Jeremias, *Theology*, I, 268–272; G. N. Stanton, *Gospels*, 249; Bruce, *John*, 63; Carson, *John*, 164; Garnet, 'Baptism,' 49–65; Witherington, *Wisdom*, 72; Ashton, *Understanding*, 340; Milne, *John*, 61; Morris, *John*, 151; Kim, *Son*, 15–37; idem., *Exposition*, 49–50; Longenecker, *Christology*, 86; I. H. Marshall, *Christology*, 63; idem., 'Contemporary,' 81; C. F. D. Moule, *Christology*, 12f; Beasley-Murray, 'Christology,' 31; Dodd, *Interpretation*, 245f; M. Wilcock, *Psalms 73–150*, 32; Ridderbos, *John*, 92–93; T. W. Manson, 'Son,' 143.
[417] Kim, *Son*, 17–18. Cf. Ezek 1:26–28; Dan 7:1–14; 4 Ezra 13; 1 En. 37–71 (*the Similitudes of Enoch*); b. Hag. 15; 3 En.
[418] Kim, *Son*, 20–25. See also, J. J. Collins, 'Man,' 448–466; T. B. Slater, 'Son,' 183–198. Also, Kim recognizes that there is also a possibility that Jesus could have started to interpret creatively the heavenly figure van rbk in Dan 7:13ff as the Son of God and the Messiah, without any connection with these traditions (p. 26). See also, Hengel, *Christology*, 104–108; N. T. Wright, *Victory*, 512–519. On the other hand, it is generally thought that 'the Son of Man' had never been used as a title for a messianic or eschatological figure at the time of Jesus. Cf. Moule, *Christology*, 11; I. H. Marshall, 'Contemporary,' 73; B. Lindars, 'Re-Enter,' 58; F. F. Bruce, 'Background,' 50–70, esp. 66.
[419] Kim, *Son*, 18–19; idem., *Exposition*, 49–50.
[420] Kim, *Son*, 26–29; Hengel, *Son*, 47–48; Borgen, 'Agent,' 129–132.

and *Conf. Ling.* 146–147, in which Jacob-Israel is honoured as the central figure, that is, the inclusive representative through whom the sons of God could reach the throne of glory. The *merkabah* traditions on Jacob-Israel in these documents are commonly based on the heavenly figure כבר נאש in Dan 7:13. Here, Jacob-Israel was recognized not only as an individual but also as the inclusive representative and the embodiment of the nation Israel in Judaism at the time of Jesus. Because of this, Kim holds that there is a possibility of messianic expectation in connection with the heavenly figure כבר נאש ('one like a son of man') of Dan 7:13 in early Second Temple Judaism.[421] He[422] assumed that even if it is not certain if Jesus was aware of this messianic interpretation about the heavenly figure כבר נאש of Dan 7:13, Jesus himself creatively used 'the Son of Man' as a self-designation, depending on the heavenly figure of Dan 7:13.

Moule[423] also held that Dan 7 was the decisive reference, emphasizing the definite article in 'the' Son of Man, which expressly refers to 'one like a human being' in Daniel's vision. Therefore, through the sayings of 'the Son of Man,' Jesus seemed to say that he is the heavenly figure, כבר נאש who appeared in Daniel's vision, to fulfil God's plan of salvation on earth at the eschatological time. Kim concludes that:

> with 'the' Son of Man he [Jesus] intended to reveal his mission in terms of gathering or, as it were, creating, God's eschatological people who, represented or embodied in him as their head, would be elevated (or made) God's sons.[424]

Kim's argument has been introduced in detail since the inclusive representative concept and the *merkabah* tradition in the OT and Judaism

---

[421] Kim, *Son*, 30–31. Independently, J. F. McGrath, *Apologetic*, 168–169, who argues that the 'one like a son of man' in Dan 7 could be understood as a messianic figure not in the pre-Christian period but in the pre-Johannine period.

[422] Kim, *Son*, 32–36. See also Marshall, *Christology*, 72, 75f; M. D. Hooker, *Son*; Kim, *ibid.*, 9–14; Jeremias, *Theology*, I, 258.

[423] Moule, *Christology*, 11–13; *idem.*, 'Son,' 277–279; Kim, *Son*, 32–35; J. A. Fitzmyer, 'Contribution,' 85–113; *idem.*, 'Son,' 143–160. See also Garnet, 'Baptism,' 49–50. *Contra*. G. Vermes, 'Use,' 310–328; Lindars, 'Re-Enter,' 52–72; R. J. Bauckham, 'Son,' 23–33; Casey, *Son*, 224–239; *idem.*, 'General,' 21–56; *idem.*, 'Idiom,' 164–182, who claims that the Aramaic expression, *Bar Enasa* means regularly 'man,' or 'human being' regardless of the presence of a determinative, and any speaker used it when he generally designates himself, or something about himself. The Son of Man is just the circumlocutory replacement of 'I,' or 'me.' However, recently, this linguistic argument by Vermes, Casey and Lindars has again been criticized in detail by P. Owen and D. Shepherd, 'Speaking,' 81–122. Cf. 3.1. The Authenticity, Origin and Meaning of the Son of Man of Ra, *Christological*.

[424] Kim, *Son*, 36 ([] added by this writer).

are crucial to our discussion concerning Jacob and 'the Son of Man' in John 1:51.

In relation with our discussion about 'Jacob-Israel' and 'the Son of Man' in the light of the *merkabah* tradition based on Dan 7, the importance of the *merkabah* tradition on Jacob-Israel in *'The Prayer of Joseph'* and Philo (*Conf. Ling.* 146–147) has to be re-emphasized. That is, the *merkabah* tradition in Jacob-Israel was already present at the time of the NT, before it was adopted and used in the targumic and rabbinic literature.

So far, we have discussed that the tradition of Jacob-Israel frequently appearing in the targumic and rabbinic literature was developed from the *merkabah*–vision tradition, and the tradition of a heavenly figure כבר נאש was based on the *merkabah*–vision tradition as well. Kim[425] supposed that if both of the targumic and rabbinic traditions concerning Jacob and the tradition of a heavenly figure (כבר נאש) are a part of the same *merkabah*–vision tradition, it is very probable that Jacob could be replaced by 'the Son of Man' in John 1:51. He [426] says that Jacob-Israel was the inclusive representative of the nation Israel in Jewish literature, particularly in the targumic and rabbinic traditions based on Gen 28:12, and thus Jesus 'the Son of Man' replacing Jacob-Israel is the real inclusive representative of the new Israel in John 1:51. This idea accords with Dan 7:13ff, in which the heavenly figure was depicted as the inclusive representative of the ideal Israel, the saints of the Most High at the eschatological time. The concept of corporate personality is one of some unique concepts of Ancient Israel in understanding the relationship of Israelites to one another and to Yahweh. Robinson said that, 'the whole group, including its past, present, and future members, might function as a single individual through any one of those members conceived as representative of it.'[427] In particular, this corporate personality concept is intimately connected with the fundamental conception of the covenant.[428] Concerning this, we have Dodd's excellent description:

> Jacob, as the ancestor of the nation of Israel, summarizes in his person the ideal Israel *in posse*, just as our Lord, at the other end of the line, summarizes it *in esse* as the Son of Man. For John, of course, 'Israel' is not the Jewish nation, but the new humanity,

---

[425] Kim, *Origin*, 255; idem., *Son*, 82–83; idem., *Exposition*, 50–51.
[426] Kim, *Son*, 83; idem., *Exposition*, 50–51; Michel, *NIDNTT*, III, 630.
[427] H. W. Robinson, *Corporate*, 25. Cf. Gen 4:15, 24; Exod 20:5; 21:23–25; Deut 13:12ff; 21:1ff; 25:5ff (Levirate marriage); 2 Sam 21. See also J. W. Rogerson, 'Corporate,' 1–16; Holwerda, *Jesus*, 34.
[428] Robinson, *Corporate*, 34.

reborn in Christ, the community, of those who are 'of the truth', and of whom Christ is king. In a deeper sense he is not only their king, he is their inclusive representative: they are in him and he in them.[429]

Here, the *merkabah*–vision tradition based on Jacob-Israel in the targumic and rabbinic literature and on the heavenly figure van rbk in the OT and Jewish apocalyptic literature can be recognized in the light of the eschatological salvation of God. In Dan 7:13–14,[430] the heavenly figure coming with the clouds of heaven was given authority, glory and sovereign power from the Ancient of Days. It means that the Danielic heavenly figure was enthroned on one of the thrones set among the heavenly assembly and was worshipped by all peoples of every language. His dominion is everlasting and his kingdom will never be destroyed. Thus, the Danielic heavenly figure is *ontologically* none other than the divine Son of the Ancient of Days (God, the Most High).[431]

Furthermore, in Dan 7:18–28, the meaning of the vision shown in Dan 7:1–14 was explained to Daniel three times. Even though the saints of the Most High will be oppressed by four continuous gentile kingdoms, they will eventually receive the kingdom from the Most High and possess the glory of God. In other words, the true people of God will be enthroned with God at the end-time. This enthronement of the saints of the Most High was symbolically described through the picture of the enthronement of the heavenly figure with 'the Ancient of Days' in Dan 7:13–14. So, the heavenly figure enthroned as the Son of the Ancient of Days is *functionally* the inclusive representative of the saints of the Most High.[432] Here, the headship of the Danielic Son of Man figure as the divine Son of God (the Ancient of Days, the Most High) and the inclusive representative of faithful Israel (the corporate son) is based on Israel's sonship (cf. the firstborn concept) to God in Exod 4:22–23 (Ps 80).[433]

Furthermore, if it is considered that the dual concepts (the son/firstborn of God and the servant of God including the priesthood) in Exod 4:22–23; 19:5–6 were applied to Davidic prince in Yahweh's covenant to David (2

---

[429] Dodd, *Interpretation*, 246. Cf. Whitacre, *John*, 75–76.
[430] See 3.2.1. Dan 7:13 of Ra, *Christological*.
[431] Moule, *Christology*, 24–27; Kim, *Son*; idem., *Exposition*, 51; G. R. Beasley-Murray, 'Christology,' 33–34; J. W. Pryor, 'Johannine,' 341–351, esp. 350; Howton, 'Son,' 237; Ham, 'Son,' 73; H. Ridderbos, *John*, 92–93.
[432] Robinson, *Corporate*, 29; Kim, *Exposition*, 51–52.
[433] Kim, *Son*, 30 says that 'Exod 4:22 is the text which stands behind all those *merkabah* texts that speak of Israel on (or beside) the heavenly throne as the 'firstborn'.' Also, see Hengel, *Son*, 48; 3.2.2. Ps 80:17 of Ra, *Christological*.

Sam 7:12–16; Pss 2:7; 89; 110:1, 4) and even to the Davidic messianic-suffering servant figure in Isaiah (cf. Isa 9:1–7; 11:1–16; 42:1–9; 52:13–53:12; 55:3; 61:1–11), we can assume some probability that the enthronement of the Danielic Son of Man figure (as the Son/firstborn of God) beside the Ancient of Days' throne in Dan 7:9–14 (Ps 80:17) alludes to the enthronement of David or the Davidic messianic King as the Son/firstborn of God (cf. 4QpsDanA*a*; Dan 9:24–26; *Midr. Ps* 2:9 on Ps 2:7).[434] Most importantly, if the writer's setting for the vision given to Daniel is the Babylonian captivity of Judah, the enthronement of the heavenly figure as the inclusive representative of the people of God can naturally be recognized as God's promise concerning the restoration of his true people. This restoration, following continuous oppression by four gentile kingdoms, is the eschatological restoration (or new exodus). As in the Daniel vision, the *merkabah* tradition in Ezek 1 given to Ezekiel in the circumstance of the Babylonian exile could be also interpreted in the light of the eschatological new exodus.[435]

Further, the *merkabah* tradition of Jacob-Israel in the targumic and rabbinic literature could be understood in the light of the same soteriological thought as the *merkabah* vision shown to Daniel, that is, the restoration of the exiled people of God, the new exodus. Kim[436] points out that, as the inclusive representative of the nation Israel, Jacob-Israel's enthronement on the *merkabah* of God, was the expression of covenant theology. It pictured the ultimate destiny of Israel on the basis of her covenant with God. Through the picture of the enthronement of Jacob Israel, the nation Israel expressed her expectation that she would ultimately experience the supreme glory, richness and sovereign power of God on the basis of the covenant of God. This hope existed even though the descendants of Jacob were afflicted and exiled by gentile kingdoms on earth. This had been prefigured by Jacob, the forefather of the nation Israel, who had been expelled by Esau[437] and caused to wander in the wilderness.[438]

---

[434] Kim, *Son*, 15–37; idem., *Exposition*, 52. Also, G. R. Beasley-Murray, 'Interpretation,' 44–58; idem., *Jesus*, 26–35, 68; C. Ham, 'Son,' 74; Hengel, *Christology*, 60; T. W. Manson, *Servant-Messiah*, 73–74; Moule, *Christology*, 24–27; Jeremias, *Theology*, I, 269–272; Longenecker, *Christology*, 86; R. D. Rowe, 'Daniel's,' 71–96; Pitre, *Tribulation*, 54–55; Ridderbos, *John*, 93; McGrath, *Apologetic*, 168–169. Contra Marshall, 'Contemporary,' 73–74; Lindars, 'Re-Enter,' 58; Fitzmyer, 'Son,' 153ff; C. Colpe, *TDNT*, VIII, 423; Stanton, *Gospels*, 251.
[435] The beginning of the exile of Judah to Babylon was described as the leaving of the glory of God from the Temple in Ezek 10, and the restoration, the new exodus of Israel to the promised land from Babylonian exile was pictured by the return of the glory of God to the eschatological Temple in Ezek 43.
[436] Kim, *Exposition*, 48–49, 51–53. See also, Robinson, *Corporate*, 34.
[437] See the next note, and n. 443, for the detail of the symbolic meaning of Esau in the OT.

Thus, Kim [439] concludes that in John 1:51 Jesus argued that he, as the Danielic Son of Man (Dan 7), will sit on the throne of God rather than Jacob-Israel whom rabbis regarded as siting on the throne of God on the basis of Gen 28:12. Rabbis in the targumic-rabbinic sources expected the Jews as the physical descendants of Jacob-Israel to be enthroned on the heavenly throne (cf. the restoration of Israel) in the end time. But this rabbinic thought is rejected by Jesus, who argued that the eschatological faithful people of God, who will be created by Jesus the Son of Man and confess him as 'the Son of God and the King of Israel' (like Nathanael), will be sitting on the throne of God. The real Israel, the real people of God will receive the kingdom of God, the eternal life.

This expectation of the nation Israel can be seen in another Jewish tradition concerning Jacob's vision. Recently, Kugel[440] has considered 'The Ladder of Jacob,' a document in Pseudepigrapha literature. It is an elaboration of the story of Jacob's vision at Bethel in Gen 28:11–22. This document concentrates on a ladder consisting of 12 steps, and on 24 human faces (or statues) standing on both sides of each step of the ladder. On the top of the ladder, there is 'the face (*prosopon*) of a man' carved out of fire. God was standing above its highest face. The angels of God ascended and descended on it (the Ladder). In chapter 5 of the document, Sariel, the archangel, explained to Jacob the meaning of the vision. The ladder means this age. The 12 steps are the periods of this age. The 24 human statues on both sides of the 12 steps of the ladder represented the kings of the lawless nations (cf. the kings of gentile empires) of this age.[441] The descendants of Jacob will suffer desolation and exile (5:7; 6:2). Because of the sins of Jacob's descendants, their palace and Temple will be deserted and they will be exiled in a strange land and be afflicted with slavery and wounds every day

---

[438] Cf. R. P. Carroll, 'Deportation,' 63–84 says that 'Deportation and diaspora are constitutive of the Jewish identity as it begins to emerge and evolve in the biblical narratives. The Bible is the great metanarrative of deportation, exile and potential return.' (p. 64). In particular, J. C. VanderKam, 'Exile,' 89 points out that the concept of exile in the OT is interwoven with the covenant theology. Cf. Deut 4:23–31; Neh 9:6–37; Ezra 9:6–15. Also, J. Neusner, 'Return,' 222, argues that the paradigm of 'exile and return' appeared in every Judaism. See also B. Halpern-Amaru, 'Exile,' 131–132, who says that 'The third patriarch (Jacob) experiences the powerlessness of the exiled stranger outside the Land when he resides with Laban in Haran (Gen 32:4)…A new cycle begins with the descent of Jacob and his family to Egypt where the Israelites, like their forefathers, experience the life of the stranger-in-exile as a fore-history to beginning their venture with the covenant making and the Land.'
[439] Kim, *Exposition*, 52–53.
[440] Kugel, 'Ladder,' 209–227. See also Milikowsky, 'Exile,' 272–279. Cf. *Exod R.* 32:7; *Lev R.* 29:2; *Pesiqta R. Kah.* 23.
[441] Cf. Kugel, 'Ladder,' 212 n. 10 interprets angels' four ascents on the ladder in the light of Daniel's vision about the rises/falls of Babylonia, Media, Greece and Rome (cf. Dan 2:36–40; 7:3–27), which could be found in later Jewish literature (e.g., *4 Ezra* 12:11–36; *2 Bar.* 39:2–6).

by the four ascents of this age. After that, Jacob's descendants in exile will be freed by God and inherit the Land promised to Jacob at the eschaton (1:9; 6:1–2).

Here, the restoration of Jacob's descendants is expressed by the destruction of the kingdom of Esau and the people of Moab. Generally, the Roman Empire was symbolized by Esau in the Jewish literature of the Second Temple era.[442] However, Kugel[443] argues that in this document, Esau's symbolism means the eschatological enemy of Israel. In particular, the destruction of Esau and Moab was described as the dawn of the new era, the new exodus in Jer 48–49 and Isa 34; 63.

However, it has to be noted in this document that the story of Jacob's vision was modified in the light of exile and exodus. By reflecting the Egyptian bondage of the descendants of Jacob and the first exodus with God's plagues performed through Moses against the Egyptians (chapter 6), this text discloses the expectation of the new exodus. We cannot be certain the story of Jacob's vision had the background of exile and restoration in Gen 28. Even so, there is a strong probability that Jacob's vision was later interpreted by the Second Temple Jewish literature in the light of exile and exodus or new exodus.[444]

Furthermore, one of Jesus's common phrases, ἀμὴν ἀμήν in John 1:51 could support the background of the new exodus. Observing that ἀμήν used only by Jesus in the Four Gospels has no parallel in all the Jewish literature and in the NT, and that double forms (e.g. ἀμὴν ἀμήν) appeared 25 times only in the Fourth Gospel, Jeremias[445] argues that ἀμήν is one of the words which were creatively used by Jesus about himself. In particular, Beasley-Murray[446] thinks that ἀμὴν ἀμήν in John 1:51 could be based on Isa 65:16, thus showing that Jesus has the authority of God. If Beasley-Murray is correct, this could also be considered in the light of the new exodus.

---

[442] Cf. Kugel, 'Ladder,' 214.
[443] Kugel, 'Ladder,' 224. Cf. It needs to be noted that Jacob-Israel was depicted as the covenant people, and Esau and his descendants (e.g., Edomite, Amalekites, Agagite, Haman) were symbolically referred to as the enemy against the covenant people in the OT; Exod 15:15; 17:14–16; Num 20:14–21; Exod 17; 1 Sam 15; Esther 3:10.
[444] Cf. Milikowsky, 'Exile,' 265–296, who says that 'There is a strong tendency in rabbinic literature to see the entire Second Temple period as part of the larger period of exile and subjugation, which began with the Babylonian conquest of Jerusalem and which, for a Rabbis, still endured. The vassalage of Israel to foreign powers during the Second Temple period meant that God's favour had not yet returned to Israel and they were still in exile, in spite of the existence of both the Temple and some level of political sovereignty at varying times.' (pp. 278–279).
[445] Jeremias, *Theology*, I, 35–36.
[446] Beasley-Murray, *John*, 21. Cf. Rev 3:14.

To sum up, the background to Jesus's prophetic promise, given in response to Nathanael's confession in terms of the Davidic covenant, could be Gen 28:12 and Dan 7:13–14 (cf. Ps 80:17), which might be understood in the light of the *merkabah*-vision tradition in the OT and the targumic and rabbinic literature. The central idea of the *merkabah* tradition is the enthronement of the heavenly figure כבר נאש as the Son/firstborn of God (the Ancient of Days, the Most High) in Dan 7:13–14, namely, as the symbolic, inclusive representative of the faithful Israel, the Saint, the corporate son of the Most High. Thus, the enthronement of the heavenly figure (Jacob-Israel, the *eikon* engraved (sitting) of the heavenly throne) means the enthronement of the people of Israel, a figure of the restoration (the new exodus) of Israel from exile in gentile kingdoms. These ideas are based on the sonship (firstborn) of Israel (Exod 4:22–23) and the enthronement of the Davidic messianic king (2 Sam 7:12–16; Pss 2:7; 89; 110:1, 4; Isa 9:1–7; 11:1–16; 55:3; 61:1–11).

2.5 Conclusion

Our discussion of John 1:19–51 leads us to the following conclusions. Firstly, John the Baptist, on the basis of Isa 40:3, understood himself as the forerunner for Yahweh's return and the restoration of his exiled people in Isa 40–66. Also, on the basis of Ezek 36:24–25, he offered water baptism to prepare for the renewing bestowal of the Spirit administered by Jesus, the Coming One, in the light of the eschatological-new exodus.

Secondly, the Passover Lamb is presented as the most likely background to the lamb of God, supported by the centrality of the Passover theme and by the Son of God (v. 34), alluding to death of the firstborn or paschal lamb in Exod 4:22–23. Further, the Johannine Lamb could be based on the Isaianic suffering servant (the Davidic messianic king), the agent of the new exodus in Deutero-Isaiah. Furthermore, the Lamb may depend on the concept of the apocalyptic lamb who is the same figure as the Davidic messianic king/firstborn/the paschal lamb (Rev 5:5–10; 1:5–7).

Thirdly, the Spirit's coming down and remaining upon Jesus points to the fulfilment of God's promise to pour out the Spirit upon the coming Davidic messianic king-suffering servant of Yahweh. This is set against the background of Isa 11:1; 42:1; 61:1 and Ezek 36:25–27, and to the announcement of the arrival of the promised eschatological salvation: the new exodus and new creation. Further, the Son of God, based on Exod 4:22–23; 2 Sam 7:12–16; Pss 2:7; 89; Isa 42:1; 9:1–7; 11:1–16; 55:3; 61:1–11, means the fulfilment of Yahweh's promises to King David, the same figure as the Deutero-Isaianic suffering servant of the Lord who will fulfil the eschatological salvation. This is clearly supported by Nathanael's confession of Jesus as the Son of God and the King of Israel.

Finally, in v. 51, as the Son of Man, Jesus's prophetic promise could be based on Gen 28:12 and Dan 7:13–14 (cf. Exod 4:22–23), which might be understood in the light of the *merkabah*-vision tradition in the OT and the targumic and rabbinic literature. Jesus says that he—as the replacement of Jacob-Israel—is the new Israel, the inclusive representative of the true people of God. As the Son of Man, Jesus will fulfil the eschatological salvation of God, confirming Nathanael's testimony about Jesus himself, and proclaiming that he is the bringer of the new exodus in the light of the fulfilment of the Davidic covenant.

Chapter 3: Water into Wine Miracle John 2:1–11

3.1 Introduction

The miracle of Jesus changing water into wine at the wedding banquet in Cana is recorded only in John. Some commentators have interpreted this miraculous sign as connected with heathen myths rather than with the OT. Bultmann[447] argued that the miracle was not based on a historical tradition concerning Jesus's ministry but taken from a Greek myth, the legend of Dionysus, and applied to Jesus. Hengel[448] also says that the wine-god of Dionysian myth originated from a Phoenician (Palestinian) background and was later adopted in wine-god myths of the countries around Palestine. Accordingly, he argues that, since the myth had a long Palestinian background, it is not right to say that the Johannine wine miracle was influenced by or was adopted from heathen legend for a missiological purpose. Furthermore, after pointing out some heathen parallels in Greco-Roman literature, Dodd[449] assumed that, without the recognition of the pagan origin of this motif, a similar folk-tale tradition concerning wine miracles was adopted and adapted by the primitive Christian tradition about the miracle. He[450] assumes this miracle was probably developed from the parables of 'the new wine and the old skins' in the Synoptic Gospels (cf. Matt 9:17; Mark 2:22; Luke 5:37). Nevertheless, he[451] thinks the most appropriate clue about the origin of the wine miracle can be found in Philo's allegorical interpretation of the story of Melchizedek, the self-existent priest-logos, who brought out bread and wine to Abram in Gen 14:18.

The weakness of Bultmann and Hengel's position is that the Dionysian legend does not describe a miraculous story of water changing to wine. Beasley-Murray[452] sees the Dionysian wine miracle and any explanation

---

[447] Bultmann, *John*, 118f; E. Lohse, 'Miracles,' 68

[448] Hengel, 'John 2:1–11,' 111–112; *idem.*, *Christology*, 315–316, 331; Koester, *Symbolism*, 81; Polhill, 'John 1–4,' 450–451. *Contra* Witherington, *Wisdom*, 78, who argues that, in adopting Dionysian rites, this wine miracle has two goals; on the one hand, to persuade the Jews by showing that the wine made by Jesus surpassed the Jewish ceremonial water, and, on the other hand, to evangelize the Greeks by introducing Jesus giving stronger life than Dionysus.

[449] C. H. Dodd, *Historical*, 224f. Cf. Pliny, *Nat. Hist.* 2.231; 31.16; Diodorus Siculus 3.66; Pausanias 6.26.1–2; Plutarch, *Lysander*, 28.4; Ovid. *Metamorphoses*, 13.650ff. See also B. Lindars, 'Parables,' 320.

[450] Dodd, *Historical*, 224f; Polhill, 'John 1–4,' 450–451.

[451] Dodd, *Interpretation*, 298ff. Cf. *Leg. Alleg.* 3.79ff; *Somn.* 2.249; *Quod Deus Immut.* 158 on Num 20:17–20; *Leg. Alleg.* 1.84; *Somn.* 2.183, 190; *Fuga* 166. See also Lindars, *John*, 127; Barrett, *John*, 188–189. Cf. Euripides, *Bacchae* 704–707; Athenaeus 1.61 (34a); Irenaeus, *Adv. Haer.* 1.13.2.

[452] Beasley-Murray, *John*, 35–36. See also Morris, *John*, 155; Brown, *John I-XII*, 101; Polhill, 'John 1–4,' 450–451; Carson, *John*, 167; C. Brown, *NIDNTT*, III, 918–922; J. Behm, *TDNT*, I, 342–343.

based on Philo's interpretation concerning the story of Melchizedek to be irrelevant to this passage in John. Furthermore, such a theory of origin for this passage becomes unnecessary when we recall that the OT has rich resources concerning vine-wine motifs, connected to messianic expectation. These frequently include a marriage motif set against the background of Yahweh's covenant restoration to the exiled Israel. If we bear this in mind, we will find that this Johannine narrative of Jesus making wine reflects the OT[453] rather than heathen sources such as the Dionysian legend.

Interestingly, in Ps 80 [79 in the LXX]:8–13 (cf. Isa 5:1–7; Amos 9:15), Israel is a vine brought out of Egypt and placed in the promised land.[454] This alludes to the first exodus and the establishment of the covenant relationship between Yahweh and Israel. In Isa 5:1–7, Israel is symbolized as the vineyard and Yahweh as the vinedresser.[455] Here, the covenant relationship between Yahweh and Israel was symbolically described with pictures of the vineyard; the yielding of bad and wild grapes rather than ripe and juicy grapes denotes Israel's failure within that covenant.[456] In Isa 27:2–6 (cf. Ezek 17), the people of God are collectively called by their inclusive forefather's name, Jacob-Israel, with the picture of vine, which will take root, bud and blossom and fill all the world with grapes in the end time. This picture often appeared in the Prophets.

In particular, the superabundance of wine was characterized as the blessing given to Judah in Gen 49:11, and this also seems to influence the development of the Davidic messianic expectation in the eschatological era.[457] The abundance of wine testified to the abundance of Yahweh, which is a distinctive characteristic of the eschatological messianic age. The idea of the abundance of wine was further developed in Judaism,[458] so that even the decoration in the Herodian Temple reflected the importance of the motif.[459] Its importance is carried through to Jesus's parable of the vine in John 15:1–11, in which he applies the image of true vine to himself. Here,

---

[453] Cf. Brown, *John I-XII*, 101–102, who finds the background of the Johannine wine miracle in the feeding miracle of Elijah (1 Kings 17), and the oil miracle and the feeding miracle of Elisha (2 Kings 4), although there is little evidence for the link as such.
[454] Burge, 'Territorial,' 391–395, esp. 392.
[455] Burge, 'Territorial,' 393.
[456] Cf. Jer 2:21; 5:10; 12:11–12; Ezek 15:1–18; 17:1–10; 19:10–14; Hos 10:1; *Sir.* 24:27; *2 Bar.* 29:5; 39:7. See Brown, *NIDNTT*, III, 918; Behm, *TDNT*, I, 342, who shows how the vine tree was metaphorically applied in the OT and Jewish documents: 1) to Israel in Hos 10:1; Jer 2:21; Ezek 15:1ff; 19:10ff; Ps 80:9ff; *Lev R.* 36 on Lev. 26:42; 2) to the Messiah in *2 Bar.* 39:7; 3) to Wisdom in *Sir.* 24:17.
[457] Cf. T. D. Alexander, 'Messianic,' 19–39, esp. 32–39; G. J. Wenham, *Genesis 16–50*, 477–479.
[458] Cf. *2 Bar.* 29:5; 39:7. See C. Brown, *NIDNTT*, III, 918.
[459] Cf. Josephus, *War* 5.210.

Israel is now pictured as a branch which had to be attached to the true vine to get its life, a radical departure from the OT, in which Israel was itself the vine or the vineyard.[460]

> The crux for John 15 is that *Jesus is changing the place of rootedness for Israel*. The commonplace prophetic metaphor (the Land as vineyard, the people of Israel as vines) undergoes a dramatic shift. God's vineyard, the land of Israel, now has only one vine (ἄμπελος), Jesus. The people of Israel cannot claim to be planted as vines in the land; they cannot be *rooted* in the vineyard unless first they are *grafted* into Jesus. Other vines are not true (15:1). Branches that attempt to live in the land, the vineyard, which refuse to be attached to Jesus will be cast out and burned (15:6). In John 15 we are given a completely new metaphor; God the vinedresser now has one vine growing in his vineyard. And the only means of attachment to the land is through this one vine, Jesus Christ.[461]

Jesus is the true vine to which the disciples, as branches, must be attached (grafted on); thus Jesus is the inclusive representative (the firstborn) of the new covenant people of God; the new Israel who replaces the old Jacob-Israel (cf. John 1:51).[462] Therefore, Jesus's miraculous sign concerning wine at the wedding banquet at Cana has to be discussed against the background of the OT and Judaism in general.

3.2 The Wedding Background (Cf. John 3:22–36)

Bruce[463] suggested that Jesus's attendance at the wedding feast could be interpreted as his approval of the divine ordinance of marriage. However, the wine miracle reflects something fundamentally more than that. To begin with, it has to be noted that this miracle was performed against the background of a wedding feast. In the OT, and in particular in the Prophets, the wedding imagery frequently symbolized the covenant relationship between Yahweh and his people.[464] In this OT imagery,

---

[460] Cf. In Matt 21:33–46; Mark 12:1–12, the parable of the tenants may show that Israel was metaphorically denoted as the vineyard. Also, Jesus says that the new wine will be drunk in the kingdom of God of the new era in Matt 26:29; Mark 14:25; Luke 22:18. Further, in regard to the new era brought by Jesus, the parable of the new wine and the old skins could show the importance of the wine motif of the OT in Matt 9:17; Mark 2:22; Luke 5:37.

[461] Burge, 'Territorial,' 393 (original emphasis). Cf. Rom 11:17–24. In particular, Hengel, *Christology*, 315 argues for an interrelationship between the wine miracle in John 2:1–11 and the true vine in John 15.

[462] Kim, *Exposition*, 61.

[463] Bruce, *John*, 68. See also Carson, *John*, 168.

[464] Cf. Song; Hos; Isa 25:6; 54:4–10; 49:18; 62:4–5; Jer 2:2; 3:1–14; 5:7; 13:26–27; Ezek 16:1–63; 23:1–49.

Yahweh was the bridegroom and his covenantal community Israel the bride. Accordingly, the rebellion of Yahweh's covenant people Israel against him was described as spiritual adultery. W. Günther correctly says that:

> Hosea was the first to express the people's apostasy as harlotry and a breach of the marriage bond between God and Israel, and he did it more clearly than any other (Hos 1ff.; cf. Jer 2:2, 10, 25; 3:1–25; Ezek 16; 23, Isa 50:1). His own act in marrying a harlot at the divine behest (Hos 1:2) was symbolic of Yahweh's relationship with Israel.[465]

In the context of Israel's exile by Yahweh and his prophetic promise of the restoration of his people Israel in the Prophets, the marriage motif was often used to explain the healing of the broken covenant relationship between Yahweh and his people (cf. Isa 54:4–10).[466] Especially in Jer 31:31–33, Yahweh promised to make a new covenant with the whole house of Israel, which would be different from the covenant made with their forefathers at the time of the first exodus. Here, Yahweh reminded them of his covenantal relationship with their forefathers through husband-wife imagery. He emphasized that the covenant community of the first exodus broke the covenant, even though he was a husband to them. The promise of this new covenant was expressed through the imagery of marriage in the light of the new exodus.

In the rabbinic sources, following the OT, the covenant at Sinai is described as a marriage between Yahweh as bridegroom and Israel as bride. Here, the Torah was thought of as a marriage contract, and Moses was the friend of the bridegroom.[467] In Song of Songs, for example, R. Akiba interpreted the relationship in this way.[468] In particular, rabbis following the OT expected that the final renewal of the covenant between God and Israel would be fulfilled in the messianic age.[469]

In the NT, this symbolic picture was again adopted to disclose the identity and the work of Jesus in the light of eschatological salvation. Jesus expressed the meaning and glory of the messianic era by the imagery of the

---

[465] W. Günther, *NIDNTT*, II, 576–577. See also E. Stauffer, *TDNT*, I. 653–654; H. Reisser, *NIDNTT*, II, 583.

[466] See Howard-Brook, *Becoming*, 79; Günther, *NIDNTT*, II, 585; Dodd, *Interpretation*, 297. Cf. Isa 54:4–10; 49:18; 62:4–5; 25:6.

[467] Stauffer, *TDNT*, I, 654. Cf. *Deut R.* 3 (200d); *Pirqe R. Eliezer* 41; *Mek. Exod* on 19:7. See Str-B, I, 969f; II, 393.

[468] Cf. *Mek. Exod* on 15:2.

[469] Stauffer, *TDNT*, I, 654. Cf. *Exod R.* 15 on 12:2; *Lev R.* 11 on 9:1. See Str-B, I, 517.

wedding or the wedding feast.[470] Jesus himself testified that he was the bridegroom (Mark 2:19) and this was confirmed by John the Baptist (John 3:29). The bride of the messianic wedding feast is the new community of the new covenant (1 Cor 6:14f). The most powerful example of the marriage motif in the NT can be found in the wedding feast of the Lamb of God at the end of the age (Rev 19; 20; 22).

The bridegroom at the wedding feast of Cana was obliged to provide enough wine and food for the guests;[471] but unexpectedly, the wine was running out. In this hopeless situation, instead of the bridegroom, Jesus supplied the best wine through miraculous means. This sign shows not only the creative power of Jesus but also sets him forth as the true bridegroom,[472] even though, in fact, Jesus is not the bridegroom in the wedding. Here, the couple remian subsidiary in the episode; Jesus is the main character. Lindars assumes that, in John 3:29ff, Jesus's words followed by John the Baptist's last testimony about him, [473] could mean that: 'the time of the wedding-feast has arrived in the new order which he himself has inaugurated.'[474] He further argues that there is an intimate relationship between the wine miracle at Cana and John 3:22–36. If so, Carmichael is correct in saying that, 'Jesus himself is to be thought of as a bridegroom. He, after all, provided the outstanding wine.'[475] Asserting that 'on the third day' in v. 1 reflects Yahweh's bestowal of the Torah to the exodus community with the revelation of the glory of Yahweh to Israel at Sinai (cf. Exod 19:16–20; 24:16–17), and that this covenant is often described as the wedding between Yahweh and Israel, Coloe [476] argues that the true

---

[470] Stauffer, *TDNT*, I, 654–655; Witherington, *Wisdom*, 78; Günther, *NIDNTT*, II, 585; Lindars, *John*, 125; Milne, *John*, 66; Dodd, *Interpretation*, 297; Manson, *Servant-Messiah*, 67. Cf. Matt 5:6; 8:11–12; 9:15; 25:10ff; Luke 5:35; 12:36ff; 22:15–18; Mark 2:19; John 3:29; 1 Cor 6:14ff; 2 Cor 11:2; Eph 5:22–32; Rev 19:7–9; 21:2; 22:17–20.

[471] According to Brown, *John I-XII*, 98, the wedding feast generally lasted for one week. Cf. Judge 14:12; *Tob.* 11:19; Str-B, I, 517. See also Bultmann, *John*, 115 n. 6; R. H. Williams, 'Mother,' 684, who says that 'in this circumstance, running out of wine represents a loss of honour, since it makes it evident to all that the groom lacks both material and social resources.'

[472] Coloe, *Dwells*, 69.

[473] Stauffer, *TDNT*, I, 654–655; Günther, *NIDNTT*, II, 585; Howard-Brook, *Becoming*, 79; Carson, *John*, 211; Coloe, *Dwells*, 69; Ng, *Symbolism*, 60. Contra Bultmann, *John*, 173 n. 11, who rejected the presence of the marriage motif in John 3:22–36.

[474] Lindars, *John*, 125. See also Jones, *Symbol*, 77, 83.

[475] Carmichael, *Creation*, 74. See also K. T. Cooper, 'Best,' 379.

[476] Coloe, *Dwells*, 69; Lee, *Narratives*, 36; Kim, *Exposition*, 70–71. F. J. Moloney, 'John 2:13–22' 445 assumes that the 'in three days' of the Temple incident in John 2:19–20 relates to Exod 19:16, that is, the establishment of the covenant on Sinai. The meaning of 'on the third day' will be further discussed in connection with the establishment of the new covenant and the new exodus, which results in the creation of the new-eschatological people of God, that is, the new

bridegroom appearing at Cana changed water for Jewish purification rituals into the abundant fine wine of the messianic banquet. This, he says, signifies the fulfilment of the promises in Isa 25:6 and 55:1–2. There is thus a clear parallel between the wedding/covenant imagery in the OT and the miracle here under consideration (cf. also John 3:29). Carson also thinks that the marriage motif appearing in both Old and New Testaments cannot be neglected:

> We cannot imagine that John the Baptist was ignorant of the many Old Testament passages that depict Israel or the faithful within Israel as the bride of the Lord (e.g. Isa 62:4–5; Jer 2:2; Hos 2:16–20) …. Jesus may allude to the same heritage of understanding in Mark 2:19. The Evangelist could not have been unaware of the fact that the post-resurrection church would picture Christ as the bridegroom and his church as the bride - the continuation and transformation of the Old Testament theme (e.g. 2 Cor 11:2; Eph 5:25–27; Rev 21:2, 9; 22:17). The joy of the 'best man' belongs to the Baptist, *and it is now complete.*[477]

Yahweh's bride rejoices in Yahweh as the bridegroom of Israel who will be enthroned as the everlasting King and build the kingdom of peace in Zion at the time of eschatological salvation or new exodus.[478] Jeremias[479] points out that the wedding or the wedding banquet was one of the common symbols denoting the dawn of the time of salvation in the OT. In particular, Isa 61 and 62 use the marriage imagery to express the extreme happiness and gladness of the renewed covenant relationship between Yahweh and Israel in terms of the out-pouring of the Spirit, the preaching of good news, and the making of an everlasting covenant with Israel. This is set in the light of the restoration, the new exodus of the exiled Israel. The Baptist's last testimony about Jesus introduces the marriage motif reflecting the covenant relationship between Jesus and the new Israel, emphasising: the joy of the Baptist in the coming of Jesus the bridegroom; the limitless bestowing of the Spirit; the speaking of the words of God; and the giving of eternal life to those who believe in the Son. All this is to be understood in the light of the salvation of the eschatological new exodus.

Furthermore, in the Fourth Gospel, the miracle continues over into the Temple incident, taking place against the background of the feast of the

---

Temple, in the narrative of Jesus's action in the Temple of John 2:12–25. Cf. 4.5. 'In Three Days' of this work

[477] Carson, *John*, 211 (original emphasis).
[478] Günther, *NIDNTT*, II, 585.
[479] Jeremias, *Theology*, I, 96–108, esp. 105–106.

Passover. This needs to be considered with reference to the crucifixion and resurrection of Jesus as the paschal lamb, the only Son (firstborn) of God. Concerning the peculiar displacement of the Temple incident in the Fourth Gospel (compared to the Synoptics), Beasley-Murray assumes the Fourth Evangelist intended to theologically emphasize specific aspects of the event in connection with the wine miracle.

> By this conjunction of the sign of Cana and the cleansing of the Temple he has created a diptych to form a prelude to his story of the ministry of Jesus .... The chapter has a programmatic significance: *whoever understands the miracle of the wine and the cleansing of the Temple has the key to the ministry, death, and resurrection of Jesus and their outcome in the salvation of the kingdom and existence of the Church.*[480]

The majority of Johannine theologians consider that 'my hour' (v. 4) frequently mentioned by Jesus, points to the hour of his death, resurrection and exaltation to glory.[481] Moreover, 'on the third day' (v. 1) indicates, in the context of early church history, the day revealing the glory of Jesus in the crucifixion (vv. 11, 19).[482] That is to say, the glory brought out from this sign alludes to the glory which will be revealed at the crucifixion of Jesus.[483] This recalls the great theophany on Sinai after the exodus event (Exod 19–20; 33–34). Furthermore, if 'my hour' is related to Jesus's crucifixion through which the wine of the kingdom of God is available to the world, then the wine offered by his miracle is also connected to the life bestowed through his death and symbolized by the blood of Christ shed for the redemption of humanity on the cross (cf. John 19:34; John 6:52–58). Accordingly, this wine could be linked to the wine of the Eucharist.[484]

---

[480] Beasley-Murray, *John*, 31 (original emphasis). Cf. Bultmann, *John*, 112.
[481] Cf. John 12:23–24; 7:6, 8, 30; 8:20; 13:1; 16:32; 17:1. Bruce, *John*, 70; Carson, *John*, 171–172; Beasley-Murray, *John*, 34–35; idem., *Life*, 95; Morris, *John*, 160; Bultmann, *John*, 121; Tasker, *John*, 56; Smith, *John*, 84; Cooper, 'Best,' 366; Koester, *Symbolism*, 162; Polhill, 'John 1–4,' 451. Carmichael, *Creation*, 67–78 understands 'my hour' to mean the new birth, i.e. the resurrection of Jesus, compared to the old birth from Mary. This comparison between 'my hour' and the old birth from Mary seems to go too far, although 'my hour' may be related to the crucifixion and resurrection of Jesus and Jesus's resurrection could be understood in the light of the new birth or the new creation. Also, Carmichael speculatively claims that the wine miracle is related to the creation of trees bearing fruit with seed in it (Gen 1:9–13).
[482] Whitacre, *John*, 79; Brown, *John I-XII*, 97; Lindars, *John*, 124; Dodd, *Interpretation*, 300; Koester, *Symbolism*, 162.
[483] Throckmorton, *Creation*, 99.
[484] Beasley-Murray, *John*, 36; idem., *Life*, 96; Throckmorton, *Creation*, 100; Cooper, 'Best,' 378–379; Hengel, 'John 2:1–11,' 89, 102; Dodd, *Interpretation*, 298; Brown, *John I-XII*, 99; Polhill, 'John 1–4,' 451. *Contra* Morris, *John*, 160; Smith, *John*, 87; Barrett, *John*, 189; Loshe, 'Miracles,' 68 n. 13.

To sum up, this wine miracle hints not only at the creative power of Jesus but also at the identity of Jesus as the true bridegroom (John 3:29). This wedding motif and the wedding banquet were common symbols to denote: initially the covenantal relationship between Yahweh and his people in the light of the covenant at Sinai; and later also of the new covenant spoken of as a new exodus by the Prophets.

3.3 The New Order and Creation

Why did Jesus's mother Mary tell him about the shortage of wine (v. 3)?[485] Further, why did she, without hesitation, tell the servants to do whatever he ordered them (v. 5)? Bruce[486] suggests that Mary asked Jesus to do something about the shortage of wine at the wedding banquet because she already knew his resourcefulness could be relied upon. Carson[487] assumes that, since, at that time, she was probably a widow, she relied upon him, the firstborn family provider and patron. Williams[488] points out that marriage in Jewish society was not only the union between a bride and a bridegroom but also the union of two families and of their honour. This honour was maintained by reciprocal relationship or cooperation within the community, which was performed by the patron, who was in charge of everything for a dependent family and slaves. Williams assumes Jesus was a patron in Mary's family because of the death of Joseph and so she depended on him. The bridegroom at a wedding at Cana was in the crisis of losing his honour because of the shortage of wine for the wedding feast. Williams[489] thinks that, in this circumstance, Mary at least was convinced that Jesus as a patron should do something to help the family of the bridegroom to keep their honour, and thereby to enhance the honour of Jesus's family. This is possible in the light of the social-historical background.

Given such a situation, Jesus ordered the servants to fill the six stone water jars, which were used by the Jews for ceremonial cleansing. Afterwards, according to his order, the jars were filled with water to the brim. Then, he told them to draw some out and take it to the master of the banquet. The water was changed into the best wine. Here, even though, in fact, it is not clear which water was changed into wine in the passage, Barrett assumes it is natural to think that all the water in the six water jars was changed into

---

[485] Michaels, *John*, 49 says Jesus's negative response to Mary's request in v. 4 means he has to follow the will of God the Father and is not forced to do something according to mankind's will. See also Milne, *John*, 64; Whitacre, *John*, 79; Throckmorton, *Creation*, 97; Carson, *John*, 171.
[486] Bruce, *John*, 69.
[487] Carson, *John*, 169–170.
[488] Williams, 'Mother,' 683–685.
[489] Williams, 'Mother,' 686.

wine.⁴⁹⁰ This miraculous sign, in which the entire water in the six water jars for Jewish ceremonial washing was turned into abundant wine of superior quality, could denote that the water of the old order of Jewish purification was replaced by the wine of the new order, provided by Jesus, in the light of the messianic age.⁴⁹¹ Therefore, Cooper says:

> the recognition of the superior quality of Jesus' wine is intended to depict the superiority of the new covenant over the old (cf. 2 Cor 3:1–18, Heb 8:13). The fact that the stone jars were Jewish purification vessels (2:6) may even suggest a new mode of cleansing under the new covenant, spiritual and not physical, real and not typical; cf. Ezek 36:22–29.⁴⁹²

Pointing out the importance of the lawsuit motif in Isa 40–55 in understanding the Fourth Gospel, Lincoln⁴⁹³ argues that this wine sign reflects, in advance, the significance of Jesus's identity and work, to replace the Jewish purification by the joyful new life provided by him.

Now, we shall concentrate on the serialization of days in 1:29, 35, 43; 2:1. Some Johannine commentators⁴⁹⁴ think that this sequence of days only reflects the memories of the people who met Jesus, and has nothing to do with the first creation in Gen 1:3–2:3. Some⁴⁹⁵ criticize the argument that 'on the third day' in John 2:1 is connected with Jesus's resurrection in the light of the start of the new creation. However, some peculiarities need to be recognized in regard to the distinctiveness of the Fourth Gospel, which, after all, begins its preface with a mirroring of the creation narrative and emphasizes the creative work of the Logos. Therefore, there is a strong

---

⁴⁹⁰ Barrett, *John*, 192. See also Morris, *John*, 161; Michaels, *John*, 49; Brown, *John I-XII*, 100, 192; Lindars, *John*, 130; H. Seesemann, *TDNT*, V, 164; Cooper, 'Best,' 378. However, Bruce, *John*, 71 thinks that only the water drawn from the well after the filling of the six jars was turned into wine, on the basis of the argument, in which, here, the verb avntle,w just means 'drawing water from a well.' Tasker, *John*, 55, says that only the water that the servant took out from the water jars and delivered to the master of the banquet, was changed into wine.
⁴⁹¹ Cf. Bruce, *John*, 71–72; idem., *Second*, 135; Carson, *John*, 173–175; Smith, *John*, 85; Beasley-Murray, *John*, 35–36; Morris, *John*, 162; Kim, *Exposition*, 69, 72; Koester, *Symbolism*, 162–163; Polhill, 'John 1–4,' 450–451; Ng, *Symbolism*, 68–69; Howard-Brook, *Becoming*, 79 says that the six stone jars symbolized the first one week in the Fourth Gospel. However, this is far from clear.
⁴⁹² Cooper, 'Best,' 377.
⁴⁹³ A. T. Lincoln, *Truth*, 15.
⁴⁹⁴ Cf. Bruce, *John*, 55 n. 54.
⁴⁹⁵ Smith, *John*, 82; Bruce, *John*, 68; Carson, *John*, 167. In particular, Michaels, *John*, 46 says that 'on the third day' just means a short period. Whitacre, *John*, 78–79, who also understands 'on the third day' in the light of Jesus's crucifixion and resurrection, denies that 'on the third day' could be assumed in terms of a 'seven-day cycle,' with relevance to John 1:19–51, symbolizing the beginning of the new creation.

possibility of the new creation motif appearing in this wine miracle at Cana. This sequence of days appears only in this part of the Fourth Gospel. In particular, the Gospel places the Temple incident at the beginning of Jesus's public ministry rather than at its end. If all of these aspects are considered, there seems to be a theological intention in this serialization. Pointing out that a wedding feast could be a long-standing Jewish symbol of the new age, Trudinger[496] claims that 'on the third day' reflects the crucifixion and resurrection of Jesus. That is the true resurrection, the new life in Christ. In connection with this, Carson says that:

> The week of days climaxing in the miracle at Cana may provide an echo of creation-week (Gen 1). That means the miracle itself takes place on the seventh day, the Sabbath. Jesus' performance of redemptive work on the Sabbath is later in this Gospel (5:16ff; 7:21–24; 9:16) given the most suggestive theological treatment in the New Testament, apart from Hebrews 4. (p.168) …. It may also hint at the 'new creation' theme … his glory would be revealed in greatest measure in his cross, resurrection and exaltation, but every step along the course of his ministry was an adumbration of that glory. (p.175)[497]

Furthermore, the motif of the creation (re-creation) will be further supported by the term 'it is finished,' Jesus's last words on the cross in John 19:30. Hengel[498] assumes that in regard to Ἐν ἀρχῇ in John 1:1, 'finished' (τετέλεσται) at the end of Jesus's life in John 19:28–30 alludes to the completion of creation in Gen 2:2. The mission for which Jesus was commissioned by God the Father has been completed by his death on the cross (cf. John 17:4). This salvation work of God was described in the imagery of the new creation, or eschatological salvation. Dodd [499] understands this wine miracle in terms of 'the new beginning,' and holds that this concept of 'the new beginning' can be found in 2 Cor 5:17 as well. Thus, this wine miracle could be understood as the new creation, the fulfilment of the new exodus in Isa 65:17.

---

[496] L. P. Trudinger, 'Third,' 42–43. See also, Howard-Brook, *Becoming*, 77; Lightfoot, *John's*, 108; Lindars, *John*, 124; Brodie, *John*, 172–173.

[497] Carson, *John*, 168, 175. See also Morris, *John*, 114; Brown, *John I-XII*, 106; T. Barrosse, 'Seven,' 507–516; Howard-Brook, *Becoming*, 77. Malina and Rohrbaugh, *John*, 60 think the miracle happened on the eighth day. On the other hand, Trudinger, 'Third,' 41–43 thinks that this miracle was performed on the sixth day. See also Barrett, *John*, 190.

[498] Hengel, 'Gospel,' 393–394. See also, Coloe, *Dwells*, 189, 197. Cf. John 4:34; 5:17, 36; 17:4.

[499] Dodd, *Interpretation*, 297. See also Throckmorton, *Creation*, 96; Lindars, *John*, 128; Brown, *John I-XII*, 106, who thinks both the beginning and the end of this one week is the same date, Wednesday.

To sum up, this miraculous sign in which the entire water in the six jars for Jewish ceremonial washing was turned into abundant wine of superior quality could illustrate that the water of the old Jewish purification was replaced by the wine of the new messianic age. In particular, the serialization of days in John 1:29–2:1 could indicate a new creation motif.

3.4 The Eschatological Richness of the Messianic Era

Against the background of Nathanael's testimony about Jesus in the light of a Davidic king Messiah in John 1:49, and of the prophetic promise of Jesus confirming his confession (1:51), the abundance of wine supplied by Jesus at the wedding banquet at Cana needs to be considered in connection with eschatological salvation. Through the OT and some extra-biblical Jewish sources of the intertestamental period, the imagery of abundant wine was widely understood to relate to the Jewish expectations of the Messiah.

The importance of Jacob's prophetic blessing to Judah in Gen 49:8–12 was widely linked with the expected Messiah.[500] In Gen 49:10, the staff and the sceptre symbolized a kingly authority, and from between his feet referred to Judah's descendants. Wenham[501] states that this passage speaks of the coming of the Davidic messianic leader, a lion's cub from Judah, for all the tribes. Wenham continues by saying that the expected blessing in the messianic day was compared to an abundant harvest of grapes. The prediction of Jacob's blessing to Judah was first accomplished by the rise of the Davidic monarchy and the establishment of the Davidic kingdom, and will finally be fulfilled by the enthronement of the Davidic Messiah in the eschatological era. Wenham also notes that this blessing to Judah is paradoxically reflected by the Babylonian exile of Israel in the imagery of 'lion and vine' (Ezek 19; 21). Therefore, Wenham concludes that Gen 49:8–12 provided, 'the sources of these pictures of the messianic age.'[502]

Moreover, Wilfall[503] assumes that Gen 3:15 became the basis of the messianic hope of the Davidic king, who will destroy Satan as represented by the ancient serpent, Rahab. This messianic expectation can be found in Ps 89:10. This psalm praises the establishment of the everlasting Davidic kingdom on the basis of Yahweh's covenant with David (vv. 3–4) and Yahweh's crushing of the enemy, denoted here by Rahab, at the hands of the Davidic messianic king, the firstborn of God (vv. 9–10). Moreover, Isa 51 describes the new exodus salvation of exiled Israel in Babylon as the restoration of Eden, the garden of the Lord, where the crushing of Rahab,

---

[500] Koester, *Symbolism*, 79.
[501] Wenham, *Genesis 16–50*, 477–479.
[502] Wenham, *Genesis 16–50*, 479; Hengel, *Christology*, 315.
[503] W. Wilfall, 'Gen 3:15,' 363. Cf. Alexander, 'Messianic,' 31–32.

the sea monster, will take place against the background of the crossing of the Red Sea in the first exodus. Alexander[504] also points out that the LXX interpretative translation of Gen 3:15 prefigures the victory against Satan in the messianic age, and is picked up in both the Targum and New Testament:

> And I will put enmity between you and the woman and between your sons and her sons. And it will come about that when her sons observe the Law and do the commandments they will aim at you and strike you on your head and kill you. But when they forsake the commandments of the Law you will aim and bite him on his heel and make him ill. For her sons, however, there will be a remedy, but for you, O Serpent, there will not be a remedy, since they are to make appeasement in the end, in the day (*sic*) of King Messiah. (*Tg. Neof.* on Gen 3:14b–15)[505]

This messianic expectation of Gen 49:8–12 was fulfilled in the triumph of Jesus, the Lamb of God, 'the Lion of the tribe of Judah, the Root of David' in Rev 5:5.[506] Thus Alexander[507] correctly argues that Gen 3:15 and 49:8–12 are the earliest texts that Judaism applied to the future messianic-Davidic king who would be responsible for the restoration of *'Edenic'* conditions upon earth and the overthrow of the powers of evil. The future King-Messiah, descended from the tribe of Judah, would achieve the restoration of creation. As mentioned above, the abundance of wine was used in the Prophets, especially, in Deutero-Isaiah and some Jewish sources, to illustrate the new exodus-salvation brought about by the Davidic Messiah in the eschatological time.[508]

---

[504] Alexander, 'Messianic,' 27–28. Cf. Rom 16:20; 1 Cor 15:22–28; Heb 2:14; Rev 12:1–13:1. Further, Alexander, *ibid.*, 28 n. 22 says that Jesus's calling his mother 'Woman' in John 2:4 and 19:26 reflects Eve (woman) in Gen 3:15, on the basis of the opinion of Wenham, *Genesis 1–15*, 80–81, who argues Jesus's self-designation, 'the Son of Man' reflects Gen 3:15. Brown, *John I-XII*, 109 also assumes Jesus's mother Mary was understood as the new Eve, as the mother of Messiah, and as woman, the symbol of church, against the background of Gen 3:15 and Rev 12. Brodie, *John*, 174 goes further and thinks that, here, Mary is a symbol or representative of the people of God, Israel. Cf. John 2:4; 4:21; 8:10; 19:26; 20:13, 15.
[505] Alexander, 'Messianic,' 27 n. 21. Cf. M. McNamara, *Targum Neofiti 1: Genesis*, 61.
[506] Alexander, 'Messianic,' 36 n. 52.
[507] Alexander, 'Messianic,' 19–39.
[508] Koester, *Symbolism*, 79 n. 10. Cf. Gen 27:28f; 49:8–12; Lev 26:5; Deut 28:1–4; Ps 72:16; Prov 9:5; Amos 9:13; Hos 2:24; 14:8f; Joel 2:21–4; 3:18; Mic 4:4; Zech 3:10; 8:12; 9:17; Isa 29:17; 30:23–6; 55:1–3; Jer 31:5; Ezek 34:23–31; 36:29f; *2 Bar.* 29:5; *1 En.* 10:19.

Drawing on this background, Hengel[509] says that the abundance of wine which resulted from Jesus's miraculous sign at the wedding feast in Cana symbolizes the abundance and overflowing joy brought by the Messiah in the eschatological age. He[510] points out the importance of John 15 with its reference to Jesus being the true vine as drawing on the messianic expectations in the OT and Judaism. Cooper also says that this wine miracle is associated with:

> the OT promises of supernatural agricultural abundance to be provided in the days of the Messiah .... Closely related are the promises of the fruitful vine in Messianic days .... Jesus is announcing the advent of Shiloh, who will come in such abundance of wine that he will be able to wash his clothes in it. The tension we face is the familiar NT tension between the already of eschatological fulfilment and the not yet of consummation promise.[511]

Whitacre[512] indicates that the restoration promised to Israel was clearly described in Hos 2:14–23 in the imagery of marriage and abundant wine. Further, Jesus's revealing of his glory through this miracle could also be understood in the light of the new exodus salvation in the second part of Isaiah.[513]

To sum up, the abundant wine symbolizes the abundance and overflowing gladness which was expected to be brought about by the Davidic Messiah in the eschatological new exodus. In regard to this, Gen 3:15 and 49:8–12 became the basis of the expectation of the Davidic Messiah who was responsible for the restoration of creation and the destruction of Satan (Ps 89). The messianic expectation of the Davidic king, with the promise of the coming new salvation, the new exodus, was described in terms of an abundance of wine by the Prophets, especially Deutero-Isaiah.

---

[509] Hengel, 'John 2:1–11,' 101; idem., *Christology*, 315–318. Cf. John 10:10; 15:11; 16:24. See also Jones, *Symbol*, 59; Howard-Brook, *Becoming*, 79; Michaels, *John*, 49; Milne, *John*, 64; Whitacre, *John*, 80; Tasker, *John*, 56–57; Carson, *John*, 172–173; Brown, *John I-XII*, 105; Smith, *John*, 86–87; Lohse, 'Miracles,' 68; Koester, *Symbolism*, 162; Polhill, 'John 1–4,' 450–451; Edwards, 'Christological,' 367; Beasley-Murray, *Life*, 95; Schnackenburg, *John*, I, 338; Dennis, *Gathering*, 167; Ng, *Symbolism*, 68; Jeremias, *Theology*, I, 106, who says that 'new wine' symbolizes the new era. Cf. Gen 9:20; 49:11f; Num 13:23f; Amos 9:13; Joel 3:18. J. Painter, *Quest*, 157, who says that new wine symbolically asserts the dawning of the superior eschatological age.
[510] Hengel, 'John 2:1–11,' 100; Burge, 'Territorial,' 391–395; Kim, *Exposition*, 61.
[511] Cooper, 'Best,' 364–380, quoted from 378. See also Brown, *NIDNTT*, III, 921–922.
[512] Whitacre, *John*, 80. Cf. In particular, J. A. Grassi, 'Wedding,' 133–136 even connects this wine miracle with the outpouring of the Holy Spirit at Pentecost in Acts 2.
[513] Cf. Isa 55:5; 60:1–2, 19–22; 66:18–19.

3.5 Conclusion

In the first place, this miracle has to be discussed against the background of the vine-wine motif in the OT, Judaism, and the NT, rather than heathen sources. In Ps 80 [79]:8–13, Israel is described as a vine brought out of Egypt and planted in the promised land. The imagery of the vineyard was commonly used to describe the new covenant relationship between Yahweh and his people in the Prophets. Above all, in John 15:1–11, Jesus introduces himself as the True Vine to which all the branches have to be attached to get eternal life. Here, Jesus discloses that he is the inclusive representative (the firstborn) of the new covenant people of God, the new Israel who replaces the old Jacob-Israel, the ancestor of Israel, the old covenant people of God.

Secondly, the fact that it was Jesus who supplied the best wine instead of the bridegroom could allude to Jesus being the true bridegroom (cf. John 3:29). This wedding motif and that of the wedding banquet alludes to the covenant relationship between Yahweh and his people, found not only in the covenant of the first exodus at Sinai but also of the new covenant of the new exodus foretold in the Prophets.

Thirdly, the fact that the water in the six pots for Jewish purification was changed into abundant wine of superior quality could mean that the Jewish old order was being replaced by the new order of the eschatological age, brought about by the Davidic Messiah. Also, with regard to 'in the beginning' in John 1:1 and 'it is finished' in John 19:30, the serialization of days in John 1:29–2:1 could be an indication of the importance of the new creation motif.

Fourthly, the abundance of superior wine at the wedding banquet symbolizes the abundance and overflowing gladness which was expected to accompany the Davidic Messiah in the eschatological age, as based on Gen 49:8–12. In the Prophets, the Davidic Messiah was expected to restore exiled Israel in the new exodus, which was described in the imagery of the abundance of wine, marriage, new covenant, David covenant, and the restoration of Edenic conditions. All speak of overflowing delight and the glory of Yahweh.

Chapter 4: Jesus's Action in the Temple John 2:12–25. cf. Matt 21:12–13; Mark 11:15–17; Luke 19:45–46

4.1 Introduction

The Temple incident is one of the stories found in all the Synoptic Gospels and the Fourth Gospel. Clearly, this is an important event for all four Evangelists, in terms of their understanding of the identity and works of Jesus.[514] In John, the Temple incident is linked to Jesus's Temple logion, that is, his own words about the destruction of the present Temple and the construction of a new. Here, Jesus accused the Jews of being responsible for the destruction of the Temple and claimed that he by himself would raise a new Temple.[515] The Evangliest also includes an interpretation of Jesus's words. In contrast to the Synoptics, John locates this incident at the beginning of Jesus's public ministry and, moreover, with the background of the first of the three Passovers recorded in his Gospel. According to the Synoptic Gospels, particularly Mark's Gospel (Mark 11; 14; 15), this event seems to be the main issue at Jesus's trial before the high priest and the Sanhedrin. As a result, the crucifixion of Jesus is set against the background of a crucial Jewish feast, the Passover, at the end of his public ministry.[516] The parable of the tenants in Mark 12:1–12 clearly shows that Jesus saw himself as the Son of God and that he already anticipated his death resulting from the Temple incident at the hands of the Jewish religious leaders. In John 2:17, the Evangelist shows that this Temple incident would result in the sufferings Jesus would experience in the future. That is to say, in all the four Gospels—despite the difference in chronology—the death of Jesus can be seen to have resulted from his action in the Temple court.[517]

---

[514] Kim, 'Temple,' 87–131; *idem.*, 'Interpretation,' 195–248; *idem.*, 'Stone,' 134–145; P. W. L. Walker, *Jesus*, 161–200, 296–303; Coloe, *Dwells*, 65–84.

[515] In the Synoptic Gospels, the Temple incident was separately placed from the so-called Temple logion. The Temple logion was brought not by Jesus himself but by false witnesses at the trial. Furthermore, Jesus was charged both with the destruction of the Temple and with the raising of the New Temple in Matt 26:61; Mark 14:58. cf. Matt 27:40; Mark 15:29. Cf. Coloe, *Dwells*, 66–69; Walker, *Jesus*, 5–6.

[516] Jeremias, *Theology*, I, 145 n. 1; Kim, 'Temple,' 108–115, who even claims that Jesus intentionally provoked the Temple incident to bring forth 'his prosecution and even his death' (p. 120). See also, B. F. Meyer, *Aims*, 170; Jeremias, *Theology*, I, 279–280; Hengel, *Atonement*, 7; S. S. Yoo, *Prayer*, 222.

[517] Concerning the discussion of the chronological differences about the Temple incident between the Synoptics and John's Gospel, the majority of commentators understand the records of the Synoptics to be historically accurate with John displacing it to the beginning of Jesus's public ministry in accordance with his theological aims. Cf. Bernard, *John*, I, 88–89; Lindars, *John*, 135; Bruce, *John*, 77; Beasley-Murray, *John*, 38–39; Schnackenburg, *John*, I, 341, 355; Witherington, *Wisdom*, 86; M. Sabbe, 'Cleansing,' 332–334; Throckmorton, *Creation*,' 103; Brown, *John I-XII*, 118; Michaels, *John*, 50. However, other Johannine theologians assume that

Why, in John's account, even though Jesus often went up to the Jerusalem Temple at the times of other Jewish festivals,[518] did he take this action in the Temple at the beginning of his public ministry against the background of the Passover?[519] Furthermore, why did Jesus relate his physical death and resurrection to the destruction of the Temple and its reconstruction? What could this action mean to the destiny of the Temple in Jerusalem? Does Jesus's action in the Temple symbolize the cleansing of the Temple or its destruction? In particular, since Jesus's statement concerning the building of the new Temple was interpreted as the resurrection of his body, something about the narrative of his resurrection must be considered if we are to determine what John intended by his account of the Temple incident. All these questions will be discussed in connection with the Passover-new exodus motif.

4.2 Temple Cleansing or Temple Destruction?

Much discussion has taken place as to whether the Temple incident is to be understood as signifying its cleansing or its destruction.[520] In what sense was the trading and money-changing in the Temple wrong? After all, the sacrificial system was the most important function of the Temple, and so it seemed natural that animals for the sacrificial worship had to be supplied through this kind of transaction, particularly for the convenience of the pilgrims travelling from long distances. So animal trading seems to be justified as an appropriate business, although it would not be suitable in the holy areas of the Temple. Also, because of the circumstances, the money-changing activity seemed to be necessary as a way for the Jews to pay the

---

there were two Temple incidents. Cf. Carson, *John*, 183; Morris, *John*, 166–169; C. L. Blomberg, *Historical*, 89–91; J. A. T. Robinson, *Priority*, 127–131; F. J. Moloney, 'Fourth,' 55; A. J. Köstenberger, *John*, 76–78; Milne, *John*, 68.

[518] Cf. Two other Passovers (John 6; 18–19), Tabernacle (John 7–8) and Dedication (John 10). If the Temple incident can be regarded as the cleansing of the Temple, it could be more natural to think that the incident would reasonably have happened at the feast of Dedication celebrating the cleansing of the second Temple performed by Judas the Maccabee and his brothers (cf. *1 Macc.* 4:36–60; *2 Macc* 10:1–8; *Ant.* 12: 316–322) rather than at the feast of Passover commemorating the first Exodus.

[519] Walker, *Jesus*, 163, 302; Throckmorton, *Creation*, 108; Sabbe, 'Cleansing,' 351; Drapper, 'Temple,' 270; Kim, *Exposition*, 72–73; Yoo, *Prayer*, 221; Beasley-Murray, *John*, 38–39; Coloe, *Dwells*, 84; Motyer, *Father*, 40; Polhill, 'John 1–4,' 451; L. Gaston, *Stone*, 205; Dennis, *Gathering*, 165; Menken, *Quotations*, 43.

[520] S. M. Bryan, *Jesus*, 206–225; R. Bauckham, 'Demonstration,' 72–89; E. P. Sanders, *Jesus*, 61–90; Kim, 'Temple,' 87–131; *idem.*, 'Interpretation,' 195–248, par. 223–241; C. A. Evans, 'Action,' 237–270; *idem.*, 'Predictions,' 92–150; M. D. Hooker, 'Traditions,' 7–19; D. Seeley, 'Temple,' 263–283; Walker, *Jesus*, 163–175.

Temple tax to the officials according to the order set up by God himself (cf. Exod 30:11–16).[521]

E. P. Sanders[522] argues that Jesus did not attack the sacrificial system that was the inherent function of the Temple, and the animal transactions and the money-changing business for that sacrificial worship. As Sanders has argued, if the trading and the money-changing itself was not a problem, was there any corruption in the activities of the traders and the money-changers? Some commentators[523] interpret Jesus's action as a symbolic demonstration of Temple cleansing, because there was obviously corruption and defilement of the Temple priests in these affairs. For these scholars, that was the main reason for Jesus's attack in the Temple. Sanders[524] also acknowledges the presence of some literary evidence testifying to the corruption of the Temple priests who were in charge of sacrificial worship and the raising of Temple tax. Nonetheless, because of the absence of any words from Jesus criticizing either dishonesty, corruption, or immorality of the priesthood, Sanders[525] rejects the argument that Jesus's action was targeted against the corruption of the Temple priests. He[526] concludes that Jesus did not attack the Temple, its sacrificial system, the priestly aristocracy who controlled the affairs of the Temple, or the activities of the animal traders and the money-changers. Rather, with the overturning of the tables, Jesus symbolically demonstrated that the old Temple had to be destroyed to make way for the building of the new eschatological Temple at the inauguration of the new age.[527] Therefore,

---

[521] For the Temple tax which was annually and compulsorily paid by every Jewish adult man, Tyrian coinage only was acceptable, either because of its exceptionally high purity of silver content (cf. Carson, *John*, 178; Bruce, *John*, 74; Milne, *John*, 68) or due to the absence of emperor's portraits (cf. Brown, *John I-XII*, 115; Coloe, *Dwells*, 72; Beasley-Murray, *John*, 38; Lindars, *John*, 138). The Temple tax was a fund raised for the general maintenance of the Temple (cf. Exod 38:25–28; 2 Chron 24:5–7; Neh 10:33; *Ant.* 3:174–176; *m. Sheq.* 4:2– even for the repair of the wall of Jerusalem) as well as for the provision to supply Israel's twice-daily acts of atonement (*tamid*) (cf. Exod 29:38–42; *m. Sheq.* 1:3, 6). For detailed discussion, see J. Neusner, 'Money-Changers,' 287–290; Bauckham, 'Demonstration,' 73–76; Bryan, *Jesus*, 213–217; R. H. Hiers, 'Purification,' 87 n. 19.

[522] Sanders, *Jesus*, 63–65.

[523] Jeremias, *Theology*, I, 145; Evans, 'Action,' 237–270; *idem.*, 'Predictions,' 92–150; Hooker, 'Traditions,' 7–19, par. 18–19; Witherington, *Wisdom*, 87, 90; G. Schrenk, *TDNT*, III, 243. See also Brown, *John I-XII*, 121–122.

[524] Sanders, *Jesus*, 65–66. Cf. *Ps. Sol.* 8:9–19; 17:6–8; *Test. Mos.* 6:1; *1QpHab* 12:8f; 12:10; 8:8–11; 11:4–7; *CD* 5:6–8.

[525] Sanders, *Jesus*, 66, 76. See also D. R. Catchpole, 'Triumphal,' 333.

[526] Sanders, *Jesus*, 71, 73–75, 90.

[527] Bauckham, 'Demonstration,' 87. See also Hooker, 'Traditions,' 7–19, esp. 17.

Sanders [528] understands the Temple incident as having eschatological significance.

One of Sanders' arguments, that the Temple incident is a symbolic demonstration of the destruction of the Temple and has to be understood in the light of eschatological expectations, seems to be correct. This will become clearer as we proceed. Nevertheless, this point apart, his arguments can be criticized in a number of ways.[529] Firstly, as he himself recognizes, there is documentary evidence about the corruption of the priesthood in connection with the Temple hierarchy at the time of Jesus.[530] In this respect, Jeremias[531] argues that the priests, especially the high priest Annas and his family, abused their calling by carrying on business to make profit. Supporting this is the evidence of Evans, who writes that, 'there are no texts that predict the appearance of a messianic figure who first destroys (or predicts the destruction of) the Temple and then rebuilds it.'[532] He[533] holds that Jesus's action was not a messianic demonstration symbolizing the destruction of the Temple, but a cleansing of the Temple.

Nevertheless, Jesus's Temple incident seems to symbolize the Temple's destruction on a scale beyond the dimension merely of Temple cleansing; especially when we note that in the Synoptic Gospels the doom of the Temple was clearly indicated in the prophecies of Jesus (cf. Mark 13:1f; 14:58; 15:29) which was the decisive charge at his trials.[534] The attitude of Jesus concerning the Temple and its cultic system was very negative.[535] Evans[536] shows that this was entirely justified, and concludes that, 'Jesus' action in the Temple was in all probability related to, indeed possibly the occasion for, a prophetic word against the Temple.' [537] Some

---

[528] Sanders, *Jesus*, 75–90.
[529] For detailed criticisms against Sanders' argument, see Hooker, 'Traditions,' 7–19, esp. 17; Evans, 'Action,' 237–270; Bauckham, 'Demonstration,' 72–89; Seeley, 'Temple,' 264–265.
[530] Cf. *t. Men.* 8:21–22; 13:22; *m. Sheq.* 1:3, 6, 174; 4:7; *m. Ker.* 1:7; *b. Pesah.* 57a; *Test. Mos.* 7; *Ant.* 20:181, 205–207; *War* 5:412; *2 Bar.* 10:18; *4 Bar.* 1:1, 8; 4:7f; *Apoc. Abr.* 25:1–6; 27:7; *Lam R.* 4:7 on 4:4; Str-B, I, 851f. For an excellent presentation of documentary evidence concerning the corruption of the priesthood and the expectation of the destruction of the Herodian Temple, see Evans, 'Predictions,' 92–150; J. Jeremias, *Jerusalem*, 49, 195–196; Bauckham, 'Demonstration,' 75–80; Brown, *John I-XII*, 121–122; Motyer, *Father*, 39 n. 19.
[531] Jeremias, *Theology*, I, 145; *idem., Jerusalem*, 49, 194–198; Bauckham, 'Demonstration,' 81; Evans, 'Action,' 319–344; Bryan, *Jesus*, 220; Drapper, 'Temple,' 280–281.
[532] Evans, 'Action,' 237–270, quoted from 250.
[533] Evans, 'Action,' 269.
[534] Kim, 'Temple,' 87–131, par. 118–119; *idem., Exposition*, 73.
[535] Kim, 'Interpretation,' 224–227; Walker, *Jesus*, 167; Brown, *John I-XII*, 122; Holwerda, *Jesus*, 67–70.
[536] Evans, 'Predictions,' 92–150.
[537] Evans, 'Predictions,' 140–150, quoted from 150. See *idem.*, 'Action,' 251, where he recognizes that Jer 7 quoted by Jesus himself in Mark 11:17 charges the priests and rulers of Judah with

commentators[538] assume this Temple incident alluded to the eschatological fulfilment of Zech 14:21. Beasley-Murray[539] interprets the presence of the traders in the Temple as an act which desecrated the glory of God the Father.

Thus, through the symbolic action against the money-changers, Jesus showed that the corrupted Temple and its cultic system could not escape the imminent judgement of God.[540] Bauckham interprets the over-turning of the money-changers' tables as a protest against the Temple tax itself and those who controlled the Temple treasury.[541] Further, Bryan[542] points out that the payment of the Temple tax as a ransom was connected not only to God's deliverance (or ransom) of Israel out of Egypt but also to keep God's wrath from falling on the entire community of Israel. With regard to Matt 17:24–7 (which Bryan interprets as referring to the establishment of the relationship between the eschatological King-Father and his children), he argues that the over-turning of the money-changers' tables symbolized the

---

various crimes, and contains a threat of destruction against the Solomonic Temple (vv. 9, 11, 14). Also, Hooker, 'Traditions,' 7–19, who tries to demonstrate the incident to be a cleansing (p. 18), although she recognizes the symbolic aspect of the forthcoming destruction of the Temple and the intimate relationship between its destruction and Jesus's death (pp. 7–11, 13–15). In my judgement, the argument of both commentators who assert Jesus's action in the Temple as a symbolic demonstration of Temple cleansing rather than of Temple destruction seems to result from their specific criticisms against Sanders' biased contention.

[538] Dodd, *Interpretation*, 159–160, 300; Brown, *John I-XII*, 121; C. Roth, 'Cleansing,' 174–181; Lindars, *John*, 139; Bruce, *John*, 74–75; Bryan, *Jesus*, 223–224; Drapper, 'Temple,' 280–281. *Contra* Bauckham, 'Demonstration,' 82; Koester, *Symbolism*, 82.

[539] Beasley-Murray, *John*, 39. See also Kim, 'Temple,' 121–123; *idem.*, 'Stone,' 139; Malina and Rohrbaugh, *John*, 74; Bryan, *Jesus*, 223–224. Josephus interpreted the destruction of the Temple in 70 A.D. as the judgement of God for the purification of the corrupted Temple. Cf. *Bell.* 4:323; *War* 5:412; *Apoc. Abr.* 25:1–6; 27:7.

[540] Kim, 'Temple,' 121–123; *idem.*, 'Stone,' 139; *idem.*, *Exposition*, 73; Motyer, *Father*, 39; P. Stuhlmacher, *Jesus*, 30–31, 46; Neusner, 'Money-Changers,' 287–290; Throckmorton, *Creation*, 103; Seeley, 'Temple,' 263–283, par. 276–280, who argues that the Temple incident was a literary creation by Mark himself rather than a real historical event. This, for Seeley, would imply that in the absence of the tradition of the Messiah marching against the Temple in Judaism, and of the Jews' great concern for the Temple, Mark carefully disclosed the end of the Jewish sacrificial system of the Temple by the introduction of Jesus as the Messiah cleansing the Temple rather than by more direct means. Seeley, nevertheless, deduces from the incident an intimate relationship between Jesus's death and the destruction of the Temple. Also, Hooker, 'Traditions,' 19 argues that 'sayings and actions which are basically hopeful and call for reform, repentance and renewal can easily be adapted to express judgement and execution.' Further, G. W. Buchanan, 'Symbolic,' 289–290 thinks that the Temple incident was a midrashic creation of the early church. However, the authenticity of the Temple action and the sayings about the destruction of the Temple is defended by Sanders, *Jesus*, 61, 364–365 n. 5; Bryan, *Jesus*, 206–207.

[541] Bauckham, 'Demonstration,' 73, 75–76. See also, Neusner, 'Money-Changers,' 288–290; Coloe, *Dwells*, 72–73.

[542] Bryan, *Jesus*, 215–216.

abolition of the Temple tax in the eschaton which has already been inaugurated by Jesus's appearance.[543] In addition, Watts[544] argues that the Temple incident and the merged citation from Isa 56:7 and Jer 7:11 in Mark 11:17 revealed the uselessness of the sacrificial system of the current Temple and warned about its forthcoming destruction as judgement from God.

To sum up, the incident could demonstrate that the destruction of the Temple was coming as a form of the judgement of God. This judgement involved its ultimate abolition and the replacement both of the Temple itself and of its cultic functions.[545]

4.3 The Davidic Messiah: the Son of God, the Temple Builder and the King of the Jews (Israel)

Upon Jesus's action at the Temple and his logion of John 2:16, the Jews demanded that he show a miraculous sign to prove his authority. From this it might be understood that there was some messianic expectation involved in the incident.[546] Such a messianic hope with regard to the construction of the Temple originated from 2 Sam 7:12–14. Yahweh's covenant with David in that passage was the basis not only of Jesus's Temple action and logion but also of the high priest's main charges against him, resulting in his death. Concerning this, Kim[547] agrees with Betz that the two charges against Jesus before the Sanhedrin (namely the destruction and rebuilding of the Temple, and whether Jesus was the Messiah, the Son of the Blessed One; cf. Mark 14:53–62) were largely based on 2 Sam 7.12–14a. This Davidic covenant could be summarized in three points: 1) the descendent of David

---

[543] Bryan, *Jesus*, 225–229.
[544] Watts, *Isaiah's*, 330. See also Wright, *Victory*, 493; Bauckham, 'Demonstration,' 86 n. 82, who says that 'verbal prophecies of the destruction of the Temple in Jewish literature normally refer to divine *judgement*.' (quoted from 87, original emphasis). Cf. Mic 3:12; Jer 7; 26; *Sib. Or.* 3:265–281; 4:115–118; *Apoc. Abr.* 27; *2 Bar.* 1–8; *4 Bar.* 1–4. Also, Jesus's Temple incident could be interpreted as the forthcoming divine judgement against the Temple, which was sandwiched by the narrative of Jesus's curse against the fruitless fig-tree in Mark 11:12–14, 20–21. See, W. R. Telford, *Barren*; P. W. L. Walker, 'Land,' 102–103; *idem.*, *Jesus*, 276; Bryan, *Jesus*, 223–225, 235; D. Juel, *Messiah*, 131, 198; Seeley, 'Temple,' 274; Holwerda, *Jesus*, 71–72.
[545] Lightfoot, *John's*, 112–114; Dodd, *Interpretation*, 301; Coloe, *Dwells*, 73–74; Schnackenburg, *John*, I, 356; Brown, *John I-XII*, 121–122; Morris, *John*, 178–179; Barrett, *John*, 196–197; Milne, *John*, 70; Bernard, *John*, I, 87–88; Kim, *Exposition*, 72–74; Drapper, 'Temple,' 280–281; Yoo, *Prayer*, 221; Koester, *Symbolism*, 84; McKnight, *Vision*, 7–8; Dennis, *Gathering*, 170.
[546] Morris, *John*, 174; Brown, *John I-XII*, 121–123; Michaels, *John*, 51; Schnackenburg, *John*, I, 348; Witherington, *Wisdom*, 88; Bernad, *John*, I, 92; Coloe, *Dwells*, 76; Hiers, 'Purification,' 87; Kim, 'Temple,' 110–111, 128; Jeremias, *Theology*, I, 259; G. Schrenk, *TDNT*, III, 243–244; O. Michel, *TDNT*, IV, 884; B. Gärtner, *Temple*, 106–107; Koester, *Symbolism*, 82.
[547] Kim, 'Temple,' 128; O. Betz, *What*, 87–92; Jeremias, *Theology*, I, 259; Holwerda, *Jesus*, 73; Juel, *Messiah*, 169–170; Brown, *John I-XII*, 123; Bryan, *Jesus*, 229, 235.

would forever be enthroned as a king of an everlasting kingdom established by Yahweh; 2) the Temple for Yahweh would be built by the descendent as the servant of God (cf. 1 Kings 8; 2 Chron 6); and 3) the Davidic king would be the Son/firstborn of Yahweh. This covenant was the very basis of the Davidic messianic expectation (or movement) in the OT, particularly as found in the Prophets and in Jewish literature of the Second Temple period and in the NT.[548] It is against such a messianic background that the Johannine Jesus discloses his identity by means both of the Temple incident and his words concerning the Temple (John 2:16), its destruction by the Jews and its reconstruction by himself (John 2:19). This will now be analysed in more detail.

Firstly, Jesus designated himself as 'the Son/Firstborn of God.' Jesus clearly laid claim to an authority when he mentioned the Jerusalem Temple as '*my Father's house*' (John 2:16), which reflects his self-consciousness as 'the Son of God,' a fact which seems to have provoked the Temple incident.[549] After his action in the Temple court, it was demanded of him that he should give a miraculous sign to prove his authority to be able to do such things in the holy place (John 2:18). Namely, the Jews demanded a defence of his reference to himself as 'the Son of God.'[550]

In addition, as mentioned above, his driving out the merchants and animals from the Temple court and his reference to the market (John 2:16) has

---

[548] For examples, Pss 2:7; 89:20–38; 132:11–18; Isa 11:1–9; Jer 33:14–22; Ezek 37:24–28; Zec 6:12; *4QFlor.* 1:6–8; *4QpsDan*ᵃ 1:7–9; 2:1–4; *Ps. Sol.* 17–18; *Jub.* 1:28f; *1 En.* 90:28f; *Sib. Or.* 5:414–433; *Tob.* 13:10 (12); 14:5 (7); The fourteenth Prayer of the *Eighteen Benedictions*; *Tg. Zech* 6:12; *Tg. Isa* 53:5; Luke 1:32–33; Acts 2:30; 2 Cor 6:18; Heb 1:5. Cf. Hiers, 'Purification,' 86–87 n. 20; Kim, 'Interpretation,' 229; *idem.*, 'Temple,' 124; Jeremias, *Theology*, I, 259; Evans, 'Predictions,' 137–149, particularly, who argues that the Idumean Herod's rebuilding of the luxurious third Temple (cf. luxuriously extending and re-molding of the Second Temple of Zerubbabel) could be understood in the light of Yahweh's covenant with David in Nathan's oracle of 2 Sam 7. This argument (the so-called Herodian messianism) gives further support to the intimate connection between the Davidic Messiah and the building of the (eschatological) messianic Temple on the basis of Davidic covenant at the time of Jesus. This argument is shared with Holwerda, *Jesus*, 67 and Bryan, *Jesus*, 197. See also Brown, *John I-XII*, 123; Schrenk, *TDNT*, III, 244; Michel, *TDNT*, IV, 884; Sabbe, 'Cleansing,' 340–345; Drapper, 'Temple,' 270–274.
[549] Schnackenburg, *John*, I, 347; Whitacre, *John*, 82.
[550] In the Gospel of Mark, Jesus indirectly revealed his authority and identity as 'the Son of God' by means of his counter-question concerning the origin of the authority of John's baptism (Mark 11:29–33) and the parable of the wicked tenants (Mark 12:1–12). In regard to the origin of John's baptism, Jesus implicitly hinted that his authority was given to him by God as his Son (Firstborn), the Davidic messianic King, the Isaianic suffering Servant of the Lord, on the basis of Exod 4:22–23; 2 Sam 7:12ff; Pss 2:7; 89; Isa 42:1 (cf. Isa 52:13–53:12; 9:1–7; 11:1–16; 55:3; 61:1–11). In addition, the parable, which was another of Jesus's evasive answers to the Jewish demand for a sign, hinted that Jesus would be killed as the Son of God by those same Jewish religious leaders. For this, see Kim, 'Temple,' 106, 115–117; Watt, *Isaiah's*, 110ff, 341–344; Marcus, *Way*, 61ff; Marshall, 'Reconsideration,' 326–336.

caused many scholars[551] to think that the event should be viewed as the fulfilment of Zech 14:21. According to Zech 14:16ff, all gentiles shall bring their treasures to Jerusalem to worship the King, the Lord Almighty, and to celebrate the great feast of the eschatological Tabernacle (cf. Isa 56:1–8; 60:1–22). At that messianic time, everything including the bells of the horses and the cooking pots in Jerusalem shall be holy and there will no longer be a trader in the house of the Lord Almighty.[552] The relevance of this prophecy, although the eschatological-messianic time had already been inaugurated with the coming of Jesus as the Davidic Messiah, is that, if the outer court of the Temple for the gentiles was occupied for the trade of sacrificial animals, the gentile could not worship the Lord (cf. Mark 11:17; Isa 56:7). Therefore, Jesus expelled them from the outer court.[553] Pitre says that both Jesus's action alluding to Zech 14:21 and his logion alluding to Isa 56:7 mean 'the End of the Exile and the eschatological ingathering of the gentiles.'[554] In pointing out that Zechariah is an important OT text in understanding Jesus's self-identification, Kim[555] argues that Jesus understood himself as the Davidic Messiah described in Zech 3:8–9; 4:7–10; 6:12–13, and Zech 9–14 and that he expelled the merchants and animals from the Temple court according to a prophecy in Zech 14:21 (cf. Isa 56:7).[556]

Secondly, Jesus referred to himself as the builder of the Temple, saying, 'Destroy this Temple, and I will raise it again in three days' (John 2:19). Even though he did not directly respond to the demand, he said that his authority to do such things in the Temple would be testified to by the building of a new Temple, which would be the miraculous sign demanded by the Jews. The Evangelist added an explanation about the meaning of 'the building of the Temple in three days' (John 2:21), namely that this promise denoted his physical resurrection from the dead in three days. By this

---

[551] Jeremias, *Theology*, I, 107; Dodd, *Interpretation*, 300; Bruce, *John*, 74; Carson, *John*, 179; Lindars, *John*, 139; Beasley-Murray, *John*, 39–40; Lightfoot, *John's*, 129; Roth, 'Cleansing,' 174–181; Barrett, *John*, 198; Smith, *John*, 89; Malina and Rohrbaugh, *John*, 74; Hiers, 'Purification,' 86–87; Kim, 'Temple,' 118; Pitre, *Tribulation*, 289–290; Dennis, *Gathering*, 169; L. P. Trudinger, 'Cleansing,' 330. On the other hand, Bruce, *John*, 74 and Carson, *John*, 179 think Mal 3:3 as well as Zech 14:21 influenced Jesus's Temple action. By the way, Milne, *John*, 70 and Tasker, *John*, 62 think only Mal 3:3 was the basis of Jesus's behaviour.
[552] Holwerda, *Jesus*, 75–76 thinks that this background could be related to the worship in spirit and in truth of John 4:21–24.
[553] Bruce, *John*, 75; Dodd, *Interpretation*, 300; Brown, *John I-XII*, 121.
[554] Pitre, *Tribulation*, 289–290.
[555] Kim, 'Stone,' 134–148; *idem.*, 'Temple,' 118; Hiers, 'Purification,' 84–89.
[556] Cf. a number of verses in the Fourth Gospel seem to be quoted from Zechariah in the light of a messianic fulfillment; e.g., Zech 9:9 in John 12:15, Zech 14:8 in John 7:38–39, Zech 12:10 in John 19:34.

argument, the resurrection was actually the miraculous sign that was given to the Jews. His authority and identity with regard to the Temple would be proved through his physical resurrection, which itself symbolized the raising of the Temple of God. Therefore, by means of these two references (cf. John 2:16, 19) Jesus seems to have proclaimed himself as the Davidic Messiah based upon Yahweh's covenant with David in 2 Sam 7:12–14a, which was, both in the OT and Jewish literature, repeatedly seen as the basis of the expectation of the Davidic Messiah.[557]

Furthermore, John 2:17 shows that the disciples understood Jesus's behaviour in the light of Ps 69:9a [68:9a in the LXX]: 'Zeal for your house will consume me.' This verse is quoted with just the change of the tense of a verb, 'consume' from κατέφαγέν (aorist) to καταφάγεταί (future). Several points should be observed. On the basis of some quotations from, or allusions to, Ps 69, particularly in the context of the passion of Jesus,[558] some scholars[559] rightly argue that the psalm could have been used as one of the messianic Psalms. Also, the fact that the tense of the verb of this psalm was changed from an aorist to a future seems to foreshadow that the Temple incident happened on account of his zeal for the Temple, 'the house of God.' Against the background of the Passover feast at the start and end of Jesus's Johannine ministry, his final death could also be in view when this psalm is alluded to.[560] Dennis[561] points out that the narrative is framed by a word, 'Passover,' in vv. 13, 23. So, the Passover has to be considered in interpreting Jesus's action in the Temple.

Why did the Evangelist suggest that the disciples expected Jesus's death as a result of this prophecy? Menken[562] argues that the Evangelist was indicating that the Temple incident caused the disciples to recognise the identity of Jesus as the Davidic Messiah, who would thereby be potentially

---

[557] Holwerda, *Jesus*, 70; Gärtner, *Temple*, 107.
[558] For examples, Ps 69:4 to John 15:25; Ps 69:9a to John 2:17; Ps 69:21 to John 19:28–29 (cf. Mark 15:36; Matt 27:34, 48; Luke 23:36). Cf. Ps 69:9b to Rom 15:3; Ps 69:22 to Rom 11:9; Ps 69:25 to Acts 1:20.
[559] Sabbe, 'Cleansing,' 338; Carson, *John*, 180; Brown, *John I-XII*, 124; Schnackenburg, *John*, I, 347; R. Kysar, *John*, 48–49; Barrett, *John*, 198–199; Keddie, *John*, I, 116; Bernard, *John*, I, 92. However, other scholars think this Psalm was quoted to refer to Jesus's passion in the light of the suffering of the righteous. For example, Dodd, *Interpretation*, 301; Lindars, *John*, 140; Trudinger, 'Cleansing,' 329; Freed, *Quotations*, 9.
[560] Whitacre, *John*, 85; Bruce, *John*, 75; Carson, *John*, 180; Lindars, *John*, 140; Kysar, *John*, 49; Coloe, *Dwells*, 74; Menken, *Quotations*, 40–41; Smith, *John*, 89; Bernard, *John*, I, 92; Witherington, *Wisdom*, 88; Barrett, *John*, 198–199; Throckmorton, *Creation*, 104; Freed, *Quotations*, 10.
[561] Dennis, *Gathering*, 168; Stibbe, *Storyteller*, 49; Kerr, *Temple*, 86, 207–211; Coloe, *Dwells*, 71–75; Koester, *Symbolism*, 82–85.
[562] Menken, *Quotations*, 44–45. See also Carson, *John*, 180.

involved in the same experience as the conflict which David had already had as a result of his own zeal for the Temple, the house of God, as described in the psalm. Further, Menken[563] assumes that the Christians understood that the last verse of the psalm concerning God's changing of the fate of the oppressed one signified Jesus's resurrection. Here, the changing of the tense of the verb could allude to the death of Jesus at the end of his public ministry in connection with the Temple incident.[564] In particular, Kerr[565] observes that both κατεσθίω and its Hebrew אכל in Ps 69:9 (cf. John 2:17) mean 'to eat' and 'to consume' in connection with the fire for the sacrifice of atonement (such as the whole-burnt offerings and the guilt-offering). So, Kerr[566] says that, 'there is an allusion to Jesus' death being a sacrifice,' and even argues that John 2:17 means that Jesus will be consumed as the paschal lamb. This argument could be supported by 'the Passover,' the *inclusio* of the narrative (vv. 13, 23).[567]

Furthermore, if this argument is right, Jesus is not only the Son/firstborn of God (cf. 'my Father's house' in John 2:16) but also the paschal lamb. This is supported by the idea of the firstborn/son, who is the same entity as the paschal lamb, against the background the first Passover for the exodus (cf. Exod 4:22–23; 12:1–51). The status of the firstborn in relation to God is applied to Davidic messianic King, who is responsible for building the Temple for God in 2 Sam 7:12–16; Pss 2:7; 89:26–27, who is the same figure as the Deutero-Isaianic suffering servant of the Lord in Isa 9:1–7; 11:1–16; 42:1; 53:13–53:12; 55:3; 61:1–11 (cf. Ps 89:38–51). In the light of these, the Jews' accusations against Jesus concerning his identity at his trial have to be noted. Here, Jesus admitted himself to be 'a king' (John 18:33–37; 19:12) as well as the Son of God (John 19:7). The notice, prepared by Pilate and fastened to the cross, showed that his offence as charged by Pilate was 'Jesus, the Nazarene,[568] the king of the Jews' (John 19:19). Accordingly, as

---

[563] Menken, *Quotations*, 45.
[564] Dennis, *Gathering*, 171; Beasley-Murray, *John*, 39; Kerr, *Temple*, 85; Lindars, *John*, 140; Menken, *Quotations*, 41; Schnackenburg, *John*, I, 347; Gaston, *Stone*, 206; McKelvy, *Temple*, 78; Brown, *John I-XII*, 124; Bultmann, *John*, 124.
[565] Kerr, *Temple*, 85; Dennis, *Gathering*, 172.
[566] Kerr, *Temple*, 85; Dennis, *Gathering*, 172. Cf. Exod 12:4, 7, 8, 9, 11, 44.
[567] Kerr, *Temple*, 85; Dennis, *Gathering*, 172.
[568] Coloe, *Dwells*, 171–174, 185–186, on the basis of archaeological evidence, who assumes that 'Nazareth' stems from the Hebrew נֵצֶר in Isa 11:1 (cf. Jer 23:5; 33:15), which, as the Davidic messianic designation, was a synonym of צֶמַח of Zech 6:12, who would construct the eschatological Temple of Yahweh at the end time, a title which could be reflected in 'the king of the Jews' on the placard fastened to the cross. Cf. *Tg. Isa.* 52:3; *Tg Zech* 6:12. See also J. A. Sanders, 'Matthew 2:23,' 116–128, esp. 126, 128; R. H. Gundry, *Matthew*, 40. *Contra* K. H. Rengstorf, *NIDNTT*, II, 332–334; L. Morris, *Matthew*, 49, who assumes that 'the Nazarene' or 'Nazareth' was generally a synonym for 'despised,' and argues that this title 'the Nazarene'

the Son of God, the King of the Jews, and the builder of the Temple of God, Jesus is the Davidic Messiah, the eschatological fulfilment of Yahweh's covenant to David in 2 Sam 7:12ff.

Yahweh's covenant with David in 2 Sam 7:12–14 had a strong influence on Jewish literature especially with regard to the building of the eschatological Temple and the new exodus of the exiled Israel. A clear example is found in *4QFlor*. 1:1–13, which includes the tradition that the Davidic Messiah will build the new Temple on the basis of this passage (cf. Exod 15:7; Amos 9:11).[569] Bryan[570] argues that a term בַּיִת (house) in the Hebrew Bible denoted both the Temple and the dynasty of David, but in *4QFlor* the two meanings of the term were combined into one to refer to the eschatological Temple, which meant the dynasty of David as well. For Bryan, *4QFlor*. shows the Sectarians' expectation that God will build the eschatological Temple, that is, the Davidic dynasty, through the Son of David, the Messiah.

Further, *Ps. Sol.* 17–18 claims that the restoration of the Temple will be one of the main tasks of the Messiah.[571] What has to be further noted in this document is that the Messiah's work in connection with the Temple is regarded as the fulfilment of the prediction of Nathan's oracle concerning the Son of David and the Temple based on 2 Sam 7. And interestingly, the 'branch' of Zech 6:12, who as the Son of David would build the new Temple, was directly interpreted as 'messiah' in *Tg. Zech* 6:12 where he would build the eschatological Temple.[572] Also, strangely, *Tg. Isa* 52:13 identified the servant with the Temple-builder, by renaming the servant as the Messiah, 'Behold my Servant, the Messiah.' Not only this, but also the 'pierced' or 'wounded' of Isa 53:5 was translated 'profaned' in the Targum and 'the building of a new sanctuary' was inserted as a task of the Servant/Messiah, 'and he will build the sanctuary which was profaned for our sins, handed over for our iniquities' (*Tg. Isa* 53:5).[573] These translations express the presence of the expectation of the Davidic Messiah (as the servant of the Lord) who would build the new Temple in the eschatological

---

was employed to reflect that Jesus as the Messiah would be despised. Cf. John 1:45–46; Acts 24:5. Further, Sanders, 'Matthew 2:23,' 122ff, 127–128, who also argues that 'Nazarene' in Matt 2:23 alludes to 'Nizirite' like Samson in Judges 13:4, 7; 16:17 (cf. Samuel in 1 Sam 1:11), who was divinely conceived for the deliverance of Israel from her enemy. Also, R. Pesch, 'Nazorean,' 175–176.

[569] Holwerda, *Jesus*, 66; G. J. Brooke, *Exegesis*, 134ff; Drapper, 'Temple,' 272–273; Koester, *Symbolism*, 83.

[570] Bryan, *Jesus*, 197–199. See also McKelvey, *Temple*, 50–51; Holwerda, *Jesus*, 66; Gärtner, *Temple*, 30–42; Coloe, *Dwells*, 172; Juel, *Messiah*, 172–177; Drapper, 'Temple,' 273.

[571] Sanders, *Jesus*, 82; McKelvey, *Temple*, 17–18.

[572] Coloe, *Dwells*, 171; McKelvey, *Temple*, 14–15.

[573] Coloe, *Dwells*, 171; Juel, *Messiah*, 183,189.

era, on the basis of Yahweh's covenant with David in 2 Sam 7:11–14. It is not strange if we recognize that the Davidic messianic king is the same figure as the Isaianic-suffering servant of the Lord (cf. Isa 9:1–7; 11:1–16; 42:1; 52:13–53:12; 55:3; 61:1–11).

Furthermore, in the *Eighteen Benedictions*, the fourteenth prayer connected the expectation of the rebuilding of the new Temple and Jerusalem, the restoration of the exiled Israel, with the re-establishment of the Davidic throne.[574] In *Tob.* 14:5 (cf. 13:5, 11; 14:4ff), Tobit expected the restoration of Israel, scattered amongst the gentiles, to the promised land, the rebuilding of Jerusalem and the new Temple, which would be more glorious than the first one.[575] Also, *Jub.* 1:15–17, 26, 28 set forth the restoration of Israel, the building of the new Temple, and Yahweh's everlasting dwelling in the midst of Israel.[576] In *Sib. Or.* 5:414–433 (3:294, 702–720), there is mention that Jerusalem and the new Temple, will be rebuilt by, 'a blessed man from heaven.' McKelvey, from *Sib. Or.* 3:98–104,[577] argues that the unity which humananity lost at the tower of Babel (cf. Gen 11) will be restored at the new Temple. Here, Bryan[578] feels that 'a blessed man from heaven' could be interpreted as a messianic figure. Finally, Ezekiel's vision of the perfect and glorious Temple revealed in the future seems to be reflected in *1 En.*, which refers to a heavenly Temple made by crystal in splendour and magnificence, and a heavenly throne (14:16–18, 20). Trees grow and bloom, whilst a stream flows from the heavenly Temple (26:1–2). *1 En.* 90–91 also speaks of the building of a new Temple which will be greater and loftier than the first.[579] Again, in *1 En.* 53:6, 'a transcendent redeemer figure' will build the new Temple revealed at the end of days.[580]

From this survey, it is clear that Yahweh's covenant with David had repeatedly been the basis for various expressions of the expectation of the coming of the Davidic Messiah, in the OT, particularly in the Prophets, and in other Jewish literature. The Davidic Messiah is identified as the Son of God, the King of Israel, reigning over the covenant people of God, and the builder of the Temple.

On the basis of the Davidic covenant and of the tradition of the Davidic Messiah developed from 2 Sam 7, by proclaiming himself as the Son of God and the builder of the new Temple for the eschatological era, Jesus

---

[574] Brown, *John I-XII*, 122–123; McKelvey, *Temple*, 20.
[575] Sanders, *Jesus*, 80–81; Koester, *Dwelling*, 24; McKelvey, *Temple*, 15–16; Brown, *John I-XII*, 122.
[576] Sanders, *Jesus*, 82.
[577] McKelvey, *Temple*, 18–19. See also Sanders, *Jesus*, 85.
[578] Bryan, *Jesus*, 194. cf. Sanders, *Jesus*, 87.
[579] Sanders, *Jesus*, 85; Holwerda, *Jesus*, 66; McKelvey, *Temple*, 28–30.
[580] Bryan, *Jesus*, 196.

demonstrated his self-conscious identity as the Davidic Messiah who had already inaugurated the restoration of the exiled Israel, the new exodus. Furthermore, through the quotation ('to consume') from Ps 69:9 in John 2:17 and the Passover as the *inclusio* of the narrative (vv. 13, 23), Jesus is presented not only as the Son/firstborn of God but also as the paschal lamb (cf. Exod 4:22–23; 12:1–51; Ezek 45:22–23; John 19:28–37).

4.4 The New Temple

What is the meaning of this new Temple that will be raised by Jesus's death and resurrection? As we have seen, Jesus's reference to the construction of a new Temple was interpreted by the Evangelist (John 2:21–22) in connection with Jesus's death and resurrection. That is to say, his death and resurrection is the miraculous sign that confirms the claims he made by his behaviour and words in the Temple (vv. 14–16).[581] The Johannine Jesus related the restoration of the Temple (or the construction of the new Temple) to his physical resurrection.[582] The construction of the new Temple would be witnessed by the resurrection of Jesus from the dead in three days. In other words, the construction of the new Temple has to be understood in the light of Jesus's bodily resurrection.

The Evangelist explained the building of the Temple by using the picture of Jesus's resurrection.[583] In v. 19, the verb ἐγείρω could be used not only for the building of a house (or Temple) but also for the resurrection of a physical body. Hence the Evangelist seems to refer intentionally both to Jesus's physical resurrection and the raising of the new Temple.[584] Ironically, the Jews' killing of Jesus resulted, from a theological perspective, in the destruction of the Temple, that is, the effectiveness of the Jerusalem Temple was nullified by the death of Jesus. The risen Jesus can be recognized as the new Temple, replacing the old, in other passages within John's Gospel.[585] Observing the change of terms indicating the Temple,

---

[581] Coloe, *Dwells*, 78; Dennis, *Gathering*, 175–176; Painter, *Quest*, 159–60. Cf. Matt 16:4; Matt 12:39–40; Luke 11:29–32.

[582] C. H. Bullock, 'Ezekiel,' 29; Dodd, *Interpretation*, 301; Lindars, *John*, 142; Dennis, *Gathering*, 164.

[583] Beasley-Murray, *John*, 41; Morris, *John*, 177; Coloe, *Dwells*, 82–83; Koester, *Symbolism*, 83–85; Witherington, *Wisdom*, 89; Carson, *John*, 182, who thinks that here Jesus's physical body raised from the dead is different from the body of the church, a specifically Pauline theme (cf. Rom 12:5; 1 Cor 12:2f).

[584] Brown, *John I-XII*, 120; Kysar, *John*, 49.

[585] Cf. John 1:14 says Jesus as the incarnated Word reveals the glory of God. John 7:38–39 says that the living water (the Holy Spirit) gushes out from the belly of Jesus, which seems to refer back to the living water flowing from under the Temple in Ezek 47:1–12 (cf. Joel 4:18; Zech 13:1; 14:8; Rev 21:22; 22:1–3). See Sabbe, 'Cleansing,' 344–345. Cf. Dodd, *Interpretation*, 301, 303; Lightfoot, *John's*, 114; Davies, *Gospel*, 289–290; Smith, *John*, 91; Koester, *Symbolism*, 77–85; J. D.

from ἱερόν (vv. 14–15) to ναός (vv. 19–21), Bruce takes it to mean, 'the replacement of the doomed material Temple by a new and spiritual Temple.'[586] In no way could Jesus's claim to raise a new Temple 'in three days' be interpreted as meaning the building of another physical Temple.[587]

Further, at this point, as some commentators[588] argue, the new Temple which Jesus mentions refers not only the Temple of Jesus's body resurrected from the dead, but also the community of Christ. Coloe says that, 'the idea of Temple-as-community predates the Johannine writing and has a basis in first century Jewish and Christian thinking.'[589] She presents evidence that the Qumran community regarded itself as the true sanctuary of God, which, as a living Temple, replaced the cultic functions of the then Herodian Temple (sacrifice and atonement). Nonetheless, Coloe[590] points out that the Sectarians' notion of community-as-Temple is different from the Johannine idea of community-as-Temple, in which God or the Holy Spirit is dwelling.

In the Gospel of John the OT concept of divine indwelling in the Temple is expressed in terms of Jesus himself, as the incarnated Word (cf. John 1:14, 32–34), and in the various forms of μένω in John 14–15.[591] What has to be noted in respect to our discussion about the reality of the new Temple, is the identity of 'my Father's house' first mentioned by Jesus at John 2:16 and then again in John 14:2, the place he will go after his resurrection to prepare a place for the disciples. In John 14:2, 'my Father's house' does not point to the Jerusalem Temple but to the future kingdom of God (cf. John 3:3, 5), the place where God the Father resides, which is quite different from the reality

---

M. Derrett, 'Zeal,' 90; Witherington, *Wisdom*, 85; Schnackenburg, *John*, I, 343; Brodie, *John*, 177; Bruce, *John*, 77.

[586] Bruce, *John*, 76, who says that here ἱερόν was used for the whole complex including the sanctuary proper, ancillary buildings and courts, and ναός for the sanctuary, the holy Temple proper, even though the meanings of two terms could not be classified clearly. See also, Throckmorton, *Creation*, 105–106; Dennis, *Gathering*, 168 n. 242; Michel, *TDNT*, IV, 882; Davies, *Rhetoric*, 223; W. von Meding, *NIDNTT*, III, 781–783.

[587] Bryan, *Jesus*, 233.

[588] Kim, 'Temple,' 117–131; Walker, *Jesus*, 170–171; Barrett, *John*, 201; Throckmorton, *Creation*, 107; Lightfoot, *John's*, 113–114; Dodd, *Interpretation*, 302; Davies, *Gospel*, 289–290; R. Campbell, *Israel*, 154–155.

[589] Coloe, *Dwells*, 167–170 (quoted from 170). Cf. *1 QS* 8:4–10; 9:3–6; 5:5–7; *CD* 3:18–4:10; *1QpHab* 12:3. See also, von Meding, *NIDNTT*, III, 783; Gärtner, *Temple*, 16–46; Holwerda, *Jesus*, 80–83; McKelvey, *Temple*, 47, 56; Juel, *Messiah*, 167–168; Drapper, 'Temple,' 273, 278.

[590] Coloe, *Dwells*, 168–169. See also, Walker, *Jesus*, 170–171. In regard to the divine indwelling, this seems to be not too far from the concept of Church in Paul (1 Cor 3:16–17; 2 Cor 6:16; Eph 2:21; Acts 7:48; 17:24; 1 Pet 2:4–10). *Contra* Schnackenburg, *John*, I, 350–352; Carson, *John*, 182.

[591] Koester, *Symbolism*, 84; Drapper, 'Temple,' 275, 278–279, 281. Cf. Exod 40:34; 1 Kings 8:10–11; Ezek 43:7; Joel 3:17; *11QTemple* 29:8–10. See also, Brown, *John I-XII*, 32; Dennis, *Gathering*, 79.

of the Jerusalem Temple. Whatever arguments surrounding the identity of 'my Father's house' here, it can at least be said that he is using 'Temple motif' or 'house imagery'[592] to introduce the kingdom of God (cf. father, house, rooms in John 14:2, 23). In regard to this connection between 'the kingdom of God' and a 'Temple motif' (or house motif), Gaston[593] argues that Jesus explained the kingdom of God as the new Temple, which is the community of the people of God.

Significantly, Jesus's promise concerning the preparation of a place for them in the Father's house was given with the repeated assurances of the sending of another Paraclete, the Holy Spirit, to them (cf. John 14:16, 26). With an observation that μονή (room) appears both in John 14:2 and 14:23 in connection with the Paraclete, Burge[594] argues that the former refers not to a mansion in the sky but to the presence of God the Father and God the Son with the disciples by the indwelling of the Holy Spirit. Conclusively, Coloe says that:

> The divine indwelling in the midst of a believing community makes it appropriate to speak of the community as a living Temple. The community is the House (household) of God.[595]

The new Temple, the Father's house which will be raised by Jesus, will no longer be a physical building, but the household (or family) of God the Father, the community where the divine presence dwells.[596]

Above all, in connection with the divine indwelling or the bestowing of the Holy Spirit, as Throckmorton[597] observes, in the Gospel of John, the community of Christ raised by Jesus's bestowing of the Holy Spirit to the disciples after his death and resurrection is the new Temple. In John 20:17, the resurrected Jesus as the firstborn of God called his disciples his brothers, who became the sons of God; the family of God. This issue will arise again in connection with Jesus's resurrection and the new exodus. For now it is enough to summarise that Jesus himself is the new Temple, but that the new Temple is also the community of Christ Jesus. This could be explained by means of concepts such as corporate personality, representation (headship), or mystical unity. The new Temple is defined by the body of Jesus (the firstborn) who is also the inclusive personality or the

---

[592] Coloe, *Dwells*, 159.
[593] L. Gaston, *Stone*, 229–243. Cf. S. Aalen, 'Reign,' 215–240.
[594] Burge, *Anointed*, 145; Yoo, *Prayer*, 224; R. Gundry, 'Father's,' 70.
[595] Coloe, *Dwells*, 163.
[596] McKelvey, *Temple*, 10–11 says that the expectation of the New Temple was based on Ezek 40–48 and 'the New Temple is the symbol of the new people of God.'
[597] Throckmorton, *Creation*, 107.

representative of the new covenant people of God, which has been raised with (or by) the resurrection of Jesus from the dead.[598] In particular, Campbell says that:

> Basically, the new Temple is Christ, who is Emmanuel (God with us). And yet it is Christ as the Root, the Representative, the Covenant Head, the Surety, and the Mediator, of a company which no man can number out of every kingdom, and tongue, and people, and nation (cf. Rev. 5:9; 7:9) …. This mystic organic unity, this solidarity, this identity of Christ with his people, is perhaps most clearly spoken of in the Lord's intercessory prayer.[599]

Furthermore, in connection with Ezek 37:1–14, the resurrection of Jesus from the dead means the resurrection of Israel, namely, the restoration (new exodus) of Israel from exile.[600] Thus, Jesus is raised as the inclusive representative of the new-covenant people of God (cf. John 20:17, 19–23), which could symbolically mean the inauguration of the restoration of new Israel (cf. John 1:51). This equates to the building of a new Temple.

What is of supreme importance for the Evangelist is that in building the new Temple for the new worship in the new era (cf. John 4:23–24), Jesus's death and resurrection is the indispensable event.[601] Kim[602] argues that through his death and resurrection Jesus made atonement and created the new covenant, with the intention of creating a new community, the eschatological people of God, that is, the new Temple. Morris concludes that:

> The words about rebuilding will in that case refer to their replacement by the spiritual Temple and the new covenant effected by the death and resurrection of Christ.[603]

Porter[604] interprets this Temple incident as the institution of a new Passover. If so, Jesus's action and logion imply the fulfilment of the eschatological deliverance of God that the first Passover from Egypt had represented. Thus the creation of the new-eschatological people of God,

---

[598] Brown, *John I-XII*, 124f; Barrett, *John*, 201; Brodie, *John*, 182; Lightfoot, *John's*, 114; Walker, *Jesus*, 170–171; McKelvey, *Temple*, 79; S. Kim, *Paul*, 274.
[599] Campbell, *Israel*, 155. Cf. John 13–15; 17.
[600] See 4.6. Johannine Resurrection Narrative (John 20:19–23. Cf. John 5:16–30; 11:1–44).
[601] Throckmorton, *Creation*, 104.
[602] Kim, 'Temple,' 122–126; Gaston, *Stone*, 161–243; Meyer, *Aims*, 200f; Aalen, 'Reign,' 215–240; Gärtner, *Temple*, 105–122; Juel, *Messiah*, 143–157.
[603] Morris, *John*, 178–179.
[604] Porter, 'Traditional,' 412; Whitacre, *John*, 81; Lightfoot, *John's*, 349–350; Morris, *John*, 169.

that is, the new Temple, occurs through the resurrection of Jesus from the dead.[605]

To sum up, the new Temple which will be raised by Jesus, as the Son/Firstborn of God and the Davidic Messiah, is none other than Jesus risen from the dead. Yet this new Temple is also identified as the community of the new-eschatological people of God raised on the basis of his death and resurrection. Here, Jesus who was the paschal lamb, the Son/firstborn of God, was offered (or slaughtered) as the Passover sacrifice as well as the atonement sacrifice, which established the new covenant and raised the new community (cf. John 1:29; 19:36–37).

4.5 In Three Days

The argument that the historical resurrection of Jesus has to be understood in the light of the raising of the new Temple and of the inauguration of the new exodus can also be supported by reference to the three days of John 2:19, 21. There are various arguments about the origin of the tradition; whether this tradition was added afterward by the early church on the basis of the historical fact of Jesus's resurrection from the dead on the third day, or originated earlier in the prophetic talk of Jesus himself about his own death and resurrection. J. Jeremias[606] argues that this tradition 'in three days' or 'after three days,' was initiated by Jesus himself.

Significantly, the Apostle Paul referred to the resurrection as the fulfilment of OT prophecy, 'Christ died for our sins *according to the Scriptures*, that he was buried, that he was raised 'on the third day' *according to the Scriptures*'(1 Cor 15:3–4). There is also the Emmaus road tradition, in which the risen Christ appears to two disciples and opens their minds to understand his resurrection from the dead 'on the third day' in the light of the OT (Luke 24:44–47). Jeremias notes that there was no moderate term to denote 'several,' 'a few' or 'some' in the Semitic language, hence instead of them, the expression 'three' was naturally used. He writes:

---

[605] Kim, 'Temple,' 122–126; idem., 'Interpretation,' 234–235; Juel, *Messiah*, 208; Gärtner, *Temple*, 111.

[606] Jeremias, *Theology*, I, 285–86; Bernard, *John*, I, 94. The Synoptic Gospels record that he died on the cross at the ninth hour on the Preparation day of the special Sabbath of the Passover feast (cf. Mark 15:34; Matt 27:45–46; Luke 23:44) but John's Gospel did not state clearly the exact time of it, probably happened after the sixth hour (cf. John 19:14). However, all four Evangelists agree that he was resurrected from the dead, at dawn, very early in the morning on the first day of the week, after the special Sabbath of the Passover (cf. Mark 16:2; Matt 28:1; Luke 24:1; John 20:1).

In the Old Testament the phrase 'three days' denotes an indefinite but not particularly long period time. This usage is also to be found in the 'three day' *logia*: 'after three days' means 'soon'.[607]

This argument could be supported by Jesus's words in the Gospel of John itself, where he repeatedly promised to the disciples his leaving them and then returning again in 'a little while.'[608] Beasley-Murray[609] also points out that this phrase was commonly used in connection with God's rescue of his people from their hardship. So, which texts in the OT have to be considered to understand the meaning of Jesus's resurrection from the dead 'in three days'?

Firstly, some Johannine scholars[610] seem to concentrate on Hos 6:2 as the most likely relevant passage. Hosea seems to have been an important text in the early church's understanding of the resurrection, since Hos 13:14 is directly quoted in 1 Cor 15:54–55 (cf. Isa 25:8), one of the most important texts concerning Jesus's resurrection and the expectation of general resurrection in the NT. Here, D. Stuart[611] points out that two verbs, 'revive' and 'restore' in the first two clauses in Hos 6:2, could mean 'coming back to life from the dead,' that is, 'resurrection,' and that 'on the third day' in Hos 6:2 could accord to 'in three days' in connection with Jesus's resurrection in the NT (cf. 1 Cor 15:4; Luke 24:7).

Hosea is urging Israel (Ephraim) and Judah to return to Yahweh (cf. Hos 6:4). In v. 1, Yahweh's judgment against Israel and Judah is described with the image of injury, and his restoration with the picture of healing. In v. 2, which shows that the first two clauses consist of synonymous parallels,[612] the restoration of Israel and Judah to Yahweh's presence is explained with

---

[607] Jeremias, *Theology*, I, 285. See also Brown, *John I-XII*, 123.
[608] Cf. John 16:16–19. See Jeremias, *Theology*, I, 285.
[609] Beasley-Murray, *John*, 40; idem., *Jesus*, 246–247; Goppelt, *Theology*, I, 237. Contra Schnackenburg, *John*, I, 349–350, who thinks that 'in three days' denoting a short period is different from 'on the third day' which is related to the resurrection of Jesus (cf. 1 Cor 15:4; Matt 16:21). His argument seems to be too minute. In fact, diverse expressions concerning Jesus's resurrection or his building of the New Temple were used in the NT; for example, 'in three days' (cf. Matt 26:64; Mark 14:58; 15:29; John 2:19, 21), 'on the third day' (cf. Matt 16:21; Luke 24:46; 1 Cor 15:4), 'three days later' (cf. Mark 10:34), 'three days and three nights' (cf. Matt 12:40).
[610] Goppelt, *Theology*, I, 237; Beasley-Murray, *Jesus*, 246–247; Kim, 'Interpretation,' 235; Walker, 'Land,' 107; idem., *Jesus*, 285; Lindars, *John*, 143; C. F. Evans, *Resurrection*, 48–49, who says there is an evidence that Hos 6:2 was applied to general resurrection in Rabbinic sources (cf. Str-B, I, 747). Moloney, 'John 2:13–22,' 445 assumes 'in three days' is related to the establishment of the covenant on Matt Sinai in Exod 19:16. See also Coloe, *Dwells*, 69.
[611] D. Stuart, *Hosea-Jonah*, 108, who, nevertheless, is not sure whether Hos 6:2 could be regarded as an actual prophetic promise about the resurrection of Jesus.
[612] Stuart, *Hosea-Jonah*, 108.

the images of resurrection and restoration, which could mean Yahweh's restoration of the covenant relationship with Israel and Judah. This covenant relationship was portrayed with the wedding (betrothal) motif in Hos 2:16–23 (cf. Hos 6:7). This is quite the opposite to the concept of exile, that is, Yahweh's judgment. This judgment was proclaimed with the image of injury inflicted by fierce animals in Hos 13:7–8 and, significantly with the images of the grave and death in Hos 13:14. This may be associated with the image of the grave and death in Ezek 37:1–14 (cf. Isa 25:7–8), which symbolically denoted the exiled condition of Israel and Judah. Above all, the image of resurrection from the dead was identified with the image of restoration of the covenant relationship of Israel and Judah to Yahweh in Hos 6:2.

We may conclude that the phrase, 'in three days', in Jesus's reference concerning the destruction and building of the Temple in John 2:19, denotes the physical resurrection of Jesus (John 2:22), and was based on Hos 6:2. His bodily resurrection from the dead on the third day thus reflects God's new salvation of life and victory,[613] the inauguration (or fulfilment) of the restoration of Israel,[614] the new creation of the people of God, that is the messianic-new Temple,[615] built by the Messiah in the eschatological era.

A second noteworthy passage is found in Jonah 1:17. Jesus himself mentioned his death in terms of the sign of Jonah (cf. Matt 12:39–40).[616] Jonah's experience was adopted as a type of the burial and resurrection of Jesus, who was entombed for 'three days and three nights.' In Jonah 2, some noteworthy phrases and ideas in connection with God's judgment and salvation can be recognized. Here, in Jonah 2:4, the divine judgment against Jonah's disobedience was expressed with notions of 'being banished out of the sight of Yahweh' and 'being distant from his presence (his holy Temple).' That is, the state of deportation or exile which metaphorically denotes the separation of death, that is, the depth of the grave (cf. Jonah 2:2). Jonah 2:6 took on the term 'pit' to refer to the grave or realm of the dead.[617]

Stuart[618] argues that 'three full days' (cf. three nights and three days) in Jonah 1:17 was based on the Sheol journey motif—an idea that the journey from the land of the living to Sheol (or *vice versa*) took three full days. Stuart

---

[613] Beasley-Murray, *John*, 41.
[614] C. H. Dodd, *According*, 103; Walker, 'Land,' 107; idem., *Jesus*, 285.
[615] Brown, *John I-XII*, 123; Kim, 'Interpretation,' 235.
[616] Cf. Matt 16:4; Luke 11:29–32.
[617] Stuart, *Hosea-Jonah*, 476.
[618] Stuart, *Hosea-Jonah*, 474–475.

suggests that Jonah being inside of the belly of a huge fish for three full days could denote the divine rescue back from the Underworld, that is, death. Yahweh's restoration of Jonah was expressed with images of resurrection (Jonah 2:6) and of restoration to his presence, the holy Temple (Jonah 2:9). Jonah then confesses, 'Salvation comes from the Lord.' Consequently, the reference to 'three days and three nights' in Jonah's experience could be part of the OT background to the phrase 'in three days' in John 2:19–22.

To sum up, the 'three days' of John 2:19–22, referring both to the destruction of the Temple and the construction of the new Temple, allude to Hos 6:2 and Jonah 1:17. This supports the idea that the bodily resurrection of Jesus denotes God's eschatological salvation of life and victory, the restoration, the new exodus of Israel. This results in the new creation of the eschatological people of God. In connection with this, Walker says:

> Jesus has taken a verse which originally referred to the restoration or revival of Israel and applied it instead to himself as Israel's Messiah. Israel's destiny was integrally bound up with the destiny of her representative Messiah .... Thus divine vindication would not come for Jerusalem in some form of restoration or political independence. On the contrary, it had already come for Jesus himself in his resurrection. There would be an end to the exile, but it would be accomplished through the Messiah entering into divine judgement and then emerging victorious in being raised from the death.[619]

Here, Jesus's death and resurrection, symbolized by his Temple incident and his words, would inaugurate the restoration of Israel; that is, God's eschatological salvation for Israel. In other words, the events disclose Jesus as the Son/firstborn of God and the Davidic Messiah (the inclusive representative), who would build the eschatological-new Temple, that is, the new eschatological people of God.

4.6 Johannine Resurrection Narratives (John 20:19–23; 11:1–44. Cf. John 5:16–30)

We have seen that the words of Jesus in John 2:19 and the Evangelist's interpretation of them in John 2:21, contribute to an understanding of the meaning of the raising of the new Temple and of the relationship between

---

[619] Walker, *Jesus*, 285; Dodd, *According*, 103, who says that 'the resurrection of Christ *is* the resurrection of Israel of which the prophets spoke.' (original emphasis).

the new Temple and the resurrection of Jesus.[620] The account of Jesus's teaching given to the disciples after his resurrection has to be considered in the light of this picture of resurrection taken over from the OT. 'The Scripture' that the Evangelist mentioned in John 2:22 points to certain OT texts concerning the resurrection from the dead.[621] The Gospel as a whole contains a number of references to resurrection.[622] In particular, we note that in John 20:19–22, Jesus's behaviour and words are a significantly distinctive record found only in the Fourth Gospel. Some commentators[623] observe that John's Gospel portrays Jesus's death and resurrection in the coming of the Holy Spirit. In this respect, some valuable remarks concerning Jesus's resurrection and the new Temple can be found in connection with his impartation of the Holy Spirit, his greeting of peace, and the bestowal of the authority for the forgiving and retaining of sin. Before discussing these in John 20, we need to note the resurrection of Lazarus from the dead in John 11:43–44, regarding the restoration (the new exodus) and the new Temple in connection with Jesus's death and resurrection (John 11:50–53).

4.6.1 The Raising of Lazarus from the Dead (John 11:43–44).

Kim[624] argues that the resurrection of Lazarus from the dead in John 11:43–44 first indicates Jesus's death and resurrection. It further reveals the climax of all the Johannine signs, showing that it is his death and resurrection that gives humanity life. In particular, that Jesus called Lazarus out from the tomb could allude to the resurrection of the nation Israel from the dead, by the word of the Lord[625] proclaimed by the Prophet Ezekiel in Ezek 37:1–14. In Ezek 37:12–13, the restoration (new exodus) of Israel from exile is explained by the picture that Yahweh opens the exiled Israel's graves and brings them forth from their graves. Dennis[626] observes that ἐξέρχομαι (go/come out) in John 11:44 (cf. 'come out' (δεῦρο ἔξω) in John 11:43) alludes to the release of the nation Israel from the bondage in Egypt. Further,

---

[620] Dodd, *Interpretation*, 301; Throckmorton, *Creation*, 107, who also argues that the community of Christ raised by Jesus's bestowal of the Holy Spirit to the disciples after his death and resurrection is itself the very New Temple.
[621] Cf. John 20:1–9; 1 Cor 15:3–5; Luke 24:45–46. See Lindars, *John*, 144.
[622] Cf. John 5:21–29; 6:39–40, 44, 54; 11:39–44; 20:1–23.
[623] Burge, *Anointed*, 134–135, 148; Kim, *Exposition*, 218–219; Brown, *John XIII–XX1*, 951; Barrett, *John*, 557; Hoskyns, *Fourth*, 532–533; Beasley-Murray, *John*, 383; idem., *Life*, 80.
[624] Kim, *Exposition*, 58; Dennis, *Gathering*, 231–244; Beasley-Murray, *John*, 201; Carson, *John*, 419; Milne, *John*, 171; Whitacre, *John*, 294.
[625] Cf. Whitacre, *John*, 293.
[626] Dennis, *Gathering*, 232; Motyer, *Father*, 136–137. Cf. Exod 12:31, 41; 13:3, 5, 10; 16:3, 6; 20:1; Deut 4:45, 46; 9:7; 16:3, 6.

Dennis[627] points out that this exodus motif is reflected in God's promise of the national restoration of Israel from exile in the Prophets. Thus, he[628] argues that the resurrection of Lazarus must be understood in the light of the restoration of Israel from exile (cf. Isa 26:19; Ezek 37).

B. Osborne[629] contrasts Lazarus emerging with linen strips and the napkin on his face in John 11:44 and Jesus's resurrection having left behind linen bands and the napkin folded separately in the tomb in John 20:6–7. Then, he interprets this difference in connection with Isa 25:6–8. For Osborne, that Lazarus comes forth from the tomb with his face still covered with a cloth means that he is still under the power of the death, and thus even though Lazarus has been brought to life, he will die again. However, the resurrected Jesus removes the cloth from his face, for he has conquered death and will never die again. Osborne argues that Jesus removing the napkin from his face means the fulfilment of the prophecy of Isa 25:6–8. That is, Jesus, with his resurrection, has swallowed up death for ever (Isa 25:7–8). The same idea is also found in Hos 13:14.

The thought of Isa 25:6–8 (cf. Hos 13:14) is alluded to in 1 Cor 15:54–56. Death came into the world through a man, Adam (Gen 3:1–21. cf. 1 Cor 15:20–22). Jesus Christ who has been raised from the dead is the firstfruit (ἀπαρχή) of those who have fallen asleep. Thus, the resurrection could be thought as the restoration of the old creation; that is, a new creation. Yahweh's victory against death, namely, his swallowing of death, the curse (consequence) of sin, is used to express his redemption (deliverance, restoration) of Israel and all nations (Isa 25:6–8; Hos 13:14).[630]

The narrative that Jesus raised Lazarus from death confirms Jesus's proclamation in John 11:25–26, 'I am the resurrection and the life.'[631] That is, Jesus as the Logos, the only Son of God, is the life-giver, and so the creator of the old and new creation. Martha confessed him as the Son of God, the Christ, in John 11:27. Also, the narrative of the resurrection of Lazarus could be related to John 5:25–29,[632] where Jesus introduces himself as the Danielic Son of Man, namely, the Son of God. The resurrection of Lazarus is a sign to show that Jesus, as the Son of God, the Danielic Son of Man and

---

[627] Dennis, *Gathering*, 232 n. 98. Cf. Isa 11:16; Jer 16:14–15; Zech 10:10–11.
[628] Dennis, *Gathering*, 237, 243–244; N. T. Wright, *Resurrection*, 116.
[629] B. Osborne, 'Napkin,' 437–440; Beasley-Murray, *John*, 195.
[630] See Watts, *Isaiah 1–33*, 329, 331–333; Motyer, *Isaiah*, 209–210; Stuart, *Hosea-Jonah*, 207. Cf. Gen 2:17; Rom 3:23; Heb 2:15; Rev 21:4; 22:3. Cf. Dennis, *Gathering*, 233.
[631] Milne, *John*, 172.
[632] Beasley-Murray, *John*, 195; Carson, *John*, 418; Whitacre, *John*, 293; Michaels, *John*, 204. Cf. John 6:38–40, 44, 53–57.

Christ, will bring about the restoration (new exodus, resurrection) of Israel from exile, through his death and resurrection.

This argument is supported by Caiaphas's prophecy and the Evangelist's interpretation of it in John 11:49–53. Caiaphas's suggestion to kill Jesus for the people is interpreted to mean that Jesus would die not only for the Jewish nation but also for the scattered children of God, to bring them together and make them one. Jesus, the firstborn/only Son of God, will, vicariously and representatively, die for nation of Israel, and bring about the 'gathering of the dispersed children (sons) of God into one' (v. 52). In particular, Dennis[633] argues that the narrative of the Temple incident in John 2:14–22 is related to Caiaphas's prophecy in John 11:47–52.

Also, since Jesus as the Son/firstborn of God is the inclusive representative of the eschatological people (children, sons) of God against the background of the Passover (cf. John 11:55), his resurrection symbolically means the resurrection (restoration) of the new-eschatological children of God. Dennis says that:

> Lazarus' resurrection therefore is an anticipation of the restoration of the children of God, or the creation of a new people, in 11.52. Thus, the vision of Ezekiel will be fulfilled in Jesus, although in John's own unique vision of things.[634]

In particular, that Jesus's death and resurrection brought about the restoration (new exodus) of the saints from death is understood from Matt 27:52–53. Matthew shows that the death of Jesus brought about the resurrection of many holy people who were dead and buried.[635] Here, Jesus was confessed as the Son of God by the gentiles (the centurion and those with him who were guarding Jesus) in v. 54. Thus, when the tombs broke open and the bodies of many holy people in the tombs were raised, came out of the tombs, and went into the holy city (Jerusalem) — all anticipating Jesus's resurrection — the restoration of people of God is in view (see Ezek 37:12–14; Isa 26:19; Hos 6:1–2; 13:14; cf. John 5:25–29; 11:43–44; 1 Cor 15:54–56).[636] The importance of Ezek 37:1–14 will be further shown in the Johannine resurrection narrative in John 20.

---

[633] Dennis, *Gathering*, 183–187; Motyer, *Father*, 140.
[634] Dennis, *Gathering*, 244.
[635] Morris, *Matthew*, 724–725; D. Senior, 'Death,' 312–319, esp. 328; Grassi, 'Ezekiel 37:1–14,' 163; Allen, *Ezekiel 20–48*, 188.
[636] Cf. Morris, *Matthew*, 725, argues that the breaking of the tombs happened on Good Friday and the rising of the saints happened with the resurrection of Jesus on Easter Day.

4.6.2 Jesus's Breathing and Bestowing the Holy Spirit (John 20:22)

Some commentators[637] have pointed out that the distinctive behaviour of the resurrected Jesus towards the disciples in John 20:22 is a conscious allusion to Ezek 37:1–14. In Ezekiel's vision, in particular, the two-phase process of the resurrection of the dry bones on the floor of the valley alluded to the two-step process of Yahweh's creation of man in Gen 2:7, in which Yahweh firstly shaped Adam from the dust of the ground and then breathed the breath of life into his nostrils. Thus the resurrection was explained by means of a creation motif. The picture of resurrection (or new creation) was employed to explain the promise of Yahweh's restoration of Israel from the exile, the new exodus. In Isa 26:19–20 the resurrection was proclaimed in connection with the first Passover (the first exodus). Accordingly, the resurrection here denoted the restoration, the new exodus, and the new creation of the people of God on the basis of the new covenant. Also, Dan 12:2, which mentioned two kinds of resurrection, namely, one to everlasting life and the other to shame and everlasting judgement (as is reflected in John 5:28–29), embraced the imagery of resurrection to express the restoration of Israel. Finally, as discussed before, Hos 6:1–2 shows that the resurrection motif was adopted to express the promise of the restoration of Israel. All of these texts show that the picture of resurrection denoted the restoration, the new exodus, and the new creation of the people of God on the basis of the new covenant.

It is with regard to these motifs of resurrection appearing in the OT and Judaism[638] that we should now turn to John 20:22, where Jesus breathed on the disciples and bestowed the Holy Spirit. Jesus's bestowal of the Holy Spirit is the fulfilment of that prophecy of the Baptist in John 1:32–34.[639] Above all, the majority of Johannine commentators[640] agree that this Johannine Pentecost is connected with concepts of creation and new creation (or resurrection), endorsed by the use of the very rare verb, ἐνεφύσησεν (breathed).[641] This alludes not only to ἐνεφύσησεν in Gen 2:7 (LXX)

---

[637] Allen, *Ezekiel 20–48*, 188; Bullock, 'Ezekiel,' 30; J. A. Grassi, 'Ezekiel 37:1–14,' 164.
[638] Cf. 4Q521. 1.2.1–14; *Test. Jud.* 23–25; the second prayer of the *Eighteen Benedictions*; *b. Sanh.* 92b; *Pirqe R. Eliezer* 33–34; 2 *Macc.* 7; 4 *Macc.* 17–18.
[639] Lindars, *John*, 611.
[640] Burge, *Anointed*, 125–126 n. 53; Lindars, *John*, 611; Bruce, *John*, 392; E. Stauffer, *TDNT*, II, 536; M. Turner, *Holy*, 91–92; J. D. G. Dunn, *Baptism*, 180; Barrett, *John*, 570; idem., 'Holy,' 3; Beasley-Murray, *John*, 381; idem., *Life*, 79; Morris, *John*, 747; Dodd, *Interpretation*, 227; Blomberg, *Historical*, 207; C. F. Evans, *Resurrection*, 117; Bullock, 'Ezekiel,' 30; Block, *Ezekiel 25–48*, 390; Hengel, 'Gospel,' 391; idem., *Christology*, 371–372; Allen, *Ezekiel 20–48*, 188; Davies, *Rhetoric*, 149.
[641] Stauffer, *TDNT*, II, 536, who says this verb appears in John 20:22; Gen 2:7; Ezek 37:9; *Wis.* 15:11 (ἐμφυσήσαντα πνεῦμα ζωτικόν) in the LXX. See also, Dunn, *Baptism*, 180; Morris, *John*, 747;

in which God breathed the breath of life into the nostrils of Adam formed from the dust, but also to the ἐμφύσησον of Ezek 37:9 (LXX), in which, according to the command of the Sovereign Lord, Ezekiel prophesied to the wind (*ruach*= breath= Spirit) to breathe into the corpses so that they may live.

Turner[642] observes that *Wis.* 15:11, when alluding to God's creation of Adam with clay and his 'breath of life' in Gen 2:7, uses 'a living spirit' instead of 'the breath of life.' We see the same in Philo's works, particularly *Op. Mund.* 134–135, which in interpreting Gen 2:7 employs both 'breath of life' and 'divine Spirit.' And then Turner concludes that, 'it seems clear the Evangelist's use of ἐνεφύσησεν was intended to indicate that somehow through the episode Jesus actually *imparted* the Spirit of new creation.'[643] Burge[644] says that John's use of the verb in John 20:22 (cf. John 3) alluding to Gen 2:7 and Ezek 37:9 intentionally emphasizes Jesus's role as the creator who brings about eschatological rebirth. This was the OT background that Nicodemus should have been familiar with when confronted with the issue of birth from on high (John 3:3). So, the creation motif which started in John 1:3 carries through to the new creation motif in John 20:22.

Block[645] also argues that John 20:22 testifies that Ezek 37 was interpreted eschatologically and messianically, and by the in-breathing of the Spirit on the disciples Jesus constituted them as the eschatological new people of God. In connection with this, Walker[646] argues that Jesus's resurrection denotes the fulfilment of the restoration of Israel, which was eagerly expected. Bullock[647] concludes that the resurrection of Jesus resulted in the inauguration of the eschatological era and the restoration of the Temple against the background of Ezek 37; 40–48.

Lindars, *John*, 611; Barrett, *John*, 570; Hengel, *Christology*, 372 n. 33; Burge, *Anointed*, 125 n. 53. In particular, Carson, *John*, 651, argues that the verb just means exhaled or expelled a deep breath. However, Carson's argument is criticized by Turner, *Holy*, 91; Burge, *Anointed*, 117.

[642] Turner, *Holy*, 91 nn. 5–6. Cf. *Quod Det. Pot. Insid. Sol.* 80, 83; *Plant.* 18, 24, 44.

[643] Turner, *Holy*, 92 (original emphasis).

[644] Burge, *Anointed*, 125–126 n. 53; P. Beasley-Murray, *Resurrection*, 96. See also O. P. Robertson, 'New-Covenant,' 134; Turner, *Holy*, 69, 92, who thinks that the re-creative Spirit in John 3:3, 5 has the background of Ezek 36:25–27.

[645] Block, *Ezekiel 25–48*, 390. See also Lindars, *John*, 612; Beasley-Murray, *John*, 381, who says that 'one should not view this as *the beginning* of the new creation but rather as the beginning of the *incorporation of man* into that new creation which came into being *in the Christ* by his incarnation, death and resurrection, and is actualized in man by the Holy Spirit (cf. 2 Cor 5:17).' (original emphasis).

[646] Walker, 'Land,' 106.

[647] Bullock, 'Ezekiel,' 30. See also C. R. Seitz, 'Ezekiel 37:1–14,' 56.

The motif of the completion of creation (re-creation) is further supported by the last word from the cross, 'it is finished' (John 19:30). Hengel[648] notes that 'finished' (τετέλεσται) appears twice in John 19:28–30 and that, in connection with 'ἐν ἀρχῇ in John 1:1, it alludes to the completion of the work of creation in Gen 2:2. He observes that John 17:4 ('I have finished the work (ἔργον) that you gave me to do (ποιήσω) alludes to the LXX of Gen 2:2 ('And on the sixth day God finished his work (ἔργα) which he had done (ἐποίησεν). This is reflected in the work of Jesus as the Son of God in John 4:34; 5:36 (as the Son of Man). These could also allude to the ministry of the personified word of God in Isa 55:10–11.[649] The mission that Jesus was commissioned by God the Father to perform has been fulfilled by his death on the cross. The enigmatic reference to a special Sabbath and a day of rest in the grave after the death of Jesus (John 19:31) may allude not only to the first Sabbath of rest in Gen 2:2–3 but may also anticipate the eternal *Shalom* of the kingdom of God accomplished at the end of time.[650]

Furthermore, the reference to giving up his spirit at the moment of death (John 19:30. cf. John 19:34) could reflect Jesus's bestowal of the Holy Spirit to the disciples on Easter evening. With regard to this, Burge[651] argues that even though the πνεῦμα of John 19:30 means only Jesus's life force and not the Holy Spirit, it could symbolically foretell the bestowal of the Holy Spirit in John 20:22. That would imply that the gift of the Spirit was actualized with the death of Jesus.[652] The Evangelist emphasizes the intimate relationship between Jesus's bestowal of the Holy Spirit and his death and resurrection. Accordingly, Jesus's death as the paschal lamb (the firstborn of God, the Isaianic suffering servant of the Lord, the Davidic messianic king) on the cross and the out-breathing of the Holy Spirit after the resurrection, both seem to bring about the creation of the new eschatological people of God and the new exodus.

To sum up, Jesus's out-breathing of the Holy Spirit into the disciples, seen in the context of his bodily resurrection, most likely alludes to the resurrection; the new creation in Ezekiel's vision (37:1–14). This recalled Yahweh's creation of the first human being in Gen 2:7, as a means of explaining the restoration of the whole house of Israel from the exile, the new exodus.

---

[648] Hengel, 'Gospel,' 393–394; *idem.*, *Christology*, 371–372. See also Coloe, *Dwells*, 189, 197. Cf. John 4:34; 5:17, 36; 17:4.
[649] Cf. Endo, *Creation*, 240–242; Burkett, *Son*, 134–141.
[650] Cf. Hengel, *Christology*, 372 n. 33. See 4.6.2. Gift of Peace (John 20:19, 21. Cf. John 20:26).
[651] Burge, *Anointed*, 134–135.
[652] Burge, *Anointed*, 135; Brown, *John XIII-XXI*, 951; Barrett, *John*, 557; Lindars, *John*, 612; Hoskyns, *Fourth*, 532–533.

4.6.3 Gift of Peace (John 20:19, 21. Cf. John 20:26)

In John 20:19, Jesus's words, 'Peace be with you' might be regarded merely as a conventional Hebrew greeting. However, that he repeated it in the same context v. 21 and again in v. 26 in the presence of Thomas a week later, could indicate that there is another dimension present here.[653]

Firstly, Jesus's greeting of peace could be the fulfilment of the promise that he gave the disciples to bestow his peace on them, a peace that was to be different from the world's (cf. John 14:27; 16:33).[654] Interestingly, the promise concerning the bestowal of peace was given in the context not only of the promise of the sending out of the Holy Spirit but also of the promise to prepare a place for the disciples in his Father's house (John 14:2), which could be taken as associated with the building of the new Temple, which, as we have seen, was envisaged as coming about by means of his crucifixion, resurrection and exaltation (cf. John 2:16). Carson understands this *shalom* in the light of the coming of the eschatological kingdom of God and says that:

> שָׁלוֹם was also the embracing term used to denote the unqualified well-being that would characterize the people of God once the eschatological kingdom had dawned. Jesus's '*shalom*' on Easter evening is the complement of 'it is finished' on the cross, for the peace of reconciliation and life from God is now imparted.'[655]

Through the completion of the new creation (the restoration, the new exodus), the everlasting *shalom* was inaugurated.[656]

The term 'peace'[657] in the OT Scriptures seems to be a very important factor in connection with the covenant relationship between God and his people, especially when eschatological salvation is in view. In classical Greek, εἰρήνη denoted just the state of 'order and harmony' resulting from a cessation of war.[658] However, in the OT,[659] שָׁלוֹם which was generally

---

[653] Burge, *Anointed*, 126, who observes that the term (peace) appears elsewhere only in the promise (John 14:27; 16:33). Also, P. Beasley-Murray, *Resurrection*, 93–94.
[654] Morris, *John*, 583, 745; Carson, *John*, 647; Bruce, *John*, 391; P. Beasley-Murray, *Resurrection*, 94.
[655] Carson, *John*, 647. See also Beasley-Murray, *John*, 378–379; Bruce, *John*, 391.
[656] Hengel, 'Gospel,' 393–394; Coloe, *Dwells*, 197.
[657] For detail discussion, see W. Foerster and G. von Rad, *TDNT*, II, 400–417; H. Beck and C. Brown, *NIDNTT*, II, 776–783; P. J. Nel, *NIDOTE*, IV, 130–135; Kim, 'Peace,' 279–303.
[658] Beck and Brown, *NIDNTT*, II, 776; Morris, *John*, 584; Foerster and von Rad, *TDNT*, II, 400–401.
[659] Foerster and von Rad, *TDNT*, II, 402–406; Beck and Brown, *NIDNTT*, II, 777–779; Nel, *NIDOTE*, IV, 130–135; Kim, 'Peace,' 279–282.

translated εἰρήνη in the LXX,[660] stood for comprehensive well-being, such as prosperity, bodily health, contentedness, good relations between nations or men, and salvation.[661] All of which, as Yahweh's gifts, were only given by Yahweh under the condition of right relationship between him and his people, Israel. Morris[662] argues that 'right relationship with God' itself was the very meaning of peace in the OT. This right relationship, that is *shalom*, generally resulted from the covenant established by Yahweh, or its renewal, 'the covenant of peace' and the restoration of the relationship between Yahweh and his people.[663] In regard to this, Beck and Brown mention that:

> the message concerning the renewal of the covenant of peace blossoms into the promise of the universal and everlasting peace, and the coming of the day of salvation is frequently linked with the Prince of peace (Isa 9:5, 6), who as God's anointed (Isa 61:1, 2) is the bringer and founder of the kingdom of peace.[664]

In addition, the eschatological peace of God would be established by an agent, the Davidic Messiah, who as the King (or Prince) of peace will reign with righteousness and peace, and as the shepherd will guide God's covenantal people to everlasting peace.[665] The Qumran community also assumed they already enjoyed the eschatological peace for themselves.[666] Peace seems to have been understood as the blessing of God at the time of the eschatological salvation. What has to be noted is that *shalom* was the main subject of the messages proclaimed against the background of Yahweh's promise of the restoration of Israel. In Isaiah, the promise of peace was proclaimed by means of the image of the new creation of heaven and earth symbolising the restoration of Israel in exile.[667]

Above all, Foerster[668] defines εἰρήνη in the NT as the state of final fulfilment and the normal state of the new creation resulting from the eschatological salvation brought about by the historical reconciliatory work of Jesus on the

---

[660] Beck and Brown, *NIDNTT*, II, 777; Kim, 'Peace,' 279.
[661] Beck and Brown, *NIDNTT*, II, 777–778. For example, Pss 38:3; 73:3; Isa 43:7; 57:18; Gen 26:29; 1 Kings 5:26; Judge 4:17; 1 Chron 2:17, 18; Jer 29:11. In particular, Kim, 'Peace,' 279, says that *shalom* could be translated salvation.
[662] Morris, *John*, 584.
[663] Cf. Num 25:12; Isa 54:10; Ezek 34:25; 37:26ff.
[664] Beck and Brown, *NIDNTT*, II, 779. See also Nel, *NIDOTE*, IV, 132; Kim, 'Peace,' 280–281.
[665] Kim, 'Peace,' 281; Foerster and von Rad, *TDNT*, II, 405–406; Nel, *NIDOTE*, IV, 132. For examples, Isa 9:6ff; 11:1ff; Mic 5:1ff; Jer 23:5f; Ezek 34:23ff; 37:24ff; *Ps. Sol.* 17f; *4 Ezra* 12:31–34; 13:1–13, 21–50; *2 Bar.* 29:73; 40:1–3; 4QpsDanA^a; *Sib. Or.* 3:653; 5:108ff, 417ff, 431; *1 En.* 46:51–53; *Test. Jos.* 19; *Test. Lev.* 18.
[666] Cf. *1 QS* 2:4; 4:7; *1 QH* 7:15; 15:16; 18:30. See Beck and Brown, *NIDNTT*, II, 779.
[667] Cf. Isa 11:6–9; 62:1–9; 65:17–25.
[668] Foerster, *TDNT*, II, 412–415.

cross. That is, peace in the NT is the salvation of Jesus. With regard to this, Kim[669] argues that Jesus understood his identity and work on the basis of Isa 61:1–2, as seen in his preaching in the synagogue in Nazareth on the Sabbath day (Luke 4:18f) and also in his answer to the disciples sent by John the Baptist (Matt 11:5; Luke 7:22). This shows that Jesus recognized the fulfilment of *shalom* (the eschatological salvation) as his special messianic task. Also, his works such as exorcism, healings and preaching the gospel were themselves the actualization of *shalom*/salvation of the kingdom of God which he proclaimed. Thus, Jesus's works concerning healing or exorcism, particularly on the Sabbath day, could be understood in the light of the *shalom* to be established by the Davidic Messiah.

It should be added that Isa 61:1–3 is a vital text for understanding the descent of the Holy Spirit as it is linked with the new exodus of Israel in exile.

In connection with the question of 'peace' we might add that the disciples' great joy when they met Jesus risen from the dead may refer back to the promise of John 16:20–22.[670] Here, Beasley-Murray[671] understands 'the joy' as 'a fundamental blessing of the kingdom of God' against the background of some Isaianic texts. If he is right, it could be said more correctly that the 'joy' mentioned in these Isaianic texts are associated with the restoration (new exodus) of Israel from exile.[672]

To sum up, Jesus's proclamation (greeting) of εἰρήνη disclosed his identity as the King of peace, the Davidic Messiah who has established the kingdom of everlasting peace, as a part of the restoration of Israel in exile.

4.6.4 Forgiving and Retaining Sin (John 20:23)

The meaning of the verse should be understood in the context of Jesus's commission of the disciples (v. 21) to continue his work in the world and of his bestowal of the Holy Spirit to enable them in the task (v. 22). Concerning the meaning of this verse, Beasley-Murray says that:

> It entails therefore the double context of the continuance of the mission of Jesus through his disciples in the world, and the continuance of that mission through the Holy Spirit to the world in

---

[669] Kim, 'Peace,' 283–284.
[670] Morris, *John*, 746; Bruce, *John*, 391; Beasley-Murray, *John*, 379.
[671] Beasley-Murray, *John*, 379. Cf. Isa 25:6–9; 54:1–5; 61:1–3. Also, P. Beasley-Murray, *Resurrection*, 91.
[672] Cf. Isa 49:8–13; 51:11; 52:7–10.

and with the disciples .... With the double context, there is a double aspect of the mission: that of declaring salvation and judgment.[673]

That is, the mission of Jesus will be continued by his disciples under the guidance of the Holy Spirit. Here, Carson[674] indicates that the passive voice being forgiven or not means that forgiveness and retention of sin is by divine authority. Thus, those who respond to the gospel as proclaimed by the disciples are forgiven by God. Bruce[675] assumes that Jesus's words here concerning the authority of forgiving sin and retaining sin have the same meaning as the binding and loosing of Matt 16:19 and 18:18, and that all of these passages allude to Isa 22:22. References to, 'the key of the house of David,' and 'open and shut' in Isa 22:22 may also be reflected in Rev 1:18; 3:7.[676] The context of Matt 16:19 could then help us in understanding the meaning of the narrative of Jesus's action and words on Easter evening.

Even though there has clearly been extensive disagreement over the meaning of 'this rock,'[677] what needs to be noted is the connection with the discussion about the building of the new Temple through Jesus's death and resurrection. Morris[678] observes that all these promises concerning the building of his church and her victory against the gates of Hades are in the future tense. In Matthew, it is from this point onwards that Jesus began to tell of his death and resurrection and it seems likely that there is a link between the two themes. Jesus's promise concerning the authority of binding and loosing was given to the apostles as the nucleus of the church of the future in the context of the building of the church through his own death and resurrection.[679] In John 20:21–23, the apostles were given

---

[673] Beasley-Murray, *John*, 383. See also Beasley-Murray, *Life*, 118; Carson, *John*, 655; S. E. Hansen, 'Forgiving,' 24–32, esp. 28.

[674] Carson, *John*, 655. See also Bruce, *John*, 392; Brown, *John XIII-XX1*, 1040; P. Beasley-Murray, *Resurrection*, 96–97.

[675] Bruce, *John*, 392. See also Morris, *Matthew*, 425–426; Lindars, *John*, 612; Beasley-Murray, *John*, 383; *idem.*, *Life*, 118; Blomberg, *Historical*, 267; P. Beasley-Murray, *Resurrection*, 97; Jeremias, *Theology*, I, 238, who particularly argues that these kinds of pairs of opposite words (cf. 'forgiving and retaining,' and 'binding and loosing') which are used in Semitic language to describe the totality, denote the total authority of the messenger, and the authority concerning 'forgiving and retaining of sin' is based on the judge's authority to acquit and to pronounce guilty. See also J. Jeremias, *TDNT*, III, 751. However, Morris, *Matthew*, 426 thinks this metaphor of 'binding and loosing' was based rather on the authority of Rabbis who could decide whether a certain behaviour would be permitted or forbidden according to the laws.

[676] Bruce, *John*, 392; Morris, *Matthew*, 425; C. H. Peisker and C. Brown, *NIDNTT*, II, 726–729; D. Müller and C. Brown, *NIDNTT*, II, 729–734; Jeremias, *TDNT*, III, 744–753.

[677] Morris, *Matthew*, 423–424, who, in detail, criticizes the Catholic arguments, in which the 'rock' points to Peter and only the church built upon Peter is the true church.

[678] Morris, *Matthew*, 425.

[679] As mentioned before, John 20:22, in recalling Gen 2:7 and Ezek 37:9, was meant to symbolize Jesus's new creation of humankinds as God's people by the gift of the Holy Spirit

authority concerning forgiving and retaining of sins by the resurrected Jesus as representatives of the church, the new Temple built by his death and resurrection as foretold in John 2:19–22, and we have seen that this new Temple constitutes the very community of the people of God, created by the inspiration of the Holy Spirit bestowed by Jesus after his resurrection from the dead.

Returning to Matt 16:19 (cf. Isa 22:22; Rev 3:7; 1:18), we next note the 'key' imagery there used. This image is associated with the theme of sovereignty. The bearing of the key figuratively means the possession of full authorization both in the OT and later Jewish literature.[680] Jeremias[681] considers that 'the keys of the kingdom of heaven' (Matt 16:19) are no different from the key of David in Rev 3:7. As mentioned, both 'the keys of the kingdom of heaven' in Matt 16:19 and 'the key of David' in Rev 3:7 make the same allusion to 'the keys of the house of David' in Isa 22:22, in which the announcement that the Lord gave to Eliakim the authority of the keys of the house of David had originally nothing to do with messianic expectation. Nevertheless, Isa 22:22 was interpreted typologically, christologically, and messianically in Rev 3:7,[682] by reference to the identity of Jesus Christ resurrected from the dead. Jesus as the Davidic Messiah, who possesses the key of David, has full sovereignty over the eschatological kingdom of God, that is, the eschatological salvation of God. In this respect, in Rev 1:18, Jesus Christ who was dead and then resurrected and has the keys of death and Hades denotes not only that he has the full sovereignty over death and Hades, that is, the authority of judgment and condemnation, but also according to Jeremias, 'he has the power to open the doors of the world of the dead and to summon the dead to resurrection.'[683] Jesus's authority over death and Hades is indirectly

---

and accordingly it can hardly be limited to the disciples. Cf. M. Turner, 'Concept,' 32–33 and Morris, *John*, 750, contend that the authority was given to the community. This opinion was followed by Hansen, 'Forgiving,' 27–28 and Burge, *Anointed*, 120. However, Jeremias, *TDNT*, III, 752–753 argues the authority was given to the Apostles rather than the community. Also, Brown, *John XIII-XXI*, 1033–1035.

[680] Jeremias, *TDNT*, III, 744–750, esp. 750.

[681] Jeremias, *TDNT*, III, 749.

[682] Müller and Brown, *NIDNTT*, II, 730; Jeremias, *TDNT*, III, 747–749; G. K. Beale, *Revelation*, 284. Cf. particularly, in later Rabbinic literature, Isa 22:22 was interpreted as granting 'teaching authority' (Str-B, I, 741), and this thought can be found in Matt 23:13; Luke 11:52. Moreover, Isa 22:22 was reinterpreted in *Tg. Isa* 22:22 as follows; 'I will place the key of the *sanctuary* and the authority of the house of David in his hand; and he will open, and none shall shut; and he will shut, and none shall open.' This is quoted from D. E. Aune, *Revelation:1–8*, 235 (original emphasis). This document shows that the sanctuary was identified with the house of David.

[683] Jeremias, *TDNT*, III, 746–747, who argues that τὰς κλεῖς τοῦ θανάτου καὶ τοῦ ᾅδου has to be interpreted as a possessive genitive ('keys of personified death and Hades') rather than an objective genitive ('keys to death and the world of the dead'). However, Beale, *Revelation*, 214–

reflected in Matt 16:18 as well. Accordingly, Jesus, the Davidic Messiah, has the authority not only over the everlasting kingdom of God but also over death and judgment.

Another aspect of the 'key' image is related to the motif of the house or Temple, which also seems to be important in understanding the identity of the kingdom of God. In Matt 16:19, the building of Jesus's church was metaphorically described by the construction on the rock. Moreover, Jesus's possession of the keys of the kingdom of heaven in Matt 16:19 pictures him as the master of the house or Temple.[684] We might note in this connection also Matt 23:13 and Luke 11:52, in which Jesus fiercely accused the teachers of the law and Pharisees, and figuratively used the imagery of door and key in connection with the kingdom of heaven.[685]

The imageries (cf. door/gate, watchman/doorkeeper, sheep-pen/house) are clearly found in John 10:1–21, where Jesus proclaimed himself as 'the gate for the sheep,' 'the gate' through which whoever enters will be saved, and 'the good shepherd' who according to his will lays down his life for his sheep. This Johannine passage can be understood in the light of Ezek 34:1–31 (cf. Zech 11:4–17; 13:7–9). [686] Above all, in Ezek 34:23–31, Yahweh promises that he will place his servant David to be the shepherd, the king among Israel, and he will make a covenant of peace with them against the background of the restoration of Israel from exile (cf. Ezek 37:24–28). Carson[687] thinks that thief and robbers in John 10:1, 8, 10 could be regarded as the religious leaders (cf. the Pharisees in John 9:39–40) or messianic pretenders. Furthermore, this imagery of house (Temple) was adopted as a metaphor for the kingdom of heaven (or God) before Jesus's crucifixion in John 14:2–3 (cf. John 2:16; John 3:5).

Therefore, in connection with the key imagery (cf. the door/gate imagery as well) of Matt 16:19; Rev 3:7; John 10:1–3, 9 (cf. Isa 22:22; Rev 1:18), Jesus's commission concerning the authority of forgiving and retaining of sin in John 20:23 denotes certain important issues: the announcement of judgment on unbelievers, and the promise of forgiveness to believers through the proclamation of the gospel but also the very identity of Jesus. He, as the Davidic Messiah, has sovereignty over death and Hades, the power of resurrection, and the authority over the kingdom of heaven, expressed in

---

215 thinks both interpretations may be possible, which means that 'Christ has authority over this realm, and figuratively this realm is in his possession.'

[684] Müller and Brown, *NIDNTT*, II, 732.

[685] Müller and Brown, *NIDNTT*, II, 730; Jeremias, *TDNT*, III, 750.

[686] Carson, *John*, 381; Beasley-Murray, *John*, 168, who also thinks that 'door' alludes to Ps 118:20 (*ibid.*, 169–170). Also, *idem.*, *Life*, 42.

[687] Carson, *John*, 381–382; Beasley-Murray, *John*, 168–169.

the evocative OT language of house, key, and Temple. In particular, Brunson[688] points out that forgiveness is an essential prerequisite for the restoration of Israel from exile, and argues that the message of forgiveness commissioned to the disciples is effecting the restoration, the creation of a new community in John 20:23.

To sum up, the two resurrection narratives (the resurrection of Lazarus and Jesus and his encounter with the disciples) in John 11:43–44; 20:5–6, 19–22 allude to the imagery of resurrection which is used to describe the restoration (the new exodus) of Israel from exile in Ezek 37:1–14 (cf. Isa 25:5–7; 26:19–20; Dan 12:2; Hos 6:1–2; 13:14). Jesus, through his death and resurrection, creates the new covenant people (children, sons) of God; the building of the new Temple. Thus, Jesus who will die as the Firstborn (the paschal lamb) of God and thus bring about the restoration of Israel from exile and the gathering of the scattered children (sons) of God is the very Davidic messianic King who builds the eschatological new Temple in three days (John 2:19–21).

4.7 Conclusion

In the Johannine Temple incident and its Temple logion, Jesus proclaimed himself as the Davidic Messiah; the Son/firstborn (the paschal lamb) of God in John 2:16. Further he portrays himself as the builder of the Temple (or the new Temple) in John 2:19, in recollection of Yahweh's covenant with David in 2 Sam 7:12–14.

The new Temple which will be raised by Jesus as the Davidic Messiah is none other than his physical body who will be resurrected from the dead after three days. Further, since Jesus as the Son/firstborn of God is the inclusive representative of the new Israel, the new-covenant people of God, his resurrected body is itself also the community of the new eschatological people of God. This is metaphorically identified with the new Temple, raised on the basis of his death and resurrection, who was offered as the vicarious, redemptive atoning sacrifice on which the new covenant was established; the firstborn (paschal lamb) of God and the Isaianic suffering Servant-Davidic messianic king.

Thus, Jesus's bodily resurrection means the creation of the new eschatological people (children, sons) of God, the building of the eschatological new Temple, bringing about the restoration (new exodus) of Israel from exile. This has been further disclosed by the studies of 'in three

---

[688] Brunson, *Psalm 118*, 166–167. Cf. Isa 1:25–27; 4:3–4; 53:4–12; Jer 31:31–33; Ezek 36:24–29, 33; 37:23–28. In John 16:5–15, particularly, the works of ὁ παράκλητος, the Spirit of truth, were described in detail in regard to sin, righteousness and judgment.

days,' 'Lazarus's resurrection narrative' (John 11:43–44) and 'Jesus's resurrection narratives' (John 20:19–23). These allude to some OT resurrection passages such as Ezek 37:1–28; Isa 25:5–7; 26:19–20; Dan 12:2; Hos 6:1–2; 13:14.

Chapter 5: Jesus and Nicodemus (John 3:1–21) and, Jesus and John the Baptist (John 3:22–36)

5.1 Introduction

The third chapter of the Gospel of John can be divided into two sections, vv. 1–21 and vv. 21–36. The first section, vv. 1–21, can again be separated into two parts: the conversation between Jesus and Nicodemus in vv. 1–15 and the commentary (vv. 16–21) provided by John the Evangelist, which leads more deeply into the meaning of the preceding dialogue.[689] The main subject of Jesus's conversation with Nicodemus is the new birth (or new creation).[690] The narrative pattern of the first section seems to be repeated in the second section.[691] That is to say, the second section, vv. 22–36 also divides into two parts: the conversation between John the Baptist and his disciples in vv. 22–30 and the Evangelist's theological commentary that uncovers the meaning of the Baptist's previous farewell testimony to Jesus in vv. 31–36.[692] The Baptist's dialogue with his disciples concerning baptisms in the first part of the second section develops into a wedding motif (bride, bridegroom and the best man) and results in the reference to the inauguration of the new age.

---

[689] Carson, *John*, 185; Smith, *John*, 93; Bennema, *Power*, 168; Lee, *Narratives*, 38, who argues that the reference that, in v. 2, *at night*, Nicodemus came to Jesus who is the light of the world, at the beginning of the first section, seems to form an *inclusio* with the mention in v. 21, at the end of the first section, which says that whoever lives by the truth *comes into the light*. And Burge, *John*, 118 n. 12, points out that, in vv. 13–15, the Son of Man, an important title of Jesus is distinctively used only by Jesus himself, and another crucial Johannine title, 'the only Son' in v. 16, and 'believe in the name' in v. 18 and 'live by the truth' in v. 21 are used not by Jesus but by John the Evangelist. See also, D. Williford, 'John 3:1–15,' 452; Witherington, *Wisdom*, 99; Bernard, *John*, I, 117. However, others think that vv. 16–21 are spoken by Jesus (e.g., Z. C. Hodges, 'Coming,' 319).

[690] Bennema, *Power*, 168, who says 'the image of birth that becomes… one of John's symbols for eternal life.' Also, Lee, *Narratives*, 36.

[691] G. M. Burge, *John*, 113; F. J. Moloney, *John*, 104.

[692] Carson, *John*, 185; Westcott, *John*, I, 57, 60; Bernard, *John*, I, 117; Whitacre, *John*, 98; Moloney, *John*, 104; Burge, *John*, 113; Witherington, *Wisdom*, 110; Morris, *John*, 215; Smith, *John*, 106; Bruce, *John*, 96. Some commentators (e.g., Lee, *Narratives*, 41; Brown, *John I-XII*, 159–160) argue that the speaker in the passage is Jesus, and other commentators (e.g., J. Wilson, 'Integrity,' 34–41) John the Baptist. Also, there are some arguments about the position of vv. 31–36. Schnackenburg, *John*, I, 380ff, claims that the passage has to be disposed between v. 12 and v. 13, and Bultmann, *John*, 131–133 and Bernard, *John*, I, 123, between v. 21 and v. 22. However, these arguments are criticized by Dodd, *Interpretation*, 309; Brown, *John I-XII*, 160; Morris, *John*, 209; Malina and Rohrbaugh, *John*, 90; Smith, *John*, 106.

Some commentators [693] argue that both sections show a literary and thematic unity. Burge in particular contends that:

> chapter 3 is built with two halves, each containing structurally similar features. As the evangelist weaves the chapter together, he concentrates on similar theological themes and literary symmetries to make it a unified whole.[694]

This argument is supported by the observation that both main sections finish with the Evangelist's emphasis on the significance of Jesus's work to bring salvation. Which is expressed by eternal life, and on the other hand on God's condemnation or God's wrath upon anyone who rejects Jesus, the only Son (μονογενής) of God, and his salvation. Therefore, the third chapter of John's Gospel will be considered under two sections: Jesus and Nicodemus in vv. 1–21 and Jesus and John the Baptist in vv. 22–36 and examined respectively in the light of the paschal-new exodus motif.

5.2 Jesus and Nicodemus John 3:1–21

From this section, some questions can be raised such as; what is the origin of the notion of the new birth? Another controversial question is what the word, 'water,' means in John 3:5. What is the relationship between water and the Spirit in connection with the new birth? Also, what is meant by 'entering the kingdom of God' in regard to the new exodus motif? In particular, the fact that Nicodemus came to Jesus at night should receive our attention, because chapter 3:1–21 closes with the sharp contrast of the two concepts of light and darkness (cf. John 1:4–9). Further in John 13:30 the Evangelist narrates how Judas went out into the night following his betrayal of Jesus, the light of the world (cf. John 8:12; 1:4). In connection with the subject of light and darkness, another related theme is 'the Son of Man' being lifted up (vv. 13–15) who was 'the only Son' given (or sent) to the world by God (vv. 16–18), and in whom was eternal life and eternal condemnation. All these motifs will be researched with regard to the paschal-new exodus motif.

---

[693] Lee, *Narratives*, 38; Carson, *John*, 185; Burge, *John*, 113; Beasley-Murray, *Life*, 94; Moloney, *John*, 89–90, 104.

[694] Burge, *John*, 120; Beasley-Murray, *Life*, 94; Moloney, *John*, 89–90, who also claims that both sections (esp. vv. 12–15 and vv. 31–35) commonly testify to Jesus as the unique revealer of the heavenly world. See also, Brown, *John I-XII*, 159–160; F. J. Moloney, *Son*, 44–45; Williford, 'John 3:1–15,' 451–461; Polhill, 'John 1–4,' 452.

5.2.1 The Origin of the Idea of the New Birth

5.2.1.1 Some Arguments

Concerning the question of the origin of the concept of the new birth, several arguments have been suggested.[695] Firstly, some[696] assume that the idea of the new birth originated from Gnosticism, mystic religions, or pagan religions. For example, Barrett[697] contends that both the idea and the terminology regarding rebirth and supernatural begetting originated not from the OT and Judaism, but from Hellenistic religions and that the notion of rebirth can be found in Gnostic sources, such as *Hermetic tractate* XIII: 1–3. However, there was a primitive gospel tradition such as the sayings about entering and receiving the kingdom of God in Matt 18:3 (cf. Mark 10:15; Luke 18:17). Under the influence of Hellenistic religion, in which the concepts of rebirth and supernatural begetting are common, this primitive gospel tradition developed into the distinctive Christian idea of regeneration. Thus, Barrett concludes that the Evangelist borrowed a phrase 'the kingdom of God' from the language of Judaism and the term 'regeneration' (γεννηθῇ ἄνωθεν) from the language of Hellenism. These were adopted in expressing a distinctive concept of Christian salvation which was neither Jewish nor Hellenistic. It is necessary here, to point out that in Barrett's argument the notions of regeneration and supernatural begetting are based not on the OT and Judaism, but on Hellenistic-Gnostic religions. Witherington[698] also thinks that since the concept of a spiritual rebirth was very common in the Greco-Roman world; the Evangelist might have used the birth concept originating from Hellenistic-Gnostic religions, for a mixed Jewish and gentile audience in the Diaspora. From the context of the chapter of John's Gospel, Carson[699] also presumes the possibility that those who listened to Jesus's teaching about the new birth could understand it against the background of these kinds of Gnosticism, mystic religions, and pagan religions.

Nevertheless, Carson [700] argues these ideas could not have been an appropriate origin of the new birth in John's Gospel. Goppelt[701] says the

---

[695] Cf. Carson, *John*, 189–190, who has classified scholars' opinions about the basis of a new birth in John 3:1–10 into four categories.
[696] Barrett, *John*, 206–207; Witherington, *Wisdom*, 95. Cf. Carson, *John*, 189.
[697] Barrett, *John*, 207–208. Cf. Apuleius, *Metamorphoses*, XI.
[698] Witherington, *Wisdom*, 95.
[699] Carson, *John*, 189. Cf. Burge, *John*, 115, who assumes that the idea of a divine birth is quite common in a Hellenistic backdrop and Judaism at that time was completely Hellenised, and so Jesus's mention of a divine birth could have been understood in the light of the language of non-Jewish faith.
[700] Carson, *John*, 190; Schnackenburg, *John*, I, 376.

concept of the new creation in John's Gospel has not grown up on the soil of syncretism but on the basis of creation typology, expressed by ἐκ θεοῦ ἐγεννήθησαν in John 1:13.

Secondly, it is suggested that this notion was grounded in Judaism,[702] such as the Jewish idea that a proselyte newly baptized into Judaism was regarded as a new-born baby. Another possible interpretation is that within Jewish thought, the daily offerings have the effect of making Israel like a one-year-old child.

However, the former, relating to a newly baptized proselyte, has to be understood as just referring to the legal status of the converts and so it does not have any concept of birth.[703] Also, the latter concerning the daily sacrifices is connected not with the birth concept but with the cleansing from sin.[704] Since this Johannine idea of the new birth is a comprehensive, complete renewal of the whole person bestowed 'from above,' it has nothing to do with these Jewish notions.

Thirdly, some commentators[705] imagine that this Johannine concept of 'the kingdom of God' and 'the new birth' originated from a synoptic tradition that the disciples must become like little children to enter (or to receive) the kingdom of heaven in Matt 18:3 (cf. Mark 10:15; Luke 18:17). As mentioned earlier, Barrett[706] thinks that under the influence of the regeneration idea in Hellenistic religion, this synoptic tradition developed into the distinctive Christian concept of regeneration of John's Gospel.

However, Beasley Murray[707] says that the Johannine tradition in John 3:3 is independent of the Synoptic tradition in Matt 18:3 and is 'an adaptation of the eschatological hope of a new creation.'[708] Matt 18:3 emphasizes an indispensable condition that the disciples should humble themselves to trust in God for their salvation like little children, but John 3:3-8

---

[701] Goppelt, *Typos*, 182; C. D. Osburn, 'Exegetical,' 136; Beasley-Murray, 'John 3:3, 5,' 167; idem., *John*, 47; L. Belleville, 'Born,' 137 n. 73, who points out that ἀναγεννηθῆναι in *Tractate* 13 of the *Hermetica* is theologically pantheistic but the concept of the new birth (or rebirth/ ἀναγένεσις) in John's Gospel is monotheistic.
[702] E.g., *b. Yeb.* 22a, 48b, 62a, 97b. Cf. Str-B, II, 420–423. Cf. Carson, *John*, 189; Barrett, *John*, 206; Morris, *John*, 190; Malina and Rohrbaugh, *John*, 82; Osburn, 'Exegetical,' 133; Bruce, *John*, 82.
[703] Carson, *John*, 189; Barrett, *John*, 206; Burge, *John*, 115; Malina and Rohrbaugh, *John*, 82; Witherington, *Wisdom*, 95; Dodd, *Interpretation*, 303–304; Belleville, 'Born,' 137.
[704] Carson, *John*, 189; Barrett, *John*, 206.
[705] Bultmann, *John*, 135; Barrett, *John*, 206–207; Lindars, *John*, 150; idem., 'Synoptic,' 287–294; Brown, *John I-XII*, 143; Michaels, *John*, 55; J. W. Pryor, 'John 3.3, 5,' 71–95, esp. 72; Dodd, *Historical*, 358–359; Marshall, *Luke*, 682.
[706] Barrett, *John*, 206–207.
[707] Beasley-Murray, 'John 3:3, 5,' 168
[708] Beasley-Murray, *Life*, 92–93; idem., 'John 3:3, 5,' 167; Dodd, *Interpretation*, 304.

emphasizes, 'the need for transformation, for new life from another realm, for the intervention of the Spirit of God.'[709]

On the other hand, some theologians[710] interpret this synoptic tradition not to mean children's humility or purity but the re-building of the father-son-relationship between God and the disciples. Therefore, the requirement to enter the kingdom of God is to be his children (or sons), able to call him ἀββά ὁ πατήρ[711] as. For example, Manson[712] suggests that Jesus's teaching about the necessity of becoming like children to enter the kingdom of God in Matt 18:3 could be understood in the light of the usage of ἀββά ὁ πατήρ in Rom 8:15; Gal 4:6. In particular, Jeremias[713] translates ἐὰν μὴ στραφῆτε καὶ γένησθε ὡς τὰ παιδία, οὐ μὴ εἰσέλθητε εἰς τὴν βασιλείαν τῶν οὐρανῶν (Matt 18:3) as 'unless you become like children again, you will not reach the *basileia* of God.' Following Manson's argument, Jeremias claims that '"become a child again" means: to learn to say ἀββᾶ again ... putting one's whole trust in the heavenly Father, returning to the Father's house and the Father's arms,' in the light of repentance (cf. Luke 15:11–32). Further, Jeremias says that:

> Wherever people are won over by the good news and join company with the new people of God, they leave the world of death for the world of life.... Now they belong under the reign of God; a new life is beginning which consists in a new relationship to God and a new relationship to man. The most important characteristic of the new life, more important than anything else, is *the new relationship to God*.[714]

This argument by Jeremias and Manson is quite reasonable. This is not too far from the concept of becoming children of God through being born of God in John 1:12–13 and the idea of the birth of water and the Spirit to enter the kingdom of God in John 3:3–5.

Nonetheless, the argument that the concept of the entry into the kingdom of God through the new birth in John 3 originated from the Synoptic tradition is not very persuasive.

---

[709] Carson, *John*, 190; Bruce, *John*, 82; Belleville, 'Born,' 137.
[710] Jeremias, *Theology*, I, 155–156, 180–181; T. W. Manson, *Teaching*, 331; Kim, 'Interpretation,' 232.
[711] Cf. Mark 14:36; Rom 8:15; Gal 4:6. On ἀββα, see Jeremias, *Theology*, I, 61–68; G. Kittel, *TDNT*, I, 5–6.
[712] Manson, *Teaching*, 331.
[713] Jeremias, *Theology*, I, 155–156.
[714] Jeremias, *Theology*, I, 178 (original emphasis).

5.2.1.2 Old Testament and Jewish Background

Fourthly, and above all, both Jesus's rigid demand concerning the new birth in John 3:7 and his reprimand of Nicodemus for his lack of knowledge about the new birth in John 3:10 must be noted. Since Nicodemus did not understand exactly Jesus's meaning about the new birth, Jesus explained in detail the meaning and necessity of new birth in John 3:5–8.[715] In particular, Jesus's emphasis in John 3:7 suggests that the notion of the new birth was neither new and unexpected, nor incomprehensible to Nicodemus as an Israelite.[716] Also, in John 3:10 Jesus is surprised that Nicodemus, as an expert of the Law of Israel and the OT, did not understand what he meant.[717] In other words, it denotes that Jesus's idea of new birth in realtion to seeing the kingdom of God had already been revealed in the OT, so that it might have been expected in Judaism in the time of Jesus. It could also be thought that Jesus's explanations for Nicodemus in John 3:5–8 would have been linked to familiar references from the OT. If the OT is the origin of Jesus's understanding, then no other sources than the OT needs to be examined. Therefore, following this claim, we shall concentrate on three verses (vv. 5, 6, 8) in the light of the OT.

5.2.1.2.1 The Birth of Water and the Spirit (v. 5)

Firstly, the entry into the kingdom of God and its requirement of the birth of water and the Spirit cited in v. 5 was offered to Nicodemus as the first consideration. If this is based on the OT, then it should have been clear to Nicodemus, but unfortunately it was not. If this assertion that Jesus's supplementary comment in v. 5 was originally built on the OT is right, from which OT reference (or references) did the concept of the new birth appear in connection with 'water and the Spirit'?

Some commentators[718] recognize that the use of 'water and the Spirit' as the agent of the new birth in John 3:5 is based on John's familiarity with Isa 44:3–5. This OT passage could be important to a fuller understanding of the dialogue with Nicodemus.

---

[715] D. W. B. Robinson, 'Born,' 16; Bruce, *John*, 84.
[716] Moloney, *John*, 94.
[717] Schnackenburg, *John*, I, 367; Carson, *John*, 190; Köstenberger, *John*, 84; M. Fallon, *John*, 98; Moloney, *John*, 94; S. M. Schneiders, 'Born,' 192–193; Barrett, *John*, 211; Milne, *John*, 76; Lindars, *John*, 154; Whitacre, *John*, 89; D. I. Block, 'Prophet,' 40; Smith, *John*, 96, who, observing that Jesus interestingly used a definite article (ὁ διδάσκαλος τοῦ Ἰσραήλ) in v. 10, interprets that this means that Nicodemus was 'the great, universally recognized, teacher.'
[718] Z. C. Hodges, 'Water,' 217; W. Russell, 'Holy,' 231–232; Burge, *John*, 116; Jones, *Symbol*, 75; Brown, *John I-XII*, 140; Schnackenburg, *John*, I, 370; Milne, *John*, 79; Dunn, *Baptism*, 192; Moloney, *John*, 94; Dennis, *Gathering*, 286 n. 202. *Contra* Bennema, *Power*, 170 n. 38.

> For I will pour water on the thirsty land, and streams on the dry ground; I will pour out my Spirit on your offspring, and my blessing on your descendants. They will spring up like grass in a meadow, like poplar trees by flowing streams. One will say, 'I belong to the Lord'; another will call himself by the name of Jacob; still another will write on his hand, 'The Lord's,' and will take the name Israel. (Isa 44:3–5)

Here, both water and the Spirit are referred to together. Isa 44:3 shows a parallel between v. 3a ('I will pour water on the thirsty land, and streams on the dry ground') and v. 3b ('I will pour out my Spirit on your offspring, and my blessing on your descendants'). That Israel would receive miraculous new life by the Spirit of Yahweh was promised to her using the pictures of the surprising growth of plants and well-watered fertility through the out-pouring of water from on high.[719] Yahweh's bestowal of the Spirit on Israel's offspring in exile leads them to confess themselves as belonging to the people of God (cf. v. 5). Above all, what has to be noted is that the image of the out-pouring of water on the thirsty land was metaphorically employed to describe the promise of the out-pouring of Yahweh's Spirit upon the nation of Israel. Thus, water is a symbol of the Spirit, through whom Yahweh would impart new life to Israel. Here, the function of water effused *from above* has to do with the life-giving power of the Spirit poured out from on high.[720] This argument could be further supported in that the water Jesus mentioned in John 3:5 is not water 'from below' used by the Pharisees, but water 'from above (ἄνωθεν)' that only God can send (cf. John 3:3).

Furthermore, in this chapter of Isaiah, Yahweh emphatically introduces himself not only as the creator of Jacob and the heavens and the earth; the living God, compared with idols who have no life. But, also as the great redeemer of Israel, who is the first and the last (cf. Isa 44:2, 6, 21–22, 24). Yahweh promised Israel her restoration to Jerusalem and the Temple in Isa 44:26–28.

> The Lord ... who says of Jerusalem, 'It shall be inhabited,' of the towns of Judah, 'They shall be built,' and of their ruins, 'I will restore them,' who says to the watery deep, 'Be dry, and I will dry up your streams,' who says of Cyrus, 'he is my shepherd and will accomplish all that I please; he will say of Jerusalem, 'Let it be

---

[719] Motyer, *Isaiah*, 342–343; Watts, *Isaiah 34–66*, 144–145.
[720] Hodges, 'Water,' 217, says that 'The image of the Holy Spirit as a divine effusion from on high is a prominent one in biblical thought.' Cf. Isa 32:15–17; Ezek 39:29; Joel 2:28; Acts 2:17 (cf. 2:33); Tit 3:5–6.

> rebuilt,' and of the Temple, 'Let its foundations be laid.' (Isa 44:26–28)

Therefore, what has to be emphasized is that the metaphor of the outpouring of water in the desert was symbolically used to depict Yahweh's out-pouring of the Spirit upon Israel in exile. This function of water as the symbol of the life-giving Spirit as expressed in Isa 44:3–5 frequently appeared not only in the OT but is also found in the NT.[721]

In particular, a vivid portrayal of water as the life-giving power is presented in Ezek 47:1–12, in which the water coming out from under the threshold of the Temple toward the east revived everything it touched. In addition, this image of water is crucial in explaining the function of the Holy Spirit in John's Gospel itself (cf. John 4:14; 7:38). Accordingly, this could support the appropriation of Isa 44:3–5 as an OT background of water and Spirit in John 3:5. Here, the miraculous new life by the Spirit poured out from on high was intimately connected with Yahweh's restoration of Israel in exile, and Jerusalem and the Temple which had been ruined before.[722] In other words, the new life given by the Spirit of Yahweh was used as a picture for the restoration, the new exodus of Israel from exile.

Secondly, as almost all Johannine commentators recognize,[723] Ezek 36:25–27 has to be considered as a primary OT text for the concept of the new birth with water and the Spirit in John 3:5.

> For I will take you out of the nations; I will gather you from all the countries and bring you back into your own land. I will sprinkle clean water on you, and you will be clean; I will cleanse you from all your impurities and from all your idols. I will give you a new heart and put a new spirit in you; I will remove from you your heart of stone and give you a heart of flesh. And I will put my

---

[721] Burge, *John*, 116; Dunn, *Baptism*, 192; Robinson, 'Born,' 19. Cf. Isa 55:1–3; Jer 2:13; 17:13; Zech 14:8; Ezek 47:1–12; John 4:14; 7:37–39; Rev 22:1–2, 17.
[722] Dennis, *Gathering*, 286.
[723] Goppelt, *Typos*, 182–183; Carson, *John*, 188, 195; Ng, *Symbolism*, 74; Beasley-Murray, *John*, 49; idem., 'John 3:3, 5,' 168–169; Köstenberger, *John*, 84; Fallon, *John*, 98; Williford, 'John 3:1–15,' 455; Burge, *John*, 116; Moloney, *John*, 94; F. P. Cotterell, 'Nicodemus,' 241; Blomberg, *Historical*, 93; Schneider, 'Born,' 192–193; Hodges, 'Water,' 219; Russell, 'Holy,' 231; Jones, *Symbol*, 75 n. 117; Milne, *John*, 76; Schnackenburg, *John*, I, 370–371; Robinson, 'Born,' 19; Turner, *Holy*, 69; Bruce, *John*, 84; Howard-Brook, *Becoming*, 88; Brown, *John I-XII*, 140–141; Bennema, *Power*, 170–171; P. Borgen, 'Son,' 147 n. 51; Dennis, *Gathering*, 286; Whitacre, *John*, 89; K. Grayston, 'Misunderstands,' 10, who, nevertheless, strangely interprets Jesus's words as follows; 'Jesus in effect invites Nicodemus to abandon Jewish expectation of the kingdom of God (which of course is never mentioned again in the Gospel) and to adopt the Greek expectation of rebirth.' (p. 11). *Contra* Witherington, *Wisdom*, 97; Michaels, *John*, 61.

Spirit in you and move you to follow my decrees and be careful to keep my laws. You will live in the land I gave your forefathers; you will be my people, and I will be your God. (Ezek 36:24–28)

This passage clearly shows the combination of water and the Spirit. The central message of this passage was Yahweh's promise that his people, Israel, having been scattered in many countries would be *restored* into the land that he had given to their forefathers. The promise that the new exodus will be fulfilled by Yahweh himself was strongly emphasized with three parallel lines in Ezek 36:24.[724] This promise was again assured with the restoration of Israel to the Land given to their ancestors in Ezek 36:28.

I will take you out of the nations,

I will gather you from all the countries,

I will bring you back into your own land. (v. 24)

You will live in the land I gave your forefathers. (v. 28)

Another point is that the restoration of Israel from exile will be accompanied by a wholesale transformation of the nation of Israel in Ezek 36:25–27. As Block[725] interprets, the wholesale renewal of the Israelites accomplished by Yahweh was pictured by three images.

The first image is the purification of the Israelites from all their impurities and all their idols with clean water (v. 25). To begin with, this expression of the purification with the sprinkling of pure water alluded to the ritual cleansings in Num 19:9–22.[726] Actually, the verb (זרק/ῥαίνω) is most frequently used in regard to the sprinkling of blood in the OT.[727] Also, concerning the sprinkling of blood, a sevenfold sprinkling of blood to make atonement on the Day of Atonement has to be considered, in spite of using a different verb, נזה, which was rendered by ῥαίνω in the LXX (cf. Lev 16:14, 15, 19).[728] So, Hunzinger claims that, 'It is evident that the predominant

---

[724] Block, *Ezekiel 25–48*, 353, who observes that the new exodus motif often appears in Ezekiel; 11:17; 20:34–35, 41–42; 28:25; 29:13; 34:13; 36:24; 37:12, 21; 39:27. See also, Allen, *Ezekiel 20–48*, 179.

[725] Block, *Ezekiel 25–48*, 354–357.

[726] V. P. Hamilton, *NIDOTTE*, I, 1153; Zimmerli, *Ezekiel 2*, 249. Cf. G. André, *TDOT*, IV, 163.

[727] Zimmerli, *Ezekiel 2*, 249; Hamilton, *NIDOTTE*, I, 1153–1154. Cf. the burnt offering (Lev 1:5, 11; 8:19; 9:12; 2 Kings 16:15; 2 Chron 30:16; Ezek 43:18), the peace offering (Lev 3:2, 8, 13; 9:18; 17:6; 2 Kings 16:13), the sin/purification offering (2 Chron 29:22), the guilt offering (Lev 7:2, 14). According to André, *TDOT*, IV, 162–163, this verb (זרק) in the light of sacramental contexts was used twenty-five times with blood, three times with water, and once with dust.

[728] G. R. Beasley-Murray, *NIDNTT*, I, 224. Schnackenburg, *John*, I, 370–371 nn. 74–75, who assumes that Ezek 36:25–26 was employed in connection with the Day of Atonement in some rabbinic sources. For example, Rabbi Akiba declared, using the authority of Ezek 36:25,

thought connected with sprinkling is that of cleansing and expiation, as in the leading chapters Lev 16 and Num 19.'[729]

Furthermore, in connection with the establishment of the new covenant promised in Ezek 36:28 (cf. God and God's new (or renewed) people), the sprinkling (זרק) could refer back to Moses; reflecting both his initial sprinkling with half of the blood of young bulls on the altar (Exod 24:6) and then his subsequent sprinkling of the rest of the blood on the assembly of the people of Israel (Exod 24:8). This followed the reading of the Book of the Covenant during the ceremony to establish the old covenant at Sinai following the exodus from Egypt.[730] Thus, the purification of Israel from all her impurities and all her idols by sprinkling clean water on Israel was probably a reminder of the 'priestly cleansing rituals and blood sprinkling ceremonies' performed in the OT.[731] Block says that:

> In the present context, the issue is not simply an external ceremonial cleansing accompanying the internal renewal described in vv. 26–27, but a wholesale cleansing from sin performed by Yahweh, a necessary precondition to normalizing the spiritual relationship between Yahweh and his people.[732]

Here, Yahweh adopted the language of cultic purification as a symbol for forgiveness and spiritual cleansing.[733] What has to be noted is that in Ezek 36:16–23, the fundamental reason that Israel had to be exiled among the nations was the defilement of God's name because of Israel's sins, such as, blood-shedding and idol worship (cf. Ezek 36:18–19; 37:23; 39:21–29; 2 Kings 21:1–18). Because of the defilement of Israel, Yahweh's holy name was profaned. So, the restoration of Yahweh's holy name would be

---

'Blessed are you, the children of Israel. By whom are you purified, and who cleanses you? Your father in heaven.' (*m. Yom.* 8.9); *Exod R.* 15 (76c) says that 'If the Israelites have fallen into sin on account of the evil urge within them, and repent and do penance, God forgives their sins every year (on the Day of Expiation) and renews their hearts so that they may fear him, as it is written: I will give you a new heart, Ezek 36:26.' (quoted by Str-B, IV, 474). Also, see W. Zimmerli, *Ezekiel 2*, 249.

[729] C.-H. Hunzinger, *TDNT*, VI, 980; Beasley-Murray, *NIDNTT*, I, 224–225.

[730] Hunzinger, *TDNT*, VI, 980–981; Hamilton, *NIDOTTE*, I, 1154; Beasley-Murray, *NIDNTT*, I, 225.

[731] Block, *Ezekiel 25–48*, 354. Cf. Exod 24:6; 29:4; Lev 1:5, 11; 16:4, 24, 26; Num 8:7; 19:11–19.

[732] Block, *Ezekiel 25–48*, 354–355. See also, Zimmerli, *Ezekiel 2*, 249; Allen, *Ezekiel 20–48*, 179.

[733] Köstenberger, *John*, 84; Blomberg, *Historical*, 93; Robinson, 'Born,' 19; Schnackenburg, *John*, I, 370, says that 'Hence Jesus' words to Nicodemus are not concerned directly with baptism, but with the new creation by the Spirit of God.' Also, Hunzinger, *TDNT*, VI, 980, who rightly says that 'In an obvious figure of speech Ez 36:25 (זרק/ῥαίνω) speaks of God's eschatological action…. Like the restoration of Israel (v. 24), the gift of a new heart of flesh (v. 26) and the gift of the Spirit (v. 27), God's cleansing sprinkling is an act of eschatological re-creation of the people of God,' followed by Beasley-Murray, *NIDNTT*, I, 225.

achieved through the purification of Israel from all her impurities and idolatry by the sprinkling of water. Since the exile of Israel resulted from her sins, the restoration of Israel was intimately related with the forgiveness of her sins.[734]

The second image is the putting of the new Spirit, the Spirit of Yahweh within the Israelites (vv. 26-27). Through an exegesis of Ezek 36:26-27, Block[735] observes that v. 26a ('I will give to you a new heart; and a new spirit I will put within you') is paralleled to vv. 26b-27 ('I will remove from you your heart of stone and give you a heart of flesh. And I will put my Spirit within you'). Here, Yahweh's giving 'a new heart' to Israel in v. 26a was further explained 'as a removal of the heart of stone from their flesh and its replacement with a heart of flesh' in v. 26b. And the placing of 'a new spirit' within Israel in v. 26a was identified with the putting of Yahweh's Spirit within Israel in v. 27. In other words, the new spirit infused within Israel was the same as Yahweh's Spirit, which animates and vivifies Israel. This vivifying effect of the infusion of the Spirit of Yahweh is described as a radical revitalization of the nation in exile. This promise of Yahweh's infusion of his Spirit within Israel was vividly portrayed by the vision of the resurrection of dry bones scattered on the floor of the valley, which were identified with Israel and Judah in exile, narrated in Ezek 37:1-14. Thus, Block[736] argues quite rightly that Ezek 37:1-14 is a dramatic exposition regarding the notion of the animating power of the Spirit of Yahweh, introduced in Ezek 36:26-27.

The third image is that Yahweh would give 'a new heart' to Israel in exile. This is also given within the context of Yahweh's promise of the new exodus. Yahweh would establish the new covenant with Israel, in which she would be renewed and thus be created as the new people of Yahweh (v. 28). The expression of 'the new heart' which Yahweh would give Israel (v. 26a) is stated as the removal of the heart of stone from their flesh and its replacement with a heart of flesh in v. 26b.[737] The similar idea of the new heart can also be found in Jer 31:31-34, in which Yahweh announced the new covenant which would be made with the house of Israel and with the house of Judah.[738] Block points out that: 'Jeremiah and Ezekiel obviously

---

[734] Wright, *Victory*, 268-274; Brunson, *Psalm 118*, 166-167.
[735] Block, 'Prophet,' 38-39; *idem.*, *Ezekiel 25-48*, 356.
[736] Block, 'Prophet,' 39; Bruce, *John*, 84; Bennema, *Power*, 170-171; Dennis, *Gathering*, 286, 293. The importance of Ezek 37:1-14 in understanding Jesus's words offered in John 3:8 will be argued later in 5.2.1.2.3. The Mystery of the Birth of the Spirit (v. 8).
[737] Block, 'Prophet,' 39; Zimmerli, *Ezekiel 2*, 249, who observes that *b. Sukk.* 52a says that 'stone is one of the seven names of the evil inclination.'
[738] Zimmerli, *Ezekiel 2*, 248-249; Carson, *John*, 195; Block, *Ezekiel 25-48*, 356-357.

have the same covenant renewal in mind, but what Jeremiah attributes to the divine Torah, Ezekiel ascribes to the infusion of the divine *ruah*.'[739] And the restoration of both Judah and Israel in exile appeared in Ezek 37:15–28 as well.[740] Here, Yahweh's gift of 'a new heart' to Israel is accomplished by the infusion of the divine Spirit within Israel. Consequently, a new heart and a new spirit put within the Israelites moves them to follow Yahweh's decrees and to keep his laws. Thus, in the OT and Jewish literature, the Spirit generally appears as God's agent bestowing life to humankind; not only in the first creation, but also in the new creation in the context of the restoration of Israel or of the eschatological era.[741]

Some commentators[742] recognize that Ezek 36:25–27 is an important text in relation to the eschatological expectation of the spiritual cleansing and renewal in Jewish literature. Brown[743] says that the thought of the new creation/birth through the Spirit, which results in 'becoming of the children of God' is found in *Jub.* 1:23–25. If Brown's argument is right, these are not too far from the ideas of 'born of God' in John 1:13 and of the new creation/birth in John 3:3, 5.

Also, *Test. Jud.* 24:2–3 shows that, as a blessing of the Holy Father, the Spirit (of grace) from on high will be poured out upon the sons of Judah, and thereby they shall be sons in truth and will walk in all the Father's decrees. This text seems to partly allude to Ezek 36:26–27. In chapters 23–25 of the *Test. Jud.*, the resurrection at the end of the restoration of Israel, which is a picture of the new birth/new creation, will be quickened by the out-pouring of the Holy Spirit from on high.

Above all, Qumran Sectarians also waited for an eschatological cleansing by the Spirit at the end times, expressed by the symbolism of water-sprinkling, with performing cleansing rituals with water. Zimmerli [744]

---

[739] Block, *Ezekiel 25–48*, 356–357.
[740] Block, 'Prophet,' 41, who says that 'The emphasis in the present text, as in the broader context of Ezekiel 34–39 in general, is on national renewal and revival, not individual regeneration.'
[741] Cf. Gen 2:7; 6:3; Isa 32:15; 44:3–5; Jer 31:28ff; Ezek 11:19; 36:25–27; 37:9–10; 39:29; Joel 2:28–29; *Jub.* 1:23; 34:14; *Ps. Sol.* 18:5; *Test. Jud.* 24:3; 1QS 4:20f. In particular, VanGemeren, 'Spirit,' 81–102, concentrates on the work of the Spirit of God in the passage of Joel 2:18–32, and says that 'The very mission of the Spirit of God is eschatological. He is the agent of restoration…' (p. 82). Also, Schnackenburg, *John*, I, 370; Carson, *John*, 195; Brown, *John I-XII*, 140.
[742] Turner, *Holy*, 69; Zimmerli, *Ezekiel 2*, 249; Schnackenburg, *John*, I, 370–371; Beasley-Murray, *NIDNTT*, I, 225; idem., *John*, 49; Dennis, *Gathering*, 287; Bennema, *Power*, 171,
[743] Brown, *John I-XII*, 140; Schnackenburg, *John*, I, 370; Dennnis, *Gathering*, 287; Turner, *Holy*, 69; Bennema, *Power*, 171.
[744] Zimmerli, *Ezekiel 2*, 249; Hodges, 'Water,' 218–219; Brown, *John I-XII*, 140; Dennis, *Gathering*, 288; Dunn, *Baptism*, 192; Bennema, *Power*, 171.

admits that the promise in *1 QS* 4:21f reflected the ideas of the Ezekiel text. In *1 QS* 4:19–23, even though the sectarians performed proselyte baptism with water, which was modified from Ezek 36, they expected purification from all wicked deeds and all abomination and injustice, not with water but with the pouring of the spirit of holiness, or the spirit of truth, or the spirit of purification.[745] They regarded purifying water as just a symbol of the cleansing work of the Spirit, in its three aspects. Another important thing which is worthy of noting in this Qumran text is that, in line with the hope of the restoration of Israel from exile in Ezek 36:25–27, the Qumran community's expectation of eschatological cleansing by the Spirit was related to the establishment of an everlasting covenant and the restoration of the glory of Adam. Also, *1 QS* 3:6–9 shows that, with the mention of purification and sanctification by the sprinkling of clean water, they expected that all their sins and iniquities would be expiated by the Spirit of holiness.[746]

Furthermore, Schnackenburg[747] introduces some rabbinic sources which reflect the importance of the Ezekiel passage. Goppelt[748] also assumes that the Jewish idea in *Cant. R.* 1 on 1:1 that a proselyte who entered Judaism was considered to be like a new born child, originated from OT prophecy, especially Ezek 36.

Köstenberger[749] claims that Ezek 36:25–27 is also reflected in Titus 3:5 as well as John 3:5. Even though Marshall[750] points out a difference between Ezek 37:25–27 and Titus 3:5 in that, in the Ezekiel text, cleansing and renewal are distinct, he admits that in the passage of Titus the two phrases ('the washing of rebirth' and 'renewal by the Holy Spirit') describe 'one and the same event from different angles ... cleansing seen as a new beginning or transformation and renewal brought about by the Holy Spirit.'

---

[745] Hodges, 'Water,' 218–219, who says that 'God's purifying work within man's heart in the time of eschatological consummation was being expressed as a kind of effusion of water, which was nothing less than the impartation of a holy spirit.' Also, Brown, *John I-XII*, 140; Dunn, *Baptism*, 192; Schnackenburg, *John*, I, 370; Beasley-Murray, *NIDNTT*, I, 225, who even admits that 'The Sectaries also awaited an eschatological cleansing at the end of the times, expressed under the symbolism of sprinkling,' although he strongly argues that water in John 3:5 points to water baptism, Christian baptism. Also, Ng, *Symbolism*, 74–75; France, 'Baptist,' 102; Dennis, *Gathering*, 289.

[746] Dennis, *Gathering*, 288, who also argues that 4QDibHam^a [*The Words of the Heavenly Luminaries^a*] 5:11–6:3 presents 'the purification function of the Spirit in the context of restoration.' (p. 287).

[747] Schnackenburg, *John*, I, 370–371. cf. *m. Yom.* 8.9; *Exod R.* 15 (76c) (cf. Str-B, IV, 474); *Exod R.* 41 (98a) (cf. Str-B, IV, 847f).

[748] Goppelt, *Typos*, 182–183

[749] Köstenberger, *John*, 84.

[750] I. H. Marshall, *Pastoral*, 316–322, esp. 318–321 (quoted from 321).

Therefore, likewise, these combinations of 'ritual purification with the sprinkling of cleansing water,' 'the new generation (or the new birth or the new creation),' and 'renewal' as works by the Holy Spirit often appear in the OT, Judaism and the NT.[751] The appropriateness of this argument that the new birth of water and the Spirit in John 3:5 alludes to Ezek 36:25–27 will be further supported by the OT backgrounds of the other ideas mentioned by Jesus in John 3:6, 8.

5.2.1.2.2 Physical Birth and Spiritual Birth (v. 6)

In v. 6, Jesus compared the birth of (water and) the Spirit to physical birth. As flesh can give birth to flesh, so the Spirit can give birth to spirit.[752] The contrast between flesh and spirit is based not on the dichotomy of body and soul which is consistent in Greek philosophy, nor the dualism of flesh and spirit in Platonism or Gnosticism, but on the principle of biblical theology concerning the origin of mankind.[753] Here, the antithesis between flesh and spirit does not represent the two different orders of being, the lower and the higher of human nature,[754] but the distinction between the weakness and mortality of the human creature on earth and the life-giving power of the Spirit of God.[755] Robinson[756] argues that the contrast of two kinds of births in v. 6 alluded to the creation of human beings in Gen 2:7. This birth motif of Gen 2:7 is repeatedly reflected in other OT passages and other Jewish documents.[757]

John's Gospel also testifies to this truth: 'The Spirit gives life; the flesh counts for nothing' (John 6:63). This means that without the indwelling of the breath (Spirit) of God, human beings have no life in themselves. Life is given from above by the Spirit of God. Also, this verse could show that just as human beings are born naturally, so the birth from the Spirit is absolutely necessary in regard to the kingdom of God. As, through a natural fleshly birth, human beings becomes members of an earthly family, to become members of the family of God they have to receive spiritual life.

---

[751] Marshall, *Pastoral*, 316, 322; Beasley-Murray, *Life*, 94; Burge, *John*, 116; Dunn, *Baptism*, 192; Carson, *John*, 195; Schnackenburg, *John*, I, 370; Robinson, 'Born,' 19.
[752] Lee, *Narratives*, 62.
[753] Schnackenburg, *John*, I, 372; Robinson, 'Born,' 17; Brown, *John I-XII*, 141.
[754] Bernard, *John*, I, 131; Dodd, *Interpretation*, 295.
[755] Schnackenburg, *John*, I, 372; Brown, *John I-XII*, 131; Beasley-Murray, *John*, 49; Barrett, *John*, 210; Carson, *John*, 196.
[756] Robinson, 'Born,' 17.
[757] For examples, Gen 6:3; Job 32:8; 33:4; 34:14f; Ps 104:29f; Eccles 12:7; Isa 31:3; *1 QS* 9:7; *1 QH* 4:29; 7:17; 8:31; 9:16; 10:23; 15:17; 18:21f. Schnackenburg, *John*, I, 372; Robinson, 'Born,' 17; Brown, *John I-XII*, 140.

This is accomplished by a birth from above, a birth of the Spirit.[758] This idea has been already suggested in the Prologue (John 1:12–13).[759] Above all, it must be noted that there is a contrast between natural and spiritual birth which originates from the motif of creation, especially Gen 2:7. Furthermore, the importance of this creation motif in Gen 2:7 in John 3:6 could be secondarily demonstrated by the mystery of the birth of the Spirit, which is described by the imagery of the blowing of the wind in John 3:8.

5.2.1.2.3. The Mystery of the Birth of the Spirit (v. 8)

This OT background of new birth can be further supported by the observation of some commentators that Jesus's explanation of the mystery of the new birth in John 3:8 is grounded in Gen 2:7[760] or Ezek 37:1–14.[761] There has been some argument about the exact meaning of τὸ πνεῦμα which appears in John 3:8. Bernard[762] claims that the term has to be translated 'the Spirit' because the context of the main focus of this dialogue was about the birth of the Spirit. However, other commentators[763] argue that the word means both 'wind' and 'spirit' as a wordplay or a double meaning which could be one of John's distinctive expressions. This claim could be appropriate in that both πνεῦμα in Greek and רוח in Hebrew have three different connotations, breath, wind and spirit. However, Carson [764] understands τὸ πνεῦμα to mean 'wind' in connection with the expression, 'You *hear its sound*, but you cannot tell where it comes from or where it is going.' In the OT and Jewish thought, the image of wind, which is essentially invisible and powerful, is used to describe the incomprehensibility and mysteriousness of the divine intervention.[765] Since

---

[758] Bruce, *John*, 85; Brown, *John I-XII*, 138.

[759] J. A. Trumbower, *Born*, 75; Carson, *John*, 196;

[760] Brown, *John I-XII*, 140; Lee, *Narratives*, 46; Howard-Brook, *Becoming*, 89.

[761] Bruce, *John*, 84–85; Robinson, 'Born,' 17; Carson, *John*, 195; Whitacre, *John*, 88–89; Robertson, 'New-Covenant,' 134.

[762] Bernard, *John*, I, 106–108; J. D. Thomas, 'Translation,' 219–224, esp. 221–223, who at first surveyed the history of the translating of the verse and assumes that 'the change from spirit to wind was brought about under the influence of the Augustinian and Calvinistic doctrines which claimed that a sinner is converted by a direct operation of the Spirit upon him without the word, and the translators were giving in to the current trend in theology,' (p. 223), and he also observes that a verb of hearing, ἀκούω taking the accusative case emphasizes 'the intellectual apprehension of the sound or noise or voice' (cf. Acts 9:4; 22:9) and the verb taking the genitive case means 'the sound of voice without accenting the sense' (cf. Acts 9:7), argues that τὸ πνεῦμα has to be translated into the Spirit rather than the wind.

[763] Brown, *John I-XII*, 131; Barrett, *John*, 210–211; Bultmann, *John*, 101 n. 4; Beasley-Murray, *John*, 45; Blomberg, *Historical*, 93.

[764] Carson, *John*, 197; Morris, *John*, 195; Milne, *John*, 76; Whitacre, *John*, 88–89; Lindars, *John*, 154.

[765] Brown, *John I-XII*, 131; Bernard, *John*, I, 107; Lee, *Narratives*, 46; Schnackenburg, *John*, I, 374; Carson, *John*, 198; Bruce, *John*, 85. Cf. Gen 1:2; Prov 30:4; Eccles 11:4; Isa 59:19; Ezek 1:4; 3:12; 37:9; *1 En.* 41:3; 60:11–12; *4 Ezra* 4:5, 9ff; *2 Bar.* 48:3–4.

this new birth takes place essentially not by human design but only by the Spirit of God, the nature and character of the process is supernatural, divinely mysterious, beyond human control and comprehension.[766]

Above all, the wind blowing without people knowing the directions of its origin and its goal, and the birth bestowed by the Spirit in John 3:8, alludes to several OT texts, such as the breath (or the Spirit) coming from the four winds, and the resurrection by the vivifying power of the breath (or the Spirit) in Ezek 37:1–14 (esp. v. 9):[767]

> Then he said to me, 'Prophesy to the breath (ἐπὶ τὸ πνεῦμα); prophesy, son of man, and say to it, 'This is what the Sovereign LORD says: Come from the four winds (ἐκ τῶν τεσσάρων πνευμάτων), O breath, and breathe into these slain, that they may live.' (Ezek 37:9 LXX).
>
> The wind (τὸ πνεῦμα) blows wherever it pleases. You hear its sound, but you cannot tell where it comes from or where it is going. So it is with everyone born of the Spirit. (John 3:9).

Furthermore, in this connection Ezek 37:1–14 is an exposition of Ezek 36:25–27,[768] which is alluded to in the birth through water and the Spirit in John 3:5. This can be strengthened by the argument that the mystery of the birth of the Spirit in John 3:8 is founded on the vision of the resurrection of the dry bones by the animating power of the breath (the Spirit) of Yahweh in Ezek 37:9. So, Carson[769] claims that the birth of water and the Spirit in v. 5 is grounded in Ezek 36:25–27 and the picture of wind and the Spirit in v. 8 alludes to Ezek 37.

On the other hand, it has been argued that Yahweh's two-step resurrection of the dry bones in the valley in Ezek 37:1–14 is also an allusion to God's two-step creation of human beings in Gen 2:7.[770] So, the resurrection motif in that passage of Ezekiel was described as the picture of the new creation built upon Gen 2:7. This close relationship between Gen 2:7 and Ezek 37:1–14 could have something to do with the argument that the birth image in John 3:6 is based on the creation idea in Gen 2:7. Thus, Brown's claim[771] that

---

[766] Barrett, *John*, 211; Milne, *John*, 76; Schnackenburg, *John*, I, 374; Whitacre, *John*, 88–89; Brown, *John I-XII*, 141; Lee, *Narratives*, 46; Carson, *John*, 197.
[767] Bruce, *John*, 84–85; Carson, *John*, 197; Whitacre, *John*, 88–89; Bennema, *Power*, 171 n. 40. Cf. Hodges, 'Water,' 217–218.
[768] Block, 'Prophet,' 39.
[769] Carson, *John*, 197.
[770] Lee, *Narratives*, 46; Brown, *John I-XII*, 140.
[771] Brown, *John I-XII*, 140; Lee, *Narratives*, 46. In particular, H. Griffith, 'Eschatology,' 387–396, esp. 391–392, who observes the importance of the creation motif in the light of eschatology in

the background of the concepts about life and Spirit (breath, wind) is the creation of human beings in Gen 2:7 cannot be lightly dismissed. In particular this picture of resurrection by the vivifying power of the Holy Spirit in Ezek 37:1–14 is distinctively echoed in John 20:19–23 (esp. v. 22), in which, after Easter, Jesus appeared to the disciples and then breathed the Spirit into them. This narrative is distinctively recorded only in John's Gospel.[772] Thus, that Ezek 37:1–14 is reflected in John 20:19–23 further supports the argument that the mystery of the birth by the Spirit in John 3:8 alludes to Ezekiel's vision of resurrection in Ezek 37:1–14. Thereby the contention must be that the new birth by water and the Spirit in John 3:5 is originally based on Ezek 36:25–27.[773]

To sum up, the birth from above in John 3:3 is based on the OT and further presented in John 3:5, 6, 8. The birth of water and the Spirit in John 3:5 alludes to Ezek 36:25–27 (cf. Isa 44:3–5). The comparison between physical birth and spiritual birth in John 3:6 alludes to creation in Gen 2:7 and the mystery of the birth by the Spirit in John 3:8 to the resurrection vision in Ezek 37:1–14, also echoed creation in Gen 2:7. Jesus's teaching about the new birth can be understood as the proclamation of the coming of the long-waited restoration, that is, the new exodus, anticipated by the Prophets in the OT.[774] What is more, in connection with the new creation as the prerequisite for entry into the kingdom of God in John 3:5, the OT and Jewish backgrounds of both 'entering' and 'the kingdom of God' could support the presence of the new exodus motif. Before discussing 'entering the kingdom of God,' we will concentrate on the identity of 'water' in John 3:5.

5.2.2 Water and the Spirit (Cf. John 3:5)

Much discussion[775] has concentrated on the identity of 'water' in John 3:5. Questions that have been addressed include: What does 'water' point to?

---

the NT and lists 'God's acts of redemption' as 're-enactments of creation' or as 'a restoration of all things.'

[772] See 4.6. Johannine Resurrection Narratives (John 20:19–23; 11:1–44. Cf. John 5:16–30).

[773] Carson, *John*, 197–198; Bruce, *John*, 84–85; Robinson, 'Born,' 17; Whitacre, *John*, 88–89; Robertson, 'New-Covenant,' 134.

[774] Cf. Brown, *John I-XII*, 140; Milne, *John*, 76; Burge, *John*, 116; Cotterell, 'Nicodemus,' 241; Belleville, 'Born,' 138–139; Carson, *John*, 195–198; Bruce, *John*, 84–85; Dennis, *Gathering*, 292–293.

[775] Belleville, 'Born,' 125–141 discusses this issue in detail. See also Carson, *John*, 191–196; Morris, *John*, 190–194; R. Fowler, 'Born,' 159; D. G. Spriggs, 'Meaning,' 149–150; Schneiders, 'Born,' 189–196; M. Pamment, 'John 3:5,' 189–190; Witherington, *Wisdom*, 97; idem., 'Waters,' 155–160; Lee, *Narratives*, 52–53; Robinson, 'Born,' 15–23; Barrett, *John*, 208–210; Beasley-Murray, *John*, 48–49; idem., 'John 3:3, 5,' 167–170; Burge, *Anointed*, 159–176; Ng, *Symbolism*, 70–75; Koester, *Symbolism*, 163–167; Hodges, 'Water,' 206–220.

What is the relationship of water and the Spirit regarding the new birth? Are both water and the Spirit two different substances or just one and the same substance? Could the birth of water and the Spirit point to two births? If not, is 'water' just a metaphor for the Spirit or the work by the Spirit?' If the word 'water' simply points to the Spirit or to the work of the Spirit, then is the use of the word 'water' redundant?

Firstly, some commentators[776] argue that water in v.5 stands for the natural birth, the physical birth, which is contrasted with the spiritual birth by the Holy Spirit. They assume that the contrast between water and the Spirit in v. 5 parallels the contrast between birth to flesh by flesh and birth to spirit by the Spirit in v. 6, and thus that water is related to birth to flesh by flesh, and the Spirit to birth to spirit by the Spirit. Their arguments can be divided into two groups. Some[777] connect water to the amniotic fluid of women and the others[778] relate water to male semen.

Secondly, some Johannine theologians [779] argue that the term denotes baptism by water. Some references to baptism or ritual washing in John 3 itself (cf. John 3:22–26) and its wider literary context (cf. John 1: 26, 33; 2:1–11; 4:1–2) have been proposed to support this argument. This argument is supported by the contrast between water-baptism by John the Baptist and Spirit-baptism by the Messiah, the man on whom the Spirit came down and remained, in John 1:26, 33.[780] Some[781] argue that water in John 3:5 means Christian baptism which denotes the prerequisite to make public entry into the Christian community in the early church period.

---

[776] Odeberg, *Fourth Gospel*, 63; Fowler, 'Born,' 159; Spriggs, 'Meaning,' 149–150; Schneiders, 'Born,' 192; Pamment, 'John 3:5,' 189–190; Witherington, *Wisdom*, 97; idem., 'Waters,' 155–160; Lee, *Narratives*, 45–47, 52; Davies, *Rhetoric*, 141–142; Morris, *John*, 192–193. Cf. Robinson, 'Born,' 20–21.

[777] Witherington, *Wisdom*, 97; idem., 'Waters,' 155–158; Spriggs, 'Meaning,' 150; Fowler, 'Born,' 159; Schneiders, 'Born,' 192; Pamment, 'John 3:5,' 189–190; Davies, *Rhetoric*, 141–142; Lee, *Narratives*, 52.

[778] Barrett, *John*, 209; Odeberg, *Fourth Gospel*, 48–71, esp. 50, 63; Strachan, *Fourth Gospel*, 134–135; Morris, *John*, 192–193.

[779] Haenchen, *John*, I, 200; Bernard, *John*, I, 104–105; Kim, *Exposition*, 77; Bruce, *John*, 84–85; Polhill, 'John 1–4,' 452–453; Burge, *John*, 115–116; idem., *Anointed*, 162–164; Moloney, *John*, 92–93, 98–99; Beasley-Murray, *Life*, 65–66, 94–95; idem., *John*, 49; idem., 'John 3.3, 5,' 168–169; Barrett, *John*, 209; Brown, *John I-XII*, 141–144; Schnackenburg, *John*, I, 369f; Lightfoot, *John's*, 116; Lindars, *John*, 152; Dunn, *Baptism*, 183–194; Koester, *Symbolism*, 163–166; Osburn, 'Exegetical,' 134–135; Brodie, *John*, 97; Smith, *John*, 95; Michaels, *John*, 56–57; Ng, *Symbolism*, 74–75; Goppelt, *TDNT*, VIII, 330; J. N. Sanders, *John*, 124; France, 'Baptist,' 102, 108–109; Hoskyns, *Fourth Gospel*, I, 230–231.

[780] Moloney, *John*, 92; Barrett, *John*, 208–209; Fallon, *John*, 97.

[781] Michaels, *John*, 57; Moloney, *John*, 93, 98–99; Westcott, *John*, I, 48–50; Koester, *Symbolism*, 165; Dodd, *Interpretation*, 309; C. H. Cosgrove, 'Place,' 522–539, esp. 530–534; France, 'Baptist,' 99–100, 107, 109.

Thirdly, some commentators[782] hold that water means the Spirit itself and quickening power or spiritual cleansing by the Spirit. Köstenberger[783] argues that 'a new heart' or 'a new spirit' was mentioned with a reality of cleansing from all impurities by sprinkling with clean water in Ezek 36:25–27 (this provides the background to the new birth in John 3). He further claims that to be born by water and the Spirit refers to, 'spiritual rebirth, metaphorically expressed by the analogy of washing with clean water.' On the other hand, Dunn[784] relates water with the life-giving operation of the Spirit in that the OT adopts the image of water to symbolize the work of God who gives human beings life. Likewise, the Johannine Jesus also uses water as a crucial image of the quickening power of the Spirit (cf. 4:14; 7:38).

As the majority of the Johannine commentators[785] recognize, and as I have argued above,[786] if the birth of water and Spirit in John 3:5 originated from Ezek 36:25–27, then the identity of water can also be understood with reference to the text of Ezekiel. As argued earlier, the picture of Yahweh's purification of Israel from all her impurities and idols by sprinkling clean water upon her in Ezek 36:25 was related to ritual cleansing. This cleansing was attained with water and blood sprinklings which were accepted in regards to atonement and covenant in the OT. Therefore, water in John 3:5 points not only to ritual cleansing with water but to blood sprinklings regarding atonement and covenant.

Watts[787] observes that, alluding to Israel's passing through the Red Sea in exodus, Isa 63 shows the descent/placement (καταβαίνω/שׁים) of the Holy Spirit (τὸ πνεῦμα/רוּחַ) with 'the coming up out of water imagery' (cf. ἀναβαίνων ἐκ τοῦ ὕδατος) against the background of the expectation of the restoration (new exodus) of Israel from exile. Watts argues that the imagery of Isa 63 is reflected in Jesus's baptism and the Baptist's baptismal work (cf. a water baptism rite) and his testimony concerning the Coming One whose

---

[782] Köstenberger, *John*, 84; Blomberg, *Historical*, 93; Dunn, *Baptism*, 193–194; Carson, *John*, 194–195; Burge, *Anointed*, 162, 166–168; *idem.*, *John*, 116; Hodges, 'Water,' 213–215; Jones, *Symbol*, 74–75; Schnackenburg, *John*, I, 370; Turner, *Holy*, 67–69; Throckmorton, *Creation*, 111–112; Belleville, 'Born,' 135–141.

[783] Köstenberger, *John*, 84; Blomberg, *Historical*, 93; Burge, *Anointed*, 162; Belleville, 'Born,' 140, who says that 'It is reasonable to assume that in ὕδωρ we have a reference to the prophetic eschatological cleansing (Ezek 36:26–27) accomplished through God's Spirit (John 3:6) — the spiritual counterpart to the Levitical rites of purification.'

[784] Dunn, *Baptism*, 189, 191–92; Hodges, 'Water,' 214; Turner, *Holy*, 68–69; Burge, *Anointed*, 167; *idem.*, *John*, 116; Throckmorton, *Creation*, 111–112; Robinson, 'Born,' 19. Cf. Isa 55:1–3; Jer 2:13; 17:13; Zech 14:8; Ezek 47:9.

[785] See 5.2.1.2. The Old Testament and Jewish Background.

[786] See 5.2.1.2.1. The Birth of Water and the Spirit (v. 5).

[787] Watts, *Isaiah's*, 103–104.

baptism is in the Spirit. This is alluded to in 1 Cor 10:1–4, where Paul compares Christian baptism with (or to) Israel's passing through the sea.[788] This argument could be supported by Mark 10:38, 45, in which Jesus related 'a ransom' to 'baptism' (cf. the imagery of the passing through water), which alludes to Israel's deliverance from Egypt via her passing through the Red Sea (cf. Exod 14:21–15:21; Isa 43:2; Zech 10:11).[789] As many commentators argue that Ezek 36:25–28 is one of the OT references for the baptism work of the Baptist in John 1:25–33 and the birth of water and Spirit in John 3:1–8, water in John 3:5 is related to cleansing/purification.

On the other hand, France[790] points out the importance of ritual washing in the OT and the Second Temple Judaism (cf. the Jewish proselytic baptism, the Baptist's community) as an initiatory water baptism to enter its community (or re-entering in the case of Qumran): 'to symbolize not only, or even primarily, the determination of the individual to lead a new life, but rather the entry into a new community. Its significance was essentially ecclesial.' Thus, as Polhill[791] recognizes, even though the argument that water refers to baptism is in danger of being developed into sacramentalism, baptism is the most probable interpretation of water. This is based upon the context in John 3–4 and the Baptist's baptismal work and his anticipation of the Coming One whose baptism in the Holy Spirit is predicted in John 1:25–33.

Hence, if the Christian baptism is excluded on account of a chronological question (cf. Matt 28:19), the most probable water rite against this background is the Baptist's water baptism.[792] Westcott[793] says that Nicodemus, a Pharisee, who questioned both the identity of John the Baptist and his reasons for performing water-baptism, would have rejected John's water baptism which was definitely sensational in Palestine at that time. Furthermore, Jesus's mention of water would have reminded

---

[788] R. Schneck, *Isaiah*, 45; Jeremias, *Theology*, I, 44; idem., *Infant*, 31–32. Cf. b. Ker. 9a; b. Yeb. 46b; Str-B, I, 85.
[789] Pitre, *Tribulation*, 412.
[790] France, 'Baptist,' 98–100, quoted from 99.
[791] Polhill, 'John 1–4,' 452.
[792] Dennis, *Gathering*, 289; Hoskyns, *Fourth Gospel*, I, 230–231; Westcott, *John*, I, 108–109; Dunn, *Baptism*, 190; Burge, *Anointed*, 163–164; idem., *John*, 116; Osburn, 'Exegetical,' 134–135; Barrett, *John*, 209; Beasley-Murray, *John*, 49; idem., 'John 3:3, 5,' 168–169.
[793] Westcott, *John*, I, 108–109; Dunn, *Baptism*, 190; Burge, *Anointed*, 163–164; idem., *John*, 116; Osburn, 'Exegetical,' 134–135; Barrett, *John*, 209; Beasley-Murray, *John*, 49; idem., 'John 3:3, 5,' 168–169; Hoskyns, *Fourth Gospel*, I, 230–231; Dennis, *Gathering*, 289 n. 213; Holland also points it out through an oral communication with this writer. Contra Turner, *Holy*, 69; Morris, *John*, 191; Carson, *John*, 193; Hodges, 'Water,' 208–209; Belleville, 'Born,' 127, who says that 'Nor does baptism fit into the overall theme in chap. 3 of spiritual birth, for it can hardly be classified as a spiritual source (ἐξ) that can effect a second birth (γεννηθῇ ἄνωθεν).'

Nicodemus of John's water baptism. Nonetheless, the birth of the Spirit, namely, the Spirit baptism is mainly emphasized in the birth of water and Spirit in John 3:5, 'the birth from above' in John 3:3 (cf. John 3:7).

5.2.3 'Entering' 'the Kingdom of God' (εἰσελθεῖν εἰς τὴν βασιλείαν τοῦ θεοῦ)[794]

Jesus talks about the requirement of new birth, the birth from above, to see the kingdom of God (John 3:3). He then proceeds to help Nicodemus understand it more clearly, explaining again about birth by water and the Spirit in order to enter the kingdom of God (John 3:5).[795] Here, the phrase 'entering' 'the kingdom of God,' or seeing the kingdom of God reflects the new exodus motif.

The phrase, 'the kingdom of God' is not as common in John's Gospel as in the Synoptic Gospels; only occurring twice in Jesus's conversation with Nicodemus. The phrase then disappears, leading some to consider that the concept of 'the kingdom of God' is not a major theme in John's Gospel. Instead, John's Gospel frequently adopts another phrase, 'eternal life' (or simply 'life'), and some commentators[796] claim that the phrase replaces 'the kingdom of God' in John.

However, in spite of its rarity, the phrase, 'the kingdom of God' and its associated concepts can be found throughout the Gospel.[797] For example, in John 1:49–50, Jesus did not reject Nathanael's confession of his being the Son of God and the King of Israel in the light of Yahweh's covenant to

---

[794] While important, space will not allow for a detailed study of the kingdom of God, see, I. H. Marshall, 'Hope,' 5–15, whose assessment of the state of studies of this subject up to the present day seems to be generally accepted. See also H. Ridderbos, *Kingdom*; Beasley-Murray, *Jesus*; Jeremias, *Theology*, I, 31–35, 96–108; H. Kleinknecht, G. von Rad, K. G. Kuhn, and K. L. Schmidt, *TDNT*, I, 564–593; B. Klappert, *NIDNTT*, II, 372–390; Goppelt, *Theology*, I, 43–76.

[795] Cf. Brown, *John I-XII*, 130 understands that 'seen' in v. 3, which means 'experience' or 'encounter' or 'participate in,' seems to be adopted to express the relationship between the revelation and the kingdom of God appropriately, both of which are mentioned by Jesus. 'See' in v. 3 is parallel to 'enter' in v. 5. That is, seeing the kingdom of God is the same as entering the kingdom of God. See also Bruce, *John*, 84; Bernard, *John*, I, 103; Morris, *John*, 189; Schnackenburg, *John*, I, 367. However, Trumbower, *Born*, 74–75, thinks that 'see and enter' do not have the same meaning but show different levels; seeing the kingdom of God and then entering the kingdom of God.

[796] J. W. Roberts, 'Observations,' 187–188; J. C. Davis, 'Johannine,' 161–169; Schnackenburg, *John*, I, 367; Milne, *John*, 73; Morris, *John*, 190; Beasley-Murray, *Life*, 2–5, 13; *idem.*, *John*, 48; *idem.*, 'John 3:3, 5,' 168; Goppelt, *Theology*, I, 45; Klappert, *NIDNTT*, II, 387–388; Bruce, *John*, 82–83; Lee, *Narratives*, 45; Barrett, *John*, 215.

[797] Hengel, *Christology*, 333–357 argues that Jesus's kingship like 'a red thread' is a key theme in the Johannine passion narrative. Cf. John 18:33, 37a, 37b, 39; 19:3, 12, 14, 15b, 15c, 19, 21a, 21b and 'the kingdom of Christ' three times (John 18:36abc). Meeks, *Prophet-King*, 19–20.

David in 2 Sam 7:11–17 and 1 Chron 17:10–15.[798] In John 6:1–15, after the crowd had seen the miraculous sign when Jesus fed them with five small barley loaves and two small fish, they intended to make him their king by force.

In John 12:12–19, the crowd of disicples who had seen Jesus raise Lazarus from the dead, and perhaps others coming for the Passover Feast who had heard about this miraculous sign, took palm branches and went out to meet him as he entered Jerusalem. Their words, 'Hosanna! Blessed is he who comes in the name of the Lord! Blessed is the King of Israel!' praised Jesus as the King of Israel.[799] Further, it must not be overlooked that Jesus had found a young donkey to ride, and the writer of John's Gospel says that this action was the fulfilment of the prophecy of Zec 9:9: 'Do not be afraid, O Daughter of Zion; see, your king is coming, seated on a donkey's colt.'

In John 18:33–37, Jesus's kingdom and his kingship are mentioned several times. In John 18:37, when Jesus was questioned before Pilate if he was the king of Jews, he clearly answered in the affirmative. In John 19:19–22, this title was written by Pilate and fastened to the cross of Jesus. Astonishingly, in John 18:36, Jesus mentioned 'my kingdom' (ἡ βασιλεία ἡ ἐμή) three times. In fact, in John 18–19, the main charge brought against Jesus at his trial in front of Pilate was concerned with his kingship.[800]

Therefore, the concept of the kingdom of Jesus (or God) can be found in the Gospel of John, although phrases such as kingdom or the kingdom of God are rare. Some questions could be considered in regard to entering the kingdom of God, but we shall concentrate only on those questions pertinent to the new exodus motif of this study.

5.2.3.1. The Kingdom of God (or Heaven in Matthew) and the new exodus

Jesus's reference to the kingdom of God can be understood against the background of the new exodus motif. In the Synoptic Gospels, in which the term 'the kingdom of God' appears very frequently, its inauguration was

---

[798] For this, see 2.4. Disciples' Testimonies and Jesus's Promise (John 1:35–51). Some scholars (e.g., Beasley-Murray, *John*, 118–119; Barrett, *John*, 330; Brown, *John I-XII*, 329–330; Schnackenburg, *John*, II, 158; Hoskyns, *Fourth Gospel*, I, 324) argue for the Davidic kingship of Jesus in John. Cf. Brunson, *Psalm 118*, 223–239, esp. 225–227, who argues for the kingship of Jesus, in light of the Isaianic Yahweh rather than the Davidic King, in John's Gospel. Also, some theologians (e.g., Meeks, *Prophet-King*, 17, 20f, 29; Anderson, *Christology*, 229–230) reject Jesus's Davidic kingship and argue for the Mosaic prophetic kingship of the Johannine Jesus. However, Meeks' argument is criticized by Brunson, *ibid.*, 229–231.

[799] Hengel, *Christology*, 336. Cf. Brunson, *Psalm 118*, 225–227 thinks that Jesus is the embodiment of Isaianic Yahweh; the Kingship of Yahweh.

[800] Hengel, *Christology*, 335, 350–351 argues that the kingdom of Christ is no different from the kingdom of God.

proclaimed by John the Baptist in the Desert of Judea (cf. Matt 3:1–3) as well as by Jesus himself from the beginning of his public ministry onwards (cf. Matt 4:17; Mark 1:15).[801] Jeremias rightly claims that the kingdom of God was 'the central theme of the public proclamation of Jesus.'[802]

Scholars[803] generally contend that the idea of the kingdom of God in the New Testament originates from the OT and Jewish Apocalyptic literature rather than from any other source. According to Kim,[804] in the OT, a standardized form of the expression of 'the kingdom of God (or heaven)' does not appear (cf. 1 Chron 28:5– 'the kingdom of the Lord over Israel') and also the references to the kingdom over which Yahweh directly reigns (or is reigning) appear only a handful of times.[805] Nevertheless, Kim argues that Yahweh was described as king about 40 times in the OT and the notion that Yahweh as king or ruler governs over heaven and earth, especially over Israel, his covenant people, is one of the main themes in the OT. In connection with this, the concept that Yahweh is to become king (or that Yahweh is reigning dynamically), often appears in the enthronement Psalms (47:8; 93:1; 96:10; 97:1; 99:1; 145:11–13).[806] In particular, the idea of Yahweh's reign over Israel is substantiated in that when David's descendants were enthroned as kings, they were proclaimed as the sons of Yahweh on the basis of his covenant to David (cf. 2 Sam 7:12–16; 1 Chron 17:7–15. cf. Pss 2; 89; Isa 9; 11).[807]

Beasley-Murray[808] in particular understands theophany, the day of the Lord, and the coming of God in Dan 7 in the OT, as the background to the idea of the kingdom of God in the NT. Beasley-Murray[809] thinks that the concept of the theophany in Israel basically originated from the appearance of Yahweh on Sinai at the exodus (Exod 19:20; Judges 5:4–5; Ps 6:7–8, 17;

---

[801] Goppelt, *Theology*, I, 44, who says that 'He (Matthew) intended thereby to emphasize that which they have in common; the difference he suggested by adding quotations from scripture (3:3; 4:15f). Historically, the preaching of the Baptist was oriented toward the 'coming One,' while the preaching of Jesus was oriented toward the coming of God, i.e., his lordship.'
[802] Jeremias, *Theology*, I, 96, 31. Also, C. C. Caragounis, 'Kingdom,' 424–425; G. R. Beasley-Murray, 'Kingdom,' 20; S. Kim, 'Proclamation,' 41; Ridderbos, *Kingdom*, 3.
[803] Beasley-Murray, *Jesus*, 3–68; Caragounis, 'Kingdom,' 420–430; Kim, 'Proclamation,' 42–46; Goppelt, *Theology*, I, 43–51; Jeremias, *Theology*, I, 32.
[804] Kim, 'Proclamation,' 42–43; Beasley-Murray, *Jesus*, 17; *idem.*, 'Kingdom,' 19; Goppelt, *Theology*, I, 45–46; Jeremias, *Theology*, I, 32, 96.
[805] cf. 1 Chron 17:14; 29:11; Pss 45:6; 47:8; 93:1; 96:10; 97:1; 99:1; 103:19; 145:11, 12, 13; Dan 2:44; 4:3, 34; Job 21.
[806] Klappert, *NIDNTT*, II, 375.
[807] Kim, 'Proclamation,' 42–43; Aalen, 'Reign,' 233–234; Klappert, *NIDNTT*, II, 376.
[808] Beasley-Murray, *Jesus*, 3–35.
[809] Beasley-Murray, *Jesus*, 6.

Deut 33:2). Beasley-Murray[810] also claims that the idea of the overthrow of the enemies of the Lord on the day of the Lord came from Israel's early historical experiences, when the nation entered the promised land and conquered its inhabitants under the Lord's leadership. Thus, Beasley-Murray says:

> The exodus event and its aftermath were of critical significance for Israel's understanding. It was precisely in connection with a series of divine interventions- the deliverance of the tribes from Egypt, their experience of theophany and the covenant with Yahweh at Sinai, and their subsequent entrance into the promised land- that the revelation of the Name was given to Moses in the desert, and through Moses to the people (cf. Exod 3:14 with 6:6–7).[811]

Marshall also argues: 'The OT had prophesied the hope of God's future action as king, and it expressed its hope on the basis of the mighty acts of God which had already been experienced especially at the exodus.'[812] That is to say, the idea of the kingdom of God in the NT originates from theophany and the day of the Lord, which are based on the mighty works of God, experienced in the historical exodus event and its aftermath.

Further, Beasley-Murray[813] argues that the greatest hope of the coming of the kingdom of God in the future is reflected not only in early pre-prophetic passages but also in the references to kingdom and Messiah of the Prophets. This is especially found in Isa 40–55 which proclaimed Yahweh's consolidation of Israel, and Dan 2 and 7 which testified to Yahweh's coming to establish his sovereignty of salvation. In the interpretation of Nebuchadnezzar's dream, Daniel announced that the God of heaven will set up in those days another kingdom over the world that will remain forever Dan 2:44. In the visionary image of Dan 7:13f, this world kingdom will be transferred to 'one like a son of man' or to the saints, the people of the Most High in the interpretative references in Dan 7:27. The Danielic Son of Man figure is ontologically the Son of God (cf. the Ancient of Days, the Most High), since he came with the clouds, was enthroned on one of the divine thrones, was given authority, glory and sovereign power from the Ancient of Days (God), and was worshipped by all peoples, nations and men of every language.

---

[810] Beasley-Murray, *Jesus*, 11–12.
[811] Beasley-Murray, *Jesus*, 18.
[812] Marshall, 'Hope,' 12.
[813] Beasley-Murray, *Jesus*, 17–35. cf. Gen 49:9ff; Num 24:3ff, 17ff; Deut 33:13ff; Isa 2:1ff; 4:1ff; 9:1ff; 11:1ff; 30:15ff; 32:1ff; Jer 23:5ff; 24:5ff, 30–31, 32, 37ff; Ezek 30:15ff; 32:1ff; 40–48. Also, Ridderbos, *Kingdom*, 5–7; Goppelt, *Theology*, I, 45–48; Carson, *John*, 188; Burge, *John*, 114; Klappert, *NIDNTT*, II, 375.

Also, the Danielic Son of Man is functionally the firstborn/Son of God, since he is symbolically the inclusive representative of the saints (sons) of the Most High. His enthronement symbolizes the enthronement of the saints of the Most High God, the Ancient of Days, which means the restoration of the saints (Israel) from the trampling and the crushing of the gentile kingdoms (Dan 7:15–28). Thus, in Dan 7, the kingdom of God, namely, the kingdom of the Danielic Son of Man is the kingdom of the saints of the Most High, which will be established by the restoration of Israel from exile. This kingdom is one that will never be destroyed.

As Beasley-Murray says, above all, the Prophet Isaiah has to be considered against the OT background of the concept of the kingdom of God. The absolute 'hymnic' naming of Yahweh as king appears in Isaiah's vision of the heavenly assembly in Isa 6:5, 'My eyes have seen the King, the Lord Almighty.' And, in Isa 9:1–7; 11:1–16 (cf. Isa 55:3), the Prophet Isaiah announced that, on the basis of Yahweh's covenant with David, Davidic descendants (a shoot/branch/root) of Jesse (the new David) will reign on the throne and over the everlasting kingdom of Yahweh.[814] Here, the Davidic descendants' reigning over Yahweh's everlasting kingdom was proclaimed against the background of the restoration of the exiled Israel. In particular, it is worth noting that John the Evangelist's testimony in John 12:40–41 that Isaiah saw Jesus's glory and spoke about him quoting Isa 6:10 in connection with the Jews' unbelief of Jesus, seems to allude to Isaiah's vision in Isa 6 of a heavenly assembly in the Temple. The Evangelist applied the kingship of the Isaianic Yahweh (Isa 6) to Jesus.

Furthermore, it should be noted that an Isaianic herald brings to the city of Jerusalem the message (or 'good tidings,' that is, 'the gospel') that 'Your God reigns' against the background of Yahweh's return to comfort (or restore) his people and to redeem Jerusalem in Isa 52:7–10 (cf. 40:9–11; 61:1–11). In particular, Mark proclaims 'the beginning of the gospel about Jesus Christ, the Son of God,' as the fulfilment of the Isa 40:3 (cf. Exod 23:20; Mal 3:1)[815] in the work of John the Baptist. This fulfilment is seen as he prepared the way for the Lord by baptising in the desert and preaching a baptism of repentance for the forgiveness of sins (Mark 1:1–4) and the coming of the

---

[814] Carson, *John*, 188; Burge, *John*, 114; Ridderbos, *Kingdom*, 5–6; Klappert, *NIDNTT*, II, 376.

[815] Generally speaking, it is accepted that Mark 1:2b-3 is a conflated citation from Exod 23:20, Mal 3:1 and Isa 40:3. Cranfield, *Mark*, 39, argues that the former part of v. 2b agrees with Exod 23:20 in the LXX, and the latter part of it with the MT of Mal 3:1, and v. 3 almost agrees with the LXX of Isa 40:3 except one variation from 'for our Lord' to 'him.' This is supported by Snodgrass, 'Stream,' 34, who says that 'there is evidence that Exod 23:20 and Mal 3:1 were connected in Judaism, such as Exod R. 32:9 and Dt R. 11:9.' Also, see Watts, *Isaiah's*, 61–90; Guelich, *Mark 1–8*, 8–12.

kingdom of God (Matt 3:1–3). All four Gospels (cf. John 1:23; Mark 1:2–4; Matt 3:1–3; Luke 3:4–6) say that Isa 40:3 is fulfilled by the Baptist's baptism work, preparing for the coming of Jesus who is the Isaianic Yahweh.[816]

Mark 1:14–15, introduces Jesus's proclamation of the coming of the kingdom of God as the proclamation of the good news of God.[817] That is to say, the inauguration of the kingdom of God *is* the good news of God. Beasley-Murray[818] argues that the good news in Mark 1:14–15 alludes to the coming of God for the redemption (deliverance) of his people in Isa 40:9 and 52:7. In Isa 40:9, the good tidings which the herald brings to Zion (Jerusalem) is a message regarding the coming of the reign of Yahweh. Mark 1:14–15, in which the good news alludes to Isa 40:9 and 52:7, is one of the most important NT references for understanding the concept of 'the coming of the kingdom of God' against the background of the new exodus motif.[819]

Also, Isa 61:1–2, in which the good news reflected the year of Jubilee in Lev 25, was quoted by Jesus himself as the fulfilment of one of Yahweh's promises regarding the restoration of Israel at the beginning of his public ministry in the Gospel of Luke (4:16–21). Accordingly, Klappert's allusion is correct:

> Put in context of announcing the new exodus, a herald now brings to the city of Jerusalem the message: 'Your God reigns' (Isa 52:7). The enthronement-Psalms do not primarily announce an eschatological event, but a present reality experienced in the cultic ceremony. The proclamation of the reign of Yahweh as an eschatological event is now associated with the historical act of the new exodus. It is not nature and the cycle of the seasons (as in

---

[816] Cf. Brunson, *Psalm 118*, argues that the Johannine Jesus is the embodiment (or presence) of the Isaianic Yahweh.

[817] Watts, *Isaiah's*, 99–100, argues that 'The parallel construction of the two adverbial participles (κηρύσσων ... καὶ λέγων) suggests that the second clause: πεπλήρωται ὁ καιρὸς καὶ ἤγγικεν ἡ βασιλεία τοῦ θεοῦ is epexegetical of the first" τὸ εὐαγγέλιον τοῦ θεοῦ.

[818] Beasley-Murray, 'Kingdom,' 20; U. Becker, *NIDNTT*, II, 107–115, esp. 108–109; G. Friedrich, *TDNT*, II, 707–737, esp. 708–709; Watts, *Isaiah's*, 96–101; Guelich, *Mark 1–8*, 12–14; Goppelt, *Theology*, I, 62–63. Cf. *Ps. Sol.* 11:1; *1QH* 18:14; *11QMelch.* 15–14; *Tg. Jer* 4:15; *Tg. Ezek* 21:12; *Tg. Isa* 53:1.

[819] Watts, *Isaiah's*, 96–101, esp. 98–99. See also Goppelt, *Theology*, I, 47. On the other hand, astonishingly, the Johannine writings (gospel and epistles) adopt neither the verb nor the noun. Concerning this, Becker, *NIDNTT*, II, 110 and Friedrich, *TDNT*, II, 717 argue that this could be explained by the distinctive theology of John, so-called present eschatology, and this concept is expressed by terms like μαρτυρέω, to witness, and μαρτυρία, witness.

Babylonia), but the historical actions of Yahweh which form the basis of his 'enthronement.'[820]

The good tidings proclaimed by an Isaianic herald, is the message that Yahweh reigns; that is, the kingdom of God is coming, and this points to the return of Yahweh to Zion. This will allow for the consolation of the exiled Israel and for the redemption of the ruined Jerusalem. In other words, in these references in Isaiah, the kingdom of God, or the reign of God was announced against the background of the restoration or the new exodus of Israel.

In Jewish literature, as in the OT, even though the idea of God's kingdom or God's kingly reign occurs quite often the phrase, the kingdom (of God) is only rarely found. On the whole, the term kingdom is used in combination with the possessive pronoun (such as 'your' or 'his') linking it to God. However, the standard form of the kingdom of God can only be found in *Wis.* 10:10. Beasley-Murray [821] points out that, in Jewish apocalyptic literature, the expectation of the visitation of God is reflected in Jewish thinking such as theophany, 'the day of the Lord,' 'on that day,' or 'at that time.' The two ages, this age and the age to come, are intimately connected with the establishment of the kingdom of God over the world. This visitation is presented as accompanying God's judgment against evil in Israel and the nations. For example, in a prayer of *Tob.* 13, [822] Tobit mentioned God's (his) kingdom (v. 1), and extolled God as the everlasting (or great) king (vv. 6, 9, 15) and 'the king of heaven' (vv. 7, 11) in connection with the restoration of Israel scattered among the gentiles.

In the Dead Sea Scrolls, in spite of the non-existence of a fixed form of the kingdom of God or heaven, God was often described as king and his kingdom was sometimes mentioned as well.[823] So, these documents testify that the kingdom of God (and its coming) was probably a key theme of the Qumran sect. In particular, regarding the kingdom of God, the good tidings, and the new exodus in the light of the year of Jubilee of Lev 25:13, like Isa 61 (cf. Luke 4:18–19), *11QMelch.* is an important text:

> This is the day of [Peace/Salvation] concerning which [God] spoke [through Isa]iah the prophet, who said, [How] beautiful upon the mountains are the feet of the messenger who proclaims peace, who brings <u>good news</u>, who proclaims salvation, who says to Zion:

---

[820] Klappert, *NIDNTT*, II, 375.
[821] Beasley-Murray, *Jesus*, 39–51; Kim, 'Proclamation,' 43–46.
[822] Jeremias, *Theology*, I, 32 n. 2.
[823] Cf. *4QShirShab*; *Masada ShirShab*; *11QShirShab*; *1QM* 6:6; 12:7; *1QSb* 4:25f; *11QMelch.* 15–24. Kim, 'Proclamation,' 43 n. 3; Jeremias, *Theology*, I, 32 n. 8; Goppelt, *Theology*, I, 50.

> Your Elohim [reigns] (Isa 52:7). Its interpretation; the mountains are the prophets ... and the messenger is the Anointed one of the spirit, concerning whom Dan[iel] said, [Until an anointed one, a prince (Dan 9:25)] ... [And he who brings] good [news], who proclaims [salvation]: it is concerning him that it is written... [To comfort all who mourn, to grant to those who mourn in Zion] (Isa 61:2–3). To comfort [those who mourn: its interpretation], to make them understand all the ages of t[ime].... In truth ... will turn away from Belial ... by the judgement[s] of God, as it is written concerning him, [who says to Zion]; your Elohim reigns, Zion is..., those who uphold the Covenant, who turn from walking [in] the way of the people.(vv. 15–25)

Here, God's kingly reign—the kingdom of God—is mentioned twice. The central message of the messenger who proclaims peace, brings good news, proclaims salvation to Zion is none other than God's kingly reign (cf. Isa 52:7). The peace and salvation which God promised through Isaiah were related to the restoration of Israel which had been exiled in Babylon. Above all, the herald who proclaims good news ('your God reigns') in Isa 52:7 is identified with 'the one anointed with the Spirit' in Isa 61:1–3 and with 'an anointed one, a prince' in Dan 9:25. Accordingly, 11QMelch. also shows that the good news, 'the kingdom of God,' which the messenger brought to Zion, was proclaimed against the background of Yahweh's return for the restoration of Israel.

Also, although there is no reference to 'the kingdom of God,' *Ps. Sol.* 11 shows that good news announced in Jerusalem involved God's mercy to the dispersed Israel and God's gathering the children of Israel from the east, the west and the north. And then, regarding the idea of 'God's kingly rule' (or kingdom) in connection with the Davidic king, the Messiah, *Ps. Sol.* 17 is another important text. In this reference, the idea of the kingdom of our God lasting forever is mentioned (v.3. cf. *Ps. Sol.* 5:18, 19). Further, the establishment of the eschatological kingdom is mentioned in *Sib. Or.* 3:766 (cf. *Sib. Or.* 3:47; *Ass. Mos.* 10:1ff).[824] In particular, the paradise described in *Sib. Or.* 3:788–794 could allude to Isa 11:6–8 which is followed by Yahweh's promise of the Davidic king, the Root of Jesse and, through him, the restoration of exiled Israel in Isa 11:10–16.

1 En. 84:2 says that, 'Your authority and kingdom abide forever and ever.' Furthermore, the eleventh petition of the *Eighteen Benedictions*, a Jewish collection of prayers uttered twice daily by pious Jews as early as Jesus's

---

[824] Jeremias, *Theology*, I, 32 n. 2; Goppelt, *Theology*, I, 48

time, is about the imminent and public establishment of God's kingdom in the world: 'Bring back our judges as before ... and be kind over us, you alone.'[825] Also, the *Kaddish* which was recited as the closing benediction at the end of the worship service in the synagogue in Jesus's time, expressed the enthusiastic Jewish expectation of the coming of the kingdom of God:

> Exalted and hallowed be his great name in the world which he created according to his will. May he let his kingdom rule in your lifetime and in your days and in the lifetime of the whole house of Israel, speedily and soon. Praised be his great name from eternity to eternity. And to this, say: Amen.[826]

Thus, Goppelt[827] claims that God's reign (or kingdom) is established with the restoration of the exiled Israel from among the gentile nations through the historical and cosmic demonstration of his mighty power.

Wis. 10:10 (cf. 6:4) which includes the standard phrase, 'the kingdom of God (βασιλείαν θεοῦ),' is a very important reference in connection with God's deliverance of the righteous from the nations who oppressed them; that is to say, the new exodus:

> When the righteous fled from his brother's wrath, she guided him in right paths, showed him *the kingdom of God* (ἔδειξεν αὐτῷ βασιλείαν θεοῦ), and gave him knowledge of holy things, made him rich in his travels, and multiplied the fruit of his labours... When the righteous was sold, she forsook him not, but delivered him from sin: she went down with him into the pit, and left him not in bonds, till she brought him *the sceptre of the kingdom*, and power against those that oppressed him: as for them that had accused him, she showed them to be liars, and gave him perpetual glory. She delivered the righteous people and blameless seed from the nation that oppressed them. (*Wis.* 10:10–15)

Here, vv. 10–12 seem to allude to Jacob's life (cf Gen 28–31) and vv. 13–14 to Joseph's life (cf. Gen 37; 39). Verse 10 reflects on Jacob's fleeing from his brother Esau, at which time he had a dream at Bethel recorded in Gen 28:10–17. The writer of the *Wisdom of Solomon* wrote that the wisdom showed the righteous (Jacob) *the kingdom of God*, instead of a stairway

---

[825] Goppelt, *Theology*, I, 49. cf. Str-B, IV, 210–223.
[826] Goppelt, *Theology*, I, 49, who argues that the Lord's prayer was influenced by the *Kaddish* and the *Eighteen Benedictions* (p. 50). See also Jeremias, *Theology*, I, 198; Ridderbos, *Kingdom*, 10; Kim, Proclamation,' 46. cf. Str-B, I, 418. Jeremias, *Theology*, I, 102, says that the term kingdom was sometimes used as a periphrasis for God as ruler in Judaism. e.g., *Tg. Isa* 24:23; 31:4; 40:9; 52:7; *Tg. Mic* 4:7; *Tg. Zech* 14:9; *Midr. Sam* 13:4 on I Sam 8:7.
[827] Goppelt, *Theology*, I, 49.

resting on the earth with its top reaching to heaven and on which the angels of God were ascending and descending. Verses 13–14 could reflect that Joseph was sold by his brothers in Gen 37, but that he was always accompanied by God in Egypt. The writer of the *Wisdom of Solomon* wrote that the wisdom did not forsake the righteous one (Joseph) who had been sold, but delivered him from sin, went down with him into the pit, and did not leave him in bonds, until she brought him the sceptre of the kingdom and power against those that oppressed him, and eventually gave him perpetual glory.

In particular, v. 14 ('till she brought him *the sceptre of kingdom and power* against those that oppressed him') alludes to Jacob's prophetic blessing to Judah in Gen 49:10, 'The sceptre will not depart from Judah, nor the ruler's staff from between his feet, until he comes to whom it belongs and the obedience of the nations is his.' Further, v. 15 says that the wisdom delivered the righteous people and blameless seed from the nation which oppressed them. From v. 16 on, through Moses, the servant of the Lord, into whose soul the wisdom entered, came deliverance of Israel from Egypt and their experiences in the wilderness are reflected in these verses.

In *Wis.* 10:10–15, close attention should be paid to both the righteous (Jacob) who fled from his brother's (Esau's) wrath and the righteous (Joseph) sold into slavery in Egypt. Both are symbolic representatives of Israel, the people of God oppressed by the nations. The kingdom of God was shown to the righteous, that is Israel, who were subjugated by the nations, and the sceptre of the kingdom and power would be given to them against their oppressors.

The references to the kingdom of God and the sceptre of the kingdom could express Israel's expectation that even though the Israelites, the righteous symbolized by the patriarchs, were oppressed by the nations at that time, they would again be delivered from the oppression of the nations. Their expectation that another eschatological deliverance for the Israelites would take place is reflected in the narratives regarding the deliverance of Israel from Egypt and their experiences in the wilderness from v. 16. If this understanding is right, the expectation regarding God's restoration of exiled Israel expressed in *Wis.* 10:10–15 is not too far from Jesus's promise in John 1:51[828] alluding to Jacob's dream in Gen 28, in which Jesus as the Son of Man is the new Israel, the symbolic representative who would bring about the restoration of Israel (Dan 7:13–28).

---

[828] For the detailed discussion of John 1:51, see 2.4.2. Allusion to Jacob's Vision and The Son of Man (John 1:51).

Accordingly, in Jewish literature, the concept of the kingdom of God can be understood in the light of the new exodus motif as well. Dennis says that '"kingdom of God" language is surely eschatological in nature and perhaps even "end of exile" language.'[829]

5.2.3.2 'Entering' (εἰσελθεῖν εἰς) and the New Exodus

We will now consider the term 'entering' (εἰσελθει/בוא) the kingdom of God in the sense of territory and community. Consideration will also be given to the argument from this viewpoint that will support the claim that entering the kingdom of God reflects the new exodus motif. The prevailing consensus[830] is that Jesus's proclamation of the kingdom of God refers, first and foremost, to God's sovereignty and secondly to his kingship to be established over the world. Jeremias further says that:

> Only in quite isolated instances in the Old Testament does *malkūt* denote a realm in the spatial sense, a territory; almost always it stands for the government, the authority, the power of a king. But this does not mean that *malkūt* is understood in an abstract way; it is always in process of being achieved. Thus the reign of God is neither a spatial nor a static concept; it is a *dynamic concept*.[831]

However, the argument for kingly reign was challenged by S. Aalen,[832] who presented a different viewpoint. According to Aalen,[833] one of the distinctive aspects of Jesus's proclamation of the kingdom of God is that he always named God not as King but as Father, and he taught his disciples to call God Father (ἀββᾶ ὁ πατήρ) (cf. Matt 6:9). This argument is supported by some references (cf. Rom 8:15; Gal 4:6). This is quite different from the idea of the kingdom of God in the OT and Judaism, in which God was mainly referred to as King and his kingship praised.[834]

---

[829] Dennis, *Gathering*, 285; Wright, *Victory*, 151; McKnight, *Vision*, 83. In particular, Beasley-Murray, *Jesus*, 275, argues that παλιγγενεσίᾳ in Matt 19:28 (cf. Luke 22:28, 30b) means 'restoration' or 'the new beginning'; the restoration of the people of the twelve tribes of Israel (cf. 1QS 4:25; *Mosis* 2.65; *Ant.* 11.66).

[830] Cf. Beasley-Murray, 'Kingdom,' 19; *idem., Life*, 2; C. L. Blomberg, 'Response,' 31; Jeremias, *Theology*, I, 98; Carson, *John*, 188; Turner, *Holy*, 69; Burge, *John*, 114; R. Bauckham, 'Kingdom,' 2; Klappert, *NIDNTT*, II, 376.

[831] Jeremias, *Theology*, I, 98.

[832] Aalen, 'Reign,' 215–240; G. E. Ladd, 'Kingdom,' 230–238; Marshall, 'Hope,' 9–12.

[833] Aalen, 'Reign,' 217–218; Marshall, 'Hope,' 9; Kim, 'Interpretation,' 231; Jeremias, *Theology*, I, 61–68, says that, 'The use of the everyday word ἀββᾶ as a form of address to God is the most important linguistic innovation on the part of Jesus' (p. 36). Cf. Luke 12:32; 22:29f (contrast Matt 19:28); Matt 13:43; 25:34.

[834] Cf. Jeremias, *Theology*, I, 66, says that '*we do not have a single example* of God being addressed as '*Abbā* in Judaism, but Jesus *always* addressed God in this way in his prayers. The only

Further, Aalen[835] proceeds to argue that the illustrations of the wedding feast and supper repeatedly adopted by Jesus to describe the kingdom of God are closely related to the idea of a room in the house and to that of the door:

> The kingdom of God is ... an idea with affinity to the local sphere. One enters it, it is like a room in a house, a hall. The meal or feast, on the other hand, stresses the idea of community. This room or house is for men who are in fellowship with God, or with his representative, Jesus, and with each other. Both sides, the room and the fellowship, are included in the idea of the house. A house is a confined area, and it forms a community. The kingdom of God is a house.[836]

In particular, Kim[837] points out that the entry into the kingdom of God in Jesus's teaching alluded to the entry into the Temple. The kingdom of God was often described as the house in which God was called Father, and the kingdom of God was also pictured with table fellowship, as in the feast and supper. He assumes that Jesus thought of the kingdom of God in terms of God as a father preparing a feast on the table in the house of God, and the people of God as his children opening the gate and the door of the house, entering the room, sitting around the table, and enjoying the feast. From this picture, he argues that Jesus connected the kingdom of God with the Temple, the house of God, in which the throne of God was located and the people of God entered and shared the fellowship of the feast with him. That is to say, Jesus thought of the kingdom of God as the new Temple, which is the new community of God created by Jesus himself.

In line with this, Marshall[838] says that the kingdom of God as a corporate entity, denotes the new Israel, the new people of God, who would be created by Jesus and ruled over by God, so it is Israel who would receive

---

exception is the cry from the cross (Mark 15:34 par Matt 27:46), and the reason for that is its character as a quotation.'

[835] Aalen, 'Reign,' 228. Cf. Matt 7:11; 22:1ff; 25:21, 23; Luke 14:16ff; 15:23, 25; 15:9; 22:30. Gate (Matt 7:13; Luke 13:24; John 10:7). Door (Luke 13:24ff); Key (Matt 16:19; 23:13; Luke 11:52).

[836] Aalen, 'Reign,' 228–229. Further, Aalen argues that the conception of the kingdom of God as a house, or as synonymous with the holy community, existed in pre-Christian Judaism as well as the NT, in connection with the Nathan prophecy (2 Sam 7:8ff; 1 Chron 17:7ff) in itself and the interpretation of the Nathan prophecy in Judaism and the NT. Aalen says that the Nathan prophecy is reflected in John 14:2 and 8:35, in which the 'house of the Father' is simply another expression for the kingdom of God (pp. 237–238).

[837] Kim, 'Interpretation,' 231–232; 'Temple,' 119; Gaston, *Stone*, 229–243; Meyer, *Aims*, 181–197; Jeremias, *Theology*, I, 168–169.

[838] Marshall, 'Hope,' 11–12; A. M. Hunter, *Testament*, 34; Blomberg, 'Response,' 35; Westcott, *John*, I, 48–50; Moloney, *John*, 98–99; Bauckham, 'Kingdom,' 1–2.

the benefits of God's rule. Thus, since in Jesus's teachings the king in the kingdom of God is ἀββα ὁ πατήρ, it is primarily concerned with the creation of the family of God.[839] That this argument for the intimate connection between the kingdom of God, that is the new Temple (my Father's house) and the new covenant people of God is correct, can be supported from John's Gospel. This is particularly seen in the crucial narrative of Jesus's cleansing of the Temple introduced in John 2:12–22 (cf. John 14:1–2).[840]

Further, Aalen[841] points out that another difference is that in the OT the establishment of the kingdom of God is a common expression (cf. Dan 2:44; 7:14, 27; 1 Kings 9:5 (LXX); *Kaddish*; *Sib. Or.* 3:767f; *Tg. Sam* 7:11), whereas in the NT, the coming of the kingdom of God and the entry into it are much more familiar phrases. Here, in connection with the entry into the kingdom of God, the verb εἰσέρχομαι is significant. As J. Schneider[842] points out, in the Septuagint, one of the usages of the term was related to the regulations (such as cultic purity and holiness) for entry into the places (the Temple or Jerusalem) dedicated to God. For example, in Isa 26:2, righteousness is required for entry through the gates of the holy city. Above all, this verb is used in connection with the entry of the people of Israel into the promised land in exodus, Leviticus, Numbers and Deuteronomy, often together with another verb κληρονομέω 'to inherit' (εἰσέλθῃς καὶ κληρονομήσῃς τὴν γῆν, e.g., Deut 6:18).

Also, in the NT, the verb is commonly used with the Temple liturgies and related regulations concerning admission to the cultic community. When used with the accompanying preposition εἰς, it is most significantly adopted in connection with Jesus's words in the Gospels regarding entry into the kingdom of God. In the NT, certain conditions for entry into the kingdom of God are variously expressed, namely, to be born of water and the Spirit (John 3:5); to become as little children (Mark 10:15); to keep the commandments (Matt 19:17); and to do the will of God (Matt 7:21). Accordingly, Schneider[843] claims that Jesus's preaching about entry into the kingdom of God in the Gospels is a similar expression to the idea in the OT of the entry of the people of Israel from Egypt into the promised land.

---

[839] Marshall, 'Hope,' 9; Jeremias, *Theology*, I, 168–169; W. H. Oliver and A. G. van Aarde, 'Community,' 379–400.
[840] For detailed discussion, see 4.4. The New Temple.
[841] Aalen, 'Reign,' 218–221.
[842] J. Schneider, *TDNT*, II, 676–678; W. Mundle, *NIDNTT*, I, 321; H. Windisch, 'Sprüche,' 163–192; Kim, 'Interpretation,' 232; Klappert, *NIDNTT*, II, 385.
[843] Schneider, *TDNT*, II, 676.

Also, H. Windisch[844] argues that the common phrase, εἰς τὴν βασιλείαν τοῦ θεοῦ εἰσελεύσονται in Jesus's teaching regarding the kingdom of God in the NT[845] originated from the Israelites being delivered out of Egypt, entering into and taking possession of the promised land (εἰσελθόντες κληρονομήσητε τὴν γῆν ἣν κύριος ὁ θεὸς τῶν πατέρων ὑμῶν δίδωσιν ὑμῖν) in the OT (Deut 4:1; 6:17f; 16:20). On the basis of this historic experience of their forefathers, its eschatological repetition was expected in Jewish apocalyptic literature. Here, the expression of entry into the kingdom of God is equivalent to the entry of Christians into eternal rest (cf. Heb 3:11, 18; 4:1ff). In line with this, Revelation says that only those whose names are written in the Lamb's book of life can enter into the holy city of the eternal world. Anything impure and anyone who does what is shameful or deceitful will be excluded from the holy city (21:27; cf. 22:14).

Thus, if the above argument is valid, Jesus's teaching about entering into the kingdom of God (εἰσελθεῖν εἰς τὴν βασιλείαν τοῦ θεοῦ) as well as its requirement (γεννηθῇ ἐξ ὕδατος καὶ πνεύματος) in John 3:5 can be understood to reflect the new exodus motif in connection with the idea of the entry of the Israelites from Egypt into the promised land.[846] In John 3:5, alluding to Ezek 36:25–28; 37:1–28, Jesus speaks of the new creation (resurrection) of water and the Spirit and the entry into the new Temple, the resurrected body of Jesus, the new covenant eschatological community of God.

5.2.4 The Heavenly Things and the Son of Man (John 3:11–15)

In relation to Jesus's teaching of the birth from above in v. 3 and his repeated explanation of it in vv. 5–8, Nicodemus could still not understand. As a result he put a question to Jesus in v. 9, 'How can these things (ταῦτα) happen?' The 'these things' relates to everything Jesus mentioned in John 3:5–8. In relation to Nicodemus' question Jesus reproved him as 'the teacher of Israel' (ὁ διδάσκαλος τοῦ Ἰσραήλ) for his ignorance concerning entering the kingdom of God through the birth of water and the Spirit, his reply which includes vv. 13–15 answers the question. The Evangelist's extended commentary in vv. 16–21 explains what Jesus has told Nicodemus.

---

[844] Windisch, 'Sprüche,' 163–192.
[845] Cf. Mark 10:23ff. pars 9:43–48=Matt 18:8f; Matt 5:20; 8:3; 7:21; John 3:5; cf. Matt 23:23, 16, 19; Luke 13:22–30=Matt 13:22–30=Matt 7:13; Matt 8:11f; Luke 14:23; Matt 22:12; 25:10ff; Rom 11:25. See, Kim, 'Interpretation,' 232; idem., 'Proclamation,' 56.
[846] Cf. Following Windisch, in the discussion of the importance of 'the Way motif' in Mark's Gospel, W. H. Kelber, Kingdom, 67ff, argues that the expression, the entry to the kingdom of God, is based on the entry of the Israelites into the promised land in Deuteronomy (cf. 1:8; 4:1; 6:19; 16:20). Also, W. M. Swartely, 'Structural,' 73–86, esp. 80, claims that ἐξέρχομαι and εἰσέρχομαι reflect Israel's exodus and entrance motifs.

This passage is quite crucial to comprehend the identity of Jesus and the meaning of his death in the Gospel of John in the light of the paschal-new exodus motif. Firstly, I will discuss what 'the earthly things' and 'the heavenly things' were in this context, and why Jesus designated them in this way. In particular, the Son of Man and his work will be interpreted in regard to 'the heavenly things' with Apocalyptic-*Merkabah* mysticism. Then the syntactical understanding of v. 13 and its emphasis concerning the Son of Man will be discussed. Also, the requirement that the Son of Man must be lifted up will be considered against the picture of the bronze snake lifted by Moses in v. 14 with special attention given to the verb ὑψωθῆναι. Furthermore, in respect to ὑψωθῆναι which alludes to Isa 52:13, the Son of Man and the suffering servant of Yahweh will be studied. Additionally, the Son of Man and the servant of Yahweh will be further examined in connection with 'the only Son' in the light of the paschal-new exodus perspective.[847]

Before we discuss the meaning of 'the earthly things' and 'the heavenly things' in v. 12, we shall consider the connotation of 'we' (cf. οἴδαμεν, λαλοῦμεν, ἑωράκαμεν, and μαρτυροῦμεν) and 'you (pl.)' (cf. λαμβάνετε) in v. 11. According to Morris,[848] Jesus's employment of the plural 'we' was very unusual, since normally he did not associate himself with people (cf. John 2:24–25). The majority of Johannine commentators[849] agree that the use of the term 'we' points to the Johannine (or Christian) community. That is, those who had experienced the birth from above (the birth of water and the Spirit) following Jesus's teaching and so could be represented by him. The other term 'you' (pl.) referred to the Jewish community which did not accept his testimony concerning the birth from above and could be represented by Nicodemus.[850] This argument could be supported by Jesus's

---

[847] At the beginning of this chapter, the first part (vv. 1–21) of the third chapter of John's Gospel was divided into two sections: Jesus's conversation with Nicodemus (vv. 1–15) and the Evangelist's commentary (vv. 16–21). However, since the two sections help to complement each other in understanding two sections and interpreting them, they will be discussed together in part.

[848] Morris, *John*, 196, following A. G. Hebert, *Form*, 46. Cf. Mark 9:40 and parallels, Matt 17:27.

[849] Lincoln, *Truth*, 66–69; J. F. McGrath, *Apologetic*, 157; De Jonge, *Jesus*, 30; J. L. Martyn, *Fourth Gospel*, 116f; C. Saayman, 'Textual,' 34–35; Burkett, *Son*, 76–78; Smith, *John*, 93; Sanders, *John*, 126; Haenchen, *John*, I, 202; Fallon, *John*, 99; Osburn, 'Exegetical,' 129. However, Williford, 'John 3:1–15,' 457, indicating the Evangelist returns to 'I' in v. 12 in spite of keeping the 'you' plural, argues that 'Perhaps the most satisfactory answer is to see vs. 11 as a continuation of the rebuttal of Nicodemus in his own words begin in vs. 10. Just as in vs. 10 Jesus picks up the 'teacher' from Nicodemus' words in vs. 2, so in vs. 11 Jesus picks up the 'we know' from vs. 2 and turns it against Nicodemus. Thus, the use of 'we' is a parody of Nicodemus' hint of arrogance.' Similarly, Ridderbos, *John*, 133.

[850] Concerning Nicodemus, see 5.2.5.3.1. Nicodemus and 'Light and Darkness' (Cf. John 3:1f, 19–21).

calling Nicodemus *'the'* teacher of Israel (ὁ διδάσκαλος τοῦ Ἰσραήλ), in which the definite article could imply that Nicodemus was the representative figure of a community, probably the Jewish community.

5.2.4.1 The Earthly Things (τὰ ἐπίγεια) (Cf. John 3:1–8)

Returning to 'the earthly things' and 'the heavenly things' in v. 12, I will first concentrate on the meaning of 'the earthly things.' As mentioned above, vv. 11–15 could be thought of as Jesus's answer to Nicodemus's question in v. 9,[851] 'How can these things happen?' In v. 10, Jesus reproves Nicodemus for his ignorance with additional teaching (vv. 5–8) concerning 'the birth from above' (v. 3). So, 'these things' connect with vv. 5–8. Thus by seeing the connection between 'these things' in Nicodemus' question (v. 9) and 'the earthly things' in Jesus's reprimand (v. 10) we can thus identify the 'earthly things'.

In the first phrase of v. 12,[852] the conditional clause (εἰ τὰ ἐπίγεια εἶπον ὑμῖν) implies fulfilment which refers to what Jesus has already mentioned, and the main clause (καὶ οὐ πιστεύετε) is about present continuous action which entails the Jewish community represented by Nicodemus not accepting Jesus's testimony. Whereas, in the second phrase of v. 12, another conditional clause (πῶς ἐὰν εἴπω ὑμῖν τὰ ἐπουράνια) does not have implications about the fulfilment of the condition, which refers to what Jesus will say in the future, and the main clause (πιστεύσετε) is the future tense which relates to what Jesus will say later. If this grammatical understanding of v. 12 is right, 'the earthly things' (τὰ ἐπίγεια) point to what Nicodemus's Jewish community did not understand or believe. That is to say, as some Johannine commentators[853] agree, 'the earthly things' mean no other than Jesus's testimony about the birth of water and the Spirit, and the mystery of the birth of the Spirit in vv. 5–8.

So, how could the birth of water and the Spirit be 'the earthly things'? Since the birth of water and the Spirit, that is, the birth from above clearly originates from God, surely this should be 'the heavenly things.' Why did Jesus designate the divine things related to the new birth as 'the earthly things'? Generally, Johannine commentators account for 'the earthly things'

---

[851] Burkett, *Son*, 77; Bultmann, *John*, 144; Carson, *John*, 202; Bruce, *John*, 89; Brown, *John I-XII*, 145.
[852] Cf. Morris, *John*, 197 n. 51.
[853] Strachan *Fourth Gospel*, 137; Burkett, *Son*, 78; Jones, *Symbol*, 73; Ridderbos, *John*, 134; Bultmann, *John*, 149; Carson, *John*, 199; Bruce, *John*, 87; Lindars, *John*, 135; Moloney, *John*, 94; Brown, *John I-XII*, 132.

in the light of 'the earthly analogies'[854] (i.e., physical birth, water and wind), or of 'the earthly events'[855] which happened on earth in spite of their divine origin from above. Barrett[856] suggests that 'the earthly things' describe the salvation in Christ with parables and 'the heavenly things' without parables. Beasley-Murray [857] argues that 'the earthly things' denote humanity's situation, being incapable of seeing the kingdom of God in the world. Further, 'the heavenly things' denote the eschatological salvation brought by the redeemer through his descent to earth and ascent to heaven via the cross. Burkett[858] understands 'the earthly things' and 'the heavenly things' as two aspects of 'eternal life.' In other words, for him, τὰ ἐπίγεια points to 'the earthly aspects' of eternal life related to the present possession on earth by the birth from above (cf. John 3:36; 5:24; 6:47, 54; 12:25). Also, τὰ ἐπουράνια to 'the heavenly aspects' of eternal life related to ascending to the kingdom in heaven and then having fellowship there with God (cf. John 12:26; 13:33–14:3; 17:24).[859]

As we have already seen,[860] Jesus's teaching about the birth of water and the Spirit and entering the kingdom of God ('the earthly things') was based mainly on Ezek 36–37. Here the crucial point is that Yahweh promised the restoration of the whole house of Israel from exile. If this understanding that Ezek 36–37 is the proper background to the birth of water and the Spirit is correct, to Nicodemus as *the teacher of Israel* who was the expert in the Scriptures, Jesus's teachings about the birth of water of the Spirit could not be a concealed mystery. Undoubtedly, since entering the kingdom of God through the birth of water and the Spirit as the eschatological new salvation has its origin in God, this is divine. Nonetheless, it was not God's hidden secret to the Jews and was his promise disclosed through the OT particularly the Prophets. This interpretation could be supported by Jesus's rigid indications to Nicodemus and the Jewish community, 'You should not

---

[854] Fallon, *John*, 99; Bruce, *John*, 87; Hoskyns, *Fourth*, I, 217; A. M. Hunter, *John*, 38; Brown, *John I-XII*, 132; Strachan, *Fourth Gospel*, 137; Davies, *Rhetoric*, 177–178.
[855] Bruce, *John*, 87; Morris, *John*, 196; Lindars, *John*, 155; Brown, *John I-XII*, 132; Carson, *John*, 199; Schnackenburg, *John*, I, 377; Bultmann, *John*, 149; Burkett, *Son*, 79–80; Bernard, *John*, I, 110–111; Saayman, 'Textual,' 37.
[856] Barrett, *John*, 212; H. Sasse, *TDNT*, I, 681. However, Burkett, *Son*, 78 points out that 'Jesus does not refer to two manners of speaking about the same subject ('in an earthly manner' and 'in a heavenly manner'), but to two categories or subjects of discourse, 'the earthly things' and 'the heavenly things.''
[857] Beasley-Murray, *John*, 50.
[858] Burkett, *Son*, 79–80.
[859] See also Schnackenburg, *John*, I, 379, who similarly thinks about 'the heavenly things'; 'the mysteries involved in the fullness of salvation, the entry of man into the heavenly world.'
[860] See 5.2.1.2. The Old Testament and Jewish Background.

be surprised at my saying' (v. 7) and 'you are the teacher of Israel and do you not understand these things?' (v. 10).

Accordingly, entering the kingdom of God through the birth of water and the Spirit was divine. However, since they were revealed through the Scripture,[861] Jesus designated them as 'the earthly things.' In regard to this argument, Brown correctly comments:

> In this case the dualism is not like flesh/spirit, for what Jesus has already said includes such a lofty subject as begetting from above by the Spirit; and therefore, 'earthly' is not derogatory. Rather, the contrast is between two types of divine action, one more heavenly and mysterious than the other.[862]

5.2.4.2 The Heavenly Things (τὰ ἐπουράνια) (Cf. John 3:12–15)

I now turn to the heavenly things. As some Johannine theologians[863] agree, the heavenly things in this context are related to Jesus's words in vv. 13–15.[864] However, their understanding of the meaning of vv. 13–15 is diverse.

---

[861] Bennema, *Power*, 175; Beasley-Murray, *John*, 49–50; Bultmann, *John*, 147–148. Cf. Burge, *John*, 117 understands Jesus's saying in v. 12 to mean that 'The signs and Scriptures are accessible here on earth, and if these cannot be understood and believed, it is not possible for profound heavenly things to be believed. People who stumble on the elemental teachings of Jesus cannot hope to grasp the deeper realities.'

[862] Brown, *John I-XII*, 132. Cf. Bruce, *John*, 87; Morris, *John*, 196–197; Lindars, *John*, 155. In connection with this kind of comparison between heaven and earth, some passages could be suggested from the OT and the Jewish documents (Cf. Prov 30:3–4; *Wis.* 9:16–18; *Bar.* 3:29; *b. Sanh.* 39a). *Wis.* 9:16–18 in particular makes a similar comparison; 'We can hardly fathom the things upon the earth... but when things are in heaven, who can search them out...except you give wisdom and send your holy spirit from on high?' Also, in this regard, *4 Ezra* 4:11, 20–21 is very instructive; 'You cannot understand the things with which you have grown up; how then can your mind comprehend the way of the Most High? ... those who dwell upon earth can understand only what is on earth, and he who is above heavens can understand what is above the height of heavens.' Ezra was seeking an answer to the question as to why Israel had been given over to the gentiles as a reproach; 'why the people whom God loved had been given to godless tribes.' (cf. v. 23). Here, the way of the Most High is considered as the heavenly secret which is difficult to comprehend in connection with the exile which Israel, the people whom God loved had been subjected to by the gentiles. See Brown, *ibid.*, 132, 145; Witherington, *Wisdom*, 98–99; Lindars, *John*, 155; Bruce, *John*, 87; Fallon, *John*, 99; Saayman, 'Textual,' 38–39; Bennema, *Power*, 178–179.

[863] Brown, *John I-XII*, 132; Bultmann, *John*, 149; Dodd, *Interpretation*, 305–307; Fallon, *John*, 99; Carson, *John*, 199; Bruce, *John*, 87; Lindars, *John*, 135; Beasley-Murray, *John*, 50; Moloney, *John*, 94; Jones, *Symbol*, 73; Williford, 'John 3:1–15,' 457; Traub, *TDNT*, V, 542; Bietenhard, *NIDNTT*, II, 195.

[864] However, Burkett, *Son*, 79–80 argues that in this context Jesus did not mention 'the heavenly aspects' of eternal life, 'ascending to the heavenly kingdom and having fellowship there with God,' because of Nicodemus' (or the Jews') incapability in understanding 'the earthly aspects' of eternal life possessing on earth after the birth from above. Saayman, 'Textual,' 44 says that without mentioning 'the mysterious content of a heavenly vision,' Jesus talked 'about the

However, we can classify the main points of vv. 13–15 as follows: the descending and ascending of the Son of Man; the necessity of the being lifted up (ὑψωθῆναι δεῖ) as the bronze serpent was lifted up by Moses; and giving eternal life to whoever believes in the Son of Man lifted up. These could be summarized as 'the works related to the Son of Man.'[865] So, why did Jesus designate 'the works of the Son of Man' as 'the heavenly things?' Here, the ἐπ- of ἐπουράνια denotes not 'upon' but 'at' and so ἐπουράνια could be rendered 'in heaven' which means 'belonging to the divine heaven.'[866] So, τὰ ἐπουράνια could mean 'the mysteries that heaven contains,'[867] or just simply 'the heavenly secrets' or 'the heavenly mysteries.' We will consider the reason why Jesus named the Son of Man's works in vv. 13–15 as 'the heavenly secrets.'

First, from the intimate relation (cf. καί) between v. 12 and v. 13, and from Jesus referring to the heavenly things in v. 12, we can ask questions such as 'by whom can the heavenly things be revealed?' and 'by which authority can a specific seer (or agent) argue to be able to reveal the heavenly things'? In respect to these questions, Johannine commentators[868] assume that v. 13 reflects the arguments of the Johannine Jesus who insisted on being the exclusive mediator of revelation about the heavenly things. They suggest that he went even further in denying the possibility of any visionary journeys to heaven in order to have access to the divine knowledge; which was a common perception in Jewish apocalyptic or *merkabah* mysticism[869] at

---

crucifixion of the Son of Man and life that those who believe can have in him.' Also, Schnackenburg, *John*, I, 361 argues that since Jesus's conversation with Nicodemus concerning the new birth finished with this negative note with Jesus's question in v. 12 and then the Evangelist's preaching or kerygmatic exposition started, 'the heavenly things' that is 'the mysteries involved in the fullness of salvation, the entry of man into the heavenly world' (p. 379) which was probably thought of by the Evangelist, have not been referred to in this context.

[865] Brown, *John I-XII*, 146; Whitacre, *John*, 90–91. Since the term, ὑψωθῆναι is thought to be a divine passive, the works of the Son of Man reflect the works of God indirectly. So, vv. 13–15 is thought of as God's works through the Son of Man.

[866] Traub, *TDNT*, V, 538–539; Bietenhard, *NIDNTT*, II, 188.

[867] Saayman, 'Textual,' 37.

[868] Odeberg, *Fourth Gospel*, 72–98; P. Borgen, 'Son,' 133–142; Meeks, *Prophet-King*, 110–111, 192–195, 235–236; Brown, *John I-XII*, 145; Morris, *John*, 198; Moloney, *Son*, 54–57; *idem.*, *John*, 100–101; Barrett, *John*, 212; Carson, *John*, 200; Beasley-Murray, *John*, 50; Strachan, *Fourth Gospel*, 138; Lindars, *John*, 156, 212; Kanagaraj, *Mysticism*, 195–196; Witherington, *Wisdom*, 100; Whitacre, *John*, 90; Saayman, 'Textual,' 39–40; Bernard, *John*, I, 111; Osburn, 'Exegetical,' 131; Bruce, *John*, 87, 99; McGrath, *Apologetic*, 157–171, esp. 157–159; Drapper, 'Temple,' 281–282; Burge, *John*, 117; Davies, *Rhetoric*, 179–180; Bultmann, *John*, 150–151; Bennema, *Power*, 176–177.

[869] Rowland, *Influence*; *idem.*, 'John 1:51,' 498–507; Kim, *Origin*, 239–253; *idem.*, *Son*, 15–37; Kanagaraj, *Mysticism*, 159–178. Cf. McGrath, *Apologetic*, 168–169. For the discussion of the Son of the Man in regard to *merkabah* mysticism, see 2.4.2. Allusion to Jacob's Vision and the Son of

that time. So what was the authority of the Johannine Jesus to be able to reveal the heavenly things (or secrets)? The answer is found in the proclamation of the Johannine Jesus as *the Son of Man, who descended from heaven* (ὁ ἐκ τοῦ οὐρανοῦ καταβάς, ὁ υἱὸς τοῦ ἀνθρώπου). It means that since Jesus was the Son of Man who descended from heaven, only he had the authority to reveal the heavenly secrets (cf. John 1:18).

Secondly, another aspect suggested by the καταβαίνω (cf. ἀναβαίνω) in v. 13 is that the Son of Man, who descended from the heavenly sphere, could be the heavenly revelation itself. That is, the Son of Man, who descended from heaven, is the embodiment of the heavenly secrets.[870] In other words, it could mean that the Son of Man, the heavenly revelation, appeared on earth (cf. John 1:14). In the pre- and post- Christian periods, the main pursuit of the seekers of *merkabah* mysticism was to see God sitting upon the throne of glory in heaven[871] (cf. the heavenly assembly in Isa 6; Dan 7. Cf. 1 Kings 22:19–23; Job 1–2), which was intimately related to knowing the divine knowledge of God's plan (or will) for Israel, consulted in the heavenly assembly. Also, central to the *merkabah*-vision traditions was אָדָם דְּמוּת כְּמַרְאֵה ('a figure like the appearance of a man') sitting on the divine throne surrounded with flame in Ezek 1:26, which developed into the figure כְּבַר אֱנָשׁ ('one like a son of man') appearing in Dan 7:13.[872] Here, there is no doubt that the Son of Man in v. 13 is also based on Dan 7:13.[873]

Accordingly, ὁ ἐκ τοῦ οὐρανοῦ καταβάς, ὁ υἱὸς τοῦ ἀνθρώπου could mean that the Son of Man, the very divine substance sitting on the glorious divine throne, which the seekers of the apocalyptic or *merkabah* mysticism pursued, descended from heaven to earth. Here, we can recognize that the second part of v. 13, ὁ ἐκ τοῦ οὐρανου καταβάς means the incarnation of the Logos, the Son of Man [874] which is clearly reflected in John 1:14. In particular, in respect to this argument, it will be significant that Isa 6, one of

---

Man (John 1:51) of this work and 3.3. The Theophany-*Merkabah* Tradition in the Jewish Apocalyptic Literature of Ra, *Christological*.

[870] Kanaragaj, *Mysticism*, 197. Cf. Odeberg, *Fourth Gospel*, 36; Lindars, *John*, 156; Bennema, *Power*, 176–177.

[871] Kanaragaj, *Mysticism*, 163, 214–247; I. Gruenwald, *Mysticism*, 31

[872] Kim, *Origin*, 239–252; idem., *Son*, 15–37.

[873] Pryor, 'Johannine,' 350–351; Ridderbos, *John*, 136; McGrath, *Apologetic*, 168–169; Kim, *Son*, 5; Borgen, 'Son,' 142–143; Bulman, 'Only,' 72–74. However, Borgen, 'Son,' 138–142, and Bulman, 'Only,' 72–73, understand the ascension as the pre-mundane ascension. Dahl, 'Johannine,' 136 says that the expression ὁ υἱὸς τοῦ ἀνθρώπου ὁ ὢν ἐν τῷ οὐρανῷ (the Son of the Man who is in heaven) in John 3:13 could be original and so is to be interpreted like John 1:51 which reflected the heavenly image seated above the throne in heaven (Ezek 1:26; Dan 7:13). Also, D. A. Black, 'John 3:13,' 65; Lindars, *John*, 156; Barrett, *John*, 213. Contra Bruce, *John*, 88; Carson, *John*, 203.

[874] Barrett, *John*, 212–213; Kanagaraj, *Mysticism*, 197, 221–224; Longenecker, *Christology*, 59. Cf. Phil 2:6–11.

the main texts of *merkabah* vision traditions, was quoted in John 12:40–41, in which the Evangelist clearly said that the glory that Isaiah had seen was the glory of Jesus.

Furthermore, ἀναβέβηκεν the verb of the main clause of v. 13 might be considered in relation to the Son of Man, because both ἀναβαίνω and καταβαίνω as a pair, on the whole, play important roles together in connection with the Son of Man in John's Gospel.[875] Accordingly, in respect to this, the verbs in v. 13 could not be an exception. Of course, ἀναβαίνω in v. 13 was used in regard to the denial proclamation against the arguments of the seekers who argued for a heavenly journey to get heavenly knowledge. Nonetheless, the verb could also enclose the meaning of the ascension of the Son of Man, who was the embodiment of the heavenly revelation. In other words, the ἀναβαίνω, as a pair with καταβαίνω, exposed the significance of the Son of Man's ascension to heaven not for the heavenly revelation but for the return (or restoration) to his heavenly glory, shared with God the Father before creation (cf. John 17:5; 6:62).

Here, in respect to the ascension of the Son of Man in John 3:13, we have to remember the heavenly figure כְּבַר אֱנָשׁ ('one like a son of man') in Dan 7:13–14, who is enthroned as the Son of the Ancient of Days. As such he is the inclusive representative of the saints of the Most High (cf. Dan 7:18–28). Here, the Danielic Son of Man figure functionally plays the role of the firstborn of God.[876] Thus, the enthronement of the heavenly figure כְּבַר אֱנָשׁ ('one like a son of man') as the inclusive representative of the people of God can naturally be recognized as God's promise regarding the restoration of the true people of God, after continuous oppression by four gentile kingdoms. Accordingly, in regard to the enthronement of the heavenly figure כְּבַר אֱנָשׁ ('one like a son of man'), the ascension of the Son of Man in John 3:13 could be understood as the enthronement (or restoration) of the heavenly Son of Man, signifying the restoration of the true people (sons) of God.[877] In addition, the distinctive picture of the ascension of the Son of Man is dramatically described in v. 14. Here, ὑψωθῆναι is another important term in interpreting the connotation of the ascension of the Son of Man in John in connection with 'the heavenly secrets.'

---

[875] Ridderbos, *John*, 135; Lindars, *John*, 156; Bernard, *John*, I, 111; B. Siede, *NIDNTT*, II, 185–186; Bietenhard, *NIDNTT*, II, 195; H. Traub, *TDNT*, V, 521–522, 526; Kim, *Son*, 5. Cf. exceptionally, the verbs John 1:51 are related to angels. Nonetheless, it will be shown that the purpose that the Son of Man in John 1:51 reflected in connection with the narrative of Jacob-Israel based on Gen 28:12 is no different from the meanings through the Son of Man who descended from heaven and then ascended to heaven in John 3:13.

[876] See 2.4.2. Allusion to Jacob's Vision and the Son of Man (John 1:51) of this work and 3.2. The (Firstborn) Son of God and the Son of Man of Ra, *Christological*.

[877] Cf. Pryor, 'Johannine,' 351; Colpe, *TDNT*, VIII, 466–447; Longenecker, *Christology*, 59–60.

5.2.4.3 Lifted up ὕψωσεν ... ὑψωθῆναι δεῖ (Cf. John 3:14; 8:28; 12:32, 34)

In v. 14, for the first time, Jesus mentions his death[878] as the Son of Man through typologically alluding to the bronze serpent put on the pole lifted up by Moses in the wilderness promised land following the first exodus from Egypt (cf. Num 21:4–9). The main point of v. 14 is that as those who had been bitten by the fiery serpents, the means of God's punishment,[879] and looked upon the bronze serpent were delivered from death; so too, those who look upon the Son of Man lifted up on the cross will be given eternal life.[880] The Israelites who looked at Moses's bronze serpent were not healed on the basis of the magical power of the bronze serpent but of the saving grace of God.[881]

So what was the reason that Yahweh instructed Moses to make a serpent as the means of healing the Israelites? Davies[882] thinks that it was based on, 'the notion that the power of dangerous creatures could be annulled by making an image of them.' S. Cho[883] further assumes that it was to teach that 'punishment' is related to God's sending the fiery serpent to punish those who murmured against him and, by contrast, healing is based on God's commanding Moses to make a bronze serpent for the sake of their recovery. It is thought that in John 3:14 the main comparison for the Son of Man was neither Moses nor the bronze snake but the lifting up.[884]

However, Burkett[885] believes that in Num 21:4–9 the bronze serpent represented the fiery serpents which bit the grumbling Israelites, causing their death, and thus was understood as the symbol of the cause of death. So, to put it on the pole symbolically meant to nullify the power of death of

---

[878] Cf. The death of Jesus is first told by the Baptist in John 1:29 ('the Lamb of God, who takes away the sin of the world'). For this, see 2.3.1. The Lamb of God (John 1:29, 36). And then, in John 2:19, Jesus himself hinted at his death in respect to The Temple Incident. For this, see Chapter Four. Jesus's Action in the Temple (John 2:12–25. cf. Matt 21:12–13; Mark 11:15–17; Luke 19:45–46).
[879] E. W. Davies, *Numbers*, 214–218; P. J. Budd, *Numbers*, 232–235.
[880] Bernard, *John*, I, 113; Schnackenburg, *John*, I, 395; Turner, *Holy*, 69; Michaels, *John*, 58–59; Beasley-Murray, *John*, 50; Bruce, *John*, 88.
[881] S. Cho, *Cultic*, 114–115; Barrett, *John*, 213–214; Lindars, *John*, 157; Brown, *John I-XII*, 133; Davies, *Numbers*, 214; T. R. Ashley, *Numbers*, 406. Bennema, *Power*, 178. Cf. *Wis.* 16:6–7; *Tg. Num* 21:8 identifies the act of looking at the bronze serpent with the act of directing one's heart to the name of the Word of the Lord. *Barnabas*, 12:5–7 interpreted the serpent as a saviour figure as a type of Christ.
[882] Davies, *Numbers*, 218; Cho, *Cultic*, 115. For example, the five golden mice story (1 Sam 6:5) and the bitter water cured by bitter wood or salt (Exod 15:25; 2 Kings 2:21).
[883] Cho, *Cultic*, 114–115.
[884] Barrett, *John*, 214; G. Bertram, *TDNT*, VIII, 610; Carson, *John*, 201; Saayman, 'Textural,' 44; Beasley-Murray, *Life*, 50; Schnackenburg, *John*, I, 395–396; Moloney, *Son*, 60.
[885] Burkett, *Son*, 121–122.

the serpents, so that those who saw it in faith were delivered from the judgement. Therefore, the serpent that was the cause of death was put on the pole so that it would be condemned on the cross. In support of his argument, Burkett suggests John 12:31–32, in which when the Son of Man is lifted up on the cross, the ruler of this world will be condemned and cast out. The ruler of this world, the power of death symbolized as a serpent,[886] is judged on the cross, resulting in life for those who believe.

In regard to the lifting up, we have to notice the meaning of the verb ὑψωθῆναι which appears four times in the context of the Son of Man in John (cf. 3:14; 8:28; 12:32, 34).[887] Generally, Johannine commentators[888] rightly agree that the ὑψόω has an intentional double meaning, the crucifixion and the exaltation to glory in heaven, although their emphasis on the senses (crucifixion or exaltation) of the verb differ from one other. Nonetheless, as Kanagaraj[889] emphasizes, the verb needs to be understood in regard to crucifixion rather than to exaltation, because the exaltation to glory happened by way of crucifixion.[890] This will be made clear by considering the contexts in which the verb was used. A clear reference concerning this argument is found in John 12:32–33, 'But I, when am lifted up from the earth, will draw all men to myself. He said this to show the kind of death he was going to die.' The words 'when I am lifted up from the earth' in v. 32 were additionally explained as referring to the crucifixion of Jesus in v. 33 (cf. v. 34).[891] Also, John 8:28 points to Jesus's crucifixion, since it was the opponents of Jesus who were to exalt him, and the most natural meaning of this was 'to crucify on the cross' rather than 'to exalt on the throne.'[892] Similarly, if we consider that ὑψωθῆναι δεῖ τὸν υἱὸν τοῦ ἀνθρώπου in John 3:14 contrasts with Moses's serpent that was lifted up upon a signal-staff (θὲς αὐτὸν ἐπὶ σημείου in the LXX Num 21:8/ ἔστησεν αὐτὸν ἐπὶ σημείου in the

---

[886] Burkett, *Son*, 121–122, says that the serpent was used as a symbol for evil, sin, or Satan in the OT, the NT, and Jewish sources. Cf. Gen 3:1ff; Isa 27:1; Luke 10:19; Rev 12:9, 14, 15; 20:2.

[887] Barrett, *John*, 214; Pryor, 'Johannine,' 350; Ham, 'Son,' 83; Bernard, *John*, I, 113.

[888] Brown, *John I-XII*, 145–146; Barrett, *John*, 214; Moloney, *Son*, 60–65; *idem.*, *John*, 95; Schnackenburg, *John*, I, 396–397; Bernard, *John*, I, 113–114; Dodd, *Interpretation*, 375–379; Pryor, 'Johannine,' 350; Beasley-Murray, *John*, 50; *idem.*, *Life*, 49–50; Milne, *John*, 77; Bruce, *John*, 88; Bertram, *TDNT*, VIII, 610; Whitacre, *John*, 90–91; Morris, *John*, 199–200; Lindars, *John*, 158; Lee, *Narratives*, 54 n. 5; Williford, 'John 3:1–15,' 458; Köstenberger, *John*, 85–86; Ridderbos, *John*, 137; Witherington, *Wisdom*, 99.

[889] Kanagaraj, *Mysticism*, 204; Brown, *John I-XII*, 145; Bernard, *John*, I, 113–114.

[890] Beasley-Murray, *Life*, 50. See also Schnackenburg, *John*, I, 394–395; Bruce, *John*, 89; Dennis, *Gathering*, 202.

[891] Brown, *John I-XII*, 145; Köstenberger, *John*, 85; Dennis, *Gathering*, 202.

[892] Kanagaraj, *Mysticism*, 204; Bertram, *TDNT*, VIII, 610; Dodd, *Interpretation*, 376.

LXX Num 21:9),[893] ὑψωθῆναι has to be literally understood in the sense of the crucifixion, since Moses's serpent cannot have been exalted to glory.

Here, we have to give proper attention to the meaning that the Son of Man must be lifted up on the cross which was probably wooden. The bronze serpent that Moses lifted up on the signal-staff was under God's curse, so it can be seen from the parallel that the Son of Man who must be lifted up on the wooden cross[894] will be under the curse of God (Deut 21:23; cf. Gal 3:13; Acts 5:30). Here, the Son of Man who descended from heaven, as the embodiment of the heavenly figure כְּבַר אֱנָשׁ ('one like a son of man') is seen sitting on the throne of glory in heaven in Dan 7:13f (cf. Ezek 1:26). Yet also, he must be crucified as the one under God's curse. These are the 'heavenly things' or 'heavenly secrets' which Nicodemus (and the Jewish community he represented) could hardly expect to accept and believe (John 3:12b, cf. 1 Cor 1:23);[895] 'How then will you believe if I speak of the heavenly things?' In addition, δεῖ ('must') with the passive tense (ὑψωθῆναι) which is normally named as divine passive, could reflect the belief that the crucifixion of the Son of Man was planned by God. Thus, that is God's will or God's secret or 'the heavenly secrets.'[896]

Furthermore, in v. 15 (ἵνα πᾶς ὁ πιστεύων ἐν αὐτῷ ἔχῃ ζωὴν αἰώνιον), it is promised that God will bestow eternal life on those who believe in the Son of Man, who was condemned on the cross by God. Of course, the curse that the Son of Man received from God was not because of himself but because of humanity. This plan of God, who gives eternal life to those who believe in the cursed Son of Man, is also one of the heavenly mysteries. This concept of the heavenly mysteries in relation to the crucified Son of Man in

---

[893] Kanagaraj, *Mysticism*, 204; Brown, *John I-XII*, 145; Moloney, *Son*, 61–62.
[894] Cf. Morris, *Galatians*, 106; F. F. Bruce, *Galatians*, 164–167, esp. 166.
[895] Cf. Bruce, *Galatians*, 166 assumes that at the beginning of his Christian career, Paul had his hostility to the followers of Jesus, with the assertions that since Jesus was crucified on the cross, he was just cursed by God. See also A. C. Thiselton, *Corinthians*, 170–171; Hengel, *Atonement*, 43–44, who points out that 'Jews would inevitably understand talk of a crucified Messiah as blasphemy, because of Deut 21:23. The Messiah of Israel could never ever at the same time be the one who according to the words of the Torah was accursed by god... This was the most obvious way to refute his messianic claim.' (p. 43).
[896] Brown, *John I-XII*, 146; Fallon, *John*, 100; Whitacre, *John*, 90–91; W. Grundmann, *TDNT*, II, 22–24; Beasley-Murray, *Life*, 51; Schnackenburg, *John*, I, 395; Bruce, *John*, 89 who indicates that in v. 14, "the Son of the Man must be lifted up" (ὑψωθῆναι δεῖ τὸν υἱὸν τοῦ ἀνθρώπου) is a similar expression to "the Son of the Man must suffer many things" (δεῖ τὸν υἱὸν τοῦ ἀνθρώπου πολλὰ παθεῖν) in Mark 8:31.

v. 14 seems to be not too far away from the concept of God's secrets in Pauline epistles (cf. 1 Cor 2:6–9).[897]

Now we will consider the verb ὑψωθῆναι in the light of the Son of Man's exaltation to glory in heaven. As mentioned earlier, in respect to the Son of Man, ὑψωθῆναι may also have a figurative meaning, 'exaltation to glory,' since the same verb refers to Jesus's exaltation to the right hand of God after Easter (cf. Acts 2:33; 5:31; Phil 2:9). Further, John's Gospel shows that the verb refers to Jesus's exaltation to heaven as well as to his crucifixion. This understanding can be supported by the verb in v. 14 and the idea of the Son of Man's ascension (ἀναβέβηκεν) to heaven in the preceding verse, v. 13.[898] Carson[899] observes that the Synoptic Gospels show that the crucifixion and the exaltation appeared separately, but John's Gospel shows that Jesus's return to the glory he had once shared with the Father before creation was fulfilled by his exaltation to the cross (John 8:28;[900] 12:32.)[901] Accordingly, by use of the verb ὑψωθῆναι δεῖ, the Johannine Jesus disclosed

---

[897] Kim, *Son*, 32 n. 64 says that 'In a theophany vision a prophetic or apocalyptic seer is taken into the assembly before God's throne and there he sees the happenings and hears the divine counsel (סוד / μυστήριον) which is to be unfolded (or realized) on earth (Amos 3:7; Jer 23:18, 22)... That Daniel is familiar with this tradition and has it as his background in ch. 7 is suggested by his definition of רז (the Aramaic equivalent to סוד / μυστήριον) in 2:28–30, 47, i.e. in the context of 2:28–29 which stands in a close connection with ch. 7 (cf. esp. 2:44f with 7:9ff).' See also Bornkamm, *TDNT*, IV, 813–824, esp. 814f; Beasley-Murray, *Jesus*, 104f; *BDB*, 691; Rowland, *Open*, 126; Bockmuehl, *Revelation*, 15f, who points out the two meanings of סוד; 'the divine council' (e.g., Jer 23:18, 22; Ps 89:8; Job 15:8; 29:4; Prov 3:32) or 'the secret plan' (Amos 3:7; Ps 25:14). On the other hand, in other Pauline Epistles (cf. Rom 11: 1–36; Eph 3:1–13; Col 1:24–29), the divine secret is related to the salvation (restoration) of the gentiles, for which the hearts of Israel became stubborn and obstinate and thus she did not accept the Gospel (cf. Jesus as Christ). This seems to be reflected in John 12:37–41 (cf. blinded and hardened), alluding to Isa 53:1; 6:10, namely, the fulfilment of Isaiah's prophecy about the obduracy of Israel in their refusal to accept the Gospel (cf. Matt 13:14f and par. Mark 4:12; Luke 8:10; Acts 28:26f). For this, see Kim, *Origin*, 94–96.
[898] Burkett, *Son*, 122.
[899] Carson, *John*, 201–202; Beasley-Murray, *Life*, 48; Burge, *John*, 117; Brown, *John I-XII*, 145–146; Pryor, 'Johannine,' 350; Schnackenburg, *John*, I, 397.
[900] Even though John 8:28 reflects that the Jewish people have crucified the Son of Man on the tree, John 8:21–22 hints the exaltation of the Son of Man and v. 23 itself demonstrates the exaltation by use of 'ἐγώ εἰμί' which is a formula of divine self-revelation of Jesus in John (cf. John 8:58; 18:6), alluding to Yahweh's self-designation in Exod 3:14 and the Second Isaiah (cf. Isa 43:25; 48;12; 52:6). By use of this title, Jesus seems to hint that his glory is Yahweh's glory, which is supported by John 12:41. For ἐγώ εἰμί, see D. M. Ball, *I Am*; P. B. Harner, *I Am*; Burkett, *Son*, 142–160; Brown, *John I-XII*, 533–538; Dodd, *Interpretation*, 93–96.
[901] Also, John 12:32-33 obviously shows the death of the Son of Man on the cross and John 12 itself repeatedly mentions his death (vv. 7, 9, 24). However, Jesus said that the Son of Man would be glorified in his death, and the time of his exaltation would dethrone and cast out Satan. Also, John 12:41 says Isaiah saw Jesus sitting on the glorious throne in the heavenly assembly (cf. Isa 6).

the heavenly things (mysteries) that the cross was not only the place of sacrifice and suffering but also the place of departure and return to the Father (cf. John 17:1–19), in other words, the place of glorification (cf. John 13:31).[902]

Here, we need to return to the subject of 'the heavenly things' in connection with the exaltation of the Son of Man. For Nicodemus (or the Jewish community) the Son of Man could be regarded as the sinner executed under the curse of God, since he was lifted up on the cross. However, God lifted the crucified Son of Man through resurrection to the glorious heavenly throne which God shared with him before creation (cf. John 1:18; 13:3; 16:28; 17:5).[903] This exaltation of the crucified Son of Man is another aspect of the heavenly things; the heavenly secrets. The exaltation (resurrection and restoration) of the Son of Man was God's vindication of his innocence and the means of his restoration to the glorious throne in heaven. Since the Son of Man is the inclusive representative of the new Israel (cf. John 1:51), the eschatological people of God, his exaltation to the throne of glory in heaven could mean the restoration of the eschatological people (sons) of God to the divine throne (cf. Dan 7:13f).[904] So, the crucifixion of the Son of Man itself was the exaltation of the Son of Man. These are the heavenly things, the heavenly mysteries.

To sum up, τὰ ἐπουράνια ('the heavenly things,' i.e., 'the heavenly secrets') in v. 12 can be defined, in respect to vv. 13–15, as all the works related to the Son of Man as the firstborn/Son of God. These being: the embodiment (incarnation in John 1:14) of the Danielic divine Son of Man (Dan 7:13f. cf. Ezek 1:26; Isa 6); the divinely cursed (condemned, lifted-up) Son of Man on the cross; and the divinely vindicated and exalted (enthroned, restored) Son of Man. Nonetheless, the essence of the heavenly secrets planned by God could be defined as the crucified Son of Man (v. 14), which is the prerequisite to bring about the earthly things, in other words, entry into the kingdom of God through the birth of water and the Spirit. The enthronement of the Son of Man who as the Firstborn/Son of God is symbolically the inclusive representative of the saints of the Most High (God) could mean the restoration of the true-eschatological people of God to the divine throne; the new exodus, the entry into the kingdom of God.

---

[902] Burge, *John*, 117.
[903] Burkett, *John*, 122–126, divides glorification into two; the first moment of glorification of the cross and the second glorification at or soon after his resurrection.
[904] Kim, *Son*, 18–19.

5.2.4.4 The Son of Man (Dan 7:13) and the servant of Yahweh (Isa 52:13–53:12)

Further consideration is required as to the question about the meaning of the crucifixion (death) of the Son of Man in John 3:14. As demonstrated above, if Jesus's reference of the Son of Man was based on the heavenly figure in Dan 7:13f, is it possible to find the ideas not only in the exaltation but also in the vicarious (or substitutionary) suffering and death of the Danielic heavenly figure in Dan 7?[905] In order to answer that question, as we have discussed above, we have to pay attention to ὑψωθῆναι.

Johannine commentators[906] generally argue for Isa 52:13 as the main linguistic background of the verb, although some[907] accept an Aramaic term (זקף)[908] and a Hebraic term (נשא)[909] as other possibilities of the linguistic background of it. So, Borgen rightly argues that John 3:14 weaves together elements 'one like a son of man' in Dan 7:13f and 'the servant of the Lord' in Isa 52:13.[910] Further, Kanagaraj[911] argues that the death of the Son of Man

---

[905] Cf. M. Hooker, *Son*, 140ff; idem., *Studying*, 58; idem., 'Use,' claims that the reference to the servanthood of the Son of Man could paradoxically be found in the saying of Dan 7, where the Son of Man was given authority to rule over others, after he as the representative of the suffering righteous is subjected to suffering and oppression. In particular, Pitre, *Tribulation*, 51–62, 399–404, regards the Danielic Son of Man figure (Dan 7:13f) as the same figure as 'an anointed one' who would be cut off against the background of the eschatological tribulation (Dan 9:24–26), and thus argues for the suffering of the Danielic Son of Man figure, which is reflected in Mark 10:45. For this, see 2.4.2. The Suffering Messianic Figure in Daniel (cf. Dan 9:24–27) of Ra, *Christological*.

[906] Beasley-Murray, *John*, 50; idem., *Life*, 49–50; Brown, *John I-XII*, 146; Carson, *John*, 201; Lindars, *John*, 157; Dodd, *Interpretation*, 375–379; Schnackenburg, *John*, I, 397; M. Pamment, 'Samaritan,' 229; Williford, 'John 3:1–15,' 458; Borgen, 'Son,' 137–138; Ham, 'Son,' 83 n. 86; Whitacre, *John*, 90–91; Dennis, *Gathering*, 324–325; M. Hengel, 'Effective,' 121–122. Cf. Isa 4:2; 5:16; 10:15; 33:10; 42:13–15; 44:23; 49:3.

[907] Beasley-Murray, *Life*, 49–50; idem., *John*, 50; Carson, *John*, 201; H. Hollis, 'Root,' 475–478; Bertram, *TDNT*, VIII, 610; Dodd, *Interpretation*, 377; Carson, *John*, 201; Brown, *John I-XII*, 146; Lindars, *John*, 157; P. Ensor, 'Glorification,' 237; Polhill, 'John 1–4,' 453; O. Betz, 'Jesus,' 79–80.

[908] Cf. Ezra 6:11, in which זקף meant 'impaled.' But, in *Tg. Job* 13:11 found in Qumran Cave II, זקף meant to be 'exalted.' For this, see Lindars, *John*, 157. Also, רום in Ps 9:13 ('You who lift me up from the gates of death') was rendered into ὑψόω and in *1 QH* 6:34; 11:12 has the meaning of 'raising from death for resurrection.' For this, see Beasley-Murray, *Life*, 49 n. 18.

[909] Cf. Gen 40:13, 19, in which נשא was used with two meanings (execution and glorification), but the LXX did not translate into ὑψόω. Cf. Dodd, *Interpretation*, 377; Beasley-Murray, *Life*, 49–50; Hollis, 'Root,' 475–478; Brown, *John I-XII*, 146.

[910] Borgen, "Son," 142–144, quoted from 144. Also, Borgen asserts that 'in Midr. Ps 2:9, where Ps 2:7 ('you are my son') was interpreted, Isa 52:13 and Dan 7:13–14 were quoted together as parallel. This shows that the word 'servant' in Isa 52:13 and 'one like a son of man' in Dan 7:13f were interchangeable, and the exaltation in Isa 52:12 means enthronement.' Furthermore, interestingly, *Tg. Isa* 52:13 interpreted the Servant as the Messiah (p. 143). See i. Midrash Ps 2:9 on Ps 2:7 of 3.3. The Theophany-*Merkabah* Tradition in the Jewish Apocalyptic Literature of Ra, *Christological*.

[911] Kanagaraj, *Mysticism*, 204; Hanson, *Prophetic*, 49

in John 3:14 recalls the Servant's vicarious suffering and death, found not only from the references of ὑψωθήσεται καὶ δοξασθήσεται in Isa 52:13, but also in the subsequent verses (Isa 52:14–15) and almost the whole of Isa 53. Then, it is not impossible to conclude that Jesus as the Son of Man based on Dan 7:13f explained his death with the picture of the suffering and death of the servant of the Lord in Isa 52:13–53:12.[912]

Cullmann[913] argues that Jesus's sayings regarding his death at the Lord's Supper on the background of the crucifixion in Mark 14:24; Matt 26:28; Luke 22:20; 1 Cor 11:24 can be classified under two headings. Firstly, 'the idea of representation,' the blood pouring out 'for', or 'instead of', (ἀντὶ/ὑπέρ) many. Then secondly 'the establishment of the new covenant,' which alludes to the works of the Deutero-Isaianic servant of Yahweh in Isa 52–53; 42:6; 49:8.

Here, it is appropriate to introduce Kim's argument[914] about Mark 10:45, where Jesus as the Son of Man disclosed the purpose of his death. This is because his self-understanding about impending death helps us understand the meaning of John 3:14 and also John 13:31–35 (where the Son of Man's imminent glorification means his death on the cross in light of the paschal setting). In John 13:1–11, when washing his disciples' feet, 'Jesus has proleptically acted out the forgiveness of the sins of his people that would take place in his atoning death.'[915] Kim[916] understands Mark 10:45 in the context of the Last Supper; καὶ γὰρ ὁ υἱὸς τοῦ ἀνθρώπου οὐκ ἦλθεν διακονηθῆναι ἀλλὰ διακονῆσαι καὶ δοῦναι τὴν ψυχὴν αὐτοῦ λύτρον ἀντὶ πολλῶν. Through a detailed analysis of the linguistic combination of כֹּפֶר תַּחַת (λύτρον ἀντὶ/ransom) in Isa 43:3f and אָשָׁם (guilt-offering) in Isa 53:10 as the background of δοῦναι τὴν ψυχὴν αὐτοῦ λύτρον ἀντὶ πολλῶν in Mark 10:45, Kim claims that Jesus as the *Ebed Yahweh* will:

> surrender himself to a substitutionary death as the guilt-offerings (אָשָׁם) for sinful Israel and all the nations and so as the ransom (λύτρον/כֹּפֶר) in order to redeem them from condemnation and death at the last judgment.[917]

---

[912] Cullmann, *Christology*, 65.
[913] Cullmann, *Christology*, 64–65.
[914] Kim, *Son*, 38–73. See 2.4.1. The Isaianic Suffering Servant of Yahweh and the Last Supper (Mark 10:45; John 13:1–35; Mark 14:22–26; Matt 26:26–30; Luke 22:14–20; cf. 1 Cor 11:23–25) and 3.4.5. Mark 10:45 (The Son of Man and the Servant of God) of Ra, *Christological*.
[915] Kim, *Son*, 48.
[916] Kim, *Son*, 38–52; Cullmann, *Christology*, 65.
[917] Kim, *Son*, 50–61, quoted from 59. See also, Michel, *NIDNTT*, III, 623–624; Watts, *Isaiah's*, 262–269; B. Lindars, 'Salvation,' 295; Bruce, 'Background,' 60–61; Jeremias, *Theology*, I, 292–293; Cullmann, *Christology*, 64–65; Hengel, *Atonement*, 36, 50; France, 'Servant,' 26–52; idem., *Jesus*,

Here, Cullmann says that it does mean that:

> The Son of Man came to fulfil the task of the *ebed Yahweh*. Jesus consciously united in his person the two central concepts of the Jewish faith, *barnasha and ebed Yahweh*.[918]

Although Kim's argument relates to the suffering and death of the Son of Man in Mark 10:45 and links with the suffering servant of Isaiah, it may help to understand the meaning of the death of the Son of Man in John 3:14; 13:31–35, as the guilt-offerings and the ransom in the light of the suffering servant of Isaiah.[919]

Jeremias [920] argues that the ὑπέρ formula (cf. περί, ἀντί) and the (παρα-) διδόναι formula regarding Christology were related to the works of the suffering servant of Yahweh disclosed in Isa 53. τὴν ψυχὴν αὐτοῦ τίθησιν ὑπὲρ τῶν προβάτων in John 10:11 could allude to אִם־תָּשִׂים אָשָׁם נַפְשׁוֹ in Isa 53:10 (HT) or דְּמַסַר לְמוֹתָא נַפְשֵׁיהּ in *Tg. Isa* 53:12.[921] Here, ὑπὲρ τῶν προβάτων in John 10:11 could allude to the sheep in Isa 53:6, which was used figuratively to denote Israel who had gone astray. Also, Jeremias [922] says that the expression αἴρειν τὴν ἁμαρτίαν in John 1:29 (cf. 1 John 3:5) reflects Isa 53:12. And, the picture that the servant of Yahweh was silent and did not open his mouth in Isa 53:7 seems to be reflected in Jesus's silence before Pilate in John 19:9 at the moment of the passion against the background of the Jewish feast, the Passover (cf. Mark 15:5; Matt 27:12, 14).[923] In particular, in

---

110ff, says that Jesus as the Son of Man (Dan 7:13), received power, glory, everlasting dominion from the Ancient of Days, whose way to this ultimate goal is through the vicarious and redemptive suffering and death of the Servant of Yahweh (Isa 53). *Contra* Hooker, *Son*, 140ff; Gundry, *Mark*, 485. On the other hand, particularly, Hooker, *Son*, 144 indicates that 'ransom (λύτρον)' in Mark 10:45 was used of God's act of deliverance by which he freed His people from bondage at the context of the first exodus and the new exodus. Cf. Exod 6:6; Deut 7:8; 9:26; Isa 43:1; 52:3; 62:12; Mic 4:10; Jer 15:21.

[918] Cullmann, *Christology*, 65.

[919] Cf. Colpe, *TDNT*, VIII, 466 says that the Evangelist's understanding of ὑψωθῆναι not only with reference to the ascension as in Acts 2:33; 5:31; Phil 2:9 but also with reference to the crucifixion, shows a counterpart to the Synoptic passion predictions.

[920] Jeremias, *TDNT*, V, 706, 710. Cf. τὴν ψυχὴν αὐτοῦ τίθησιν ὑπὲρ τῶν προβάτων in John 10:11, 15, 17; 15:13; 1 John 3:16, παραδόντος ἑαυτὸν ὑπὲρ ἐμοῦ in Gal 2:20; Eph 5:2, 25, δόντος ἑαυτὸν ὑπὲρ τῶν ἁμαρτιῶν ἡμῶν in Gal 1:4; 1 Tim 2:6; Tit 2:14, δοῦναι τὴν ψυχὴν αὐτοῦ λύτρον ἀντὶ πολλῶν in Mark 10:45; Matt 20:28, ὑπὲρ ἡμῶν πάντων παρέδωκεν αὐτόν in Rom 8:32. Jeremias says that 'In all the instances just quoted (παρα-) διδόναι is linked with the ὑπέρ formula and its variants.' Also, Cullmann, *Christology*, 64–65.

[921] Jeremias, *TDNT*, V, 708.

[922] Jeremias, *TDNT*, V, 708, 710–711. cf. ἁμαρτίαν οὐκ ἐποίησεν (Heb 9:28; 1 Pet 2:24) and also ἁμαρτίαν οὐκ ἐποίησεν (1 Pet 2:22), or ἁμαρτία ἐν αὐτῷοὐκ ἔστιν (1 John 3:5) from Isa 53:9b.

[923] Jeremias, *TDNT*, V, 712–713. Cf. Jesus is silent before the Sanhedrin in Matt 26:63; Mark 14:61 and before Herod Antipas in Luke 23:9. In particular, Jeremias, *TDNT*, V, 702, 708 argues that since טַלְיָא דַאלָהָא in Aramaic meant 'the lamb of God' and 'the servant of God,' the

respect to Isa 53:10, the term, δεῖ ('must') of ὑψωθῆναι δεῖ τὸν υἱὸν τοῦ ἀνθρώπου in John 3:14 could allude to the will (חפץ/βούλεται) of Yahweh regarding the suffering and guilt-offering death of the Servant. [924] And further, the idea that the will of Yahweh is accomplished in the Servant's hand in Isa 53:10 reflects the emphasis that Jesus the Son of Man will fulfil the will of God the Father and glorify him in John's Gospel. Above all, the idea that the servant will see his offspring (זרע/σπέρμα) through offering his Life as a guilt-offering in Isa 53:10 is reflected in John 12:24, where, in regard to his death as the Son of Man, Jesus told a parable of a kernel of wheat.

Furthermore, a close relationship between this Johannine Son of Man and the Isaianic servant of Yahweh is supported by the perspective of the covenant. In Isa 42:6 and 49:8, Yahweh proclaimed that he would make the Isaianic servant of Yahweh a covenant for the people of Israel. This is reflected in the Johannine Last Supper in John 13:31–35, in which Jesus told the disciples of the glorification of the Son of Man in connection with his impending death on the cross and gave them a new commandment (ἐντολὴν καινήν) of loving one another. In the OT and Judaism, commandment and covenant are two sides of the same coin. [925] Accordingly, that Jesus bestowed a new commandment on the disciples against the background of his death can be interpreted as that he understood his death as the sacrifice of the establishment of the new covenant.

That the Johannine Jesus is the Isaianic servant of Yahweh in regard to atonement of the guilty-offering in Isa 53:10, could be reflected in that he washed his disciples' feet (a picture of cleasnign from sin) at the moment of his imminent death and against the background of the Jewish feast Passover. Washing feet was a very unusual custom between teacher and pupils in Jewish background. So, his washing their feet could be a very powerful picture to denote him not only as the servant of Yahweh but also the servant of the new people of God in John's Gospel. In addition, that in the same text of Isaiah (42:6; 49:9) the servant of Yahweh was given as a light for the gentiles; a theme reflected in Jesus's proclamation that he is the light of the world (John 8:12; 3:19–21; 9:5; 12:35–36).

---

designation ὁ ἀμνὸς τοῦ θεοῦ in John 1:29 has the meaning of both 'the lamb of God' and 'the servant of God.' Similarly, Cullmann, *Christology*, 71.

[924] Cf. Grundmann, *TDNT*, II, 21–25; G. Schrenk, *TDNT*, I, 629–633; Hooker, *Studying*, 48 admits that when Jesus explained his suffering in terms of the Son of Man, he emphasized its necessity by use of 'must' or 'according to,' which means that Jesus's death was a part of God's plan. Cf. Mark 8:31; 9:12; 10:38, 45; 14:21, 27, 48. Also, see Dennis, *Gathering*, 325–327 (cf. μέλλω in John 11:51c); Hengel, 'Effective,' 121–122; Jeremias, *TDNT*, V, 708.

[925] Kim, *Son*, 48; J. Behm, *TDNT*, II, 124–134. Cf. Exod 19:5–8; 34:1–28; 1 Kings 11:11; Jer 31:31–34; 1 *Macc*. 1:57; 2:27; Heb 9:18f.

In particular, the importance of the Isaianic background in the Gospel of John can be shown by John 12:37–41, where the Jews did not believe in Jesus despite his many miraculous signs. The Evangelist understood this as the fulfilment of Isaiah's prophecy of Yahweh's judgment, 'blindness and deafness' in Isa 6:10.[926] And then, the Evangelist added that Isaiah said this because he saw Jesus's glory and spoke about him. This narrative was positioned between (as the Son of Man) Jesus's prophecy of his death and his washing of the disciples' feet.

To sum up, in John 3:14–15, this series of observations of John's Gospel in connection with Deutero-Isaiah (esp. Isa 52–53) can support the argument that ὕψωσεν ... ὑψωθῆναι δεῖ (cf. John 3:14; 8:28; 12:32, 34) alludes to ὑψωθήσεται καὶ δοξασθήσεται in Isa 52:13. Furthermore, Jesus himself thought that he, as the Son of Man based on Dan 7:13–14, must accomplish the work (death) of the suffering servant of Yahweh based on Deutero-Isaiah (cf. Isa 52:13–53:12). He would endure a vicarious atoning death as the guilt-offering for sinful Israel and all the nations; and so redeem them from condemnation at the last judgment. The identification between the Danielic Son of Man and the Deutero-Isaianic suffering servant of the Lord could be explained by the idea of the firstborn and the dual concepts (the firstborn/son of God and the servant of God including the priesthood. cf. Exod 4:22f; 12:1–51; 19:5f).[927] The argument that both the Danielic Son of Man and the Isaianic suffering servant of the Lord are based on the idea of the firstborn is further supported by 'the only Son' of God in John 3:16–18.

5.2.5 The Evangelist's Commentarial Interpretation (John 3:16–21)

John 3:16–21 is thought to be the Evangelist's commentarial interpretation of Jesus's conversation with Nicodemus.[928] The Evangelist first states that 'eternal life' (or 'salvation') and 'condemnation' (or 'to perish') must be seen in connection with 'the only Son' given (or sent) by God in vv. 16–18; cf. 'the Son' (τὸν υἱὸν) in v. 17 (cf. vv. 35–36), God's only Son (τοῦ μονογενοῦς υἱοῦ τοῦ θεοῦ) in v. 18. John further explains 'eternal life' (or 'salvation') and 'condemnation' (or 'the process of condemnation') by use of the motif of light and darkness in vv. 19–21.

In this section, particularly in v. 16 (cf. vv. 13ff, 17f), we will concentrate on the identity of τὸν υἱὸν τὸν μονογενῆ and his work. Focus will centre on the

---

[926] Kim, *Origin*, 32; Dennis, *Gathering*, 325–326, 328–329.
[927] See iv) Summary of the Study of '*Old Testament Christological Development.*' For detailed discussion, see 2.4.2. The Suffering Messianic Figure in Daniel (cf. Dan 9:24–26) and 3.2. The (Firstborn) Son of God and the Son of Man of Ra, *Christological*.
[928] Burge, *John*, 117–118 n. 12; Morris, *John*, 202 n. 73; Carson, *John*, 203–204; Whitacre, *John*, 92; Westcott, *John*, I, 118–119.

one who was given by God the Father, who loved the world, so that whoever believes in him should not perish but have eternal life. In particular, the passage shows the intimate interrelationship of three Christological titles (the Son of Man, the Isaianic-suffering servant of the Lord, and the only Son of God), which has been already studied in the discussion of the Christological Titles[929] on the basis of the idea of the firstborn. Subsequently, the notions of eternal life and condemnation (or wrath) will be discussed in the light of the new exodus motif. Furthermore, in connection with the motif of hardening and blindness (deafness), the ideas of light and darkness which are used to explain condemnation and eternal life will be explored with attention to some references (cf. John 8:12; 9:4f, 39; 11:9f; 12:35f, 39ff, 46). This too will be set against the background of the OT regarding the paschal-new exodus motif.

5.2.5.1 The Only Son and the Servant of Yahweh (vv. 16–18)

Some commentators [930] interpret 'the only Son', a very Johannine Christological title, in the light of the *Aqedah* theology (cf. Gen 22:12). Not enough attention has been given to the title in connection with other references, the Son of Man (Dan 7:13f) in vv. 13, 14 and the servant of Yahweh (Isa 52:13) reflected in ὑψωθῆναι in v. 14. As some have already recognized,[931] the two passages (vv. 14–15 and v. 16) are exactly parallel (cf. John 3:34, 36).

In v. 16, the Evangelist just replaced ὑψωθῆναι δεῖ τὸν υἱὸν τοῦ ἀνθρώπου (cf. v. 14) with (ὁ θεὸς) τὸν υἱὸν τὸν μονογενῆ ἔδωκεν (cf. v. 16) and just added μὴ ἀπόληται ἀλλ' (cf. v. 16) το ἵνα πᾶς ὁ πιστεύων ἐν αὐτῷ ἔχῃ ζωὴν αἰώνιον (cf. v. 15). This means that, in vv. 14–15, Jesus's words about being the Danielic Son of Man who undertakes the work of the Isaianic-suffering servant are

---

[929] See Ra, *Christological* or iv) Summary of the Study of '*Old Testament Christological Development*' of this work.

[930] Brown, *John I-XII*, 147, who argues that the statement in John 3:16 goes well with Abraham's generosity that, in Gen 22:18; *Sir.* 44:21; *Jub.* 18:15, the sacrifice of his 'only son,' Isaac was beneficial to all the nations of the world. Furthermore, for Brown, the argument about the presence of Isaac typology in John 3:16 is supported by John 19:17 in which Jesus's carrying of his own cross alludes to Isaac's bearing of the wood for the burnt offering. Also Milne, *John*, 77; Bernard, *John*, I, 118; Lindars, *John*, 159; Barrett, *John*, 216; Beasley-Murray, *Life*, 39–40; *idem.*, *John*, 51; Westcott, *John*, I, 120; Cullmann, *Christology*, 300–301; Hengel, *Atonement*, 36; *idem.*, *Son*, 11f.

[931] Brown, *John I-XII*, 147 recognized this parallel; nonetheless, he did not develop their relationship. Also, Maddox, 'Function,' 190, 192; Beasley-Murray, 'Christology,' 33f; E. D. Freed, 'Son,' 403; Burkett, *Son*, 76–111; Smith, *John*, 99; Dennis, *Gathering*, 198. Furthermore, Bulman, 'Only,' 74–75, points out that the Danielic Son of Man in John 3:13–15 is identified with the Son of God (cf. John 3:16), Christ (cf. John 20:31) and the King of Israel (cf. John 1:49) and 'the ascended Son of Man' with 'the Only Begotten Son of God.' Nevertheless, Bulman does not explore this important relationship between these titles.

being reinterpreted by the Evangelist as God's works through his τὸν υἱὸν τὸν μονογενῆ (cf. τὸν υἱὸν in vv. 17, 35–36). For the Evangelist, the Son of Man and the Isaianic servant of Yahweh could be the same entity as the only Son (or 'the Son'), in respect to Jesus's identity and his salvation works. Here, we need to consider how John reinterpreted Jesus's works (as the Son of Man and the servant of Yahweh) as the work of the only Son of God.

In vv. 16–21,[932] what should not be overlooked is the world's identity and its circumstances. For John, the world is not a reference to the neutral world between sin and righteousness, nor the natural world of trees, animals, and plants, but to the world of sinners. This world is pictured to be under the power of the darkness (cf. John 1:5–9; 3:19–21) and is antagonistic to God and his agent sent by him (cf. John 1:10–11; 7:7). Further, it has to be redeemed from sin and condemnation (cf. 1:29; 3:17; 6:51).[933] Carson[934] rightly says that the world has already been lost and condemned, and is not a neutral world which is neither sinful nor righteous. Nevertheless, this passage clearly shows that the hostile world which has already been lost and condemned is the object of the love of God. In regard to this, Jesus was later named as 'the Saviour of the world' (John 4:42; cf. 1 John 4:14). God's love is not limited to a selected few (those chosen, those privileged) but the world, 'the all-encompassing circle of men and women who inhabit this planet, people who embrace darkness habitually (3:19–21).'[935]

R. H. Gundry and R. W. Howell[936] relate 'for in this way God loved the world' (v. 16) to v. 14 ('Just as Moses lifted up the snake in the desert so the Son of Man must be lifted up'), which means God loved the world by way of determining that the Son of Man be lifted up as Moses lifted up the serpent in the wilderness (v. 14). The way that God loved the world refers to Jesus's crucifixion, portrayed as usual in John as exaltation. That God gave up his ὁ υἱός ὁ μονογενής means Jesus's incarnation and his vicarious, atoning death on the cross.[937]

---

[932] In this passage, the term, 'the world' appears five times. According to Burge, *John*, 118, 'the world' occurs 78 times in John's Gospel and 24 times in John's Epistles.
[933] Burge, *John*, 118.
[934] Carson, *John*, 207.
[935] Burge, *John*, 118; Bruce, *John*, 90.
[936] R. H. Gundry and R. W. Howell, 'Sense,' 35; Carson, *John*, 204, 206; Kim, *Exposition*, 81; Morris, *John*, 203.
[937] Schnackenburg, *John*, I, 399; Brown, *John I-XII*, 134; Haenchen, *John*, I, 205; Lindars, *John*, 159; Morris, *John*, 203; Beasley-Murray, *Life*, 39–40; Carson, *John*, 206; Westcott, *John*, I, 120.

In particular, some commentators[938] observe that a verb ἔδωκεν in John 3:16 could allude to παρεδόθη in Isa 53:6, 12. If this observation is right, it could further support the previous argument that ὑψωθῆναι of the Son of Man in v. 14 is based on the work of 'the servant of Yahweh' in Isa 52:13–53:12. Also, from this observation that v. 16 shows the combination of 'the only Son' and 'the servant of Yahweh,' we can claim that the Evangelist understands 'the only Son' as the agent who accomplishes the works of the suffering of the Deutero-Isaianic servant of Yahweh. That is to say, here, the only Son of God can be understood as the Deutero-Isaianic servant of Yahweh who will give up himself to a vicarious death as a guilt-offering for sinful Israel and all the gentiles, and so as the ransom in order to redeem them from condemnation at the last judgment. This could be another important observation in defining the relationships between 'the Son of Man,' 'the servant of Yahweh' and 'the one and only Son' in regard to our argument concerning the importance of the paschal-new exodus motif in John's Gospel.

In addition, Burge gives a passing mention concerning the statement in v. 16, which, in my opinion, seems to be another significant observation regarding the paschal-new exodus motif in John's Gospel. Pointing out that the statement that God loves the world is rare or never spoken of in Judaism, he argues that v. 16 reflects that, 'God desires to reach this world through Israel, his child.'[939] In other words, 'the only Son' could be understood in the light of the important theological idea that God had corporately elected Israel as the son of God, particularly, as his 'firstborn' (cf. Exod 4:22f; 19:5f, the priestly kingdom; 2 Pet 2:9). God's plan was for the restoration (salvation) of the gentiles, to make also them his sons (cf. Gen 12:1–3; 17:1–8). This is possible even though the title shows the unique ontological relationship between Jesus and God, reflecting God's all-encompassing love for the world (or the gentiles) by giving up his unique Son.

Furthermore, as mentioned above, the main ideas of both verses (v. 16 and v. 17) are closely parallel to each other. These verses clearly show God the Father's will to restore the world, to save it from judgement. According to

---

[938] Schnackenburg, *John*, I, 399; Brown, *John I-XII*, 134; Cullmann, *Christology*, 70. Cf. Beasley-Murray, *Life*, 39–40; Jeremias, *Theology*, I, 295–297. *Contra* Barrett, *John*, 216. In particular, Kim, *Exposition*, 80–81 points out that v. 16 shows 'the giving up formula' (=God-His Son-gives up-for our salvation') which normally comes out in connection with the love of God (cf. Rom 8:32; Gal 1:4; 2:20). Also, Brown, *John I-XII*, 134; Westcott, *John*, I, 120; Hengel, *Atonement*, 36; idem., *Son*, 11–12.

[939] Burge, *John*, 118, even though he does not seem to recognize the importance of his observation in understanding the identity of Jesus as 'the one and only Son' regarding the new exodus motif. See also J. Byron, *Slavery*, 57–58.

Kim,[940] in v. 17, the Evangelist uses 'the sending formula,' which premises the pre-existence of the Son of God. He as the agent of God was commissioned with absolute authority of God and sent to carry out his will perfectly (cf. Rom 8:3; Gal 4:4; 1 John 4:9). Therefore, if the observation that ἔδωκεν in John 3:16 alludes to παρεδόθη in Isa 53:6, 12 is right, the only Son who knows the will of God the Father perfectly (cf. John 1:18), and obeys him completely up to dying on a cross that he might give eternal life to all nations (cf. John 6:38–39), alludes to the perfect servant of Yahweh in Deutero-Isaiah (cf. Isa 52:13–53:12), who was given as the covenant for the people of Israel and as the light for the gentiles so that they could join the salvation of Yahweh (Isa 42:6; 49:8–9. cf. John 8:12; 3:19–21; 9:5; 12:35–36).

John's Gospel itself testifies that some gentiles shared the eschatological salvation through Christ's work against the background of the feast of the Passover in John 12:19–25. After Jesus had raised Lazarus from the dead, and as he entered Jerusalem, the great crowd who had come for the feast of the Passover 'took palm branches and went out to meet him shouting, "Hosanna!" "Blessed is he who comes in the name of the Lord!" "Blessed is the King of Israel!"' (cf. John 12:13), alluding to Ps 118:25–26, which is an important song regarding the expectation of the restoration of Israel.[941] By sitting upon a young donkey, Jesus fulfilled Zech 9:9. In this context, John 12:20–23 says that some Greeks among those who went up Jerusalem to worship at the feast of the Passover wanted to see Jesus and their expectation to meet him was reported to him. In regard to this, Jesus as the Son of Man compares his death with the parable of a kernel of wheat which dies and produces many seeds.

To sum up, vv. 16–18 shows that the only Son of God (τὸν υἱὸν τὸν μονογενῆ) alludes to the priestly function of the firstborn to restore the world (i.e. all the gentiles) (cf. Exod 4:22f; 19:5f) and plays the role of the Isaianic suffering servant of the Lord to restore Israel and the gentiles (cf. Isa 52:13–53:12; 42:6; 49:8–9). Also, vv. 13–18 is a documentary example to confirm the justification of our main argument: the intimate relationship of some paradoxical Christological titles, the Son/Firstborn of God (the only

---

[940] Kim, *Exposition*, 80; Hengel, *Son*, 11f; Schweizer, *TDNT*, VIII, 374–375, 386; Beasley-Murray, *Life*, 15–18; Barrett, *John*, 216; Morris, *John*, 204; Brown, *John I-XII*, 134 points out that 'send' is parallel to in 'gave' v. 16 and the same pair of 'send' and 'give' was used of the *Paraclete* in John 14:16, 26.

[941] Brunson, *Psalm 118*, who fully discussed the presence and function of Ps 118 in John's Gospel, placing particular emphasis on its interpretation in the new exodus context. Also, M. L. Strauss, *Davidic*, 312 n. 3; D. L. Bock, *Proclamation*, 122; Marshall, *Supper*, 77–78; Carson, *John*, 432; Beasley-Murray, *John*, 210.

Son of God and the beloved Son of God), the suffering servant of God, the Son of Man, and the priesthood, on the basis of the concept of the firstborn.

5.2.5.2 Eternal Life (Life/Salvation) and Condemnation (Perishing)

The term, 'eternal life' which appears three times (cf. vv. 15, 16, 36) in the third chapter of the Gospel, with 'to perish' (cf. v. 16) and 'condemnation' (cf. vv. 17–19) and 'wrath' (cf. v. 36), are important factor in understanding the Gospel of John in light of the new exodus motif. In the Gospel, the importance of the concept of eternal life (or life), can be recognized by its high usage.[942] As has been shown above,[943] the idea of the kingdom of God can be clearly found in the Gospel of John.[944] Nonetheless, compared with the Synoptic Gospels, the reference of the kingdom of God in John is quite rare (only twice). So, some commentators[945] think that, instead of the kingdom of God, the term eternal life (or life) was adopted.

John 3:13–15 says that everyone who believes in the Son of Man—who came from heaven and must be lifted up—may have eternal life. This is explained again in v. 16, which says that whoever believes in the only Son shall have eternal life, and in v. 17, which says that God sent his Son to save the world (cf. 'not being condemned' in v. 18). Also, John 3:36 says whoever believes in the Son has eternal life. Thus, it can be recognized that the phrase 'the kingdom of God' was replaced by other phrases such as 'eternal life' or 'salvation.' That is to say, even though the kingdom of God, eternal

---

[942] According to Davis, 'Johannine,' 161, the term 'life' occurs 66 times in the Johannine literature and another term 'eternal life' 17 times (John 3:15, 16, 36; 4:14, 36; 5:24, 39; 6:27, 40, 47, 57, 68; 10:28; 12:25, 50; 17:2, 3) in John's Gospel and 6 times (1:2; 2:25; 3:15; 5:11, 13, 20) in 1 Jn. See also, Keener, *John*, 329; Roberts, 'Observations,' 186; Dodd, *Interpretation*, 144 n. 1; Brown, *John I-XII*, 505–506; J. G. Van Der Watt, 'Use,' 227 concludes that 'All the evidence seems to be strongly in favour of the semantic field of ζωή αἰώνιος overlapping exactly with that of ζωή in John's Gospel, and that the absence of αἰώνιος can be explained mainly on *stylistic* basis (except in the references to God)... Ζωή αἰώνιος must be regarded as the primary and basic expression, while ζωή (alone) is used without any semantic difference.' So, Brown, *ibid.*, 508; R. W. Thomas, 'Meaning,' 199–212, esp. 204; Lightfoot, *John's*, 132; Roberts, *ibid.*, 189.
[943] See 5.2.2.1. The Kingdom of God (or Heaven) and the New Exodus.
[944] Cf. The references of 'the kingdom of God' appear in this chapter of the Gospel (cf. John 3:3, 5). And, at the trial of Jesus in the passion narrative, the conclusive moment of his mission (cf. John 18:28–19:22), the main charge was about his kingship, and he himself mentioned 'his kingdom' (cf. 'my kingdom'/ἡ βασιλεία ἡ ἐμή) three times and admitted his kingship as the response of Pilate's question about it (cf. John 18:36–37).
[945] Goppelt, *Theology*, I, 14–15, 45; Klappert, *NIDNTT*, II, 387–388; Bruce, *John*, 82–83; Roberts, 'Observations,' 186–193; Davis, 'Johannine,' 161–169; Beasley-Murray, *Life*, 2–5, 13; Bauckham, 'Kingdom,' 2; Lee, *Narratives*, 45; Barrett, *John*, 215; Dodd, *Interpretation*, 144–150.

life and salvation are not synonymous, they have the same essential function in John.[946]

So, what is the background of the term eternal life? Some commentators[947] believe that eternal life in the Gospel originates from Dan 12:2. Dodd[948] observes that in the Bible the term ζωὴ αἰώνιος appears only once in the Greek version of Dan 12:2 = לְחַיֵּי עוֹלָם which literally means 'the life of the age to come,' i.e., 'the resurrection life,' in which God will reign with righteousness and life, based on the Hebraic idea of two ages (this age and the age to come). Also, eternal life means 'the life of God,' in other words, participation in the unlimited rich life of God.[949] Eternal life means that God bestows his life on human beings who do not have divine life by nature.[950] Thus, the eternal life of the OT is different from the immortality of the soul in Greek thought. The argument that the term ζωὴ αἰώνιος is based on the LXX Dan 12:2 לְחַיֵּי עוֹלָם could be supported by John 3:14–15; 5:27, in which Jesus disclosed his identity as the Son of Man, based on Dan 7:13. Also, the notions of eternal life and eternal condemnation with the idea of the kingdom of God (Dan 2:44; 7:14, 27)[951] can be found in Dan 12:2, 'Multitudes who sleep in the dust of the earth will awake: some to 'everlasting life'(עוֹלָם לְחַיֵּי), others to shame and 'everlasting

---

[946] Roberts, 'Observations,' 187; U. E. Simon, 'Eternal,' 98; Barrett, *John*, 215; Lee, *Narratives*, 45; Polhill, 'John 1–4,' 445; Davis, 'Johannine,' 164ff. Cf. Mark 9:43–48, in which 'to enter life' has the same meaning as 'to enter the kingdom of God' and both phrases are entirely opposite to 'to go into hell' (or 'to be thrown into hell'). Also, Mark 10:17–31 (cf. Matt 19:16–30) in which all the phrases ('to inherit eternal life,' 'treasure in heaven' (i.e., with God), 'to enter the kingdom of God,' 'to be saved' and 'eternal life in the age to come') are alternatively used. Concerning this, see Klappert, *NIDNTT*, II, 387–388; Beasley-Murray, *Life*, 2–3; Thomas, 'Meaning,' 203; Davis, 'Johannine,' 164f; Goppelt, *Theology*, I, 45; Brown, *John I-XII*, 508; Lindars, *John*, 158; Bruce, *John*, 83, who points out that a term 'regeneration' (παλιγγενεσία) in Matt 19:28 is another synonym for 'the kingdom of God.' See also Beasley-Murray, *John*, 48. Cf. 1 Pet 1:23; Tit 3:5; Gal 6:15; 2 Cor 5:17.
[947] Dodd, *Interpretation*, 144; Barrett, *John*, 124; Brown, *John I-XII*, 506; Bernard, *John*, I, 116; G. Sloyan, *John*, 46; Simon, 'Eternal,' 97, 109; Keener, *John*, 328; Bruce, *John*, 89; Beasley-Murray, *Life*, 2; Kim, *Exposition*, 120–121; Lindars, *John*, 158; Roberts, 'Observations,' 192; Thomas, 'Meaning,' 203; M. Reiser, *Jesus*, 41.
[948] Dodd, *Interpretation*, 144–149; Keener, *John*, 328, who introduces some references related with the idea of 'the life of the world to come' or 'the life of the age to come' (eternal life) in Judaism and the NT; e.g., *Tob.* 12:9–10; *Ps. Sol.* 3:12; 13:11; 14:7; *2 Macc.* 7:9–14; *4 Ezra* 7:137; 14:22; Mark 10:17, 30; Matt 25:46; Acts 13:46, 48; Rom 2:7; 5:21; 6:22–23; Gal 6:8; 1 Tim 1:16; 6:12; Tit 1:2; 3:7; Jud 21 (p. 329). See also, Brown, *John I-XII*, 506. Cf. *2 Macc.* 12:43f; *1 QS* 4:7; *CD* 3:20.
[949] Kim, *Exposition*, 120–121; Beasley-Murray, *Life*, 4; Bernard, *John*, I, 116.
[950] Davis, 'Johannine,' 162, 168; Bruce, *John*, 89; Kim, *Exposition*, 81, 121; Roberts, 'Observations,' 191; Bernard, *John*, I, 116; Simon, 'Eternal,' 109; Beasley-Murray, *Life*, 4; Brown, *John I-XII*, 507; Whitacre, *John*, 91; Keener, *John*, 328; H. Sasse, *TDNT*, I, 197–209.
[951] Cf. Bruce, *John*, 83.

contempt' (לְדִרְאוֹן).' Reiser[952] argues that Dan 12:1–3 shows eschatological salvation and damnation, in which the lot of the damned is shame and everlasting contempt, whereas the lot of those who are found written in the book is everlasting life.

Two kinds of resurrection of Dan 12:2 in relation to the Danielic heavenly figure described in Dan 7:13, are clearly reflected in John 5:27–29.[953] In connection with the saying in John 5:27–29, Dodd assures us that: 'It (cf. Jesus's raising of Lazarus in John 11) certainly appears as though the Evangelist had deliberately dramatized the saying, "Those who are in the tombs will hear his voice and come forth."'[954] Also, this imagery of the coming out of the tombs on hearing the voice could reflect the resurrection of the dry bones of the valley in Ezek 37:1–14 (esp. vv. 12–13), alluding to the creation in Genesis (Gen 2:7).

In particular, in Ezek 37:12f, what has to be noted is that the exile of Judah and Israel was described as *the dead in the tombs*. As discussed earlier, the picture of resurrection (new creation) in Dan 12:2 as well as Isa 26:19; Ezek 37:1–14 was used to describe Yahweh's promise of the restoration of the Israelites from exile to the promised land.[955] Here, in Dan 12:2, the promise that some of the multitudes who sleep in the dust will be resurrected to eternal life, is reflected in the idea of eternal life in John 3:14–16, therefore, eternal life can be understood in the light of the restoration or the new exodus motif.

In particular, in connection with the idea of condemnation which is the opposite of eternal life, it seems helpful to consider a very rare term, 'everlasting contempt' (לְדִרְאוֹן) in Dan 12:2.[956] The only other reference to this term is found in Isa 66:24:[957]

> And they will go out and look upon the dead bodies of those who rebelled against me; their worm will not die, nor will their fire be quenched, and they will be loathsome (דֵּרָאוֹן) to all mankind.

---

[952] Reiser, *Jesus*, 41.
[953] Bruce, *John*, 133; Whitacre, *John*, 132; Barrett, *John*, 263.
[954] Dodd, *Interpretation*, 148.
[955] Knibb, 'Life,' 407. In particular, concerning the intimate relationship between the resurrection motif (cf. the new birth) and the new exodus motif, see 4.6. Johannine Resurrection Narratives (John 20:19–23; 11:1–44. Cf. John 5:16–30), and 5.2.1. The Origin of the Idea of the New Birth.
[956] Reiser, *Jesus*, 41.
[957] Motyer, *Isaiah*, 544; Watts, *Isaiah 34–66*, 361; J. E. Goldingay, *Daniel*, 281; Reiser, *Jesus*, 30 n. 30, who also says that in Isa 66:24 'the eternal adoration of the redeemed in the Temple' is contrasted with 'the eternal damnation of the rebels' (*ibid.*, 32).

Interestingly, a part of this passage was quoted by Jesus to describe hell (τὴν γέενναν) in Mark 9:47–48 (cf. v. 43), in which both to enter life (cf. vv. 43, 45) and to enter the kingdom of God (cf. v. 47) are alternatively mentioned and are entirely opposite to 'to go into hell' (or 'to be thrown into hell') (cf. vv. 43, 45, 47). That is to say, in Mark 9:43–48, warning against causing one of little ones to sin, the Markan Jesus repeatedly said that those who do not enter life (the kingdom of God) due to parts (hand, foot, eye) of their body causing them to sin should be thrown into hell. Here, he reminded them of the horrible reality of hell by quoting Isa 66:24.[958] Concerning this, Motyer rightly says that, 'On the lips of Jesus these verses will become the vehicle of the doctrine of eternal loss.'[959] The idea of everlasting contempt in Dan 12:2 is intimately connected with the image of the loathsome situation of the dead bodies of those who rebelled against Yahweh in Isa 66:24.

Against this background Yahweh promised to the faithful pilgrims from all the nations that their name and descendants will endure, as the new heaven and the new earth (the new creation) which Yahweh makes will endure before him (v. 22). As a result, all mankind will come and bow down before him from one New Moon to another and from one Sabbath to another (v. 23). Here, Isaiah's ending that the two feasts were perfectly kept, recalled Israel's corruptions which distressed Yahweh in Isa 1:13.[960] In v. 24, Yahweh's condemnation against those who rebelled against him was described as 'its ceaseless corruption' and 'its unending holy wrath' by use of the images of 'undying worm' and 'unquenchable fire' reciprocally. Motyer also observes that the rebellion theme is one of main themes from beginning to end in Isaiah.[961] Above all, what has to be noted in Isa 66:24 is that Yahweh's condemnation against those who rebelled against him was described by the metaphor of the horrible *death* under its ceaseless corruption and his unending wrath.

---

[958] Reiser, *Jesus*, 32 n. 31 says that the image of the undying worm and the unquenchable fire shows 'an unceasing process of torment and corruption' and the undying worm is 'a sign of eternal perdition and its pains.' See also F. Lang, *TDNT*, VI, 937; VII, 454.

[959] Motyer, *Isaiah*, 544; Reiser, *Jesus*, 146f, 147f n. 10, who says that Isa 66:24 is the basis of the ultimate punishment of sinners, which 'is connected with the idea of enduring suffering in the valley of Gehenna. This passage is the source of the 'fire' that becomes the epitome of the pains of hell; from this time on it describes Gehenna and then burns in Sheol after the latter was identified with Gehenna and became the place of eternal punishment for sinners.' Cf. *1 En.* 22; 63:10; 99:11; 103:7–8; *Jub.* 7:29; 22:22; *Ps. Sol.* 14:9; 15:10; Str-B, IV, 1075, 1095.

[960] Motyer, *Isaiah*, 543.

[961] Motyer, *Isaiah*, 544. Cf. Isa 1:2, 28; 24:20; 43:25, 27; 44:22; 46:8; 48:8; 50:1; 53:5, 8, 12; 57:4; 58:1; 59:12, 13, 20; 66:24.

What eternal condemnation was, pictured by the horrible *death* state under the unending wrath of God, could also be found in significant terms, 'to perish' (ἀπόληται) in John 3:16 and 'God's wrath' (ἡ ὀργὴ τοῦ θεοῦ) in John 3:36. Concerning the term, ἀπόλλυμι, Opeke says that:

> In contrast to σῴζεσθαι or to ζωὴ αἰςώνιος, ἀςπόλλυσθαι is definitive destruction, not merely in the sense of the extinction of physical existence, but rather of an eternal plunge into Hades and a hopeless destiny of death.[962]

Above all, Dennis[963] says that the verb ἀπόλλυμι which is opposite to the gift of eternal life (cf. John 6:33, 39, 40, 50, 51, 54, 58) means 'lostness or destruction as the result of not believing in Jesus' in John 3:16. This signifies the second exodus, as does the verb συνάγω, which denotes rescue from perishing (v. 12). Dennis[964] also points out that ἀπόλλυμι of John 10:10, 12, with the parallel to σκορπίζω (to scatter) in John 10:12 and with the shepherd discourses of the OT, alludes to, 'the dispersion and exile of Israel due in part to the corrupt leaders of Israel' (cf. Jer 23; Ezek 34–37). Furthermore, Dennis[965] says that particularly the verb ἀπόλλυμι in John 11:50 means 'the perishing of Israel in connection with Israel's experiences of dispersion and exile.' Thus, Dennis argues that ἀπόλλυμι in the OT and Jewish literature, 'describes an experience that was either parallel to or equivalent with exile/dispersion.'[966]

To sum up, we can understand that in John 3:15–18, eternal life (in connection with the resurrection motif in Dan 12:2 and Ezek 37:1–14) reflects the restoration (new exodus) motif and, further, eternal condemnation in connection with the horrible death under God's unending wrath reflects the exile motif (see Isa 66:24; Ezek 37:1–14; Dan 12:1–2).

5.2.5.3 Self-Condemnation: Hardening and Blindness (Deafness), Light and Darkness, and Nicodemus

In 3:17–18 (cf. v. 19), the terms, κρίνῃ, κρίνεται, κέκριται and ἡ κρίσις (cf. ἀπόληται in v. 16) are related to adverse judgment which means

---

[962] R. Opeke, *TDNT*, I, 396. Also, Barrett, *John*, 216 points out that 'perish' is the inevitable destiny of people or things that are separated from God, because life is only present in the Father, the Logos and the Spirit.
[963] Dennis, *Gathering*, 197f.
[964] Dennis, *ibid.*, 197.
[965] Dennis, *ibid.*, 197.
[966] Dennis, *ibid.*, 198 n. 368. For the detailed discussion of the verb ἀπόλλυμι in light of exile and dispersion in the OT and Judaism, see Dennis, *ibid.*, 89–105. Cf. Isa 11:12; 27:12f; Jer 23:1; 34:15; 1 Macc. 3:9; Bar. 3:3.

condemnation, the opposite of salvation (or eternal life).[967] By use of this parallel in vv. 16–17, the Evangelist repeatedly emphasized that the foremost purpose that God sent his only Son into the world of sinners is not to condemn the world but to save the world through him.[968] Also, in this paragraph (John 3:16–21), self-condemnation is proclaimed against those who reject eternal life (or salvation) offered through the Son of Man, the only Son of God. Some commentators[969] agree that in this passage the emphasis is not on the condemnation of God against the sinful, even hostile world, but on the eternal life (or salvation) which God offers it. Nevertheless, God's condemnation may take place inevitably against those who constantly reject the eternal life offered through the only Son whom he sent.[970] God's condemnation happens not because of his rejection of the hostile world but because of their rejection of his only Son. That is to say, they condemn themselves. This self-condemnation (or the process of self-condemnation) has been clearly explained in vv. 18–21.

To begin with, let us look at v. 18: ὁ πιστεύων εἰς αὐτὸν οὐ κρίνεται· ὁ δὲ μὴ πιστεύων ἤδη κέκριται, ὅτι μὴ πεπίστευκεν εἰς τὸ ὄνομα τοῦ μονογενοῦς υἱοῦ τοῦ θεοῦ (NASB, 'he who believes in him is not judged; he who does not believe has been judged already, because he has not believed in the name of the only Begotten Son of God.') Here, we have to pay attention to the characteristic tense of verses in v. 18.[971] From the two perfect tense verbs

---

[967] Bruce, *John*, 90; Haenchen, *John*, I, 205; Carson, *John*, 206; Morris, *John*, 205; Smith, *John*, 100; Barrett, *John*, 216.
[968] This idea is the same as the statement in John 12:47 ('I did not come to judge the world, but to save the world'). These statements seem to externally contradict the statement in John 9:39 ('For judgment I came into this world, so that the blind will see and those who see will become blind'). However, if the context of the passage (John 9:39) is considered, the meaning of it is the same as the meaning of these passages in John 3:16–18; 12:47. Actually, in John 9:39 which has the background of the dispute between Jesus and the Pharisees in regard to his healing of a man born blind, he proclaimed this self-condemnation against them who always argued from their knowledge of their own truth but did not accept his identity shown through this miraculous sign. For this, see Bruce, *John*, 90; Barrett, *John*, 216–217; Carson, *John*, 206–207; Morris, *John*, 205–206.
[969] Morris, *John*, 205; Beasley-Murray, *Life*, 21; Lindars, *John*, 159; Smith, *John*, 99–100; Bultmann, *John*, 154; Moloney, *John*, 96; Whitacre, *John*, 83–83; Bruce, *John*, 90; Burge, *John*, 118; Haenchen, *John*, I, 205; Kim, *Exposition*, 83–84; Westcott, *John*, I, 121.
[970] Bultmann, *John*, 157.
[971] Cf. Barrett, *John*, 217; Morris, *John*, 207; Brown, *John I-XII*, 134. If we compare the first main clause with the second one, we can recognize the differences between them. The first main clause, ὁ πιστεύων εἰς αὐτὸν οὐ κρίνεται shows that both 'believing in him' and 'being not condemned' are described as the present event. It could mean that as soon as he believes in him, he is presently excluded from the condemnation. However, the second main clause ὁ δὲ μὴ πιστεύων ἤδη κέκριται shows that 'not believing' is present tense and 'to have been already condemned' is perfect tense, so which could be rendered 'he who does not believe at the present time *has been already condemned.*' Also, the subordinate clause of the second main

(κέκριται πεπίστευκεν), we could understand that the second main clause and its subordinate clause ('he who does not believe *has been already condemned* because he *has not believed in* the name of the one and only Son of God') mean that those who do not believe at the present time have already been under the condemnation of God from the past until now. That is to say, before the only Son of God was sent into the world, it had already been under the condemnation of God, and thus his wrath continuously remains on those who reject the Son at the present time (John 3:36). Those who refuse to believe in the Son offered by God the Father are self-condemned. Also, this could mean that when Jesus the Son of the Man came into the world, it was not in a neutral situation between salvation and condemnation, but already under the condemnation of God.[972]

Above all, it must be noted that God gave (or sent) his only Son to the lost and condemned world, to be lifted up (in death and exaltation) so that whoever believes in him shall have eternal life, calling them out of the condemnation. This could reflect the restoration or the new exodus motif; John 5:24 'whoever hears my word and believes in him who sent me has eternal life and will not be condemned; he has crossed over from death to life' (cf. Ezek 37:1–28; Isa 26:19; Rom 6; Acts 26; Luke 1:79).[973] This argument is further supported by pictures of light and darkness in vv. 19–21.

V.19 starts with a proclamation: 'This is the condemnation.'[974] In vv. 19–20, the Evangelist explains that light has come into the world, but humanity loves darkness rather than light because their deeds were evil. Those who do evil hate the light and will not come into the light for fear that their deeds will be exposed.[975] This shows that before the light came into the world, it was totally possessed by the darkness, which as the picture for death symbolized the condemnation of God.[976] That is to say, the world was already lost and condemned. In order to give eternal life (salvation) to the already lost world, the light of life (cf. John 1:4) had to come into it. Since

---

clause ὅτι μὴ πεπίστευκεν εἰς τὸ ὄνομα τοῦ μονογενοῦς υἱοῦ τοῦ θεοῦ is perfect tense, so it could be rendered 'because he *has not believed in* the name of the only Son of God.'

[972] Carson, *John*, 207; Lindars, *John*, 159; Barrett, *John*, 216; Hodges, 'Coming,' 318f.

[973] Moloney, *John*, 96. In Ezek 37:1–28, the pictures of death (grave) and resurrection (life) are used to symbolize exile and restoration respectively. Cf. Thomas, 'Meaning,' 209 points out that in Rom 5:12–17 death is identified with condemnation, and life with acquittal or justification. C. P. Baylis, 'Meaning,' 215 says that walking in the darkness means 'abiding in death by rejecting God's message of eternal life through Christ.'

[974] Carson, *John*, 207; Lindars, *John*, 160; Barrett, *John*, 217; Morris, *John*, 206, who argues that the word denotes the *process* of judging, not the *sentence* of condemnation. Also Beasley-Murray, *John*, 51 thinks that *krisis* means 'separation and condemnation.' Cf. Bruce, *John*, 92; Haenchen, *John*, I, 205; Bultmann, *John*, 157.

[975] Lee, *Flesh*, 169.

[976] Koester, *Symbolism*, 133.

people do evil things, they love the darkness instead of the light. Further, they hated the light and would not come into the light, remaining in the darkness continuously for fear that their evil deeds would be exposed. Here, it has to be noted that the light came into the dark world in order to call people out from there to the light, alluding to the restoration (the new exodus) (cf. Eph 5:8–14; Col 1:12–13). This is the major premise of the Gospel of John not only at the beginning of the Prologue (cf. John 1:4–11) but also in this passage (cf. John 3:16–21) by use of the metaphor of light and darkness (cf. John 8:12; 9:4f; 12:35f, 46; 13:30).[977]

John's Gospel says not that both the light and the darkness have been present together in the world at the beginning, but that at first the darkness was in the world and then the light penetrated into the world of the darkness. There are only two choices to them in the dark world; whether they come out to the light from the darkness or remain in the darkness continuously.[978] By avoiding the redeemer, the light of life, and further hating him, those who have moved into the deeper darkness, expose their real identity as the sons of the darkness.[979] As a result, they confront self-incurred condemnation.[980]

In v. 21, the Evangelist writes that whoever lives by the truth comes into the light, so that it may be seen plainly that what he/she has done has been done through God. The majority of Johannine commentators feel a difficulty in understanding the meaning of v. 21.[981] What does this verse mean? Does it mean that some of those who have been lost in the dark world can do the truth through God, before they confront Jesus who as the light of life came into the world? In regard to this, some commentators[982] explain v. 21 in the light of predestinarian theology based on the doctrine of election.

---

[977] Cf. Westcott, *John*, I, 122; Bruce, *John*, 91; Barrett, *John*, 217; Baylis, 'Meaning,' 217.
[978] Beasley-Murray, *John*, 51; Hodges, 'Coming,' 319.
[979] Kim, *Exposition*, 83–84; Burge, *John*, 118; Moloney, *John*, 96.
[980] Carson, *John*, 207; Morris, *John*, 207; Moloney, *John*, 96; H.-C. Hahn, *NIDNTT*, I, 424f; Lindars, *John*, 161.
[981] For example, Hodges, 'Coming,' 314–322.
[982] Barrett, *John*, 217–218; Morris, *John*, 205, 207; Moloney, *John*, 102; Brown, *John I-XII*, 148–149; Bultmann, *John*, 159; Smith, *John*, 101; Beasley-Murray, *John*, 52; Schnackenburg, *John*, I, 543–547; Haenchen, *John*, I, 205. However, Hodges, 'Coming,' 315, points out that, in giving an example of a Samaritan woman who, although she had lived under the darkness-adultery sinful life, came to Jesus the light of the world, repented from her sinful life, and got eternal life, 'the predestinarian approach to John 3:21 in reality bypasses the fundamental difficulty and is not in fact a real solution.' So, Whitacre, *John*, 92. Hodges, *ibid.*, 318 presents John the Baptist as an example of v. 21.

Rather, this passage (vv. 20–21) seems to show that the light reveals just what a man/woman really is and what he/she always was (good or bad); whoever is good is not afraid of God and therefore comes to Jesus, the light of the world. By contrast, whoever is bad is afraid and moves away from Jesus, the light of the world, into the deeper darkness.[983] This emphasizes that Jesus as the penetrating light coming into the world exposes the reality and real identity of man/woman.[984] Nonetheless, there is a general reluctance to interpret the statement in the light of a moral standard, in which everything depends utterly on the real nature of his (or her) life.[985]

For a much clearer understanding of self-condemnation in John 3:19–21, the subjects of light and darkness and hardening and blindness have to be considered in the light of the OT and John's Gospel. These concepts are also important with regard to the study of the new exodus motif.

5.2.5.3.1 Nicodemus and 'Light and Darkness' (John 3:1f, 19–21)

The passage of John 2:23–25 could be regarded as the bridge between John 2 and John 3.[986] This is due to the reference to Jesus's performance of miraculous signs in Jerusalem at the Passover feast and thereby many people's believing in his name (cf. John 2:23); which is related to the confession of Nicodemus[987] who understood him as a teacher who had come from God, on the basis of the miraculous signs he had done (cf. John 3:2). Accordingly, John 2:23–25 is the introduction of the third chapter of

---

[983] Koester, *Symbolism*, 133.
[984] Brown, *John I-XII*, 148f; Bruce, *John*, 92; Barrett, *John*, 217f; Bultmann, *John*, 114, 159; Smith, *John*, 101; Lindars, *John*, 161.
[985] Haenchen, *John*, I, 205; Brown, *John I-XII*, 148f; Barrett, *John*, 218; Bultmann, *John*, 114; Whitacre, *John*, 92; Burge, *John*, 119; Morris, *John*, 207; Baylis, 'Meaning,' 218, who says that 'Those who reject that revelation are thereby claiming self-righteousness. It is not a question of whether one is good, but whether one will accept God's revelation and His offer of eternal life.'
[986] Lee, *Narratives*, 38; Burge, *John*, 111; Bruce, *John*, 81; Bennema, *Power*, 168.
[987] Cf. Nicodemus who appears three times in the Gospel of John (cf. John 3:1–9; 7:50–51; 19:39–42) is regarded as a Greek version of a Hebrew name Niqdimon (e.g., Smith, *John*, 93; Barrett, *John*, 204; Lindars, *John*, 149; Haenchen, *John*, I, 199). Generally, commentators think that Nicodemus is not the same figure as Niqdimon b. Gurion in Josephus (*Ant.* 14.37; an ambassador of Aristobulus to Pompey) and Talmud (*b. Gitt.* 56a; *b. Taan.* 20a; *b. Ket.* 66b; cf. Str-B, II, 413–419; Niqdimon b. Gurion, a wealthy Jerusalemite who was entrusted with supplying water to pilgrims at the great festival). In particular, R. Bauckham, 'Nicodemus,' 1–37 thinks that probably Nicodemus in John's Gospel is related with the Gurion family (cf. the Jewish ruling elite, Pharisees, teachers of the Law and extremely rich); the uncle of Naqdimon b. Gurion and brother of the famous Gurya/Gurion at whose house in Jericho the Pharisees met (p. 34). See also, Blomberg, *Historical*, 91f; Beasley-Murray, *John*, 44f. Cf. Bernard, *John*, I, 99; Brown, *John I-XII*, 129f; Lindars, *John*, 149; Morris, *John*, 186; Smith, *John*, 93; Carson, *John*, 186; Bruce, *John*, 81 who are not sure that the Johannine Nicodemus is the same figure as Niqdimon b. Gurion appearing in Josephus and Talmud.

John's Gospel and so, for the moment, he could be regarded as the representative of Jewish people introduced in John 2:23–25, who had a faith depending upon the miraculous signs and so a partial faith.[988] Also, he, as the Pharisees, the teacher of the laws, a member of the council of Sanhedrin, could be seen as the representative of the Jewish people.[989] Johannine commentators diversely reason why Nicodemus came to Jesus *at night*.[990]

Kim[991] points out that Nicodemus' nocturnal encounter means that although as the representative of the Jews, he is a prominent figure of the Jewish religion, he is just the man of the darkness. Nonetheless, generally, commentators think that the Evangelist has a theological intention in referring that Nicodemus came to Jesus *at night*, symbolically meaning that he came from the darkness to Jesus, the light of the world (John 8:12).[992] This could be supported by the fact that the section of the conversation between Jesus and Nicodemus is brought to an end with the motif of light and darkness (John 3:1–21), especially in John 3:19–21.[993] This alludes to

---

[988] Burge, *John*, 111; Bruce, *John*, 81; Howard-Brook, *Becoming*, 87; Lee, *Narratives*, 39; Polhill, 'John 1–4,' 452; Haenchen, *John*, I, 199; Bennema, *Power*, 168; Witherington, *Wisdom*, 92f; Moloney, *John*, 97.

[989] Cf. Lindars, *John*, 149; Barrett, *John*, 208; Bultmann, *John*, 133.

[990] Cf. Williford, 'John 3:1–15,' 453 n. 7; Morris, *John*, 187.

1) To meet Jesus secretly because Nicodemus was afraid of his fellow Jews (esp. the Temple authorities) who were hostile to Jesus after the Temple incident (John 2:13–22). E.g., Burge, *John*, 113; Brown, *John I-XII*, 130; Schnackenburg, *John*, I, 365f; Lindars, *John*, 149. Contra Bultmann, *John*, 133; Beasley-Murray, *John*, 47; Haenchen, *John*, I, 199.

2) To have a conversation with Jesus without being disturbed. E.g., Bauckham, 'Nicodemus,' 27–32; Beasley-Murray, *John*, 47.

3) Because the night is the proper time for visionary experiences of *Merkabah* (cf. *4 Ezra* 3:14; 6:12; 10:58f; 13:1; *2 Bar.* 36:1). E.g., Motyer, *Father*, 46 n. 47, who also says that Nicodemus is a Pharisee who longed for the heavenly knowledge through *Merkabah*. Also, Motyer points out that the ascent-descent language in John 3:13 is related with the rejection against the argument of the Jewish apocalypticists. Also, Bultmann, *John*, 133 n. 5. Cf. Some theologians (e.g., Meeks, *Prophet-King*, 295–301; idem., 'Man,' 52f; Dunn, 'John,' 322–325; W. C. Grese, 'Unless,' 678) observe the presence of the *Merkabah*-mysticism in John 3:13.

4) Because of a rabbinic custom of using the night for theological discussion. E.g., Bennema, *Power*, 168 n. 31; Blomberg, *Historical*, 92; Witherington, *Wisdom*, 94; Schnackenburg, *John*, I, 356f; Brown, *John I-XII*, 130; Smith, *John*, 94; Bultmann, *John*, 133 n. 5. Cf. Str-B, II, 420; *1 QS* 6:7. Contra Haenchen, *John*, I, 199.

[991] Kim, *Exposition*, 76; Brodie, *John*, 194; Beasley-Murray, *John*, 47; Collins, 'Representative,' 37.

[992] Carson, *John*, 186; Kim, *Exposition*, 76; Schnackenburg, *John*, I, 365f; Brodie, *John*, 194; Burge, *John*, 113f; Bennema, *Power*, 168 n. 31; Moloney, *John*, 91; J. P. Bowen, 'Coming,' 278; Lindars, *John*, 149; Witherington, *Wisdom*, 94; Morris, *John*, 187; Williford, 'John 3:1–15,' 460; Munro, 'Pharisee,' 716; Barrett, *John*, 205; Lee, *Flesh*, 168. Contra Bruce, *John*, 81 thinks that Nicodemus' nocturnal encounter with Jesus has nothing to do with any spiritual or specific meaning.

[993] Koester, *Symbolism*, 133; Smith, *John*, 93; Barrett, *John*, 205; Burge, *John*, 113f; Moloney, *John*, 91; Bennema, *Power*, 168 n. 31; Bowen, 'Coming,' 282–283; Malina and Rohrbaugh, *John*, 81. Nonetheless, Koester, *ibid.*, 134 is not sure whether Nicodemus was still in the darkness of the night or he came out of the darkness into the light, Jesus.

John 1:4–9, and recalls the creation motif of Gen 1:1–5,[994] in which the coming of Jesus into the world as the incarnate Logos is expressed as the coming of the light into darkness.[995] Also, this argument could be reversely supported by John 13, in which the comment that it was night when Judas went out from the Last supper to betray Jesus in John 13:30 could mean that he left the light of the world and went into darkness.[996]

The motifs of light and darkness or day and night are adopted in connection with Jesus's identity and his salvation work in John 9:4f; 11:9f; 12:35f, 46. In these references he compares his presence or his work in the world as light or day and his absence or his death from the world as darkness or night. Above all, in John 8:12 Jesus proclaimed himself as 'the light of the world' against the setting of the Tabernacle feast. Thus, Bowen says that:

> The theme of light and darkness runs right through John's Gospel, from chapter 1, where 'the light shines in the darkness' (1:5) to Jesus's final conversation with the disciples 'just after daybreak' (21:4). A key to understanding the role of this light is in chapter 3, where John writes: … Those who respond to the light of Jesus are those who are already turned (or turning) towards the light of God which was present before they ever encountered Jesus, enlightening all people (1:9). What they see in Jesus is the fullest expression of that light to which they were already responding in some way.[997]

---

[994] Koester, *Symbolism*, 125ff; Lee, *Flesh*, 168.
[995] Munro, 'Pharisee,' 715, who says that in John's Gospel 'light' means 'life, revelation, knowledge, understanding' but 'darkness' 'incomprehension, rejection of divine truth, and a severance from the source of life, and thus, a state of death (1:4–5, 9).' Cf. Jones, *Symbol*, 68; Brown, *John I-XII*, 130; Lindars, *John*, 149; Koester, *Symbolism*, 123–154, esp. 125f; Lee, *Flesh*, 166–196, esp. 167f, 174. For detailed studies concerning darkness (night) and light (day) in the OT, Judaism and the NT, see Hahn, *NIDNTT*, I, 420–425; H. Conzelmann, *TDNT*, VII, 423–445; J. D. Price, *NIDOTTE*, I, 479–481; II, 312–315.
[996] Kim, *Exposition*, 76; Burge, *John*, 113f; Lindars, *John*, 149; Carson, *John*, 186; Smith, *John*, 94; Munro, 'Pharisee,' 716; Lee, *Flesh*, 174; Koester, *Symbolism*, 150.
[997] Bowen, 'Coming,' 282–283; Carson, *John*, 186; Lindars, *John*, 149. Accordingly, Bauckham, 'Nicodemus,' 29–30 correctly argues that in John 3:1–9; 7:45–52, Nicodemus, even though he was sympathetic toward Jesus, did not recognize the real identity of Jesus and so did not commit himself fully to him, but, after the crucifixion in John 19:39f, he exposed his belief in Jesus publicly in bringing an enormous amount of a mixture of myrrh and aloes for the burial of Jesus, showing himself a devoted disciple of Jesus. Also, Carson, *John*, 186; Lindars, *John*, 149; Polhill, 'John 1–4,' 452; Lee, *Narratives*, 57. *Contra* Collins, 'Representative,' 37. On the other hand, some theologians interpret that an enormous amount of a mixture of myrrh and aloes brought by Nicodemus in John 19:39 hints at a royal burial for Jesus. For example, Schneiders, 'Born,' 191; Schnackenburg, *John*, III, 295–299; Brown, *John XIII-XXI*, 960; J. S. King,

Thus, Nicodemus's nocturnal encounter with Jesus in John 3:2 could be interpreted as the coming to Jesus who, as the light of the world, penetrated into the darkness possessing the world in John 3:19–21. In other words, Nicodemus came out of the darkness of death and condemnation into the light of eternal life and salvation offered by Jesus, the Son of Man (vv. 13f), the suffering servant of God (v. 14, ὑψωθῆναι δεῖ), the only Son of God (the Son/firstborn/beloved Son of God) (vv. 16ff); this is restoration to eternal life and salvation from death and judgment.

Here, reference must be made to the ninth plague (darkness) of Moses, showing Yahweh's judgment and salvation with the pictures of 'darkness and light' respectively in the OT. In Exod 10:21–29, the ninth plague is the impenetrably thick darkness which as the divine judgment covered all of Egypt for three days (cf. Ps 105:28; *Wis.* 17:1f, 21). The idea of total darkness was often used for the divine calamity of 'the Day of Yahweh' in the Prophets.[998] However, all the Israelites had light in the places where they lived, meaning the presence of the Lord. J. I. Durham says that:

> This darkness is inexplicable, comparable to nothing the Egyptians or the Israelites have ever before known, so thick as to suggest palpability, and *'eerie,'* heavy with impending calamity, וִיהִי חֹשֶׁךְ has been variously translated as darkness that could be 'felt' or 'touched.'... This darkness is חֹשֶׁךְ־אֲפֵלָה 'eerie darkness,' the darkness of calamity, quite probably divine calamity. Most of the occurrences of אֲפֵלָה refer to the unnatural and fearsome darkness of the Day of Yahweh (cf. Isa 8:22; Joel 2:1; Zeph 1:15; see also Deut 28:29; Amos 5:20; Isa 58:10; 59:9). It is unquestionably a supernatural darkness, thus all the more terrible and frightening. No man could see the person next to him, and no man could do anything to cancel or ward off the thick darkness.[999]

Fretheim[1000] argues that some references to darkness (cf. Exod 11:4; 12:12, 29–31, 42) with the tenth plague (the death of the firstborn) and the crossing

---

'Nicodemus,' 45. *Contra* Meeks, 'Man,' 149, for whom, that Nicodemus brought an enormous amount of a mixture of myrrh and aloes for the burial of Jesus means that he did not properly understand the meaning of the lifting-up of Jesus as the Son of Man.

[998] J. J. Enz, 'Afterlife,' 29–38, esp. 31f; J. I. Durham, *Exodus*, 141ff; J. L. Mackay, *Exodus*, 188–190; T. E. Fretheim, *Exodus*, 129; Hahn, *NIDNTT*, I, 422f; Conzelmann, *TDNT*, VII, 430; Price, *NIDOTE*, II, 312f; Koester, *Symbolism*, 134. cf. Isa 8:22; Joel 2:1f; Zeph 1:14f; Deut 28:29; Amos 5:20; Joel 2:10; Isa 13:9ff; 3:14f; 2:31; 58:10; 59:9; Nah 1:8; Ezek 30:18f; 32:7f.

[999] Durham, *Exodus*, 141, who also points out that the thick darkness was the divine judgment against Pharaoh who was believed in as the sun-god Kephri-Re-Atum, 'the Egyptians' light' (p. 142). Also Mackay, *Exodus*, 188–190; Fetheim, *Exodus*, 129; Enz, 'Afterlife,' 32.

[1000] Fretheim, *Exodus*, 129; Mackay, *Exodus*, 188f.

of the Red Sea (Exod 14:20f) allude to the darkness of primal chaos before the creation in Genesis. Enz[1001] thinks that in the narratives of the Day of Yahweh of the Prophets, the expressions that Yahweh executes acts of judgment whereby they will know that he is the Lord allude to the narrative of exodus (cf. Exod 7:5; 14:4, 18; Jer 4:23).

In particular, 'the eerie darkness' and 'the light of Yahweh' in Exod 10:21–29 are reflected in Isa 8:22–9:2 (cf. Isa 60:1–3), in which the unnatural and fearsome darkness as the divine judgement of the Day of Yahweh will be poured out upon those who will become enraged and curse their king and their God (cf. 'signs and symbols' in Isa 8:18). Then the people walking in the darkness have seen a great light; on those living in the land of the shadow of death a light has dawned (cf. Galilee of the gentiles in Isa 9:1), as the divine salvation, through the Davidic Messiah (cf. Isa 9:6–7).[1002] Above all, the divine salvation through the Davidic messianic King is presented as the great light in Isa 9:1–7 (cf. Isa 11:1–16; 55:3), which is reflected in the debate between the Jewish religious leaders and Nicodemus as to the identity of Jesus. This debate centred on whether or not Jesus is the Davidic Messiah, because he came from Galilee of John 7:41–52, and Jesus's proclamation that he is the light of the world (John 8:12), through which he disclosed himself as the Davidic Messiah.[1003]

Furthermore, in John 8:12, Jesus's proclamation in the vicinity of the Temple treasury (John 8:20) has to be related to four enormous lampstands erected in the women's court. These structures alluded to the pillar of fire, through which Yahweh gave the delivered Israelites light by night during the wilderness life (cf. Exod 13:20ff; 14:19f; Pss 78:14; 105:39: Neh 9:12, 19). This would fit well, since John 7–8 has the setting of the Tabernacle feast, which commemorated the wilderness life of the Israelites after the exodus.[1004] Here, 'Light indicated the divine presence in the phrase of

---

[1001] Enz, 'Afterlife,' 32.
[1002] Cf. Durham, *Exodus*, 141; Mackay, *Exodus*, 189; Fretheim, *Exodus*, 129; Enz, 'Afterlife,' 33–35, who also argues that the darkness of Exod 10:21–29 is reflected in Isa 60:1–3, in the narrative of the signs of the end of the age in Matt 24:9f, and in the narrative of the crucifixion in Matt 27:45; Mark 15:33; Luke 23:44f. Also, Hahn, *NIDNTT*, I, 425.
[1003] Koester, *Symbolism*, 138. Above all, Matt 4:16–17 is clearly a messianic interpretation of Isa 9:1–2 (see Hahn, *NIDNTT*, I, 422f; Conzelmann, *TDNT*, VII, 440f); 'the Davidic Messiah' (cf. *Tg. Isa* 9:6), who as 'the light of the nations' is the same figure as 'the suffering Servant of God' in Isa 42:6; 49:6 (cf. Luke 1:79; 2:32; Acts 26:17, 23). Further, Koester, *ibid.*, 140 argues that Jesus's distinctive words, 'I Am' (evgw, eivmi,) alludes to the name of Yahweh in Isaiah (cf. Isa 43:10) and furthermore, the light imagery in John 8 strengthens the divinity of Jesus in connection with Isa 60:1–2 ('Arise, shine, for your light has come, and the glory of the Lord has risen upon you') and Isa 60:19–20 ('the Lord will be your everlasting light') (Cf. Pss 27:1; 36:9).
[1004] Koester, *Symbolism*, 141f; Schnackenburg, *John*, II, 195f; Brown, *John I-XII*, 344; Brunson, *Psalm 118*, 313f. Cf. *m. Sukk.* 5.5; Str-B, II, 805ff.

Israel's history that was commemorated by the festival.'[1005] Koester[1006] points out that the presence of God with light and the Tabernacle recalls Zech 14:16, saying that the nations of the world come to Jerusalem to worship Yahweh the King enthroned and to celebrate the feast of Tabernacles.

5.2.5.3.2 Hardening and Blindness (Deafness) (Cf. John 12:35–50; 9:39; Isa 6:9f; Exod 4–14; Deut 29:3f)

In John 3:19–21, the process of condemnation against those who reject the light of eternal life and continuously remain in the darkness of death and condemnation, can be understood in connection with the motifs of hardening and blindness (deafness). This could allude to the hardening of Pharaoh's heart in Exod 4–14 (cf. the hardening of the Israelites' hearts in Deut 29:2–4) and the later hardening of the Israelites' hearts in Isa 6:9–10, which is quoted in John 12:37–41 (40) and reflected in John 9:39 (cf. Matt 13:15; Mark 4:12; 8:18; Luke 8:10; Acts 28:27; 1 John 2:11; Rom 9–11).[1007] Hardening and blindness (deafness) are important motifs in connection with the study of the exodus and the Isaianic new exodus or restoration in the OT.[1008]

E. Sjöberg and G. Stählin[1009] argue that Paul in Romans 9 explained the wrath of God in the light of the motif of hardening caused by sin and unbelief:

> Sin and unbelief, the two main causes of the ὀργὴ θεοῦ, are also its effect. Paul points this out in Rom 1, and it is also the meaning of Rom 9:22: God demonstrates his wrath in the hardening of the σκευή ὀργῆς which he has tolerated so long, e.g., Pharaoh, but also the Jews.

[1005] Koester, *ibid.*, 141.
[1006] Koester, *ibid.*, 141f. On the other hand, Brunson, *ibid.*, 313ff argues that 'the light of the world' of John 8:12 alludes to Ps 118:27, if it is considered that the term is proclaimed in the setting of the Tabernacle, which reminds the pilgrimage of 'the unending light of the eschatological Zechariahan Tabernacles' (Zech 14:6) and thus of Ps 118:27.
[1007] J. M. Lieu, 'Blindness,' 83–95, esp. 84f; G. D. Robinson, 'Motif,' 167–186, esp. 185; Dennis, *Gathering*, 94 n. 79; Endo, *Creation*, 222 n. 43; Carson, *John*, 377f, 447–450; Beasley-Murray, *John*, 215f. Cf. G. K. Beale, 'Exegetical,' 129–154; Enz, 'Afterlife,' 35; Lee, *Flesh*, 171f; Koester, *Symbolism*, 149.
[1008] Cf. Beasley-Murray, *John*, 216 writes that 'hardening and blindness' has a long history in biblical thought in connection with the fulfilment of God's ultimate purpose, namely, the saving history; God's hardening of Pharaoh's heart in Exodus (e.g., Exod 4:21), God's hardening of the Israelites' hearts in Deut 29:2–4; Isa 6:9–13. Cf. Mark 4:11f; Rom 9–11, esp. 11:28–31. Also, Carson, *John*, 449.
[1009] E. Sjöberg and G. Stählin, *TDNT*, V, 412–416, quoted from 413.

In particular, Beale[1010] discusses the hardening of Pharaoh's heart in Exodus 4–14 in the setting of the exodus, being alluded to in Rom 9:17–18. He observes that in the narrative of the plagues Yahweh is the ultimate cause of the hardening of Pharaoh's heart, although Pharaoh's volitional decision and accountability should not be ignored (cf. Exod 4:21; 7:3; 10:1ff). He goes on to say that the ultimate purpose of Yahweh's hardening of Pharaoh's heart is for his glory.[1011] The glorification of Yahweh or the proclamation of his name is related to the exodus of Israel, the restoration of the nations including the order of the creation.[1012] This is the reverse of the divine judgment against all creation after the Fall (Gen 3). Through this, Yahweh's name is proclaimed and Yahweh is glorified.

Concerning the motifs of hardening and blindness (deafness), we have to note Isa 6:9–10, which is reflected in some Old and New Testament texts.[1013] Watts[1014] argues that the Hebrew Text of Isa 6:9–10 shows that in Isaiah 'the messenger plays an active role in hardening and dulling so that repentance will not take place, now that the decision to destroy has been taken.' This alludes to the divine hardening of Pharaoh's heart in Exodus (cf. 8:11, 28 [15, 32]; 9:7, 34). So, in Isa 6:11f, the judicial judgment against Israel is not avoidable; the total destruction of cities, houses, and fields, and the

---

[1010] Beale, 'Exegetical,' 129–154. On the other hand, Beasley-Murray, *John*, 216 says that 'In Exodus it is frequently said that God hardened Pharaoh's heart (e.g., Exod 4:21), and as frequently that Pharaoh hardened his own heart (e.g., 8:15, 32); the relation between the two actions is never explained.'

[1011] Beale, *ibid.*, 150, who also presents three detailed reasons why Yahweh hardened Pharaoh's heart; first, 'The uniqueness of Yahweh's omnipotence would be demonstrated to the Egyptians.' (Exod 7:17; 8:6 [10], 8 [22]; 9:16; 10:1–2; 14:4, 17–18).' Secondly, 'Yahweh's acts would become a memorial in Israel and its later generations.' (10:1–2; 13:14–16).' Thirdly, 'then [Ex] 14:4, 17, 18 summarizes the whole purpose of the *Heilsgeschichte* program: it is for Yahweh's glory.' (p. 149). Furthermore, Beale, *ibid.*, 151, 151 n. 92, observes that Paul's use of ἐξεγείρω in Rom 9:17, which is synonymous with *āmad* (MT) or διατηρέω (LXX), with the metaphor of the potter-clay in Rom 9:20f, could allude to God's inciting Pharaoh's heart to disobey His command to release Israel. This verb is used with the same kind of meaning in Isa 45:13 in connection with Cyrus, on the background of the parable of the potter-clay (cf. Isa 29:16; 45:9; 64:8).

[1012] Cf. The restoration of the order of the creation could be found from Israel's crossing of the Red Sea in Exod 14–15 after the Exodus, which could allude to Yahweh's reign of the chaotic, rebellious water in the creation of Genesis. This motif often appears in the context of the new exodus (cf. Isaiah and Psalms).

[1013] Robinson, 'Motif,' 174–185; Lieu, 'Blindness,' 83–95; Endo, *Creation*, 221 n. 413; Dennis, *Gathering*, 94 n. 79; Motyer, *Isaiah*, 78f; Watts, *Isaiah 1–33*, 75. Cf. Isa 1:2–9; 29:9–24; 42:18–20; 43:8–13; 44:9–20; Pss 135:15–17; 58:3–5; John 12:40; Acts 28:27; Matt 13:15; Mark 4:12; 8:18; Luke 8:10; 1 John 2:11.

[1014] Watts, *Isaiah 1–33*, 75; Motyer, *Isaiah*, 79, who says that 'The imperative of these verses must, therefore, be seen as expressing an inevitable outcome of Isaiah's ministry (cf. 2:9).' Cf. Exod 4:21.

deportation (the exile) of Israel, so thus the land of Israel vacant and abandoned.[1015] Evans[1016] argues that, 'Isa 6:9–10 explicitly states that God hardens his people in order to prevent repentance, and so render judgment certain.' However, Motyer says that:

> He, in fact, faced the preacher's dilemma: if hearers are resistant to the truth, the only recourse is to tell them the truth yet again, more clearly than before. But to do this is to expose them to the risk of rejecting the truth yet again and, therefore, of increased hardness of heart. It could even be that the next rejection will prove to be the point at which the heart is hardened beyond recovery.[1017]

In particular, in Isa 44:9–20, Yahweh proclaims the idolaters will be like their idols, 'the idolaters know nothing, they understand nothing; their eyes are plastered over so they cannot see, and their minds closed so they cannot understand' (Isa 44:18). This could allude to the hardening of the heart of Pharaoh, who, in spite of being worshipped as a god by the Egyptians, was just a living idol, totally controlled (hardened) by Yahweh.[1018]

On the other hand, the restoration, or new exodus, of Israel from exile is expressed as the future reversal of the blindness in Isa 29:17–21; 35:5, 10; 42:6f; 43:10.[1019] In Isa 6:13b, 'the holy seed' which will be the stump in the land could be identified with the Davidic messianic king, the shoot out of the stem of Jesse in Isa 11:1 or with the remnant in Isa 4:3 (cf. 41:8; 43:5; 45:25; 53:10; 59:21; 65:9, 23; 66:22).[1020] So, Carson argues that:

> God's sovereign hardening of the people in Isaiah's day, his commissioning of Isaiah to apparently fruitless ministry, is a stage

---

[1015] Watts, *Isaiah 1–33*, 76; Motyer, *Isaiah*, 79; Robinson, 'Motif,' 174.
[1016] C. A. Evans, *Isaiah 6:9–10*, 52. Also, Beale, 'Exegetical,' 129–154.
[1017] Motyer, *Isaiah*, 79; Watts, *Isaiah 1–33*, 75; Robinson, 'Motif,' 183, 186; Beasley-Murray, *John*, 216; Carson, *John*, 447–449; Lieu, 'Blindness,' 84.
[1018] Cf. According to Beale, 'Exegetical,' 149 n. 84, 153, for the Egyptians Pharaoh was believed to be the divine incarnation of two Egyptian gods (Re and Horus), related with heart. Also 'the Egyptians viewed Pharaoh as divine and sinless while living, and believed at death he was exempt from judgment but became the god (Orisis) presiding over judgment after his death.' So, Yahweh's hardening of Pharaoh's heart was to show the Egyptians that Yahweh has the ultimate authority in controlling not only Pharaoh's divinity but also his heart.
[1019] Robinson, 'Motif,' 183 n. 45, for whom, Isa 43:8–13 says the restoration of Israel as the transition from the judicial blindness to total restoration of sight. In Isa 43:8 'the very people that Isa 6:9–10 condemned to continued blindness are to be released. The period of cursed judgment (6:11–13) is past (cf. 40:2).' Also, 'Israel is called to know, believe, and understand the sovereignty and uniqueness of Yahweh, and to act as a faithful witness to God's works. This, of course, implies the ability to see the works of God. Furthermore, Israel is called to be a worthy servant of Yahweh, and this implies the ability to hear the Master, 43:10.' (p. 181). Also, Lieu, 'Blindness,' 87.
[1020] Motyer, *Isaiah*, 80; Watts, *Isaiah 1–33*, 76.

in God's 'strange work' (Isa 28:21–22) that brings God's ultimate redemptive purpose to pass.[1021]

Above all, in Isa 42:5–9, Yahweh, as the creator of the heavens and the earth, gives life and breath to all people. His name is proclaimed and his glorification is mentioned against the background of the new exodus of Israel and the restoration of the nations. Here, Yahweh raises his servant as 'a covenant for the people' and as 'a light for the gentiles' in order to 'open eyes that are blind, to free captives from prison and to release from the dungeon those who sit in darkness' (cf. Isa 49:5–13). The new exodus (restoration) is expressed through the reversal of the imageries of blindness, enslavement (captive) and darkness. The new exodus of Israel from exile and the restoration of the nations to the sons of Yahweh, through the death of the suffering servant of Yahweh (Isa 52:13–53:12), are the proclamation of Yahweh's name and his glorification, which will not be given to the idols possessing Israel and the nations (Isa 48:11). The scope of the restoration of Yahweh who is 'the redeemer' (Isa 43:11f; Exod 3:14) and 'the first and the last' in Isa 48:12 (cf. Isa 44:6) includes all creation as well; the new exodus and the new creation.[1022] Thus, the proclamation of Yahweh's name and his glorification will be shown with the new exodus of Israel from exile and the restoration of the gentiles, including the restoration of all creation. These will be accomplished by the suffering servant of Yahweh in Isa 53, who bears the vicarious, representative, atoning, redemptive, and covenant-establishing death.

In John 2:23ff, at the Passover feast, many people saw the miraculous signs performed by Jesus and believed in his name. Nicodemus, as their representative, came to him at night and confessed him as the worker of the miraculous sign, who came from God in John 3:2. This means that Nicodemus came out of the darkness into the light of the world in John 3:21. However, there are some Jews who, in spite of seeing the miraculous signs performed by Jesus, will not believe in him as the light; instead they reject him, do not come out of the darkness into the light, and remain in the darkness continuously (John 3:19). In other words, their hearts are hardened and incur self-condemnation.

For example, John 9:1–12 presents the narrative of a sign that Jesus as the light of the world healed the eye sight of a man born blind. However, the Pharisees did not believe the healing (the sign) done by Jesus who came from God (John 9:13–34). The Pharisees 'do not remember the ancient

---

[1021] Carson, *John*, 449; Beasley-Murray, *John*, 216.
[1022] Cf. Isa 9:1–7; 11:1–16; 35:1–10; 43:14–21; 48:6f; 55:12f; 65:17–25; 66:22; John 3:16–18; Rom 8:1–39; Rev 21–22.

promises that one of the signs of the dawning of the messianic age is the restoration of sight to the blind (Isa 29:18; 35:5; 42:7).'[1023] Regarding this, in saying that Jesus himself is the Son of Man (v. 35), he proclaims that, 'For judgment I have come into this world, so that the blind will see and those who see will become blind' in John 9:37.[1024] Here, the man born blind is spiritually contrasted with the Pharisees.[1025] Carson[1026] points out that the second half 'so that the blind will see and those who see will become blind' of the verse (v. 39) alludes to Isa 6:10; 42:19 (cf. Mark 4:12).

Furthermore, in John 12:20–24, Jesus said that he would die as the Son of Man and then strongly urged the crowds to believe in him the light of the world and to become the sons of the light, with the motifs of light and darkness (John 12:35f; cf. 1 Thes 5:5; Eph 5:8). In spite of all these miraculous signs done by Jesus in front of them, the crowds would not believe in him (v. 37).[1027] This is presented as the fulfilment of the prophecy of Isaiah, by quoting Isa 53:1; 6:10 in John 12:38, 40.[1028] In particular, the Evangelist says that the reason that the Jews could not believe in Jesus is that Yahweh has blinded their eyes and hardened their heart, so they can neither see with their eyes, nor understand with their heart (Isa 6:10).

5.3 Jesus and John the Baptist (John 3:22–36)

John 3:22–36 is divided into two segments: the relationship between Jesus and the Baptist in vv. 22–30, and the Evangelist's commentary of vv. 22–30 in vv. 31–36.[1029] In this section, we will discuss the wedding motif (the bridegroom and the best man) in the light of the new exodus in the testimony stated by John in John 3:22–30. And then, the wrath of God (with

---

[1023] Carson, *John*, 375; See also Koester, *Symbolism*, 145.
[1024] Lieu, 'Blindness,' 84; Beasley-Murray, *John*, 160.
[1025] Carson, *John*, 377f; Koester, *Symbolism*, 144; Lieu, 'Blindness,' 83.
[1026] Carson, *John*, 377; Robinson, 'Motif,' 185; Lieu, 'Blindness,' 83f. Cf. Enz, 'Afterlife,' 35 argues that John 9:39 alludes to the hardening of Pharaoh's heart in Exodus.
[1027] Carson, *John*, 447 argues that the crowds who still would not believe in Jesus who had done many miraculous signs in their presence 'are like the ancient Israelites whom Moses addressed in Deut 29:3–4.' Also, Brown, *John I-XII*, 485; Dennis, *Gathering*, 94. Cf. Enz, 'Afterlife,' 35.
[1028] Carson, *John*, 448–450; Beasley-Murray, *John*, 216f; Lieu, 'Blindness,' 84–86; Robinson, 'Motif,' 185; Dennis, *Gathering*, 94 n. 79; Endo, *Creation*, 221 n. 43; Koester, *Symbolism*, 149.
[1029] Burge, *John*, 122; Moloney, *John*, 104; Beasley-Murray, *John*, 53; Carson, *John*, 212; Bruce, *John*, 96; Michaels, *John*, 66; Brown, *John I-XII*, 159f; Malina and Rohrbaugh, *John*, 90. On the other hand, Wilson, 'Integrity,' 39 says that 'John 3 can be divided into two parallel sections: vss. 1–21 and vss. 24–36 with vss. 22–24 serving as a literary bridge.' In particular, Brown, *ibid.*, 160 argues that vv. 31–36 is 'to recapitulate the whole of iii 1–30 and to summarize both the Nicodemus and the John the Baptist.' So, Moloney, *ibid.*, 111; Whitacre, *John*, 98. Malina and Rohrbaugh, *ibid.*, think that Nicodemus, the eminent Pharisee teacher in vv. 1–21 is contrasted with John the prophet who baptized in vv. 22–36. Carson, *John*, 209 argues that John 3:22–36 is the preparation to the chapter 4 of John's Gospel.

eternal life) will be discussed in connection with the new exodus motif in John 3:31–36.

5.3.1 John's Testimony to Jesus: the Best Man and the Bridegroom (John 3:22–30)

According to vv. 22–23, Jesus and his disciples went out into the Judean countryside and baptized people with water, [1030] and also the Baptist, probably with his disciples, was baptizing people with water at Aenon near Salim. [1031] From these baptismal ministries, an argument developed between some of John's disciples and a certain Jew over the matter of ceremonial washing (v. 25). [1032] And then, the envious disciples of John came to him and reported on Jesus's popularity in v. 26: 'he [Jesus] is baptizing and everyone is going to him.' Regarding this, in vv. 27–30, John spoke of his identity and his relationship to Jesus.

Firstly, John said that in v. 27, 'A man can receive only what is given him from heaven,' which, for Neyrey and Rohrbaugh, means 'God is the source of Jesus's honour and success (3:27); human beings should in no way

---

[1030] In John 4:1f, the Evangelist corrected the statement in John 4:1 ('Jesus was gaining and baptizing more disciples than John') with adding another statement in v. 2 ('in fact it was not Jesus who baptized, but his disciples'). Here, the water baptism performed by Jesus's disciples could be understood in light of the extension of John the Baptist's baptism, because some of John's disciples probably became Jesus's disciples (cf. John 1:35–42), so Jesus just allowed them to baptize people with water, even though his main concern was the baptism with the Holy Spirit (cf. Brodie, *John*, 204). For this, see Jones, *Symbolism*, 79; Bruce, *John*, 93; Morris, *John*, 209f; Brown, *John I-XII*, 151; Witherington, *Wisdom*, 108; Fallon, *John*, 107. Beasley-Murray, *John*, 52 argues that the baptism of Jesus in v. 22 is not Christian baptism nor John's baptism but a water baptism which 'oriented to the coming of the kingdom, like John's baptism it gained special significance as obedient response to him who was in the process of bringing the saving sovereignty.' Also, Dodd, *Historical*, 285f; Schnackenburg, *John*, I, 411f.

[1031] Cf. Brodie, *John*, 201f, 206 understands 'Aenon near Salim' has a theological implication; 'Springs near Peace' which is related with 'the aspect of the peace which is brought by Jesus, particularly, with the ideas of love and joy (cf. esp. 3:29–36); His [John's baptism] is a world of springs, of cleansing water, of preparatory baptism. But nearby is Jesus, the one who, as well as cleansing what is negative, brings a positive peace.' ([] added by this writer). Jones, *Symbol*, 78 observes that John was geopolitically getting away from Jerusalem the centre of Israel to the north but Jesus was achieving a more influential ministry near Jerusalem.

[1032] Cf. Carson, *John*, 210 says that there were some sects (e.g., Qumran community) doing ceremonial washing on the basis of the OT in the Jewish society at the time of Jesus, and so John's baptism was investigated by priests and Levites sent by the Jews of Jerusalem in John 1:19–22. Also, Bruce, *John*, 94; Witherington, *Wisdom*, 108. Cf. *Ant.* 18.117; *Bell.* 2.129; *t. Yad.* 2.20. However, Beasley-Murray, *John*, 52 thinks that the argument over the matter of ceremonial washing is not between Jewish baptism and John's baptism but between Jesus's baptism and John's baptism. Bultmann, *John*, 171 and J. W. Pryor, 'Baptist,' 15–26 think that the argument about the ceremonial washing took place between Jesus's disciples and John's disciples.

challenge God's sovereignty as benefactor.'[1033] Secondly, in v. 28, John again confirmed what he had said by quoting Isa 40:3 in John 1:23, 27, 'he is not the Christ but is sent ahead of him.' Thirdly, in v. 29, alluding to the marriage motif in the OT, John compares himself as the best man who just attends the bridegroom, and Jesus as the bridegroom to whom the bride belongs. Here, John testifies to Jesus as the Messiah, who is the bridegroom of the messianic community, the head of the new Israel who are flocking to him and being baptized by him (with the Spirit. cf. John 3:5, 8), by his disciples (with water) in John 3:22; 4:1f.

Schnackenburg[1034] argues that there is no reference describing the Messiah and the messianic community as the bridegroom and the bride respectively in the early Jewish document. However, this reflects a covenantal relationship between Yahweh and Israel his people in the OT, which was often expressed by the marriage relationship; the bridegroom and the bride, and which is the basis of the relationship between Christ (the bridegroom) and the church (the bride) in the NT.[1035] Bernard[1036] points out that Yahweh was described as the jealous husband of Israel in Exod 34:15; Deut 31:16; Ps 73:27 (cf. Hos 2:19).

In particular, D. I. Brewer[1037] argues that Yahweh's covenant with Israel is expressed as 'a treaty covenant' in the Pentateuch but as 'a marriage

---

[1033] J. H. Neyrey and R. L. Rohrbaugh, 'Increase,' 482

[1034] Schnackenburg, *John*, I, 416; J. Jeremias, *TDNT*, IV, 1101; Witherington, *Wisdom*, 109. However, Morris, *John*, 213f argues that these motifs (bridegroom and bride) of the relationship between Yahweh and His people in the OT were applied to the Messiah and the messianic community. Also, Michaels, *John*, 64; Brown, *John I-XII*, 156; Carson, *John*, 211; Bruce, *John*, 95.

[1035] For examples, Isa 54:5f; 61:10; 62:4f; Jer 2:2; 3:20; 7:34; 16:9; 25:10; 33:11; Ezek 16:8; 23:4; Hos 2:21; Song; 2 Cor 11:2; Eph 5:24–27, 31f; Rev 19:7; 21:2; 22:17; Matt 22:1f; 25:1; Mark 2:18f and parallels; Cf. Exod 34:15; Deut 31:16; Ps 73:27. For this, see Schnackenburg, *John*, I, 416; Milne, *John*, 80; Michaels, *John*, 64; Bernard, *John*, I, 130f; Witherington, *Wisdom*, 109; J. Jeremias, *TDNT*, IV, 1099–1106; Whitacre, *John*, 97; Carson, *John*, 211; Morris, *John*, 213f; Howard-Brook, *Becoming*, 97f; Bruce, *John*, 95; Beasley-Murray, *John*, 53; Lindars, *John*, 167; Koester, *Symbolism*, 166; Brown, *John I-XII*, 156; Polhill, 'John 1–4,' 454; Moloney, *John*, 106; Barrett, *John*, 222f; Davies, *Rhetoric*, 210; Beasley-Murray, *Life*, 105. *Contra* Burge, *John*, 122, who criticizes for the interpretation of the wedding imagery in vv. 27–30.

[1036] Bernard, *John*, I, 130. Especially, after the incident of the golden calf in Exod 32, Yahweh gave Israel the new stone tablets with the re-establishment of the covenant in Exod 34. Here, Yahweh warned her not to worship any other god because He, whose name is Jealous, is a jealous God in v. 14, and again warned her not to make a treaty with the native people in the land, for, when they prostitute themselves to their gods and sacrifice to them, they will invite her and she will be tempted into worshipping other gods lustfully (v. 15). Namely, that Israel as the people of Yahweh prostitutes herself to other gods could mean breaking the marriage covenant with Yahweh her husband.

[1037] D. I. Brewer, 'Weddings,' 1–25, esp. 3–5, who also says that Exod 21:10f is the law that Yahweh established concerning the right of a maidservant who became the wife of her master;

covenant' instead of 'a treaty covenant' in the Prophets. Also, Brewer says that the marriage covenant between Yahweh and Israel in the Prophets is not an interesting metaphor but involves all the legal requirements of a marriage covenant in the Mosaic Law, particularly, in Exod 21:10f, which is the basis of the marriage covenant between Yahweh and Israel in the Prophets (cf. Hos, the second part of Isaiah, Jer 2:2, 20–25; 3:1–18 and Ezek 16:1–63; 23:1–49). Above all, in the OT, Yahweh, the divine king of Israel is said to marry his people or the Land in Isa 62:4.[1038] Howard-Brook[1039] says that here Jesus the bridegroom is identified with Yahweh, the God of the covenant, the true God. In John's Gospel, this metaphor is clearly reflected in the miracle at Cana in 2:1–11,[1040] probably in the narrative of a Samaritan woman symbolizing the spiritual situation of the Samaritans in John 4:16–17,[1041] and in the narrative of a Jewish woman caught in adultery, symbolizing the spiritual situation of the Jews in John 8:1–11.

John introduces his identity as the best man who attends the bridegroom, waits and listens for him, and is full of joy when he hears the bridegroom's voice, and goes on to say that it is now completed in v. 29. Schnackenburg describes the functions of the best man and interprets John's sayings of v. 29 as follows:

> The 'friend of the bridegroom' is one of the two groomsmen who were entrusted with special functions at a Jewish marriage, their chief duty being to lead the bride to the bridegroom and keep watch outside the bridal chamber. The 'voice of the bridegroom' probably means the triumphal shout by which the bridegroom announced to his friends outside that he had been united to a virginal bride. This is the voice which John 'hears' and which

---

he as her husband must provide her with food, clothing and marital relationship, which is the basis of the traditional Jewish marriage contract. This is reflected in Hosea and Ezek 16 (cf. *m. Ket.* 5) (pp. 7–9). Above all, Brewer, *ibid.*, 15f concludes that 'The laws of marriage and divorce in the book of Moses were applied by the prophets to the marriage covenant of God with Israel and Judah. The revelation to Hosea was examined and re-evaluated by Jeremiah, Ezekiel and Isaiah. They all concluded that Israel was divorced, and deservedly so because she broke the terms of the marriage covenant. Judah also committed adultery, and she appeared to be divorced when she was exiled. However, there was never any formal divorce certificate, so Isaiah concluded that she only suffered a temporary separation. This means that she could be lawfully wooed by God again.' Cf. Isa 50:1– 'Where is your mother's certificate of divorce with which I sent her away?'

[1038] Bruce, *John*, 95.
[1039] Howard-Brook, *Becoming*, 98.
[1040] See 3.2. The Wedding Background (Cf. John 3:22–36). Cf. Koester, *Symbolism*, 166; Barrett, *John*, 223; Ng, *Symbolism*, 60; Howard-Brook, *Becoming*, 97f; Brown, *John I-XII*, 153; Jones, *Symbol*, 77f, 83.
[1041] See 6.3. The Betrothal Motif (John 4:16–18).

causes him to rejoice heartily- a striking picture of unselfishness quite acceptable to Semitic feeling, and chosen by John to express his joy on behalf of Jesus.[1042]

Thus, in announcing the completion of his mission as the best man for the marriage of the bridegroom and the bride, John proclaimed his subordinate position and the inauguration of the messianic new epoch. This is supported by v. 30, in which John said that: 'he must become greater; I must become less.' Here, 'must' (δεῖ) can be understood as 'the statement of divine necessity, signalling God's will that Jesus increase.'[1043]

Moloney[1044] points out that the two terms, increase and decrease, can be understood using, 'an image of the waxing and waning of the sun' indicate 'a turning point where the old gives way to the new.' Similarly, for Bultmann, John's word in v. 30 means the inauguration of the new, eschatological epoch, 'the old epoch of the world has run its course, the eschatological age is beginning.'[1045] If we consider that John's baptism ministry in the wilderness was thought as the fulfilment of Isa 40:3 in John 1:23, the inauguration of the new eschatological salvation in John's saying of John 3:30 could allude to the restoration or the new exodus of Israel and the nations in Isa 42:9; 43:18f.

5.3.2 The Evangelist's Commentarial Interpretation (John 3:31–36)

In v. 31, who are 'the one who comes from above (heaven)' and 'the one who is from the earth'? It is not difficult to recognize as Jesus 'the one who comes from above (ἄνωθεν)'[1046] and 'the one who come from heaven' in v. 31 and 'the one whom God has sent' in v. 34, indicating the heavenly origin of Jesus (cf. John 1:15; 3:13; 11:27). However, the identity of 'the one who is from the earth belongs to the earth, and speaks as one from the earth' in v.

[1042] Schnackenburg, *John*, I, 416; Witherington, *Wisdom*, 109; Jeremias, *TDNT*, IV, 1101; Bruce, *John*, 95; Beasley-Murray, *John*, 53; Polhill, 'John 1–4,' 454; Moloney, *John*, 106; Whitacre, *John*, 97. Carson, *John*, 212, pointing out that the best man was absolutely prohibited from marrying the bride in ancient Sumerian and Babylonian law (cf. Judges 14–15), interprets John's confession of v. 29 as that 'he is the last who could compete with the bridegroom, for under no circumstances is he allowed to marry the bride.' For later Jewish material on marriage practices and the friend of the bridegroom, see Moloney, *John*, 110; Barrett, *John*, 223; Beasley-Murray, *John*, 53; Schnackenburg, *John*, I, 416. Cf. Str-B, I, 45–46; 500–504; *t. Ket.* 1.4. On the other hand, Brown, *John I-XII*, 152 observes that the role of the best man of the wedding was argued by Paul in 2 Cor 11:1 and Rabbis interprets Moses playing the role of the best man in the covenantal marriage between God and Israel. Also, Bernard, *John*, I, 131.
[1043] Neyrey and Rohrbaugh, 'Increase,' 482; Barrett, *John*, 223f; Polhill, 'John 1–4,' 454.
[1044] Moloney, *John*, 110; Schnackenburg, *John*, I, 417f; Bultmann, *John*, 174.
[1045] Bultmann, *John*, 174; Ng, *Symbolism*, 60.
[1046] Cf. Carson, *John*, 212; Brown, *John I-XII*, 157 rightly thinks that ἄνωθεν means 'from above' for it is parallel with 'from heaven' in the same verse.

31 is regarded as John the Baptist[1047] or the Jews[1048] who are represented by Nicodemus the teacher of Israel, or as both John (as the Jewish prophet) and Nicodemus (as the Jewish leader).[1049] Concerning the meaning of 'from the earth,' Bruce who interprets 'the one who comes from the earth' as John the Baptist in v. 31, says that:

> There is no suggestion of evil in being 'from the earth', but rather one of limitation. Even John's witness, excellent as it was, was subject to limitation because, while he was 'a man sent from God' (John 1:6), he did not come down from heaven as the Son of Man did.[1050]

However, what has to be noted in vv. 22–30 is that John's baptismal ministry is not contrasted with Jesus's or his disciples', even though we do not know whether or not John's disciples might have thought so. At least, John admitted that his baptism and Jesus's baptism had their respective roles in the history of the eschatological salvation of God. John thought that his ministry with water was just a preparatory step to the ministry of Jesus. John explained these different ministries in terms of the wedding motif (the best man and the bridegroom). For John, Jesus's growing popularity was regarded as the inauguration of the eschatological-new salvation time; accordingly, John's work had arrived at its completion. With the parallel ('the one who comes from above is above all'… 'the one who comes from heaven is above all'), v. 31 emphasizes the heavenly origin of Jesus and the supremacy of the testimony revealed by him who had seen and listened to the heavenly things in the heavenly council.[1051] Bruce interprets v. 33 as follows:

> Jesus's witness is God's perfect truth. He is God's perfect messenger and delivers God's message perfectly. Those who accept Jesus's witness therefore attest the truthfulness of God, as though they affixed their seal to the divine message.[1052]

In v. 34, God the Father gives the Spirit without limit to the Son whom he has sent from heaven into the world, because he loves him (cf. the beloved

---

[1047] Barrett, *John*, 224f ; Brown, *John I-XII*, 161f; Michaels, *John*, 66; Whitacre, *John*, 98; Burge, *John*, 119; Bruce, *John*, 96; Carson, *John*, 212.
[1048] Moloney, *John*, 111; W. R. G. Loader, 'Central,' 189.
[1049] Burge, *John*, 119.
[1050] Bruce, *John* 96; Brown, *John I-XII*, 157f, 160f.
[1051] Beasley-Murray, *John*, 53; Bruce, *John*, 96; Burge, *John*, 119; Moloney, *John*, 106f.
[1052] Bruce, *John*, 97; Whitacre, *John*, 99; Barrett, *John*, 226.

and only Son of God in John 1:14, 18; 3:16, 18)[1053] and has placed everything in his hands, as v. 35 explains.[1054] Turner interprets v. 34 to mean that:

> the *immeasurable* gift of the Spirit (of revelation) *to* Jesus corresponds to the perfection of revelation *through* Jesus – it provides a revelation which *transcends* the Law and the Prophets.[1055]

In vv. 34–35, we can recognize the status of the heir of Jesus as the Son of God, which is intimately related with the beloved Son.[1056] That the Father loves the Son and has placed everything in his hands in v. 35 is again interpreted to mean that the Father gives the Son the authority of eternal life and God's wrath in v. 36.

This is the same authority (eternal life and eternal condemnation) given to the Son of Man, the only Son of God, and the Son in John 3:13–18 and is reflected in John 5:19–29.[1057] Here it is the Son who is the same figure as the Son of Man to whom the Father has entrusted all the power of life and judgment (vv. 21f, 25f), alluding to the authority of the 'one like a son of man' in Dan 7:13f.[1058] Carson[1059] argues that the fact that the Father gives the Spirit without measure in vv. 34–35 alludes to John's testimony in John 1:32f, 'the Spirit *comes down* upon Jesus and *remains* on him who will baptize with the Holy Spirit,' which is the fulfilment of Isa 11:2; 42:1; 61:1. So, this could mean the eschatological outpouring of the Spirit upon the Davidic-suffering Servant-Messiah of Isaiah. Also, this reflects new generation (birth) by water and the Spirit[1060] (John 3:5–8; 20:22; cf. Ezek 36:25–28; 37:1–14; Gen 2:7) and eternal life (John 3:15ff, 36).

[1053] Michaels, *John*, 66.
[1054] Burge, *John*, 123; Brown, *John I-XII*, 158, 161f; Smith, *John*, 107; Turner, *Holy*, 59; Beasley-Murray, *Life*, 65; Lindars, *John*, 170f; Whitacre, *John*, 99; Bernard, *John*, I, 125; Moloney, *John*, 111f; F. Pack, 'Spirit,' 140f; Morris, *John*, 218f, who also says that this hints that Jesus the Son will give the Spirit to those who believe in him.
[1055] Turner, *Holy*, 59 (original emphasis); Pack, 'Spirit,' 140f; Beasley-Murray, *Life*, 65; *idem.*, *John*, 53f, who also compares the immeasurable gift of the Spirit (as the Spirit of prophecy) to Jesus with the saying that the Spirit restrictedly remained on the Prophets in the saying of R. Aha (the fourth century A.D.) in *Lev R.* 15:2 on Lev 13:2. Also, see Carson, *John*, 213; Barrett, *John*, 226; Bruce, *John*, 99 n. 24; Brown, *John I-XII*, 158.
[1056] Watts, *Isaiah's*, 114; Bulman, 'Only,' 64f. Cf. Mark 12:6; Gen 21:10; 24:36; 25:5; *Tob.* 3:15. Also, see Turner, 'ΥΙΟΣ,' 113–129; Goppelt, *Theology*, I, 201; Du Plessis, 'Christ,' 29; Kim, 'Baptism,' 18; Boismard, *Moses*, 108; F. Büchsel, *TDNT*, IV, 740–741; Cullmann, *Christology*, 298.
[1057] Bruce, *John*, 97f, 128ff, who also argues that John 5:25 alludes to Isa 55:3 and Ezek 37:4 (p. 131). Also, Ezek 37:12–14 seem to be reflected in John 5:29.
[1058] Bruce, *John*, 132, who also points out that the two sorts of resurrection in John 5:28–29 allude to Dan 12:2 (p. 133). Also, Whitacre, *John*, 132; Barrett, *John*, 263.
[1059] Carson, *John*, 213; Brown, *John I-XII*, 158; Burge, *John*, 123; Bruce, *John*, 97.
[1060] Brown, *John I-XII*, 161f.

In v. 36, eternal life and the wrath of God allude to eternal life and condemnation in John 3:15–18.[1061] In particular, commentators[1062] recognize that the wrath of God as the word of judgment (like light and darkness/judgment and judging in John 3:18–21) is rare (only once in John's Gospel cf. in John's message of Matt 3:7; Luke 3:7), but its idea is based on the OT. Dennis[1063] argues that the idea that Jesus gives eternal life to those who believe him and delivers them from perishing, judgment and wrath in John 3 cannot be fully understood without knowledge of the relation between sin, wrath and restoration in the OT and Jewish literature. Dennis highlights the background of the idea of the wrath of God in Deuteronomy, in which God's anger (θυμός) and wrath (ὀργή) are related to:

> the sins of Israel, the curses of the covenant, and the dispersion of Israel from the land to the nations (cf. Deut 29:27), and the restoration of Israel reverses the consequences of the curses placed on Israel.[1064]

Above all, Barrett[1065] points out that in v. 36 the wrath of God which remains on those who reject the Son is in the present tense, as is eternal life. This indicates the state of the present progressive of the wrath of God as well as eternal life. Barrett goes on to say that it has the same meaning as 'already condemned' in John 3:18 ('whoever does not believe stands condemned already because he has not believed in the name of God's one and only Son'). Therefore, Burge rightly argues that the wrath of God in John 3:36 (vv. 19–21) means that:

> Those who reject the Son will not see life; instead, God's wrath rests on them.... Rather, it means that the world of darkness and unbelief stands under the judgment of God (Rom. 1:18ff.), and

---

[1061] Moloney, *John*, 107; Dennis, *Gathering*, 126; Brown, *John I-XII*, 159, 162. Bruce, *John*, 97 thinks that eternal life alludes to new birth and God's children of John 1:12f; 3:3ff. Barrett, *John*, 227 says that v. 36 is the climax of the chapter 3 of John's Gospel.

[1062] Moloney, *John*, 112; Fallon, *John*, 110f; Howard-Brook, *Becoming*, 98; Lindars, *John*, 171, who says that the wrath of God has an eschatological, apocalyptic background.

[1063] Dennis, *Gathering*, 126; J. Fichtner, *TDNT*, V, 396, who also says that 'The consistent linking of nouns for wrath with Yahweh, the covenant God, is of supreme theological significance. It shows that the idea of wrath is closely bound up with belief in the covenant.' Also, S. Erlandsson, 'Wrath,' 113; J. W. Locke, 'Wrath,' 225–227.

[1064] Dennis, *Gathering*, 126. Cf. 2 *Macc.* 5:19–20; 2 *Bar.* 64:4–5. Also see, Fichtner, *TDNT*, V, 400, 407; Erlandsson, 'Wrath,' 113; Locke, 'Wrath,' 226–227, 229. On the other hand, according to O. Grether and J. Fichtner, *TDNT*, V, 409, both terms θυμός and ὀργή in the LXX are used together for rendering the various Hebrew words for wrath; 200 times respectively for the wrath (anger) of God.

[1065] Barrett, *John*, 227; Bruce, *John*, 98; Brown, *John I-XII*, 159, 162; Dennis, *Gathering*, 127f; Polhill, 'John 1–4,' 453. Cf. Turner, *Holy*, 60.

those who refuse the light, who reject Jesus, remain in the darkness and thus continue to live under divine judgment.[1066]

This is in agreement with the idea of the judgement of God of the previous segment (John 3:18–21). That whoever believes in the Son has eternal life means the coming out of the wrath of God rather than the remaining under it, which could reflect the idea of the new exodus.

The motif of the new birth (new generation/creation) in John 3:1–15 can be compared to the wedding motif in John 3:22–30. Both John 3:16–21 and John 3:31–36 as the Evangelist's commentaries concern eternal life and eternal condemnation (cf. the wrath of God). In John 3:16–21, Jesus who has been sent from heaven by God the Father, introduces himself as the Son of Man, and the only Son of God. Those who believe in him will have eternal life (salvation), coming from the darkness into the light. However, those who reject him stand condemned already, remaining in the darkness. Likewise, in John 3:31–36, Jesus is introduced as the Son who comes from above (heaven) and who God the Father has sent. Eternal life which is given to whoever believes in the Son is contrasted with the wrath of God, under which the one who rejects the Son and will not see eternal life, remains.[1067]

5.4 Conclusion

From the study of the John 3:1–36 the following conclusions have been reached.

In vv. 1–8, the new birth, namely, the birth of water and Spirit is related to the new exodus motif of the OT background (cf. Ezek 36–37). Thus, water in v. 5 denotes water baptism performed in the wilderness (cf. Isa 63:10–14; 1 Cor 10:1–4), even though the role of the Spirit was emphasized. Also, in v. 5, entering and the kingdom of God have been studied in connection with the new exodus motif. This suggests entering the eschatological-new community of God, the new Temple (cf. my Father's house), raised by Jesus, the Davidic Messiah (cf. John 2:12–22; 14:1–2).

In John 3:12, 'the earthly things' refers to the new birth in vv. 1–8, revealed in the OT, and 'the heavenly things' is the works of Jesus (vv. 13–15). He as the embodiment of the Danielic Son of Man (7:13ff) bears the works of the Isaianic suffering servant of the Lord (Isa 52:13–53:12); a vicarious atoning death as a guilt-offering and ransom to restore Israel and the nations (cf.

[1066] Burge, *John*, 123; Moloney, *John*, 112; Whitacre, *John*, 99; Fallon, *John*, 111.
[1067] Cf. Polhill, 'John 1–4,' 452 says that the seemingly unrelated episodes (the conversation with Nicodemus (3:1–21) and the witness of John the Baptist (3:22–30) are knitted into a whole with the conclusion of the theme of the new life in 3:31–36.

Mk 10:45). The combination between the Danielic Son of Man and the Isaianic suffering servant of the Lord in John 3:13–15 is explained by the idea of the firstborn (Exod 4:22ff), which is supported by the only Son of God who bears the work of the Isaianic suffering servant in John 3:16–18.

In John 3:15–18, 'eternal life' alludes to Dan 12:2 (לְחַיֵּי עוֹלָם), which means the life of the age to come, or the resurrection life, reflecting the restoration (Ezek 37:1–14; Isa 26:19). Eternal condemnation alludes to everlasting contempt (לְדִרְאוֹן) in Dan 12:2; Isa 66:24, pictured as the horrible *death* under the unending wrath of God (cf. 'to perish' in John 3:16), reflecting the deportation (exile).

In John 3:16–17, God's purpose to send his only Son into the world was to save it. Nevertheless, God's condemnation will take place against those who constantly reject the eternal life offered through the Son. They condemn themselves, namely, self-condemnation. This is explained by the pictures of light and darkness alluding to hardening and blindness in John 3:18–21.

In John 3:22–30 (esp. v. 29), the Baptist explained himself as the best man and Jesus as the bridegroom. This marriage motif alludes to the covenantal relationship between Yahweh and Israel. Thus, the Baptist's testimony in John 3:29–30 discloses the inauguration of the new-eschatological salvation (restoration). John 3:31–36, like John 3:13–21, presents the heavenly origin of Jesus and the supremacy of his testimony. In John 3:33–34, the fact that the Father gives the Spirit to the Son reflects John 1:32f. alluding to the Davidic Messiah-suffering servant figure (Isa 11:2; 42:1; 61:1). In John 3:36, like John 3:16–21, eternal life is the coming out of the wrath of God, reflecting the idea of the new exodus.

Chapter 6: Jesus and the Samaritan Woman (John 4:1–42) and Jesus's Healing (John 4:43–54)

6.1 Introduction

Chapter 4 of John's Gospel can be divided into two sections: the narrative about Jesus's encounter with a Samaritan woman besides a well in Sychar, in vv. 1–42; and the narrative about Jesus's healing of a royal official's son in Capernaum in vv. 43–54. The Samaritan woman, one of the main characters in John 4:1–42, is seen as the representative of the Samaritans. Carson[1068] argues that the Evangelist purposely contrasts Nicodemus in John 3 with the Samaritan woman in John 4. Nicodemus is a man, a Jew, a ruler who is learned, powerful, respected, orthodox and theologically trained. However, the woman, in itself a cultural obstacle, is a Samaritan, a moral outcast who is unschooled, without influence, despised and capable of observing only folk religion. Nonetheless, both of them representing the Jews and the Samaritans respectively need Jesus who is the very one who fulfils the promise of the OT and thus replaces the old religious orders based on Jerusalem or Mount Gerizim.[1069]

At Jacob's well Jesus offers to give the Samaritan the gift of God, living water, a spring of water welling up to eternal life. Some Johannine commentators[1070] recognize that water symbolism appears consistently in the chapters 2, 3, 4 of John's Gospel. The water of Jewish purification and the wine of the kingdom brought by Jesus in John 2 (vv. 6ff), the water of the new generation and baptism in John 3 (vv. 5, 22–26), and the water of Jacob's well and the living water given by Jesus in John 4 (vv. 10–15).

Jesus changes the topic of the conversation from water to her marital status and discloses the reality of her infidelity. In connection with this, the woman recognizes Jesus as a prophet, and thus she brings up the issue of the place to worship God; Jerusalem or Mount Gerizim? Concerning this problem, Jesus talks about the new worship, namely, the worship of God the Father in Spirit and truth, which has nothing to do location. Beasley-

---

[1068] Carson, *John*, 216; Bruce, *John*, 104; Milne, *John*, 83; Kim, *Exposition*, 84f; Witherington, *Wisdom*, 119; *idem.*, *Women*, 57; W. Munro, 'Pharisee,' 711, 727; M. M. Pazdan, 'Nicodemus,' 145–148; Koester, 'Hearing,' 333–336; Trumbower, *Born*, 73, 79.
[1069] Carson, *John*, 216; Bruce, *John*, 104; Milne, *John*, 83; Beasley-Murray, *John*, 59; Kim, *Exposition*, 84f; Barrett, *John*, 228; Morris, *John*, 225 n. 12; Witherington, *Wisdom*, 119; Munro, 'Pharisee,' 711, 727; Koester, 'Hearing,' 333–336; Howard-Brook, *Becoming*, 104; Bennema, *Power*, 181f.
[1070] Beasley-Murray, *John*, 58; Carson, *John*, 214; Bruce, *John*, 104; Morris, *John*, 225 n. 12; Barrett, *John*, 228; Witherington, *Wisdom*, 119; Lindars, *John*, 172; C. M. Carmichael, 'Marriage,' 332–346, esp. 332; Polhill, 'John 1–4,' 454.

Murray[1071] points out that as the Temple incident in John 2:13–22 shows that the old Temple built by hands (cf. 'the old order of worship') will be replaced by the new Temple of Christ's body (cf. 'the worship of the new age initiated through the death and resurrection of Christ'). So, Jesus's saying in John 4:20–24 shows that the worship in Jerusalem and Mount Gerizim will be replaced by the worship in Spirit and truth, namely, the worship of the new age introduced by Jesus and the Holy Spirit that will be sent by him. He further discloses his identity as the very Messiah (Christ) whom the woman expected to come and to teach everything (including the true worship) to them (probably the Samaritans).

After that, the woman left her waterpot at the well and went to the town to proclaim Jesus the Messiah to her people. Meanwhile, to the disciples who came back with some food from the town and urged him to eat it, Jesus talks about his work and mission with the imagery of food. He then proceeds to explain his ministry with the harvest motif, illustrated by the restoration of the Samaritans who rush out of the town toward him. After staying with them two more days in Samaria, Jesus is confessed as 'the Saviour of the world.'

In John 4:43–54, Jesus and the disciples moved to Galilee and Cana, where he was asked by a royal official to heal his son in Capernaum. This act of healing was carried out through Jesus simply speaking the command.

In this section, we will study the gift of God, living water (vv. 1–15), the betrothal motif (vv. 16–18), the new worship (the new Temple vv. 19–26), the restoration of the Samaritans with the harvest motif and the restoration of the world (the gentiles) (vv. 27–42). This will be set against their respective OT backgrounds, the purpose is to disclose Jesus's identity and his works in the light of eschatological restoration or the new exodus. Jesus will be presented on a diverse spectrum; the new Israel replacing Jacob-Israel, the true husband, the builder of the new Temple, namely, the eschatological fulfiller as the Davidic messianic King of the Davidic covenant, the 'I Am' (ἐγώ εἰμι), the Saviour (the restorer/the deliverer/the redeemer) of the world, the true Son/servant of God.

Consideration will also be given to the narrative of Jesus's healing of a royal official's son in the second part of John 4 (vv. 43–54). Here, firstly, the significance of Jesus's own land will be discussed coupled with the meaning of the saying about the prophet who has no honour in his own home. Secondly, the miraculous signs and wonders mentioned in v. 48 will be considered in connection with their OT backgrounds. Thirdly, in

---

[1071] Beasley-Murray, *John*, 59; Witherington, *Wisdom*, 119; Coloe, *Dwells*, 86.

connection with the new creation, the new exodus / the restoration, I will discuss Jesus's identity reflected in the sign when he, in Cana of Galilee, healed the royal official's son in Capernaum by simply speaking.

6.2 The Living Water (the Gift of God) (John 4:1–15)

In v. 2, the comment, 'Although in fact it was not Jesus who baptized, but his disciples,' added by the Evangelist is given to correct the statement in John 3:22 that 'Jesus and his disciples went out into the Judean countryside, where he spent some time with them, and baptized.'[1072] In vv. 3ff, when Jesus with his disciples left Judea and went back to Galilee, he had to (δεῖ) pass through Samaria, in particular a Samaritan town called Sychar,[1073] near the plot of ground Jacob had given to his son Joseph. According to Witherington,[1074] the Galilean Jews at the time of Jesus used to make their way through Samaria as a shortcut between their home and Jerusalem to attend Jewish feasts and to return home. Here, δεῖ could signify that Jesus's passing through Samaria, namely, his encountering the Samaritan woman (and the Samaritans through her) was the fulfilment of the divine will.[1075]

In vv. 6f, Jesus who was tired from the journey sat down at Jacob's well and asked the woman to give him a drink.[1076] However, in v. 9, she asked a question in return; how he as a Jew could ask her a Samaritan woman for a drink. Concerning this, the Evangelist adds another comment, 'For Jews do not associate with Samaritans.'[1077] In v. 10, Jesus answered the woman, 'If

---

[1072] Brown, *John I-XII*, 164; Carmichael, 'Marriage,' 333; Fallon, *John*, 112, who also says that the reason that Jesus did not baptize with water was because Jesus will baptize with water and Spirit (cf. John 3:5; 1:35) which is available after his death and resurrection (cf. John 7:39). Malina and Rohrbaugh, *John*, 98 say that it is because Jesus baptizes with Spirit rather than with water.

[1073] Lindars, *John*, 178 assumes Sychar a Samaritan town in v. 5 is the modern village of 'Askar.' Also, Blomberg, *Historical*, 99; Michaels, *John*, 76. *Contra* Brown, *John I-XII*, 169 thinks that Sychar is Shechem rather than Askar. But Polhill, 'John 1–4,' 547 n. 18 is not sure that Sychar is Shechem.

[1074] Witherington, *Wisdom*, 115. Cf. *Ant.* 20.118; *War* 2.232; *Life* 269.

[1075] Witherington, *Wisdom*, 115; Grayston, 'Misunderstands,' 11; Brown, *John I-XII*, 169; Fallon, *John*, 112.

[1076] Cf. Brown, *John I-XII*, 169 observes that 'at the well' in v. 6 ['Jesus was sitting at the well' (ἐκαθέζετο οὕτως ἐπὶ τῇ πηγῇ)] literally means 'on the well.' Also, Coloe, *Dwells*, 95.

[1077] For the historical background of the hostility between the Jews and the Samaritans, see 2 Kings 17:24–41 (cf. Ezra 4; Nehemiah), in which, after Israel, the Northern kingdom was captured by Assyria and the Israelites were deported to Assyria in 722–721 B.C., Samaria, the territory of the Northern kingdom was settled by the Assyrians with their gods. Thus, the Samarians of the Northern kingdom lost their racial, religious identity as the people of Yahweh (cf. 2 Kings 17:24–41). The Samaritans had built their own Temple on Mount Gerizim in 400 B.C., but this was destroyed by John Hyrcanus in 128 B.C. For this, see Milne, *John*, 83; Howard-Brook, *Becoming*, 101f; Smith, *John*, 112; Witherington, *Wisdom*, 117f. Furthermore, the antagonistic relationship between the Jews and the Samaritans is disclosed in some Jewish

you knew the gift of God and who it is that asks you for a drink, you would have asked him and he would have given you living water.' In vv. 13f, comparing living water, the gift of God, with the water from Jacob's well, Jesus additionally said that, 'whoever drinks the water I give him will never thirst. Indeed, the water I give him will become in him a spring of water welling up to eternal life.' Here, the gift of God is no other than 'living water,' namely, 'a spring of water welling up to eternal life.'[1078] Also, the gift of God, living water, a spring of water welling up to eternal life, is bestowed to the woman by Jesus himself. So, what is the gift of God, the living water, or the spring of water welling up to eternal life? What is the OT background of the gift of God expressed in such terms?

Firstly, the living water as spring water or running water is different from water held in cisterns, alluding to Jer 2:13 (cf. Pss 36:9; 42:1f); in which the living water is metaphorically used for God by himself in the light of his covenantal relationship with his people Israel:[1079]

> The Lord declares, My people have committed two sins: They have forsaken Me, *the spring of living water*, and have dug their own cisterns, broken cisterns that cannot hold water.

In v. 6, Jacob's well is called πηγή throughout denoting a running spring or fountain, and φρέαρ throughout in vv. 11–12, meaning a cistern or an artificially dug-out well. So, Carson[1080] says that, 'it [Jacob's well] was dug out, but it is fed by an underground spring that is remarkably reliable to this day.' On the other hand, Brown thinks that the means of the two terms (*phrear, pēgē*) are not different from each other in the LXX; nonetheless,

---

documents, such as, Josephus, *War* 2.232; *Life* 269; *Sir.* 50:25f (cf. Grayston, 'Misunderstands,' 12). The Jews did not associate with the Samaritans for fear of incurring ritual defilement (*m. Sheb.* 8.10). Especially, the Jews, by defining the daughters of the Samaritans as menstruants from their cradle, regarded them in a permanent state of ceremonial uncleanness (*b. 'Erub.* 53b; *m. Nid.* 4:1. cf. H. Danby, *The Mishnah*, 803; Str-B, I, 538–560). Concerning this see Carson, *John*, 217f; Bruce, *John*, 103; Morris, *John*, 229 n. 22; Barrett, *John*, 232; Lindars, *John*, 180; Brodie, *John*, 221; Blomberg, *Historical*, 100; Polhill, 'John 1–4,' 457 n. 18; Brown, *John I-XII*, 170; Köstenberger, *John*, 88; Malina and Rohrbaugh, *John*, 99; R. G. Maccini, 'Reassessment, 35–46, esp. 38. In particular, Malina and Rohrbaugh, *John*, 98 argue that 'to associate with' added by the Evangelist in v. 9 means 'to share in common' which literally connotes to share utensils such as drinking cups or dishes, pointing out a concern for ritual purity. Also, Köstenberger, *John*, 88; Howard-Brook, *Becoming*, 101; Barrett, *John*, 232.
[1078] Morris, *John*, 230; Lindars, *John*, 181; Beasley-Murray, *John*, 60; idem., *Life*, 69.
[1079] Bruce, *John*, 104; Carson, *John*, 218f; Beasley-Murray, *John*, 60; Morris, *John*, 231; Barrett, *John*, 233; Lindars, *John*, 182f; Blomberg, *Historical*, 100; Milne, *John*, 84; Köstenberger, *John*, 90; Smith, *John*, 113; Fallon, *John*, 114; Ng, *Symbolism*, 171. Cf. Philo, *Fuga* 198.
[1080] Carson, *John*, 217 ([] added by this writer); Bruce, *John*, 102; Morris, *John*, 227f; Barrett, *John*, 234; Howard-Brook, *Becoming*, 104.

phrear (Heb. *beʾēr*) is closer to 'cistern' and *pēgē* (Heb. *ʿayin*) is closer to 'fountain,' and then argues that:

> The idea may be that in the earlier conversation which concerns natural water Jacob's well is a fountain (*pēgē*) with fresh, flowing water; but when the conversation shifts to the theme of Jesus's living water, Jesus is now the fountain (*pēgē* in vs. 14), and Jacob's well becomes a mere cistern (*phrear*).[1081]

So, in connection with 'the spring of living water' of Jer 2:13, 'the living water' or the spring of water of John 4:10, 14 is employed in the light of Yahweh's covenantal relation with the Israelites. Jesus's words that he will give the living water, the spring of water to the Samaritan woman could be understood as the restoration of the covenantal relationship with the Samaritan woman and her people.

Above all, the imagery of the living water which is given to the thirsty is frequently adopted in connection with the restoration of Israel, Isa 49:10; 44:3; 55:1; 12:3 (cf. Rev 7:16; 21:6; John 6:35; 7:37–39).[1082] In Isa 49:10, the pictures, no hunger nor thirst, and guiding and leading them beside springs of water, are used to express the restoration of Israel from exile (the captives) and the salvation of the nations through the suffering servant of Yahweh, who is the covenant for the people of Israel and the light for the gentiles.[1083]

Also, in connection with the restoration of Israel and the nations and even the creation, we have to note the importance of Isa 55:1–3 (cf. Yahweh's invitation to the thirsty to drink for free) as the OT background of water and thirst. Further Isa 55:4–5 which shows that Yahweh will make an everlasting covenant based on the promise to David (cf. 2 Sam 7:12–16) with those who respond to his invitation. However this relates not only to Israel but also the nations whom Israel does not know,[1084] and further the restoration of the creation with the motif of the new exodus (cf. Isa 55:12–13).[1085]

[1081] Brown, *John I-XII*, 170. Also see Lindars, *John*, 182; Smith, *John*, 114; A. F. Wedel, 'John 4:5–26,' 406–412, esp. 408; Polhill, 'John 1–4,' 454; Grayston, 'Misunderstands,' 11.

[1082] Carson, *John*, 220; Morris, *John*, 231; Lindars, *John*, 182f; Ng, *Symbolism*, 172–179; Blomberg, *Historical*, 100; Köstenberger, *John*, 90; Fallon, *John*, 114; Barrett, *John*, 234; Turner, *Holy*, 61f; Jeremias, *Theology*, I, 107.

[1083] Cf. Barrett, *John*, 234 relates the expression ('never thirst') in John 4:14 with the description of the time of salvation in Isa 49:10.

[1084] Cf. Carson, *John*, 220

[1085] Cf. Ng, *Symbolism*, 174; Motyer, *Isaiah*, 452–458. The intimate relationship between Isa 55 and John 4 will be presented by the study of Jesus's saying in John 4:34, alluding to Isa 55:10–11.

In particular, in Isa 44:3 (cf. Isa 32:15–20; Ezek 36:25ff; Joel 2:28–32; 3:17f; Rev 7:16), the pictures that Yahweh pours water on the thirsty land and streams on the dry grounds are metaphorically used to express Yahweh's pouring out his Spirit on the offspring of Israel and his blessing on descendants of Israel.[1086]

> For I will pour water on the thirsty land, and streams on the dry ground; I will pour out my Spirit on your offspring, and my blessing on your descendants…. One will say, 'I belong to the Lord'; another will call himself by the name of Jacob; still another will write on his hand, 'The Lord's,' and will take the name Israel. (Isa 44:3, 5)

This means the restoration of Yahweh's covenantal relation with Israel, Yahweh and his people.[1087]

Furthermore, concerning the OT background of the living water giving eternal life in John 4:10, 14, we have to pay attention to Ezek 47:8–9 (vv. 1–12) (cf. Zech 14:8).[1088] Here Ezekiel saw the vision of the water gushing out from under the threshold of the Temple toward the east. The water was coming down from under the south side of the Temple, south of the altar toward the eastern region and goes down into the Arabah, where it enters the Sea (the Dead Sea).[1089] The water flowing from the Temple makes the salty water of the Dead Sea fresh and the Sea is filled with 'every living creature.' 'The arrival of the living water from the Temple revives the Dead Sea, which results in the profuse multiplication of fish.'[1090] The imagery that the living water gushing out from the Temple makes the Dead Sea like a fresh water lake is related to the restoration of Israel's relationship with God.[1091] Also, in Zech 14:8, on the day of Yahweh, living water will flow out from Jerusalem, half to the eastern sea and half to the western sea, which is

---

[1086] Carson, *John*, 220; Milne, *John*, 84; Burge, *Anointed*, 96–99; Ng, *Symbolism*, 176; Turner, *Holy*, 61f; Schnackenburg, *John*, I, 431f; Coloe, *Dwells*, 94; Koester, *Symbolism*, 171f.
[1087] Ng, *Symbolism*, 176.
[1088] Carson, *John*, 219; Morris, *John*, 231; Barrett, *John*, 233; Lindars, *John*, 182f; Blomberg, *Historical*, 100; Smith, *John*, 113; Turner, *Holy*, 61; Ng, *Symbolism*, 177–179; Dennis, *Gathering*, 178, 181; Coloe, *Dwells*, 94. Cf. Block, *Ezekiel 25–48*, 696–705, who argues that Ezekiel's vision of the stream is reflected in John 7:38, however, interprets the verse to mean that the rivers of living water shall flow out of the believer not out of the Christ.
[1089] Block, *Ezekiel 25–48*, 693f argues that הַיָּמָּה הַמּוּצָאִים meaning 'the sea of stagnant waters' refers to the stagnant nature of the Dead Sea, which is occasionally called the Sea of Arabah in Deut 4:49; Josh 3:16; 12:3; 2 Kings 14:25. That the Sea is identified with the Dead Sea is supported by the topographical names, En-gedi and En-eglaim in v. 10, which are located on opposite sides of the Dead Sea (p. 695). Allen, *Ezekiel 20–48*, 277, 279.
[1090] Block, *Ezekiel 25–48*, 695; See also Allen, *Ezekiel 20–48*, 279.
[1091] Block, *Ezekiel 25–48*, 701; Coloe, *Dwells*, 96; Ng, *Symbolism*, 177; Dennis, *Gathering*, 178, 181.

the same tradition of the renewal of the paradisal stream, alluding to Gen 2:10–14.[1092]

Beasley-Murray[1093] points out that in Judaism the absolute necessity of water for life is diversely applied; most frequently to the laws (cf. Str-B, II, 433–436; *CD* 3:16f; 6:4–11; 19:34), also to wisdom (cf. *Sir.* 24:21–31; *1 En.* 48:1; 49:1; *1 QH* 8:1–21; Prov 13:14; 18:4) or to *Logos*(*Somn.* 2.242), to even the Holy Spirit (*Tg. Isa* 44:3; *1 QS* 4:20ff). Philo, in interpreting Jer 2:13, defines God as, 'the most ancient of all fountains, the fountain of life, the everlasting fountain of life' in *Fuga* 198. Smith[1094] observes that *Odes of Solomon* 11:6–8 (cf. 6:8–18; 28:15; 30:1–7) show examples of a very similar metaphor about water as in John 4. Fallon[1095] says that in the *Targum* about Num 21:16–18, the Israelites including the Samaritans believed Jacob's well to be the gift of God and a miraculous and inexhaustible source of water, which is in accord with the symbolic meaning of the narrative of John 4. In particular, Brown[1096] argues that the Johannine tradition of living (flowing) water welling up eternal life in John 4 is related to the *Palestinian Targum* of Gen 28:10 concerning the well of Haran, saying that: 'After *our ancestor Jacob* had lifted the stone from the mouth of the well, the well rose to its surface and overflowed, and was *overflowing* twenty years.'

Yahweh's invitation to the thirsty to buy the waters, wine, and milk without money and without cost in Isa 55:1 (cf. Isa 49:10) could be reflected in the idea of 'the gift of Yahweh' in John 4:10. This is also reflected in Rev 21:6, in which the giver who gives the thirsty the drink without cost from the spring of the water of life is introduced as the Alpha and the Omega, the Beginning and the End (Rev 21:7), which alludes to the name of

---

[1092] Ng, *Symbolism*, 178f; Dennis, *Gathering*, 178, 181. Cf. Turner, *Holy*, 61.
[1093] Beasley-Murray, *John*, 60; Morris, *John*, 230 n. 26; Barrett, *John*, 233; Lindars, *John*, 183f; Blomberg, *Historical*, 100; Milne, *John*, 84; Whitacre, *John*, 103; Smith, *John*, 113; Fallon, *John*, 114; Witherington, *Wisdom*, 118f, 382 n. 7; Turner, *Holy*, 61f; Coloe, *Dwells*, 93f; Brown, *John I-XII*, 178f, who points out that the law was regarded as the gift of God in Judaism. Also, Dunn, *Baptism*, 187; Koester, *Symbolism*, 170; Ng, *Symbolism*, 172; Dennis, *Gathering*, 177f.
[1094] Smith, *John*, 113; Barrett, *John*, 233.
[1095] Fallon, *John*, 112; Coloe, *Dwells*, 92. Cf. Rabbinic sources have traditions of a travelling well; for example, with Jacob in *Pirqe R. Eliezer* 35 or with the people of Israel in *Num R.* 19:25.
[1096] Brown, *John I-XII*, 170f (original emphasis); Coloe, *Dwells*, 91. Also, Brown, *ibid.*, points out that there is no proper OT background for Jacob's well and thinks that Jacob's well in John 4 is based on the narrative of Jacob and the well of Haran in Gen 28. On the other hand, Pamment, 'Samaritan,' 222 observes that not Jacob's well but his field was mentioned in Gen 33:18; 48:22; Josh 24:32. Bruce, *John*, 105 thinks that the mention that Jesus will give the living water (a spring of water welling) reminds the Samaritan woman of the tradition about the overflowing from the buckets of Taheb (the Samaritan counterpart to the Jewish Messiah) in the Samaritan liturgy for the Day of Atonement, which is based on Balaam's oracle in Num 24:7. Also, Carson, *John*, 220.

Yahweh, the great redeemer in Isaiah (cf. Isa 41:4; 44:6; 48:12; 43:10).[1097] That the phrase, 'the gift of God,' namely, 'the living water' in John 4:10, 14 is applied to the Holy Spirit is found in the Gospel itself (cf. John 7:37–39; 6:35) and in other NT references (cf. Acts 8:20; 2:38; 10:45; 11:17; Heb 6:4).[1098] The Johannine Jesus is identified as 'the eschatological bringer of such abundant divine provision' in John 4:10, 14 and John 7:38–38, particularly, disclosing that the living water is the emblem of the Holy Spirit.[1099]

In John 7:38–39, in alluding to Yahweh's invitation to the thirsty in Isa 55:1, Jesus invites people at the end of the Tabernacle feast: 'If anyone is thirsty, let him come to me and drink. Whoever believes in me, as the Scripture has said, streams of living water will flow from within him.' And then, in John 7:39, the Evangelist explains that by 'streams of living water,' Jesus meant the Holy Spirit, whom those who believed in him were later to receive.[1100] In particular, the connection between John 7:37 and Isa 55:1–2 can be supported by the debate caused by Jesus's invitation among the Jews who argue if he is the Christ, the descendant of David in John 7:40–43, which

---

[1097] Beale, *Revelation*, 1055ff.
[1098] Milne, *John*, 70; Dunn, *Baptism*, 187; Koester, *Symbolism*, 172; Brown, *John I-XII*, 179, who says the gift of the Holy Spirit as a mark of the messianic era. Also, Jeremias, *Theology*, I, 76–85.
[1099] Köstenberger, *John*, 90; Brown, *John I-XII*, 179; Bennema, *Power*, 181f; Burge, *Anointed*, 90; Koester, *Symbolism*, 171f; Turner, *Holy*, 61f; Throckmorton, *Creation*, 115; Dunn, *Baptism*, 188; Drapper, 'Temple,' 282; Beasley-Murray, *Life*, 69; Ng, *Symbolism*, 172, 174ff.
[1100] According to Burge, *Anointed*, 89–91, the interpretation of John 7:37-38 is divided into two groups, depending on the position of a period (after πινέτω or εἰς ἐμέ) and on the identity of αὐτοῦ (pointing 'believer' or 'Jesus'). **First,** Eastern Interpretation, following Origen, Athanasius and the Greek fathers, understands that a period is placed after πινέτω (let him drink) and that ὁ πιστεύων is regarded as the suspended subject of the quotation, and thus 'the believers to be the source of living water.' For examples, Carson, *John*, 321–329; Turner, *Holy*, 62; idem., 'Concept,' 24–42, esp. 29–31. **Secondly,** Western (following Justine, Hippolytus, Tertullian, Irenaeus) or Christological Interpretation, understand that a period is placed after εἰς ἐμέ (in me) and thus ὁ πιστεύων is the subject of πινέτω and accordingly the stream of living water in the quotation is related only to Jesus Christ. Namely, the Christ is the source of the living water. For example, Beasley-Murray, *Life*, 69; Burge, *ibid.*, 90, supporting the Christological interpretation, writes that 'No where in John or the NT is the believer said to be the source of living water. Such distribution (which v. 39 describes as the Spirit) is strictly a divine prerogative.' Burge further argues that the Johannine Jesus offers the Samaritan woman his living water (John 4:10; John 6:35; 7:37–38) and only Jesus is the source of the Spirit (John 20:22; cf. 14:16), and John 19:34 ('a sudden flow of blood and water' from Jesus's side) is an 'unavoidable allusion to what is predicted here' and Rev 22:1–2 says that the living water flows from the thrones of God and the Lamb. Furthermore, Burge, *ibid.*, 91 thinks that the living water of John 7:37–39 which is based on Isa 43:19; 44:3; Zech 14:8; Ezek 47:1–11 means the messianic visions and the expectations of the coming age, and the living water also alludes to the rock of Num 20:8ff, from which Moses let water gush out in the wilderness (cf. Isa 43:20; 44:3; 48:21; Ps 78:15f; 105:40f; 1 Cor 10:4); 'Jesus is the rock from the midst of which living water will flow. He is the messianic bearer of God's Spirit and wisdom.' Also, Dennis, *Gathering*, 181.

could allude to the reference of David in Isa 55:3; Yahweh will make an everlasting covenant with Israel, based on his faithful love promised to David.[1101]

Thus, Carson rightly says that the living water namely, a spring of water welling up to eternal life in John 4 is:

> the satisfying eternal life mediated by the Spirit that only Jesus, the Messiah and Saviour of the world, can provide.... The 'living water'...Jesus gives bans thirst forever in the one who drinks it. This thirst is not for natural water, but for God, for eternal life in the presence of God; and the thirst is met not by removing this aching desire but by pouring out the Spirit. Indeed, this water *will become in him a spring of water welling up to eternal life* (v.14) – clearly a reference to the Spirit who alone gives life (6:63).[1102]

Barrett further comments that:

> The 'water' is pre-eminently the Holy Spirit, which alone gives life (cf. 6.63). It proceeds from the side of the crucified Jesus [cf. John 19:34]; it is the agent of the generation of Christians; and it forms the fountain of life which for ever springs within Christians, maintaining their divine life.[1103]

This argument that Jesus will give the Holy Spirit, the gift of God, the living water which will be a spring of water welling up eternal life could be supported from Ezekiel's vision. In that the life-giving water gushing out from the eschatological Temple becomes a river and flows to the Dead Sea to revive it as in the vision recorded in Ezek 47:1–12.[1104] That Jesus is the new Temple through whom the Holy Spirit, the life-giving water, gushes out, is reflected in Jesus's Temple incident of John 2:19–21 (if one interprets

---

[1101] On the other hand, that Jesus's mention in John 6:35 alludes to Isa 55:1 could be supported by John 6:37–40 (cf. John 4:34), which is related with Isa 55:10–11. For this, see Burkett, *Son*, 131f; Endo, *Creation*, 241f; Turner, *Holy*, 63, who says that the discourse about bread and drink in John 6 is based on Exod 16:4, 15 and Isa 54–55, and especially Isa 54:13 is quoted in John 6:45 and Isa 55:1 explains the subjects of bread and refreshing drink in John 6:35.

[1102] Carson, *John*, 219f (original emphasis); Beasley-Murray, *John*, 60; idem., *Life*, 69; Morris, *John*, 230f; Barrett, *John*, 233f; Michaels, *John*, 70; Milne, *John*, 84; Whitacre, *John*, 103; Kim, *Exposition*, 87f; Köstenberger, *John*, 90; Smith, *John*, 113; Fallon, 115; Brown, *John I-XII*, 179; Carmichael, 'Marriage,' 340; Munro, 'Pharisee,' 720; Lindars, *John*, 183; Bruce, *John*, 105; Burge, *Anointed*, 87f; Turner, *Holy*, 61f; Throckmorton, *Creation*, 115; Dunn, *Baptism*, 187f; Koester, *Symbolism*, 171. Cf. Jeremias, *Theology*, I, 82.

[1103] Barrett, *John*, 233f ([] added by this wirter); Throckmorton, *Creation*, 115; Dunn, *Baptism*, 187; Beasley-Murray, *Life*, 69; Coloe, *Dwells*, 96.

[1104] Coloe, *Dwells*, 95, interprets, pointing out that ἐπὶ τῇ πηγῇ (dative) in John 4:6 means 'on [or upon] the well,' that Jesus as the new eschatological Temple (cf. John 2:19–21) sat down upon the rock of the lid of the Jacob's well. Also, Brown, *John I-XII*, 169.

the resurrected body of Jesus as the new eschatological Temple). Then, with his words in John 4:21–24, Jesus defines the new eschatological worship, namely, worshipping God the Father in truth and the Spirit.[1105]

In John 4:10, 13f, the living water (spring water) has to be understood in the meaning of drinking giving or restoring life rather than cleansing or bringing purification.[1106] Nonetheless, the imagery of drinking the Spirit like living water is not different from the baptism in the Spirit (cf. John 1:33; 3:5; Ezek 36:25; 1 Cor 12:13), or the breathing the Spirit into the body/the birth of the Spirit (cf. John 3:5–8; 6:63; 20:22; 1 Cor 15:45; Gen 2:7; Ezek 37:1–14).[1107]

On the other hand, we can recognize the comparison between Jacob-Israel and Jesus-the new Israel in the narrative. A similar comparison to this can be found in John 1:51, in which Jesus as the Son of Man the inclusive representative of the new Israel (the 12 disciples), namely, the new eschatological people of God, will replace Jacob-Israel; the inclusive representative of the 12 tribes of Israel, the people of God in the OT. In John 4, the patriarch Jacob-Israel[1108] who was the inclusive forefather of the 12 tribes of Israel, gave his well of Sychar in Samaria to his sons and his flock and herds (vv. 6, 12). However, those who drink the water from Jacob's well will be thirsty again (v. 13). In contrast, Jesus is greater than Jacob-Israel (cf. v. 12) and gives living water to those who ask. Thus, whoever drinks the living water that Jesus gives him/her will never thirst. The water Jesus gives him/her will become in them a spring of water welling up to eternal life (v. 14). Here, the water that Jacob gave from his well is contrasted with the living water that Jesus will give.[1109] That the water from Jacob's well cannot solve the problem of thirst, is contrasted with the fact

---

[1105] Turner, *Holy*, 61–63; Coloe, *Dwells*, 94; Ng, *Symbolism*, 178; Dennis, *Gathering*, 178; Drapper, 'Temple,' 282. Cf. The meaning of the new worship in Spirit and truth in John 4:19–26 will be studied in next section, 6.4. The New Worship / The New Temple.

[1106] Dunn, *Baptism*, 187; Michaels, *John*, 70 (cf. 1 Cor 12:13). Also, Brown, *John I-XII*, 179f; Coloe, *Dwells*, 96.

[1107] Brown, *John I-XII*, 179f; Munro, 'Pharisee,' 720; Polhill, 'John 1–4,' 455; Lindars, *John*, 183; Grayston, 'Understands' 12. Cf. Michaels, *John*, 70; Throckmorton, *Creation*, 115; Burge, *Anointed*, 87f.

[1108] Whitacre, *John*, 103 points out that Jacob-Israel was the central figure to the covenant identity of the 12 tribes of Israel as the people of God, which was important not only for the Jews but also for the Samaritans as the covenantal people of God. So, 'Jesus' superiority to Jacob means that both Judaism and Samaritanism have been superseded in Jesus.' (p. 104). Also, Lindars, *John*, 182; Wedel, 'John 4:5–26,' 408; Coloe, *Dwells*, 86

[1109] Lindars, *John*, 183 observes that 'whoever drinks' (ὃς δ' ἂν πίῃ -aorist subjunctive) in v. 14 'makes it perfectly plain that a single draught is meant, as opposed to the frequentative participial construction [πᾶς ὁ πίνων ἐκ τοῦ ὕδατος τούτου διψήσει πάλιν] of the last verse [v. 13]. It is only necessary to drink once.' ([]added by this writer).

that the living water (a spring of water) given by Jesus quenches thirst permanently and leads to eternal life.[1110]

6.3 The Betrothal Motif (John 4:16–18)

In John 4:16, the fact that the Samaritan woman has had the five husbands is allegorically interpreted in connection with 2 Kings 17:24, 30–32, 41 (cf. *Ant* 9.14.3 §288), in which the five foreign races from Mesopotamia and Assyria had been transported to settle in Samaria, bringing the seven gods.[1111] Thus some commentators claim the five husbands of the woman in the past symbolize the seven gods being served by the Samaritans in the past, and her sixth man who was not her husband is interpreted to be Yahweh the one true God who was not husband of the Samaritans. The Samaritan woman who had a marital infidelity problem is seen as the symbolic representative of the ethnically mixed and religiously tainted Samaritans.

However, this allegorical interpretation has been criticized by other commentators,[1112] who, pointing out that the transported settlers in 2 Kings 17 served not five gods but seven gods and furthermore not one by one but simultaneously. They argue that it is just a factual statement showing her marital disorder and Jesus's omnipotence to penetrate her personal life. Thus it is right to criticize the argument that the five previous husbands of the woman correspond to the seven (or five) gods brought by the five foreign tribes transported in Samaria.[1113]

Nonetheless, it has to be noted that Jesus has some purpose in abruptly changing the subject from Jacob's well and the living water offered by him to her marriage life. He further exposes her disgraceful marital disorder, 'You are right when you say you have no husband. The fact is, you have had five husbands and the man you now have is not your husband' (vv. 17f). Here, we can recognize that the narrative discloses not only the marital infidelity of the Samaritan woman, but also the covenantal infidelity of the

---

[1110] Whitacre, *John*, 104; Smith, *John*, 114.
[1111] Hoskyns, *Fourth*, I, 242f. Cf. Brodie, *John*, 223; Kim, *Exposition*, 86; Howard-Brook, *Becoming*, 106f; Dodd, *Interpretation*, 313; Carmichael, 'Marriage,' 332–346; J. H. Neyrey, 'Traditions,' 426; C. R. Koester, 'Saviour,' 665–680, esp. 669; *idem.*, *Symbolism*, 49f; Fallon, *John*, 113, 116.
[1112] Carson, *John*, 221, 232f; Bruce, *John*, 107; Beasley-Murray, *John*, 61; Morris, *John*, 235; Lindars, *John*, 185ff; Lee, *Flesh*, 174f; Bernard, *John*, I, 143f; Haenchen, *John*, I, 221, 227; Brown, *John I-XII*, 171; Wedel, 'John 4:5–26,' 409; Schnackenburg, *John*, I, 420f; Bultmann, *John*, 188 n. 3; Coloe, *Dwells*, 97; J. D. M. Derrett, 'Samaritan,' 254ff, who allegorically interprets the 'five' in the five previous husbands of the woman as the five senses dominating over her, which were represented by the five kings of Canaan (cf. Joshua 10:5, 16, 22f). Grayston, 'Misunderstands,' 13 argues that her marital life just shows the actual fact of sexual perversion.
[1113] Cf. Brodie, *John*, 223

Samaritans in connection with Yahweh, the fountain of living water (Jer 2:13).[1114]

This argument could be supported by the following conversation about the worship of God in vv. 20–24. Here Jesus first points out the inappropriateness of the Samaritan worship, even though both the worship by the Jews in Jerusalem and the worship by Samaritans in Mount Gerizim will be replaced by the worship in Spirit and truth.[1115] Here, the worshipping of God could be related with the restoration of the covenantal relationship between God and the Samaritans (and the Jews as well).

Concerning this, we have to note Jer 2:1–13 (cf. the contrast between cistern water and the fountain of living water), which is one of the important OT references concerning the spring of living water in John 4:5–15. In Jer 2:1–13, Yahweh reminded the house of Jacob-Israel of her being the bride (the lover) of Yahweh the bridegroom. However, she strayed so far from Yahweh (who brought her up out of Egypt and led her through the barren wilderness into the promised land to eat her its fruits and rich produce), and followed worthless idols, Baal, and defiled the Land and made Yahweh's inheritance detestable. Israel forsook Yahweh, the spring of living water, and dug her own cisterns, broken cisterns that cannot hold water (Jer 2:13). So, Jer 2:1–13 may provide an OT background in understanding Jesus's disclosing the woman's marital infidelity in the setting of the conversation of Jacob's well and the living water in John 4:5–18, and his pointing out that her people the Samaritans worship what they do not know in John 4:20–24. Concerning this, Carmichael says that:

> he recalls, for example, the early history of God's relationship with Israel in terms of a bridegroom with a bride (Jer 2:2). Israel, however, had become a harlot, bowing down to the Baals, and unable, because of her uninhibited desires, to restrain her thirst for lovers (Jer 2:20–5). We recall that the water that Jesus offers the Samaritan woman, whose history of love affairs is similar, will

---

[1114] Schnackenburg, *John*, I, 420f, 433; Brown, *John I-XII*, 171; Lindars, *John*, 185ff; Davies, *Rhetoric*, 210f; Coloe, *Dwells*, 97–99; Barrett, *John*, 235, who thinks that the argument that the five husbands of the Samaritan woman symbolize the five gods brought by the settlers in Samaria, who were transported by Assyria, can be explained by Josephus, *Ant.* 9.14.3 §288, saying that the five gods were brought in Samaria. cf. Koester, 'Saviour,' 669, 669 nn. 11–12.

[1115] Koester, 'Saviour,' 669; Carmichael, 'Marriage,' 338f nn. 23f, who also thinks that Jesus's words ('Your Samaritans worship what you do not know') in v. 22 mean the apostasy of the Samaritans against Yahweh. Also, Koester, *Symbolism*, 49f observes that Jesus's conversation with the woman in John 4:22–24 used plural forms of speech (cf. our fathers (Samaritans), you people (Jews), you people (Samaritans), you people (Samaritans)), which mean that the Samaritan woman represents the Samaritan worshippers and Jesus the Jewish worshippers (p. 50).

prevent her from ever thirsting again. Equally interesting is that Jeremiah in the midst of his indictment of Israel's love life in chs. 2 and 3 raises the fundamental objection that Israel has forsaken its fountain of living waters, God, and hewed out cisterns that can hold no water (2:13). The Johannine context is decidedly reminiscent in that reference to a divine fountain of living water co-exists with mention of the woman's love life.[1116]

In the OT, the covenantal relationship between Yahweh and Israel his people is frequently expressed with the motif of a wedding (bridegroom and bride) or marriage (husband and wife). Thus Israel's religious apostasy against Yahweh is compared with the marital infidelity of Israel as the bride or the wife to Yahweh as the bridegroom or the husband[1117] (cf. Hos 2:2, 7, 16; Jer 2:1–13; 3:1–22; Ezek 16:1–52; 23:1–49). Furthermore the restoration of the covenantal relationship between Yahweh and Israel is compared with the motif of remarriage or wedding in the setting of the restoration or the new exodus of Israel from the exile (Isa 54:1–9; 61:10; 62:4f; John 3:29; Rev 19:1–10). Thus, pointing out that Jesus and the woman play the roles of the bridegroom and the bride respectively, Carmichael argues that:

> The Samaritan woman has served to recall the first break-up of the original Israelite community, but Jesus's approach to her as a Jew symbolizes in turn the movement toward reunion.... The evangelist feels comfortable in working with the notion of Jesus as a divine being who is involved in a love relationship with a woman because he can interpret precedents in the prophetic tradition of Hosea, Ezekiel and Jeremiah.[1118]

The argument for the presence of the wedding motif in the narrative of Jesus's encounter with the Samaritan woman could be supported by the courtship motif at a well. Some commentators[1119] recognize that Jesus's encounter with the woman at Jacob's well is to be understood in the light of the encounters between a man and a woman at a well in the OT (cf. Gen

---

[1116] Carmichael, 'Marriage,' 339; Howard-Brook, *Becoming*, 106f (cf. *War* 1.21.1 §403). Also, Koester, 'Saviour,' 675f; idem., *Symbolism*, 49; Munro, 'Pharisee,' 720f.
[1117] Koester, 'Saviour,' 669; Davies, *Rhetoric*, 210f; Coloe, *Dwells*, 99.
[1118] Carmichael, 'Marriage,' 341f. In particular, Munro, 'Pharisee,' 721 indicates that 'That the woman, though attached to a man, 'has no husband' means, for whatever reason, that she is available for Jesus to 'woo.''
[1119] Collins, 'Representative,' 38; Pamment, 'Samaritan,' 222; Koester, *Symbolism*, 48f; idem., 'Saviour,' 668 n. 9; Brodie, *John*, 217f; Smith, *John*, 111; Witherington, *Wisdom*, 118; Carmichael, 'Marriage,' 332–346; Howard-Brook, *Becoming*, 106, 113f; J. D. M. Derrett 'Samaritan,' 253; Polhill, 'John 1–4,' 455; Munro, 'Pharisee,' 721; Bennema, *Power*, 182; Coloe, *Dwells*, 86 n. 5, 97f.

24:11–20; 29:1–14; Exod 2:15–22). This argument could be further strengthened in that Jesus is introduced as the bridegroom in John's Gospel. Koester[1120] points out that Jesus hints at his role of the bridegroom in John 2:1–12 and also he is clearly identified as the bridegroom by the Baptist in John 3:29.[1121]

6.4 The New Worship/The New Temple (John 4:19–26)

Since Jesus is actually a Jew and the woman regarded him as the prophet on the basis that he knew her past and present marriage life exactly (cf. v. 29), she raised with him the problem about the place of worship Jerusalem or Mount Gerizim. This had always caused controversy between the Jews and the Samaritans (v. 20).[1122] Regarding the question raised by the woman, in vv. 21–24 Jesus says the coming of the time when God the Father will be worshipped by the true worshippers in spirit and in truth, having nothing to do with the place of worship, neither on this mountain (Gerizim) nor in Jerusalem on Mt. Zion. The new worship to God the Father is not restricted by the specific places.[1123]

6.4.1 Worship God the Father in Spirit and in Truth (vv. 23–24)

In vv. 22–24, Jesus says that the true worshippers will worship God the Father in spirit and truth through the eschatological works of Jesus. In v. 24, it is said that, since God is spirit, his worshippers must worship him in spirit and in truth. If so, what does it mean to worship God the Father in spirit and in truth? What does 'spirit and truth' mean? Some diverse arguments are suggested concerning the meanings of spirit and truth. Also, what does 'God is spirit' mean? Morris[1124] interprets God is spirit in v. 24 to mean that: 'Jesus is not saying, "God is one spirit among many"; rather his meaning is "God's essential nature is spirit."' Whitacre[1125] argues that the worship in spirit vv. 23f means the 'worship with one's innermost self, at one's centre, one's heart,' namely, 'it is centred deeper, in the spirit,' and the worship in truth is the 'worship as who one really is, with no hypocrisy, falseness, deception.'

[1120] Koester, *Symbolism*, 48f; Witherington, *Wisdom*, 118; Howard-Brook, *Becoming*, 114; Derrett, 'Samaritan,' 253; Munro, 'Pharisee,' 721; Coloe, *Dwells*, 98; Carmichael, 'Marriage,' 332–336 (Prov 5:15; cf. Prov 9:17; *Tg. Cant.* 4.12).
[1121] Koester, 'Hearing,' 327–348; Coloe, *Dwells*, 86 n. 5.
[1122] Morris, *John*, 237; Lindars, *John*, 187; Blomberg, *Historical*, 101; Michaels, *John*, 71. Cf. In Deut 27:3 of the Samaritan version of the Pentateuch, Mount Gerizim was appointed as the place for building the altar to the Lord, although in the MT the altar was set up on Ebal.
[1123] Carson, *John*, 226; Beasley-Murray, *John*, 61; Holwerda, *Jesus*, 76.
[1124] Morris, *John*, 240; Bruce, *John*, 110f; Carson, *John*, 225.
[1125] Whitacre, *John*, 106; Morris, *John*, 239–240; Bruce, *John*, 110f.

However, Polhill[1126] argues that, in Greek terms, 'God is spirit' does not mean the incorporeity of God, but represents the life-giving power of God, as seen in the Hebrew Scriptures. Also, Carson[1127] recognizes that the spirit in the OT is 'renovative, creative, life-giving' (as in John 3:5; 7:38–39), and 'God is spirit,' as in the parable about the wind in John 3:8, which means that, 'God is invisible, divine as opposed to human (cf. 3:6), life-giving and unknowable to human beings unless he chooses to reveal himself (cf. 1:18).' Brown[1128] argues that the 'spirit' in 'worshipping God in spirit and in truth' in vv. 23f means the Holy Spirit of God, rather than the spirit of man, who is given by Jesus to those who believe in him (cf. John 7:39; 3:3, 5, 8).

And, for Brown,[1129] the 'truth' in 'worshipping in spirit and in truth' means Jesus who introduces himself as 'the truth' in John 14:6, in the sense that he reveals God's truth to people (John 8:45; 18:37; 1:17f), and thus, the Holy Spirit is called the Spirit of Truth (cf. John 14:17; 15:26). Accordingly, Carson rightly says that worshipping God the Father in spirit and truth means:

> essentially God-centred, made possible by the gift of the Holy Spirit, and in personal knowledge of and conformity to God's Word-made-flesh, the one who is God's 'truth', the faithful exposition and fulfilment of God and his saving purpose.... The worshippers whom God seeks worship him out of the fullness of the supernatural life they enjoy ('in spirit'), and on the basis of God's incarnate Self-Expression, Christ Jesus himself, through whom God's person and will are finally and ultimately disclosed ('in truth'); and these two characteristics form on matrix, indivisible.[1130]

Carson[1131] understands Jesus's words 'a time is coming and has now come' to mean the hour of his cross, resurrection and exaltation (as in John 16:32), or to the situation introduced by his passion and exaltation (cf. John 12:23; 13:1; 17:1). The true worship will be fulfilled by Jesus, who is the true

---

[1126] Polhill, 'John 1–4,' 455; Beasley-Murray, *John*, 62; Barrett, *John*, 238f; Throckmorton, *Creation*, 114; Carson, *John*, 225.

[1127] Carson, *John*, 225; Throckmorton, *Creation*, 114.

[1128] Brown, *John I-XII*, 180; Throckmorton, *Creation*, 114; Michaels, *John*, 72.

[1129] Brown, *John I-XII*, 180, who says that 'In fact, one could almost regard 'Spirit and truth' as a hendiadys equivalent to 'Spirit of truth.' Also, Barrett, *John*, 238; Michaels, *John*, 77.

[1130] Carson, *John*, 225f; Beasley-Murray, *John*, 62; idem., *Life*, 70; Brown, *John I-XII*, 180; Lindars, *John*, 179; Whitacre, *John*, 107; Holwerda, *Jesus*, 76; Smith, *John*, 117; Polhill, 'John 1–4,' 456; Wedel, 'John 4:5–26,' 409; Kim, *Exposition*, 85; Milne, *John*, 89.

[1131] Carson, *John*, 223; Barrett, *John*, 236; Brodie, *John*, 223; Beasley-Murray, *John*, 61–62; idem., *Life*, 70; Dennis, *Gathering*, 180f; Polhill, 'John 1–4,' 455; Lindars, *John*, 188.

Temple (cf. John 2:19–22), the resurrection and the life (cf. John 11:25). His passion and exaltation is the great turning point, because on the basis of this the Holy Spirit is bestowed (cf. John 7:37–39).[1132]

Here, the imagery that Jesus, as the new Temple replacing the Jerusalem Temple, will give the Holy Spirit (cf. John 20:22; Gen 2:7; Ezek 37:1–28); the living water giving eternal life could also remind us of the eschatological Temple of Ezekiel (cf. John 4:10, 13f; 7:37ff; Ezek 47:1–12; Zech 14:8). This is reflected in the narrative about the living water in John 4:10, 13f; 7:37ff. Dennis argues that in the context of the true 'place' of worship in John 4:20f:

> the living water' in 4:10, 11, 14 echoes the waters issuing out from under the restored, eschatological Temple in Ezek 47:1–2 and probably also the 'living water' flowing from the restored Jerusalem in Zech 14:8. John's emphasis that the 'living water' brings eschatological 'life' (zwh,) in 4:14 would have found particular inspiration from Ezek 47:9–13 where the waters that flow from the eschatological Temple bring 'life' (za,w) to all living things (Ezek 47:9–12), reminiscent of a renewed Eden, and mark the boundaries for the restored 'twelve tribes' (v.13). The Qumran Text 11Q18 (*Description of the New Jerusalem*) frag. 24:1 clearly draws upon Ezek 40–48 when it associates 'living water'(מיך חייך) with the eschatological New Jerusalem and Temple.[1133]

Further, Dennis[1134] points out that the living water in vv. 1–14 and the true Temple in vv. 20–24 alludes to Joel 3:18 (LXX 4:18). This verse suggests that in the day of Jerusalem's restoration, water (all the fountains of Judah) shall flow from the Temple, the house of God. For Dennis, in *Eccl R.* 1:8, the eschatological Prophet like Moses was expected to bring up water in fulfilment of Joel 3:18, and *1 En.* 26:1–6 shows the expectation of a stream of water flowing from the centre of the earth (cf. Ezek 38:12), the new Eden, the eschatological Zion. Dennis[1135] points out that for the Samaritan woman or for the audience of John's Gospel, Jesus was introduced as the eschatological locus, or place of the divine presence for the restored Israel,

---

[1132] Carson, *John*, 244; Beasley-Murray, *Life*, 70; Dennis, *Gathering*, 180f; Brown, *John I-XII*, 180.
[1133] Dennis, *Gathering*, 178; Coloe, *Dwells*, 94f; Keener, *John*, 604; Brown, *John I-XII*, 180f; Ng, *Symbolism*, 177–179; Cf. Polhill, 'John 1–4,' 454; Drapper, 'Temple,' 282, who even assumes that the imagery of the water flowing from the Temple is related to the water gushed out the rock by Moses in the wilderness (cf. Num 20:11; Deut 8:15; 1 Cor 10:4). Koester, *Symbolism*, 169 assumes that 'Jesus' comments are reminiscent of the way the prophet Moses miraculously provided water for Israel in the desert, which would be appropriate for the one who fulfilled the Samaritan hope for a Moses-like messiah.'
[1134] Dennis, *Gathering*, 178 n. 298; Ng, *Symbolism*, 178f.
[1135] Dennis, *Gathering*, 178f; Motyer, *Father*, 41; Ng, *Symbolism*, 177.

namely, the true place of worship, which is the answer against the question where is the true place of worship.

> Jesus is here presented as the true realization of both the Samaritan 'place' and well traditions, as well as the true realization of Jewish expectation concerning the Temple (the τόπος). The place of true worship, the locus of the true messianic community, is no longer tied to a geographical place, but rather to Jesus himself. The essential theme then of 2:13–22 has been resumed in 4:23–24. Thus, in the context of Samaria, the depiction of Jesus as the true divine 'place' of worship (4:23–24; cf. 2:21) and the one who provides true eschatological water suggests that Jesus is here portrayed as creating a new, restored, eschatological Samaria/Israel, who will worship in spirit and truth through Jesus himself, who is the true Temple (2:21; 4:23–24).[1136]

Dennis[1137] argues that the same ideas, the living water flowing from the true Temple in John 4:10, 13f are found in the words of Jesus's invitation of John 7:37–39, alluding to Ezek 47:1–12; Zech 14:8. In John 7:37–39, Jesus is introduced as the source of the stream of water, which is clearly mentioned as the Holy Spirit,[1138] in the setting of the Jewish feast Tabernacle. Kerr argues that:

> [it] is not in opposition to Judaism, but an answer to the trauma that had overtaken it with the destruction of the Temple. Jesus is the eschatological Temple in Ezek. 47:1–11 (cf. 2.21 where the Temple is specifically identified with Jesus' body), and it is from this Temple that the rivers of living waters shall flow. He is the fulfilment of Zech 14:8 and Ezek. 47:1–11.[1139]

[1136] Dennis, *Gathering*, 179f, quoting McGrath, *Apologetic*, 206; Lee, *Narrative*, 76; Ng, *Symbolism*, 177 says that 'the water imagery is compounded with the Temple theme, a liturgical element reflecting the hope of the nation for restoration.'

[1137] Dennis, *Gathering*, 181; Kerr, *Temple*, 239–241; Coloe, *Dwells*, 133; Menken, *Quotations*, 187–202; Beasley-Murray, *John*, 114–116; Brown, *John I-XII*, 327.

[1138] Dennis, *Gathering*, 181; Menken, *Quotations*, 202; Carson, *John*, 324; Brown, *John I-XII*, 320–323. In particular, Dennis, *ibid.*, 181–182 n. 317 says that the water-drawing festival as the central rite of the Tabernacle feast includes 'a procession from the pool of Siloam to the Temple where the priests would pour out water at the base of the altar' (cf. *m. Mid.* 2.7; *m. Sukk.* 4.9; *t. Sukk.* 48ab), which is related with Ezek 47; Zech 14 in *t. Sukk.* 3.3–10.

[1139] Kerr, *Temple*, 241. Also, F. J. Moloney, *Belief*, 102 says that 'The members of the Johannine community, living their Christian lives after the destruction of the Jerusalem Temple, are able to look to the presence of the risen Lord as their 'Temple.''

6.4.2 The Son/Firstborn of God the Father, the New Temple (or the Builder of the New Temple), and 'Death and Resurrection'

It is necessary to note from vv. 21–23 that Jesus called God the Father three times. If it is considered that the 'time' or 'hour' was twice mentioned to point to his death, resurrection, and exaltation, thus bringing about the advent of the new worship order, Jesus disclosed his death as the Son of God, who would build the new Temple, actually his resurrection body (cf. John 2:19–21). That Jesus as the Son of God will build the new Temple could reflect the identity of Jesus as the eschatological fulfiller of Yahweh's covenant to David in 2 Sam 7:12–16.

This idea could be reflected in 'salvation is from the Jews' in v. 22. Beasley-Murray[1140] interprets these words to mean that God has chosen the Jews through whom the Messiah will come and bring the salvation for the world. Bruce[1141] observes that, 'salvation is from the Jews' alludes to Gen 49:10. Lindars[1142] also points out that salvation (deliverance) based on God's promise to the Jews reminds us of the messianic prophecy of Isaiah (cf. Isa 9; 11; 45:8, 17). If these interpretations concerning, 'salvation is from the Jews' are right, Yahweh's covenant promised to David in 2 Sam 7:12–16 has to be noted. Hence this interpretation is in accord with the argument that Jesus who as the Son of God will build the (new eschatological) Temple is none other than the Davidic prince in the eschatological time.

Furthermore, the words, 'salvation is from the Jews' could be understood to mean not that the Jews themselves are the origin of salvation but that God's salvation was first given to the Jews but is not restricted to them. God's salvation will be given through the Jews to the Samaritans and even to the gentiles, by the Saviour of the world (John 4:42). This, as has been frequently presented above in our main arguments, could allude to Exod 4:22f; 19:5f, in which God corporately elected Israel as the firstborn/son of God and the servant of God including the priesthood. It was those, through whom God wanted to call (or restore) the gentiles the sons of God, on the setting of the exodus, the Passover, and the Sinai covenant. These dual concepts were applied to the Davidic prince based on Yahweh's covenant to David (2 Sam 7:12–16; Pss 2:7; 89), whose responsibility is the building of the Temple. This is further reflected in the Deutero-Isaianic suffering servant (including the sonship to Yahweh) in Isa 52:13–53:12, who is the

---

[1140] Beasley-Murray, *John*, 62; Bruce, *John*, 110; Lindars, *John*, 188f; Morris, *John*, 238f; Michaels, *John*, 72. On the other hand, Blomberg, *Historical*, 101 points out that 'salvation is from the Jews' in v. 22 shows that it is not right to argue for the presence of the anti-Semitism in the Gospel of John. Also, Motyer, *Father*, 213; Pamment, 'Samaritan,' 223.
[1141] Bruce, *John*, 110.
[1142] Lindars, *John*, 188f.

same figure as the new David (or the Davidic messianic King) in Isa 9:1–7; 11:1–16; 55:3; 61:1–11. This is set against the background of the restoration of Israel from the exile and the salvation for the nations.

Accordingly, for the Johannine Jesus, the Jews were collectively approved as the successor to the dual titles given to the Israelites in the OT.[1143] If this is right, Jesus who as the Son/firstborn of God and as the Davidic messianic King, with giving the Holy Spirit through his death and resurrection, is presented to create the eschatological community including the Jews and the Samaritans (cf. Ezek 37:1–28[1144]) and even the nations. He is also the centre of the true worship in the Spirit and truth; the building of the new eschatological true Temple bringing about the eschatological salvation (the restoration or the new exodus) for the world.

Furthermore, Endo[1145] mentions the connection between John 4:22 and Isa 2:3, pointing out that John 6:45 alludes to Isa 54:13:

> It should be noted that the coming of the תורה or דבר־יהוה is expected in an eschatological context (Isa 2:3–5; 51:4–5; Mic 4:1–3). John 4:22 understands that Isa 2:3 was fulfilled by the coming of the Son of God. John 6:45 also argues that Isa 54:13 (i.e. an eschatological hope that his people shall be taught by God) was fulfilled.

The expectation that the coming Messiah will explain everything to the Samaritans in v. 25 could allude to the eschatological hope reflected in Isa 2:3 (cf. Mic 4:1–3). Here, it is prophesied that in the last days Mt Zion, the mountain of the Lord's Temple will be established as chief among the mountains and all nations will stream to it and many peoples from all the nations will go up to the mountain of the Lord. They will go to the house of the God of Jacob, the Jerusalem Temple, and it is here that the Lord will teach the peoples his ways so that they may walk in his paths. Here, Zion is presented as the place from which the law will go out, and Jerusalem as the

---

[1143] Cf. Pamment, 'Samaritan,' 225f observes that in John's Gospel 'the king of the Jews' is not different form 'the king of Israel,' and Nicodemus was called as 'the ruler of the Jews' in John 3:1 and as 'the teacher of Israel' in John 3:10.

[1144] Cf. The vision of the two-step's resurrection of dry bones on the floor of the valley with breathing in with the Holy Spirit in Ezek 37:1–14, alluding to the creation of Adam in Gen 2:7, means the restoration of Judah and Israel (the Samaritans, Ephraim) from the exiles; the unification of the two countries to make one nation under one king, David, the establishment of a covenant of peace (cf. an everlasting covenant) between Yahweh and them, and the building of Yahweh's sanctuary (Yahweh's dwelling place) among them forever in Ezek 37:15–28.

[1145] Endo, *Creation*, 224, 219f n. 40.

place from where 'the word of the Lord' will go out.[1146] The similar idea to Isa 2:3 could be found in Isa 51:4–5: 'The law will go out from me [Yahweh]; my justice will become a light to the nations ... my salvation is on the way,' and 54:13, 'All your sons will be taught by the Lord,' which Jesus alludes to in John 6:45.[1147]

6.4.3 A Prophet (v. 19), the Messiah (the Christ) and 'I Am' (ἐγώ εἰμι) (vv. 25–26)

In John 4:19, on the basis that Jesus knew the details of her marriage life (vv. 29, 39), the woman acknowledged him as a prophet.[1148] In vv. 25–26, the Samaritan woman said that she knew the Messiah would come and explain to the Samaritans everything on worship. Concerning this, Jesus declares, ἐγώ εἰμι ὁ λαλῶν σοι. From the woman's mention in v. 25 (cf. vv. 29, 39), we can recognize that there was the expectation of the coming of the Messiah among the Samaritans at the time of Jesus and that for them one of the functions of Messiah was teaching the truth or revealing it, especially concerning worship.

For some commentators,[1149] the reference to Messiah (Christ) in v. 25 is a reference to the Samaritans' Messiah, namely, Taheb, the Restorer or the

---

[1146] Cf. Isa 2:2–4 is clearly alluded to in Mic 4:1–3 in the setting of the restoration of Israel (the Daughter of Zion, the Daughter of Jerusalem) from the exile (cf. Mic 4:6–5:21), with the establishment of Davidic Messiah from Bethlehem Ephrathah, the clans of Judah (cf. Mic 5:2).
[1147] Endo, *Creation*, 220 n. 40.
[1148] Cf. Bruce, *John*, 108 thinks that 'a prophet' is probably Taheb, the prophet like Moses, the messianic figure for the Samaritans in connection with Deut 18:15–18; 34:10. Also, Morris, *John*, 236; Lindars, *John*, 187. However, Carson, *John*, 221 argues that in view of v. 25, the prophet that the woman mentioned concerning Jesus in v. 19 could not be clearly related to Taheb, the prophet like Moses, the second Moses, the messianic figure for the Samaritans. Similarly, Barrett, *John*, 236, who also assumes there was no reference saying that the Messiah, even though he would teach the gentiles (cf. Str-B, II, 348), has the function of teaching in Judaism (p. 239). Also, Carson, *John*, 226. On the other hand, Beasley-Murray, *John*, 62f argues that the function of Taheb the Samaritan Messiah as the revealer of the truth is disclosed in v. 29 (cf. vv. 19, 39), saying that the woman testified Jesus as the Messiah in that Jesus disclosed her marriage life exactly.
[1149] Bruce, *John*, 111; Carson, *John*, 226; Barrett, *John*, 239; Blomberg, *Historical*, 101; Beasley-Murray, *John*, 62f; Schnackenburg, *John*, I, 441; Michaels, *John*, 73; Whitacre, *John*, 105, 107; Fallon, *John*, 117; Morris, *John*, 241 nn. 61ff; Witherington, *Wisdom*, 117; Polhill, 'John 1–4,' 456; Howard-Brook, *Becoming*, 109; Collins, 'Representative,' 39 n. 50; Coloe, *Dwells*, 102, who argues that according to *Ant.* 18.85–88, the Samaritans at the time of Jesus had the messianic expectation which had nothing to do with David but with the prophet like Moses; Taheb. Also, Brown, *John I-XII*, 171f; Koester, *Dwelling*, 55–59; *idem.*, 'Saviour,' 673; Neyrey, 'Traditions,' 419–437, esp. 428; Dennis, *Gathering*, 159–161. Dennis, *ibid.*, 161, 177 argues that John 4:4–26 contains the Samaritan tradition, namely, Jesus is presented as the fulfilment of Samaritan messianic expectation; 1) the well at the foot of Mount Gerizim (vv. 4–5) and the defence of the patriarch Jacob and his well (v. 12), 2) the question of legal purity (v. 9), 3) the prophet like Moses (v. 19) and Mount Gerizim as the holy places (v. 20).

Revealer of the truth; a Prophet like Moses, on the basis of Deut 18:15–18. In particular, it is thought that Taheb would reveal the truth to restore true belief in God and the true worship to God.[1150] For example, Coloe[1151] says that Taheb was regarded as the eschatological figure who would restore the tabernacle vessels, which were believed to have been buried by Moses on Mount Gerizim. Further, Dennis[1152] says that in *2 Macc.; Life of Jeremiah; 4 Bar.*, the prophet Jeremiah hid the Temple vessels on Mount Sinai and Moses was expected to reveal them in the end. Thus, Dennis[1153] points out that the traditions of the restoration of the hidden vessels of the tabernacle (for the Samaritans) or of the Temple (for the Jews) are related with the expectation of 'the return of the divine presence and favour' and with the gathering and restoration of the people of God.

Some[1154] argue that the Evangelist or the Johannine Jesus were influenced by the Samaritan theology or adopted it for the salvation of the Samaritans. However, this argument remains questionable, because, in saying that 'salvation is from the Jews' in v. 22, the Johannine Jesus clearly accepted the correctness of the worship of the Jews rather than the Samaritans, even though after his coming the importance of the Jerusalem Temple as a place to worship God would be finished: 'neither on this mountain nor in Jerusalem' (v. 21).[1155] This could mean the inauguration of the new order of

---

[1150] Coloe, *Dwells*, 101; Koester, 'Saviour,' 673; *idem.*, *Dwelling*, 56; Neyrey, 'Traditions,' 428; Dennis, *Gathering*, 159; Meeks, *Prophet-King*, 250.

[1151] Coloe, *Dwells*, 101; Neyrey, 'Traditions,' 428, who also, pointing out that the household gods (i.e., local idols) of Raban, Rachel's father in Gen 31:19, 34 were believed to be buried by Jacob in Shechem in the shadow of Mount Gerizim (cf. Gen 35:4), argues that there were the traditions of the expectation of the restoration of the hidden vessels (Moses' tabernacle vessels or Jacob's household gods) by 'the eschatological prophet who would restore true worship there as the rightful place.' And, according to Dennis, *Gathering*, 160, a teacher called *Marqah* in *Memar Marqah* a Samaritan literature of the fourth century taught that the concealment of the tabernacle vessels on Mount Gerizim was caused by the Israelites' evils and apostasy (*M.M.* 5.2.120) and the hidden vessels as the eschatological blessing will be revealed on Mount Gerizim again, in which Moses was described as the eschatological deliverer, the Taheb, the restorer of the tabernacle and cult in the day of restoration. Also, Koester, *Dwelling*, 57.

[1152] Dennis, *ibid.*, 159.

[1153] Dennis, *ibid.*, 159, who also says that 'The connection between a new revelation of the tabernacling presence of God on Mount Gerizim, the restoration of the cult, and the eschatological restoration of Israel – all by the agency of a messiah figure – is well established in Samaritan traditions from the first century to the fourth century. In addition, it appears that Deut 18:18 was the basic text for the Samaritan Messiah or Taheb.' (pp. 160f). Also, Koester, *Dwelling*, 56–57; *idem.*, 'Saviour,' 673; Neyrey, 'Traditions,' 428. Cf. *Ant.* 18; *M.M.* 4.3.89.

[1154] For example, Dennis, *Gathering*, 161, 177; E. D. Freed, 'Samaritan,' 243.

[1155] Carson, *John*, 237; Pamment, 'Samaritan,' 225 says that 'The Fourth Evangelist presents Jesus as a Jew who shares Jewish attitudes to Samaritan religion, whose own country is Judea, but who is rejected by his own countrymen and accepted by Samaritans. John shows no particular knowledge of Samaritan belief, as far as we can tell. Instead of confessing Jesus as

worship with the coming of Jesus, the reality of the Temple (cf. the new Temple in John 2:19–21), and thus the cessation of the function of the Temple as the centre of the old order of the worship.[1156] Smith[1157] rejects the argument that the Messiah mentioned by the woman in v. 25 was the Samaritans' messianic figure, and argues instead that Jesus's answer concerning the correct place of worship shows that Jesus agreed with the Jews on the messianic expectation based on the Pentateuch, the Prophets and the Psalms rather than with the Samaritans, which was based only on the Pentateuch (see John 1:41, 45, 49; 20:31); Jesus was the Davidic messianic king rather than Taheb.

In v. 26, Jesus declared that he himself as the very messianic figure the woman was expecting: ἐγώ εἰμι, ὁ λαλῶν σοι. Some commentators[1158] understand that ἐγώ εἰμι of Jesus's saying in v. 26 means that Jesus affirmatively disclosed his identity as the Messiah against the woman's expectation about the coming of the Messiah (the Christ) who will explain everything to them (the Samaritans). Furthermore, it could have something

---

the Taheb, as we would expect, in John 4, the Samaritans confess Jesus as 'a prophet', 'the Messiah', and 'the Saviour of the world', using the language either of Jews or of pagans.'

[1156] Kim, *Exposition*, 85.

[1157] Smith, *John*, 115f. Also, Collins, 'Representative,' 39 n. 50 thinks that the Evangelist added the Messiah title to the confession of the woman's messianic expectation (Taheb, the one awaited by the Samaritans). Pamment, 'Samaritan,' 223, thinks that the confession that the Samaritan woman believed Jesus as the prophet in John 4:19 is not different from the confession that the man born blind accepted Jesus who had healed him as the prophet in John 9:17, and also points out that the confession that Jesus was the prophet coming into the world was often mentioned in John's Gospel and the Evangelist used the title as a Jewish confession (cf. John 6:14; 1:21; 7:40). Accordingly, Pamment even argues that 'The Fourth Evangelist was familiar with OT traditions which were interpreted eschatologically, but does not point to a special knowledge of Samaritans' traditions. On the contrary, even the Samaritans woman does not express a specific Samaritan belief.' (p. 223). Furthermore, Pamment argues that the Christology of John's Gospel is not familiar with Mosaic typology; 'As far as the influence of Moses legends on Johannine christology is concerned, in comparison with Matthew, John seems to make little use of a Moses typology. Even when Moses is mentioned, Jesus's role is compared not with that of Moses, but with that of the serpent (3:14) or with that of the manna (6:25ff).' (p. 227). Cf. Longenecker, *Christology*, 64 says that 'by the first century BC, ... the term 'Messiah' had come to be something of a *terminus technicus* for the Anointed One who would be God's deliverer in days of eschatological consummation.' Cf. *Ps. Sol.* 17:32; 18:5, 7; Qumran Scrolls (cf. 4QFlor.); The Eighteen Benedictions (cf. the fourteenth song); *Targum*; *4 Ezra* 12:32; *2 Bar.* 29:3; 30:1; *1 En.* 48:10; 52:4. Longenecker, *ibid.*, 67 observes that Jesus disclosed himself as the Messiah in three passages; 1) the narrative of Peter's confession and Jesus's response (Matt 16:13–20; Mark 8:27–30; Luke 9:18–21), 2) the narrative of the trial before the high priest Caiaphas (Matt 26:57–66; Mark 14:53–64) and before Pilate (Mark 27:11–14; Mark 15:2–5; Luke 23:3; John 18:33–38), and 3) the narrative of the conversation with the Samaritan woman (John 4:25–26).

[1158] Barrett, *John*, 239; Lindars, *John*, 191; Michaels, *John*, 77; Witherington, *Wisdom*, 121; Carson, *John*, 227.

to do with Yahweh's self-designation in Exod 3:14 and the Second Isaiah (cf. Isa 41:4; 43:10; 45:18; 52:6).[1159] Whitacre states that:

> his [Jesus's] use of *egō eimi* here is primarily self-designation, but it conceals yet deeper revelation since it is God's own self designation as I AM (cf. comment on 8:58). Thus, Jesus identifies himself as the awaited Messiah of the Samaritans, but he does so in language that hints he is God's own presence, the Jewish God who brings the living water of salvation, who indeed *is* 'the spring of living water' (Jer 2:13).[1160]

Coloe[1161] also interprets Jesus's mention of ἐγώ εἰμι as the form of the divine revelation based on Deutero-Isaiah (41:4; 43:10; 52:6), which meant that the woman's messianic expectation was not enough. For Coloe, in using the ἐγώ εἰμι, Jesus disclosed that he is the incarnated Yahweh who revealed himself as ἐγώ εἰμι to Moses (Exod 3:14), and thus is far greater than the prophet (v. 19), the Davidic Messiah (v. 25), Jacob (v. 12). Further, Coloe[1162] points out that here Jesus as 'I Am' is the true bridegroom to the Samaritans as well as to the Jews. Lincoln[1163] says that ἐγώ εἰμι is used as Yahweh's self-designation in the setting of the trial motif (who is the true God?) in Deutero-Isaiah. Thus, the 'I Am' is Yahweh's self-designation revealed to Moses in connection with his redemption of Israel from Egyptian slave-bondage in the setting of the exodus (Exod 3:14). The title is again adopted as Yahweh's self-designation to reveal his promise of the advent of the redemption (restoration) of Israel in exile in Deutero-Isaiah (Isa 41:4; 43:10; 45:18; 52:6), thus, the new exodus. Yahweh's self-designation of these OT references of the exodus and the Isaianic new exodus was applied to the Johannine Jesus by himself in connection with his eschatological

---

[1159] Coloe, *Dwells*, 102; Lincoln, *Truth*, 40f, 44; Morris, *John*, 241; Beasley-Murray, *John*, 62; Brodie, *John*, 224; Bultmann, *John*, 192; Milne, *John*, 85; Whitacre, *John*, 107; Smith, *John*, 118; Collins, 'Representative,' 39; Fallon, *John*, 117; Munro, 'Pharisee,' 719; Pazdan, 'Nicodemus,' 147; Brown, *John I-XII*, 172; Harner, *I am*, 47; Howard-Brook, *Becoming*, 109, who says that Jesus's own title, ἐγώ εἰμι is reversely the fulfilment of the mention of the Baptist in John 1:20 ('I am not the Christ; ἐγὼ οὐκ εἰμὶ ὁ χριστός).

[1160] Whitacre, *John*, 107 (original emphasis, [] added by this writer); Brodie, *John*, 224. Cf. Lindars, *John*, 191.

[1161] Coloe, *Dwells*, 102. For the discussion that the Johannine Jesus is the incarnated Yahweh or the presence of Yahweh, see Brunson, *Psalm 118*.

[1162] Coloe, *Dwells*, 105.

[1163] Lincoln, *Truth*, 40f, who says that 'a self-designation of Yahweh as the one true God that is characteristic of Deutero-Isaiah. The claim is made that, unlike other gods, Yahweh has existed from the beginning and is the only God and Saviour Israel has known.... In the final trial speech against the nations in 45:18–25, Yahweh is introduced as the Creator God who has not spoken in secret, as the 'I am' (LXX 45:19– ἐγώ εἰμι ἐγώ εἰμι) who proclaims the truth.'

deliverance (redemption, restoration, new exodus). This is also reflected in the food motif and the harvest motif in John 4:27–42.[1164]

6.5 The Restoration of the Samaritans (John 4:27–42)

6.5.1 Jesus's Food and Work, and the True Son/Servant of God (vv. 27–34)

In John 4:25f, when the Samaritan woman said that the coming Messiah will explain to the Samaritans everything concerning true worship, Jesus disclosed that he was the Messiah. After this conversation, in vv. 28ff, she left her water jar behind and went back to the town and testified that a man who told her everything she had ever done was the Messiah. Following her report, the people of Sychar came out to Jesus. Here, some different interpretations have been suggested concerning why she left her water jar behind. It could mean that she left it in hurrying to testify that she had met the Messiah.[1165] Also, it could have a symbolic meaning: 'it indicates also the depth of her response to the Revealer's call: having found a new form of living water, she leaves behind her the symbol of her former preoccupation.'[1166]

Meanwhile, in vv. 31–34, the disciples who had returned with some food from the Samaritan town urged Jesus to eat the food. But Jesus said that he had food to eat that they knew nothing about and explains what the food is in v. 34, where the imagery of food is used to emphasize his doing the will of God the Father and finishing his work.

The majority of Johannine commentators[1167] argue that the imagery of food in doing the will of God in v. 34 alludes to Deut 8:3. In the OT, Israel was collectively called not only the son/firstborn of God, but also the servant of

---

[1164] Cf. Dennis, *Gathering*, 180 points out that 'it should not go unnoticed that the Samaritan narrative combines the two most dominate restoration motifs in Jewish literature: the restoration of the 'place,' or the Temple, and the gathering of true Israel in the eschatological harvest (4.35–36).'

[1165] Milne, *John*, 86; Smith, *John*, 119; Barrett, *John*, 240; Brodie, *John*, 224, who also points out that the leaving of the waterpot is related to the conventional betrothal motif, like Rebecca in Gen 24:28. Similarly, Derrett, 'Samaritan,' 257. On the other hand, Lindars, *John*, 193 thinks that the leaving of the water pitcher means that she would come back and it could show that the story was not finished. Also, Howard-Brook, *Becoming*, 110.

[1166] Brodie, *John*, 224. Bruce, *John*, 115, as to that the Samaritans believed in Jesus as the Saviour of the world in v. 39, argues that 'The living water which the woman received from Jesus had certainly become an overflowing fountain in her life, and others were coming to share the refreshment that she had begun to enjoy.'

[1167] Carson, *John*, 228; Bruce, *John*, 113; Beasley-Murray, *John*, 63; Dodd, *Historical*, 325f; Barrett, *John*, 240; Brown, *John I-XII*, 173; Fallon, *John*, 118; Michaels, *John*, 74; Whitacre, *John*, 110; Smith, *John*, 120; Lindars, *John*, 194, who also argues that the subject concerning the bread (the manna) in the wilderness is well known to John, as a form of the teaching from heaven, which was dealt with at length in John 6.

God through the death of the firstborn son (the paschal lamb) on the Passover night (Exod 4:22f; Hos 11:1; Jer 31:9, 20; cf. Exod 19:5f), and thus Israel should have obeyed Yahweh (the will of Yahweh) in the wilderness. However, in particular, Israel failed in relation to the food to eat and the water to drink. Recalling the failures of their forefathers in the wilderness, Moses emphasized not only living by bread alone but also living by every word that comes from the mouth of God in Deut 8:3.

Also, as some commentators [1168] recognize, Jesus's statement about the relationship of food to doing God's will, recalling Deut 8:3, is reflected in the narrative of the temptation of Jesus (Matt 4:4; Luke 4:4). In the narrative of Jesus's baptism with the descending of the Spirit of God upon him (Matt 3:13–17; Mark 1:9–11; Luke 3:21–22), through the voice from heaven, he was officially proclaimed as the Son of God and the suffering servant of God, alluding to Exod 4:22f; Ps 2:7; Isa 42:1. He was then led by the Spirit of God into the wilderness to be tempted by the devil and fasted forty days and forty nights, which typologically alludes to the life of Israel as the corporate son/firstborn of God in the wilderness for 40 years after the exodus. In Matt 4:3, the devil tempted Jesus who was hungry after fasting for 40 days: 'If you are the Son of God, tell these stones to become bread.' Here, it must be noted that the first temptation of the devil is related to bread to eat and to Jesus's status as the Son of God. Jesus's answer in Matt 4:4 recalling Deut 8:3 alludes to Israel's status as the corporate firstborn son of God based on Exod 4:22f. Although Israel who had been collectively given the dual position (the firstborn son and servant of God), they still failed to obey him concerning bread in the wilderness. Yet Jesus, who also has dual status as the Son of God and the Isaianic suffering servant of God, perfectly obeyed God concerning bread in the wilderness, quoting Deut 8:3. Thus if John 4:34 alludes to Deut 8:3, Barrett correctly argues that Jesus's words about doing God's will being his food in v. 34 means that: 'Jesus does what Israel of old should have done.' [1169]

The idea that Jesus as the only Son of God accomplished the will of the Father who sent him is clearly reflected in John 3:16–17. In John's Gospel (and in the Synoptic Gospels), it has been repeatedly emphasized that Jesus the Son of God was sent to finish the work given to him by his Father (John

---

[1168] Carson, *John*, 228; Beasley-Murray, *John*, 63; Dodd, *Historical*, 325f; Barrett, *John*, 240; Lindars, *John*, 194; Brown, *John I-XII*, 173; Fallon, *John*, 118; Michaels, *John*, 74; Whitacre, *John*, 110; Smith, *John*, 120; Morris, *John*, 244 n. 73, who also points out that the other temptations recorded in the Synoptic Gospels are reflected in Jesus's refusal to become the king of Israel intended by the Jews in John 6:15 and his refusal to perform the miracle asked by his brothers in 7:3ff.

[1169] Barrett, *John*, 240; Whitacre, *John*, 110; Howard-Brook, *Becoming*, 111.

5:36; 6:38; 8:29; 9:3–4; 10:25, 32, 37–38; 14:10; 17:4; 19:30).[1170] In particular, Morris[1171] observes that a term, τελειώσω (to finish) of 'to finish his work' is the same word family as τετέλεσται 'It is finished' in John 19:30, which, regarding the accomplishment of the salvation work commissioned by God the Father, was used by Jesus on the cross. Whitacre[1172] writes that to partake of spiritual nourishment is to share the life of God (John 6:53–58), and that Jesus's obedience to the will of God through the crucifixion disclosed the life of God to us.

In particular, Endo observes that the combination of 'to do' (ποιήσω) and 'to accomplish' (τελειώσω) in John 4:34 appears only three times in the NT (John 4:34; 5:36; 17:4). All of these references are related to the work of the Son of God. Further, Endo notes that the combination of the two terms appears six times in the OT (Ps 37:7; Dan 8:12, 24; 11:36; Isa 55:11; 1 Chron 31:21) and only in Isa 55:11 are the terms used in connection with the work of God. Thus in presenting the similarity between John 4:34 and Isa 55:11,[1173] Endo argues that:

> John 4:34 depicts the ministry of the Son as the food (βρῶμα), which may be contrasted to the water in John 4:14 (see John 6:35). The motifs of both food and water appear in Isa 55:1–2 and 10 as the things which God would offer to the people in the end time. It should be noted that similarly, the ministry of the word of God (which is personified) in Isa 55:11 is depicted by the imagery of food and water (Isa 55:10). Therefore, it is possible to conclude that the description of the ministry of the Son of God in John 4:34 may allude to the figure of the word of God in Isa 55:11.[1174]

[1170] Cf. Carson, *John*, 228; Fallon, *John*, 118;
[1171] Morris, *John*, 245 n. 80; Wedel, 'John 4:5–26,' 410; Fallon, *John*, 118; Whitacre, *John*, 110.
[1172] Whitacre, *John*, 110.
[1173] Endo, *Creation*, 240. Cf. My food is *to do* (ἵνα ποιήσω) *the will* of him who *sent* me, and *to accomplish* (τελειώσω) his work (John 4:34) / It (Word) shall *do* (עשה) that which *I will*, and *accomplish* (והצליח) the thing for which I *sent* it (Isa 55:11).
[1174] Endo, *Creation*, 240f. Also, Endo, *ibid.*, 241f argues that Isa 55:11 is reflected in John 6:22–58, and the motifs of food and water of Isa 55:1–2 in John 6:27, 35 (cf. John 6:53–56), and the descent motif of Isa 55:10–11 in John 6:33, 38, 50–51, 58 (cf. the figure of descending Manna' in Ps 78:23–25). In particular, Endo, *ibid.*, 242 points out that 'life-giving motif' in John 6 means the dynamic aspect of the work of the word of God and the personified word of God appears in the contexts of creation and end, being described as the agent fulfilling the will of God (cf. *4 Ezra* 6:38, 43; *2 Bar.* 54:3; 56:4). Endo, *ibid.*, continues to say that the Johannine Jesus argues that the will of the Father is to give the life to the world (cf. John 3:16; 6:39–40; 12:50; 5:21, 26) and the work of the Son is to fulfil the will of the Father, and Isa 55:11 is reflected in John 4:34; 6:33, 38. Smith, *John*, 120 thinks that Isa 55:2 is alluded to in Jesus's statement about the food with the fulfilment of the will of God in John 4:32, 34. See also Burkett, *Son*, 131f, who argues that John 6:27–71 alludes to Isa 55:1–11 thematically and literally.

Therefore, we could say that Jesus's comparing doing the will of God and finishing his work with the nourishment of food in John 4:34 alludes not only to Deut 8:3 (in the setting of the wilderness after the exodus), but also to Isa 55:11 (in the setting of the restoration or the new exodus).

6.5.2 The Harvest Motif (vv. 35–38)

In v. 35, Jesus says, 'Do you not say, 'Four months more and then the harvest'? I tell you, open your eyes and look at the fields! They are ripe for harvest.' Here, 'Four months more and then the harvest' is normally thought to be a proverbial saying, rhythmical prose, which has a Semitic basis.[1175] On the other hand, it can be interpreted to mean that this incident happened in December or January, 4 months before the harvest time.[1176] This argument is supported by Guilding[1177] who argues that the synagogue lectionary cycles read during this time included Exod 1:1–2:25; Joshua 24; Isa 27:6ff; Ezek 20, which constitute the background of this Johannine passage. Guilding also thinks that Exod 2:15ff includes the story of Moses and the well in Midian, and Exod 3:12 'you shall serve God upon this mountain' (Mount Horeb, cf. John 4:20) is reflected in the narrative of Jesus's conversation with the Samaritan woman.

However, Carson disagrees,[1178] suggesting that the late evidence for the synagogue lectionary cycles means they cannot be applied to verse 35. Further he submits that the parallel Guilding presents is not proper, because the well in the exodus cycle is not in Samaria but in Midian, and the mountain is not Gerizim but Horeb. Carson thinks that Jesus's word in v. 35 means actually:

> there are four months remaining until harvest, but in the salvation-historical plane the harvest has already begun. He himself is engaged in that harvest; that is part and parcel of the work the

---

[1175] Bruce, *John*, 114; Lindars, *John*, 195; Beasley-Murray, *John*, 63; Wedel, 'John 4:5–26,' 411; Morris, *John*, 246; Blomberg, *Historical*, 103; Schnackenburg, *John*, I, 449; Michaels, *John*, 74. Cf. A. W. Argyle, 'John 4:35,' 247f, who understands it in the light of the iambic rhythm of a Greek statement. *Contra* Carson, *John*, 229; Barrett, *John*, 241; Smith, *John*, 120.

[1176] Cf. According to Morris, *John*, 246, the agricultural year consists of six two-month periods; seedtime, winter, spring, harvest, summer, the time of extreme heat. The interval from the end of seedtime to the beginning of harvest would be normally four months, although the time difference between sowing and reaping is six months (cf. Str-B, II, 438–440). Also, see Schnackenburg, *John*, I, 449; Lindars, *John*, 195; Barrett, *John*, 241; Beasley-Murray, *John*, 63; Smith, *John*, 120; Whitacre, *John*, 111; Michaels, *John*, 74.

[1177] A. Guilding, *Fourth*, 206–211.

[1178] Carson, *John*, 229; Bruce, *John*, 114; Beasley-Murray, *John*, 63.

Father gave him to do (v. 34). On this reading, the gap between *sowing* and harvest has not yet been introduced (cf. vv. 36–38).[1179]

In v. 35b, the crop that is ready for harvest in this context refers to the Samaritans. Its focus was those who had listened to the testimony of the woman and then rushed out of the town to Jesus (cf. vv. 29f).[1180]

In v. 36, 'Even now the reaper draws his wages, even now he harvests the crop for eternal life' could mean that harvest time has already arrived, the reaper who has been already employed is busy harvesting the crop and so there is no interval between sowing and harvest.[1181] Above all, it has to be noted that the harvest imagery is a common eschatological symbol in Scripture.[1182]

Furthermore, some commentators[1183] recognize that Jesus's saying in v. 36b, 'the sower and the reaper may be glad together' alludes to 'the reaper will be overtaken by the plowman and the planter by the one treading grapes' in Amos 9:13. Here Yahweh's eschatological salvation is vividly symbolized in the imagery of the abundant harvest of grapes and the plentiful new wine flowing from the mountains and the hills. Amos 9:10–15 shows that in the day of Yahweh's salvation and judgment he will restore David's fallen throne and his kingdom so that they will possess the remnant of Edom and all the nations that bear Yahweh's name (vv. 11–12). In Amos 9:14–15, Yahweh promises the restoration of Israel from the exile. In particular, Amos 9:15 shows the new exodus, alluding to the first exodus, in the imagery of planting Israel symbolized by a vine brought out of Egypt in the promised land (cf. Ps 80:1–19).

Also, Brown[1184] thinks that 'the sower and the reaper may be glad together' could allude to, 'the abundance of crops shall be so great that the idle

---

[1179] Carson, *John*, 230 (original emphasis); Fallon, *John*, 119; Whitacre, *John*, 111; Bultmann, *John*, 196ff; Bruce, *John*, 114; Lindars, *John*, 195f; Barrett, *John*, 241; Smith, *John*, 120.
[1180] Carson, *John*, 230; Bruce, *John*, 114; Howard-Brook, *Becoming*, 111; Witherington, *Wisdom*, 122; Morris, *John*, 247; Brown, *John I-XII*, 182; Whitacre, *John*, 111.
[1181] Barrett, *John*, 241; Lindars, *John*, 196; Whitacre, *John*, 111; Michaels, *John*, 74; Smith, *John*, 120; Bultmann, *John*, 196–198; Beasley-Murray, *John*, 63.
[1182] For example, Ps 126:5f; Isa 9:3; 27:12; Joel 3:13; Amos 9:13; Mark 4:1–9, 13–20, 26–29; Matt 3:12; 13:24–30; 9:37f; Luke 3:17; 10:2; Rev 14:14–16; *2 Bar.* 70:2; *4 Ezra* 4:30–32. Lindars, *John*, 196; Beasley-Murray, *John*, 63; Carson, *John*, 230; Blomberg, *Historical*, 103; Howard-Brook, *Becoming*, 111; Morris, *John*, 248; Barrett, *John*, 242; Brown, *John I-XII*, 181; Fallon, *John*, 119; Malina and Rohrbaugh, *John*, 101; Michaels, *John*, 58, 74; Jeremias, *Theology*, I, 106; Smith, *John*, 120; J. Miranda, *John*, 174f; Whitacre, *John*, 111.
[1183] Carson, *John*, 230; Morris, *John*, 248; Barrett, *John*, 242; Brown, *John I-XII*, 182; Fallon, *John*, 119; Michaels, *John*, 58, 74; Miranda, *John*, 174f; Howard-Brook, *Becoming*, 111; Whitacre, *John*, 111; Coloe, *Dwells*, 109.
[1184] Brown, *John I-XII*, 182.

intervals between the agricultural seasons will disappear' in Lev 26:5. In addition, Whitacre[1185] points out that the thought of the fulfilment of God's will was developed with an eschatological subject, the imagery of harvest, which usually denotes the coming judgment of God in the OT (cf. Joel 3:13) and also is used as the imagery that God gathered (restored) the people of Israel scattered among the gentiles (cf. Isa 27:12).

In Isa 27:12f, by using the imagery of harvest, Yahweh says that he will gather the Israelites one by one from the flowing Euphrates to the Wadi of Egypt in the eschatological time. Also, with the blowing of a great trumpet in the eschatological time, those who were perishing in Assyria and those who were exiled in Egypt will be restored and worship him in the Jerusalem Temple on Mount Zion. Howard-Brook,[1186] thinking that the harvest imagery in John 4:35f is related to the picture presented in Isa 27:12f, argues that:

> 'Those who were lost in the land of Assyria' include, of course, the very Samaritans who are on their way to Jesus, who supplants the 'holy mountain of Jerusalem.'

So, Howard-Brook[1187] asserts that Isaiah's prophecy in Isa 27:12f is about the expectation of the reconciliation between the Samaritans and the Jews, which is fulfilled in the light of the Johannine community.

On the other hand, Coloe[1188] assumes that the abundant food produced by the living water gushing out of the Temple in Ezekiel's vision in Ezek 47:1–

[1185] Whitacre, *John*, 111; Coloe, *Dwells*, 109, who also points out that the harvest imagery in the past history of Israel was used to describe the gathering of people in the end time, when Yahweh's judgment brought out joy and blessing (cf. Isa 9:3; 27:12; Joel 3:18) or condemnation and punishment (cf. Isa 18:3–6; Jer 51:3; Joel 3:11–15).
[1186] Howard-Brook, *Becoming*, 111.
[1187] Howard-Brook, *Becoming*, 111f.
[1188] Coloe, *Dwells*, 108. Cf. See R. Bauckham, '153 Fish,' 271–284, esp. 278–282, who, using numerical techniques of literary composition, argues that the miraculous catch of 153 fish in John 21:11 alludes to Eglaim (עֶגְלַיִם) of Ezek 47:10; 'The passage tells how the stream of water that will issue from the new Temple will flow down to the Dead Sea, turning it into a fresh water lake, where people will stand on the shore fishing all the way from the spring of Gedi (En-gedi) to the spring of Eglaim (En-eglaim): 'It will be a place for the spreading of nets; its fish will be of a great many kinds' (Ezek 47:10).... Thus, the 153 fish of John 21:11 constitute a reference to Eglaim in Ezekiel 47:10 and at the same time are to be understood as signifying 'the children of God,' since this phrase has the same numerical value (153) as the word Eglaim.' (pp. 278f). Bauckham, *ibid.*, 279f, additionally strengthens this argument with the connection that 'as the Scripture says, 'From his breast shall flow rivers of living water' (ποταμοὶ ἐκ τῆς κοιλίας αὐτοῦ ῥεύσουσιν ὕδατος ζῶντος) of John 7:38 alludes to Ezek 47:1 (also to Zech 14:8; Ps 78:16) and 'one of the soldiers pierced his side (πλευρὰν) with a spear, and at once blood and water came out' in John 19:34 alludes to 'water coming out from under the south

12 alludes to a bountiful harvest already ripe for reaping in John 4:35–38. Furthermore, Coloe[1189] argues that the harvest imagery could allude to the description of the eschatological blessings of Joel 3:18. One of the important aspects of the blessing is the unification of the divided relation between Israel (Samarians) and Judah, and the gathering of the people of Israel scattered among the nations (cf. Isa 60:4; 11:11; 27:12f; Jer 23:3; 29:14; Ezek 20:34; 37:21). Here, Coloe points out that unification between Israel and Judah was one of the eschatological expectations of Ezek 37:15–22, in which Yahweh will build the everlasting sanctuary among them (cf. Ezek 37:26), namely, the new Temple. Following this unification and blessing the inheritance of the unified Israel will spread to the nations: 'They shall eat with you in their inheritance in the midst of the tribes of Israel' (Ezek 47:22 LXX). Thus, Coloe[1190] argues that all these expectations are fulfilled by Jesus's encounter with the Samaritan woman, and as a result even with the Samaritans.

> The eschatological background to the imagery of the harvest, supports the understanding of 'living waters,' having their background in Ezekiel's vision of the waters of eschatological salvation, flowing from the new Temple which God will provide. The Temple waters and the abundance that they produce provide a natural continuity between the Johannine images of water, food and harvest. The gift Jesus promised in vv. 7–15 is shown to be already operative in vv. 31–38. These two sections are balanced in a creative tension around the central verse (19–26) where Jesus proclaims, 'the hour is coming and now is' (v. 23), for in Jesus's presence in Samaria the Father is already active and seeking true worshippers.[1191]

In addition, in Ezek 37:22–28, the one nation based on the unification of Israel and Judah will be ruled over by one king, David, the new David, the

---

end of the threshold of the Temple' in Ezek 47:1, which could be more literally translated 'from below the right-hand shoulder (כתף) of the Temple.'

[1189] Coloe, *Dwells*, 109.

[1190] Coloe, *Dwells*, 109, who also points out that the targumic version of Jacob's blessing to Judah is similar to John 4; 'In the Targums, Jacob's final blessing to Judah is given lengthy elaboration, emphasizing that the future Messiah will come from the line of Judah, and will usher in a time of fruitful abundance.' (p. 110). Cf. 'I shall compare you Judah, to a lion's whelp... Kings shall not cease from among those of the house of Judah...until the time King Messiah shall come, to whom the kingship belongs... How beautiful is the King Messiah who is to arise from the house of Judah. The mountains will become red from his vines and the vats from wine: and the hills will become white from the abundance of grain and flocks of sheep.'(*Tg. Neof. Gen* 49:9–12).

[1191] Coloe, *Dwells*, 111.

servant of Yahweh, forever. Yahweh will make a covenant of peace with the restored people of Israel and Judah, which will be an everlasting covenant, and thus Yahweh will be their God and they the people of Yahweh. Yahweh will put his sanctuary (the Temple) among the restored people of God forever and thus he will dwell among them forever. Then the nations will know that Yahweh makes Israel holy.

Above all, Dennis[1192] points out that the harvest imagery of John 4:36 is conceptually related to the fruit bearing of John 12:24, even though the parable of the death of the kernel of wheat in John 12:24 which explains the effect of Jesus's death in the light of producing many seeds is different from that of the reaper in John 4:36 who gathers fruit for eternal life. Dennis says as follows:

> The 'gathering of fruit' in the harvest that is now ready for reaping in 4.35–38 clearly refers to the harvest among the Samaritans; they are the 'fruit' that is being gathered in Jesus' ministry (4:39). Thus, it appears that the eschatological gathering and unification of Israel is beginning in the context of Samaria, the 'bringing in' of the historical tribes of the North or Ephraim.[1193]

In v. 37, Jesus says that, 'Thus, the saying "One sows and another reaps" is true.' The majority of Johannine theologians[1194] regard the saying as a proverb, and think that it alludes to some OT references.[1195] These OT passages generally refer to pessimistic meanings, such as cynicism, depression, threat of judgement, punishment, the inevitable and tragic inequality of life; one sows but receives no reward, while another reaps what he has now sowed. However, Jesus uses the saying in an optimistic sense in John 4:37.[1196] Beasley-Murray says that:

> By contrast Jesus uses the saying to indicate the difference of roles in the service of the kingdom of God. The part that each plays is

---

[1192] Dennis, *Gathering*, 203. Cf. Morris, *John*, 248f says that the sowing has to be understood in the light of the crucifixion of Jesus, the very one sowing seeds in John 12:24.
[1193] Dennis, *Gathering*, 203.
[1194] Smith, *John*, 121; Carson, *John*, 230; Bultmann, *John*, 198; Bruce, *John*, 114f; Beasley-Murray, *John*, 64; Michaels, *John*, 74; Lindars, *John*, 196; Blomberg, *Historical*, 103; Brown, *John I-XII*, 182f; Wedel, 'John 4:5–26,' 411; Howard-Brook, *Becoming*, 112; Whitacre, *John*, 111f. *Contra* Barrett, *John*, 242 argues that the proverb in v. 37 is not Jewish but Hellenistic, which is proper paralleled to Aristophanes, *Equites*, 392; Philo, *Leg. Alleg.* 3.227.
[1195] Lev 26:16; Deut 20:6; 28:30; Mic 6:15; Job 31:8; Judges 6:3; Eccles 2:18–21; Cf. Matt 25:24, 26; 1 Cor 3:6
[1196] Beasley-Murray, *John*, 64; Carson, *John*, 230; Bruce, *John*, 114f; Lindars, *John*, 196; Blomberg, *Historical*, 103; Brown, *John I-XII*, 182f; Wedel, 'John 4:5–26,' 411; Howard-Brook, *Becoming*, 112; Whitacre, *John*, 111f; Michaels, *John*, 74.

important for the mission of the kingdom in the world, and each worker may rejoice in the success that 'the Lord of the harvest' give to their labours.[1197]

Interestingly, in Joshua 24:13, when the Israelites freed from the Egyptian bondage occupied the promised land, the opposite pictures were presented as the divine blessings for them: they were given the land on which they did not toil and cities they did not build and they lived in them and ate from vineyards and olive groves that they did not plant. In Isa 65:21–22, Yahweh's chosen ones reap the fruits of what they have sown—a divine blessing in the setting of the eschatological salvation (new creation/the restoration of the creation).[1198]

In v. 38, Jesus says that he sent (ἀπέστειλα) the disciples to reap what they have not worked for. Here, the tense of ἀπέστειλα is aorist, which means that the disciples have already been sent in the past. So, when have they been sent to harvest what they did not sow? In John's Gospel, there is no specific mention of this. Brown[1199] argues that this has to be interpreted in the light of the post-resurrectional mission, or in the light of the mission of the disciples given by Jesus during his public ministry, which has not been recorded in John's Gospel but in the Synoptic Gospels.

Jesus continues, 'others have done the hard work, and you have reaped the benefits of their labour.' Here, the 'you' whom Jesus sent and who have reaped the benefits of others' labour are clearly the disciples. However, the identity of the 'others' is not clear. The 'others' who have done the hard work, probably sowing seeds, are diversely thought to be Jesus, or the Samaritan woman, or the Prophets,[1200] in the OT, or John the Baptist and his followers. In this context the 'others,' namely, the sowers, are Jesus and the woman, and the disciples are the reapers.[1201] However, Morris[1202] argues

---

[1197] Beasley-Murray, *John*, 64.
[1198] Cf. Whitacre, *John*, 112.
[1199] Brown, *John I-XII*, 183. Also, Whitacre, *John*, 112–113; Beasley-Murray, *John*, 64. On the other hand, Schnackenburg, *John*, I, 452 explains this as the earthly Jesus's looking into the future.
[1200] Lindars, *John*, 197.
[1201] Witherington, *Wisdom*, 122; Morris, *John*, 248f; Smith, *John*, 121.
[1202] Morris, *John*, 248f. Brown, *John I-XII*, 183f thinks that the 'others' (the sowers) are Jesus and the Baptist. Barrett, *John*, 242 thinks that the sower and the reaper is the same figure, namely, Jesus, because Jesus sowed seeds in his conversation with the woman and the believing Samaritans are the fruits that Jesus harvested. Similarly, Whitacre, *John*, 111, who also says that the sower is God the Father (cf. John 4:34) who gives or leads the believers to Jesus, who thus is the reaper (cf. John 6:37ff, 44, 65; 10:29; 17:6). Also, Schnackenburg, *John*, I, 447, 451; Michaels, *John*, 75, who argues that in v. 34 God the Father is the sower and Jesus as the

that the Christ is the sower if the sowing is understood in connection with the parable of the death of a kernel in John 12:24, denoting the crucifixion.

6.5.3 The Saviour of the World and the Restoration of the World (vv. 39–42; cf. John 1:29, 34; 3:16–17)

As recorded in vv. 39–42, many of the Samaritans who listened to the woman's testimony believed in Jesus and urged him to stay with them. After Jesus stayed with them two days, many more Samaritans became believers and confessed that Jesus really was 'the Saviour of the world' in John 4:42. What is the origin of the title and its meaning? Pamment[1203] argues that in the OT God was called the one who brings salvation, but was not called the Saviour nor was the title applied to the Messiah. However, for Pamment, 'the Saviour of the world' was applied to Hadrian the Roman Emperor, and thus 'the Saviour of the world' in John 4:42; Luke 2:11; Acts 5:31; 13:23; Eph 5:23; Phil 3:20; 1 John 4:14, is not a Jewish title but Hellenistic. Also, Koester[1204] observes that 'the Saviour of the world' was not a common messianic title in Judaism or Samaritanism of the first century, but saviour was often used in the Greco-Roman world, and 'the Saviour of the world' was exclusively applied to the Roman Emperor. Thus, for Koester,[1205] the use of the term for Jesus in v. 42 was intended to bring about Jesus's imperial association:

> when the Samaritans called him 'the Saviour of the world,' they used a title that was associated not with Samaritan or Jewish messianic expectations but with worldwide dominion. They recognized that Jesus transcended national boundaries; like Caesar he was a figure of universal significance.[1206]

Barrett[1207] observes that in the OT God is called the Saviour, because he is characteristically the one who saves his people; the Messiah is sometimes described as the one who saves Israel in later Judaism. However, it is not the Messiah but God who is emphasized as the Saviour in the Jewish documents of NT times (cf. Str-B, I, 67–70), and in Hellenistic sources the

---

fulfiller of the will of God is the reaper, reflected in vv. 39–42, however, for Michael, the 'others' are related to the woman and the Samaritans.

[1203] Pamment, 'Samaritan,' 224. Also, Malina and Rohrbaugh, *John*, 102 point out that the Savour is used to gods, heroes, and even emperors who provided their devotees or adherents with rescue from some difficult situation in the Greco-Roman world and 'the Savour of the world' is applied to Hadrian in the second century AD, and thus Jesus who is confessed with the title in v. 42 means the 'rescuer of all Israel, including that branch of Israel considered a bastard offshoot by Judeans.'

[1204] Koester, 'Saviour,' 665–680, esp. 665–667.

[1205] Koester, 'Saviour,' 667; Howard-Brook, *Becoming*, 113.

[1206] Koester, 'Saviour,' 668.

[1207] Barrett, *John*, 244; Carson, *John*, 232.

Saviour is applied to divine or semi-divine deliverers and 'the Saviour of the world' to Roman Emperors. Accordingly, Barrett argues that 'the Saviour of the world' in v. 42 is based on Hellenistic literature, including the concept of salvation of the OT (the Messiah of Judaism).

Beasley-Murray[1208] observes that the Jews did not apply this title to the Messiah but to God, and then argues that this title as a divine title often occurs in Deutero-Isaiah (e.g., Isa 43:3, 11; 45:21–22; 63:8–9). The title is applied to Jesus in Acts 5:31; 13:33; Phil 3:20, meaning that Jesus is, 'the representative of God the Saviour, and the Mediator of the kingdom of God, which means salvation and life.'

Above all, Yahweh is introduced as the Saviour in Isa 43:3, 11. In v. 3, Yahweh reminds Israel of his identity as, 'your God, the Holy One of Israel, your Saviour who gives Egypt for your ransom (כָּפְרְ), Cush and Seba in your stead (תַּחְתֶּיךָ).' In vv. 5–7, Yahweh promises that his chosen people (sons and daughters) scattered (exiled) among the gentiles will be restored, alluding to the redemption based on the first exodus. In vv. 8–13, Israel was elected as the eyewitness and the servant to testify to Yahweh and his works to all the peoples. Yahweh presents himself as the one who is the unprecedented, unparalleled, unique God: 'I, even I, am Yahweh, and apart from Me there is no saviour' (אָנֹכִי יְהוָה וְאֵין מִבַּלְעָדַי מוֹשִׁיעַ׃ Isa 43:11). Yahweh's name in v. 11 alludes to Yahweh's self-designation disclosed to Moses in connection with his plan for the deliverance and redemption of Israel from the slavery of Egypt. In vv. 14–15, Yahweh again presents himself as, 'your Redeemer, the Holy One of Israel, Yahweh, your Holy One, Israel's Creator, your King.' By recalling the crossing of the Red Sea (cf. Exod 14) in vv. 16–17, Yahweh promises that he will bring about the new salvation, namely, the new exodus, for Israel in vv. 18–21.

In addition, in Isa 45:20–21, Yahweh presents himself as the Saviour: 'There is no God apart from me, a righteous God and a Saviour; there is no other.' Yahweh then demands that they (the people scattered among the nations) turn to him and be saved (restored). Furthermore, in Isa 63:7–14, in alluding to the first exodus event, Yahweh who has chosen Israel as his people, sons, introduces himself as their Saviour (vv. 8–9) and is confessed as their Father in v. 16.

[1208] Beasley-Murray, *John*, 65.

Lindars[1209] also thinks that Jesus who is confessed as, 'the Saviour of the world' by the Samaritans is not only the Messiah in Jewish expectation but also the universal Saviour, and rightly argues that:

> This word is applied to God in Deutero-Isaiah, e.g. Isa 43:3, referring to the divine activity in the exodus and the coming return from exile, which is a repetition of it. It is as the agent of a new exodus that it might be applied to Jesus.[1210]

Accordingly, that the title 'the Saviour of the world' is applied to Jesus in connection with the restoration of the Samaritans could be understood in the light of Yahweh's salvation plan in Isaiah. In Isaiah he promises that Judah and Israel (Samaria) in exile will be restored and even the nations will be saved through the suffering servant of Yahweh, the light for the gentiles, the Davidic messianic king. The title, 'the Saviour of the world,' reflects the salvation plan of Yahweh who first elected Israel as the corporate son/firstborn/servant/priest, through whom to restore the nations as his sons in Exod 4:22f; 19:5f. The idea of the salvation of the world reflected in the title, 'the Saviour of the world' is presented in John 1:29, 34 as 'the Lamb of God,' namely, the Son of God, who takes away the sin of the world. This is also represented in John 3:16–17 in that God will save (give eternal life to) the world through his only Son. Acts 1:8 further illustrates this point in that the resurrected Jesus commanded the disciples to become his witnesses in Jerusalem, and in all Judea, and Samaria, and to the ends of the earth.[1211]

6.6 Jesus's Healing of a Royal Official's Son (John 4:43–54)

6.6.1 A Prophet in His Own Country

After staying in the Samaritan town for two days, Jesus and his disciples left for Galilee. On the way, Jesus pointed out that, 'a prophet has no honour in his own country' (v. 44). When Jesus arrived in Galilee, the Galileans initially welcomed him. The Evangelist added the reason for this welcome in v. 45, because they had seen all (probably, miraculous signs) that he had done in Jerusalem at the Passover Feast, alluding to John 2:23. The Evangelist's reference may suggest that, although they welcomed him,

---

[1209] Lindars, *John*, 198, who also assumes that since the title was widely used to pagan deities in the NT era, Christians were reluctant to use the title for Jesus in the early stage, but the title was often applied to Jesus in the Pastoral Epistles, namely, in the gentile mission of the early church.

[1210] Lindars, *John*, 198.

[1211] Carson, *John*, 232. Cf. Barrett, *John*, 244 says that 'the Saviour of the world' confessed by the Samaritans means that God will save the world through Jesus, which is fulfilled by Jesus's obedience to the will of God.

they believed in him simply on the basis of the miraculous signs. The Galileans' faith in Jesus is thus superficial and insufficient.

Concerning the apparent contradiction between Jesus's saying in v. 44, 'a prophet is rejected in his own country,' and the Galileans' welcoming him in v. 45, some different arguments about the meaning of 'hometown' or 'homeland' (πατρίς) have been suggested. Possible suggestions are: Galilee (esp. Nazareth), [1212] Jerusalem, [1213] Judea [1214] or heaven. [1215] As some commentators[1216] recognize, in the context of vv. 43–45 and in the Gospel of John (cf. John 1:45; 2:1; 7:3, 41, 52; 19:19), Galilee, especially Nazareth, is presented as the hometown of Jesus. Thus, the πατρίς of Jesus denotes Galilee, Nazareth. Furthermore, in comparison with Samaria where Jesus was believed in and confessed as the Saviour of the world in vv. 39–42, although the Galileans welcomed him, their faith based on the miraculous signs performed in Jerusalem at the Passover feast (cf. John 2:23–25) is superficial and insufficient.[1217] Also, if we consider that Jesus reprehends the royal official as the representative of the Galileans dependence on miraculous signs and wonders in vv. 47f[1218] and that they later reject Jesus in John 6:66,[1219] the πατρίς of Jesus in v. 44 is related to Galilee (Nazareth).

On the other hand, the atmosphere that Jesus is, superficially and insufficiently, believed in, is recognized not only in Galilee but also in Judea, especially Jerusalem, the centre of inherited Jewish religion (cf. John

---

[1212] Carson, *John*, 234–237, esp. 235f; Schnackenburg, *John*, I, 462; Brown, *John I-XII*, 187; Morris, *John*, 253; Beasley-Murray, *John*, 73; Freed, 'Samaritan,' 243; Koester, *Symbolism*, 51; J. W. Pryor, 'John 4:44,' 254–263, esp. 263; Witherington, *Wisdom*, 126; Whitacre, *John*, 114. Cf. Howard-Brook, *Becoming*, 114.
[1213] Dodd, *Interpretation*, 352; Davies, *Gospel*, 323; Barrett, *John*, 245f; Lindars, *John*, 200f; Smith, *John*, 122f; Michaels, *John*, 79; Blomberg, *Historical*, 105. Cf. Howard-Brook, *Becoming*, 114.
[1214] Westcott, *John*, I, 77f; Hoskyns, *Fourth*, I, 259f; Barrett, *John*, 245f; Bruce, *John*, 116; W. A. Meeks, 'Galilee,' 163–166; Fallon, *John*, 120; Pamment, 'Samaritan,' 224; Smith, *John*, 122f; Howard-Brook, *Becoming*, 114; Witherington, *Wisdom*, 126; Whitacre, *John*, 114; Blomberg, *Historical*, 105; Brodie, *John*, 228. Cf. Carson, *John*, 235f; Koester, *Symbolism*, 51; Pryor, 'John 4:44,' 263.
[1215] Lightfoot, *John's*, 35. *Contra* Carson, *John*, 235; Lindars, *John*, 201.
[1216] Carson, *John*, 235f; Beasley-Murray, *John*, 73; Morris, *John*, 253; Brown, *John I-XII*, 187; Pryor, 'John 4:44,' 262; Freed, 'Samaritan,' 243.
[1217] Carson, *John*, 235f; Whitacre, *John*, 114; Witherington, *Wisdom*, 126; Howard-Brook, *Becoming*, 114; Köstenberger, *John*, 90; Smith, *John*, 122f; Pryor, 'John 4:44,' 260; Koester, *Symbolism*, 51; Morris, *John*, 254; Brown, *John I-XII*, 187.
[1218] Witherington, *Wisdom*, 128; Carson, *John*, 236; Pryor, 'John 4:44,' 262f.
[1219] Cf. In the setting of the feeding miracle in Galilee of John 6, after the discourse about eating the flesh of Jesus (the Son of Man) and drinking his blood, many of his disciples including the Jews (probably, the Galileans, cf. John 6:41f) rejected Jesus and his teaching, and left him. Above all, Pryor, 'John 4:44,' 260 points out that the superficiality and inadequacy of the acceptance of the Galileans is reflected in John 6:26, 41, 52, 60, 66. Cf. Pamment, 'Samaritan,' 224f.

2:23–25). Also, Jesus was opposed or rejected by the Jews, especially in Jerusalem (John 1:11; 4:1–3; 6:64f; 7:1–9; 12:36–43. cf. Luke 13:33f; Isa 53:1; 6:10).[1220] Pryor says that:

> It is significant that in this final scene which begins with 12:12, John consistently uses ὄχλος (12:12, 17, 18, 29, 34); and there can be no doubt that when the marvel of unbelief is recorded in terms of quotations from Isaiah 53 and 6, the Jewish people as a whole are in mind. Israel, gathered together to celebrate the Passover, has rejected its Messiah. From this wider perspective on rejection in John 1–12, the meaning of 4:44 can now be approached.[1221]

Accordingly, Jesus's hometown or homeland (πατρίς) is Galilee and Judea, including Jerusalem, contrasted with Samaria, where Jesus was believed in as the Saviour of the world.[1222]

So, what does Jesus's reference in v. 44 mean? Does it mean that Jesus understands himself as a prophet or the Prophet like Moses based on Deut 18? Here, the saying commonly appears in the Synoptic Gospels (Matt 13:57; Mark 6:4; Luke 4:24 cf. *Thomas* 31).[1223] In fact, Jesus was called, 'the prophet' (cf. John 4:19; 6:14; 7:40; 9:17; Mark 21:11; Luke 24:19; cf. John 7:52) and the Baptist was questioned whether he was 'the Prophet' in connection with his baptismal work (cf. John 1:21, 25). These could encourage us to assume that the Prophet in the time of Jesus was expected as an eschatological figure on the basis of Deut 18:15, an assumption supported in that Jesus was clearly confessed as 'the prophet like Moses' in Acts 3:22; 7:37. Above all, John 4:44 shows that Jesus applied the title of, a prophet, to himself in that he would be rejected by his hometown or by his own house. This could therefore disclose that Jesus would think of himself as a prophet, or as a prophet like Moses based on Deut 18:15; 34:10.

Nonetheless, the suffering and rejection that Moses (including prophets) received from Israel the people of God in the settings of the exodus and the wilderness hardly explains Jesus's suffering and death perfectly. This is because Moses did not bear vicarious death for atonement (as a guilt offering) and redemption (ransom). Thus, the saying about a prophet who

---

[1220] Carson, *John*, 235–237; Bruce, *John*, 116; Barrett, *John*, 246; Lindars, *John*, 201; Brodie, *John*, 228; Michaels, *John*, 79; Howard-Brook, *Becoming*, 114; Smith, *John*, 122f; Blomberg, *Historical*, 105; Pryor, 'John 4:44,' 257; Marshall, *Luke*, 188. Cf. Luke 4:16–30.
[1221] Pryor, 'John 4:44,' 260.
[1222] Carson, *John*, 235f; Whitacre, *John*, 114; Witherington, *Wisdom*, 126; Koester, *Symbolism*, 51; Pryor, 'John 4:44,' 262f. Cf. Brown, *John I-XII*, 187.
[1223] Bruce, *John*, 116; Morris, *John*, 253; Barrett, *John*, 246; Lindars, *John*, 200; Michaels, *John*, 82; Smith, *John*, 122f; Pryor, 'John 4:44,' 254.

has no honour in his own home in John 4:44 could be based on general suffering and rejection that a prophet received in the OT and Judaism rather than on the unique experience that Moses encountered.[1224] Above all, the saying that, 'a prophet has no honour in his own home' in John 4:44 could allude to John 1:11, 'he [the Logos] came to that which was his own, but his own did not received him,' which denotes that Jesus was rejected by his own people.

6.6.2 The Healing of the Royal Official's Son and βασιλικός

In vv. 46–54, Jesus moved to Cana in Galilee, where he had turned the water into wine (cf. John 2:1–11), and there he met a certain royal official whose son lay sick at Capernaum. The official begged him to come down to Capernaum and to heal his son, who was close to death. Concerning this, in saying that, 'Unless you people see miraculous signs and wonders, you (pl) will never believe' (v. 48), Jesus reproached the official, and then healed his son, declaring in v. 50, 'You may go. Your son will live.'

It is thought that the narrative of the healing of a certain royal officer's son (υἱός) in John 4:46–54 is different from the narrative of the healing of a Roman centurion's servant (or son, παῖς) in Mark 8:5–13 (δοῦλος in Luke 7:1–10).[1225] However it could be that they are just two different traditions (records) of one and the same healing incident.[1226] For example, Beasley-Murray argues that:

> In view of these parallels the common notion that the Evangelist was responsible for modifying a straightforward narrative by his insertion of vv. 48–49 is to be queried; the motifs and vocabulary are akin to synoptic traditions and are likely to have existed in that handed on to the Evangelist.[1227]

Above all, in connection with the relationship between the two healing narratives, there are some arguments about the identity of the royal official (βασιλικός) in vv. 46f. The argument surround his nationality; was he a Jew or a Roman (or a gentile), and a royal official or a person of royal blood?

[1224] Cf. Strauss, *Davidic*, 280f. K. H. Rengstorf, *TDNT*, VII, 245 n. 304 says that 'The saying about the prophet who has no honour in his own country is perhaps taken by John in the sense that there is something quite inappropriate about calling Jesus a prophet.'
[1225] Bruce, *John*, 117; Michaels, *John*, 65, 82; Carson, *John*, 234; Morris, *John*, 254–255; Witherington, *Wisdom*, 127; Milne, *John*, 90f; Köstenberger, *John*, 91; Smith, *John*, 125.
[1226] Beasley-Murray, *John*, 71; Dodd, *Historical*, 188–195, esp. 194; Schnackenburg, *John*, I, 471–475; Bultmann, *John*, 294–295; Lindars, *John*, 198f; Brown, *John*, 193f; Lohse 'Miracles,' 65f; Malina and Rohrbaugh, *John*, 107; Collins, 'Representative,' 40; Fallon, *John*, 121; Blomberg, *Historical*, 107; A. H. Mead, 'John 4:46–53,' 71; Barrett, *John*, 245.
[1227] Beasley-Murray, *John*, 71. Also, Lindars, *John*, 198f.

Witherington[1228] assumes that the βασιλικός could mean a royal official or a person of royal blood. However, here it refers to a royal official who worked for Herod Antipas who as the tetrarch of Galilee (from 4 BCE to 39 CE) was popularly called a king (Mark 6:14, 22; Matt 14:9). According to Witherington,[1229] the term was applied to officers who served Herod as recorded in Josephus (*Life* 400ff). Whitacre[1230] thinks that it is not clear whether the royal official is a Jew or a gentile. However, Mead[1231] argues that it is not necessary to assert that the man was a Jew but it is probable that the royal official as a gentile centurion could serve Herod Antipas. In particular, Koester[1232] regards the βασιλικός as a non-Jewish royal official, because Galilee was ruled by Herod Antipas, who was not a Jew but an Idumaen. For Koester, Antipas, who as the vassal of the Roman emperor employed his officials and soldiers not only from the Jews but also from the gentiles who allied themselves with the Romans. Thus, there is a possibility that the Johannine royal official as one who serves Herod Antipas could be a gentile. Also, if he was the same person as the gentile centurion in the Synoptic Gospels, it could be in accord with the confession of the Samaritans in v. 42 that Jesus was, 'the Saviour of the world.'

Nonetheless, the two narratives are quite different from each other, except for healing at a distance (cf. the healing of the Syrophoenician woman's daughter in Matt 15:21–28; Mark 7:24–30).[1233] Morris argues that:

> The most notable difference, perhaps, is in the attitude of the man seeking healing. In the Synoptists when Jesus proposes going to his home, the centurion strongly opposes the idea and utters his notable words about his giving of commands and having them carried out without being present, whereas here the man asks Jesus to come to his home and when Jesus makes a comment without

---

[1228] Witherington, *Wisdom*, 128, 383 n. 11; Brown, *John I-XII*, 190; Smith, *John*, 125; Bruce, *John*, 117; Whitacre, *John*, 114f; Milne, *John*, 91; Howard-Brook, *Becoming*, 117; Köstenberger, *John*, 90; A. H. Mead, 'John 4:46–53,' 71; Collins, 'Representative,' 41; Fallon, *John*, 120; Malina and Rohrbaugh, *John*, 107, who think that the βασιλικός refers to 'a royal personage, such as a member of the Herodian family' in connection with vv. 51, 53.

[1229] Witherington, *Wisdom*, 128, 383 n. 11; Brown, *John I-XII*, 190. However, Michaels, *John*, 82 argues that the term was not used for Roman soldiers.

[1230] Whitacre, *John*, 114f; Michales, *John*, 79. On the other hand, Bruce, *John*, 117 thinks that there is no clear evidence that the royal official was a gentile. Also, Carson, *John*, 234; Morris, *John*, 255. Further, Collins, 'Representative,' 41 argues that the royal official who is not the same figure as the centurion in the Synoptic Gospels was a high official in the employ of the Herodian court.

[1231] Mead, 'John 4:46–53,' 71; Fallon, *John*, 120.

[1232] Koester, *Symbolism*, 52. Brown, *John I-XII*, 190.

[1233] Morris, *John*, 254f; Carson, *John*, 233f; Witherington, *Wisdom*, 127; Smith, *John*, 125; Michaels, *John*, 82. Cf. See Schnackenburg, *John*, I, 471–475; Beasley-Murray, *John*, 71.

indicating a move he utters a peremptory 'Sir, come down....' The two attitudes are very different. Despite the verbal parallels the two stories are distinct.[1234]

Accordingly, the two narratives, the healing of the royal official's son in John 4:46–54 and the healing of the centurion's servant in Matt 8:5–13; Luke 7:1–10, denote the traditions of totally different healing incidents.

6.6.3 Miraculous Signs and Wonders

Now, we will think about the background of miraculous signs and wonders. Following the royal official's request for Jesus to come down to Capernaum and to heal his son, Jesus replied, 'Unless you people see miraculous signs and wonders, you will never believe' (v. 48). Here, it is necessary to investigate the OT background of the 'miraculous signs and wonders' (σημεῖα καὶ τέρατα) and their meaning. Generally, Johannine commentators think that the concept of miraculous signs and wonders is based on the works of Moses in the setting of the exodus.[1235] The combination of 'miraculous signs and wonders,' which appears once in John's Gospel, is a conventional expression for the great acts of God in the deliverance of the exodus (cf. Exod 7:3f; Deut 4:34; 6:22).[1236] Also, the combination of, 'miraculous signs and wonders' associated with the exodus and Moses is found in Acts 7:36 and is related to messianic expectation of the new age (cf. the apocalyptic contexts).[1237]

Generally, signs (אות, σημεῖον) function as proof of divine authorization of prophets (cf. Exod 3:12; 1 Sam 10:1-9), especially as the divine authority of Moses in the exodus narratives (cf. Exod 4:1–9, 17, 30).[1238] So, Smith argues that:

[1234] Morris, *John*, 255.
[1235] According to Rengstorf, *TDNT*, VII, 210f, אות, a corresponding term to σημεῖον, appears 79 times in the HT, about half of all the references (39 times) are in the Pentateuch and about quarter of the references (19 times) in the major prophets (Isaiah, Jeremiah, Ezekiel), and אות is closely related to מופת in Exod 7:3; Deut 4:34; 6:22; 7:19; 13:2f; 26:8; 28:46; 29:2; 34:11; Isa 8:18; 20:3; Jer 32:20f; Pss 78:43; 105:27; 135:79; Neh 9:10, which as a corresponding term to τέρας occurs 36 times in the HT. The combined expression (אות and מופת) appears in the plural (σημεῖα καὶ τέρατα) and both terms are together found especially in Deuteronomy (9 references).
[1236] Lindars, *John*, 203; Lohse, 'Miracles,' 66 n. 6; Howard-Brook, *Becoming*, 118; Brown, *John I-XII*, 191; Smith, *John*, 126; Dennis, *Gathering*, 94 n. 80; M. J. J. Menken, 'Christology,' 313f; Enz, 'Afterlife,' 35; Brunson, *Psalm 118*, 161; Rengstorf, *TDNT*, VII, 216, 221, 244. Cf. *Bar.* 2:11; *Wis.* 10:16; *Mosis* 1.95; *Spec. Leg.* 2.218.
[1237] Lindars, *John*, 203; Smith, *John*, 126; Rengstorf, *TDNT*, VII, 240f. Cf. Acts 2:19, 22, 43; 4:30; 5:12; 6:8; 7:36; 14:3; 15:12; 2 Cor 12:12; Matt 24:24; Mark 13:22.
[1238] Smith, *John*, 94; Beasley-Murray, *John*, 33; Dennis, *Gathering*, 94 n. 80; Pamment, 'Samaritan,' 229; Rengstorf, *TDNT*, VII, 212.

The expectation to which the signs of Jesus correspond may have more to do with the prophets like Moses (Deut 18:15–22) than the Davidic Messiah, who was not expected to perform such deeds.[1239]

Brunson[1240] also recognizes that the signs of John's Gospel allude to the events of the exodus. Nevertheless, he argues that, the great majority of sign references from exodus through Deuteronomy were related not to Moses but to Yahweh. As a result the Johannine Jesus who took the first exodus as the model for much of his ministry may be intent not so much on reproducing the signs and works of Moses as on associating his signs and works with those of Yahweh (ἐγώ εἰμι):

> In evoking the works/signs parallels to Moses it was no doubt John's intention to take the reader back to the exodus and portray Jesus as the leader of a new or second exodus. However, the Johannine Jesus associates his ministry principally with the Father, not with Moses.... In many of the exodus parallels to Jesus' ministry it is the works of Yahweh that Jesus reproduces: It is Yahweh who opened the Red Sea, guided Israel with the pillar of fire, gave the Law, instituted the first covenant, healed those who looked at the serpent, and provided bread and water in the wilderness. If the people grumbled against Moses, they did so even more against God.... Jesus' ministry in this sense makes it clear that one greater than Moses has come, one whose works and signs are those of the Father. The signs and works terminology evokes primarily the salvific acts of God on behalf of his people and presents Jesus as the one who will bring about a new deliverance and salvation, leading his people from bondage, through the wilderness, to a new promised land.... In the first exodus Moses was an instrument of God's pleasure. But Jesus is the 'Ἐγώ εἰμι (cf. Exod 3:14) who is one with the Father, has authority in himself, and reproduces the signs and works of Yahweh.[1241]

[1239] Smith, *John*, 94; Dennis, *Gathering*, 94 n. 80; Rengstorf, *TDNT*, VII, 240ff, 244f.

[1240] Brunson, *Psalm 118*, 161f.

[1241] Brunson, *Psalm 118*, 162–163. Cf. John 5:18; 8:58; 10:33, 36; 19:7, where Jesus identifies his works to God's works, which is the reason that the Jews tried to kill him. Cf. Menken, 'Christology,' 313f; Rengstorf, *TDNT*, VII, 216, 221, 257, who argues that the description of Jesus as the prophet (cf. John 4:19; 6:14; 7:40; 9:17) and his divine foreordination as the Passover Lamb of eschatological redemption (cf. John 1:29, 36) in John's Gospel typologically allude to the age of Moses with the redemption from bondage in Egypt. Nonetheless, Rengstorf recognizes that the signs performed by Jesus in John's Gospel present Jesus as the one more than a new Moses, 'For Jesus acts as God, and therein He shows Himself to be the Son of God.' (p. 257).

Also, ἐγώ εἰμι (אָנֹכִי אָנֹכִי) is a very important self-designation of Yahweh in connection with the restoration or new exodus of Israel from exile in Deutero-Isaiah (cf. Isa 43:11). In particular, Beasley-Murray points out that, 'it [σημεῖον] also denotes events that herald things to come, especially in relation to the eschatological future (e.g. Isa 7:10–16).'[1242] Regarding this, above all, we have to note John 20:30f, in which the Evangelist clearly wrote the purpose of the record of some collections of Jesus's miraculous signs:

> Jesus did many other miraculous signs in the presence of his disciples, which are not recorded in this book. But these are written that you may believe that Jesus is the Christ, the Son of God, and that by believing you may have life in his name.

Rengstorf[1243] argues, concerning the references to Jesus's sign (cf. John 2:23; 3:2; 6:2, 26; 9:16) and the summary references to Jesus's performing a great numbers of signs (cf. John 11:47; 12:37; 20:30), that these signs were, 'the kind of miracles expected with the dawn of the messianic age, cf. the saying in Isa 35:5 (Matt 11:5; Luke 7:22).' In other words, the miracles recorded in John's Gospel have messianic distinction; for examples, the miracle at the wedding in Cana of Galilee in John 2:11, the second miracle at Cana of Galilee in John 4:46, 54, the feeding miracle in Galilee in John 6:14, the raising of Lazarus in 12:18, the healing of the man born blind in 9:1ff, and, the healing of the lame man on the Sabbath in 5:1ff. For Rengstorf,[1244] the raising of the dead and the healings in John are typical wonders of the messianic age, and the feeding miracle and the wine miracle correspond to the expectation of the abundance of the messianic age. Thus, Rengstorf[1245] rightly says that Jesus's miraculous signs related to the messianic age based on the OT are in accord with the reference in John 20:30f.

Furthermore, Bryan[1246] argues that a sign the Jews demanded Jesus to show was related not to a sign testifying Jesus as the Messiah (cf. the divine

---

[1242] Beasley-Murray, *John*, 33 ([] added by this writer); Pamment, 'Samaritan,' 229. Cf. Isa 8:18; 20:3.
[1243] Rengstorf, *TDNT*, VII, 245f. Lohse, 'Miracles,' 72; Beasley-Murray, *John*, 33; Lindars, *John*, 132.
[1244] Rengstorf, *TDNT*, VII, 246.
[1245] Rengstorf, *TDNT*, VII, 246.
[1246] For the detailed discussion of the relationship between signs and restoration, see Bryan, *Jesus*, 21–45. For example, the Qumran community understood healing and raising of the dead as divine works in 4Q521 (p. 24). The rebels being raised at the time of Jewish wars interpreted a number of unusual phenomena in the light of Scripture and concluded that they were signs of God's immediate intervention; 'the appearance of a sword-shaped star and of a comet, a light which shone around the altar for half an hour during Passover, a heifer which, while being led to sacrifice, gave birth to a lamb, the opening of the heavy eastern gate of the Temple's inner court of its own accord, the appearance in the clouds of a commotion of

authorization). For Bryan, the sign was, however, to bring about the new salvation (the eschatological restoration) like the exodus, in the setting that the Jews at the times of the Second Temple believed wonders (miracles) as signs of the eschatological restoration of Israel, according to a typological pattern based on the first exodus.

The expected signs cannot have been mere confirmation of the prophet's authenticity; rather, they were signs which would effect deliverance in the manner of the theophanic miracles of the exodus/conquest. It is my contention that the sign prophets provide firm evidence for the expectation in the first century of a belief that the arrival of the time of fulfilment would be accompanied by a particular sort of sign. Such a sign would not merely authenticate the prophetic claim but actually began to effect eschatological deliverance and judgement. In other words, *the demand for a sign emerged from a specific expectation*. If viewed in this light the sign requested by the Pharisees and/or the crowds need not be one of messianic or even prophetic authentication. Rather, they sought a sign which by close analogy with one of God's great redemptive acts in the time of the exodus and conquest unmistakably demonstrated the truth of Jesus's claim that the time of fulfilment had come.[1247]

In particular, this argument could be supported by Jesus's Temple incident in the setting of the Jewish Passover feast in John 2:13-22. Concerning Jesus's action and his *logion* in the Temple court, when the Jews demanded of Jesus, 'what miraculous sign can you show us to prove your authority to do all this?' Jesus answered them by predicting the destruction of the Temple by the Jews and the raising of the new Temple by Jesus himself in

---

chariots and soldiers, and the experience by a number of priests serving in the Temple during Pentecost of a great quake accompanied by a loud noise and followed by the voice of multitude saying, 'We are departing hence' (*J. W.* 6.289-300).' (pp. 24f). The community regarded the living in the wilderness based on Isa 40 as the preparation for the way of Yahweh's eschatological deliverance for Israel in *1QS* 8:12-15 (p. 28). In particular, some sign prophets in Josephus are presented as the impostors or deceivers who led multitudes into the wilderness promising signs of freedom (*War* 2.259; *Ant.* 20.167). For example, a magician called Theudas, purporting to be a prophet, led many into the wilderness in 45 or 46 BCE, promising to part the Jordan (*Ant.* 20.97). An Egyptian who, claiming to be a prophet, led a multitude of common people commanded the collapse of the walls of Jerusalem, alluding to the falling of the walls of Jericho (*Ant.* 20:169-172; *War* 2.261-263). An impostor under the rule of Festus (cf. 61 CE) tempted a number of people into the wilderness with promise of freedom and rest (*Ant.* 20.188). (pp. 30f). Cf. Rengstorf, *TDNT*, VII, 225.

[1247] Bryan, *Jesus*, 39 (original emphasis), who also claims that his argument could be supported by the narrative of the feeding miracle in John 6, in which the Jews, after experiencing the miracle, asked a sign, namely, a miracle bringing about the deliverance of Israel; 'The crowds expected a particular type of sign – a miraculous act which by manifest correspondence with God's action for Israel during the time of the Exodus provided clear attestation that God was again at work in effecting the deliverance of his people.' (pp. 39-40).

three days. This was commented on by the Evangelist to mean his physical death and resurrection, which will raise the new eschatological Temple, namely, the eschatological covenantal community of God. Jesus as the Son/firstborn of God, in being killed by the Jews and then risen by God the Father, will build the new eschatological Temple; the Davidic messianic King, namely, the eschatological fulfiller of the Davidic covenant of 2 Sam 7:12–16 (cf. Pss 2:7; 89), who is simultaneously the same figure as the Deutero-Isaianic suffering servant (Isa 9:1–7; 11:1–16; 42:1–9; 52:13–53:12; 55:1–3; 61:1–11). As such his vicarious, atoning, covenantal death will not only bring about the restoration or the new exodus of Israel from exile, but also restore the gentiles as the sons of God (cf. the light to the gentiles in Isa 42:6; 49:6). This is supported by the Markan version of the Temple incident in Mark 11:17, saying that, 'My house will be called a house of prayer for all nations,' alluding to Isa 56:7 (vv. 1–8) (cf. 2 Kings 8:1–61; 2 Chron 6:1–42). Thus, this is the very sign Jesus will show to the Jews.

On the other hand, Howard-Brook[1248] points out that Jesus's reproof of the multitude's belief depending on miraculous signs and wonders in v. 48 alludes Pharaoh's unbelief, in spite of seeing miraculous signs and wonders performed by Yahweh in Exod 7:3f. In particular, Dennis argues that the rejection of Jesus's signs by the Jews and their religious leaders in John's Gospel alludes to the disobedience of Israel in Deut 29:2–9:

> Thus, Jesus' sign ministry in John has a Deuteronomistic character designed to call Israel to faith in the Messiah. The rejection of the messianic signs by many of the *Ioudaioi* and their leaders echoes the disobedience of Israel in Deut 29:2–9, a disobedience that will, if continued, keep Israel under the curses of the covenant (continued destruction, dispersion, and loss of the true divine 'place').[1249]

6.6.4 The Meaning of Jesus's Healing Miracle

The royal official repeatedly begged Jesus to come down to Capernaum to heal his son who was close to death (vv. 47, 49). However, Jesus did not come down directly to the boy. Instead at Cana he replied that, 'Your son will live' (v. 50). The life of the boy is restored from the brink of death by the word of Jesus. Jesus performed a sign whereby he himself gave life to the almost dead boy by his word, which presents him as the giver of life. Thus, Michaels rightly says that the sign:

> makes the point that Jesus' words are life-giving words. The restoration of the physical life and health of the government

---

[1248] Howard-Brook, *Becoming*, 118; Brown, *John I-XII*, 191.
[1249] Dennis, *Gathering*, 94.

official's son illustrates and reinforces Jesus' promises made earlier at Jerusalem (3:15–16) and in Samaria (4:14, 36). To some degree it also anticipates his self-revelation as giver of life in the following chapter (5:19–26).[1250]

The reference to the 'sign' in v. 54 (the second miraculous sign in connection with the wine miraculous sign in Cana in John 2:1–11) could point beyond itself to the deeper meanings of Jesus's identity and mission. The boy's restored health (life) is a sign pointing to the life in Jesus;[1251] Jesus is the life, the resurrection, the creative word (*Logos*) of God, which is the main subject from the beginning (cf. John 1:1–4) to the end (cf. John 20:31) of John's Gospel.[1252] Concerning the claim that this healing miraculous sign was related to the wine miraculous sign (John 2:1–11) in v. 46, Carson says that:

> The one who transformed water into wine, eclipsing the old rites of purification and announcing the dawning joy of the messianic banquet, is the one who continues his messianic work, whether he is rightly trusted or not, by bringing healing and snatching life back from the brink of death (cf. Is 35:5–6; 53:4a [cf. Matt 8:16–17]; 61:1).[1253]

Thus, the healing by the word of Jesus alludes to the power of the creative word of God in Genesis (esp. Gen 1:1–31; 2:7),[1254] reflected in the creation work of the Logos in the Prologue of the Gospel (John 1:1–4). Further it relates to the recreation work (new creation/eternal life) of the resurrected Jesus after Easter in John 20:22, alluding to Ezek 37:1–14 (cf. Gen 2:7), meaning the restoration or the new exodus of Judah and Israel from exile (Ezek 37:15–28).

6.7 Conclusion

In this chapter, we have studied the narrative of Jesus's encounter with a Samaritan woman in John 4:1–42 and his healing of a royal official's son in John 4:43–54. The narrative in John 4:1–42 is about the restoration of the Samaritans, disclosed with the living water motif (vv. 1–15), the betrothal

---

[1250] Michaels, *John*, 81; Throckmorton, *Creation*, 117; Lindars, *John*, 198; Fallon, *John*, 120f; Collins, 'Representative,' 41; Brodie, *John*, 226; Polhill, 'John 1–4,' 456.
[1251] Polhill, 'John 1–4,' 456.
[1252] Cf. Brown, *John I-XII*, 197 says that 'In Johannine thought the life ... given to the boy remains on the level of a sign of the eternal life that Jesus will give after his resurrection.' Cf. the bread of life in John 6, the living water in John 7:37–39, the light of life in John 8:12, 51; 10:10, 28 (*ibid.*, 198).
[1253] Carson, *John*, 238; Bruce, *John*, 117.
[1254] Cf. Throckmorton, *Creation*, 117.

motif (vv. 16-18), the new worship (or the new Temple) (vv. 19-26), the food motif (vv. 32-34), and the harvest motif (vv. 35-42).

In John 4:1-15 (cf. John 7:37-39), the reference to Jesus giving the Samaritan woman 'living water,' symbolizing the Holy Spirit as the means of the restoration of covenantal relationship of the Samaritans (represented by her) to Israel (Jer 2:13; Isa 49:10; 44:3; Ezek 47:1-12; Zech 14:8; Joel 2:28-32).

In vv. 16-18, Jesus's encounter with the woman at the well reflects the courtship (betrothal) motif in the OT (cf. Gen 24:11-20; 29:1-14; Exod 2:15-22). This symbolizes the restoration of the covenantal relationship between Yahweh and Israel (cf. Hos 2:2, 7, 16; Jer 2:1-13; Ezek 16:1-52; 23:1-49; Isa 54:1-9; 61:10; 62:4f).

In vv. 19-26, Jesus discloses that the true worship in Spirit and truth will be fulfilled by him who is the true Temple (cf. 2:19-22). He is the source of the stream of living water symbolizing the Holy Spirit (cf. John 4:10, 13f; 7:37ff; 20:22; Ezek 37:1-28), recalling the eschatological Temple in Ezekiel (Ezek 47:1-12; cf. Zech 14:8; Joel 3:18). Further he is the builder of the new Temple, the Davidic Messiah based on 2 Sam 7:12-16. In v. 22, 'Salvation is from the Jews' could mean that the Jews are the successor of Israel (cf. Exod 4:22f; 19:5f), through whom the gentiles would be restored as the sons of God. It could mean that the world will be saved through the Davidic Messiah, who will come through the Jews (Gen 49:10; 2 Sam 7:12-16; Ps 2:7; 89; 110; Isa 9:1-7; 11:1-16). In v. 26, Jesus declared himself the Messiah who will restore the true worship of God. Here, he discloses his identity with ἐγώ εἰμι, Yahweh's name revealed in the setting of the exodus (cf. Exod 3:14) and the Deutero-Isaianic new exodus (cf. Isa 41:4; 43:10; 45:18; 52:6).

In v. 34, the imagery of food as doing the will of God the Father and finishing his work, alluding to Deut 8:3, presents Jesus as the true Son/servant of God (cf. Exod 4:22f; 19:5f; Hos 11:1). Also, the combination of 'to do' and 'to accomplish' alluding to Isa 55:11 discloses Jesus as the figure of 'the word of God' bringing about the new exodus.

The harvest motif in John 4:35-38 (cf. vv. 35-42) presents the eschatological restoration of Israel (the Samaritans) scattered among the gentiles (cf. Isa 27:12f), and the unification of Israel and Judah (cf. Isa 11:11-12; Ezek 37:21). In v. 42, Jesus is, 'the Saviour of the world,' the name of Yahweh who saves his people, the divine designation concerning the restoration of Israel in Deutero-Isaiah (Isa 43:3, 11; 45:21f; 63:8f). Also, the title shows Yahweh's plan to restore the nations (the world) through Israel, his firstborn/servant/priest (Exod 4:22f; 19:5f; cf. John 1:29; 3:16ff).

In John 4:46–54, Jesus's healing of a royal official's son presents him as the life, the life-giver, the creative word of God in creation and in the restoration (resurrection, cf. Ezek 37:1–28).

Chapter 7: Conclusion

In conclusion, as we have explored the firstborn and its Christological significance for the Johannine Jesus and his saving work, we have seen that themes related to the paschal-new exodus/firstborn motif are abundantly reflected in the narratives of John 1–4. We have found diverse Christological titles based on the idea of the firstborn in the baptism (John 1:19–34); Nathanael's confession and Jesus's promise (John 1:47–51; cf. Gen 28:12; Dan 7:13f); the heavenly things related to the works of the Son of Man (John 3:13–16). Also, in the wine miracle and the wedding motif (John 2:1–12; 3:28–30); Jesus's action and his saying in the Temple set against the background the Passover feast in John 2:13–23 were found distinct paschal/firstborn motifs.

In particular, it has been shown that resurrection (the new creation) is an important theme in John in connection with the restoration or new exodus themes, which allude to the creation. These continued to be found in the birth of water and Spirit (that is, the new birth, the birth from above, the making of the children of God) and entry into the kingdom of God in the narrative of Jesus's conversation with Nicodemus (John 3:1–15; 1:12–13). Judgment (perishing) and eternal life (salvation) were discussed with the motif of light and darkness alluding to hardening and blindness in John 3:16–21. This paschal-new exodus/firstborn motif was also found in the 'living water' (the Holy Spirit) discussion, the betrothal motif, the predicted new worship (that is, worship of the Father in Spirit and Truth) and the restoration (the harvest motif) of the Samaritans as the children of God in John 4:1–42; and lastly Jesus's healing of the official's son in John 4:43–54.

Above all, it has been shown that the Johannine Logos, who is introduced as the only Son of God and as the Son of Man in John's Gospel (cf. John 1:14, 18, 51; 3:13–18), probably alludes to the idea of the firstborn and the Danielic Son of Man figure (based on the idea of the firstborn). It is this figure who fulfils the calling of the Deutero-Isaianic suffering servant of the Lord for the restoration of Israel from exile and for the salvation of the gentiles as the sons of God. Also, the Johannine Logos is based on the creative and eschatological Word of God in Isa 55:11 (cf. John 6:22–71; 4:34). In John 6:22–71, the work of the Son of Man as the Son of God is described as the work of the personified and hypostatized Word of God in Isa 55:10–11. This is set against the background of the restoration (the new creation), alluding to the creation through the word of God in Genesis (cf. the restoration of the creation).

It has been shown that the Johannine Jesus, as the Logos, the only Son of God and the Danielic Son of Man, is ontologically the divine Son enthroned on one of the heavenly thrones. As such he as the Danielic Son of Man, namely, as the symbolic inclusive representative of the Saints of the Most High (the Ancient of Days), will be enthroned on one of the heavenly thrones. That is, the Johannine Jesus will functionally accomplish the restoration (ascension) of the Israelites from exile to the throne of God through the work (death) of Isaianic suffering servant of Yahweh. This is accomplished by his bearing a vicarious atoning death as the guilt-offering for sinful Israel and all the nations, and so as the ransom in order to redeem them from condemnation at the last judgment.

Further investigation has revealed that the Johannine Jesus is the eschatological fulfilment of the Davidic covenant (2 Sam 7:12–14; Ps 2:7; 89). He, as the Son of God, the firstborn/paschal lamb, and the King of Israel, builds the eschatological new Temple through his vicarious atoning redemptive death and resurrection. This set against the background of the Passover feast (John 2:13–22; 1:49), which is the work of the Isaianic suffering servant of the Lord (the same figure the Davidic Messiah. cf. Isa 11:2; 42:1; 61:1), upon whom the Holy Spirit descended and thus will baptize people with the Holy Spirit (John 1:32–33; 3:5–8, 34; 20:22; Ezek 37:1–14). Also, he is the true Temple, the eschatological locus of the true worship, the source of the flowing of the living water (the Holy Spirit). That is, the bestower of the living water symbolizing the Holy Spirit (John 4:10, 14; 7:37–39; Ezek 47:1–12; Zech 14:8; Joel 3:18); the establisher of the new worship order, namely, the worship of the Father in the Holy Spirit and the Truth (John 4:23–24); the making (creation/restoration) of the children of God, the new Temple, the eschatological community of the people of God. The building of the new eschatological Temple is related to the expectation for the new exodus, which will be brought about by the Davidic Messiah.

Consideration was given to the Johannine Jesus as the replacement of Jacob-Israel who was the inclusive forefather of the Israelite nation, the people of God in the OT. As such he is the inclusive representative of the new Israel, the community of the true people of God in the eschatological time (John 1:51; 4:12–14; 15:1–8). This is also based on the concept of the firstborn.

It has also been shown that the Johannine Jesus as the Son of God has made God the Father known to the world (gentiles) and has fulfilled the purpose (will) of God the Father for the salvation and restoration of the world (cf. John 1:14, 18; 3:16; 6:38f, 46). This shows the perfect sonship/servanthood/priesthood of the Johannine Jesus, alluding to the dual status (the concept of the firstborn) given to Israel (cf. Exod 4:22f; 19:5f).

Finally it has been shown that the Johannine Jesus is presented as the embodiment (incarnation) of Yahweh. This is reflected in, 'the name' (cf. John 1:12; 3:18), which alludes to Yahweh's name revealed to Moses and set against the background of the exodus. Further it alludes to the Deutero-Isaianic Yahweh's name set against the background of the restoration or the new exodus, reflected in a Johannine Christological title (ἐγώ εἰμι cf. John 4:26; 6:35; 8:12).

Conclusively, it has been shown that the paschal-new exodus motif is an important prism for interpreting John's Gospel and Johannine Christology.

Bibliography

Aalen, S. "'Reign' and 'House' in the Kingdom of God in the Gospels,' *NTS* 8 (1961/62), 215–240.

_____. *NIDNTT*, II, 44–48.

Ackroyd, P.R. *Exile and Restoration: A Study of Hebrew Thought of the Sixth Century BC*. London: SCM, 1968.

Albright, W.E. *New Horizons in Biblical Research*. London: OUP, 1966.

Alexander, A.B. 'The Johaninne Doctrine of the Logos,' *ExpT* 36 (1924/25), 394–399, 467–472.

Alexander, T.D. 'Messianic Ideology in the Book of Genesis,' *The Lord's Anointed: Interpretation of Old Testament Messianic Texts*, eds. P.E. Satterthwaite, R.S. Hess, and G.J. Wenham. Carlisle: Paternoster; Grand Rapids: Baker Books, 1995, 19–39.

Allen, L.C. *Ezekiel 1–19*. WBC 28; Dallas, Texas: Word Books, 1994.

_____. *Ezekiel 20–48*. WBC 29; Dallas, Texas: Word Books, 1990.

Allison (Jr), D.C. *The New Moses: A Matthean Typology*. Minneapolis: Fortress, 1993.

Anderson, B.W. 'Exodus Typology in Second Isaiah,' *Israel's Prophetic Heritage: Essays in Honor of J. Muilenburg*, eds. B.W. Anderson and W. Harrelson. London: SCM; New York: Harper, 1962, 177–195.

_____. *From Creation to New Creation: Old Testament Perspective*. Minneapolis: Fortress Press, 1994.

Anderson, P.N. *The Christology of the Fourth Gospel: Its Unity and Disunity in the Light of John 6*. Valley Forges, PA: Trinity Press International, 1996.

André, G. *TDOT*, IV, 162–165.

Argyle, A.W. 'A Note on John 4:35,' *ExpT* 82 (1971), 247–248.

Ashley, T.R. *The Book of Numbers*. Grand Rapids: Eerdmans, 1993.

Ashton, J. *Studying John: Approaches to the Fourth Gospel*. Oxford: Clarendon, 1998.

_____. *Understanding the Fourth Gospel*. Oxford: Clarendon, 1991.

Aune, D.E. *Revelation 1–5*. WBC 52; Dallas: Word, 1997.

Baer, D. A. and Gordon, R.P. *NIDOTTE*, II, 211–218.

Ball, D.M. *I Am in John's Gospel*. JSNTSupp 124; Sheffield: SAP, 1996.

Barrett, C.K. *The Gospel According to St. John*. 2nd ed.; Philadelphia: Westminster, 1978.

_____. 'The Holy Spirit in the Fourth Gospel,' *JTS* 1 (1950), 1–14.

_____. 'The Lamb of God,' *NTS* 1 (1955), 210–218.

_____. 'The Old Testament in the Fourth Gospel,' *JTS* 48 (1947), 155–169.

Barrosse, T. 'The Seven Days of the New Creation in St. John's Gospel,' *CBQ* 21 (1956), 507–516.

Bartels, K.H. *NIDNTT*, II, 723–725.

Bauckham, R. *'Jesus' Demonstration in the Temple,' Law and Religion: Essays on the Place of the Law in Israel and Early Christianity by members of the Ehrhardt Seminar of Manchester University*, ed. B. Lindars. Cambridge: James and Clarks and Co, 1988, 72–89.

_____. 'Kingdom and Church According to Jesus and Paul,' *HBT*, 18/1 (1996), 1–26.

_____. 'Nicodemus and the Gurion Family,' *JTS* 47 (1996), 1–37.

_____. 'The 153 Fish and the Unity of the Fourth Gospel,' in *The Testimony of the Beloved Disciple: Narrative, history, and Theology in the Gospel of John*. Grand Rapids: Baker Academic, 2007, 271–284.

_____. 'The Son of Man: 'A Man in My Position' or 'Someone,'' *JSNT* 23 (1985), 23–33.

Baylis, C.P. 'The Meaning of Walking 'in the Darkness' (1 John 1:6),' *BS* 149 (1992), 214–222.

Beale, G.K. 'An Exegetical and Theological Consideration of the Hardening of Pharaoh's Heart in Exodus 4–14 and Romans 9,' *TrinJ* 5 (1984), 129–154.

_____. *Revelation: A Commentary on the Greek Text*. Carlisle: Paternoster; Grand Rapids: Eerdmans, 1999.

Beasley-Murray, G.R. 'John 3:3, 5: Baptism, Spirit and the Kingdom,' *ExpT* 97 (1986), 167–170.

_____. 'The Interpretation of Daniel 7,' *CBQ* 45 (1983), 44–58.

_____. 'The Kingdom of God and Christology in the Gospels,' *Jesus of Nazareth Lord and Christ: Essays on the historical Jesus and New Testament Christology*, eds. J.B. Green and M.T. Turner. Carlisle: Paternoster; Grand Rapids: Eerdmans, 1994, 22–36.

_____. 'The Kingdom of God in the Teaching of Jesus,' *JETS* 35 (1992), 19–30.

_____. *Baptism in the New Testament.* Carlisle: Paternoster, 1997.

_____. *Gospel of Life: Theology in the Fourth Gospel.* Peabody: Hendrickson, 1995.

_____. *Jesus and the Kingdom of God.* Carlisle: Paternoster; Grand Rapids: Eerdmans, 1986.

_____. *John.* WBC 36; Waco, Texas: Word Books, 1987.

_____. *NIDNTT*, I, 224–225.

Beasley-Murray, P. *The Message of the Resurrection.* Leicester: IVP, 2000.

Beck, H. and Brown, C. *NIDNTT*, II, 776–783.

Becker, U. *NIDNTT*, II, 107–115.

Behm, J. *TDNT*, I, 342–343.

_____. *TDNT*, II, 124–134.

Belleville, L. 'Born of Water and Spirit: John 3:5,' *TrinJ* 1 (1980), 125–141.

Bennema, C. *The Power of Saving Wisdom: An Investigation of Spirit and Wisdom in Relation to the Soteriology of the Fourth Gospel.* WUNT 2/148; Tübingen: Mohr Siebeck, 2002.

Bernard, J.H. *The Gospel according to St John*, I. ICC; Edinburgh: T&T Clark, 1928.

Bertram, G. *TDNT*, VIII, 602–620.

Betz, O. 'Jesus and Isaiah 53,' in *Jesus and the Suffering Servant: Isaiah 53 and Christian Origins,* eds. W.H. Bellinger and W.R. Farmer. Harrisburg, PA: Trinity Press International, 1998, 70–87.

_____. *What Do We Know About Jesus?* trans. M. Kohl. London: SCM, 1968.

Bietenhard, H. *NIDNTT*, II, 188–196.

Black, D.A. 'The Text of John 3:13,' *GTJ* 6/1 (1985), 49–66.

Block, D.I. 'The Prophet of the Spirit: The Use of *RWH* in the Book of Ezekiel,' *JETS* 32/1 (1989), 27–49.

_____. *The Book of Ezekiel: Chapters 25–48.* Grand Rapids: Eerdmans, 1997.

Blomberg, C.L. 'A Response to G.B. Beasley-Murray in the Kingdom,' *JETS* 35 (1992), 31–36.

_____. *The Historical Reliability of John's Gospel.* Leicester: Apollo, 2001.

Bock, D.L. *Proclamation from Prophecy and Pattern: Lucan Old Testament Christology*. JSNT Supp 12; Sheffield: SAP, 1987.

Bockmuehl, M.N.A. *Revelation and Mystery in Ancient Judaism and Pauline Christianity*. Grand Rapids and Cambridge: Eerdmans, 1997.

Boismard, M.-É. *Moses or Jesus: An Essay in Johannine Christology*, trans. B.T. Viviano. Leuven: Leuven University Press, 1993.

Borgen, P. 'Creation, Logos and the Son: Observations on John 1:1–18 and 5:17–18.' *EA* 3 (1987), 88–97.

_____. 'God's Agent in the Fourth Gospel,' *Logos was the True Light and Other Essays on the Gospel of John*. Trondheim: Tapir Publisher, 1983, 121–132.

_____. 'Logos was the True Light,' *NovT* 14 (1972), 115–130.

_____. 'Observations on the Targumic Character of the Prologue of John,' *NTS* 16(1970), 288–295.

_____. 'The Son of Man Saying in John 3:13–14,' *Logos was the True Light and Other Essays on the Gospel of John*. Trondheim: Tapir Publisher, 1983, 133–148.

_____. *Bread From Heaven: An Exegetical Study of the Concept of Manna in the Gospel of John and the Writings of Philo*. NovT Supp 10; Leiden: Brill, 1965.

_____. *Logos was the True Light and Other Essays on the Gospel of John*. Trondheim: Tapir Publisher, 1983.

Bornkamm, G. *TDNT*, IV, 813–824.

Bowen, J.P. 'Coming to Faith in the Gospel of John,' *Anvil* 19 (2002), 277–283.

Bredin, M.R.J. 'The Influence of the Aqedah on Revelation 5:6–9,' *IBS* 18 (1996), 26–43.

Bretscher, P. 'Exodus 4.22–23 and the Voice from Heaven,' *JBL* 87 (1968), 301–311.

Brewer, D.I. 'Three Weddings and a Divorce: God's Covenant with Israel, Judah and the Church,' *TynB* 47 (1996), 1–25.

Brodie, T.L. *The Gospel According to John: A Literary and Theological Commentary*. Oxford and New York: OUP, 1993.

Brooke, G.J. *Exegesis at Qumran: 4QFlorilegium in Its Jewish Context*. Sheffield: JSOT, 1985.

Brown, C. *NIDNTT*, II, 186–187.

_____. *NIDNTT*, III, 918–922.

Brown, R.E. *The Gospel According to John I-XII*. The Anchor Bible 29; Garden City: Doubleday, 1966.

_____. *The Gospel According to John XIII-XX1*. The Anchor Bible 29A; Garden City: Doubleday, 1970.

Bruce, F. F. *New Testament History: Historical Foundation of the New Testament Story*. London: Thomas Nelson, 1977.

_____. 'Our God and Saviour,' The Saviour God: Comparative Studies in the Concept of Salvation presented to Edwin Oliver James by Colleagues and Friends to Commemorate his Seventy-fifth Birthday, eds. S.G.F. Brandon. Manchester: Manchester University Press, 1963, 51–66.

_____. 'The Background to the Son of Man Sayings,' in *Christ The Lord: Studies in Christology presented to D. Guthrie*, eds. H.H. Rowdon. Leicester: IVP, 1982, 50–70.

_____. Second Thoughts on the Dead Sea Scrolls. Exeter: Paternoster, 1961.

_____. *The Epistle to the Galatians: A Commentary on the Greek Text*. NIGTC; Grand Rapids: Eerdmans; Exeter: Paternoster, 1982.

_____. *The Gospel of John*. Grand Rapids: Eerdmans, 1994.

Brunson, A.C. *Psalm 118 in the Gospel of John: An Intertextual Study on the New Exodus Pattern in the Theology of John*. WUNT 2/158; Tübingen: Mohr Siebeck, 2003.

Bryan, S.M. *Jesus and Israel's Traditions of Judgment and Restoration*. SNTSMS 117; Cambridge: CUP, 2002.

Buchanan, G.W. 'Symbolic Money-Changers in the Temple?' *NTS* 37 (1991), 280–290.

Büchsel, F. *TDNT*, IV, 737–741.

Budd, P.J. *Numbers*. WBC 5; Word Books: Waco, 1984.

Bullock, C.H. 'Ezekiel, Bridge between the Testaments,' *JETS* 25/1 (1982), 23–31.

Bulman, J.M. 'The Only Begotten Son,' *CTJ* 16/1 (1981), 56–79.

Bultmann, R. 'The history of Religions Background of the Prologue to the Gospel of John,' *The Interpretation of John*, ed. J. Ashton. IRT 9; London: SPCK; Philadelphia: Fortress, 1986, 18–35.

_____. *TDNT*, I, 689–719.

_____. *The Gospel of John: A Commentary*, trans. G. R. Beasley-Murray. Oxford: Basil Blackwell, 1971.

_____. *Theology of the New Testament*, II, trans. K. Grobel. London: SCM, 1955.

Burge, G.M. 'Territorial Religion, Johannine Christology, and the Vineyard of John 15,' *Jesus of Nazareth Lord and Christ: Essays on the historical Jesus and New Testament Christology*, eds. J.B. Green and M. Turner. Grand Rapids: Eerdmans; Carlisle: Paternoster, 1994, 384–396.

_____. *John: The NIV Application Commentary*. Grand Rapids: Zondervan, 2000.

_____. *The Anointed Community: The Holy Spirit in the Johannine Tradition*. Grand Rapids: Eerdmans, 1987.

Burkett, D. *The Son of Man in the Gospel of John*. JSNT Supp 56; Sheffield: SAP, 1991.

Burney, C.F. *The Aramaic Origin of the Fourth Gospel*. Oxford: Clarendon, 1922.

Burrow, E.W. 'Did John the Baptist Call Jesus 'Lamb of God'?' *ExpT* 85 (1973/74), 245–247.

Byron, J. *Slavery Metaphors in Early Judaism and Pauline Christianity: A Traditio-historical and Exegetical Examination*. WUNT 2/162; Tübingen: Mohr Siebeck, 2003.

Campbell, R. *Israel and the New Covenant*. Philadelphia: Presbyterian and Reformed Pub., 1954.

Caragounis, C.C. 'Kingdom of God / Kingdom of Heaven,' *Dictionary of Jesus and the Gospels*, eds. J.G. Green, S. McKnight and I.H. Howard. Downer's Grove, IL: IVP, 1998, c. 1992, 417–430.

Carey, G.L. 'The Lamb of God and Atonement Theories,' *TynB* 32 (1981), 97–122.

Carmichael, C.M. 'Marriage and the Samaritan Woman,' *NTS* 26 (1979/80), 332–346.

_____. *The Story of Creation: Its Origin and Its Interpretation in Philo and the Fourth Gospel*. Ithaca and London: Cornell University Press, 1996.

Carroll, R.P. 'Deportation and Diasporic Discourses in the Prophetic Literature,' *Exile: Old Testament, Jewish, and Christian Conceptions*, eds. J.M. Scott. Leiden: Brill, 1997, 63–84.

Carson, D.A. 'John and the Johannine Epistles,' *It Is Written: Scripture Citing Scripture: Essays in Honour of B. Lindars*, eds. D.A. Carson and H.G.M. Williamson. Cambridge: CUP, 1988, 245–264.

_____. *The Gospel According to John.* Grand Rapids: Eerdmans; Leicester: IVP, 1991.

Casey, M. 'General, Generic, and Indefinite: The Use of the Term 'Son of Man' in Aramaic Sources and in the Teaching of Jesus,' *JSNT* 29 (1987), 21–56.

_____. 'Idiom and Translation: Some Aspects of the Son of Man Problem,' *NTS* 41 (1995), 164–182.

_____. 'Where Wright is Wrong: A Critical Review of N.T. Wright's Jesus and the Victory of God,' *JSNT* 69 (1998), 99–100.

_____. *The Son of Man: The Interpretation and Influence of Daniel 7.* London: SPCK, 1979.

Catchpole, D.R. 'The Triumphal Entry,' *Jesus and the Politics of his Day*, eds. E. Bammel and E.F.D. Moule. Cambridge: CUP, 1984, 319–334.

Cheon, S. *The Exodus Story in the Wisdom of Solomon: A Study in Biblical Interpretation.* JSPS Supp 23; Sheffield: SAP, 1997.

Chilton, B.D. and Davies, P. 'The Aqedah: A Revised Tradition History,' *CBQ* 40 (1978), 514–546.

Chilton, B.D. 'Isaac and the Second Night: A Consideration,' *Bib* 61 (1980), 78–82.

Cho, S. *The Cultic Image of Seraph and Nehushtan in the Bible in Light of Ancient Near Eastern World.* Ph.D. Dissertation, the University of Hebrew, 1994.

Clark, G.H. *The Johannine Logos.* Nutley, N.J: Presbyterian and Reformed Publishing, 1972.

Collins, J.J. 'The Son of God Text from Qumran,' *From Jesus to John: Essays on Jesus and New Testament Christology in Honour of Marinus de Jonge*, eds. M.C. De Boer. JSNT Supp 84; Sheffield: JSOT Press, 1993, 65–82.

_____. 'The Son of Man in First-Century Judaism,' *NTS* 38 (1992), 448–466.

_____. *The Scepter and the Star: The Messiah of the Dead Sea Scrolls and Other Ancient Literature.* Anchor Bible Reference Library; New York: Doubleday, 1996.

Collins, R.F. 'The Representative Figures of the Fourth Gospel-1,' *DR* 94 (1976), 26–46.

Coloe, M.L. *God Dwells with Us: Temple Symbolism in the Fourth Gospel.* Collegeville: Liturgical Press, 2001.

Colpe, C. *TDNT*, VIII, 430–477.

Conzelmann, H. *TDNT*, VII, 423–445.

Cooper, K.T. 'The Best Wine: John 2:1–11,' *WTJ* 41 (1979), 364–380.

Cosgrove, C.H. 'The Place Where Jesus Is: Allusions to Baptism and the Eucharist in the Fourth Gospel,' *NTS* 35 (1989), 522–539.

Cotterell, F.P. 'The Nicodemus Conversion: A Fresh Appraisal.' *ExpT* 96 (1985), 237–242.

Cranfield, C.E.B. *The Gospel According to Saint Mark: An Introduction and Commentary.* Cambridge: CUP, 1974.

Cullmann, O. 'Jesus the Word (lo,goj),' *The Christology of the New Testament*, trans. S.C. Guthrie and C.A.M. Hall. London: SCM, 1977, 249–269.

_____. *The Christology of the New Testament*, trans. S.C. Guthrie and C.A.M. Hall. London: SCM, 1977.

Culpepper, R. A. 'The Pivot of John's Prologue,' *NTS* 27 (1980/81), 1–31.

Dahl, N.A. 'The Johannine Church and History,' *Current Issues in the New Testament Interpretation: Essays in Honour of O.A. Piper*, eds, W. Klassen and G.F. Synder. New York: Harper and Row, 1962, 124–142.

Dahms, J.V. 'Isaiah 55:11 and the Gospel of John,' *EQ* 53 (1981), 78–88.

Danby, H. (trans.) *The Mishnah.* Oxford: Clarendon, 1933.

Daube, D. *The Exodus Pattern in the Bible.* London: Faber and Faber, 1963.

Davies, E.W. *Numbers.* NCBC; Grand Rapids: Eerdmans, 1995.

Davies, M. *Rhetoric and Reference in the Fourth Gospel.* JSNT Supp 69; Sheffield: JSOT Press, 1992.

Davies, P.R. 'Passover and the Dating of the Aqedah,' *JJS* 30 (1979), 59–67.

Davies, W.D. 'Reflections on Aspects of the Jewish Background of the Gospel of John,' *Exploring the Gospel of John in Honor of D. Moody Smith*, eds. R.A. Culpepper and C.C. Black. Louisville KT: Westminster John Knox Press, 1996, 43–64.

Davies, W.D. *The Gospel and the Land: Early Christianity and Jewish Territorial Doctrine.* Sheffield: JSOT Press, 1994.

Davis, J.C. 'The Johannine Concept of Eternal Life as a Present Possession,' *RQ* 27 (1984), 161–169.

Deeks, D. G. 'The Prologue of St. John's Gospel,' *BTB* 6 (1976), 62–78.

Dennis, J.A. *Jesus' Death and the Gathering of True Israel: The Johannine Appropriation of Restoration Theology in the Light of John 11:47–52*. WUNT 2/217; Tübingen: Mohr Siebeck, 2006.

Dennison, J.T. 'The Exodus and the People of God,' *BT* 171 (1977), 6–32.

Derrett, J.D.M. 'The Samaritan Woman's Pitcher,' *DR* 102 (1984), 252–261.

_____. 'The Zeal of the House and the Cleansing of the Temple,' *DR* 95 (1977), 79–94.

_____. *Law in the New Testament*. London: Darton, Longman and Todd, 1970.

Dodd, C.H. 'The Old Testament in the New,' *The Right Doctrine from the Wrong Texts?: Essays on the Use of the Old Testament in the New*, ed. G.K. Beale. Grand Rapids: Baker Books, 1994, 167–181.

_____. *According to the Scripture: The Substructure of New Testament Theology*. London: Nisbet, 1952.

_____. *Historical Tradition in the Fourth Gospel*. Cambridge: CUP, 1965.

_____. *Interpretation of the Fourth Gospel*. Cambridge: CUP, 1953.

Drapper, J.A. 'Temple, Tabernacle, and Mystical Experience in John,' *Neot* 31/2 (1997), 263–288.

Du Plessis, I.J. 'Christ as the 'Only Begotten,'' *Neot* 2 (1968), 22–31.

Dunn, J.D.G. 'Incarnation,' The Christology and The Spirit: Collected Essays of J.D.G. Dunn, Vol. I. Christology. Cambridge and Grand Rapids: Eerdmans, 1998, 30–47.

_____. 'Jesus and the Kingdom: How Would his Message have been Heard?' in *Neotestamentica et Philonica: Studies in Honour of Peder Borgen*, eds. D.A. Aune, T. Seland and J.H. Ulrichsen. NovT Supp 106; Leiden; Boston: Brill, 2003, 3–36.

_____. 'Paul's Understanding of the Death of Jesus,' *Reconciliation and Hope: Essays presented to L.L. Morris on his 60th Birthday*, ed. R. J. Banks. Exeter: Paternoster, 1974, 125–141.

_____. *Baptism in the Holy Spirit: A Re-examination of the New Testament Teaching on the Gift of the Spirit in Relation to Pentecostalism Today*. Philadelphia: Westminster Press, 1970.

_____. 'Let John be John; A Gospel for Its Time,' *The Christology and The Spirit: Collected Essays of J.D.G. Dunn, Vol. I. Christology*. Cambridge and Grand Rapids: Eerdmans, 1998, 345–375. Originally published in *Das Evangelium und die Evanelien. Vorträge vom Tübingen Symposium 1982*, ed. P. Stuhlmacher. Tübingen: Mohr, 1982, 309–339 = *The Gospel and the Gospels*, ed. P. Stuhlmacher. Grand Rapids: Eerdmans, 1991, 293–322.

_____. *Christology in the Making: A New Testament Inquiry into the Origin of the Doctrine of the Incarnation*. London: SCM, 1980.

Durham, J.I. *Exodus*. Waco, Tex: Word Books, 1987.

Edwards, R.B. 'ΧΑΡΙΝ ΑΝΤΙ ΧΑΡΙΤΟΣ (John 1:16): Grace and the Law in the Johannine Prologue,' *JSNT* 32 (1988), 3–15.

_____. 'The Christological Basis of the Johannine Footwashing,' *Jesus of Nazareth Lord and Christ: Essays on the historical Jesus and New Testament Christology*, eds. J.B. Green and M. Turner. Grand Rapids: Eerdmans; Carlisle: Paternoster, 1994, 367–383.

Endo, M. *Creation and Christology: A Study on the Johannine Prologue in the Light of Early Jewish Creation Accounts*. WUNT 2/149; Tübingen: Mohr Siebeck, 2002.

Ensor, P.W. 'The Glorification of the Son of Man: An Analysis of John 13:31–32,' *TynB* 58/2 (2007), 229–252.

Enz, J.J. 'The Afterlife of the Ninth Plague (Darkness) in Biblical Literature,' *The New Way of Jesus: Essays Presented to H. Charles*, ed. W. Klassen. Newton: Faith and Life Press, 1980, 29–38.

_____. 'The Book of Exodus as a Literary Type for the Gospel of John,' *JBL* 76 (1957), 208–215.

Erlandsson, S. 'The Wrath of YHWH,' *TynB* 23 (1972), 111–116.

Evans, C. A. *Word and Glory: On the Exegetical and Theological Background of John's Prologue*. JSNT Supp 89; Sheffield: SAP, 1993.

_____. 'Jesus and the Continuing Exile of Israel,' *Jesus and the Restoration of Israel: A Critical Assessment of N.T. Wright's Jesus and the Victory of God*, ed. C.C. Newman. Downers Grove: IVP, 1999, 77–100.

_____. 'Jesus' Action in the Temple Cleansing or Portent of Destruction,' *CBQ* 51 (1989), 237–270.

_____. 'Predictions of the Destruction of the Herodian Temple in the Pseudepigrapha, Qumran Scrolls, and Related Texts,' *JSP* 10 (1992), 89–147.

_____. *To See and Not Perceive: Isaiah 6:9–10 in Early Jewish and Christian Interpretation*. Sheffield: JSOT Press, 1989.

Evans, C.F. *Resurrection and the New Testament*. London: SCM, 1970.

Fallon, M. *The Gospel according to Saint John*. Kensington (Australia): Chevalier Press, 1998.

Fichtner, J. *TDNT*, V, 395–409

Fishbane, M. *Text and Texture: Close Reading of Selected Biblical Text*. New York: Schoken, 1979.

Fisk, B.N. 'Offering Isaac Again and Again: Pseudo-Philo's Use of the Aqedah as Intertext,' *CBQ* 62 (2000), 481–507.

Fitzmyer, J.A. 'The Contribution of Qumran Aramaic to the Study of the New Testament,' *NTS* 20 (1973/74), 382–407 (Cf. This article was reprinted in *A Wandering Aramean: Collected Aramaic Essays*. Missoula: Scholars Press, 1979, 85–113).

_____. 'The New Testament Title 'Son of Man' Philologically Considered,' *A Wandering Aramean: Collected Aramaic Essays*. Missoula: Scholars Press, 1979, 143–160.

_____. 'The Sacrifice of Isaac in Qumran Literature,' *Bib* 83 (2002), 211–229.

_____. *The Semitic Background of the New Testament: Combined Edition of Essays on the Semitic Background of the New Testament and A Wandering Aramean: Collected Aramaic Essays*. Grand Rapids and Cambridge: Eerdmans, 1997.

Foerster, W. and von Rad, G. *TDNT*, II, 400–420.

Forestell, J.T. *The Word of the Cross: Salvation as Revelation in the Fourth Gospel*. Rome: Biblical Institute Press, 1974.

Fowler, R. 'Born of Water and the Spirit (John 3:5),' *ExpT* 82 (1971), 159.

France, R.T. 'Jesus the Baptist?' *Jesus of Nazareth Lord and Christ: Essays on the historical Jesus and New Testament Christology*, eds. J.B. Green and M. Turner. Grand Rapids: Eerdmans; Carlisle: Paternoster, 1994, 94–111.

_____. 'The Servant of the Lord in the Teaching of Jesus,' *TynB* 19 (1968), 26–52.

_____. *Jesus and the Old Testament*. London: Tyndale, 1971.

_____. *The Gospel of Mark: A Commentary of Greek Texts*. NIGTC; Grand Rapids: Eerdmans; Carlisle: Paternoster, 2002.

Freed, E.D. 'Did John Write his Gospel Partly to Win Samaritan Converts?' *NovT* 12 (1970), 241–256.

_____. '*Ego Eimi* in John 1:20 and 4:25,' *CBQ* 41 (1979), 288–291.

_____. 'The Son of Man in the Fourth Gospel,' *JBL* 86 (1967), 402–409.

_____. *Old Testament Quotations in the Gospel of John*. NovT Supp 11; Leiden: Brill, 1965.

Fretheim, T.E. *Exodus: Interpretation- A Bible Commentary for Teaching and Preaching*. Louisville: John Knox Press, 1991.

Friedrich, G. *TDNT*, II, 707–737.

Fries, G. *NIDNTT*, III, 1081–1087.

Garnet, P. 'The Baptism of Jesus and the Son of Man Idea,' *JSNT* 9 (1980), 49–65.

Gärtner, B. *The Temple and the Community in Qumran and the New Testament*. Cambridge: CUP, 1965.

Gaston, L. *No Stone on Another: Studies in the Significance of the Fall of Jerusalem in the Synoptic Gospels*. Leiden: Brill, 1970.

Glasson, T.F. *Moses in the Fourth Gospel*. London: SCM, 1963.

Goldingay, J.E. *Daniel*. WBC 30; Dallas, Word Book, 1989.

Goppelt, L. *TDNT*, VIII, 314–333.

_____. *Theology of The New Testament* Vol. I, trans. J.E. Alsup. Grand Rapids: Eerdmans, 1981.

_____. *Theology of The New Testament Vol. II: The Variety and Unity of the Apostolic Witness to Christ*, trans. J.E. Alsup. Grand Rapids: Eerdmans, 1982.

_____. *Typos: The Typological Interpretation of the Old Testament in the New*, trans. D.H. Madvig. Grand Rapids: Eerdmans, 1982.

Grassi, J.A. 'Ezekiel 37:1–14 and the New Testament,' *NTS* 11 (1964/65), 162–164.

_____. 'The Wedding at Cana (John 2:1–11): A Pentecostal Meditation?' *NovT* 14 (1972), 131–136.

Grayston, K. 'Who Misunderstands the Johannine Misunderstandings?' *SB* 20 (1989), 9–15.

Grese, W.C. 'Unless One is Born Again: The Use of a Heavenly Journey in John 3,' *JBL* 107 (1988), 677–698.

Grether, O. and Fichtner, J. *TDNT*, V, 409–412.

Griffith, H. 'Eschatology Begins with Creation,' *WTJ* 49 (1987), 387–396.

Grigsby, B.H. 'The Cross as an Expiatory Sacrifice in the Fourth Gospel,' *JSNT* 15 (1982), 51–80. This article was again published in *The Johannine Writings*, eds. S.E. Porter and C.A. Evans. Sheffield: SAP, 1995, 69–94.

Gruenwald, I. *Apoclyptic and Merkabah Mysticism*. Leiden: Brill, 1980.

Grundmann, W. *TDNT*, II, 21–25.

Guelich, R.A. *Mark 1–8:26*. WBC 34 A; Dallas: Words Books, 1989.

Guilding, A. *The Fourth Gospel and Jewish Worship: A Study of the Relation of St John's Gospel to the Ancient Jewish Lectionary System*. Oxford: Clarendon, 1960.

Gundry, R.H. 'In My Father's House are Many monh,' (John 14:2),' *ZNW* 58 (1967), 68–72.

_____. *Mark: A Commentary on his Apology for the Cross*. Grand Rapids, Eerdmans, 1993.

_____. *Matthew: A Commentary on his Handbook for a Mixed Church under Persecution*. 2nd ed; Grand Rapids: Eerdmans, 1994.

Gundry, R.H. and Howell, R.W. 'The Sense and Syntax of John 3:14–17 with Special Reference to the Use of 'ou[twj....w[ste' in John 3:16,' *NovT* 41 (1999), 24–39.

Günther, W. *NIDNTT*, II, 575–577.

Haenchen, E. *John 1: A Commentary on the Gospel of John Chapters 1–6*, trans. R.W. Funk. Philadelphia: Fortress Press, 1984.

Hagner, D.A. *Matthew 1–13*. WBC 33A; Dallas: Word Books, 1993.

Hahn, H.-C. *NIDNTT*, I, 421–425.

Halpern-Amaru, B. 'Exile and Return in Jubilees,' *Exile: Old Testament, Jewish, and Christian Conceptions*, eds. J.M. Scott. Leiden: Brill, 1997, 127–144.

Ham, C. 'The Title 'Son of Man' in the Gospel of John,' *SCJ* 1/2 (1998), 67–84.

Hamilton, V.P. *NIDOTTE*, I, 1153–1154.

Hansen, S.E. 'Forgiving and Retaining Sin: A Study of the Text and Context of John,' *HBT* 19 (1997), 24–32.

Hanson, A.T. 'John 1:14–18 and Exodus xxxiv,' *NTS* 23 (1976/1977), 90–101.

_____. 'John's Use of Scripture,' *The Gospels and the Scriptures of Israel*, eds. C.A. Evans and W.R. Stegner. JSNT Supp 104; Sheffield: SAP, 1994, 358–379.

_____. *The Prophetic Gospel: A Study of John and the Old Testament*. Edinburgh: T&T Clark, 1991.

Harner, P.B. 'Creation Faith in Deutero-Isaiah,' *VT* 17 (1967), 298–306.

_____. *The 'I Am' of the Fourth Gospel: A Study in Johannine Usage and Thought*. Facet Books; Philadelphia: Fortress, 1970.

Harris, E. *Prologue and Gospel: The Theology of the Fourth Evangelist*. JSNTSupp. 107; Sheffield: SAP, 1994.

Harris, M. J. and Brown, C. *NIDNTT*, III, 811–816.

Harris, M.J. *Jesus as God: The New Testament Use of Theos in Reference to Jesus*. Grand Rapids, Mich: Baker Book House, 1992.

_____. *NIDNTT*, III, 1171–1215.

Harris, R. *The Origin of the Prologue to St John's Gospel*. Cambridge: CUP, 1917.

Harrison, E.F. 'A Study of John 1:14,' *Unity and Diversity in the New Testament Theology: Essays in Honour of G. E. Ladd*, eds. R. A. Guelich. Grand Rapids: Eerdmans, 1978, 23–36.

Harstine, S. *Moses as a Character in the Fourth Gospel: A Study of Ancient Reading Technique*. JSNT Supp 229; Sheffield: SAP, 2002.

Hayward, C.R.T. 'The Sacrifice of Isaac and Jewish Polemic Against Christianity,' *CBQ* 52 (1990), 292–306.

Hebert, A.G. *The Form of the Church*. London: Faber and Faber, 1944.

Hengel, M. 'The Interpretation of the Wine Miracle at Cana: John 2:1–11,' *The Glory of Christ in the NT: Studies in Christology in Memory of G.B. Caird*, eds. L.D. Hurst and N.T. Wright. Oxford: Clarendon, 1987, 83–112.

_____. 'The Old Testament in the Fourth Gospel,' *The Gospels and the Scriptures of Israel*, eds. C.A. Evans and W.R. Stegner. JSNT Supp 104; Sheffield: SAP, 1994, 380–395.

_____. 'The Old Testament in the Fourth Gospel,' *HBT* 12 (1990), 19–41.

_____. *Judaism and Hellenism: Studies in Their Encounter in Palestine during the Early Hellenistic Period*, Vol. I, II, trans. J. Bowden. London: SCM, 1974.

_____. *Studies in Early Christology*. Edinburgh: T&T Clark, 1995.

_____. *The Atonement: The Origin of the Doctrine in the New Testament*, trans. J. Bowden. London: SCM, 1981.

_____. *The Son of God: The Origin of Christology and the History of Jewish-Hellenistic Religion*, trans. J. Bowden. London: SCM, 1976.

Hengel, M. with the collaboration of D.P. Bailey, 'The Effective History of Isaiah 53 in the Pre-Christian Period,' in *The Suffering Servant: Isaiah 53 in Jewish and Christian Sources*, eds. B. Janowski and P. Stuhlmacher, trans. D.P. Bailey. Grand Rapids: Eerdmans, 2004, 75–146.

Hiers, R.H. 'Purification of the Temple: Preparation for the Kingdom of God,' *JBL* 90 (1972), 82–91.

Hill, C.E. 'The Identity of John's Nathanael,' *JSNT* 67 (1997), 45–61.

Hodges, Z.C. 'Coming to the Light – John 3:20–21,' *BS* 135 (1978), 314–322.

_____. 'Water and Spirit-John 3:5,' *BS* 135 (1978), 206–220.

Holland, T.S. *Contours of Pauline Theology: A Radical New Survey of the Influence on Paul's Biblical Writings*. Fearn: Mentor, 2004.

_____. *The Paschal-New Exodus Motif in Paul's Letter to the Romans with Special Reference to Its Christological Significance*. Ph.D Dissertation, the University of Wales, Lampeter, 1996.

Hollis, H. 'The Root of the Johannine Pun- u`ywqh/nai,' *NTS* 35 (1989), 475–478.

Holwerda, D.E. *Jesus and Israel: One Covenant or Two?*. Grand Rapids: Eerdmans; Leicester: Apollos, 1995.

Hooker, M. D. 'The Johannine Prologue and the Messianic Secret,' *NTS* 21 (1974/75), 40–58.

_____. 'Did the Use of Isaiah 53 to Interpret his Mission Begin with Jesus?' *Jesus and the Suffering Servant: Isaiah 53 and Christian Origins*, eds. W.H. Bellinger and W.R. Farmer. Harrisburg, Pennsylvania: Trinity Press International, 1998, 88–103.

_____. 'Traditions about the Temple in the Sayings of Jesus,' *BJRL* 70 (1988), 7–19.

_____. *Studying the New Testament*. Southampton: Epworth Press, 1989.

_____. *The Son of Man in Mark: A Study of the Background of the Term 'Son of Man' and its Use in St Mark's Gospel*. London: SPCK, 1967.

Hoskyns, E. *The Fourth Gospel* (ed. by F.N. Davey): 2 Vols. London: Faber and Faber, 1940.

Howard, J.K. 'Passover and Eucharist in the Fourth Gospel,' *SJT* 20 (1967), 329–337.

Howard-Brook, W. *Becoming Children of God: John's Gospel and Radical Discipleship*. Maryknoll, New York: Orbis Books, 1999.

Howton, D.J. 'Son of God in the Fourth Gospel,' *NTS* 10 (1963/64), 227–237.

Hunter, A.M. *According to John*. London: SCM, 1968.

_____. *Introducing the New Testament*. London; SCM, 1957.

Hunzinger, C.-H. *TDNT*, VI, 976–984.

Jeremias, J. 'The Revealing Word,' *The Central Message of the New Testament*. London; SCM, 1965, 71–90.

_____. *Infant Baptism in the First Four Centuries*, trans. D. Cairns. London: 1960.

_____. *Jerusalem in the Time of Jesus: An Investigation into Economic and Social Conditions during the New Testament Period*, trans. F.H. and C.H. Cave. London: SCM, 1969.

_____. *New Testament Theology*, I, trans. J. Bowden. London: SCM, 1971.

_____. *TDNT*, I, 185–186.

_____. *TDNT*, I, 338–341

_____. *TDNT*, III, 744–753.

_____. *TDNT*, IV, 848–873.

_____. *TDNT*, IV, 1099–1106.

_____. *TDNT*, V, 677–717.

_____. *The Eucharistic Words of Jesus*, trans. N. Perrin. London: SCM, 1973.

Johnston, G. The Spirit-Paraclete in the Gospel of John. Cambridge: CUP, 1970.

Jones, I.H. 'Disputed Questions in Biblical Studies: 4 Exile and Eschatology,' *ExpT* 112 (2000), 401–405.

Jones, L.P. *The Symbol of Water in the Gospel of John*. JSNT Supp 145; Sheffield: SAP, 1997.

Jonge, M. de. *Jesus: Stranger from Heaven and Son of God- Jesus Christ and the Christians in Johannine Perspective*. Missoula: Scholars Press, 1977.

Juel, D. *Messiah and Temple: The Trial of Jesus in the Gospel of Mark*. Missoula: Scholars Press, 1977.

Kanagaraj, J.J. *Mysticism in the Gospel of John: An Inquiry into Its Background*. JSNT Supp 158; Sheffield: Sheffield Academic Press, 1998.

Kasemann, E. *New Testament Questions of Today*. London: SCM, 1969.

Keck, L.E. 'The Spirit and the Dove,' *NTS* 17 (1970/71), 41–67.

Keddie, G.J. *A Study Commentary on John: Vol. 1 Chapters 1–12*. Darlington: Evangelical Press, 2001.

Keener, C.S. *The Gospel of John: A Commentary*. Peabody: Hendrickson, 2003.

Kelber, W.H. *The Kingdom in Mark: A New Place and a New Time*. Philadelphia: Fortress Press, 1974.

Kerr, A.R. *The Temple of Jesus' Body: The Temple Theme in the Gospel of John*. JSNT Supp 220; Sheffield: SAP, 2002.

Kim, S. 'Interpretation of Jesus' Death in the New Testament,' *Essays on Jesus and Paul*. 2nd ed.; Seoul: Chammal, 1993, 195–248. The English version of the article was lectured in 'The 1993 Harold John Ockenga Lectures' at Gorden-Conwell Theological Seminary. South Hamilton, Mass. on 8th-12th, Feb, 1993.

_____. 'Jesus and the Temple,' *ACTSTJ* 3(1988), 87–131.

_____. 'Jesus- The Son of God, the Stone, the Son of Man, and the Servant: The Role of Zechariah in the Self-Identification of Jesus,' in *Tradition and Interpretation in the New Testament*, eds. G.F. Hawthorne and O. Betz. Grand Rapids: Eerdmans; Tübingen: J.C.B. Mohr. Paul Siebeck, 1987, 134–148.

_____. 'Jesus' Baptism and Trials,' *Essays on Jesus and Paul*. 2nd ed.; Seoul: Chammal, 1993, 13–39.

_____. 'Jesus' Proclamation of the Kingdom of God and Christian's Political Reality,' *Essays on Jesus and Paul*. 2nd ed.; Seoul: Chammal, 1993, 89–118.

_____. 'Peace in the New Testament,' *Essays on Jesus and Paul*. 2nd ed.; Seoul: Chammal, 1993, 279–303.

_____. *Exposition of John's Gospel*. Seoul: Tyrannus, 2002.

_____. *Paul and the New Perspective: Second Thoughts on the Origin of Paul's Gospel*. Grand Rapids and Cambridge: Eerdmans, 2002.

_____. *The Origin of Paul's Gospel*. Grand Rapids: Eerdmans, 1981.

_____. *The Son of Man as the Son of God*. Grand Rapids: Eerdmans, 1985.

King, J.S. 'Nicodemus and the Pharisees,' *ExpT* 98 (1986), 45.

Kittel, G. *TDNT*, I, 5–6.

_____. *TDNT*, II, 242–255.

Klappert, B. *NIDNTT*, II, 372–390.

_____. *NIDNTT*, III, 1087–1117.

Kleinknecht, H. *TDNT*, IV, 77–91.

Kleinknecht, H., von Rad, G., Kuhn, G.K., and Schmidt, K.L. *TDNT*, I, 564–593.

Knibb, M.A. 'Life and Death in the Old Testament,' *The World of Ancient Israel*, ed. R.E. Clements. Cambridge: CUP, 1993, 395–415.

_____. 'The Exile in the Literature of the Interestamental Period,' *HeyJ* 17 (1976), 253–272.

Koester, C.R. 'Hearing, Seeing, and Believing in the Gospel of John,' *Bib* 70 (1989), 327–348.

_____. 'Messianic Exegesis and the Call of Nathanael (John 1:45–51),' *JSNT* 39 (1990), 23–34.

_____. "The Saviour of the World' (John 4:42),' *JBL* 109 (1990), 665–680.

_____. *Symbolism in the Fourth Gospel: Meaning, Mystery, Community*. Minneapolis: Fortress, 1995.

_____. *The Dwelling of the God: The Tabernacle in the Old Testament, Intertestamental Jewish Literature, and the New Testament*. Washington: Catholic Biblical Association of America, 1989.

Köstenberger, A.J. *Encountering John: The Gospel in historical, Literary, and Theological Perspective*. Grand Rapids: Baker Academic, 1999.

Kruijf, T.C. de. 'The Glory of the Only Son (John 1:14),' *Studies in John presented to Professor Dr. J.N. Sevenster: On the Occasion of his Seventieth Birthday*, ed. M.C. Rientsma. NovT Supp 24; Leiden: Brill, 1970, 111–123.

Kugel, J. 'The Ladder of Jacob,' *HTR* 88 (1995), 209–227.

Kurz, W.S. 'Intertextual Permutations of the Genesis Word in the Johannine Prologues,' *Early Christian Interpretation of the Scriptures of Israel*, eds. C.A. Evans and J.A. Sanders. JSNT Supp 148; Sheffield: SAP, 1997, 179–190.

Kysar, R. *John*. ACNT; Minneapolis, Minn.: Augsburg Publishing House, 1986.

_____. *The Fourth Evangelist and his Gospel: An Examination of Contemporary Scholarship*. Minneapolis: Augsburg, 1975.

Ladd, G.E. 'The Kingdom of God- Reign or Realm?' *JBL* 81 (1962), 230–238.

Lamarche, P. 'The Prologue of John' *The Interpretation of John*, ed. J. Ashton. IRT 9; London: SPCK; Philadelphia: Fortress, 1986, 36–52.

Lang, F. *TDNT*, VI, 928–952.

_____. *TDNT*, VII, 456–457.

Lee, D. *Flesh and Glory: Symbolism, Gender and Theology in the Gospel of John*. New York: Crossroad, 2002.

_____. *The Symbolic Narratives of the Fourth Gospel: The Interplay of Form and Meaning*. JSNT Supp 95; Sheffield: JSOT Press, 1994.

Lieu, J. M. 'Gnosticism and the Gospel of John,' *ExpT* 90 (1979), 233–237.

_____. 'Blindness in the Johannine Tradition,' *NTS* 34 (1988), 83–95.

Lightfoot, R.H. *St John's Gospel: A Commentary*, eds. C.F. Evans. Oxford: Clarendon, 1956.

Lincoln, A.T. *Truth on Trial: The Lawsuit Motif in the Fourth Gospel*. Peabody, MA: Hendrickson, 2000.

Lindars, B. 'John and the Synoptic Gospels: A Test Case,' *NTS* 27 (1980/81), 287–294.

_____. 'Re-Enter the Apocalyptic Son of Man,' *NTS* 22 (1975/76), 52–72.

_____. 'Salvation Proclaimed VII. Mark 10:45: A Ransom for Many,' *ExpT* 93 (1982), 292–295.

_____. 'The Place of the Old Testament in the Formation of New Testament Theology,' *The Right Doctrine from the Wrong Texts?: Essays on the Use of the Old Testament in the New*, ed. G.K. Beale. Grand Rapids: Baker Books, 1994, 137–145.

_____. 'Two Parables in John,' *NTS* 16 (1969/70), 318–329.

_____. *The Gospel of John*. NCB; London: Oliphants, 1977.

Link, H.-G. *NIDNTT*, II, 476–484.

Loader, W.R.G. 'The Central Structure of Johannine Christology,' *NTS* 30 (1984), 188–216.

Locke, J.W. 'The Wrath of God in the Book of Isaiah,' *RQ* 35/4 (1993), 221–233.

Lohse, E. 'Miracles in the Fourth Gospel,' *What about the New Testament?: Essays in Honour of Christopher Evans*, eds. M. Hooker and C. Hickling. London: SCM, 1975, 64–75.

Longenecker, B.W. *The Triumph of Abraham's God: The Transformation of Identity in Galatians*. Edinburgh: T&T Clark, 1998.

Longenecker, R.N. *The Christology of Early Jewish Christianity*. London: SCM, 1970.

Longman, T. (III) and Reid, D.G. *God is a Warrior*. Carlisle: Paternoster, 1995.

Lund, N.W. 'The Influence of Chiasmus upon the Structure of the Gospels,' *ATR* 13 (1931), 41–46.

Maccini, R.G. 'A Reassessment of the Woman at the Well in John 4 in Light of the Samaritan Context,' *JSNT* 53 (1994), 35–46.

MacGregor, G.H.C. *The Gospel of John*. London: Hodder and Stoughton, 1949.

Mackay, J.L. *Exodus: A Mentor Commentary*. Fearn, Ross-Shire: Christian Focus Publications, 2001.

Maddox, R. 'The Function of the Son of Man in the Gospel of John,' in *Reconciliation and Hope: New Testament Essays on Atonement and Eschatology Presented to L.L. Morris on his 60th Birthday*, ed. R.J. Banks. Exeter: Paternoster, 1974, 186–204.

Malina, B.J. and Rohrbaugh, R.L. *Social-Science Commentary on the Gospel of John*. Minneapolis: Fortress, 1998.

Manson, T.W. 'The Johannine Logos Doctrine,' *On Paul and John: Some Selected Theological Themes*, ed. M. Black. London: SCM, 1963, 136–160.

_____. 'The Son of Man in Daniel, Enoch and the Gospels,' in *BJRL* 32 (1950), 171–193.

_____. *The Servant-Messiah: A Study of the Public Ministry of Jesus*. Grand Rapids: Baker Book House, 1984.

_____. *The Teaching of Jesus: Studies of Its Form and Content*. Cambridge: CUP, 1955.

Marcus, J. *The Way of the Lord: Christological Exegesis of the Old Testament in the Gospel of Mark*. Edinburgh: T&T Clark, 1993.

Marshall, I.H. 'An Assessment of Recent Developments,' *The Right Doctrine from the Wrong Texts?: Essays on the Use of the Old Testament in the New*, ed. G.K. Beale. Grand Rapids: Baker Books, 1994, 195–216. This article was originally published in *It Is Written: Scripture Citing Scripture: Essays in Honour of B. Lindars*, eds. D.A. Carson and H.G.M. Williamson. Cambridge: CUP, 1988, 1–21.

_____. 'Incarnational Christology in the New Testament,' *Christ The Lord: Studies in Christology presented to D. Guthrie*, ed. H.H. Rowdon. Leicester: IVP, 1982, 1–16.

_____. 'Lamb of God,' *Dictionary of Jesus and the Gospels*, eds. J.B. Green, S. McKnight and I.H. Marshall. Leicester: IVP, 1992, 432–434.

_____. 'Son of God or Servant of Yahweh?- A Reconsideration of Mark 1:11,' *NTS* 15 (1968/69), 326–336.

_____. 'The Development of the Concept of Redemption in the New Testament,' *Reconciliation and Hope: New Testament Essays on Atonement and Eschatology Presented to L.L. Morris on his 60th Birthday*, ed. R.J. Banks. Exeter: Paternoster, 1974, 153–169.

_____. 'The Hope of a New Age: The Kingdom of God in the New Testament,' *Themelios* 11 (1985), 5–15.

_____. 'The Son of Man in Contemporary Debate,' *EQ* 42 (1970), 67–87.

_____. *A Critical and Exegetical Commentary on The Pastoral Epistles*. ICC; Edinburgh: T&T Clark, 1999.

_____. *Last Supper and Lord's Supper*. Carlisle: Paternoster, 1997.

_____. *The Gospel of Luke: A Commentary on the Greek Text*. NIGTC; Grand Rapids: Eerdmans; Carlisle: Paternoster, 1995.

_____. *The Origins of New Testament Christology*. Updated edition. Leicester: Apollos, 1990.

Martyn, J.L. *History and Theology in the Fourth Gospel*. Nashville: Abingdon, 1979.

McGrath, J.F. *John's Apologetic Christology: Legitimation and Development in Johannine Christology*. SNTSMS 111; Cambridge: CUP, 2001.

McKelvy, R.J. *The New Temple: The Church in the New Testament*. Oxford: OUP, 1969.

McKnight, S. *A New Vision for Israel: The Teachings of Jesus in National Context*. Grand Rapids and Cambridge: Eerdmans, 1999.

McNamara, M. 'Logos of the Fourth Gospel and Memra of the Palestinian Targum (Exod 12^{42}),' *ExpT* LXXIX (1967/68), 115–117.

_____. *Targum Neofiti 1: Genesis*. The Aramaic Bible 1A; Edinburgh: T&T Clark, 1992.

Mead, A.H. 'The basiliko.j in John 4:46–53,' *JSNT* 23 (1985), 69–72.

Meeks, W.A. 'The Man from Heaven in Johannine Sectarianism,' *JBL* 91 (1972), 44–72.

_____. 'Galilee and Judea in the Fourth Gospel,' *JBL* 85 (1966), 159–169.

_____. *The Prophet-King: Moses Traditions and the Johannine Christology.* NovT Supp 14; Leiden: Brill, 1967.

Menken, M.J.J. 'The Christology of the Fourth Gospel: A Survey of Recent Research,' *From Jesus To John: Essays on Jesus and New Testament Christology in Honour of Marinus de Jonge*, ed. M.C. De Boer. JSNT Supp 84; Sheffield: SAP, 1993, 292–320.

_____. 'The Quotation from Isa 40:3 in John 1:23,' *Bib* 66 (1985), 190–205.

_____. *Old Testament Quotations in the Fourth Gospel: Studies in Textual Form.* Kampen: Kok Pharos Publishing House, 1996.

Meyer, B.F. *The Aims of Jesus.* London: SCM, 1979.

Michaelis, W. *TDNT,* VII, 368–394.

Michaels, J.R. *John.* NIBC; Peabody: Hendrickson Publishers; Carlisle: Paternoster, 1998.

Michel, O. *NIDNTT,* III, 607–613, 613–634, 634–648.

_____. *TDNT,* IV, 880–890.

Milikowsky, C. 'Notions of Exile, Subjugation and Return in Rabbinic Literature,' *Exile: Old Testament, Jewish and Christian Conceptions*, ed. J.M. Scott. JSJ Supp 56; Leiden: Brill, 1997, 265–296.

Miller, Ed. L. 'The Johannine Origin of the Johannine Logos,' *JBL* 112 (1993), 445–457.

Milne, B. *The Message of John.* BST; Leicester: IVP, 1993.

Miranda, J. *Being and the Messiah: The Message of St. John.* Maryknoll, NY: Orbis Books, 1977.

Moloney, F.J. 'Reading John 2:13–22: The Purification of the Temple,' *RB* 97 (1990), 432–453.

_____. 'The Fourth Gospel and the Jesus of history,' *NTS* 46 (2000), 42–58.

_____. *Belief in the Word: Reading John 1–4.* Minneapolis: Fortress Press, 1993.

_____. *The Gospel of John.* Collegeville: Liturigical Press, 1998.

_____. *The Johannine Son of Man.* 2nd ed.; Roma: Libreria Ateneo Salesiano, 1978.

Morris, L. *Galatians: Paul's Charter of Christian Freedom*. Leicester: IVP, 1996.

_____. *The Gospel according to John*. Rev. Ed., NICNT; Grand Rapids: Eerdmans, 1995.

_____. *The Gospel according to Matthew*. Grand Rapids: Eerdmans; Leicester: IVP, 1995.

Motyer, J.A. *The Prophecy of Isaiah*. Leicester: IVP, 1995.

Motyer, S. *Your Father The Devil?: A New Approach to John and 'the Jews'*. Carlisle: Paternoster, 1997.

Moule, C.F.D. 'A Note on 'Under the Fig Tree' in John 1:48, 50,' *JTS* 5 (1954), 210–211.

_____. 'The Son of Man': Some of the Facts,' *NTS* 41 (1995), 277–279.

_____. *The Origin of Christology*. Cambridge, London, New York and Melbourne: CUP, 1978.

Müller, D. and Brown, C. *NIDNTT*, II, 729–734.

Mundle, W. *NIDNTT*, I, 320–324.

Munro, W. 'The Pharisee and the Samaritan in John: Polar or Parallel?' *CBQ* 57 (1995), 710–728.

Nel, P.J. *NIDOTE*, IV, 130–135.

Neufeld, D. "And When That One Comes': Aspects of Johannine Messianism,' *Eschatology, Messianism and the Dead Sea Scrolls*, eds. C.A. Evans and P.W. Flint. Grand Rapids: Eerdmans, 1997, 120–140.

Neusner, J. 'Exile and Return as the history of Judaism,' *Exile: Old Testament, Jewish, and Christian Conceptions*, eds. J.M. Scott. Leiden: Brill, 1997, 221–237.

_____. 'Money-Changers in the Temple: The Mishnah's Explanation,' *NTS* 35 (1989), 287–290.

Neyrey, J.H. 'Jacob Traditions and the Interpretation of John 4:10–26,' *CBQ* 41 (1979), 419–437.

_____. 'The Jacob Allusions in John 1:51,' *CBQ* 44 (1982), 586–605.

Neyrey. J.H. and Rohrbaugh, R.L. 'He Must Increase, I Must Decrease' (John 3:30): A Cultural and Social Interpretation,' *CBQ* 63 (2001), 465–483.

Ng, W.Y. *Water Symbolism in John*. New York: Peter Lang, 2001.

Nixon, R.E. *The Exodus in the New Testament*. London: Tyndale Press, 1963.

Nolland, J. *Luke 1–9:20*. WBC 35A; Dallas: Word Books, 1989.

O'Neill, J.C. 'The Lamb of God in the Testaments of the Twelve Patriarchs,' *JSNT* 2 (1979), 2–30.

Odeberg, H. *The Fourth Gospel: Interpreted in its Relation to Contemporaneous Religious Currents in Palestine and the Hellenistic-Oriental World*. Amsterdam: B. R. Grüner 1968.

Oliver, W.H. and van Aarde, A.G. 'The Community of Faith as Dwelling-Place of the Father: basilei,a tou/ qeou/ as 'Household of God' in Johannine Farewell Discourse(s),' *Neot* 25 (1991), 379–400.

Opeke, A. *TDNT*, I, 394–397.

Osborne, B. 'A Folded Napkin in an Empty Tomb: John 11:44 and 20:7 Again,' *HeyJ* 14 (1973), 437–440.

Osburn, C.D. 'Some Exegetical Observations on John 3:5–8,' *RQ* 31 (1989), 129–138.

Owen, P. and Shepherd, D. 'Speaking Up for Qumran, Dalman and the Son of Man: Was *Bar Enasha* a Common Term of 'Man' in the Time of Jesus?' *JSNT* 81 (2001), 81–122.

Pack, F. 'The Holy Spirit in the Fourth Gospel,' *RQ* 31/3 (1989), 139–148.

Painter, J. *The Quest for the Messiah: The history, Literature and Theology of the Johannine Community*. Edinburgh: T&T Clark, 1991.

_____. 'Christology and the history of the Johannine Community in the Prologue of the Fourth Gospel,' *NTS* 30 (1984), 460–474.

Pamment, M. 'Is There Convincing Evidence of Samaritan Influence in the Fourth Gospel?' *ZNW* 73 (1982), 221–230.

_____. 'John 3:5: Unless One is Born of Water and the Spirit, he Cannot Enter the Kingdom of God,' *NovT* 25 (1983), 189–190.

Pao, D. *Acts and the Isaianic New Exodus*. WUNT 2/130; Tübingen: Mohr Siebeck, 2000.

Pazdan, M.M. 'Nicodemus and the Samaritan Woman: Contrasting Models of Discipleship,' *BTB* 17 (1987), 145–148.

Peisker, C.H. and Brown, C. *NIDNTT*, II, 726–729.

Pesch, R. 'He will be called a Nazorean: Messianic Exegesis in Matthew 1–2,' *The Gospels and the Scriptures of Israel*, eds. C.A. Evans and W.R. Stegner. JSNT Sup 104; Sheffield: SAP, 1994, 129–178.

Pitre, B. *Jesus, The Tribulation, and the End of the Exile: Restoration Eschatology and the Origin of the Atonement.* Tübingen: Mohr Siebeck; Grand Rapids: Baker Academic, 2005.

Polhill, J.B. 'John 1-4: The Revelation of True Life,' *RE* 85 (1985), 445-457.

Porter, S.E. 'Can Traditional Exegesis Enlighten Literary Analysis of the Fourth Gospel?: An Examination of the Old Testament Fulfillment motif and the Passover Theme,' *The Gospels and the Scriptures of Israel*, eds. C.A. Evans and W.R. Stegner. JSNT Supp 104; Sheffield: SAP, 1994, 396-428.

Price, J.D. *NIDOTTE*, I, 479-481.

_____. *NIDOTTE*, II, 312-315.

Pryor, J.W. 'Jesus and Israel in the Fourth Gospel- John 1:11', *NovT* 32 (1990), 210-218.

_____. 'John 3.3,5: A Study in the Relation of John's Gospel to the Synoptic Tradition,' *JSNT* 41 (1991), 71-95.

_____. 'John 4:44 and the *Patris* of Jesus,' *CBQ* 49 (1987), 254-263.

_____. 'John the Baptist and Jesus: Tradition and Text in John 3:25,' *JSNT* 66 (1997), 15-26.

_____. 'Of the Virgin Birth or the Birth of Christian?: The Text of John 1:13 Once More,' *NovT* 27 (1985), 296-318.

_____. 'The Johannine Son of Man and the Descent-Ascent motif,' in *JETS* 34/3 (1991), 341-351.

Ra, K. *Old Testament Christological Development.* London: Apostolos: Forthcoming.

Reiser, M. *Jesus and Judgment: The Eschatological Proclamation in Its Jewish Context*, trans. L.M. Maloney. Minneapolis: Fortress, 1997.

Reisser, H. *NIDNTT*, II, 587-589.

Rengstorf, K.H. *NIDNTT*, II, 332-334.

_____. *TDNT*, VII, 200-269.

Ridderbos, H. *The Coming of the Kingdom*, trans. H. de Jongste. Philadelphia: Presbyterian and Reformed Publishing Company, 1962.

_____. *The Gospel According to John: A Theological Commentary.* Grand Rapids: Eerdmans, 1997.

Ringwald, A. *NIDNTT*, I, 176-180.

Rissi, M. 'John 1:1-18: The Eternal Word,' *Interpretation* 31 (1977), 394-401.

Roberts, J.W. 'Some Observations on the Meaning of 'Eternal Life' in the Gospel of John,' *RQ* 7 (1963), 186–193.

Robertson, O.P. 'A New-Covenant Perspective on the Land,' *The Land of Promise: Biblical, Theological and Contemporary Perspectives*, eds. P. Johnston and P. Walker. Downers Grove, IL: IVP/Apollos, 2000, 121–141.

Robinson, D.W.B. 'Born of Water and Spirit: Does John 3:5 refer to Baptism?' *RTR* 25 (1966), 15–23.

Robinson, G.D. 'The Motif of Deafness and Blindness in Isaiah 6:9–10: A Contextual, Literary, and Theological Analysis,' *BBR* 8 (1998), 167–186.

Robinson, H.W. *Corporate Personality in Ancient Israel*, rev. ed. with a New introduction by C.S. Rodd. Edinburgh: T&T Clark, 1981.

Robinson, J.A.T. 'Elijah, John and Jesus: An Essay in Detection,' *NTS* 4 (1957/58), 263–281.

_____. 'The Relation of the Prologue to the Gospel of St. John,' *NTS* 9 (1962/63), 120–129.

_____. *The Priority of John*. London: SCM, 1985.

Robinson, J.M. 'Gnosticism and the New Testament,' *Gnosis: Festschrift für Hans Jonas*, eds. B. Aland and U. Bianchi. Göttingen: Vandenhoek and Ruprecht, 1978, 125–143.

_____. 'The Johannine Trajectory,' *Trajectories through Early Christianity*, eds. J. M. Robinson and H. Koester. Philadelphia: Fortress Press, 1971, 232–268.

Rogerson, J.W. 'The Hebrew Concept of Corporate Personality: A Re-examination,' *JTS* 21 (1970), 1–16.

Rosenberg, R.A. 'Jesus, Isaac, and the Suffering Servant,' *JBL* 84 (1965), 381–388.

Roth, C. 'The Cleansing of the Temple and Zech 14:21,' *NovT* 4 (1960), 174–181.

Rowe, R.D. 'Is Daniel's 'Son of Man' Messianic?' in *Christ the Lord: Studies in Christology presented to D. Guthrie*, ed. H.H. Rowdon. Leicester: IVP, 1982, 71–96.

Rowland, C.C. 'John 1:51, Jewish Apocalyptic and Targumic Tradition,' *NTS* 30 (1984), 498–507.

_____. *The Influence of the First Chapter of Ezekiel on Jewish and Early Christian Literature*. Ph.D Dissertation, the University of Cambridge, 1974.

_____. *The Open Heaven: A Study of Apocalyptic in Judaism and Early Christianity*. London: SPCK, 1982.

Russell, W. 'The Holy Spirit's Ministry in the Fourth Gospel,' *GTJ* 8/2 (1987), 227–239.

Saayman, C. 'The Textual Strategy in John 3:12–14: Preliminary Observations,' *Neot* 29/1 (1995), 27–48.

Sabbe, M. 'The Cleansing of the Temple and the Temple Logion,' *Studia Neotestamentica: Collected Essays*. Peeters: Leuven University Press, 1991, 331–354.

Sabourin, L. 'Who was Begotten of God (John 1:13),' *BTB* 6 (1976), 86–90.

Sanders, E.P. *Jesus and Judaism*. Philadelphia: Fortress Press, 1985.

Sanders, J.A. 'Nazwrai/oj in Matthew 2:23,' *The Gospels and the Scriptures of Israel*, eds. C.A. Evans and W.R. Stegner. JSNT Supp 104; Sheffield: SAP, 1994, 116–128.

Sanders, J.N. *A Commentary on the Gospel according to St John*, edited and completed by B.A. Mastin. London: Adam and Charles Black, 1977.

Sasse, H. *TDNT*, I, 197–209, 677–681.

Schlier, H. *TDNT*, I, 352–353.

Schnackenburg, R. *The Gospel according to St John*, I, trans. K. Smyth, C. Hastings et al. London: Burns and Oates, 1968.

_____. *The Gospel according to St John*, II, trans, K. Smyth, C. Hastings et al. London: Burns and Oates, 1980.

_____. *The Gospel according to St John*, III, trans, K. Smyth, C. Hastings et al. London: Burns and Oates, 1982.

Schneck, R. *Isaiah in the Gospel of Mark*, I-VIII. Vallejo: BIBAL Press, 1994.

Schneider, J. *TDNT*, II, 666–684.

Schneiders, S.M. 'Born Anew,' *TT* XLIV (1987), 189–196.

Schrenk, G. *TDNT*, I, 629–637.

_____. *TDNT*, III, 221–283.

Schweizer, E. *TDNT*, VIII, 363–392.

Scott, J.M. (ed.), Exile: Old Testament, Jewish, and Christian Conceptions. JSJ Sup 56; Leiden: Brill, 1997.

_____. (ed.), Restoration: Old Testament, Jewish, and Christian Perspectives. JSJ Sup 72; Leiden: Brill, 2001.

_____. 'And then All Israel Will BE Saved (Rom 11:26),' *Restoration: Old Testament, Jewish, and Christian Perspectives*, ed. J. M. Scott. JSJ Sup 72; Leiden: Brill, 2001, 489–526.

_____. 'Exile and the Self-Understanding of Diaspora Jews in the Greco-Roman Period,' *Exile: Old Testament, Jewish, and Christian Conceptions*, ed. J.M. Scott. Leiden: Brill, 1997, 173–218.

_____. 'For as Many as are of Works of the Law are Under a Curse' (Galatians 3.10),' *Paul and the Scripture of Israel*. JSNT Supp 83; Sheffield: SAP, 1993, 187–213.

Seeley, D. 'Jesus' Temple Act,' *CBQ* 56 (1993), 263–283.

Seesemann, H. *TDNT*, V, 162–166.

Seitz, C.R. 'Ezekiel 37:1–14,' *Interpretation* 46 (1992), 53–56.

Senior, D. 'The Death of Jesus and the Resurrection of the Holy Ones (Mt 27:51–53),' *CBQ* 38 (1976), 321–319.

Sidebottom, E.M. *The Christ of the Fourth Gospel*. London: SPCK, 1961.

Siede, B. *NIDNTT*, II, 184–186.

Simon, U.E. 'Eternal Life in the Fourth Gospel,' in *Studies in the Fourth Gospel*, ed. F.L. Cross. London: Mowbrays, 1957, 97–109.

Sjöberg, E. and Stählin, G. *TDNT*, V, 412–416.

Sklba, R.J. 'Until the Spirit from on High is poured out on us (Isa 32:15): Reflections on the Role of the Spirit in the Exile,' *CBQ* 46 (1984), 1–17.

Slater, T.B. 'One like a Son of Man in First-Century CE Judaism,' *NTS* 41 (1995), 183–198.

Sloyan, G. *John: Interpretation*. Atlanta: John Knox Press, 1988.

Smalley, S.S. 'Salvation Proclaimed VIII. John 1:29–34,' *ExpT* 93 (1982), 324–329.

_____. *John: Evangelist and Interpreter*. 2nd ed.; Carlisle: Paternoster, 1998.

Smith, D.M. *John*. ANTC; Nashville: Abingdon, 1999.

Smith, R.H. 'Exodus Typology in the Fourth Gospel,' *JBL* 81 (1962), 329–342.

Snodgrass, K.R. 'Reading and Overreading the Parables in Jesus and the Victory of God,' *Jesus and the Restoration of Israel: A Critical Assessment of*

N.T. Wright's *Jesus and the Victory of God*, ed. C.C. Newman. Downers Grove: IVP; Carlisle: Paternoster, 1999, 61–76.

_____. 'Streams of Tradition Emerging from Isaiah 40:1-5 and Their Adaptation in the New Testament,' *JSNT* 9 (1980), 24–45.

Spriggs, D.G. 'Meaning of 'Water' in John 3:6,' *ExpT* 85 (1974), 149–150.

Staley, J. 'The Structure of John's Prologue: Its Implication for the Gospel's Narrative Structure,' *CBQ* 48 (1986), 241–264.

Stanton, G.N. *The Gospels and Jesus*. Oxford: OUP, 2002.

Stauffer, E. *TDNT*, I, 648–657.

_____. *TDNT*, II, 536–537.

Stern, D.H. *Restoring the Jewishness of the Gospel: A Message for Christians*. Clarksville, MD: Jewish New Testament Publications, 1988.

Stibbe, M.W.G. *John as a Storyteller: Narrative Criticism and the Fourth Gospel*. Cambridge: CUP, 1992.

Strachan, R.H. *The Fourth Gospel: Its Significance and Environment*. London: SCM, 1960.

Strauss, M.L. *The Davidic Messiah in Luke-Acts: The Promise and its Fulfilment in Lukan Christology*. JSNT Supp 110; Sheffield: SAP, 1995.

Stuart, D. *Hosea-Jonah*. WBC 31; Waco: Word Books, 1987.

Stuhlmacher, P. *Jesus of Nazareth, Christ of Faith*, trans. S.S. Schatzmann. Peabody, MA: Hendrickson Publisher, 1993.

Stuhlmueller, C. 'The Theology of Creation in Second Isaiah,' *CBQ* 21 (1959), 429–467.

Swancutt, D.M. 'Hungers Assuaged by the Bread from Heaven: 'Eating Jesus' as Isaian Call to Belief: The Confluence of Isaiah 55 and Psalm 78 (77) in John 6:22–71,' *Early Christian Interpretation of the Scriptures of Israel: Investigations and Proposals*, eds. C.A. Evans and J.A. Sanders. JSNT Supp 148; Sheffield: SAP, 1997, 218–215.

Swartely, W.M. 'The Structural Function of the Term 'Way' (*Hodos*) in Mark's Gospel,' *The New Way of Jesus: Essays Presented to Howard Charles*, ed. W. Klassen. Kansas: Faith and Life Press, 1980, 73–86.

Tasker, R.B.G. *The Gospel according to St. John*. Leicester: IVP; Grand Rapids: Eerdmans, 1999.

Telford, W.R. *The Barren Temple and the Withered Tree: A Redaction-Critical Analysis of the Cursing of the Fig-Tree Pericope in Mark´s Gospel and Its Relation to the Cleansing of the Temple Tradition.* JSNT Supp1; Sheffield: JSOT Press, 1980.

Thiselton, A. C. *NIDNTT*, III, 874–902.

_____. *The First Epistle to the Corinthians : A Commentary on the Greek Text.* NIGTC; Grand Rapids: Eerdmans; Carlisle: Paternoster, 2000.

Thomas, J.D. 'A Translation Problem- John 3,' *RQ* 24 (1981), 219–224.

Thomas, R.W. 'The Meaning of the Terms 'Life' and 'Death' in the Fourth Gospel,' *SJT* 21 (1968), 199–212.

Throckmorton (Jr), B.H. *Creation by the Word: A Study of the Idea of Creation in Second Isaiah and the Gospel According to John.* Boston: United Church Press, 1968.

Traub, H. *TDNT*, V, 509–543.

Trudinger, L.P. 'An Israelite in Whom There is no Guile: An Interpretive Note on John 1:45–51,' *EQ* 54 (1982), 117–120.

_____. 'On the Third Day There was a Wedding at Cana: Reflections on St John 2:1–12,' *DR* 104 (1986), 41–43.

_____. 'The Cleansing of the Temple: St John's Independent, Subtle Reflections,' *ExpT* 108 (1997), 329–330.

Trumbower, J.A. *Born From Above: The Anthropology of the Gospel of John.* Tübingen: J.C.B. Mohr, 1992.

Tsumura, D.T. *NIDOTTE*, IV, 160–166.

Turner, C.H. 'O` UIOS MOU O` AGAPHTOS,' *JTS* 27 (1926), 113–129.

Turner, M.M.B. 'Atonement and the Death of Jesus in John – Some Questions to Bultmann and Forestrell,' *EQ* 62/2 (1990), 99–122.

_____. 'The Concept of Receiving the Spirit in John's Gospel,' *VoxE* 10 (1977), 24–42.

_____. *The Holy Spirit and Spiritual Gifts in the New Testament Church and Today.* Rev. ed.; Peabody: Hendrickson Publishers, 1998.

Valentine, S.R. 'The Johannine Prologue: A Microcosm of the Gospel,' *EQ* 68 (1996), 291–304.

Van Der Watt, J.G. 'The Use of VAIWNIOS in the Concept ZWH VAIWNIOS in John's Gospel,' *NovT* 31/3 (1989), 217–228.

VanderKam, J.C. 'Exile in Jewish Apocalyptic Literature,' *Exile: Old Testament, Jewish, and Christian Conceptions*, eds. J.M. Scott. Leiden: Brill, 1997, 89–109.

VanGemeren, W.A. 'The Spirit of Restoration,' *WTJ* 50 (1988), 81–102.

Vermes, G. 'The Use of vn rb/avn rb in Jewish Aramaic,' *An Aramaic Approach to the Gospels and Acts*, eds. M. Black. Oxford: Clarendon, 1967, 310–328.

_____. *Scripture and Tradition in Judaism*. Leiden: Brill, 1961.

_____. *The Complete Dead Sea Scrolls in English*. London: Penguin, 1997.

von Meding, W. *NIDNTT*, III, 781–785.

von Rad, G. *TDNT*, II, 238–242.

_____. *TDNT*, II, 402–406.

_____. *TDNT*, II, 843–849.

_____. *TDNT*, V, 502–509.

Walker, P.W.L. 'The Land and Jesus Himself,' *The Land of Promise: Biblical, Theological and Contemporary Perspectives*, eds. P. Johnston and P. Walker. Downers Grove, IL: IVP/Apollos, 2000, 100–120.

_____. *Jesus and the Holy City: New Testament Perspectives on Jerusalem*. Grand Rapids and Cambridge: Eerdmans, 1996.

Walker, W.O. 'John 1:43–51 and 'the Son of Man' in the Fourth Gospel,' *JSNT* 56 (1994), 31–42.

Watts, J.D.W. *Isaiah 1–33*. WBC 24; Waco: Word Books, 1985.

_____. *Isaiah 34–66*. WBC 25; Waco: Word Books, 1987.

Watts, R.E. 'Consolation or Confrontation? Isaiah 40–55 and the Delay of the New Exodus,' *TynB* 41 (1990), 31–59.

_____. *Isaiah's New Exodus and Mark*. WUNT 2/88; Tübingen: Mohr Siebeck, 1997.

Wedel, A.F. 'John 4:5–26 (5–42),' *Interpretation* 31 (1977), 406–412.

Wenham, G.J. *Genesis 1–15*. WBC 1; Waco, Texas: Word Books, 1987.

_____. *Genesis 16–50*. WBC 2; Waco, Texas: Word Books, 1994.

Westcott, B.F. *The Gospel According to St. John: The Greek Text with Introduction and Notes*, I, II. London: John Murray, 1908.

Whitacre, R.A. *John*. Leicester and Downers Grove: IVP, 1999.

Wilcock, M. *The Message of Psalms 73–150*. BST; Leicester: IVP, 2001.

Wilfall, W. 'Gen 3:15 – A Protevangelium?' *CBQ* 36 (1974), 361–365.

Wilkinson, D. *The Message of Creation: Encountering the Lord of the Universe*. Leicester: IVP, 2002.

Williams, R.H. 'The Mother of Jesus at Cana: A Social-Science Interpretation of John 2:1–12,' *CBQ* 59 (1997), 679–692.

Williford, D. 'John 3:1–15– *gennêthênai anôthen*: A Radical Departure, A New Beginning,' *RE* 96 (1999), 451–461.

Wilson, J. 'The Integrity of John 3:22–36,' *JSNT* 10 (1981), 34–41.

Wilson, R.McL. 'Philo and the Fourth Gospel,' *ExpT* 65 (1953/54), 47–49.

Windisch, H. 'Die Sprüche vom Eingehen in das Reich Gottes,' *ZNW* 27 (1928), 163–192.

Witherington, B. 'The Waters of Birth: John 3:5 and 1 John 5:6–8,' *NTS* 35 (1989), 155–160.

_____. *John's Wisdom: A Commentary on the Fourth Gospel*. Louisville: Westminster John Knox Press, 1995.

_____. *Women in the Ministry of Jesus: A Study of Jesus' Attitudes to Women and Their Roles as Reflected in his Earthly Life*. Cambridge: CUP, 1987.

Wright, N.T. *Jesus and the Victory of God*. London: SPCK, 1996.

_____. *The New Testament and the People of God*. London: SPCK, 1993.

_____. *The Resurrection of the Son of God*. London: SPCK, 2003.

Yamauchi, E.M. 'Some Alleged Evidences For Pre-Christian Gnosticism,' *New Dimensions in New Testament Studies*, eds. R.N. Longenecker and M.C. Tenney. Grand Rapids: Zondervan, 1974, 46–70.

_____. *Pre-Christian Gnosticism: A Survey of the Proposed Evidences*. Grand Rapids: Baker, 1983.

Yoo, S.S. *Let's Go back to Jesus' Prayer*. Seoul: Kyujang, 2000.

Young, F.W. 'A Study of the Relation of Isaiah to the Fourth Gospel,' *ZNW* 46 (1955), 215–233.

Zimmerli, W. *Ezekiel 2: A Commentary on the Book of the Prophet Ezekiel, Chapters 25–48*, trans. J.D. Martin. Philadelphia: Fortress Press, 1983.

www.ingramcontent.com/pod-product-compliance
Lightning Source LLC
Chambersburg PA
CBHW071232230426
43668CB00011B/1397